Mobile Networks and Cloud Computing Convergence for Progressive Services and Applications

Joel J.P. Rodrigues
Instituto de Telecomunicações, University of Beira Interior, Portugal

Kai Lin
Dalian University of Technology, China

Jaime Lloret
Universidad Politecnica de Valencia, Spain

A volume in the Advances in Wireless Technologies and Telecommunication (AWTT) Book Series

Information Science REFERENCE
An Imprint of IGI Global

Managing Director:	Lindsay Johnston
Production Manager:	Jennifer Yoder
Publishing Systems Analyst:	Adrienne Freeland
Development Editor:	Allyson Gard
Acquisitions Editor:	Kayla Wolfe
Typesetter:	Deanna Jo Zombro
Cover Design:	Jason Mull

Published in the United States of America by
Information Science Reference (an imprint of IGI Global)
701 E. Chocolate Avenue
Hershey PA 17033
Tel: 717-533-8845
Fax: 717-533-8661
E-mail: cust@igi-global.com
Web site: http://www.igi-global.com

Library of Congress Cataloging-in-Publication Data

Mobile networks and cloud computing convergence for progressive services and applications / Joel J.P. Rodrigues, Kai Lin, and Jaime Lloret, editors.
       pages cm
 Includes bibliographical references and index. Summary: "This book is a fundamental source for the advancement of knowledge, application, and practice in the interdisciplinary areas of mobile network and cloud computing, addressing innovative concepts and critical issues"-- Provided by publisher.
   ISBN 978-1-4666-4781-7 (hardcover) -- ISBN 978-1-4666-4782-4 (ebook) -- ISBN 978-1-4666-4783-1 (print & perpetual access) 1. Cloud computing. 2. Mobile computing. 3. Computer networks. I. Rodrigues, Joel, 1972- II. Lin, Kai, 1979- III. Lloret Mauri, Jaime.
 QA76.585.M63 2014
 004.67'82--dc23
                                   2013028694

This book is published in the IGI Global book series Advances in Wireless Technologies and Telecommunication (AWTT) (ISSN: 2327-3305; eISSN: 2327-3313)

British Cataloguing in Publication Data
A Cataloguing in Publication record for this book is available from the British Library.

Advances in Wireless Technologies and Telecommunication (AWTT) Book Series

Xiaoge Xu
The University of Nottingham Ningbo, China

ISSN: 2327-3305
EISSN: 2327-3313

MISSION

The wireless computing industry is constantly evolving, redesigning the ways in which individuals share information. Wireless technology and telecommunication remain one of the most important technologies in business organizations. The utilization of these technologies has enhanced business efficiency by enabling dynamic resources in all aspects of society.

The **Advances in Wireless Technologies and Telecommunication Book Series** aims to provide researchers and academic communities with quality research on the concepts and developments in the wireless technology fields. Developers, engineers, students, research strategists, and IT managers will find this series useful to gain insight into next generation wireless technologies and telecommunication.

COVERAGE

- Cellular Networks
- Digital Communication
- Global Telecommunications
- Grid Communications
- Mobile Technology
- Mobile Web Services
- Network Management
- Virtual Network Operations
- Wireless Broadband
- Wireless Sensor Networks

IGI Global is currently accepting manuscripts for publication within this series. To submit a proposal for a volume in this series, please contact our Acquisition Editors at Acquisitions@igi-global.com or visit: http://www.igi-global.com/publish/.

Titles in this Series

For a list of additional titles in this series, please visit: www.igi-global.com

Multidisciplinary Perspectives on Telecommunications, Wireless Systems, and Mobile Computing
Wen-Chen Hu (University of North Dakota, USA)
Information Science Reference • copyright 2014 • 274pp • H/C (ISBN: 9781466647152) • US $175.00 (our price)

Mobile Networks and Cloud Computing Convergence for Progressive Services and Applications
Joel J.P. Rodrigues (University of Beira Interior, Portugal) Kai Lin (Dalian University of Technology, China) and
Jaime Lloret (Polytechnic University of Valencia, Spain)
Information Science Reference • copyright 2014 • 306pp • H/C (ISBN: 9781466647817) • US $180.00 (our price)

Research and Design Innovations for Mobile User Experience
Kerem Rızvanoğlu (Galatasaray University, Turkey) and Görkem Çetin (Turkcell, Turkey)
Information Science Reference • copyright 2014 • 352pp • H/C (ISBN: 9781466644465) • US $190.00 (our price)

Cognitive Radio Technology Applications for Wireless and Mobile Ad Hoc Networks
Natarajan Meghanathan (Jackson State University, USA) and Yenumula B. Reddy (Grambling State University, USA)
Information Science Reference • copyright 2013 • 370pp • H/C (ISBN: 9781466642218) • US $190.00 (our price)

Evolution of Cognitive Networks and Self-Adaptive Communication Systems
Thomas D. Lagkas (University of Western Macedonia, Greece) Panagiotis Sarigiannidis (University of Western
Macedonia, Greece) Malamati Louta (University of Western Macedonia, Greece) and Periklis Chatzimisios (Al-
exander TEI of Thessaloniki, Greece)
Information Science Reference • copyright 2013 • 438pp • H/C (ISBN: 9781466641891) • US $195.00 (our price)

Tools for Mobile Multimedia Programming and Development
D. Tjondronegoro (Queensland University of Technology, Australia)
Information Science Reference • copyright 2013 • 357pp • H/C (ISBN: 9781466640542) • US $190.00 (our price)

Cognitive Radio and Interference Management Technology and Strategy
Meng-Lin Ku (National Central University, Taiwan, R.O.C.) and Jia-Chin Lin (National Central University, Tai-
wan, R.O.C.)
Information Science Reference • copyright 2013 • 354pp • H/C (ISBN: 9781466620056) • US $190.00 (our price)

Wireless Radio-Frequency Standards and System Design Advanced Techniques
Gianluca Cornetta (Universidad San Pablo-CEU, Spain) David J. Santos (Universidad San Pablo-CEU, Spain) and
Jose Manuel Vazquez (Universidad San Pablo-CEU, Spain)
Engineering Science Reference • copyright 2012 • 422pp • H/C (ISBN: 9781466600836) • US $195.00 (our price)

www.igi-global.com

701 E. Chocolate Ave., Hershey, PA 17033
Order online at www.igi-global.com or call 717-533-8845 x100
To place a standing order for titles released in this series, contact: cust@igi-global.com
Mon-Fri 8:00 am - 5:00 pm (est) or fax 24 hours a day 717-533-8661

Editorial Advisory Board

Table of Contents

Detailed Table of Contents

Chapter 1
Jorge E. F. Costa, University of Beira Interior, Portugal
Joel J. P. C. Rodrigues, Instituto de Telecomunicações, University of Beira Interior, Portugal

Mobile devices have gained great importance in the daily lives of people. Smartphones and tablet computers make people's lives easier by being more useful and offering more capabilities and services for a plethora of activities. Those devices include various sensing modules for collecting location information related to navigation, gravity, and orientation, which bring a diversity and intelligent ubiquitous mobile experience to users. In this chapter, cloud computing and mobile cloud computing are addressed in order to give insight about the topic and offer an important overview for this book. The diverse research definitions of these emerging technologies and contributions to enhance users' lives are considered. Furthermore, the technologies and identified advantages to improve and justify the strong use of mobile cloud are discussed. Relevant mobile cloud computing applications are presented, showing good results and a promising future for mobile cloud computing technologies.

Chapter 2
Yi Xu, Auburn University, USA
Shiwen Mao, Auburn University, USA

Leveraging Mobile Cloud Computing (MCC), resource-poor mobile devices are now enabled to support rich media applications. In this chapter, the authors briefly review basic concepts and architecture of mobile cloud computing, and focus on the technical challenges of MCC for multimedia applications. Specifically, they discuss how to save energy, ensure Quality of Experience (QoE), deal with stochastic wireless channels, support security and privacy, and reduce network costs for rich media applications. Prototypes, ongoing standardization efforts, and commercial aspects are also reviewed. The authors conclude this chapter with a discussion of several open research problems that call for substantial research and regulation efforts.

Chapter 3

Scott Fowler, Linköping University, Sweden

Today, mobile tools, such as smartphones and tablets, have become primary computing devices for many users. One mobile tool to satisfy this is the 4G network technology LTE (Long-Term Evolution)-Advanced. These mobile tools are resource-poor due to limited battery life. Mobile Cloud Computing (MCC) is intended to provide services to mobile users by supplementing the resource-paucity of mobile devices (i.e. off-loading tasks/data on the Internet and providing the resources to a local client on-demand). However, despite LTE-Advanced's improved network quality, much needs to be done before MCC can reach its true potential. This chapter characterizes key challenges for deployment of MCC with 4G: device battery lifetime, latency, quality of service/experience, and handover. Statistical modeling is a powerful tool to address these issues. Once MCC with 4G network behavior is characterized, it is translated into the future development of innovative mobile technologies for a wide variety of new applications.

Chapter 4

Sattar B. Sadkhan, University of Babylon, Iraq
Nidaa A. Abbas, University of Babylon, Iraq

Wireless networks are inherently more vulnerable than their wired counterparts. In addition, complications arise in the presence of node mobility and dynamic network topology. Moreover, intermittent connectivity, whether caused by mobility or periodic node sleep, brings about additional challenges. At the same time, node resource constraints make direct adoption of existing security solutions difficult, if not impossible. Wireless Communication Network Security and Privacy analyze important problems in the realms of wireless networks and mobile computing. The Security aspects relate to authentication, access control and authorization, nonrepudiation, privacy and confidentiality, integrity, and auditing. Privacy is an essential feature of any product or service.

Chapter 5

Hero Modares, University of Malaya, Malaysia
Jaime Lloret, Universidad Politecnica de Valencia, Spain
Amirhossein Moravejosharieh, University of Canterbury, New Zealand
Rosli Salleh, University of Malaya, Malaysia

Cloud computing is a new and promising technology that is transforming the paradigm of traditional Internet computing and probably the whole IT industry. Cloud computing is predicted to expand in the mobile environment leveraging on the rapid advances in wireless access technologies. These mobile applications are built around mobile cloud computing techniques and models. In the Mobile Cloud environment, users can remotely store their data as well as enjoy high quality on-demand cloud applications without the limitations of having to purchase and maintain their own local hardware and software. However, data security is still a major concern and is the main obstacle preventing cloud computing from being more widely adopted. This concern originates from the fact that sensitive data stored in the public clouds is managed by commercial service providers who might not be totally trustworthy. As such, there are several security and privacy issues that need to be addressed. This chapter gives an overview on the cloud computing concept followed by a description on mobile cloud computing and the different security issues pertinent to the mobile cloud computing environment.

Chapter 6

Gianmarco Baldini, Joint Research Centre – European Commission, Italy
Pasquale Stirparo, Joint Research Centre – European Commission, Italy

Information systems and wireless communications are becoming increasingly present in the everyday life of citizens both from a personal and business point of view. A recent development in this context is Mobile Cloud Computing (MCC), which is the combination of Cloud Computing and pervasive mobile networks. Ensuring the preservation of privacy can be difficult in MCC. Therefore, this chapter provides an overview of the main challenges in ensuring privacy in MCC and surveys the most significant contributions from the research community. The second objective of the chapter is to introduce and describe a new framework for privacy protection based on the concepts of Virtual Object (VO) and Composite Virtual Object (CVO), where data are encapsulated and protected using a sticky policy approach and a role-based access model. The proposed iCore framework is compared to the privacy challenges described in the first objective.

Chapter 7

Zhili Sun, University of Surrey, UK
Yichao Yang, University of Surrey, UK
Yanbo Zhou, University of Surrey, UK
Haitham Cruickshank, University of Surrey, UK

Mobile cloud computing is a new computing paradigm to integrate cloud computing technology into the mobile environment. It takes full advantages of cloud computing with great potential to transform a large part of the IT industry. The objectives of mobile cloud computing are to meet user demand, efficiently utilize a pool of resources, including mobile network, storage, and computation resources, and optimize energy on mobile devices. Here, the authors review the current mobile cloud computing technologies, highlight the main issues and challenges for the future development, and focus on resource management. Then, combining the current agent architectures and resource optimization strategies, they present an agent-based resource management to deal with multiple data and computation intensive applications of user demand. The chapter offers a promising solution of selecting the best service provider and efficiently utilizing mobile network resources given the user's request constraint.

Chapter 8

Claudio Estevez, Universidad de Chile, Chile

Cloud computing is consistently proving to be the dominant architecture of the future, and mobile technology is the catalyst. By having the processing power and storage remotely accessible, the main focus of the terminal is now related to connectivity and user-interface. The success of cloud-based applications greatly depends on the throughput experienced by the end user, which is why transport protocols play a key role in mobile cloud computing. This chapter discusses the main issues encountered in cloud networks that affect connection-oriented transport protocols. These issues include, but are not limited to, large delay connections, bandwidth variations, power consumption, and high segment loss rates. To reduce these adverse effects, a set of proposed solutions are presented; furthermore, the advantages and disadvantages are discussed. Finally, suggestions are made for future mobile cloud computing transport-layer designs that address different aspects of the network, such as transparency, congestion-intensity estimation, and quality-of-service integration.

Qi Wang, University of the West of Scotland, UK

James Nightingale, University of the West of Scotland, UK

Runpeng Wang, Beijing Foreign Studies University, China

Naeem Ramzan, University of the West of Scotland, UK

Christos Grecos, University of the West of Scotland, UK

Xinheng Wang, University of the West of Scotland, UK

Abbes Amira, University of the West of Scotland, UK

Chunbo Luo, University of the West of Scotland, UK

Mobile multimedia computing has become ubiquitous in everyday life. However, mobile device users involved in resource-demanding visual applications such as video streaming often encounter performance degradations due to their mobile devices' intrinsic constraints in processing power, storage, and battery capacity. Cloud computing can be explored to circumvent such problems thanks to the vast resources available in the cloud. Mobile video cloud computing has thus emerged as an important research and development topic to achieve high-performance, innovative networked video applications. This chapter discusses the recent advances in mobile video cloud technologies and applications. The authors investigate mobile video cloud systems starting with the various mobile cloud paradigms and then present challenges and solutions of mobile video cloud management for mobility, context, and security. Furthermore, the authors examine the latest video coding standards and explore methods based on parallelisation and scalability for their optimised application over mobile clouds, followed by three highlighted mobile cloud video applications including streaming, transcoding, and gaming. Finally, future directions in this area are envisioned.

Fragkiskos Sardis, Middlesex University, UK

Glenford Mapp, Middlesex University, UK

Jonathan Loo, Middlesex University, UK

Advances in Mobile and Cloud technologies have redefined the way we perceive and use computers. Mobile devices now rely on Cloud technology for storage and applications. Furthermore, recent advances in network technology ensure that mobile devices in the future will have high-bandwidth connectivity at all times. This drives the incentive of doing all the processing and storage in the Cloud and using mobile devices to access the services. In this chapter, the authors argue that always-on connectivity along with increased demand of Cloud services will contest the Internet backbone and create problems in the management of Cloud resources. Client mobility is also a factor that should be taken into account when providing Cloud services to mobile devices. The authors therefore propose a new service delivery architecture that takes into account client mobility as well as the distance between clients and services in order to manage Cloud and network resources more efficiently and provide a better Quality of Experience for the user.

Mobile Cloud Computing (MCC) integrates cloud computing into the mobile environment and overcomes obstacles related to performance (e.g., bandwidth, throughput) and environment (e.g., heterogeneity, scalability, and availability). Quality of Service (QoS), such as end-to-end delay, packet loss ratio, etc., is vital for MCC applications. In this chapter, several important approaches for performance evaluation in MCC are introduced. These approaches, such as Markov Processes, Scheduling, and Game Theory, are the most popular methodologies in current research about performance evaluation in MCC. QoS is special in MCC compared to other environments. Important QoS problems with details in MCC and corresponding designs and solutions are explained. This chapter covers the most important research problems and current status related to performance evaluation and QoS in MCC.

Earlier this century there was a crisis among the major Web companies. Berners-Lee started the concept of semantics for the Web. The large academic centers began to create tools to support the dissemination and research associated with their work; the collaborative networks emerged. Taking advantage of this new concept and seeking to attract new users to the Web, social networks began to emerge with a single purpose: to enable new users to customize data. Startups represent this new concept of the Web of the 21st century. In this sense, cloud computing, as well as energy efficiency should represent the biggest advances of this decade, enabling the growth of new market niches. This, along with the need for integration and mobility, is the object of study in this chapter.

This book chapter presents the integration of widely available technologies to bridge the gap between mobile devices and their computational rich surrounding environments. Taking as common glue Cloud Storage systems, new interaction between devices becomes more natural. The processing of files can be transparently executed on nearby computers, taking advantage of better hardware and saving mobile devices power. In this chapter, the authors present a novel resource evaluation mechanism, which allows a finer evaluation and more precise comparison of remote resources, leading to fewer wasted resources and better use of those resources. The use of remote resources can be performed by means of processing offloading, executing complete application on remote devices or by relocation of mobile classes. Both methods resort to the presented resource evaluation mechanism. Monolithic applications are transformed (with information from a configuration file) into distributed application, where some components execute on remote devices: nearby computers (to take advantage of existing human-computer interaction devices) or on the cloud (to speed processing). Processing offloading is accomplished by executing on nearby computers applications compatible with the one on the mobile device. This speeds that processing task (better CPU, better interaction devices), reducing the mobile device's power consumption.

Kayhan Zrar Ghafoor, Koya University, Iraq

Marwan Aziz Mohammed, Koya University, Iraq

Kamalrulnizam Abu Bakar, Universiti Teknologi Malaysia, Malaysia

Ali Safa Sadiq, Universiti Teknologi Malaysia, Malaysia

Jaime Lloret, Universidad Politecnica de Valencia, Spain

Recently, Vehicular Ad Hoc Networks (VANET) have attracted the attention of research communities, leading car manufacturers, and governments due to their potential applications and specific characteristics. Their research outcome was started with awareness between vehicles for collision avoidance and Internet access and then expanded to vehicular multimedia communications. Moreover, vehicles' high computation, communication, and storage resources set a ground for vehicular networks to deploy these applications in the near future. Nevertheless, on-board resources in vehicles are mostly underutilized. Vehicular Cloud Computing (VCC) is developed to utilize the VANET resources efficiently and provide subscribers safe infotainment services. In this chapter, the authors perform a survey of state-of-the-art vehicular cloud computing as well as the existing techniques that utilize cloud computing for performance improvements in VANET. The authors then classify the VCC based on the applications, service types, and vehicular cloud organization. They present the detail for each VCC application and formation. Lastly, the authors discuss the open issues and research directions related to VANET cloud computing.

Tae-Gyu Lee, Korea Institute of Industrial Technology, Korea

Previous medical services for humans provided healthcare information using the static-based computing of space-constrained hospitals or healthcare centers. In contrast, current mobile health information management computing and services are being provided so that they utilize both the mobility of mobile computing and the scalability of cloud computing to monitor in real-time the health status of patients who are moving. In addition, data capacity has sharply increased with the expansion of the principal data generation cycle from the traditional static computing environment to the dynamic computing environment. This chapter presents mobile cloud healthcare computing systems that simultaneously leverage the portability and scalability of healthcare services. This chapter also presents the wearable computing system as an application of mobile healthcare.

Eraldo Guerra, Center of Advanced Studies and Systems of Recife, Brazil

Felipe Furtado, Federal University of Pernambuco (UFPE), Brazil

This chapter is about the study of treatments for autistic children and interventions of entertainment games with the purpose of developing a technological solution in order to promote a better adaptation between the autistic children and treatment, consequently showing better results in a shorter period of time. The multidisciplinary software for Autism treatment is being developed. It is based on PECs, ABA, and TEACCH methods, and it uses ludic games and activity interventions. Before applying technology to autism treatment, a deep study about autistic children is made. This way, concepts such as customization and the use of Kinect, Mobile (WP7), and Cloud Computer technologies take part as a stimulator system, since they are responsible for intensifying cognitive development and reducing the patient's excitement, aggressiveness, and irritability.

Chapter 17

Charalampos Dimoulas, Aristotle University of Thessaloniki, Greece

Andreas Veglis, Aristotle University of Thessaloniki, Greece

George Kalliris, Aristotle University of Thessaloniki, Greece

Cloud Computing is one of the most rapidly evolving technologies available today that offers the possibility of multimedia content exploitation with rich media experience. Cloud computing users have the flexibility to enjoy media content independently of time and space. Multimedia cloud computing encompasses technology, multimedia data, and community contribution, offering augmented multimodal interaction and advanced processing services to the users. Mobile multimedia resources can now be accessed through the cloud practically at anytime and from anywhere, facing contemporary demands for information access and process, thus perfectly matching to the nature of news media. Such features are very favorable in online journalism and specifically in news reporting services. This chapter presents technological and application-oriented trends in cloud-based mobile news reporting both at journalists' (news producers) and users' (news consumers) sides. Future and emerging perspectives, such as ubiquitous and pervasive computing, incorporating context and location-aware services in semantic interaction modes, are also described from the news-reporting point of view.

Preface

With the rapid development of mobile networks and cloud computing technology, Mobile Cloud Computing (MCC) is attracting great attention from academia, industry, and government. MCC is the combination of cloud computing and mobile networks to bring benefits to mobile users, network operators, as well as cloud providers. As there are more than six billion mobile phone subscribers worldwide, mobile cloud computing has the potential to have a profound effect on the wireless industry and on our society. The book briefly reviews basic concepts and hot topics of mobile cloud computing and focuses on the technical challenges of MCC. It tries to take account of developments and trends that are taking place in the area of MCC and it offers a comprehensive and integrated approach to related issues. The objective of this book is to introduce the applications and techniques for mobile networks and cloud computing. After reading it, you will understand what these techniques are and appreciate their strengths and applicability.

The book is aimed at the reader who is interested in the theories and techniques of mobile cloud computing and related research questions. It will also be of interest to information professionals who need to become acquainted with this new technology and to all those who wish to gain a detailed technical understanding of what issues MCC involves. It is written for computer and network practitioners, developers, information technology managers, specification writers, patent examiners, and curious lay people, as well as students and professors, who need an easy-to-read book to begin related research of MCC.

The book is organized in layers that make the ideas accessible to reader who are interested in grasping the basics, as well as accessible to those who would like more depth of treatment, along with full details on the techniques covered. It is formed by 17 chapters. Chapter 1 addresses cloud computing and mobile cloud computing in order to give an insight about the topic and offer an important overview for the whole book. The technologies and identified advantages to improve and justify the strong use of mobile cloud are both discussed. Chapter 2 introduces the basic concepts and the state of the art of mobile cloud media, and discusses several open research problems associated with it. Specifically, it discusses relevant hot questions like energy saving methods, quality of experience assurance, management for stochastic wireless channel, security and privacy support, and so on. Chapter 3 characterizes critical challenges for deployment of MCC with 4G network technology LTE-Advanced: device battery lifetime, latency, quality of service/experience, and handover. A power tool of statistical modeling is applied to help research these issues in this chapter. Chapter 4 investigates the different technologies and networking of wireless communication, the security methods used in wireless networks, and the types of attacks against secure wireless communication networks. It also displays a variety of challenges in security and privacy of wireless communication networks.

Data security is a major concern and is the main obstacle preventing mobile cloud computing from being more widely adopted. Chapter 5 first gives an overview of the cloud computing concept followed by a description of mobile cloud computing and the different security issues pertinent to the mobile cloud computing environment. Chapter 6 provides an overview of the main challenges in ensuring privacy in

MCC and surveys the most significant contributions from the research community. The other objective of this chapter is to introduce and describe a new framework for privacy protection-based concepts - Virtual Object (VO) and Composite Virtual Object (CVO), where data are encapsulated and protected using a sticky policy approach and a role-based access model.

Quality of Service (QoS) is special in MCC compared to other environments. Chapter 10 argues that always-on connectivity along with increased demand of Cloud services will congest the Internet backbone and create problems in the management of Cloud resources. A new service delivery architecture is proposed to manage Cloud and network resources more efficiently and provide a better quality of experience for the user. Chapter 11 covers several important approaches for performance evaluation in MCC. These approaches, such as Markov processes, scheduling, and game theory, are the most popular methodologies in current research about performance evaluation in MCC. Important QoS problems with details in MCC and corresponding designs and solutions are also explained in this chapter. Chapter 7 presents an agent-based resource management to deal with multiple data and computation-intensive applications of user demand. It offers a promising solution by selecting the best service provider and efficiently utilized mobile network resource given the user's request constraint. Chapter 8 discusses the main issues like large delay connections, bandwidth variations, power consumption, and high segment loss rates encountered in cloud networks and which affect connection-oriented transport protocols. In the end, this chapter gives some suggestions for future mobile cloud computing transport-layer designs that address different aspects of the network. Chapter 9 describes the recent advances in mobile video cloud technologies and applications and makes deep and detailed discussion of the mobile video cloud system, mobile video cloud management for mobility, context and security, etc. Chapter 12 introduces and describes a new paradigm of the Internet combined with energy management: new models and tools to aid the integration of data. Chapter 13 presents the integration of widely available technologies to bridge the gap between mobile devices and its computation-rich surrounding environments. A novel resource evaluation mechanism is presented, which allows a finer evaluation and a more precise comparison of remote resources, leading to fewer wasted resources and better use of those resources. Chapter 14 performs a survey of state-of-the-art vehicular Cloud computing as well as the existing techniques that utilize Cloud computing for performance improvements in Vehicular Ad Hoc Networks (VANET). The VCC is classified based on the applications, service types, and vehicular Cloud organization. Chapter 15 presents mobile cloud healthcare computing systems that simultaneously leverage the portability and scalability of healthcare services. This chapter also presents the wearable computing system as an application of mobile healthcare. Chapter 16 offers a proposal for multidisciplinary software for people with autism. The multidisciplinary software for Autism treatment is being developed. It is based on PECs, ABA, and TEACCH methods, and it uses ludic games and activity interventions. Chapter 17 aims at presenting technological and application-oriented trends in cloud-based mobile news reporting both for journalists' (news producers) and users' (news consumers). Future and emerging perspectives, such as ubiquitous and pervasive computing, incorporating context and location-aware services in semantic interaction modes, are also described from the news-reporting point of view.

Joel J. P. C. Rodrigues
Instituto de Telecomunicações, University of Beira Interior, Portugal

Kai Lin
Dalian Universiy of Technology, China

Jaime Lloret
Universidad Politécnica de Valencia, Spain

Acknowledgment

The editors of the book *Mobile Networks and Cloud Computing Convergence for Progressive Services and Applications* would like to thank to all the authors for their ideas and the excellent work of their chapters. We appreciate the originality of their works. Moreover, we would like to express our deep appreciation to the editorial advisory board for their excellent review of the book chapters. The editors acknowledge the remarkable collaboration and the effort of all the reviewers to ensure the technical quality of this book.

Finally, this book is the result of great teamwork. For this, we would like to thank all the efforts of IGI Global.

Joel J. P. C. Rodrigues
Instituto de Telecomunicações, University of Beira Interior, Portugal

Kai Lin
Dalian Universiy of Technology, China

Jaime Lloret
Universidad Politécnica de Valencia, Spain

Chapter 1
Mobile Cloud Computing:
Technologies, Services, and Applications

Jorge E. F. Costa
Instituto de Telecomunicações, University of Beira Interior, Portugal

Joel J. P. C. Rodrigues
Instituto de Telecomunicações, University of Beira Interior, Portugal

ABSTRACT

Mobile devices have gained great importance in the daily lives of people. Smartphones and tablet computers make people's lives easier by being more useful and offering more capabilities and services for a plethora of activities. Those devices include various sensing modules for collecting location information related to navigation, gravity, and orientation, which bring a diversity and intelligent ubiquitous mobile experience to users. In this chapter, cloud computing and mobile cloud computing are addressed in order to give insight about the topic and offer an important overview for this book. The diverse research definitions of these emerging technologies and contributions to enhance users' lives are considered. Furthermore, the technologies and identified advantages to improve and justify the strong use of mobile cloud are discussed. Relevant mobile cloud computing applications are presented, showing good results and a promising future for mobile cloud computing technologies.

1. INTRODUCTION

A wide range of potential mobile cloud applications has being recognized in the literature. These applications fall into different areas such as image processing, natural language processing (e.g., SIRI by Apple), sharing global positioning system (GPS), sharing Internet access, sensor data applications, querying, multimedia search, among others (Fernando, Loke, & Rahayu, 2013). Mobile cloud computing overcomes obstacles related to the performance, environment, and security issues identified on the above-mentioned powerful applications.

DOI: 10.4018/978-1-4666-4781-7.ch001

Smartphone and tablet devices are increasingly involved in the people daily life. They become one of the most effective and convenient tools for anytime and anywhere communications. Cho and Kim referred by (Mirusmonov, Changsu, Yiseul, & Jongheon, 2012) states that, in 2013, about 40% of all Internet traffic will be assigned to smartphones. Mobile devices have accumulated rich experience to their users through several services and mobile applications, which run on the devices or on remote servers via third Generation (3G) or common wireless technologies. On this way, mobile cloud computing will be a main branch of the development of cloud computing in the near future. The client of mobile cloud computing can also enjoy the interest of new Internet without the limitation of fixed equipment (Weiguang & Xiaolong, 2011). According to the study performed by Juniper Research (Holden, 2013), cloud computing based mobile software and applications are expected to rise 88% annually from 2009 to 2014.

In the literature, is not available a standard definition for mobile cloud computing. Nevertheless, several suggestions are available and the importance of the topic is evident. The MCCF (2013) refers mobile cloud computing to an "infrastructure where both the data storage and the data processing happen outside of the mobile device. Mobile cloud applications move the computing power and data storage away from mobile devices into the cloud, bringing applications and mobile computing to not just smartphone users but a much broader range of mobile subscribers". Han and Gani (2012) mention that previous mobile device-based intensive computing, data storage, and mass information processing have been transferred to 'cloud' and, thus, the requirements of mobile devices in computing capability and resources have been reduced. Therefore, the developing, running, and using mode of mobile applications have been totally changed. Thus, mobile cloud computing appears as a combination of two technologies: mobile computing and cloud computing (Christensen, 2009; Liu, Moulic, & Shea, 2010). In other words, the computing and major data processing phases have been migrated to the 'cloud'. In (Kadu, Bhanodiya, & Samvatsar, 2012; Zhong, Wang, & Wei, 2012), authors consider mobile cloud computing as a 3+ combination – the combination of mobile computing, mobile Internet, and cloud computing. Zhong et al. (2012) distinguish mobile computing from mobile cloud computing. They consider mobile computing as just resources exchange and sharing, unlike the nature of mobile cloud computing is the ability to provide valuable, accurate, and real-time information for any user at anywhere and anytime.

Given the importance of this topic, this book addresses innovative concepts and critical issues in the emerging field of mobile cloud computing. This chapter overviews the mobile cloud computing topic and elaborates about its technologies, services, and applications offering an important insight about them. The most relevant and updated issues related with the topic are considered, based on a deep review of the related literature.

The rest of the chapter is organized as follows. Section 2 presents a background and overviews the related work on cloud computing including its definition, architecture and corresponding services and deploying models, and an insight about its advantages. Mobile cloud computing is elaborated in Section 3 while mobile cloud technologies are described in Section 4. Section 5 discusses the major mobile cloud computing challenges. Applications and future trends of mobile cloud computing are studied in Section 6. Section 7 summarizes the chapter.

2. CLOUD COMPUTING OVERVIEW

The main idea behind cloud computing is not new. John McCarthy in the early 1960s already envisioned that computing facilities would be provided to general public like an utility (Zhang, Cheng, & Boutaba, 2010). However, after Google's CEO Eric

Schmidt used the word to describe the business model of providing services across the Internet, in 2006, the term really started to gain popularity. Since then, the term cloud computing has been used mainly as a marketing term in a variety of contexts to represent many different ideas. Because of this large variety, recently, there has been work on standardizing the definition of cloud computing, emerging the definition from The National Institute of standards and Technology (NIST) as it covers all the essential cloud computing aspects.

Cloud computing is a model for enabling convenient, on-demand network access to a shared pool of configurable computing resources (e.g., networks, servers, storage, applications, and services) that can be rapidly provisioned and released with minimal management effort or service provider interaction (Mell & Grance, 2011).

The main reason for the existence of different perceptions of cloud computing comes from the fact that cloud computing is not a new technology, but rather a new operations model that brings together a set of existing technologies to run business in a different way. In other words, it means that most of the technologies used on cloud computing, such as, grid computing, utility computing virtualization, and services are not new.

The architecture of a cloud-computing environment can be divided into the following four layers: the hardware, the infrastructure layer, the platform layer and the application layer, as may be seen in Figure 1. The hardware layer is responsible for managing the physical resources of the cloud, including physical servers, routers, switches, power, and cooling systems. In practice, the hardware layer is typically deployed in data centers. A data center usually contains thousands of servers that are organized in racks. The infrastructure layer, also known as the virtualization layer, creates a pool of storage and computing resources by partitioning the physical resources using virtualization technologies, such as Xen

(XenSourceInc, 2013), KVM (KMV, 2013), VMware (VMware, 2013), or Parallels (Gmb, 2013). The infrastructure layer is an essential component of cloud computing since many key features, such as dynamic resource assignment are only made available through virtualization technologies. The platform layer considers operating systems and application frameworks. The main objective of the platform layer is to minimize the burden of deploying applications directly into virtual machines containers. The application layer is performed by the current cloud applications. Different from traditional applications, cloud applications can leverage the automatic-scaling feature to achieve better performance, availability, and lower operating costs.

Cloud computing is based on and employs a service-driven model. It means that hardware and platform-level resources are provided as services on an on-demand basis. Conceptually, every layer of the above-described architecture can be deployed as a service to the corresponding above-layer. In practice, clouds offer services that can be grouped into three main categories: software as a service (SaaS), platform as a service (PaaS), and infrastructure as a service (IaaS) (Guan, Ke, Song, & Song, 2011; Han & Gani, 2012).

Infrastructure as a Service (IaaS) provides the option to run on-demand computational resources, usually in terms of virtual machines. The cloud owner who offers IaaS is so called an IaaS provider. Examples of IaaS providers include Amazon EC2 (Amazon Web Services, 2013), GoGrid (GoGrid, 2013), and Flexiscal (Flexiscale, 2013).

Platform as a Service (PaaS) assist users to develop, design, experiment, and host applications into the cloud. Examples of PaaS providers include Google App Engine (Google, 2013a), Microsoft Windows Azure (Microsoft, 2013), and Force.com (salesforce.com, 2013).

Software as a Service (SaaS) offers software solutions to users. Examples of SaaS providers include Salesforce.com (salesforce.com, 2013) or Rackspace (Rackspace, 2013).

Figure 1. Illustration of the cloud computing architecture

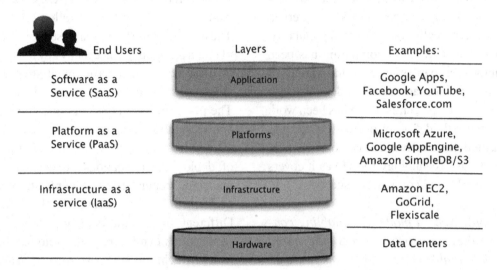

When moving an enterprise application to a cloud environment there are many issues that should be considered. In order to offer an adjusted "cloud" for each demand, the following four types of cloud can be considered, each one with its own benefits and drawbacks:

1. **Public Clouds:** A cloud in which service providers offer their resources as services to the general public. Multi-tenant solutions are employed in a provider, leveraging highly available and redundant platforms to deliver services to end-users over the Internet.
2. **Private Clouds:** Private clouds are designed for exclusive use by a single organization (client). A private cloud may be created and managed by the client or by external providers. This type of cloud offers the highest degree of control over performance, reliability, and security. However, it does not offer several benefits as the public one, such as no up-front capital costs.
3. **Hybrid Clouds:** A hybrid cloud is a combination of public and private clouds. In a hybrid cloud, part of the service infrastructure runs in private clouds while the remaining part are performed in public clouds.

4. **Virtual Private Cloud:** Virtual private cloud is also known as Community cloud. It is an alternative solution to address the limitations of both public and private clouds.

Cloud-based services are provided on-demand, scalable, device-independent, and reliable. The core technology of cloud computing is centralizing computing, services, and specific applications as an utility to be sold as a service like water, gas, or electricity to users (Han & Gani, 2012). The emergence of cloud computing presents a tremendous impact on the information technology (IT) industry over the past few years where large companies, such as Google, Amazon, or Microsoft strive to provide more powerful, reliable, and cost-efficient cloud platforms (Zhang *et al.*, 2010). Business enterprises seek to reshape their business models to gain benefit from this new paradigm. Indeed, cloud computing provides several compelling features that make it attractive to business owners, as shown in the following paragraphs.

No up-front investment: Cloud computing uses a pay-as-you-go pricing model. A service provider does not need to invest in the infrastructure to start gaining benefit from cloud computing. It simply rents resources from the cloud according to its own needs and pay for the usage. Thereby allowing companies to start small and increase hardware resources only when there is an increase in their needs.

Lowering operating cost: Resources in a cloud environment can be rapidly allocated and de-allocated on demand. It is the ability to pay for use of computing resources on a short-term basis as needed (for instance, processors by hour and storage by day) and release them as needed, thereby rewarding conservation by letting machines and storage go when they are no longer in use.

Highly scalable: The appearance of infinite computing resources available on demand, quickly enough to follow load surges. A service provider can easily expand its service to large scales in order to handle rapid increase in service demands (e.g., flash-crowd effect). This model is sometimes called surge computing (Armbrust *et al.*, 2009).

Easy access: Services hosted in a cloud are generally Web-based. Therefore, they are easily accessible through a variety of devices with Internet connection, even fixed or mobile.

Reducing business risks and maintenance expenses: The outsourcing service is already known by most of IT enterprises. This type of service used by cloud provider shifts its business risks to infrastructure providers who should have better expertise, knowledge, and may be better equipped for managing these risks. In addition, a service provider can cut down the hardware maintenance and the staff training costs.

Currently, it is possible to split the available applications in two main different approaches: Offline applications and Online applications. Most of the applications available for current mobile devices belong to the online category. The applications run on a client, which processes the presentation and business logic layer locally on mobile device with data downloaded from backend systems. The synchronization between a client and backend system is periodical. Online approach assumes the connection between mobile devices and Internet is available most of the time. The Online

approach dreams and try to play a crucial role enabling the next generation mobile applications. It is so called the application mobility, which is the act of moving application between hosts during their execution. Basically, application mobility performs the migration during the application execution from one device to another allowing and giving to the user an immediate access (Ahlund, Mitra, Johansson, Ahlund, & Zaslavsky, 2009; Koponen, Gurtov, & Nikander, 2004).

3. MOBILE CLOUD COMPUTING

It is considered that mobile cloud computing is at its infancy and, as above-mentioned, its definition still under discussion in the community. There are several proposals available in the related literature and, mainly, different research groups and experts mentions two main approaches for the "mobile cloud" concept.

Generally, the term mobile cloud computing refers to the execution of an application on a remote resource rich server, while a mobile device acts like a thin client connecting to the remote server such as wireless networks and 3G. In this context, mobile cloud computing is the information what a mobile device will get. This concept is also known by Agent-client scheme, which tries to help and to overcome limitations of mobile devices, in particular, the processing power and data storage (Guan et al., 2011). Then, it refers to performing computing activities (data storage and processing) in a cloud infrastructure and let mobile devices being simple terminals to access services. This centralized approach presents the advantage that mobile devices do not need to possess a powerful computing capacity. However, its drawback comes from the fact that users strongly depend from the network infrastructure and its performance (Anh-Dung, Senac, & Ramiro, 2011).

Another approach considers mobile devices as resource providers of the cloud performing a mobile peer-to-peer network. This approach is also known as Collaborated scheme or Ad-hoc scheme. This scheme regards mobile devices as part of a cloud environment. Cloud server may assume the function of controller and scheduler to manage the collaboration among devices. Then, this second approach defines mobile cloud computing as performing computing activities on a mobile platform. A mobile cloud network is an infrastructure extension to the traditional cloud infrastructure where mobile devices are service clients but also part of the cloud, providing hardware and software resources. Mobile clients interact using the same old way with a cloud service provider. This means that they use native mobile applications or embedded browser applications.

Mobile cloud computing is also based on cloud computing concepts. This means that mobile cloud presents certain requirements that should be assembled in a cloud environment, such as self-services on-demand, broad network access, resource pooling, rapid elasticity, and measured services. To sum up, the mentioned characteristics allow a consumer provisioning computing capabilities including server time, network storage, the use of heterogeneous client platforms, the rapidly and elastically provisioned capabilities, and the automatic control in a level of abstraction appropriate to the type of service (e.g. storage, processing, bandwidth, and active user accounts). It is extremely versatile, capable, and exciting technology that offers many benefits to organizations and users overcoming the limitations seen today.

4. MOBILE CLOUD TECHNOLOGIES

Currently, data storage capabilities of mobile devices are increasing fast but their battery lifetime seems to even decrease compared to older less capable models (Kovachev, Tian, & Klamma, 2012; K. Kumar & Yung-Hsiang, 2010). Thus, an important issue to be solved is related with energy conservation, which should be a priority on mobile

devices. Several known power-conservation techniques include turning off the handheld computing device screen when it is not needed, optimizing input/output (I/O) (Govil, Chan, & Wasserman, 1995), slowing down the CPU (Helmbold, Long, & Sherrod, 1996), among others. Furthermore, processing and memory capability also present several limitations. Therefore, in order to overcome these limitations several opens issues are identified and new technologies may appear: Partition and Offloading. Following, several approaches are considered in order to address the most relevant technologies on mobile cloud computing.

Partition

Partition scheme is used to statically divide a program into server and client tasks in order to reduce the energy consumed by the program (Li, Wang, & Xu, 2001). Currently, these applications running on weak devices are defined at the beginning which part will be statically partitioned between a weak device and a server running in a cloud. Two representative applications partitions are as follows. First, most of applications processing is performed at servers (in a cloud environment) and the end-user device runs simple tasks such as user interfaces, acting such as a thin client. For example, Facebook (Facebook, 2013) and Twitter (Twitter, 2013) clients belong to this category. Second, most of applications processing is performed at the client as exhibited in interactive and graphics-intensive games. These different partitions incur different costs (e.g., execution time, energy consumption, etc.) (Chun & Maniatis, 2010). Giurgiu *et al.* (Giurgiu, Riva, Juric, Krivulev, & Alonso, 2009) develop an application middleware that can automatically distribute different layers of an application between a device and a server while optimizing several parameters. The core of this approach is a module to manage automatically and dynamically decision-making when and which application parts should be offloaded in order to achieve the best performance or the minimal cost.

Offloading

The contemporary mobile devices do not depend on local applications. Unlike local applications, smartphones or tablet computers let data centers and Internet servers handle part of users' daily data processing tasks. Services such as weather information, instant messaging, social media, eMail, and also document processing are delivered through Web-based applications that run entirely or partially on a remote server. It is the offloading technology (Karthik Kumar, Liu, Lu, & Bhargava, 2013).

It is easy to highlight the enormous advantages that some remote processing tasks facilities offload all the processing tasks from mobile devices. Thus, the low/limited mobile devices processing power and memory capability are hidden by the desktop computers, which, currently, are much more powerful. Offloading or augmented execution refers to a technique of computation, memory, and battery. Such applications, which can adaptively be split and partially offloaded are called *elastic mobile applications*. Basically, this model of elastic mobile applications enable the developers the illusion as whether he/she is programming virtually more powerful mobile devices than current capabilities. Additionally, elastic mobile applications can run as stand-alone mobile applications but also use external resources adaptively. Parts of an application are executed remotely is decided at runtime based on resources availability. Differently to traditional client/server applications that include static code partitioning, the data and business logic on offload applications is performed at a development phase (Kovachev et al., 2012).

Offloading of a mobile computing task is a tradeoff between the energy used for local processing and the energy required for task offloading, uploading its data and downloading the result, if necessary (Lagerspetz & Tarkoma, 2011). Lagerspetz and Tarkoma (2011) express the offloading energy trade-off with the Equation (1).

$$E_{trade} = E_{local} - E_{delegate} > 0 \qquad (1)$$

where E_{local} is the energy consumed for complete local execution and $E_{delegate}$ is the energy consumed from the perspective of a mobile device if the task is offloaded. If E_{trade} is greater than zero, then there is an energy benefit for delegating the task to the cloud. The authors break down this primary equation and explain all the process on their evaluation to understand which and what applications and environments can benefit of offloading. With the performance analysis and measurements, they proposed the following guidelines:

1. Tasks with little or no data should always be offloaded;
2. Tasks with heavy computation requirements can be offloaded;
3. Tasks that require secondary data transfers of greater length than required by offloading should be offloaded.

They provide an excellent example: indexing of HTML documents or PDFs. These files contain references and links to other documents of the same type and other resources on the Internet. While it would require a lot of energy and time for the mobile device to download, index, and rank these documents, the cloud is well connected to the Internet and has a virtually unlimited energy supply. So these types of tasks are best offloaded to the cloud.

Both Approaches (Partition and Offloading)

In several cases, some authors considered the use of the both technologies, partition and offloading. In C. Wang and Li (2004), the authors developed a program partition scheme, which determines whether and how to offload the computation of a given program. They first collected profiling information of computation time and data sharing at the level of procedure calls. Based on that, the authors created a cost graph for the given program and applied a task mapping algorithm to statically divide the program into server tasks and client tasks such that the energy consumed by the program is minimized.

5. CHALLENGES OF MOBILE CLOUD COMPUTING

Mobile computing presents several constraints and for a given cost and technology level, considerations of weight, power, size, and ergonomics will exact a penalty in computational resources, such as, processor speed, memory size, and disk capacity (Satyanarayanan, 1996). The properties previously described include several limitations of mobile devices, which will be described in the following subsections. Almost all the innovations come from the necessity. Then, mobile cloud computing become more useful after solving several identified issues. Mobile cloud computing services are deployed in mobile wireless environments incorporating several challenges (Guan *et al.*, 2011; Jing, Helal, & Elmagarmid, 1999).

Network Latency and Limited Bandwidth in a Mobile Network

Network latency and limited bandwidth is the first challenge that mobile cloud computing needs to face. The transmission channel, due to the intrinsic nature and constraints of wireless networks and devices, is a true challenge when it comes to rich-Internet and immersive mobile applications. Examples of these applications include online gaming, image retrieval, voice recognition, and augmented reality that require high processing capacity. These instances will probably continue to be processed locally, limited to smartphones and tablets computers hardware. Several authors already studied solutions, such as, downstream data peak reduction or optimization of upstream packetization overhead (Simoens, De Turck, Dhoedt, & Demeester, 2011).

Various Access Scheme in Mobile Environment

Mobile cloud computing should be deployed in a heterogeneous access scenario with different radio access technologies, such as, GPRS, 3G, WLAN, and WiMax. Constant and speedy Internet connectivity must be ensured in mobile cloud computing. Following the directive that mobile devices should always be connected to a cloud anytime and anywhere. Under this challenge, mobile cloud computing can explore at the HTML5 technology which realized the solution by enabling data caching through a mobile device and this turns it possible for several cloud applications to continue working in case of interrupted connectivity.

Elastic Application Models

Cloud computing services are scalable since mobile cloud computing uses cloud computing technologies, gains that characteristic by inheritance. It is assumed that scalable means that specific applications can run as an usual mobile application, but they can also reach transparently remote computing resources. Thus, elastic application models should be proposed to solve fundamental processing problems faced at mobile devices.

Security and Privacy

Nowadays, both personal and professional life gains a mutual space and not only in cloud computing but also in every area of technology, security and privacy is a key issue. Usually, users prove their identities with digital credentials, typically passwords and digital certificates. If some of those data are stolen or someone manages to use fake credentials, the cloud would present serious problems. To improve mobile cloud computing is necessary to include resolutions to the lack of computing power to execute sophisticated security algorithms (Guan *et al.*, 2011).

Table 1. Challenges and solutions of mobile cloud computing

Challenges	Solutions
Limitations of mobile devices	Virtualization and Image, Task migration
Quality of communication	Bandwidth upgrading, Data delivery time reducing
Division of applications services	Elastic application division mechanism

Table 1 presents a summary, identifying several challenges and including the corresponding proposed solutions to mobile cloud computing.

6. APPLICATIONS AND FUTURE TRENDS OF MOBILE CLOUD COMPUTING

Mobile applications gain increasing importance in a global mobile market. Due to devices limitation, such as storage or network bandwidth, developers have used and taken advantages of the cloud computing technology. Currently, it is possible to find several mobile applications already connected to a cloud, such as Apple iCloud (Apple, 2013), Google's Gmail for Mobile (Google, 2013c), and Google Goggles (Google, 2013b). In these applications, all the computation tasks are performed on cloud and mobile devices play role purely as thin clients. In the following, mobile cloud applications are identified and briefly described, illustrating the popularity of the topic and the vast plethora of interested areas.

Image Processing

In terms of image processing, as the natural language processing, has been a topic under intensive research and has been yielded significant results for the community. In Cheng, Balan, and Satyanarayanan (2005), the authors focus on experiments on an optical character recognition (OCR),

called GOCR (Schulenburg, 2013), a text to audio synthesizing tool, called Festival-Lite (Black & Lenzo, 2013), and a language translation tool, called Pangloss-Lite (Frederking & Brown, 1996). These three types of applications are highly useful for mobile users. For example, a foreign traveller can take an image of a museum sign, perform OCR on it to extract the words, and then translate the words into a known language using a language translator. The results presented by the authors show that data decomposition could greatly improve application latency by 85%, in some cases, compared with using just a single remote execution server. Another research work (Huerta-Canepa & Lee, 2010) uses a different philosophy, which is more similar and more coherent with the mobile cloud definition. Recent research connect via Internet to a remote server, would mean that use roaming data, which is too expensive. Instead, a user device scans for nearby users/devices who are also interested to read the description and request sharing their mobile resources and the task may be executed collaboratively. Those who are interested in this common processing task create an ad hoc network together, and this mobile cloud is able to extract the text and, then, translate it to the native language. An example of this application may be applied in a museum; however, this can be applied to many situations in which a group is involved in an activity together.

Education

Cloud education or cloud learning is a new and emerging concept associated with cloud computing (Hirsch & Ng, 2011; Kim, Song, & Yoon, 2011). In Minjuan and Ng (2012), the authors define cloud learning as a shared pool of learning courses, digital assets, and resources, which instructors and learners can access via computers, laptops, TVs, or mobile devices. They found some characteristics of cloud learning, which include storage and sharing, universal accessibility, collaborative interactions, and learner centered.

Jian (2010) summarizes the characteristics and models of traditional mobile learning, analyzes the features of cloud computing, and clarifies the development superiority of the mobile learning model in a cloud computing environment. The author concludes that cloud computing provides a new solution to mobile learning and its obvious advantage promotes the popularization and development of mobile learning.

Assisted Healthcare

With the advance of information and communication technologies, current healthcare systems are being transformed from a traditional scenario that requires manual care and monitoring for an advanced scenario where patients are automatically monitored and get fast emergency response using mobile sensing technologies, wireless sensor networks, and sophisticated back-end emergency processing centers (Kern & Jaron, 2003; Wells, 2003). In Hoang and Lingfeng (2010), the authors proposed a new solution (called Mobile Cloud for Assistive Healthcare - MoCAsH) that includes a cloud platform designed to deal with different issues, such as, deployment difficulty in grid technologies, network selection limitations, power limitations of mobile devices, and context-sensitive data and applications that are relevant for an assistive healthcare infrastructure. The proposed MoCAsH relies on intelligent mobile agents and context-aware sensor records for monitoring and power/resource-saving.

Filtering Content

Mobile devices can be seen as tools that can be used in diverse environment and enable applications for collecting a plethora of context-aware data. In order to provide suitable services, the context-ware reasoning technique has been studied to provide better services for users considering users' context and personal profile information in mobile environments (Biegel & Cahill, 2004; Hess & Campbell, 2003; Khungar & Riekki, 2004; Tao, Pung, & Da Qing, 2004). Furthermore, several recommendation techniques have been studied to provide the most relevant information depending on users' information and user's context. Recently, many studies based on ubiquitous environment are progressing and context is collected various elements like time, location, companion, condition, etc. They are used to perform the recommendation estimation about items, improving certainly the recommendation accuracy. Chang et. al. (2012) propose a recommendation technique that considers resource usage frequency, context location, and time. The information can be collected to the mobile cloud computing by mobile phones, PDAs, watches, shoes, among others.

Sharing GPS/Navigation

Location based applications (LBAs) present some inherent limitations surrounding energy and such as example is the global position system (GPS). It is well known for being extremely power-hungry (Ma, Cui, & Stojmenovic, 2012). Experiments have shown that GPS is able to run continuously for 9 hours only, while Wi-Fi and GSM can be sustained for 40 and 60 hours, respectively. In the last few years, researchers tried to amend this issue and created the dynamic tracking. The basic idea of being dynamic comes from the fact that it tries to minimize the frequency of needed position updates by only sampling positions (generally, with GPS) when the estimated uncertainty in a position exceeds the accuracy threshold (Kj *et al.*, 2011; Kj *et al.*, 2009; Zhuang, Kim, & Singh, 2010). Another example is Rate-Adaptive Positioning System (RAPS) (Paek, Kim, & Govindan, 2010). It uses a collection of techniques to cleverly determine when GPS should be turned on. RAPS uses the location-time history of the user to estimate user velocity and adaptively, and turn ON the GPS only when the estimated uncertainty in a position exceeds the accuracy threshold. To make this approach to be more efficiently, RAPS estimates user movement using a duty-cycled accelerometer, and utilizes Bluetooth communication to reduce position uncertainty among neighbor devices. The authors evaluated RAPS through real-world experiments using a prototype deployment and showed that it increases the battery lifetime. In (Vallina-Rodriguez & Crowcroft, 2011), is presented ErdOS, a user-centered energy-aware operations systems that extends the battery life of mobile devices by exploiting opportunistic access to resources in nearby devices using social connections between users. To perform their studies, authors chose the scenario of the natural park in the Arctic Circle. The dataset contains Bluetooth scans and GPS reading of 17 conference attendees during a day and the results show that is possible to save up to 11% of energy by sharing GPS readings (Angin, Bhargava, & Helal, 2010).

Sensor Data Applications

Most mobile devices are equipped with sensors (e.g. accelerometer and a GPS). Usually, GPS receptor, accelerometer, light sensor, microphone, thermometer, clock, and compass are considered. Most of them are used for gaming or ambient assisted living solutions. For instance, Lopes, Vaidya, and Rodrigues (2011) use the mobile device accelerometer for numerous applications, such as tracking objects or elderly people monitoring. They proposed and presented an application tool based on an accelerometer, called SensorFall, to detect and report the acceleration caused by a fall movement. After, the application sends alerts in a form of SMS or phone call.

Multimedia Search

Multimedia has been seen as a topic that presents lots of potential moving to the mobile cloud or just the cloud. Under commercial use, can be found several applications that are vastly used by mobile users. Google Goggles (Google, 2013b) is one of them. It allows users taking a picture and

search over the Google databases and had access to innumerous resources/information about the place, the object, or even similar images. Shazam (Shazam Entertainment, 2013) and SoundHound (SoundHound, 2013) are a music identification services for mobile devices, which searches for similar songs in a central database using a piece of the music. In Lagerspetz and Tarkoma (2011), the authors proposed a global cloud-assisted search, which can alleviate mobile device processing and energy usage in several ways. They analyzed the trade-off between local and remote processing from the viewpoint of energy use, taking into account the energy used for transferring the task from the local system to a remote service. When weakly connected to the network, a mobile device should offload computationally expensive tasks and delay offloading data intensive tasks. When a WLAN hotspot with sufficient bandwidth available is detected; data intensive tasks may be offloaded. The experiments indicate about 97.6% improvement in a basic indexing scenario with English text files. Furthermore, it shows that cloud-assisted search can be enhanced with various social networking and collaborative filtering solutions.

Mobile Gaming

Mobile gaming possibilities changed in 2006-2007 with the introduction of the first generation of smartphones (Feijoo et. al., 2012). With the appearance of the iPhone (late 2007) the mobile gaming changed dramatically. This smartphone allowed a combination of new possibilities in the handset, such as touch screen, motion sensor, enhanced display, heavy storage, and high-quality audio, among others. The ubiquitous connection to the network bring many innovations, including application stores, playing online while moving, multi-player games, and more advantages.

Cloud gaming is a new kind of service which combines the successful concepts of cloud computing and online gaming (Jarschel, Schlosser, Scheuring, & Hoßfeld, 2013). The service essentially moves the processing power required to render a game away from the user device into a data center. Traditionally only multiplayer games use a network where clients are connected to a server, which controls the game environment, receives input commands and sends out status updates. In cloud gaming the entire user experience, or even in part, must be delivered through the network.

Nowadays, games are the worst "enemy" of mobile devices batteries life. In research, are found several improvements to increase the performance and battery lifetime using a cloud. Several studies show that manufacturing industry moves forward slowly (battery capacity grow by only 5% annually (Ma *et al.*, 2012). So, games run in a cloud environment and gamers only interact with the screen interface on their devices. Lamberti and Sanna (2007) proposed a streaming-based system where a cluster of PCs equipped with accelerated graphics cards, managed by the Chromium software, was able to handle remote visualization sessions based on MPEG video streaming involving complex 3D models. Chromium allows complex 3D geometries to be rendered at high frame rates, increasing the number of rendering nodes. The authors obtain MPEG streams displayable at 30 ftp at the client side and consider that represents a crucial step in an ongoing effort to build a comprehensive client-server 3D rendering framework. Allowing mobile users to interact with intensive graphics without noticing that most of the processing is done on a remote server. Cuervo et al. (2010) present MAUI, a system that enables fine-grained energy-aware offload of mobile code to the infrastructure. MAUI uses offloading and partition techniques to maximize energy savings with minimal programmer effort. A number of experiments to evaluate the energy used for game applications with 3G network and Wi-Fi network were conducted. Instead of offloading all the codes to the cloud for processing, MAUI partitions the application codes in runtime based on the costs of network communication at the mobile device to maximize the energy savings depending on

network connectivity. In their evaluation, the authors demonstrate that MAUI improves the performance of two different aspects: *i*) increases energy reduction significantly for mobile devices (saves 27% for several games and, in a particular case, a chess game, reduce about 45%) and *ii*) improves the game refresh rate, which increases from 6 to 13 frames per second). Summarizing MAUI, the code is offloaded to a remote server only if MAUI predicts that remote execution ends up savings energy.

In Chu, Song, Wong, Kurakake, and Katagiri (2004), a seamless application framework, called the Roam system, is presented. Roam system was developed to build multi-platform applications that can are executed on heterogeneous devices and allows users to move a running application among heterogeneous devices in an effortless manner. Differently from the above-mentioned system (MAUI), the Roam system is based on an application partitioning into components and it automatically selects the most appropriate adaptation strategy for the target platform. The authors evaluate the system creating several multi-platform Roam applications, such as Chess game and a Connect4 game. In S. Wang and Dey (2010), the authors propose a rendering adaptation technique, which can adapt the game rendering parameters to satisfy the mobile cloud gaming communication and several constraints. Experiments demonstrate the proposed rendering adaptation techniques and the mobile cloud approach are feasible. Ensuring protection against wireless network conditions and the server computation scalability provides an acceptable mobile gaming user experience.

7. CONCLUSION

This chapter overviews mobile cloud computing and presents the most relevant insights about the topic. The diverse definitions of mobile cloud computing are introduced because the related literature still have different proposals about the topic. However, the concepts are closer and the increasing interest by the research community is significant given the enormous potential of these technologies. Cloud computing were considered in order to establish a bridge to mobile cloud computing, considering the used technologies (partition and offloading) and who/when can be useful. Subsequently, several applications and future trends were explored, presented, and discussed. These applications address distinct areas showing that mobile cloud computing is already used and a plethora of applications already available in online stores are useful for people's daily life.

ACKNOWLEDGMENT

This work has been partially supported by the *Instituto de Telecomunicações*, Next Generation Networks and Applications Group (NetGNA), Portugal, and by national funding from the *Fundação para a Ciência e a Tecnologia* (FCT) through the PEst-OE/EEI/LA0008/2011 project.

REFERENCES

Ahlund, A., Mitra, K., Johansson, D., Ahlund, C., & Zaslavsky, A. (2009). *Context-aware application mobility support in pervasive computing environments*. Paper presented at the 6th International Conference on Mobile Technology, Application Systems. Nice, France.

Amazon Web Services. (2013). *Amazon elastic compute cloud (Amazon EC2), cloud computing servers*. Retrieved 22 March 2013, from http://aws.amazon.com/ec2/

Angin, P., Bhargava, B., & Helal, S. (2010). *A mobile-cloud collaborative traffic lights detector for blind navigation*. Paper presented at the Mobile Data Management (MDM). New York, NY.

Anh-Dung, N., Senac, P., & Ramiro, V. (2011). *How mobility increases mobile cloud computing processing capacity*. Paper presented at the Network Cloud Computing and Applications (NCCA). New York, NY.

Apple (2013). *iCloud*. Retrieved 22 March 2013, from http://www.apple.com/icloud/

Armbrust, M., Fox, A., Griffith, R., Joseph, A. D., Katz, R. H., Konwinski, A., & Zaharia, M. (2009). *Above the clouds: A Berkeley view of cloud computing*. Berkeley, CA: EECS Department, University of California..

Biegel, G., & Cahill, V. (2004). *A framework for developing mobile, context-aware applications*. Paper presented at the Pervasive Computing and Communications, 2004. New York, NY.

Black, A. W., & Lenzo, K. A. (2013). *FLITE: A small fast run-time synthesis engine*. Retrieved March 2013, from http://www.speech.cs.cmu.edu/flite/

Chang, H., Kang, Y., Bae, Y., Ahn, H., & Choi, E. (2012). Filtering technique on mobile cloud computing. *Energy Procedia*, *16*, 1305–1311. doi:10.1016/j.egypro.2012.01.209.

Cheng, J., Balan, R. K., & Satyanarayanan, M. (2005). *Exploiting rich mobile environments*.

Christensen, J. H. (2009). *Using RESTful web-services and cloud computing to create next generation mobile applications*. Paper presented at the 24th ACM SIGPLAN Conference Companion on Object Oriented Programming Systems Languages and Applications. Orlando, FL.

Chu, H.-H., Song, H., Wong, C., Kurakake, S., & Katagiri, M. (2004). Roam, a seamless application framework. *Journal of Systems and Software*, *69*(3), 209–226. doi:10.1016/S0164-1212(03)00052-9.

Chun, B.-G., & Maniatis, P. (2010). *Dynamically partitioning applications between weak devices and clouds*. Paper presented at the 1st ACM Workshop on Mobile Cloud Computing Services: Social Networks and Beyond. San Francisco, CA.

Cuervo, E., Balasubramanian, A., Cho, D.-K., Wolman, A., Saroiu, S., Chandra, R., & Bahl, P. (2010). *MAUI: Making smartphones last longer with code offload*. Paper presented at the 8th International Conference on Mobile Systems, Applications, and Services. San Francisco, CA.

Entertainment, S. (2013). *Welcome to Shazam*. Retrieved 22 March 2013, from http://www.shazam.com

Facebook (2013). Retrieved 22 March 2013, from http://www.facebook.com

Feijoo, C., & Jos, G-L., Mez-Barroso, & Ramos, S. (2012). Mobile gaming: Industry challenges and policy implications. *Telecommunications Policy*, *36*(3), 212–221. doi:10.1016/j.telpol.2011.12.004.

Fernando, N., Loke, S. W., & Rahayu, W. (2013). Mobile cloud computing: A survey. *Future Generation Computer Systems*, *29*(1), 84–106. doi:10.1016/j.future.2012.05.023.

Flexiscale (2013). *Flexiant cloud computing services, cloud software and cloud hosting provider*. Retrieved from http://www.flexiscale.com

Frederking, R. E., & Brown, R. D. (1996). *The pangloss-lite machine translation system*. Paper presented at the ExpandingMT Horizons. Montreal, Canada.

Giurgiu, I., Riva, O., Juric, D., Krivulev, I., & Alonso, G. (2009). *Calling the cloud: Enabling mobile phones as interfaces to cloud applications*. Paper presented at the ACM/IFIP/USENIX 10th International Conference on Middleware. Urbana, IL.

Gmb, H. P. I. H. (2013). *Virtualization and automation solutions for desktops, servers, hosting, SaaS - Parallels*. Retrieved 22 March 2013, from http://www.parallels.com/

GoGrid. (2013). *Deploy public, private or dedicated cloud servers in minutes*. Retrieved 22 March 2013, from http://www.gogrid.com

Google. (2013a). *Google app. engine*. Retrieved 22 March 2013, from http://developers.google.com/appengine/

Google. (2013b). *Google goggles*. Retrieved 22 March 2013, from http://www.google.com/mobile/goggles/

Google. (2013c). *Google mobile*. Retrieved 22 Mar 2013, from http://www.google.com/mobile/mail

Govil, K., Chan, E., & Wasserman, H. (1995). *Comparing algorithm for dynamic speed-setting of a low-power CPU*. Paper presented at the 1st Annual International Conference on Mobile Computing and Networking. Berkeley, CA.

Guan, L., Ke, X., Song, M., & Song, J. (2011). *A survey of research on mobile cloud computing*. Paper presented at the Computer and Information Science (ICIS). New York, NY.

Han, Q., & Gani, A. (2012). *Research on mobile cloud computing: Review, trend and perspectives*. Paper presented at the Digital Information and Communication Technology and it's Applications (DICTAP). New York, NY.

Helmbold, D. P., Long, D. D. E., & Sherrod, B. (1996). *A dynamic disk spin-down technique for mobile computing*. Paper presented at the 2nd Annual International Conference on Mobile Computing and Networking. New York, NY.

Hess, C. K., & Campbell, R. H. (2003). An application of a context-aware file system. *Personal and Ubiquitous Computing*, *7*(6), 339–352. doi:10.1007/s00779-003-0250-y.

Hirsch, B., & Ng, J. W. P. (2011). *Education beyond the cloud: Anytime-anywhere learning in a smart campus environment*. Paper presented at the Internet Technology and Secured Transactions (ICITST). New York, NY.

Hoang, D. B., & Lingfeng, C. (2010). *Mobile cloud for assistive healthcare (MoCAsH)*. Paper presented at the Services Computing Conference (APSCC). New York, NY.

Holden, W. (2013). *Juniper research - Mobile telecoms research*. Retrieved from http://www.juniperresearch.com

Huerta-Canepa, G., & Lee, D. (2010). *A virtual cloud computing provider for mobile devices*. Paper presented at the 1st ACM Workshop on Mobile Cloud Computing Services: Social Networks and Beyond. San Francisco, CA.

Jarschel, M., Schlosser, D., Scheuring, S., & Hoßfeld, T. (2013). Gaming in the clouds: QoE and the users' perspective. *Mathematical and Computer Modelling, 57*(11–12), 2883–2894. doi:10.1016/j.mcm.2011.12.014.

Jian, L. (2010). *Study on the development of mobile learning promoted by cloud computing*. Paper presented at the Information Engineering and Computer Science (ICIECS). New York, NY.

Jing, J., Helal, A. S., & Elmagarmid, A. (1999). Client-server computing in mobile environments. *ACM Computing Surveys, 31*(2), 117–157. doi:10.1145/319806.319814.

Kadu, C., Bhanodiya, P., & Samvatsar, M. (2012). Review of challenges in accessing cloud services through mobile devices. *International Journal of Scientific & Engineering Research, 3*(11).

Kern, S. E., & Jaron, D. (2003). Healthcare technology, economics, and policy: An evolving balance. *IEEE Engineering in Medicine and Biology Magazine, 22*(1), 16–19. doi:10.1109/MEMB.2003.1191444 PMID:12683057.

Khungar, S., & Riekki, J. (2004). *A context based storage for ubiquitous computing applications*. Paper presented at the 2nd European Union Symposium on Ambient Intelligence. Eindhoven, The Netherlands.

Kim, S., Song, S.-M., & Yoon, Y.-I. (2011). Smart learning services based on smart cloud computing. *Sensors (Basel, Switzerland), 11*(8), 7835–7850. doi:10.3390/s110807835 PMID:22164048.

Kj, M. B., Bhattacharya, S., Blunck, H., & Nurmi, P. (2011). *Energy-efficient trajectory tracking for mobile devices*. Paper presented at the 9th International Conference on Mobile Systems, Applications, and Services. Bethesda, MD.

Kj, M. B., Langdal, J., Godsk, T., & Toftkj, T. (2009). *EnTracked: Energy-efficient robust position tracking for mobile devices*. Paper presented at the 7th International Conference on Mobile Systems, Applications, and Services. Krakow, Poland.

KMV. (2013). *Kernal based virtual machine*. Retrieved 22 March 2013, from http://www.linux-kvm.org/page/MainPage

Koponen, T., Gurtov, A., & Nikander, P. (2004). *Application mobility with host identity protocol*. Paper presented at the Identifier/Locator Split and DHTs. Helsinki, Finland.

Kovachev, D., Tian, Y., & Klamma, R. (2012). *Adaptive computation offloading from mobile devices into the cloud*. Paper presented at the Parallel and Distributed Processing with Applications (ISPA). New York, NY.

Kumar, K., Liu, J., Lu, Y.-H., & Bhargava, B. (2013). A survey of computation offloading for mobile systems. *Mobile Networks and Applications, 18*(1), 129–140. doi:10.1007/s11036-012-0368-0.

Kumar, K., & Yung-Hsiang, L. (2010). Cloud computing for mobile users: Can offloading computation save energy? *Computer*, *43*(4), 51–56. doi:10.1109/MC.2010.98.

Lagerspetz, E., & Tarkoma, S. (2011). *Mobile search and the cloud: The benefits of offloading.* Paper presented at the Pervasive Computing and Communications Workshops (PERCOM Workshops). New York, NY.

Lamberti, F., & Sanna, A. (2007). A streaming-based solution for remote visualization of 3D graphics on mobile devices. *IEEE Transactions on Visualization and Computer Graphics*, *13*(2), 247–260. doi:10.1109/TVCG.2007.29 PMID:17218742.

Li, Z., Wang, C., & Xu, R. (2001). *Computation offloading to save energy on handheld devices: A partition scheme.* Paper presented at the 2001 International Conference on Compilers, Architecture, and Synthesis for Embedded Systems. Atlanta, GA.

Liu, L., Moulic, R., & Shea, D. (2010). *Cloud service portal for mobile device management.* Paper presented at the e-Business Engineering (ICEBE). New York, NY.

Lopes, I., Vaidya, B., & Rodrigues, J. P. C. (2011). Towards an autonomous fall detection and alerting system on a mobile and pervasive environment. *Telecommunication Systems*, 1–12. doi: doi:10.1007/s11235-011-9534-0.

Ma, X., Cui, Y., & Stojmenovic, I. (2012). Energy efficiency on location based applications in mobile cloud computing: A survey. *Procedia Computer Science*, *10*, 577–584. doi:10.1016/j.procs.2012.06.074.

MCCF. (2013). *Mobile cloud computing forum.* Retrieved from http://www.mobilecloudcomputingforum.com/

Mell, P., & Grance, T. (2011). The NIST definition of cloud computing (draft). *NIST Special Publication*, *800*, 145.

Microsoft. (2013). *Windows Azure.* Retrieved 22 March 2013, from http://www.microsoft.com/azure

Minjuan, W., & Ng, J. W. P. (2012). *Intelligent mobile cloud education: Smart anytime-anywhere learning for the next generation campus environment.* Paper presented at the Intelligent Environments (IE). New York, NY.

Mirusmonov, M., Changsu, K., Yiseul, C., & Jongheon, K. (2012). *Mobile cloud computing: The impact of user motivation on actual usage.* Paper presented at the Computing and Networking Technology (ICCNT). New York, NY.

Paek, J., Kim, J., & Govindan, R. (2010). *Energy-efficient rate-adaptive GPS-based positioning for smartphones.* Paper presented at the 8th International Conference on Mobile Systems, Applications, and Services. San Francisco, CA.

Rackspace, U. I. (2013). *Open cloud computing.* Retrieved 22 March 2013, from http://www.rackspace.com

salesforce.com. (2013). *Salesforce platform.* Retrieved 22 March 2013, from http://www.salesforce.com/platform

Satyanarayanan, M. (1996). *Fundamental challenges in mobile computing.* Paper presented at the Fifteenth Annual ACM Symposium on Principles of Distributed Computing. Philadelphia, PA.

Schulenburg, J. (2013). *GORC.* Retrieved from http://jocr.sourceforge.net/

Simoens, P., De Turck, F., Dhoedt, B., & Demeester, P. (2011). Remote display solutions for mobile cloud computing. *Computer*, *44*(8), 46–53. doi:10.1109/MC.2011.70.

SoundHound. (2013). *SoundHound - Instant music search and discovery*. Retrieved 22 March 2013, from http://www.soundhound.com

Tao, G., Pung, H. K., & Da Qing, Z. (2004). *A middleware for building context-aware mobile services*. Paper presented at the Vehicular Technology Conference, 2004. New York, NY.

Twitter (2013). Retrieved from http://www.twitter.com

Vallina-Rodriguez, N., & Crowcroft, J. (2011). *ErdOS: Achieving energy savings in mobile OS*. Paper presented at the Sixth International Workshop on MobiArch. Bethesda, MD.

VMware. (2013). *VMWareESXServer*. Retrieved 22 May 2013, from http://www.vmware.com/products/esx

Wang, C., & Li, Z. (2004). A computation offloading scheme on handheld devices. *Journal of Parallel and Distributed Computing, 64*(6), 740–746. doi:10.1016/j.jpdc.2003.10.005.

Wang, S., & Dey, S. (2010). *Rendering adaptation to address communication and computation constraints in cloud mobile gaming*. Paper presented at the Global Telecommunications Conference (GLOBECOM 2010). New York, NY.

Weiguang, S., & Xiaolong, S. (2011). *Review of mobile cloud computing*. Paper presented at the Communication Software and Networks (ICCSN). New York, NY.

Wells, P. N. T. (2003). Can technology truly reduce healthcare costs? *IEEE Engineering in Medicine and Biology Magazine, 22*(1), 20–25. doi:10.1109/MEMB.2003.1191445 PMID:12683058.

XenSourceInc. (2013). *XenServer*. Retrieved from http://www.xensource.com

Zhang, Q., Cheng, L., & Boutaba, R. (2010). Cloud computing: State-of-the-art and research challenges. *Journal of Internet Services and Applications, 1*(1), 7–18. doi:10.1007/s13174-010-0007-6.

Zhong, L., Wang, B., & Wei, H. (2012). *Cloud computing applied in the mobile Internet*. Paper presented at the Computer Science & Education (ICCSE). New York, NY.

Zhuang, Z., Kim, K.-H., & Singh, J. P. (2010). *Improving energy efficiency of location sensing on smartphones*. Paper presented at the 8th International Conference on Mobile Systems, Applications, and Services. San Francisco, CA.

KEY TERMS AND DEFINITIONS

Cloud Computing: Model for enabling convenient, on-demand network access to a shared pool of configurable computing resources.

Mobile Cloud Computing: Combination of two technologies: mobile computing and cloud computing.

Offloading: Tradeoff between the energy used for local processing and the energy required.

Partition: Scheme to statically divide a program into server and client tasks in order to reduce the energy consumed.

Chapter 2
Mobile Cloud Media:
State of the Art and Outlook

Yi Xu
Auburn University, USA

Shiwen Mao
Auburn University, USA

ABSTRACT

Leveraging Mobile Cloud Computing (MCC), resource-poor mobile devices are now enabled to support rich media applications. In this chapter, the authors briefly review basic concepts and architecture of mobile cloud computing, and focus on the technical challenges of MCC for multimedia applications. Specifically, they discuss how to save energy, ensure Quality of Experience (QoE), deal with stochastic wireless channels, support security and privacy, and reduce network costs for rich media applications. Prototypes, ongoing standardization efforts, and commercial aspects are also reviewed. The authors conclude this chapter with a discussion of several open research problems that call for substantial research and regulation efforts.

1. INTRODUCTION

Mobile cloud computing is a new technology of increasing interest from industry, academia, and government. Cloud computing makes it possible to provide infrastructure, platform, and software as services for users from any computer with an Internet connection. Mobile cloud computing then extends such services to mobile devices. As there are six billion mobile phone subscribers world-

wide (Wikipedia, Mobile Phone), mobile cloud computing has the potential to have far-reaching impacts in the wireless industry and in our society.

Last decades have witnessed tremendous increase in the popularity of video and interactive video (such as video conferencing and online gaming). With the prosperity of mobile devices, there are huge interests for people to watch video and play online games on mobile devices. According to Cisco's recent study (Cisco 2013), among all the mobile data traffic across the world, 66.5% of them will be video related by 2017. This number

DOI: 10.4018/978-1-4666-4781-7.ch002

was 51% by the end of 2012. As mobile devices are limited by speed, memory and energy, they could not support rich media applications, were it not for cloud applications and services. It is forecasted that cloud applications will account for 84% of total mobile data traffic in 2017, compared to 74% at the end of 2012. These facts tell us that as the gap between the demand from users and capability from mobile devices never gets smaller, we have to resort to cloud computing for providing rich media application on mobile devices.

Although cloud computing is envisioned to bring rich media applications to mobile devices, several key challenges need to be addressed to fully harvest the high potential of mobile cloud computing. As the battery life of mobile device is rather limited, how to save energy is of great importance. Inherent from wireless communications, mobile cloud computing is characterized by limited bandwidth and large network latency. The intermittent network connection may also cause big problems for many cloud based applications. In face of fluctuating wireless networks and longer response time, how to ensure acceptable user experience is quite challenging. The open air interfaces make mobile cloud computing more susceptible to malicious attacks, and the distributed storage in the cloud may also result in privacy issues. Last but not least, online gaming or video streaming usually take an extended period of time and transmit a large amount of data, which may easily consume a user's data budget. The consumers may need to pay a lot to the wireless networking service provider. The relatively high network costs may prevent some consumers from using mobile cloud computing. In this chapter, we briefly review basic concepts and architecture of mobile cloud computing, and then focus on the technical challenges of MCC for multimedia applications. Specifically, we discuss how to save energy, ensure quality of experience (QoE), deal with stochastic wireless channel, support security and privacy and reduce network costs for rich media applications. Prototypes,

ongoing standardization efforts and commercial aspects are also reviewed. Finally, we discuss several open research problems in mobile cloud computing that call for substantial research and regulation efforts.

The remainder of this chapter is organized as follows. Section 2 discusses the basic concepts and architecture of mobile cloud computing. We discuss technical challenges and review proposed solutions of MCC for multimedia application in Section 3. Section 4 reviews prototyping, ongoing standardization efforts and commercial aspects. Open research problems are discussed in Section 5. Section 6 concludes this chapter.

2. BACKGROUND OF MOBILE MULTIMEDIA CLOUD

2.1. Mobile Computing

Generally speaking, mobile computing can be regarded as a combination of the enabling technologies, network infrastructures, software applications and electronic devices that enable access to the Internet at any time and any place. From a narrower point of view, mobile computing offers great flexibilities to access network services and helps to eliminate the time and place restrictions imposed by wired networks and traditionally fixed electronics.

Mobile computing directly benefits from the advances of wireless communication technologies. The enabling technologies include Wireless Local Area Network (WLAN) technologies such as Wi-Fi (IEEE 802.11 series), cellular technologies such as Long Term Evolution (LTE), Bluetooth, satellite communications, Femtocell, etc. With the development of these technologies and the deployment of network infrastructures, mobile device such as smartphone, tablet computer, GPS, etc. is enabled to connect to the Internet and run all kinds of software. Typical applications include mobile browser, mobile online gaming, positioning, and location-based services, etc.

Mobility is well supported by mobile computing. However, inherited from wireless communications, mobile computing has several limitations as follows.

- **Low Computational Capacity:** Due to the size limit of mobile devices, the computational capacity of mobile computing is one of the bottlenecks to further assist people's lives.
- **Intermittency of Network Connection:** Intermittency is of great concern for mobile computing since wireless networks are more susceptible to disconnection.
- **Low Bandwidth:** Since wireless networks usually have much lower bandwidth than their wired counterparts, bandwidth of mobile computing is another limitation.
- **Limited Power:** To support mobility, mobile device surely has limited power supply.
- **Security and Privacy Issue:** Since the wireless communications are conducted open in the air, mobile computing has higher risk of security and privacy leak.

2.2. Cloud Computing

In a broad sense, cloud computing can be regarded as the process of provisioning and consumption of computational resources in the Internet. Some of the vendors and experts consider cloud computing as an updated version of utility computing. Essentially, in cloud computing, computational resources are offered as a service in the cloud, which has a complex infrastructure and often denoted using a symbol of cloud.

The service model of cloud computing falls into three categories:

1. Infrastructure as a Service (IaaS), where computers and/or other resources are offered as service to users,

2. Platform as a Service (PaaS), where computing platforms (in the form of operating system, database, web server, or some programming environment) are provided as service to users, and

3. Software as a Service (SaaS), where computer software is provided as service for users.

Key features of cloud computing include the following.

- **Super Powerful Computing:** Since thousands of servers and computers can be pooled together in a complex structure, the cloud works as a super computer that is capable of massive computing. For instance, according to a recent report (Teicher 2012), Google Cloud has at least 1 million servers cumulatively, which are deployed worldwide.
- **Agility and Instant Elasticity:** For instance, the infrastructure provided by cloud computing service provider allows you to carry out computational intensive application instantly without waiting for new hardware.
- **Scalability:** The service of cloud computing is scalable and on-demand. The resources are provided on fine-grained and self-service basis in real-time. For instance, a business owner can request specific amount of storage which well fits his business demand.
- **Virtualization:** Basically, the cloud can be regarded as a virtual network of resources, which contains numerous servers and storage centers. Data processing or storage can be easily migrated from the end user to the cloud and from one server in the cloud to the other.
- **Low Cost:** Since the infrastructures are shared and the usage is on-demand, the cost is greatly reduced.

2.3. Mobile Cloud Computing

By integrating mobile computing and cloud computing, mobile cloud computing inherits the advantages of both technologies. Mobile cloud computing can be simply viewed as cloud computing for mobile devices. More specifically, data storage and data processing for mobile users can be outsourced to the cloud. In this way, mobility is well supported while the capability of mobile devices is greatly enhanced by the cloud. This technique is often termed as "offloading." For instance, the basic idea in (Zhu, 2012, January) is that based on packet delivery statistics, a media proxy at the cloud is envisioned to calculate the optimal media adaptation decisions on behalf of the mobile devices, which may be too difficult to carry out locally in the mobile device. This idea can be regarded as one of the applications of offloading. It is claimed in (Chun, 2009, May) that, the proposed architecture and approach therein is the first to have the whole smartphone image

and the application code replicated and run with least modifications in powerful virtual machine (VM) replicas.

The basic mobile cloud computing concept is illustrated in Figure 1. Computation tasks running on the users' mobile device (e.g., laptops, smartphones, tablets etc.) can be offloaded to the cloud via all kinds of wireless internet access methods (e.g., Wi-Fi, 3G networks, 4G networks, Femtocell, etc.).

Inside the cloud, the system contains two categories of servers (Wu, 2011, June): NFS (Network File System) storage servers and computing servers. The cloud consumer and cloud provider communicate via the Broker, while the Request Monitor listens to the requests and forwards them to the SLA Negotiator. NFS Scheduler is responsible for the content placement onto the NFS clusters. VM Scheduler carries out VM provisioning, which is tracked by VM Monitor. Service is charged based on a per time unit rate

Figure 1. Illustration of the basic mobile cloud computing concept

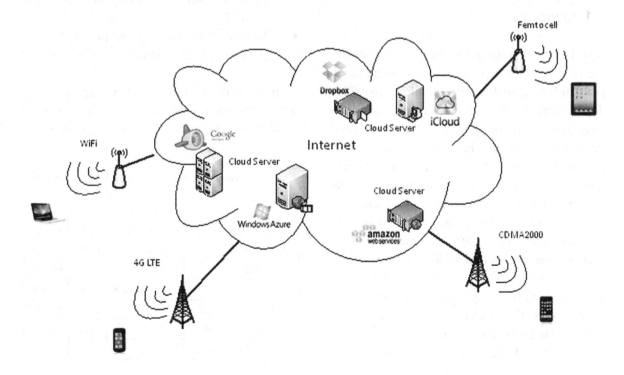

for the rental fees of the VMs to run application and the storage cost to use the NFS cluster.

A brief summary of the advantages of mobile cloud computing is given as follows.

- The computational burden on mobile devices is reduced, since the complicated data processing and massive data storage can be perform in the cloud.
- The battery life of mobile devices can be extended, since computing-intensive applications can be migrated to and carried out by the cloud.
- The reliability of mobile applications is reinforced. Since data is stored on multiple servers in the cloud, even if some data are lost in the mobile device, there are still backup copies in the cloud. Furthermore, when the battery of mobile device dies, the application can still be running without interruption in the cloud.

3. TECHNICAL CHALLENGES

3.1. Overview

Mobile cloud computing is designed to cater for the demand of more convenient access and more powerful computation for mobile users. The deployment of mobile cloud computing is still at its early stage. In this section, we briefly discuss the challenges need to be addressed and review proposed solutions. Briefly speaking, these challenges mainly stem from the limitation of mobile devices and unreliable wireless connections.

On one hand, although the computational capability, storage and battery life of mobile devices such as smartphones have been greatly enhanced during recent years, they are still comparatively weak in contrast with computers and more powerful servers. For instance, it is still difficult to run the popular Multiplayer Online Role Playing Game such as World of Warcraft (WoW) on mo-

bile devices. The storage space of mobile device is rather limited in contrast to PC. See Table 1 for an illustration of the disparity. And many mobile devices, especially smartphones need to be charged almost daily.

Meanwhile, mobile cloud computing relies on wireless networks (e.g., 3G and Wi-Fi) to transmit and receive data. Compared with fixed and wired networks, wireless networks have limited bandwidth, probably longer latency, and intermittent connectivity. Moreover, in the presence of many mobile devices, the bandwidth allocated to each device is further reduced, and network latency can go up and waiting time can be further increased.

In conclusion, the following technical challenges need to be addressed to fully harvest the high potential of mobile cloud computing for multimedia applications.

- How to offload computing tasks?
- How to save energy?
- How to cope with the limited bandwidth, intermittent connectivity and longer latency?
- How to ensure the quality of experience (QoE)?
- How to ensure security and privacy?
- How to minimize network service cost?

It is worth noting that rather than being independent, these challenges are interrelated to each other and even conflict with each other. For

Table 1. Comparison of mobile devices and the computers

Product	CPU (GHz)	RAM	Storage
Apple iPhone5	1.2 (dual-core)	1 GB	64 GB
Apple iPad	0.97 (dual-core)	1 GB	64 GB
Apple MacBook Pro	2.6 (quad-core)	8 GB	768 GB
Samsung Galaxy S III	1.5 (dual-core)	2 GB	16 GB
Samsung Galaxy Tab 2	1 (dual-core)	1 GB	32 GB
Samsung Series 7 Gamer	2.3 (quad-core)	16 GB	1.5 TB

instance, we could save energy by scheduling communications only when the user's signal is comparatively strong. But in that case, the user may have to wait for a long period of time or need to change his/her location to get a better channel. The delay will be unbearable in that case. And many aspects of the system is related to energy saving, even security assurance (Oberheide, 2008, June). Thus, many existing studies try to seek an optimal tradeoff between several objectives.

3.2. Energy Saving

One of the greatest challenges for mobile cloud computing is related to energy. In fact, limited battery life has been found as the biggest complaint for smart phones (Wen, 2011).

Generally, two main factors contribute to the energy problem: one is relatively limited battery capacity; the other is the soaring demand for energy-hungry applications (Cuervo, 2010, June). On one hand, although batteries last much longer than decades before with the advancement of new technologies, it is unlikely that the limited power supply problem for mobile devices would disappear in the near future. On the other hand, the ever-increasing user demands such as ubiquitous access, mobile online gaming, mobile video streaming, etc., only add fuel to the flame. One experiment carried out in (Cuervo, 2010, June) showed that it only took one hour and twenty minutes to drain the battery of an HTC Fuze running heavy task applications.

3.2.1. To Offload or Not To Offload?

Assisted by the cloud, multimedia applications can be either carried out in the mobile device or in the cloud. Executing the computing-intensive applications surely consumes lots of power of the mobile device. One may think that all the computing-intensive applications should be offloaded to and executed in the cloud. However, bulky data transmission, especially under unfavorable wireless channel conditions, could also consume a large amount of energy.

Therefore, given the size of the data packet L, the wireless channel condition and the application completion deadline T (i.e., the time before which the application must be completed otherwise users will lose patience), there is an optimal policy to determine where to execute current application so that the energy consumption of the mobile device is minimized. That is, if mobile execution consumes less power, then execute the application in the mobile device, and vice versa.

Y. Wen, et al investigated this problem in (Wen, 2011). For mobile execution, the energy consumption for each operation is proportional to the square of voltage supply (i.e., V^2), which is further proportional to the CPU clock frequency f. So the energy consumption per operation is given by:

$$\varepsilon_{op} = kf^2, \tag{1}$$

where k is a capacitance parameter. So if the application is carried out in the mobile device, the energy consumption can be minimized via optimally scheduling the CPU clock frequency which can be obtained by solving:

$$\varepsilon_m^* = \min_{\varphi \in \Psi} \{\varepsilon_m(L, T, \varphi)\}, \tag{2}$$

where φ is a chosen clock frequency and $\Psi = \{f_1, f_2, ..., f_w\}$ is the clock frequency vector. Recall that L is the data packet size and T is the application completion deadline.

For cloud execution, the energy consumption at the mobile device is related to the data transmission rate and the channel condition, which can be modelled as:

$$\varepsilon_t(s, g, n) = \lambda \frac{s^n}{g}, \tag{3}$$

where s denotes the transmission rate, g denotes the channel condition, λ denotes the energy coefficient, and n denotes the monomial order which ranges from 2 to 5 depending on the modulation scheme. So if the application is offloaded to the cloud, the energy consumption can be minimized through optimally scheduling the transmission data rate by solving:

$$\varepsilon_c^* = min_{\phi \in \Phi} \mathbb{E}\{\varepsilon_c (L, T, \phi)\}, \qquad (4)$$

where ϕ is a chosen data rate and $\Phi = \{s_1, s_2, ..., s_T\}$ is the data rate vector.

Solving these optimization problems, the followings results are found in (Wen, 2011).

$$\varepsilon_m^* \propto T^{-2}, \; \varepsilon_m^* \propto L^3. \qquad (5)$$

$$\varepsilon_c^* \propto T^{-(n-1)}, \; \varepsilon_c^* \propto L^n. \qquad (6)$$

With given data size, delay deadline and wireless channel condition, the optimal execution policy can be readily figured out. For instance, for an application profile $L=800bits$, $T=400ms$, when $n=5$ mobile execution consumes 13 times energy than cloud execution.

From another perspective, (Cuervo, 2010, June) also studied the problem of whether or not to offload so as to minimize energy cost. Previously, there were mainly two kinds of approaches for offloading. The first one relied on the programmer to specify how to partition a program and which states need to be offloaded adaptively. The second approach was to migrate the entire application to the cloud infrastructure. The first one was fine-grained and could lead to considerable energy savings. The second one saved less energy but reduced the burden on the programmer. In order to combine these benefits, MAUI was proposed in (Cuervo, 2010, June), which enabled fine-grained code offload to maximize energy savings with minimal burden on the programmer.

Specifically, in the architecture of MAUI, programmers annotate the methods of application that can be offloaded for remote execution in accordance with some rules (e.g., code that implements the application's user interface should not be marked as remotable). MAUI constantly measures the network condition and estimates the bandwidth and latency. When a remote server is available, MAUI uses its solver to determine the cost (e.g., number of states needs to be transferred) and benefit (e.g., number of CPU cycles saved) of offloading each option, and then makes a decision.

The evaluations show that MAUI saves approximately 90% energy for a face recognition application, 27% energy for a video game and 45% energy for a chess game. Besides, MAUI reduces 90% latency for a face recognition application, 75% latency for a video game and up to 62.5% latency for a chess game. Finally, MAUI successfully runs a Spanish to English translation application by leveraging cloud to overcome the memory limitation of the smartphone.

3.2.2. Wi-Fi or 3G?

With the evolution of wireless networks and mobile devices, mobile devices (e.g., iPhone5 and iPad) are enabled to upload any data such as videos and photos or offload any application simultaneously via Wi-Fi and 3G networks. Then there comes another question: which connection to use for the communication tasks?

In many circumstances (e.g. users are at home or office), the signal strength of Wi-Fi is much stronger than that of 3G networks. Hence, Wi-Fi usually outperforms 3G networks with respect to data rate and energy saving performance. An experiment carried out in (Cuervo, 2010, June) showed that smartphones may consume three times more energy using 3G than using Wi-Fi with 50 ms RTT (Round Trip Time); or even five times more energy using 3G than using Wi-Fi with 25 ms RTT. If an HTC Fuze phone (with a 1,340 mAH battery) keeps downloading a 100 kB file over 3G networks, its battery dies within 2 hours.

However, 3G networks provide ubiquitous acccss while the coverage of Wi-Fi is much more limited. In a broader sense, the signal strength from 3G networks could be much higher than that from any Wi-Fi depending on the location of the mobile device. Therefore, the balance between Wi-Fi and 3G networks could shift from side to side depending on time and location. It is important to investigate how to dynamically assign the packets to Wi-Fi and 3G networks, adjust the packet transmission duration, and control the transmission power on each interface according to the current channel conditions, so that the overall energy consumption of a mobile device is minimized. This interesting problem is discussed in (Wen, 2011, December).

The design objective is to minimize the overall energy consumption by optimally allocating packets to two interfaces (Wi-Fi and 3G) and scheduling the transmission durations given the wireless conditions, while satisfying a delay requirement. The formulated convex optimization problem in (Wen, 2011, December) is decoupled into two sequential sub-problems and then solved. Two interesting insights from the results are as follows.

- The optimal packet allocation policy depends on the noise power ratio of the two interfaces, which follows a "water-filling" pattern.
- For each interface, transmit the packets with equal duration while filling up the delay limit.

3.2.3. What to Do without Wi-Fi?

From the previous discussions, we know that Wi-Fi is a preferable choice if it is at favorable conditions. The questions are what can we do if Wi-Fi is unavailable? (Aggrawal, 2010, August) shows that even when only cellular networks are

available, we could still use aggregation, compression, and scheduling to reduce the energy cost.

Observing that cellular radio incurs significant delay and energy overhead when switching between the idle state and the active state, sending data to mobile device in intermittent spurts would consume much more energy. Thus, it is proposed to merge the data spurts into a single and sustained burst.

On the other hand, compression is often employed between the cloud-based proxy and the mobile device to reduce the transmission overhead. However, the overall energy saving may not be achieved without considering the overhead of decompression. The authors of (Aggarwal, 2010, August) thus proposed an asymmetric dictionary-based redundancy elimination technique with minimal decompression overhead. The bandwidth savings readily translate into energy savings. Since six times higher energy could be consumed with a weak signal than that with a strong signal, a scheduling mechanism is also introduced in (Aggarwal, 2010, August).

These techniques were implemented in a prototype called Stratus. The test results showed that 50% energy saving could be achieved for web browsing, and 35% energy saving could be achieved for media streaming using aggregation and scheduling. A demo is available at (Microsoft Research, 2011).

3.3. Ensuring QoE

Mobile devices have been able to display videos for several years. As video streaming is one-way communications, video conferencing and online gaming are essentially interactive two-way multimedia communications with tight delay constraints, which is a more challenging problem. We choose online gaming as an example for mobile cloud media application due to the following reasons:

- It is likely to be a popular application in mobile media cloud, where computational intensive online games can be enabled to run at mobile devices with assistance from the mobile could,
- Most online games are interactive applications requiring tight response time and synchronization among multiple users, and
- Most online games are video based and are computation/storage/communication-intensive, requiring QoS/QoE provisioning.

Conventionally, people play interactive multimedia and multiple player online games on their desktops or laptops. Recently, there are tremendous interests to extend these computation-intensive and latency-sensitive games on mobile devices. However, the challenge is, with the current PC-based gaming architecture, the storage and computation tasks are mostly carried out by the client's device, while mobile devices are not able to perform resource-intensive tasks. As a result, currently most online games for mobile devices are light, single-player based, involving a low-level of multimedia and providing limited user experience.

The good news is by leveraging cloud, the limitations of mobile device could be readily overcome, making interactive multimedia online gaming feasible for mobile devices. Furthermore, users can start playing a greater number of games without waiting for large files to be downloaded to the mobile device. (This approach also helps to protect the game software as the games are never downloaded to the clients.)

We focus on the users' experience. Note that QoS (Quality of Service) is from the designer's perspective, which emphasizes the technical parameters such as delay, packet loss, Peak Signal-to-Noise Ratio (PSNR), etc. QoE (Quality of Experience) is from the end user's experience, which is subjective. Different users could have different experiences towards the same content and parameters.

3.3.1. Gaming QoE Modelling

In (Wang, 2009, November), a cloud server based mobile gaming model was presented. The basic idea is to put the computational burden on cloud servers, while mobile devices just communicate the gaming commands to the servers. Their prototype implementation demonstrated the feasibility of mobile cloud online gaming.

Although there have been many efforts trying to model and understand video streaming and delivery over wireless networks, video quality metrics (e.g., PSNR) cannot be directly applied to model the QoE of mobile online gaming. Mobile online gaming is, by nature, highly interactive and extremely delay-sensitive two-way communications. The authors in (Wang, 2009, November) have identified various objective and subjective factors affecting cloud mobile gaming user experience (MGUE). For more general (wireless) video quality assessment, readers are referred to (Chikkerur, 2011; Moorthy, 2010; Seshadrinathan, 2010). The impacts of network factors are also examined in (Dobrian, 2011; Oran, 2013).

In addition to these factors, game genre also plays an important role in determining the QoE. For instance, racing game like Need for Speed (NFS) has much more stringent requirement of response time than role play game such as WoW.

Nevertheless, to make the model tractable, not all the factors are included in the model. Specifically, only Game Genre, System Configuration (including the codec, resolution, and frame rate), PSNR, Delay, and Packet Loss are included. As to quantify the QoE, Game Mean Opinion Score (GMOS), which is a subjective score system ranging from 1 (unacceptable) to 5 (excellent), is adopted. The GMOS model is

$$GMOS = f(Game, Config, PSNR, Delay, Loss). \quad (7)$$

According to the ITU-T E-model, it is further formulated as

$$GMOS = 1 + 0.035R + 7 \times 10^{-6}R(R - 60)(100 - R), \quad (8)$$

where

$$R = 100 - I_C(Game, Config) - I_P(Game, PSNR) - I_D(Game, Delay) - I_L(Game, Loss).$$

We refer interested readers to (Wang, 2009, November) for further details on I_C, I_P, I_D, and I_L including their meanings and values.

Then subjective tests were conducted in (Wang, 2009, November). 21 students and staff from UCSD, who had experiences of playing these games, attended the study and provided assessment of their gaming experience. Then, all the parameters were determined using linear regression technique. The model obtained was further validated by another group consisting of 15 participants.

3.3.2. Dealing with Fluctuating Wireless Bandwidth and Busy Cloud Server

Although the QoE model is developed for cloud-assisted online gaming in Section 3.3.1, it still remains unanswered how to maximize the QoE under practical settings. For instance, the wireless bandwidth assigned may not be sufficient, which may result in longer delay of transmission and higher packet loss ratio. And the cloud server may be too busy to assist one particular user at a given time, which may also result in longer delay and slower rendering frame rate. All these negative impact could finally result in an unacceptable user experience. To maximize the QoE (e.g., using the model given in Section 3.3.1), these two important problems, i.e., the fluctuating wireless bandwidth

and available server computing resource are addressed in (Wang, 2010, December).

There are basically two kinds of costs associated with cloud assisted mobile online gaming:

1. The Communication Cost (CommC), which is the bit rate of game video;
2. The Computation Cost (CompC), which is the GPU utilization.

On one hand, game video content complexity greatly affects the video bit rate, so CommC can be reduced by bringing down the video complexity. On the other hand, frame time has great impact on CompC and frame time is limited by the bottleneck processor. Thus, CompC can be reduced by alleviating bottleneck processor load.

Going one step further, four parameters are identified to have impacts on CommC and CompC:

1. Realistic Effect (including color depth, anti-aliasing, texture filtering and lighting mode),
2. Texture Detail (downsample rate),
3. View Distance, and
4. Environment Detail.

So a 4-tuple rendering setting variable S(Realistic Effect, Texture Detail, View Distance, Environment Detail) can be defined. Given all the feasible values of S, their corresponding CommC and CompC are measured by a desktop server with NVIDIA GeForce 8300 graphic card. And there are two opportunities that can be exploited. The first one is by removing unimportant objects in the game video to reduce the video complexity and bottleneck load, and hence CommC and CompC. The other one is to scale CommC and CompC by scaling texture detail and environment detail.

Gaining these understandings, an adaptation level matrix and its corresponding cost matrix can be constructed. Given current network and cloud server condition, we could use a level selection algorithm to adapt the game video rendering setting to maximize QoE. For instance, if the network RTT is detected as being greater than a threshold, the algorithm lower the CommC level by 1 by adjusting S from $S(H,0,60,Y)$ to $S(M,2,300,N)$, meaning from (High Realistic Effect, 0 downsample rate, 60-meter View Distance, Enable Environment) to (Medium Realistic Effect, 2 downsample rate, 300-meter View Distance, Not Enable Environment).

Experiments conducted on a commercial UMTS network demonstrate that the proposed rendering adaptation scheme makes cloud mobile gaming feasible and robust against varying wireless channel and server occupation, hence maximizing the mobile game user experience.

3.3.3. Dealing with High Response Time

While mobile cloud brings online gaming to mobile devices, it also brings about new problems. One of the new problems is probably longer response time, since game commands and videos need to travel through the stochastic wireless channel. On account of much more stringent requirement of response time for online gaming, the risk needs to be well investigated.

In (Wang, 2010, March), the Response Time (RT) is identified as the period from the time one game command is issued to the time the resulting game video is properly displayed. That is:

$$RT = D_{UL} + D_S + D_{DL} + D_C, \qquad (9)$$

where D_{UL} is network uplink delay, D_S is the server delay, D_{DL} is the network downlink delay, and D_C is client delay (including client playout delay and decoding delay). Using the model developed in Section 3.3.1, the RT threshold for Excellent user experience (RT_E) and Acceptable user experience (RT_A) can be calculated. For instance, $RT_E = 280ms$ and $RT_A = 440ms$ for WoW; $RT_E = 200ms$ and $RT_A = 320ms$ for NFS; $RT_E = 160ms$ and $RT_A = 240ms$ for PES (Pro Evolution Soccer). Since delays related to server and decoding video

are mainly fixed, D_{UL}, D_{DL} and D_{PL} are used for minimizing RT.

Given the values of RT_A and RT_E, the user acceptable downlink delay threshold (D_{DL}^{TH}) and uplink delay threshold (D_{UL}^{TH}) can be obtained. Then a set of application layer optimization techniques (including a downlink rate-selection algorithm, an uplink delay optimization technique and a client playout delay adaptation algorithm) is designed to ensure acceptable gaming response time and video quality, and thus acceptable user experience.

Experiments carried out in noisy network conditions, loaded network conditions and mobility conditions validate the efficacy of the proposed techniques.

3.3.4. Scheduling of Multiple Gaming Sessions

With the cloud mobile gaming framework discussed above, users are enabled to play rich media internet game on smartphones and tablets. However, previous discussions are mainly focused on the gaming experience for one single user. Popular online games like WoW have several hundreds of thousands players online at the same time. When there are too many simultaneous requests, even if a powerful cloud server could afford the assistance, the wireless network will surely fall short of capability. A proper scheduling mechanism thereby should be introduced to support multiple gaming sessions while ensuring acceptable user experience. To this regard, WCS (Wireless Cloud Scheduler) is proposed in (Wang, 2012, June).

For each game session, a particular wireless network (denoted as m) and a cloud server (denoted as n) is assigned. The $MGUE(m,n)$ can be then calculated using the model discussed in Section 3.3.1. To quantify the cloud service cost, four parameters are identified, which are RT_A (Acceptable Response Time Threshold, as defined previously), CMG_{Comp} (Computing Resource Requirement),

$CMG_{Storage}$ (Storage Space Requirement), and $CMG_{DataRate}$ (Video Data Rate Requirement). With given computing price P_C, storage price P_S, and network price P_N, the cloud service cost ($Cost_{Cloud}$) can be formulated as

$$Cost_{Cloud} = P_C \times CMG_{Comp} + P_S \times CMG_{Storage} + P_N \times CMG_{DataRate}. \qquad (10)$$

Another importance metric is the Schedule Rate, which represents the percentage of users actually being served. For instance, if there are 1000 requests from users, but only 700 of them are being served, then the Schedule Rate is 70%.

The main objectives of the scheduling algorithm are three-fold:

1. Satisfying the QoE requirements of game video by keeping $MGUE(m,n) \geq 3.0$ (Wang, 2009, November),
2. Reducing the cloud service cost by keep $Cost_{Cloud}$ low, and
3. Provisioning as high schedule rate as possible.

The basic idea of the scheduling algorithm is as follows. Firstly, for user i, figure out the possible solution set PS by satisfying three constraints:

1. $Bandwidth(m) > CMG_{DataRate}$,
2. Server n supports the requested game genre, and
3. $MGUE(m,n) \geq 3.0$.

If set PS is empty for user i, this user cannot be scheduled. Otherwise, choose the optimal channel m^* and cloud server n^* by maximizing the preset utility function $F(m,n)$.

To further enhance the performance, a joint scheduling-adaptation algorithm is also proposed in (Wang, 2012, June). Typically, adaptation techniques in (Wang, 2010, December; Wang, 2010, March) are employed so that users' communication and computation requests are adjusted adaptively

in light of the stochastic wireless channel. Simulation results show that with WCS, the schedule rate is enhanced while the average cloud service cost is minimized and the $MGUE$ maximized.

Considering that some system parameters, such as user demand rate and server service time, may not be available to the scheduler, a Blind Scheduling Algorithm (BSA) is developed in (Zhou, in press). Specifically, the BSA is formulated as a stochastic minimization problem with fairness ensured. BSA routes the new users to the server whose weighted idle time is the longest, then assigns the available server according to the fairness on idle time. It is demonstrated that BSA is asymptotically optimal in minimizing the steady-state waiting time of all the users. In the Halfin-Whitt heavy traffic (HWHT) regime, the heterogeneous server system outperforms its homogeneous MSP counterpart in terms of the user waiting time.

3.4. Other Challenges

3.4.1. Stochastic Wireless Networks

The challenges related to wireless networks have been considered in the previous discussions. For instance, (Wen, 2011) and (Wen, 2011, December) investigate the energy consumption and delay deadline tradeoff; (Wang, 2010, March) is particularly about latency. The impact of network RTT and wireless link throughput on cloud-assisted video streaming is studied in (Zhu, 2012, January). The relationship between the RTT and energy consumption is also considered in (Cuervo, 2010, June). The problem formulation of (Wang, 2010, March) has taken into consideration wireless network, network condition, delay, and packet loss rate.

Although wireless networks are not as stable or fast as wireline networks, it could serve as a supplement when the wireline network is too crowded. Although Content Delivery Networks (CDNs) have been employed to reduce the Internet bandwidth consumption, videos played out on mobile device must additionally go through the wireless carrier core network (CN) and Radio Access Network (RAN). A video aware wireless cloud, which enables caching of video at (e) NodeBs at the edge of the RAN is proposed, so that most video requests can be served from the RAN caches, instead of constantly fetching from the Internet CDNs. To enhance the wireless video cloud, a hierarchical caching structure is proposed in (Ahlehagh, 2012, June) to supplement the caches at the edge of RAN.

Another interesting example is (Miao, 2011, November), which investigates the resource allocation problem for cloud assisted free viewpoint video (FVV) for mobile devices. FVV, which enables the user to generate new views of a dynamic scene from any 3D position by interactively adjusting the viewpoint, requires large bandwidth to transmit video. Given the limited computation and battery life of mobile devices, it is highly challenging to enable FVV for mobile devices over cellular networks. However, remote rendering using cloud computing represents a promising solution. From the QoE perspective, users mainly care about visual quality and interaction delay. To enjoy optimal visual quality, the entire FVV rendering is proposed to perform in the cloud. To achieve minimal delay, it is proposed to carry out local rendering on the mobile device for the novel view while waiting for the requested view to come. To minimize the total distortion for the

entire viewing period, a rate allocation optimization problem is formulated and solved. Experiments are conducted on Network Emulator for Windows toolkit and HTC HD (QUALCOMM(R) 7201A 528MHz CPU and 288 MB memory) using 3D video BookArrival, which validate that the proposed solution can substantially improve the video quality on mobile devices.

It's worth noting that with the advancement of 4G wireless networks, some of these challenges may be partially alleviated. The IMT-Advanced specifies that the peak rate requirement for 4G systems is 100 Mbps for high mobility communications (e.g., users in a moving car) and 1 Gbps for low mobility communications (e.g., pedestrians) (Wikipedia, IMT Advanced). Table 2 compares the throughput and HDTV support of evolving wireless networks. Furthermore, compared with Wi-Fi, 4G networks have comparable speed but much broader coverage, which would be highly desirable for mobile cloud applications.

3.4.2. Security and Privacy Issues

The open air transmissions of mobile devices are more vulnerable to malicious programs and attacks. It is of pivotal importance to protect the data of mobile cloud computing applications. Apple co-founder Steve Wozniak recently expressed his doubts about cloud computing, saying that "the more we transfer everything onto the web, onto the cloud, the less we're going to have control over

Table 2. Mobile TV support for various mobile networks

Mobile Network	2G	3G/UMTS	3.5G/HSDPA	LTE
Cell throughput	236 Kbps	258-260 Kbps	0.5-4.2 Mbps downlink 0.6-1.7 Mbps uplink	100 Mbps downlink 50 Mbps uplink
TV throughput	Initially 50 Kbps then 80 Kbps	250 Kbps	250 Kbps	300 Kbps, 650 Kbps, 1.5 Mbps
Streaming capacity per cell	2 users max (not adapted to live streaming)	Limited for live HDTV	Depends on user location in the radio cell (users at cell borders are impacted)	More cell capacity for the streaming (>200 users per cell)
HDTV	No support	Supported at 384 Kbps	Supported	1.5 Mbps

it." As a matter of fact, Steve Wozniak is not the only person who doubts the security and privacy of the cloud. Security and privacy issues could be the biggest obstacle that keeps mobile cloud computing from prevailing.

In addition to the inherent vulnerabilities from wireless transmissions, mobile cloud computing is also susceptible to many new forms of attacks when offloading applications to be executed in the cloud, employing distributed storage of files, and accessing the cloud content from different mobile devices.

As the mobile cloud getting more popular, the security issue becomes more and more important. However, mobile devices may not be feasible to run sophisticated computation-intensive anti-virus programs on the mobile device, due to computational and power constraints. Again, we have to resort to the cloud to detect potential vulnerabilities and threats. A virtualized in-cloud security service for mobile devices is presented in (Oberheide, 2008, June). Experiments carried out on Nokia's N800 and N95 demonstrate three important benefits of the proposed framework: better detection of malicious software, reduced on-device resource consumption, and reduced on-device software complexity.

Privacy is also an important issue. For instance, a user's uploaded file may be used by the service provider without notice ahead. There comes the tricky issue that who owns the uploaded files. Take a look at Google's terms of service last modified on March 1, 2012 (Google, 2012):

When you upload or otherwise submit content to our Services, you give Google (and those we work with) a worldwide license to use, host, store, reproduce, modify, create derivative works (such as those resulting from translations, adaptations or other changes we make so that your content works better with our Services), communicate, publish, publicly perform, publicly display and distribute such content.

As a result, a user may have no idea what the service provider might do with the data.

For game vendors, as discussed, mobile cloud helps to protect the game software, since only outputs in response to user inputs are downloaded to the clients. However, game vendors should work collaboratively with network vendors to prevent full game downloading.

3.4.3. Network Service Cost

As wireless network service such as 4G LTE is usually more expensive than traditional wireline Internet access or Wi-Fi, network service cost is also a concern for mobile cloud users. If a user watches lengthy movies or playing online games for a long period of time, the data-usage bill could prohibit him from further participation. Effective compression schemes could be adopted to reduce the data volume, while scalable coding could be used for users to choose from different media formats that are suitable for the device (e.g., screen size) and budget. Alternatively, (Wang, 2012, June) proposes to use WCS and the joint-scheduling-adaptation algorithm to reduce the cloud service costs. Table 2 therein provides a real-world illustration.

3.4.4. Video Related Challenges

Many mobile cloud media applications involve streaming of various videos over a wireless network. The challenges from video encoding perspective should also be addressed. There have been considerable work on video coding and streaming related issues. For example, (Schwarz, 2007) provides an overview of extending H.264/AVC towards Scalable Video Coding (SVC). (Ohm, 2012) compares the main video coding standards of several generations including H.262/MPEG-2, H.263, MPEG-4, H.264/MPEG-4 AVC (Advanced Video Coding), and HEVC (High Efficiency Video Coding). (Sodagar, 2011) provides an overview of recent development for MPEG DASH based video streaming. (Thang, 2012) studies the problem of adaptive streaming using MPEG DASH.

For video related applications, not only the wireless channel is stochastic, so does the data rate of the video traffic. With buffering, the video variability can be reduced (Van Der Auwera, 2009). In addition, smart scheduling can help to further reduce the video variability and overcome the wireless link variations (Shao, 2012; Zhang, 2010; Zhou 2010).

4. PROTOTYPE, STANDARDIZATION AND COMMERCIAL ASPECTS

Following the discussions of the theoretic parts, it is more convincing to see what we have in reality. In this section, we review the prototypes, ongoing standardization efforts and some commercial aspects of mobile cloud media.

4.1. Prototype

With the support of cloud, Stratus is presented in (Aggarwal, 2010, August). It comprises a cloud based proxy on the Windows Azure platform and a client proxy on a Windows Mobile phone with the objective of reducing mobile device energy consumption.

Employing multiple virtualized malware detection engines in cloud, (Oberheide, 2008, June) successfully implements security software on mobile phones of Nokia N800 and N95.

MAUI is presented and implemented in (Cuervo, 2010, June), which also aims at reducing energy costs and making smartphones longer. Typically, the system contains an HTC Fuze smartphone running Windows Mobile 6.5 (.NET Compact Framework v3.5), and a dual-core desktop with a 3 GHz CPU and 4 GB of RAM running Windows 7 (.NET Framework v3.5). A computation-intensive face recognition application, a voice based language translation application

which requires much RAM and a latency-sensitive video game are all successfully launched.

Melog is presented in (Li, 2010, October). By analyzing GPS data and photos taken in the travel, realtime automatic blogging is enabled. Typically, the estimated time of creating a travel blog is about 15 seconds and it is almost negligible for a micro-blog.

Muse is presented in (Yu, 2011, December). Experiments carried out demonstrate that Muse can reduce loading time, network traffic and response latency of remote display and interaction. More specifically, Muse could play the webpage version of "Angry Bird" with interactive performance at a resolution of 1024*768 with a 1 Mbit/s wireless connection.

AMVSC framework is proposed and implemented in (Chen, 2012, December), which focuses on the adaptive mobile video streaming in the cloud. The system consists of a virtual server with 6 virtual CPU cores (2.66 GHz) and 32 GB memory, and a smartphone Samsung Galaxy II running Android 4.0. Data service is provided by a LTE network. AMVSC shows that cloud computing brings significant improvements to mobile device for video streaming.

Realizing that GPS is not able to provide sufficient location based information in densely populated cities (e.g., New York, Hong Kong), (Ye, 2010, October) proposes a mobile cloud-assisted location search technique. By shooting a video about the surrounding buildings and sending it to the cloud, users will be returned with a summary of the location and services available from the cloud. Effectiveness of the proposed technique on a small scale trial is validated remaining large scale video repositories like YouTube for future work.

In (Vartiainen, 2010, December), a photo sharing service named Image Exchange is designed and implemented in Nokia95 with Symbian S60 platform. Image Exchange automatically backs up all the user's images into the cloud and synchronizes all the other data related to the photos.

Two user studies are carried out to evaluate Image Exchange. And the results show that current design of Image Exchange provides positive user experience, although it could be further enhanced to fully utilize the cloud.

By taking advantage of the graphics rendering contexts (e.g., pixel depth, rendering viewpoints, camera motion, etc.), (Shi, 2011, November) introduced a 3D image warping assisted real-time video coding method. By implementing the proposed method in a 3D tank battle game, it is shown experimentally that the proposed technique could achieve more than 2 dB quality improvements.

(Wang, 2009, December; Wang, 2010, December; Wang, 2010, March) also implement the proposed ideas in each paper for the cloud-assisted mobile online gaming. Specifically, the wireless network used is either HSDPA networks or 802.11g WLAN deployed in UCSD, and the game server located in the authors' lab in UCSD. Resource-intensive 3D game like PlaneShift and online multiple user game like WoW are successfully launched and played in mobile devices.

4.2. Standardization

There are many standards organizations attempting to establish cloud standards for end users and vendors, such as the Distributed Management Task Force (DMTF), the IEEE, the Storage Networking Industry Association (SNIA), the Open Data Center Alliance, the European Telecommunications Standards Institute (ETSI), and the standards consortium OMG, among others. So far, each of these groups has been working on certain aspect of cloud computing, and there is a compelling need for a holistic set of standards that can be widely accepted.

For instance, SNIA announced the formation of the Cloud Storage Initiative (CSI) on Oct. 12, 2009, which specifically targeted at the emerging cloud storage market for both commercial and consumer environments. It was announced on Oct. 16, 2012 that the Cloud Data Management Interface (CDMI) specification, the first industry-developed open standard specifically for data storage as a service as part of cloud computing, had been designated as an International Standard (IS) by the Joint Technical Committee 1 (JTC 1), a joint effort of the International Organization for Standardization (ISO) and the International Electrotechnical Commission (IEC) for standardization in the field of Information Technology.

Another ongoing effort made by the Open Cloud Manifesto, intends to initiate a conversation that will bring together the emerging cloud computing community (both cloud users and cloud providers) around a core set of principles. Although IBM is in the list of supporting companies for Open Cloud Manifesto, other big names such as Apple, Google, Microsoft, Amazon, Dropbox, Salesforce, etc. are not included in the list at this time. Full list available at http://www.opencloudmanifesto.org/supporters.htm

One may notice that the standardization process of cloud computing is moving forward slowly, largely due to the immaturity of the cloud market. It might need another several years to develop a comprehensive standard suite. Although wireless or mobile organizations (e.g., ETSI) and companies (e.g., Cisco, Huawei, ZTE in DMTF, and CSI of SNIA) are actively participating in the standardization process, there is a lack of standards and specifications specially designed for mobile cloud computing.

4.3. Commercial Aspects

For a general discussion of the impact of cloud on mobile multimedia, readers are referred to (Moustafa, 2012). Launched in Oct. 2011, iCloud of Apple Inc. mainly provides cloud storage and cloud data backup service for its users. It allows users to store and access documents, music, photos, calendars, contacts, etc. from any Apple device. iCloud can also be used as a synchronization solution if you have multiple devices, whether they are mobile or not.

Two more useful features enabled by iCloud are Find My iPhone and Find My Friends. When a device is missing, Find My iPhone helps to locate the device on the map, remotely lock the device and even remotely wipe all the personal data. Visualization of real-time locations on the map is a rather computation-intensive application. By leveraging iCloud, one may easily keep track of family and friends on the map.

Google Cloud has more than 1 million servers worldwide. Google Drive is a cloud-based service for file storage and synchronization launched in Apr. 2012. It now hosts Google Docs, which allows users to collaboratively editing documents, spreadsheets, presentation, etc. in real-time. Google Drive also allows upload and access of other kinds of files such as photos and videos. The uploaded files are kept in the cloud and can be accessed from all kinds of devices including mobile devices.

SkyDrive is a cloud-based file storage service provided by Microsoft. It is part of the Windows Live service and allows users to upload files, share them with friends, and make them public. SkyDrive web interface is built on HTML5, the fifth revision of the HTML standard and a potential candidate for cross-platform mobile applications.

Another company providing cloud-based storage service is Dropbox. Table 3 presents a brief comparison of the available cloud storage services.

Facebook also provides cloud-based multimedia service. Users usually take pictures and then upload them through computers, smartphones and tablet PCs to Facebook, and access these pictures from some device later. According to a recent report (Gary Pageau, 2011), Facebook was holding 4\% of all the photos taken throughout the human history (i.e., about 140 billion photos). Since there were 3.5 trillion photos, Facebook was actually holding 140 billion photos. And this number has been ever increasing.

A consortium including Universal Studios, Warner Bros. Entertainment, Microsoft, Huawei, Cisco, Samsung, SONY, Adobe, Walmart, Bestbuy, etc. launchned the UltraViolet service recently (Lawton, 2012) with the slogan "Your Movies in the Cloud." Typically, UltraViolet is a digital-rights authentication and cloud-based licensing system. The cloud stores customer owned digital movies and TV shows in an online library, providing the freedom to watch movies and TV shows anywhere, using computers, TVs, tablets and smartphones.

Onlive is a company offering cloud gaming platform and a cloud desktop system. The cloud gaming platform is available using various systems including Android and iOS (both are operating systems for mobile devices). Since the data and games are rendered, synchronized, and stored on Onlive's servers, even the low-end device is enabled to play even the most resource-hungry game, as long as the device can access internet (for data delivery) and play video (for game rendering). The full list of supporting games by Onlive can be found at: (Wikipedia, List of OnLive video games).

To make video games as easily accessible as movies and music, Gaikai (recently acquired by Sony Computer Entertainment) leverages the cloud to allow users to play high-end PC and console video games rendered on remote server via

Table 3. Comparison of mobile cloud storage products

Company	Product	Storage (GB)	Price ($/year)
Apple	iCloud	5/15/25/55	0/20/40/100
Google	Google Drive	5/15/100/16,000	0/29.88/59.88/9,599.88
Microsoft ‚	SkyDrive	7/27/57/107	0/10/25/50
Dropbox	Dropbox	2/100/200/500	0/99/199/499

internet streaming. Wikipad is the first mobile-only device for Gaikai service since May 2012. Gaikai also has developed a prototype iPad application for playing the WoW using cloud streaming recently (Lawton, 2012).

The last example is Otoy. By using the rendering power of the cloud, Otoy also aims to develop an infrastructure for using high-end graphics applications on many devices including the mobile ones. For instance, Otoy is working with Autodesk to run 3D modeling and animation software on mobile devices (Lawton, 2012).

5. RESEARCH DIRECTIONS

Although highly promising, mobile cloud computing for multimedia applications is still in its infancy. There are many unsolved problems need to be investigated to fully harvest its potential. In this section, we discuss several potential research directions.

- Previous works on energy saving mainly care about the energy consumption on the client side (i.e., mobile device). However, for the sake of green communication, joint optimization by considering the energy consumption on both the cloud and client side should be investigated.
- The packet scheduling problem was discussed in (Wen, 2011, December) when Wi-Fi and 3G networks are available. Further studies can be conducted when more options, such as Femtocell and 4G networks, are available.
- Existing works rarely discuss High Definition (HD) video streaming under bandwidth constrained wireless networks while taking costs and energy into account, while it is expected that the demands for HD videos will also increase quickly in the near future.

- As (Wang, 2012, June; Zhou, in press) mainly consider new requests, the problem of how to adapt the scheduled session to the dynamic changes of wireless network, in order to maximize the QoE, remains an interesting problem.
- With more and more video applications being developed, security issues regarding particular scenarios, such as video conferencing, should be investigated.
- Routing is also an important topic in mobile cloud computing, e.g., how to find a suitable server in the cloud and how to access the server via a multi-hop wireless access network.

6. CONCLUSION

Mobile cloud computing can be leveraged to enable multimedia applications on mobile devices. This chapter focuses on the technical part of the enabling technologies and discusses the challenges from several aspects such as energy saving, QoE ensuring, etc. Real world prototypes, standardization efforts and commercial aspects are also reviewed. A discussion of open research problems is presented to conclude this chapter.

ACKNOWLEDGMENT

Shiwen Mao's research is supported in part by the US National Science Foundation (NSF) under Grants CNS-0953513 and CNS-1247955, and through the NSF Broadband Wireless Access and Applications Center (BWAC) at Auburn University. Any opinions, findings, and conclusions or recommendations expressed in this material are those of the author(s) and do not necessarily reflect the views of the NSF.

REFERENCES

Advanced, I. M. T. (n.d.). *Wikipedia.* Retrieved March 8 2013, from http://en.wikipedia.org/wiki/IMT_Advanced

Aggarwal, B., Spring, N., & Schulman, A. (2010). *Stratus: Energy-efficient mobile communication using cloud support.* Paper presented at the meeting of ACM SIGCOMM. New Delhi, India.

Ahlehagh, H., & Dey, S. (2012). *Hierarchical video caching in wireless cloud: Approaches and algorithms.* Paper presented at the meeting of IEEE ICC. Ottawa, Canada.

Chen, M. (2012). *AMVSC: A framework of adaptive mobile video streaming in the cloud.* Paper presented at the Meeting of IEEE GLOBECOM. Anaheim, CA.

Chikkerur, S., Sundaram, V., Reisslein, M., & Karam, L. J. (2011). Objective video quality assessment methods: A classification, review, and performance comparison. *IEEE Transactions on Broadcasting, 57*(2), 165–182. doi:10.1109/TBC.2011.2104671.

Chun, B., & Maniatis, P. (2009). *Augmented smartphone applications through clone cloud execution.* Paper presented at the Meeting of the 12th Conference on Hot Topics in Operating Systems. Monte Verità, Switzerland.

Cisco. (2013). *Cisco visual networking index: Global mobile data traffic forecast update.* February 6 2013, from http://www.cisco.com/en/US/solutions/collateral/ns341/ns525/ns537/ns705/ns827/white_paper_c11-520862.html

Cuervo, E., Balasubramanian, A., Cho, D., Wloman, A., Saroiu, S., Chandra, R., & Bahl, P. (2010). *MAUI: Making smartphones last longer with code offload.* Paper presented at the Meeting of the 8th International Conference on Mobile Systems, Applications, and Services. San Francisco, CA.

Dobrian, F., Sekar, V., Awan, A., Stoica, I., Joseph, D., & Ganjam, A. … Zhang, H. (2011). *Understanding the impact of video quality on user engagement.* Paper presented at the ACM SIGCOMM. Toronto, Canada.

Google. (2012). *Google terms of service.* Retrieved March 1 2012, from http://www.google.com/intl/en/policies/terms/

Lawton, G. (2012). Cloud streaming brings video to mobile devices. *IEEE Computer, 45*(2), 14–16. doi:10.1109/MC.2012.47.

Li, H., & Hua, X. (2010). *Melog - Mobile experience sharing through automatic multimedia blogging.* Paper presented at the Meeting of ACM MCMC. Firenze, Italy.

List of OnLive Video Games. (n.d.). *Wikipedia.* Retrieved March 19 2013, from http://en.wikipedia.org/wiki/List_of_OnLive_video_games

Miao, D., Zhu, W., Luo, C., & Chen, C. (2011). *Resource allocation for cloud-based free viewpoint video rendering for mobile phones.* Paper presented at the meeting of ACM MM. Scottsdale, AZ.

Microsoft Research. (2011). *Stratus: Energy-efficient mobile communication using cloud support.* Retrieved September 27 2011, from http://research.microsoft.com/apps/video/default.aspx?id=158653

Mobile Phone. (n.d.). *Wikipedia.* Retrieved March 26 2013, from http://en.wikipedia.org/wiki/Mobile_phone

Moorthy, A. K., Seshadrinathan, K., Soundararajan, R., & Bovik, A. C. (2010). Wireless video quality assessment: A study of subjective scores and objective algorithms. *IEEE Transactions on Circuits and Systems for Video Technology, 20*(4), 587–599. doi:10.1109/TCSVT.2010.2041829.

Moustafa, H., Marechal, N., & Zeadally, S. (2012). Mobile multimedia applications delivery technologies. *IEEE IT Professional, 14*(5), 12–21. doi:10.1109/MITP.2012.46.

Oberheide, J., Veeraraghavan, K., Cooke, E., Flinn, J., & Jahanian, F. (2008). *Virtualized in-cloud security services for mobile devices*. Paper presented at the Meeting of the First Workshop on Virtualization in Mobile Computing. Breckenridge, CO.

Ohm, J.-R., Sullivan, G. J., Schwarz, H., Tan, T. K., & Wiegand, T. (2012). Comparison of the coding efficiency of video coding standards—Including high efficiency video coding (HEVC). *IEEE Transactions on Circuits and Systems for Video Technology*, 22(12), 1669–1684. doi:10.1109/TCSVT.2012.2221192.

Oran, D. (2013). Video quality assessment in the age of internet video: Technical perspective. *Communications of the ACM*, *56*(3), 90. doi:10.1145/2428556.2428576.

Pageau, G. (2011). Facebook now hosts 4 percent of all photos ever taken: Report. *PMA Newsline*. September 22, 2011, from http://pmanewsline.com/2011/09/22/facebook-now-hosts-4-percent-of-all-photos-ever-taken-report/#.UI2aAM-Wk680

Schwarz, H., Marpe, D., & Wiegand, T. (2007). Overview of the scalable video coding extension of the H.264/AVC standard. *IEEE Transactions on Circuits and Systems for Video Technology*, *17*(9), 1103–1120. doi:10.1109/TCSVT.2007.905532.

Seshadrinathan, K., Soundararajan, R., Bovik, A. C., & Cormack, L. K. (2010). Study of subjective and objective quality assessment of video. *IEEE Transactions on Image Processing*, *19*(6), 1427–1441. doi:10.1109/TIP.2010.2042111 PMID:20129861.

Shao, D., Ding, L., Yang, F., Qian, L., & Fang, X. (2012). A novel queue scheduling scheme for video transmission over IEEE 802.11e WLAN. *Advances on Digital Television and Wireless Multimedia Communications*, *331*, 355–362. doi:10.1007/978-3-642-34595-1_49.

Shi, S., Hsu, C., Nahrstedt, K., & Campbell, R. (2011). *Using graphics rendering contexts to enhance the real-time video coding for mobile cloud gaming*. Paper presented at the meeting of ACM MM. Scottsdale, AZ.

Sodagar, I. (2011). The MPEG-DASH standard for multimedia streaming over the internet. *IEEE MultiMedia*, *18*(4), 62–67. doi:10.1109/MMUL.2011.71.

Teicher, J. G. (2012). The brain of the beast: Google reveals the computers behind the cloud. *WBUR*. Retrieved October 17, 2012, from http://www.wbur.org/npr/163031136/the-brain-ofthe-beast-google-reveals-the-computers-behind-the-cloud

Thang, T. C., Ho, Q.-D., Kang, J. W., & Pham, A. T. (2012). Adaptive streaming of audiovisual content using MPEG DASH. *IEEE Transactions on Consumer Electronics*, *58*(1), 78–85. doi:10.1109/TCE.2012.6170058.

Van Der Auwera, G., & Reisslein, M. (2009). Implications of smoothing on statistical multiplexing of H.264/AVC and SVC video streams. *IEEE Transactions on Broadcasting*, *55*(3), 541–558. doi:10.1109/TBC.2009.2027399.

Vartiainen, E., & Väänänen-Vainio-Mattila, K. (2010). *User experience of mobile photo sharing in the cloud*. Paper presented at the Meeting of ACM MUM. Limassol, Cyprus.

Wang, S., & Dey, S. (2009). *Modeling and characterizing user experience in a cloud server based mobile gaming approach*. Paper presented at the Meeting of IEEE GLOBECOM. Honolulu, HI.

Wang, S., & Dey, S. (2010). *Rendering adaptation to address communication and computation constraints in cloud mobile gaming*. Paper presented at the Meeting of IEEE GLOBECOM. Miami, FL.

Wang, S., & Dey, S. (2010). *Addressing response time and video quality in remote server based internet mobile gaming*. Paper presented at the meeting of IEEE WCNC. Sydney, Australia.

Wang, S., Liu, Y., & Dey, S. (2012). *Wireless network aware cloud scheduler for scalable cloud mobile gaming*. Paper presented at the meeting of IEEE ICC. Ottawa, Canada.

Wen, Y., Zhang, G., & Zhu, X. (2011). *Lightweight packet scheduling algorithms for content uploading from mobile devices to media cloud*. Paper presented at the Meeting of IEEE GLOBECOM Workshops. Houston, TX.

Wen, Y., Zhang, W., Guan, K., Kilper, D., & Luo, H. (2011). *Energy-optimal execution policy for a cloud-assisted mobile application platform (Tech. Rep.)*. Singapore: Nanyang Technological University..

Wu, Y., Wu, C., Li, B., Qiu, X., & Lau, F. (2011). *CloudMedia: When cloud on demand meets video on demand*. Paper presented at the meeting of IEEE ICDCS. Minneapolis, MN.

Ye, Z., Chen, X., & Li, Z. (2010). *Video based mobile location search with large set of SIFT points in cloud*. Paper presented at the Meeting of ACM MCMC. Firenze, Italy.

Yu, W., Li, J., Hu, C., & Zhong, L. (2011). *Muse: A multimedia streaming enabled remote interactivity system for mobile devices*. Paper presented at the Meeting of ACM MUM. Beijing, China.

Zhang, H., Zheng, Y., Khojastepour, M. A., & Rangarajan, S. (2010). Cross-layer optimization for streaming scalable video over fading wireless networks. *IEEE Journal on Selected Areas in Communications, 28*(3), 344–353. doi:10.1109/JSAC.2010.100406.

Zhou, L., & Wang, H. (2013). Toward blind scheduling in mobile media cloud: Fairness, simplicity, and asymptotic optimality. *IEEE Transactions on Multimedia*. doi:10.1109/TMM.2013.2241044.

Zhou, L., Wang, X., Tu, W., Muntean, G., & Geller, B. (2010). Distributed scheduling scheme for video streaming over multi-channel multi-radio multi-hop wireless networks. *IEEE Journal on Selected Areas in Communications, 28*(3), 409–419. doi:10.1109/JSAC.2010.100412.

Zhu, X., Zhu, J., Pan, R., Prabhu, M. S., & Bonomi, F. (2012). *Cloud-assisted streaming for low-latency applications*. Paper presented at the Meeting of International Conference on Computing, Networking and Communications. Maui, HI.

KEY TERMS AND DEFINITIONS

Energy Efficiency: The goal to reduce the amount of energy required to provide products and services (from Wikipedia.com).

Mobile Cloud Computing: The combination of cloud computing and mobile networks to bring benefits for mobile users, network operators, as well as cloud providers (from Wikipedia.com).

Mobile Online Gaming: Users playing online games through their wireless devices.

Mobile Video Streaming: Transmission of a video while playing it out at the receiver before the entire video is downloaded for mobile users.

Offload: to transmit network traffic from other connections, to reduce the load on the original connection.

Quality of Experience: An objective measure of a user's experiences with a service.

Standardization: The process of developing and implementing technical standards (from Wikipedia.com).

Chapter 3
Addressing Fundamental Challenges in Mobile Cloud Computing with 4G LTE–Advanced

Scott Fowler
Linköping University, Sweden

ABSTRACT

Today, mobile tools, such as smartphones and tablets, have become primary computing devices for many users. One mobile tool to satisfy this is the 4G network technology LTE (Long-Term Evolution)-Advanced. These mobile tools are resource-poor due to limited battery life. Mobile Cloud Computing (MCC) is intended to provide services to mobile users by supplementing the resource-paucity of mobile devices (i.e. off-loading tasks/data on the Internet and providing the resources to a local client on-demand). However, despite LTE-Advanced's improved network quality, much needs to be done before MCC can reach its true potential. This chapter characterizes key challenges for deployment of MCC with 4G: device battery lifetime, latency, quality of service/experience, and handover. Statistical modeling is a powerful tool to address these issues. Once MCC with 4G network behavior is characterized, it is translated into the future development of innovative mobile technologies for a wide variety of new applications.

INTRODUCTION

The mobile cloud ecosystem is rapidly evolving globally. Meanwhile, an increasing number of operators are now offering cloud-based services with 4th generation long-term evolution advanced (4G

DOI: 10.4018/978-1-4666-4781-7.ch003

LTE-Advanced) in mind. 4G LTE's higher bandwidth capabilities, nearly ubiquitous broadband access and improved quality of user experience have the potential to deliver the innovative cloud-based mobile multimedia services with fast, cost-effective, accessible, and scalable deployment. To maximize its potential, research needs to be conducted for Mobile Cloud Computing (MCC) with 4G.

Without the development of 4G technologies, emergence of MCC would not be substantiated or vice versa. 4G systems enable ultra-broadband Internet access to mobile devices thereby handling cloud offloading, whereas 4G counts on cloud computing to manage resource-demanding applications. The key contribution of MCC with 4G is the capacity for advanced multimedia services which demands large amount of resources. To achieve optimal mobile multimedia cloud services, there are several challenges to overcome.

In this chapter, we will discuss the following fundamental challenges in MCC with 4G: maximizing device battery lifetime, improving interaction latency, provisioning of the quality of service/experience (QoS/QoE), and providing seamless handover. Our objective is to understand these challenges and explore the means to address them.

BACKGROUND

Today's Mobile Communications. The advancement of mobile technologies has profoundly affected our lives. It is a rapidly growing trend that more users are becoming dependent on the mobile tools as their primary computing devices, replacing the traditional stationary hardware (Mei 2011), while the mobile-only Internet population is projected to grow up to 788 million people worldwide by 2015 (Rao 2011); hence the impact of the mobile communication market on the global economy is obvious. Now the features for handling multimedia (images, videos, music, and other media) are integrated into the smartphones, and thus the potential for mobile communication keeps expanding.

However, there is a major obstacle for further development and that is the resource-paucity of portable devices. Even though mobile hardware keeps evolving, they will always be resource-poor relative to stationary hardware (Satyanarayanan 2009). The reason is that, first, battery technologies for mobile devices only allow limited computing

power on a portable lightweight package, and second, the processing power and the memory of mobile hardware are much smaller than those of traditional desktops and laptops. This presents another challenge for a mobile device to execute resource-hungry user applications. Hence, a logical and obvious solution is to leverage cloud computing. With cloud computing, the resource intensive applications can be stripped out of the mobile devices and out-sourced for remote execution over the Internet.

Cloud computing: Cloud computing has become an important paradigm for delivering shared resources on-demand (e.g., infrastructure, platform, software, and so on), to a user's devices (e.g. computer or mobile device), over the Internet (Garg 2011), just like other utilities (e.g. water, electricity and gas). End-users can access cloud applications through a web browser on the desktop computer or on their mobile device. While the software and data is stored on servers at an unknown remote location, the end-users can receive the same, or better, level of service and performance, as if the software programs were installed on their local computing device. Synergy between these features of cloud computing and mobility of portable handsets is termed Mobile Cloud Computing.

Mobile Cloud Computing: When the cloud works together with mobile networks, all the data and complicated computing modules can be processed in the cloud and thus, mobile devices do not require a powerful configuration such as high CPU speed and large memory capacity. Usage of the mobile cloud can grow with the development of mobile applications (apps) as Apple states: "There's an app for that®". MCC is expected to become the leading mobile application development/deployment strategy, and some mobile cloud apps have already been in use, such as mobile Gmail and Google Maps. The cloud app-users can access applications from a cloud-based location via their handset's browser, which enables richer functions with less handset resource consumption.

Another advantage is that mobile cloud apps can be created on cloud-based platforms and delivered to any device whereas in case of non-cloud apps, different versions of one application have to be built for each device. Therefore, Mobile Cloud Computing Industry Outlook Report: 2011-2016 predicts that mobile cloud will change the life of consumers and enterprises beyond what can be conceived today (Visiongain 2011).

4G technologies in mobile cloud environment: Data rates of 4G (fourth generation) technologies (i.e. peak data rates of LTE-Advanced is 1Gb/s) have already exceeded DSL (digital subscriber line) and other broad band technology competitors such as cable (e.g Hybrid Fiber-Coax), although fiber optics based broadband network architectures such as FTTH (fiber-to-the-home) and PON (passive optical network) can still provide higher speed than 4G technologies by10-fold. Ever since the world's first publicly available LTE service was launched in Stockholm and Oslo in 2009, LTE has gained popularity and is anticipated to become the first truly global mobile phone standard. The current LTE (specified in the 3GPP Release 8 and 9 document series) is commonly referred to as 4G wireless service in the market. LTE specifies several standardized quality channel indicator (QCI) values with characteristics preconfigured for the network elements. The set of standardized QCIs and their characteristics are reviewed and summarized in (3GPP 2008), where the QCI table can be found. Technically speaking, it does not satisfy the requirement defined by ITU-R organization, and thus in some cases, classified as pre-4G. The LTE-Advanced standard, on the other hand, satisfies the requirements to be 4G and the standardization was finalized in 2011. The higher access speed of 4G enables a unique opportunity to offer new revenue-generating services. Not surprisingly, an increasing number of operators are now offering cloud-based services with 4G LTE-Advanced in mind. LTE-Advanced's higher bandwidth capabilities, nearly ubiquitous broadband access and improved quality of user

experience have the potential to deliver the innovative cloud-based new mobile multimedia services with fast, cost-effective, accessible, and scalable deployment.

However, much needs to be done before the MCC can reach its true potential. The following sections will discuss on the main obstacles we need to overcome and explore the possible solutions for the issues.

CHALLENGES IN MCC WITH 4G LTE-ADVANCED

Emergence of MCC cannot be substantiated without 4G technologies, or vice versa. 4G systems enable mobile-ultra broadband Internet access to mobile devices such as smartphones and tables and thus can handle Cloud offloading, while 4G relies on Cloud computing to manage resource-hungry applications (e.g. multimedia). The key contribution of MCC with 4G is the capacity for advanced multimedia services such as gaming, mobile TV, video, and 3D television which demands large amount of resources. Here, we will discuss on the challenges and issues to tackle in order to maximize the effectiveness of MCC with 4G. The main obstacles include the device battery lifetime, interaction latency, the resulting quality of service/experience (QoS/QoE), and handover problems. In the first section, we will briefly summarize each problem. Then, we will examine the state-of-the-art, what have been done and is currently being done, to address the above issues. The possible solutions, approaches, and suggestions for the groundwork of MCC with 4G implementation will be discussed at the end to conclude this section.

Issues, Controversies, Problems

Energy efficiency: For all MCC scenarios, energy consumption in battery-powered devices is a key issue (Raicu 2005, Kumar 2010). One aspect of the argument is that cloud computing enables computation by off-loading from the device and thereby reducing energy consumption of the mobile device. For example (Othman 1998) simulated the system and found that, under certain conditions, 20% energy savings would be achieved. However, the remote computing in the cloud consumes substantial energy for wireless communication. Therefore, it is important to identify optimal proportion of local (mobile device) and remote (cloud) computing, taking account communication energy for offloading and device computing energy.

There are additional elements which would affect the break-even point between communication energy for offloading and device computing energy. For instance, newer standards for wireless communication, LTE-Advanced include energy efficiency requirements. The mobile device by itself can have a scheduling mechanism for energy efficiency, in which the device goes through awake/sleep cycles with the machine turning off automatically when it is not used (Fowler 2011, Mushtaq 2012, Fowler 2012a, Sunggeun 2012, Jia-Ming 2013). How such functions in LTE-Advanced improve the gross energy usage should be investigated to maximize MCC's potential for energy efficiency.

Latency: Interaction latency refers to the delay that users experience between generating some input and seeing the result on their display (Simoens 2011). This delay is inevitable in MCC since the mobile device must communicate with the server even for the most trivial operations. It is particularly problematic as users are accustomed to the responsive interface of traditional desktop applications and will expect same level of interactivity in Mobile communications.

In cloud architecture, remote display protocol data needs to traverse numerous links and multiple network elements, each of which introduce additional propagation and transmission delays to the end-to-end path. Moreover, the wireless mobile setting induces additional transmission delays

due to the limited bandwidth. This limited bandwidth, however, is expected to improve over time. LTE-Advanced, for example, sets the bandwidth requirement of the downlink at 100Mbit and the uplink at 50Mbit. Thus, bandwidth-related latency, *per se*, can be reduced to a certain degree. Nonetheless, there will *always* be a trade-off between latency and other aspects of networking, such as energy efficiency, security, and manageability (Fowler 2008, 2011, 2012a, Sunggeun 2012, Jia-Ming 2013, Puttonen 2012). Thus, mobile cloud latency under new wireless communication standards needs to be addressed.

Quality of service/experience (QoS/QoE): QoS technologies have been developed and deployed to overcome several constrains in computer networks, including low throughput, packet-drop, bit errors latency, jitter, and out-of-order delivery. As mobile cloud services are often affected by many specific factors including hardware and software limitations of mobile handsets, signal strength of mobile networks, mobility of mobile users, provisioning of QoS assurance in mobile cloud environment requires more advanced mechanisms.

Current cloud algorithms select the best operator based on the traditional static QoS parameters such as end-to-end delays (Zhu 2012, Distefano 2012, Hassan 2011). Instead, mobile cloud should consider adaptive mechanisms (Fowler 2012b, Ma 2011, Song 2011) in the regulation process. While the traditional QoS parameters are used to objectively measure the network quality, a more recent concept, called Quality of experience (QoE) has become commonly used to represent user perception. Cloud-based QoE metrics should include parameters involved in the quality of the user experience such as delay before first image (the time it takes to see the first image of a streaming flow), video fluidity (i.e. average number of frames per second) and its variance, stream breakdown times, coding quality, and the size of the video stream window.

Although the up-and-coming LTE-Advanced has its own QoS features, it does not consider either cloud-based adaptive regulation mechanisms or QoE parameters. Implementation of QoE with LTE-Advanced in cloud environment is a new field to be explored.

Handover: Advanced wireless broadband systems such as 3G and 4G are designed seamless handover in mind (reference Handover Measurement in Mobile Cellular Networks: Analysis and Applications to LTE). The mechanism is that the mobile devices can simultaneously scan multiple adjacent cells operating in a common frequency band. As the number of cells that a mobile device can scan per given time is increased, subsequently, the handover performance is improved. Despite such effort, handover is one of the inherent mobile network challenges and constant improvement of network design and optimization is inevitable.

In contrast to wired network using physical connection, the data transfer rate in MCC environment is dynamically changing and bandwidth consistency are not always ensured. Continuous service in mobile communications is achieved by supporting handover from one cell to another. Handover is initiated either by crossing a cell boundary or by deterioration in quality of the signal in the current channel. Thus, poorly designed handover schemes will lead a dramatic decrease in QoS/QoE (Fowler 2006, Taleb 2012).

Typically in cloud, data center and resource in Internet service provider are remotely located from end users, especially from mobile device users. Thus in MCC, the network latency delay in last mile is inevitably larger than traditional wired network. Furthermore, several factors including dynamically changing application throughput and user mobility will also lead to bandwidth fluctuation and network overlay.

Another MCC specific challenge, Off-loading of the tasks can also contribute for network handover delay. Meanwhile, to ensure minimal handover interruption time, LTE-Advanced has robust general minimum radio resource management requirements. LTE's Mobility support for user equipment (UE) in connected-state comprises

of two types of handover procedures: backward handover and Radio Link Failure (RLF) handover, and both procedures require the source Enhanced Node B or base station (eNB) to prepare a target cell for handover concurrently with the handover decision. Despite the improved features of LTE system for optimal handover, limitations still exist such as high latency, handover procedure unreliability, high outage probability and data lost (Yuan 2012, Nguyen 2011, Deng 2012, Shayea 2012). Thus, interaction between the advanced handover techniques for LTE system and the unique handover challenges in MCC environment should be studied. The question is "How to achieve seamless handover in wireless mobility provided by LTE-Advanced and MCC, which comes with constantly changing environment with dynamically fluctuating traffic behavior?"

State-of-the-art: The development of both MCC and 4G network are at their infancy stage. Therefore, major groundwork has to be done to be ready for the expected popular use. In the long run, our ultimate goal is to maximize the resource utilization of MCC and improve QoS/QoE, which is a prerequisite for future development of wireless based technologies with resource-intensive applications such as e-commerce, e-learning, e-health with mobility or even intelligent transportation system for the future traffic safety. One way to achieve this, the first step will be to characterize the network behavior of MCC by modeling/simulating 4G wireless network LTE-Advanced in the cloud environment. It allows addressing fundamental MCC challenges; managing limited device battery lifetime, minimizing interaction latency, assuring QoS/QoE, and providing seamless handover. In other words, we intend to answer the question "How much work to be off-loaded to cloud to maximize energy efficiency, speed and user experience"

We will divide the strategies into four blocks: developing a cloud network model that can be used to evaluate mobile cloud network behavior, designing and evaluating the energy efficient protocols for optimal energy usage in MCC with 4G LTE-Advanced, evaluating 4G wireless network protocols in cloud environment to identify potential bottleneck for QoS/QoE implementation, evaluating handover protocols in 4G wireless network in cloud environment to achieve seamless handover with the connection quality.

We now look into the state-of-the-art in relation to the previous four strategies.

1. State-of-the-art in relation to the development of a cloud network model which can be used to evaluate mobile cloud network behavior.

Despite rapidly growing popularity of the mobile Internet, MCC research is still in its infancy. Only a few projects have rolled out just recently, but none of them has described end-to-end network behavior of MCC to the best of our knowledge. For example, FP7 funded projects CLOUD4all (CLOUD4all 2013) and I2Web (I2Web 2013) aim to address improvement of user interface but do not consider the whole cloud networks. In spite of their large cost, effort, and time consumed for real MCC measurements, those approaches are not feasible for evaluating end-to-end network behavior.

Instead, we propose to construct a cloud network model to evaluate wireless-to-wireless, wireless-to-wired, and wired-to-wired networks, which reflects the whole picture of the end-to-end cloud network topology. A generic model for mobile cloud network allows a person to study and address wide range of MCC challenges associated with the usability. Furthermore, once the work is done, the developed model can be utilized among the MCC research community since the modeling approach is flexible, appliable, and cost and time effective.

2. State-of-the-art in relation to designing energy efficient protocols for optimal energy usage in mobile cloud with 4G LTE-Advanced.

Energy efficiency and green network in mobile network has become a *hot* area of research. Especially, driving force towards MCC is to resolve the intrinsic mobile Internet challenge, i.e. handling resource-hungry rich data with resource -poor mobile devices. However, the focus of the research has been either targeting energy-efficiency in the cloud network topology only or the mobile device itself only. In either case, the main assumption is that outsourcing energy-consuming tasks to the cloud would dissolve the energy issues in mobile devices. The energy required for transferring and receiving data between mobile device and cloud network has not been considered. For example EuroCloud (EuroCloud 2013) and TREND (TREND 2013) aim to design energy efficient cloud network, while C2Power (C2Power 2013) aim to improve mobile devices' energy-saving with MCC in mind.

The LTE-BE-IT: LTE Advanced for Network Behaviour Energy and Intelligent Transportation Systems (LTE-BE-IT 2013) project has also focused on the energy-saving in 4G technology. We have studied Discontinuous Reception (DRX) mechanism for power-saving in LTE system (Fowler 2011, Fowler 2012a, Bhamber 2013). In the project, we have developed semi-Markov analytical model to study both adjustable and fixed sleep cycle to achieve energy-efficiency.

The next step for progressing MCC is to find out the trade-off between out-sourcing and local computing in the mobile device in terms of energy required for each case. "How much work to be done locally by mobile device, and how much to be outsourced to cloud?" to answer such questions, the end-to-end MCC network model is an attractive (time- and cost- effective) and effective (flexible, appliable and yet accurate) method.

3. State-of-the-art in relation to the evaluation of the 4G wireless network protocols in cloud environment to identify potential bottleneck for QoS/QoE implementation.

Few projects have addressed QoE implementation in MCC today, since both QoE and MCC are quite new concepts. Fit4Green (Fit4Green 2013) aim to study the trade-off between service quality and energy in cloud, but their focus is not on wireless network or QoE. On the other hand, Monica (Monica 2013) and MobileCloud (MobileCloud 2013) aim to address service quality in MCC, but tradeoffs between energy and QoS/QoE is not considered. Furthermore, in the above three projects, the quality measurement is limited to QoS and not QoE, thus user perception is out of there scope.

The LTE-BE-IT (Fowler 2011, Fowler 2012a, Bhamber 2013) project have focused on the scheduling in 4G mobile device LTE-Advanced for provisioning of QoS/QoE. Since the target of the project was on scheduler in the mobile device and not on its interaction with cloud, a logical progression of the research is to study how mobile device and cloud network interact with each other thereby causing delay and quality degradation. To achieve this, one should aim to identify potential bottleneck in end-to-end mobile cloud network. Since the bottleneck could reside literally anywhere, e.g. within wireless device, at wireless connection, and inside the cloud network, the end-to-end mobile cloud model would be a powerful tool. In addition, using the proposed modeling approach, we will be able to study the trade-off between energy-saving and QoS/QoE provisioning in MCC, and the knowledge can be directly translated into usability of MCC.

4. State-of-the-art in relation to evaluation of handover protocols in 4G wireless network in cloud environment to achieve seamless handover with the connection quality.

Handover delay has always been a big obstacle in mobile communications and many approaches have been proposed and applied to date. Given the sharp growth of mobile Internet along with MCC, it is expected that we would encounter with unique challenges yet unseen to achieve seamless handover (Liu 2012). The main MCC specific concern is response time constraint during handover when executing application which resides in cloud and not in mobile device. Application partitioning in cloud can also be a cause of response time delay. The delay is more noticeable especially dealing with real-time applications such as video, voice and on-line games.

Ironically, consumers expect more from these applications with MCC. Nonetheless, handover issues in MCC have not been explored yet, while several projects have addressed handover with 4G networks. For example, CROSSFIRE (CROSSFIRE 2013) aims to study handover with LTE but does not consider interaction with energy-saving or cloud network, while C2POWER (C2POWER 2013) aims to study handover with energy-saving in general wireless network but does not consider 4G technology or interaction with cloud network.

Here, we propose to evaluate handover protocols in LTE-Advanced in mobile cloud network utilizing the model proposed in the following section (Solutions and Recommendations). By modifying the *single-cell* end-to-end mobile cloud network model into *multiple-cell* model, one can simulate handover in MCC rather simply.

The basic knowledge obtained on handover in MCC can be extended to a variety of applications such as Vehicle-to-infrastructure and vehicle-to-vehicle communication (V2X). There should be considerable amount of handover in V2X due to its dynamically changing environment. V2X has acquired considerable attention from both academia and industry because it holds the potential to improve road safety and decrease vehicle energy usage (e.g. fuel), and companies such as Ford (Ford 2012), Honda (Honda 2012), Audi (Audi 2012), GM (GM 2012), BMW (BMW 2012), etc are using LTE in there models.

Solutions and Recommendations

To address the fundamental MCC with 4G challenges (device battery lifetime, interaction latency, QoS/QoE, seamless handover), characterization of the end-to-end network behavior of MCC is a necessary first step. To achieve this, we will propose modeling/simulation of LTE in a Cloud environment. Here, we will detail the approaches according to the previously described four blocks of the work process.

1. Approaches to develop a Cloud Network model which can be used to evaluate Mobile cloud network behavior.

Modeling is a useful method because it is cost effective and has the flexibility to accommodate large numbers of tests, compared to using real equipment. Especially, because of the complexity of the cloud network architecture, it is not feasible to have a dedicated system running in a lab environment for performance testing. More realistically, simulation and modeling can be utilized to predict cloud capacity and network behavior (e.g. response time and resource utilization at various arrival rates), which will provide valuable information on the system architecture in order to capture bad designs and potential performance hotspots. Therefore, we propose to develop a flexible model based on a statistics-based analytical approach to conduct a series of tests. Indeed, one should not ignore the importance of validating the modeling results on real cloud network equipment.

Recommendation 1: Model a cloud system architecture using statistical model based on Queueing theory/Markov chain.

Advantage of modeling via statistical model: It is extremely time-consuming to run a simulation with detailed features. To by-pass this problem, statistical models can be applied, since well-designed Queueing Theory/Markovian-based models provide relevant results within a short time (Kleinrock 1975). Although several assumptions need to be made in statistical models, the outcomes are generally comparable to the ones from a complete detailed simulator that eliminates the need for any assumptions. Typically, Markov models can be readily integrated within analytical models of queuing systems (Bhamber 2013, Fowler 2012a). Such queueing models can then be utilized for computing performance metrics, inexpensively, accurately, and rapidly. This provides a quantitative methodology for energy efficiency, QoS/QoE evaluation, and a wide range of additional performance testing in the cloud under future research.

Advantage of developing a generic mobile cloud model: A few groups have proposed cloud or cloud mobile model via statistical models based on Queueing theory/Markov Chain, but they are limited to studying specific applications, e.g., single type of traffic, such as only-voice or only-video (Khazaei 2012), or specific behavior of wireless devices, such as mobility and uplink effects (Tursunova 2012). Such models are not flexible enough to characterize the overall picture of 4G multimedia in a cloud network. Therefore we propose to develop a generic cloud network model integrating Queueing theory/Markov Chain which can be utilized for a wide variety of tests, including multimedia (e.g. video plus audio, game) in a 4G LTE context. Once the model is developed, it can be utilized to study MCC for various applications.

Recommendation 2: Adjust the model based on the actual LTE measurement data.

Preliminary studies of our group have gathered the actual measurement data from LTE equipment for capturing real LTE traffic behavior. Such empirical measurement data can be utilized for adjusting the analytical model by modulating elements such as the number of processors, service time, and waiting time. By incorporating this process, the model will become more realistic and reliable to predict LTE behavior in the mobile cloud.

2. Approaches to design energy efficient protocols for optimal energy usage in mobile cloud with 4G LTE-Advanced.

The question to be asked for achieving energy efficiency in the mobile cloud environment is: "How much work should be off-loaded to the cloud, and how much should be executed by the mobile device itself?" Adding LTE network to the Mobile cloud topology is equivalent to finding a break-even point between energy-efficiency and energy-consumption in both cloud and LTE. Trade-offs need to be made through extensive evaluation in the following complex issues.

Energy saving effects includes:

- Off-loading computation to the cloud network, which reduces the burden of mobile devices.
- Out-sourcing to cloud for execution of the instructions on the device.
- LTE's power-saving protocols including Discontinuous Reception (DRX) and Discontinuous Transmission (DTX).

Energy-consuming potential includes:

- Transmission energy, which is required for bidirectional communication (sending/receiving) between mobile device and cloud network for off-loading computation.
- LTE-Advance's capacity for handling higher data rate and wider range of traffic types, due to the increased bandwidth, leads to higher demand for energy.

The following recommendations 1 through 3 will address the trade-off between cloud off-loading computing and energy-efficiency.

Recommendation 1: Develop algorithms to make decisions whether the off-loading computing or local computing is preferable.

The algorithms should perform energy calculations for: Cost of sending transfer request, Cost of receiving a reply, Cost of transferring a job, Cost of migration of a job, and Cost of executing a job on a mobile device. Since the main objective of off-loading computation by cloud is to conserve battery power on a mobile device, jobs should only be migrated if the amount of power consumption with migration of the job is less than that with local job execution by the device.

Recommendation 2: Test energy consumption under the developed algorithms

The parameters to be considered including; Available bandwidth, Job size, Power consumed by the CPU to execute a job on the mobile device, and Power consumed to transmit and receive messages.

The variables that need to be considered here are; Available bandwidth, Packet size of request message, Packet size of transfer reply, Packet size of the returned result, Size of the job to be transferred, Power remaining on the mobile device, Power consumed transmitting packets(s), Power consumed receiving packets(s), and Power consumed to execute a job on the mobile host. One can also evaluate the algorithm using the real measurement data of LTE as a reference.

Recommendation 3: Apply the LTE-DRX parameters to the developed mobile cloud model, so as to maximize power saving without incurring network re-entry and packet delays.

Wireless standard LTE and LTE-Advanced employs power saving mechanisms, e.g., turning off the radio antenna for the longest time possible, while staying connected to the network. LTE/ LTE-Advanced power-saving protocols include DRX and DTX, both of which involve reducing the transceiver duty cycle while inactive operation. Thus, DRX/DTX operates with a cost; the mobile device's data throughput is reduced in proportion to the power savings. Our group have recently investigated the LTE DRX mechanism with adjustable and non-adjustable DRX cycle and modeled it with bursty packet data traffic using a semi-Markov process (Fowler 2012a, Bhamber 2013), in which we demonstrated differentiated performance between the adjustable LTE DRX and the non-adjustable LTE DRX, a trade-off relationship between the power saving and wake-up delay performance, and a validation of four DRX parameters (active, inactive, light sleep, and deep sleep) on output performance via the analytical model (Figure 1). Using such DRX model, one can analyze the trade-off of off-loading versus local device computing.

Figure 1(top) (Fowler 2012a) depicts a model for the LTE Discontinuous Reception (DRX) mechanism with adjustable and non-adjustable DRX cycles using a semi-Markov process tested with bursty packet data traffic for Powering Saving as the Inactivity Timer (T_I) increases. Figure 1(bottom) (Fowler 2012a) shows the performance differences between adjustable and non-adjustable DRX in the Inactivity Timer (T_I), the Short Cycle Timer, and the Long Cycle Timer, in terms of the power saving factor and wakeup delay. The figures indicate power saving factors and wakeup delay in the DRX Inactivity Timer, with either adjustable or non-adjustable DRX, by means of a Semi-Markov model. The analytical model shows that there is a trade-off between energy saving and

Figure 1. LTE power saving and delay

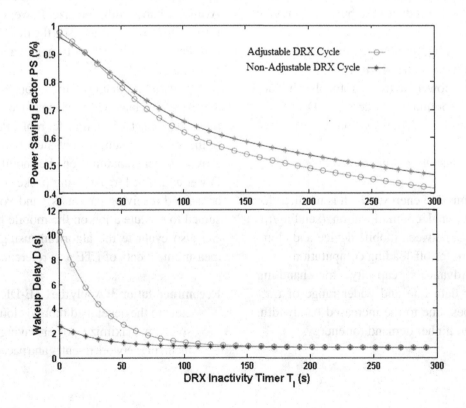

delay (or latency) for DRX. There is a need to investigate the trade-off relationship of off-loading versus local device computing in a mobile cloud with 4G LTE.

3. Approaches to evaluate the 4G wireless network protocols in cloud environment to identify potential bottleneck for QoS/QoE implementation.

Traditionally, QoS is achieved by managing delays, jitter, fairness and packet loss rate. However, as 4G LTE is intended to provide real-time, delay-sensitive multimedia, a different type of quality assurance is needed, namely, Quality of Experience (QoE). QoE is a measurement of how well a system or an application meets the user's expectations such as degradation in voice or video quality, whereas QoS focuses on standard quantitative performance from a network perspective. QoE is directly related to QoS; therefore one can map the objective QoS measurements (e.g. delay, packet loss and jitter) into the user's perception QoE, through an appropriate set of tools and processes (Truong 2012). There are many QoS/QoE factors that directly affect the performance of network components and mobile devices. Scheduling and power saving are two main factors in QoS/QoE provisioning for multimedia applications since these applications demand more radio resources and power. Scheduling is a process of allocating the physical resources among mobile devices thereby guaranteeing QoS/QoE for multimedia service.

In the LTE-mobile cloud, scheduling can be performed within the LTE wireless network and at the interface between the wireless and the cloud network, which is called the cloud broker. As enhanced multimedia is a key feature of LTE, real-time (RT) and nonreal-time (NRT) traffic needs to be scheduled in LTE. A scheduler, therefore, is a vital element of an LTE system. The scheduling mechanism, which is unique to LTE, is known as PDCCH (Physical Downlink Control Channel). The PDCCH contains all scheduling control information, including Downlink (DL) resource allocation, Uplink (UL) grants, PRACH (Physical Random Access Channel) responses, UL power control commands, and common scheduling assignments for signaling various messages, such as system information. In the cloud network, the cloud broker acts as a middle component between users and resources and tries to search for the best resources which fit the user requirements as measured by the QoE. The resource scheduler in the cloud broker discovers possible relevant resources, monitors whether QoS/QoE is met or not, mediates any mismatched requirements, and selects the best resources across multiple cloud service providers that match the incoming request.

However, the scheduling process in the LTE and the cloud are separate entities and not coordinated with each other. Therefore, in the whole picture of LTE-Mobile cloud architecture, there will be several spots that represent potential bottlenecks. Hence, one should aim to identify these QoS/QoE bottlenecks. Additionally, one can investigate the trade-off between QoS/QoE and energy efficiency in the scheduler. We will present the following recommendations.

Recommendation 1: Design energy-aware scheduler in LTE utilizing simulation data.

LTE system's scheduling decisions on how to treat RT and NRT can be made on the basis of two parameters, namely QoS and the so-called Channel Quality Indicator (CQI). Using these parameters, we will propose a scheduler that improves the QoS for multimedia service (e.g. one that minimizes packet delay). A traditional scheduling scheme aims to maximize the overall system throughput while keeping fairness, delay, and packet loss rate within QoS requirements. In addition to that, we will propose a new scheduling technique which also features energy efficiency. In order to balance QoS against power consumption, a delay energy trade-off has to be performed, since traffic transmission rate and power consumption are directly related.

The challenge is that the energy-efficient scheduler has to assign the radio resources in such a way as to minimize the energy consumption by the mobile device, while the QoS/QoE of the connections is maintained. Previously, we have designed an energy-aware LTE downlink scheduler for VoIP-only traffic (Figure 2). As a complement to the previous work, we can design a scheduler which will handle multi-media traffic as well.

Despite increasing power savings, our scheduling approach sustains the level of packet delay. Similar outcomes were also observed in other QoS parameters, including Packet loss ratio, Throughput fairness index and System throughput (data not shown). Complementary to the preliminary study that tested the scheduler for VoIP-only traffic, we will design an opportunistic scheduler which can handle multimedia traffic as well.

Figure 2(a) (Mushtaq 2012) depicts a new QoS-aware downlink scheduling algorithm for delay sensitive traffic (VoIP). The scheduler uses an opportunistic approach that calculates the priorities of the user equipment (UE) and assigns resources based on the following features: Channel condition, Average throughput, UE buffer status, GBR (guaranteed bit rate)/non-GBR

Figure 2. (a) Average packet delay vs. power saving; and (b) Throughput fairness index vs. power saving

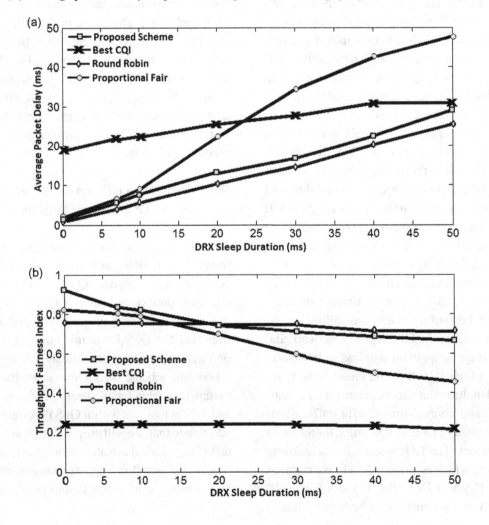

traffic, UE DRX status and packets delay at the eNB buffer. Figure 2(b) (Mushtaq 2012) depicts the correlation between the QoS Degradation parameter (expressed as average packet delay in milliseconds) versus the Power-Saving factor (expressed as DRX sleep duration in milliseconds), simulated with two traditional schedulers (Proportionally Fair and Best CQI) and our opportunistic scheduler. Despite increasing power savings, our scheduling approach sustains the level of packet delay. Similar outcomes were also observed in other QoS parameters, including Packet loss ratio, Throughput fairness index and System throughput. Complementary to the preliminary study that tested the scheduler for VoIP-only traffic, we will design an opportunistic scheduler which can handle multimedia traffic as well. Figure 2(b) shows that initially the Proposed Scheme performs significantly well, but its fairness index reduces and goes below RR after 20 ms sleep duration. When the sleep duration increases, packet delays increase and scheduler tries to compensate this by giving more resources to the UE which packet is getting closer to the delay threshold. As a result, some UEs have higher throughput and some experience lower throughput. The Figure clearly shows that the RR has the highest performance index as compared to the Proposed Scheme but the RR did not provide sufficient data rates for UEs to satisfy its QoS requirements,

Recommendation 2: Implement the developed schedulers in the mobile cloud model and identify bottlenecks in relation to the delay-energy trade-off.

The cloud broker's basic function is to choose the best provider in the upstream based on the knowledge of who offers the Potential candidates for a QoS/QoE bottleneck include the limited wireless bandwidth, the network backbone between the LTE network and the cloud broker, and the virtualized systems inside the cloud. We will also

investigate the trade-off between energy efficiency and QoS/QoE in this context.

4. Approaches to evaluate handover protocols in 4G wireless network in cloud environment to achieve seamless handover with the connection quality.

In the real world, users would demand seamless services in MCC, especially with real-time data traffic such as voice, online games, and video. Thus, MCC should support seamless handover to mobile users regardless of their *locations* and *movements*. Therefore, one should investigate effective strategies for seamless handover in MCC while maximizing the effects of 4G network. Utilizing the model developed, we can evaluate the handover protocols for 4G LTE with mobile cloud network. One can modify the *single-cell* end-to-end mobile cloud network model into *multiple-cell* model. This way, one can model more realistic MCC environment and analyze handover in MCC with a relatively simple procedure.

Recommendation 1: Address the bottlenecks in handover model and develop effective MCC topology.

To achieve this, one can investigate the impact of handover by comparing the measurements in single-cell vs. multiple-cell handover model. First, we will develop an end-to-end MCC network multiple-cell model. Continuation from the previous approaches and recommendations, we can simply apply the knowledge for developing multiple-cell model for studying handover. Second, one can compare the energy saving data obtained in single-cell model, vs. multiple-cell handover measurement data. Similarly, one can compare the QoS/QoE single-cell data obtained in single-cell model with the measurements in handover model. The parameters to be considered in the algorithm in previous approaches and recommendations can be also applied. The approach

Figure 3. Predicting handover performance when UE moving

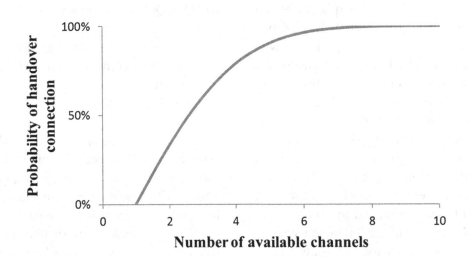

allows us to characterize handover delay in MCC and to identify handover bottleneck(s) (Figure 3). Once the bottleneck(s) of handover delay are identified, we should be able to present an efficient end-to-end MCC network handover topology. We can test the topology in more dynamic and realistic traffic model in Recommendation 2.

Figure 3 depicts prediction for fail or success of handover connectivity, or blocking probability, by utilizing Erlang loss formula. Assumptions to be made include:

- An unsuccessful handover as a result of the channel in target cell being busy, being not queued or not retried.
- Handover requests are independent and following a position process, and
- Average throughput (or average delay) are exponentially distributed based on Markovian system.

Despite the usage of MCC, connectivity will still decrease if the channel resources in need are not available. Therefore, there is a need to develop a *multiple-cell* model to improve QoS/QoE handover performance in an end-to-end MCC.

Recommendation 2: Apply traffic density data into handover model to characterize realistic MCC network environment with vehicle transportation.

Here, we will utilize the handover model to characterize MCC networks with vehicle transportation. This segment of work should be multidisciplinary i.e. mobile telecommunication, Intelligent Transportation System and Math. Our multidisciplinary team has been studying traffic density/behavior in the currently ongoing project. We are planning to integrate the traffic data into the proposed handover model in LTE-MCC network. Simulation tools available for traffic behavior (vehicle density, mobile user density and speed) include Aimsun, Visum/Vissim, and contram. The approach is unique because the traffic/handover model allows us to evaluate 4G LTE performance in a high mobility and density.

Figure 4 demonstrate that a queuing theory model of this kind can be used to describe the number of channels needed to serve a specific combination of number of vehicles and the amount of traffic they request. The model was designed to predict wireless capacity required between UE (vehicle in this scenario) and Enhanced Node B or base station BS (eNB). Optimal number of

Figure 4. Optimal number of channels for effective handover

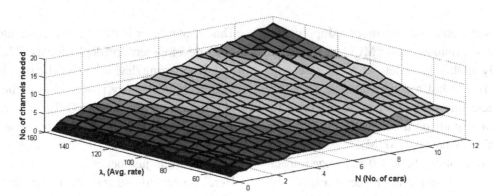

channels (z-axis) required in relation to the average packet arriving rate- λ (y-axis) and number of the cars in traffic-N (x-axis) in a LTE-Advanced network is depicted. By using the following set values, $\beta_i = 0.01$ and $t_i = 100$ms based on (Pedersen 2009) for Equation (3). Figure 4 shows acceptable level for a voice communication.

The Equation (4) was derived based on the following steps. First, the traffic is assumed to have a position arrival rate. The probability of having no jobs waiting on connection upon arrival and the probability of no having a connection available (seeing m jobs on arrival, where m is the number of servers) are only depending on the number of servers m and the traffic intensity ρ. The probability that there are no jobs in service, P_0, and the probability of all servers' connections being busy, P_m, is given by (Kleinrock 1976):

$$P_0(m,\rho) = \left[\frac{(m\rho)^m}{m!(1-\rho)} + \sum_{n=0}^{m-1} \frac{(m\rho)^n}{n!} \right]^{-1} \quad (1)$$

The probability of all servers' connections (we refer them to Channels) being busy (refer to as Erlang-C) is given by (Kleinrock 1976)

$$P_q = P_m(m,\rho) = \frac{(m\rho)^m}{m!(1-\rho)} P_0 \quad (2)$$

In the case with no priority, the traffic intensity ρ is defined as

$$\rho = \frac{N\lambda}{m\mu} \quad (3)$$

The number of channels/servers needed to serve N number of customers, each requesting data with a packet-rate of λ, in such a way that 1-β_i of the requested packets will be served within time t_i, is given by:

$$P_q e^{-(m\mu - N\lambda)t_i} < \beta_i \Rightarrow m > \frac{\log\left(\frac{1}{\beta_i} P_q\right) + N\lambda t_i}{\mu t_i} \quad (4)$$

The specific value of βi and t_i depends on what service (i) we are considering. Such values are for different services described in (Pedersen 2009).

FUTURE TRENDS

The knowledge obtained from proposed approaches to address groundwork for MCC with 4G can be directly applied to variety of MCC research. Particularly, the last recommendation on MCC with vehicle transportation can be extended to a new area of study on Intelligent transportation and machine to machine (M2M).

In the near future, there will be a huge impact of M2M to the transportation sector, especially to a future Vehicle-to-Vehicle, Vehicle-to-Device, Vehicle-to-Infrastructure (V2X) core system. More specifically, a research consortium consists of automotive electronics engineer should integrate the knowledge of LTE-Advanced networks, innovations such as self-organizing femto-cells, traffic shaping and heterogeneous/vertical roaming across different radio access technologies in order to improve the performance of cloud-based vehicular applications.

The idea behind is that vehicles can serve as wireless gateways that manage/collect data from devices or sensors deployed in vehicles and highway infrastructure which utilize 4G cellular devices as the last-mile wide-area connection to the cloud network. How 4G will manage devices/sensors which are utilizing short range radio access technologies (e.g. Wi-Fi) as the last yard connection is the question to be asked.

Furthermore, the basic knowledge obtained from the modeling approach to capture the end-to-end network behavior of MCC with 4G can be extended into the following academic and industrial multidisciplinary research projects in the future, for example, Development of technologies for coordinated scheduling between the 4G LTE network and the cloud broker, Development of cloud broker scheduling algorithms for the *Green Cloud* and energy-efficiency for data centers, Investigation of mobility and seamless hand-over in the mobile cloud network, and Implementation of mobile cloud in multimedia visualization.

CONCLUSION

This chapter described the fundamental challenges in the development and deployment of MCC with 4G; maximizing device battery lifetime, improving interaction latency, provisioning of the quality of service/experience (QoS/QoE), and providing seamless handover. In general, the research on MCC with 4G is at its infancy stage, and only a few projects just began to tackle these issues. Here, we considered statistical modeling as one of the robust tool to address these issues and proposed several strategies to achieve the goals. We classified the strategies into the following four blocks; Approaches to develop a cloud network model which can be used to evaluate mobile cloud network behavior, Approaches to design energy efficient protocols for optimal energy usage in mobile cloud with 4G LTE, Approaches to evaluate the 4G wireless network protocols in cloud environment to identify potential bottleneck for QoS/QoE implementation, and Approaches to evaluate handover protocols in 4G wireless network in cloud environment to achieve seamless handover with the connection quality.

In conclusion, such groundwork towards the deployment of MCC with 4G will provide the opportunity for the development of innovative technologies and applications. Since the challenges in MCC discussed here are intrinsic and continuous research effort is required, study on mobile cloud network behavior is relevant for even the future generation of mobile technologies.

REFERENCES

3GPP Technical Specification 23.203. (2008). *Policy and charging control architecture* (Release 8). Retrieved April 21, 2013, from www.3gpp.org

Audi. (2012). Retrieved February 14, 2013, from http://www.greencarcongress.com/2012/03/audi-connect-20120309.html#more

Bhamber, R. S., Fowler, S., Braimiotis, C., & Mellouk, A. (2013). Analytic analysis of LTE/LTE-advanced power saving and delay with bursty traffic. In *Proceedings of the IEEE International Conference on Communications (ICC)*. IEEE.

BMW. (2012). Retrieved February 14, 2013, from http://bimmermania.com/blog/2012/07/12/bmw-connecteddrive-blitzkrieg-includes-lte-connectivity -android-compatibility-and-new-idrive-touch/

C2Power. (2013). *Cognitive radio and cooperative strategies for power saving in multi-standard wireless devices*. Retrieved February 14, 2013, from http://www.ict-c2power.eu/over_objs.htm

CLOUD4all. (2013). Retrieved February 14, 2013, from http://cloud4all.info/

CROSSFIRE. (2013). *Uncoordinated network strategies for enhanced interference, mobility, radio resource, and energy saving management in lte-advanced networks*. Retrieved February 14, 2013, from http://gain.di.uoa.gr/crossfire/

Deng, B., Wang, W., & Li, Y. (2012). A novel low complexity cell search algorithm for TD-LTE advanced system. In *Proceedings of the IEEE International Conference on Wireless Communications, Networking and Mobile Computing (WiCOM)*. IEEE.

Distefano, S., & Puliafito, A. (2012). Cloud@Home: Toward a volunteer cloud. *IEEE IT Professional, 14*(1), 27–31. doi:10.1109/MITP.2011.111.

EuroCloud. (2013). *Energy-conscious 3D server-on-chip for green cloud*. Retrieved February 14, 2013, from http://www.eurocloudserver.com/

Fit4Green. (2013). *Federated IT for a sustainable environmental impact*. Retrieved February 14, 2013, from http://www.fit4green.eu/

Ford. (2012). Retrieved February 14, 2013, from http://www.indiandrives.com/fords-new-mobile-app-promises-to-speed-up-car-charging.html

Fowler, S. (2011). Study on power saving based on radio frame in LTE wireless communication system using DRX. In *Proceedings of the IEEE Globecom Workshop*. IEEE.

Fowler, S., Bhamber, R. S., & Mellouk, A. (2012). Analysis of adjustable and fixed DRX mechanism for power saving in LTE/LTE-advanced. In *Proceedings of the IEEE International Conference on Communications (ICC)*. IEEE.

Fowler, S., & Zeadally, S. (2006). Fast handover over micro-MPLS-based wireless networks. In *Proceedings of the 11th IEEE Symposium on Computers and Communications (ISCC)*. IEEE.

Fowler, S., Zeadally, S., & Mellouk, A. (2008). Quality of service support for MPLS-based wired-wireless domains. In A. Mellouk (Ed.), *End-to-End Quality of Service Engineering in Next Generation Heterogeneous Networks* (pp. 309–345). London, UK: Wiley/ISTE Publishing..

Fowler, S., & Zhang, X. (2012). Ubiquitous fair bandwidth allocation for multimedia traffic on a WiMAX mesh network with multi-channels. *International Journal of Ad Hoc and Ubiquitous Computing, 9*(4). doi:10.1504/IJAHUC.2012.047009.

Garg, S. K., Versteeg, S., & Buyya, R. (2011). SMICloud: A framework for comparing and ranking cloud services. In *Proceedings of the Fourth IEEE International Conference on Utility and Cloud Computing*. IEEE.

GM. (2012). Retrieved February 14, 2013, from http://www.greencarcongress.com/2012/01/onstar-20120110.html#more

Hassan, M. M., Song, B., & Huh, E. (2011). Distributed resource allocation games in horizontal dynamic cloud federation platform. In *Proceedings of the IEEE 13th International Conference on High Performance Computing and Communications (HPCC)*, (pp. 822-827). IEEE.

Honda. (2012). Retrieved February 14, 2013, from http://www.greencarcongress.com/2012/04/ibm-20120412.html#more

I2Web. (2013). *Inclusive future internet web services*. Retrieved February 14, 2013, from http://services.future-internet.eu/index.php/I2WEB

Jia-Ming, L., Chen, J.-J., Cheng, H.-H., & Tseng, Y.-C. (2013). An energy-efficient sleep scheduling with QoS consideration in 3GPP LTE-advanced networks for internet of things. *IEEE Journal on Emerging and Selected Topics in Circuits and Systems, 3*(1), 13–22. doi:10.1109/JET-CAS.2013.2243631.

Khazaei, H., Misic, J., & Misic, V. (2012). Performance analysis of cloud computing centers using M/G/m/m + r queueing systems. *IEEE Transactions on Parallel and Distributed Systems, 23*(5), 936–943. doi:10.1109/TPDS.2011.199.

Kleinrock, L. (1975). Queueing systems: Vol. I. *Theory*. New York: Wiley..

Kleinrock, L. (1976). Queueing systems: Vol. II. *Computer applications*. New York: Wiley..

Kumar, K., & Yung-Hsiang, L. (2010). Cloud computing for mobile users: Can offloading computation save energy?. *IEEE Computer, 43*(4).

Liu, L., Yang, F., Wang, R., Shi, Z., Stidwell, A., & Gu, D. (2012). Analysis of handover performance improvement in cloud-RAN architecture. In *Proceedings of the IEEE International Conference on Communications and Networking in China* (CHINACOM) (pp. 850-855). IEEE.

LTE-BE-IT. (2013). *LTE-advanced for network behaviour, energy and intelligent transportation systems*. Retrieved February 14, 2013, from http://webstaff.itn.liu.se/~scofo47/WebPage%20LTE-BE-IT/

Ma, R. K. K., Lam, K., & Wang, C.-L. (2011). eXCloud: Transparent runtime support for scaling mobile applications in cloud. In *Proceedings of the IEEE International Conference on Cloud and Service Computing* (CSC) (pp. 103-110). IEEE.

Mei, C., Taylor, D., Wang, C., Chandra, A., & Weissman, J. (2011). *Mobilizing the cloud: Enabling multi-user mobile outsourcing in the cloud* (TR 11-029). Retrieved February 10, 2013, from http://www-users.cs.umn.edu/~jon/papers/11-029.pdf

MobileCloud. (2013). *Future communication architecture for mobile cloud*. Retrieved February 14, 2013, from http://www.utwente.nl/ctit/research/projects/international/fp7-ip/mobilecloud.doc/

MONICA. (2013). *Mobile cloud computing: Networks, services and architecture*. Retrieved February 14, 2013, from http://www.fp7-monica.eu/

Mushtaq, M. S., Shahid, A., & Fowler, S. (2012). QoS-aware LTE downlink scheduler for VoIP with power saving. In *Proceedings of the IEEE 15th International Conference on Computational Science and Engineering* (CSE). IEEE.

Nguyen, V. M., Chen, C. S., & Thomas, L. (2011). Handover measurement in mobile cellular networks: analysis and applications to LTE. In *Proceedings of the IEEE International Conference on Communications (ICC)*. IEEE.

Othman, M., & Hailes, S. (1998). Power conservation strategy for mobile computers using load sharing. *ACM Mobile Computing and Communication Review, 2*(1), 44–50. doi:10.1145/584007.584011.

Pedersen, K. I., Kolding, T. E., Frederiksen, F., Kovács, I. Z., Laselva, D., & Mogensen, P. E. (2009). An overview of downlink radio resource management for UTRAN long-term evolution. *IEEE Communications Magazine, 47*(7), 86–93. doi:10.1109/MCOM.2009.5183477.

Puttonen, J., Virtej, E., Keskitalo, I., & Malkamaki, E. (2012). On LTE performance trade-off between connected and idle states with always-on type applications. In *Proceedings of the IEEE 23rd International Symposium on Personal Indoor and Mobile Radio Communications* (PIMRC) (pp. 981-985). IEEE.

Raicu, I., Schwiebert, L., Fowler, S., & Gupta, S. K. S. (2005). Local load balancing for globally efficient routing in wireless sensor networks. *International Journal of Distributed Sensor Networks, 1*(2), 163–185. doi:10.1080/15501320590966431.

Rao, M. (2011). *Mobile Africa report 2011: Regional hubs of excellence and innovation.* Retrieved February 10, 2013, from http://www.mobilemonday.net/reports/MobileAfrica_2011.pdf

Satyanarayanan, M., Bahl, P., Caceres, R., & Davies, N. (2009). The case for VM-based cloudlets in mobile computing. *IEEE Pervasive Computing/IEEE Computer Society [and] IEEE Communications Society, 8*(4), 14–23. doi:10.1109/MPRV.2009.82.

Shayea, I., Ismail, M., & Nordin, R. (2012). Advanced handover techniques in LTE-advanced system. In *Proceedings of the IEEE International Conference on Computer and Communication Engineering* (ICCCE). IEEE.

Simoens, P., De Turck, F., Dhoedt, B., & Demeester, P. (2011). Remote display solutions for mobile cloud computing. *IEEE Computer, 44*(8), 46–53. doi:10.1109/MC.2011.70.

Song, H., Bae, C.-S., Lee, J.-W., & Youn, C.-H. (2011). Utility adaptive service brokering mechanism for personal cloud service. In *Proceedings of IEEE Military Communications Conference* (MILCOM) (pp. 1622-1627). IEEE.

Sunggeun, J., & Qiao, D. (2012). Numerical analysis of the power saving in 3GPP LTE advanced wireless networks. *IEEE Transactions on Vehicular Technology, 61*(4), 1779–1785. doi:10.1109/TVT.2012.2187690.

Taleb, T., & Ksentini, A. (2012). QoS/QoE predictions-based admission control for femto communications. In *Proceedings of the IEEE International Conference on Communications* (ICC) (pp. 5146-5150). IEEE.

TREND. (2013). *Towards real energy-efficient network design.* Retrieved February 14, 2013, from http://www.fp7-trend.eu/

Truong, T. H., Nguyen, T. H., & Nguyen, H. T. (2012). On relationship between quality of experience and quality of service metrics for IMS-based IPTV networks. In *Proceedings of the IEEE International Conference on Computing and Communication Technologies, Research, Innovation, and Vision for the Future* (RIVF). IEEE.

Tursunova, S., & Young-Tak, K. (2012). Realistic IEEE 802.11e EDCA model for QoS-aware mobile cloud service provisioning. *IEEE Transactions on Consumer Electronics, 58*(1), 60–68. doi:10.1109/TCE.2012.6170056.

Visiongain. (2011). *Mobile cloud computing industry outlook report: 2011-2016.* Retrieved February 10, 2013, from http://www.visiongain.com/Report/737/Mobile-Cloud-Computing-Industry-Outlook-Report-2011-2016

Yuan, S., Tao, L., & Win, M. Z. (2012). Neighboring cell search for LTE systems. *IEEE Transactions on Wireless Communications, 11*(3), 908–919. doi:10.1109/TWC.2012.011012.100089.

Zhu, Q., & Agrawal, G. (2012). Resource provisioning with budget constraints for adaptive applications in cloud environments. *IEEE Transactions on Services Computing, 5*(4), 497–511. doi:10.1109/TSC.2011.61.

Chapter 4
Privacy and Security of Wireless Communication Networks

Sattar B. Sadkhan
University of Babylon, Iraq

Nidaa A. Abbas
University of Babylon, Iraq

ABSTRACT

Wireless networks are inherently more vulnerable than their wired counterparts. In addition, complications arise in the presence of node mobility and dynamic network topology. Moreover, intermittent connectivity, whether caused by mobility or periodic node sleep, brings about additional challenges. At the same time, node resource constraints make direct adoption of existing security solutions difficult, if not impossible. Wireless Communication Network Security and Privacy analyze important problems in the realms of wireless networks and mobile computing. The Security aspects relate to authentication, access control and authorization, nonrepudiation, privacy and confidentiality, integrity, and auditing. Privacy is an essential feature of any product or service.

WIRELESS COMMUNICATION NETWORKING AND TECHNOLOGIES

Wireless communications have become a very interesting sector for the provision of telecommunication services. Mobile networks are available almost anytime and anywhere. The popularity of wireless handheld devices is high. The services offered are strongly increasing. They vary from simple communication services to applications for

DOI: 10.4018/978-1-4666-4781-7.ch004

special and sensitive purposes such as electronic commerce, medical services and digital cash (Thurwachter, 2002).

Due to low cost, low power consumption, flexible, no physical infrastructure and easy to deploy, wireless communications have been an admired research area over the past few years with tremendous growth in the population of wireless users. Nowadays, there are number of wireless technologies on hand for long range applications like cellular mobile, satellite communications, Radio Frequency (RF), and short range applications such as Bluetooth, Infrared (IR), Near Field Communication (NFC), ZigBee, Ultra Wide Band (UWB). These short range wireless technologies are being used in many wireless networks like wireless local area networks (WLAN), wireless body area networks (WBANs), wireless personal area networks (WPANs), and, ad-hoc network (Tachikawa, 2002).

The IEEE 802.11 standard for wireless local area networks (also known as Wi-Fi) currently supports multiple over-the-air modulation techniques in the 2.4 GHz and 5 GHz frequency bands with speeds between 11 and 540 Mbit/s. In the most common setup, the infrastructure mode, a computer or a mobile phone connects to an access point, which offers further connection to the fixed Internet. The area covered by a single access point is known as a hotspot. The IEEE 802.11 standard also allows for mesh networks and for peer-to-peer (wireless ad hoc) connections (Chen, 2007).

In future wireless protocols and communication environments (networks), the security will play a key role in transmitted information operations. Cryptography is an essential part of today's users' needs, hence recent and future wireless communication systems have special needs for cryptography. Most of the widely used wireless communication systems support all different types of encryption. The user can select the best-suited algorithm for the needs of the application (McCabe, 2007).

Examples of Wireless Technologies

In this subsection we will give some examples of the well known wireless technologies, which have wide applications in many important fields.

Wi-Fi: To connect two devices wirelessly, we would typically require a Wi-Fi setup in which a router broadcasts a network and our devices - may be a PC, phone, laptop, or TV - all connect to the router. The router in turn, acts as starting point, enables the connected devices to communicate with each other. Opposed to this conventional

way, with Wi-Fi Direct, compatible devices can be connected directly through generating their own wireless network. While most devices across gadget categories (TV, Printers, etc.) have Wi-Fi connectivity built-in as an option. Wi-Fi Direct will be the easiest way to share data. Wi-Fi, refers to interoperable implementations of the IEEE 802.11 Wireless LAN standards certified by the Wi-Fi Alliance (Abu-Rgheff, 2007).

Cellular Network: A cellular network is a radio network distributed over land areas called cells, each served by at least one fixed-location transceiver, known as a cell site or base station. In a cellular network, each cell uses a different set of frequencies from neighboring cells, to avoid interference and provide guaranteed bandwidth within each cell. When joined together these cells provide radio coverage over a wide geographic area. This enables a large number of portable transceivers (e.g., mobile phones, pagers, etc.) to communicate with each other and with fixed transceivers and telephones anywhere in the network, via base stations, even if some of the transceivers are moving through more than one cell during transmission. Cellular networks offer a number of advantages over alternative solutions (Agrawal & Zeng, 2003):

- Flexible enough to use the features and functions of almost all public and private network.
- Increased capacity.
- Reduced power use.
- Larger coverage area
- Reduced interference from other signals

In a cellular radio system, a land area to be supplied with radio service is divided into regular shaped cells, which can be hexagonal, square, circular or some other regular shapes, although hexagonal cells are conventional. Each of these cells is assigned multiple frequencies $(f_1 - f_n)$ which have corresponding radio base stations. The group of frequencies can be reused in other cells, provided that the same frequencies are not reused in adjacent neighboring cells as that would cause interference. The increased capacity in a cellular network, compared with a network with a single transmitter, comes from the fact that the same radio frequency can be reused in a different area for a completely different transmission. If there is a single plain transmitter, only one transmission can be used on any given frequency. Unfortunately, there is inevitably some level of interference from the signal of the other cells which use the same frequency. This means that, in a standard FDMA system, there must be at least a one cell gap between cells which reuse the same frequency (Nicopplitidis & Pomportsis, 2003).

Bluetooth Technology: Bluetooth is a wireless transferring technology that enables short-range wireless connections between desktop and laptop computers, personal digital assistants (PDAs), cellular phones, printers, scanners, digital cameras and even home appliances. Bluetooth wireless technology is gradually becoming a popular way to replace existing wireline connections with short-range wireless interconnectivity. It is also an enabling technology for new types of applications. The principle of Bluetooth (a chipset) is to transfer information and voices at the frequency of ISM Band from 2400–2480 MHz from fixed and mobile devices, creating personal area networks (PANs) with high levels of security. Bluetooth technology was originally intended to be a wireless replacement for cables and wires between things like phones and headsets or computers, keyboards and mice. Every Bluetooth technology devices do come with a standard address to connect one-to-one or one-to-seven (to form a Pico-net), with transferring range up to 10 meters (100 meters to follow), using low power radio. Bluetooth do not only possess high transfer rate of 1MB/s, it also could be encrypted with pin code (Gehrmann & Smeets, 2004). With hopping rate of 1600 hops per second, it's difficult to be intercepted and is less interrupted by electromagnetic wave.

With Bluetooth, it is feasible to have several interesting usage scenarios like the following (Anand, 2003):

- Electronic identity validation by simply walking through a doorway with your phone in your pocket.
- Using a multipurpose PDA to purchase electronic tokens or tickets which are "punched" as you drive or walk by a sensor.
- Doctors automatically know the identity of emergency care patients who carry Bluetooth-enabled identification cards. Because Bluetooth chips are always on and seeking other Bluetooth devices, a doctor can call up a patient's information in a central database by toting another Bluetooth-enabled device.

WiMAX: WiMax(Worldwide Interoperability for Microwave Access) is a wireless communications standard designed to provide 30 to 40 megabit-per-second data rates, with the 2011 update providing up to 1 Gbit/s for fixed stations. WiMAX is wireless a technology based on the IEEE 802.16 specifications to enable the delivery of last-mile wireless broadband access as an alternative to cable and DSL. The design of WiMAX network is based on the following major principles (Mahmoud, 2007):

- **Spectrum:** Able to be deployed in both licensed and unlicensed spectra.
- **Topology:** Supports different Radio Access Network (RAN) topologies.
- **Interworking:** Independent RAN architecture to enable seamless integration and interworking with WiFi, 3GPP and 3GPP2 networks and existing IP operator core network.
- **IP Connectivity:** Supports a mix of IPv4 and IPv6 network interconnects in clients and application servers.

- **Mobility Management:** Possibility to extend the fixed access to mobility and broadband multimedia services delivery.

The WiMAX technical working group is defining MAC and PHY system profiles for IEEE 802.16a and HiperMan standards. The MAC profile includes an IP-based version for both wireless MAN (licensed) and wireless HUMAN (licence-exempt). IEEE Standard 802.16 was designed to evolve as a set of air interfaces standards for WMAN based on a common MAC protocol but with physical layer specifications dependent on the spectrum of use and the associated regulations. As the first 4G wireless technology, WiMAX combines the performance of Wi-Fi with the range and quality of service (QOS) of a carrier-grade cellular technology. WiMAX can provide broadband wireless access (BWA) up to 30 miles (50 km) for fixed stations, and 3-10 miles (5 - 15 km) for mobile stations. In contrast, the Wi-Fi/802.11 wireless local area network standard is limited in most cases to only 100-300 feet (30-100m) (Gavrilovska & Prasad, 2006).

Examples of Wireless Networking

Wireless Personal Area Networks (WPAN): A low-range wireless network which covers an area of only a few dozen metres. This sort of network is generally used for linking peripheral devices (like printers, cellphones, and home appliances) or a personal assistant (PDA) to a computer, or just two nearby computers, without using a hard-wired connection. There are several kinds of technology used for WPANs. The main WPAN technology is Bluetooth (Arslan & Di Benedetto, 2006).

Wireless Local Area Networks (WLAN): This type provides wireless network communication over short distances using radio or infrared signals instead of traditional network cabling. A WLAN typically extends an existing wired local area network. WLANs are built by attaching a device called the access point (AP) to the edge of the

wired network. Clients communicate with the AP using a wireless network adapter similar in function to a traditional Ethernet adapter. Wireless LANs offer the following productivity, convenience, and cost advantages over wired networks (Wang & Poor, 2003):

- **Mobility:** Wireless LAN systems can provide LAN users with access to real-time information anywhere in their organization. This mobility supports productivity and service opportunities not possible with wired networks.
- **Installation Speed and Simplicity:** Installing a wireless LAN system can be fast and easy and can eliminate the need to pull cable through walls and ceilings.
- **Reduced Cost-of-Ownership:** While the initial investment required for wireless LAN hardware can be higher than the cost of wired LAN hardware, overall installation expenses and life-cycle costs can be significantly lower. Long-term cost benefits are greatest in dynamic environments requiring frequent moves and changes.
- **Scalability:** Wireless LAN systems can be configured in a variety of topologies to meet the needs of specific applications and installations. Configurations are easily changed and range from peer-to-peer networks suitable for a small number of users to full infrastructure networks of thousands of users that enable roaming over a broad area.

Wide Area Network (WAN): A network that covers a broad area (i.e., any telecommunications network that links across metropolitan, regional, or national boundaries) using private or public network transports. Business and government entities utilize WANs to relay data among employees, clients, buyers, and suppliers from various geographical locations. In essence, this mode of telecommunication allows a business to effectively carry out its daily function regardless of location. The Internet can be considered a WAN as well, and is used by businesses, governments, organizations, and individuals for almost any purpose imaginable (Schwartz, 2005).

Related terms for other types of networks are personal area networks (PANs), local area networks (LANs), campus area networks (CANs), or metropolitan area networks (MANs) which are usually limited to a room, building, campus or specific metropolitan area (e.g., a city) respectively. A WAN spans a large geographic area, such as a state, province or country. WANs often connect multiple smaller networks, such as local area networks (LANs) or metro area networks (MANs). The world's most popular WAN is the Internet. Some segments of the Internet, like VPN-based extranets, are also WANs in themselves. WANs generally utilize different and much more expensive networking equipment than do LANs. Key technologies often found in WANs include SONET, Frame Relay, and ATM (Comaniciu & Poor, 2005).

Wireless Mesh Networks (WMN): Wireless communication technologies are going through swift progression. Wireless Mesh Networks is drawing attention due to its characteristics, such as (Ahmad, 2005):

- Easiness and low cost network deployment,
- Easiness of network reconfiguration,
- Reduction in wired links,
- Robust communication,
- Spectrum reuses efficiency,
- Network capacity improvement, and so on.

A basic WMN consists of mesh routers and mesh clients. There are three main types of WMNs determined by their structural design and deployment configuration, which are:

- **Infrastructure Mesh:** Its architecture comprises of mesh routers creating an infrastructure for clients. The mesh routers

create links which configure and heal themselves, and some mesh routers with gateway functionalities connect to the internet through access routers (ARs) (Agrawal & Zeng, 2003).

- **Client Mesh:** Its architecture is a peer-to-peer mesh networking among clients. Mesh routers are not required in this architecture because mesh clients do all the routing and configurations themselves.

- **Hybrid Mesh:** Its architecture combines infrastructure and client meshing. Mesh clients are able to access the mesh network through the mesh routers or through peer-to-peer communication with other mesh clients.

Cloud Computing Networking: Cloud computing is the set of elements, networks, storage area, solutions, and connections that incorporate to produce different aspects of computing as a service. Cloud computing involve the shipping of program, functions, and storage area over the online. It can be provided whenever and wherever a person needs a particular assistance. The service can be either individual elements or complete systems. The delivery is according to person need. There are four crucial features of cloud processing. They involve (Al-Omari & Sumari, 2010):

- Versatility and the ability to scale up and down,
- Program development connections (APIs),
- Stipulating and automatic payments, and
- Metering of assistance utilization in a pay-as-you-go style.

Cloud processing comes in different forms, such as (Chen, 2007):

- Public clouds are with regards to the standard cloud processing style, in which a company creates options, such as programs and storage area, available to town over the online. Public cloud services may be free or offered on a pay-per-usage basis.

- Personal cloud is functions managed just for 1 company or organization. They can be handled internal or by a third-party and organized internal or on the outside.

- A combination of public and personal cloud (hybrid cloud). This structure of two or more clouds that remain unique agencies but are limited together. Hybrid clouds are connected in a way that allows programs and details to be shifted easily from one implementation program to another. Each form of cloud computing services is employed either independently or in combination with others.

The Network

Clouds generally refer to wide area networks (WANs) such as the Internet, but can also refer to a private cloud, which is a company's own network. However, the term "cloud computing" most always refers to the public Internet and not to private networks as shown in Figure 1.

SECURITY AND PRIVACY METHODS OF WIRELESS COMMUNICATION NETWORKS

Security and privacy of user, application, device, and network resources and data are increasingly important areas of network architecture and design. Security is integrated within all areas of the network and impacts all other functions on the network. For the proper functioning of security within a network, it is crucial that the relationships among security mechanisms, as well as between the security architecture and other component architectures, be well understood (Xiao & Du, 2009).

Network security is defined here as the protection of networks and their services from unauthorized access, modification, destruction, or disclosure. It provides assurance that the network performs its critical functions correctly and that there are no harmful side effects. Network privacy is a subset of network security, focusing on protection of networks and their services from unauthorized access or disclosure. This includes all user, application, device, and network data. Whenever the term network security is used

Figure 1. The cloud networking

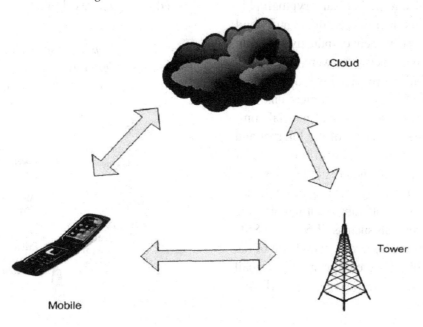

in this book, it includes all aspects of network privacy as well (Olakanmi, 2012). Security in the network needs to protect network resources from being disabled, stolen, modified, or damaged. This includes protecting devices, servers, users, and system data, as well as the users' and organization's privacy and image.

Overlaying security onto a developed network was an acceptable approach in the past. Today, however, security must be integrated into the network from the beginning in order for the network to meet the needs of the users and for security to provide adequate protection.

The introduction of wireless data communications at the beginning of the 20th century has resulted in an increasing interest in cryptology due to the following reasons (Boncella, 2002):

- The growth of both business and military communications as a consequence of this technology, which allowed for global communications in seconds rather than weeks.
- It is obvious that wireless communications are as easy to intercept for an adversary as for the legitimate receiver.

This resulted in a wide deployment of mechanical and electromechanical cryptographic devices in the first half of the 20th century and a growing interest in their cryptanalysis. From the 1960s, computer networks were built up for data communication over fixed wired networks; the protection of these communications was mainly restricted to military and financial communications. The popularity of the Internet and the World Wide Web resulted in broad use of cryptography for e-commerce and business applications. The underlying enabling technologies are inexpensive fast software cryptography and open security protocols such as TLS (SSL), SSH and IPsec as introduced in the second half of the 1990s. In spite of this development, only a small fraction of the Internet traffic is encrypted (Prttig, & Davide, 2002).

The first analog mobile phones provided no or very weak security, which resulted in serious embarrassment. The European GSM system designed in the late 1980s provided already much better security, even if many flaws remain; these flaws did not stop the system from growing to more than 2 billion subscribers in 2006. Most of these flaws have been addressed in the 3GSM system, but even there no end-to-end protection is provided.

The concepts of security and privacy are not easy to distinguish as they on one hand overlap in certain areas and on the other are not always combinable as shown in Figure 2. Security always involves trades. It costs money, convenience, functionality and sometimes, freedoms like liberty or privacy (Lashkari & Samadi, 2009).

The important security requirements that must be considered in wireless networks are:

- Confidentiality of the communicated information. There are clear advantages in end-to-end confidentiality, that is, between the sender and receiver across heterogeneous networks. However, most wireless connections continue over a fixed network, and confidentiality protection is often restricted to the wireless link.

Figure 2. Overlapping of security and privacy in information technology

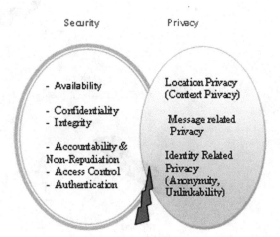

- Data Authentication should also be provided as well as protection against replay. In order to achieve data confidentiality, data authentication and replay protection, authenticated encryption should be used. Such service requires the establishment of a secret key between the mobile terminal and the network.

- Access Control; in order to limit access to authorized user and/or for billing purposes, most wireless services require access control. On the other hand, the mobile terminal wants to make sure that it is connected to a legitimate access point (Sklavos & Xinmiao, 2007).

There are several security mechanisms available today and many more on the horizon. However, not all mechanisms are appropriate for every environment. Each security mechanism should be evaluated for the network it is being applied to, based on the degree of protection it provides, its impact on users' ability to do work, the amount of expertise required for installation and configuration, the cost of purchasing, implementing, and operating it, and the amounts of administration and maintenance required (Sklavos & Xinmiao, 2007).

Encryption/Decryption

While other security mechanisms provide protection against unauthorized access and destruction of resources and information, encryption/decryption protects information from being usable by the attacker (Elminaam & Hadhoud, 2009). Encryption/decryption is a security mechanism where cipher algorithms are applied together with a secret key to encrypt data so that they are unreadable if they are intercepted. Data are then decrypted at or near their destination. This is shown in Figure 3.

As such, encryption/decryption enhances other forms of security by protecting information in case other mechanisms fail to keep unauthorized users from that information. There are two common types of encryption/decryption: public key and private key. Software implementations of public key encryption/decryption are commonly available. Examples include data encryption standard (DES) private key encryption, triple DES private key encryption, and Rivest, Shamir, and Adleman (RSA) public key encryption. Public key infrastructure (PKI) is an example of a security infrastructure that uses both public and private keys. Public key infrastructure is a security infrastructure that combines security mechanisms, policies, and directives into a system that is targeted for use across unsecured public networks

Figure 3. Encryption/Decryption of network traffic

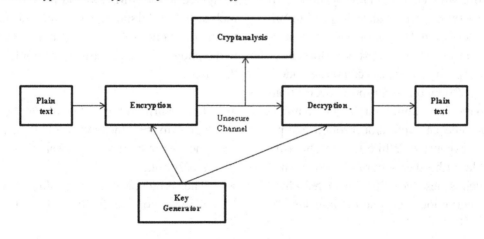

(e.g., the Internet), where information is encrypted through the use of a public and a private cryptographic key pair that is obtained and shared through a trusted authority. PKI is targeted toward legal, commercial, official, and confidential transactions, and includes cryptographic keys and a certificate management system. Components of this system are:

- Managing the generation and distribution of public/private keys
- Publishing public keys with UIDs as certificates in open directories
- Ensuring that specific public keys are truly linked to specific private keys
- Authenticating the holder of a public/private key pair

PKI uses one or more trusted systems known as Certification Authorities (CA), which serve as trusted third parties for PKI. The PKI infrastructure is hierarchical, with issuing authorities, registration authorities, authentication authorities, and local registration authorities.

Another example is the secure sockets library (SSL). Secure sockets library is a security mechanism that uses RSA-based authentication to recognize a party's digital identity and uses RC4 to encrypt and decrypt the accompanying transaction or communication. SSL has grown to become one of the leading security protocols on the Internet. One trade-off with encryption/decryption is a reduction in network performance. Depending on the type of encryption/decryption and where it is implemented in the network, network performance (in terms of capacity and delay) can be degraded from 15% to 85% or more. Encryption/decryption usually also requires administration and maintenance, and some encryption/decryption equipment can be expensive. While this mechanism is compatible with other security mechanisms, trade-offs such as these should be considered when evaluating encryption/decryption (Elminaam & Hadhoud, 2010).

Mobile Phone Systems Security

The only security service offered by the first generation of mobile phone systems was a secret user identifier that was sent in clear over the network, similar to user name and password in a computer system. Very quickly cloning attacks were launched: criminals simply captured the secret and reprogrammed it into their own phones, thus allowing them to place phone calls at the expense of another user. This resulted in the development of advanced security services for the second generation mobile systems (GSM and IS-95); these services were further improved for the third generation systems (Gerkis, 2006).

GSM Security

The security goals of the GSM system are user identity confidentiality, user identity authentication, user data confidentiality and signaling information confidentiality. These security goals (except for the first one) are achieved by running an authenticated key agreement (AKA) protocol between the mobile phone and the base station. This protocol requires a long term secret or key that is stored in a smart card called the Subscriber Identity Module (SIM). A smart card is a small tamper resistant microprocessor that can securely store secrets and perform cryptographic computations (Xiao, Chen & Du, 2009). The key is computed in the SIM card and forwarded to the mobile phone. All subsequent communication between the phone and the base station is encrypted in the phone. There are still some problems with this protocol:

- For security reasons it would not be appropriate to store the keys Ki of all the users in the base stations or to forward these keys to a base station.
- The protocol does not offer subscriber identity confidentiality. Indeed, by eaves-

dropping the wireless link one can obtain the possibility to trace a mobile phone.

- The AKA protocol authenticates the SIM card to the network, which is not the same as authenticating the user of the mobile phone to the network. User authentication can be achieved by a locally verified PIN code (Anand, 2003).

The weaknesses of the GSM security system can be classified into three classes:

- Weaknesses of cryptographic algorithms,
- Lack of protection against active attacks (a cryptographic protocol weakness), and
- Architectural weaknesses.

Wireless LAN Security

The security goals of the IEEE 802.11 security architecture are entity authentication, authorization, data confidentiality and data integrity. Note that anonymity of users with respect to third party is not a requirement. Security is offered at the data link layer. The first solution included in the 1999 standard IEEE 802.11 was the Wired Equivalent Privacy (WEP) Very quickly multiple security flaws were discovered in WEP, resulting in the adoption in 2002 of Wi-Fi Protected Access (WPA) as an intermediate solution by the industry consortium Wi-Fi Alliance. In 2004, IEEE ratified the 802.11i standard, also known as WPA2, that resolves the security weaknesses of WEP (Olakanmi, 2012).

The WEP protocol is an optional security protocol for IEEE 802.11 that intends to offer authenticated encryption at the data link layer. The encryption is provided by the stream cipher RC4 and the data authentication is implemented using a MAC computed with a linear function CRC-32 (Cyclic Redundancy Check). RC4 is a stream cipher that stretches a short key K (40 or 104 bits) to a long key stream to be added to the data. WEP offers the choice between open systems (without authentication of the mobile nodes) or a shared key protocol. No key management is provided, hence each access point uses a single key shared by its user that has to be installed manually and is thus updated infrequently.

The 40-bit key size is too small; the cost of recovering such a key is very low. A 104-bit key offers sufficient long-term protection, but in some implementations it is derived from a short password resulting in weak security. A linear MAC algorithm does not offer any data integrity: one can add an arbitrary string to the plaintext and compute the correction that needs to be added to the MAC value without knowing any secret. If modifications are inserted in the packet headers, the packet will be decrypted by the access point and may be diverted to a machine of the attacker's choice.

WEP can be implemented to provide more protection against authentication spoofing through the use of Shared Key Authentication (SKA). However, SKA creates an additional vulnerability. Because SKA makes visible both a plaintext challenge and the resulting ciphertext version, it is possible to use this information to spoof authentication to a closed network (Boncella, 2002).

Wi-Fi Protected Accesses (WPA)

WPA is a short term solution for WEP that was developed in 2002 in anticipation of the 2004 publication of the IEEE 802.11i standard (WPA2). As WPA had to be compatible with the deployed hardware with limited computational power, it kept using RC4, but replaced the CRC-32 with a stronger MAC algorithm with a 64-bit result called Michael.

The Michael algorithm had to execute in less than 5 cycles per byte and even if it is much more secure than CRC-32 it is known to have weaknesses (Robert J. Boncella, 2002). The Temporal Key Integrity Protocol (TKIP) doubles the IV space to 48 bits with sequencing rules and adds a mechanism to derive per-packet WEP keys from a temporal secret key, the MAC address of the device and the packet sequence number. This ensures unique keys even if multiple nodes share the same secret key. The temporal key is derived from the pair-wise master key (PMK) and is changed every 10,000 packets. The PMK is computed either from a manually installed pre-shared key (typical for home networks) or from a key established using the EAP protocol.

WPA allows the use of the IEEE 802.1X framework for port based network access control; this protocol authenticates user or devices and allows for establishment of the PMK key. This framework is based on the Extensible Authentication Protocol (EAP) that supports multiple authentication methods, such as smart cards, one-time password tokens, Kerberos, and public key authentication. When a mobile node requests access, the access point opens a port only for EAP packets to an authentication server (e.g., RADIUS or Diameter) on the fixed network. All other traffic is blocked at the data link layer. After successful entity authentication, the access point will allow normal traffic (Sen, 2009).

Personal Area Network (Bluetooth) Security

The Bluetooth authenticated key agreement protocol is rather complex. Each Bluetooth device generates at first power-up a unit key, which is stored in non-volatile memory. The key is generated as a function of the 48-bit Bluetooth address and a random number. All data sent between A and B is encrypted using the key stream generated by E0. Note also that devices can be configured to operate without any security. The security of the Bluetooth protocol could be improved substantially by using password-based authenticated key exchange (PAKE) protocols (Sreedhar & Kasiviswanath, 2010); these protocols prevent off-line PIN guessing attacks, but require public-key operations that are more expensive than the symmetric cryptographic operations used in Bluetooth (Sklavos & Xinmiao, 2007).

WIRELESS NETWORKS ATTACKING METHODS

Passive Attack Methods

Wireless communication takes place on unlicensed public frequencies. Anyone can use these frequencies. This makes protecting a wireless network from passive attacks more difficult. A passive attack occurs when someone listens to or eavesdrops on network traffic. Armed with a wireless network adaptor that supports promiscuous mode, the eavesdropper can capture network traffic for analysis using easily available tools, such as Network Monitor in Microsoft products. A passive attack on a wireless network may not be malicious in nature (Sreedhar & Kasiviswanath, 2010).

If the network administrator has been kind enough to provide a clue about the company in the SSID or is not encrypting traffic with WEP, the potential eavesdropper's job has been made a lot easier. Using a tool such as Netstumbler is only a preliminary step for the attacker. After discovering the SSID and other information, the attacker can connect to the wireless network to sniff and capture network traffic. This network traffic can reveal a lot of information about the network and the company that uses it. For example, looking at the network traffic, the attacker can determine what DNS servers are being used, the default home pages configured on browsers, network names, logon traffic, and so on. The attacker can use this information to determine if the network is of sufficient interest to proceed further with other attacks. Furthermore, if the network is using WEP, the attacker can, given enough time, capture a sufficient amount of traffic to crack the encryption.

Netstumbler works on networks that are configured as open systems. This means that the wireless network indicates that it exists and will respond with the value of its SSID to other wireless devices when they send out a radio beacon with an "empty set" SSID. This does not mean, however, that wireless network can be easily compromised, if other security measures have been implemented. To defend against the use of Netstumbler and other programs to detect a wireless network easily, administrators should configure the wireless network as a closed system. This means that the AP will not respond to "empty set" SSID beacons and will consequently be "invisible" to programs such as Netstumbler which rely on this technique to discover wireless networks. However, it is still possible to capture the "raw" 802.11b frames and decode them through the use of programs such as Ethereal and WildPacket's AiroPeek to determine this information. As well, RF spectrum analyzers can be used to discover the presence of wireless networks. Notwithstanding this weakness of closed systems, you should choose wireless APs that support this feature (Padmavathi & Shanmugapriya, 2009).

We should note that on the wireless side, APs are half-duplex devices and work just like other half-duplex devices, such as hubs and repeaters. This means that all the devices on the network can potentially see all the traffic from other devices. The only defense against sniffing on a wireless network is to encrypt Layer 2 and higher traffic whenever possible through the use of WEP, VPNs, SSL, Secure Shell (SSH), Secure Copy (SCP), and so on. Some of these defensive strategies will be more effective than others, depending on the circumstances.

Active Attacking Methods

Once an attacker has gained sufficient information from the passive attack, the hacker can then launch an active attack against the network. There are a potentially large number of active attacks that a hacker can launch against a wireless network. For the most part, these attacks are identical to the kinds of active attacks that are encountered on wired networks. These include, but are not limited to, unauthorized access, spoofing, and

Denial of Service (DoS) and Flooding attacks, as well as the introduction of Malware and the theft of devices. With the rise in popularity of wireless networks, new variations of traditional attacks specific to wireless networks have emerged along with specific terms to describe them, such as "drive-by spamming" in which a spammer sends out tens or hundreds of thousands of spam messages using a compromised wireless network.

Spoofing occurs when an attacker is able to use an unauthorized station to impersonate an authorized station on a wireless network. A common way to protect a wireless network against unauthorized access is to use MAC filtering to allow only clients that possess valid MAC addresses access to the wireless network. The list of allowable MAC addresses can be configured on the AP, or it may be configured on a RADIUS server that the AP communicates with. However, regardless of the technique used to implement MAC filtering, it is a relatively easy matter to change the MAC address of a wireless device through software to impersonate a valid station (Anand, 2003).

Once the attacker has authenticated and associated with the wireless network, he/she can then run port scans, use special tools to dump user lists and passwords, impersonate users, connect to shares, and, in general, create havoc on the network through DoS and Flooding attacks. These DoS attacks can be traditional in nature, such as *a* ping flood, SYN, fragment, or Distributed DoS (DDoS) attacks, or they can be specific to wireless networks through the placement and use of Rogue Access Points to prevent wireless traffic from being forwarded properly.

Man-in-the-Middle Attacks

Placing a rogue access point within range of wireless stations is wireless-specific variation of a man-in-the-middle attack. If the attacker knows the SSID in use by the network and the rogue AP has enough strength, wireless users will have no way of knowing that they are connecting to an unauthorized AP. Using a rogue AP, an attacker can gain valuable information about the wireless network, such as authentication requests, the secret key that may be in use, and so on. Often, the attacker will set up a laptop with two wireless adaptors, in which one card is used by the rogue AP and the other is used to forward requests through a wireless bridge to the legitimate AP. With a sufficiently strong antenna, the rogue AP does not have to be located in close proximity to the legitimate AP. So, for example, the attacker can run the rogue AP from a car or van parked some distance away from the building. However, it is also common to set up hidden rogue APs (under desks, in closets, etc.) close to and within the same physical area as the legitimate AP (Padmavathi & Shanmugapriya, 2009).

Jamming Attacking Methods

Jamming is a special kind of DoS attack specific to wireless networks. Jamming occurs when spurious RF frequencies interfere with the operation of the wireless network. In some cases, the jamming is not malicious and is caused by the presence of other devices, such as cordless phones, that operate in the same frequency as the wireless network. In a case like this, the administrator must devise and implement policies regarding the use of these devices, such a banning the use of Bluetooth devices, or choose wireless hardware that uses different frequencies. Intentional and malicious jamming occurs when an attacker analyzes the spectrum being used by wireless networks and then transmits a powerful signal to interfere with communication on the discovered frequencies. Fortunately, this kind of attack is not very common because of the expense of acquiring hardware capable of launching jamming attacks (Çakıro, & Çetin, 2010).

Access Control Attacking Methods

These attacks attempt to penetrate a network by using wireless or evading WLAN access control measures, like AP MAC filters and 802.1X port access controls. The different types of this attack are (Sreedhar & Kasiviswanath, 2010):

- **War Driving:** Discovering wireless LANs by listening to beacons or sending probe requests, thereby providing launch point for further attacks.
- **Rogue Access Points:** Installing an unsecured AP inside firewall, creating open backdoor into trusted network.
- **Ad Hoc Associations:** Connecting directly to an unsecured station to circumvent AP security or to attack station.
- **MAC Spoofing:** Reconfiguring an attacker's MAC address to pose as an authorized AP or station.
- **802.1X RADIUS Cracking:** Recovering RADIUS secret by brute force from 802.1X access request, for use by evil twin AP.

Confidentiality Attacking Methods

These attacks attempt to intercept private information sent over wireless associations, whether sent in the clear or encrypted by 802.11 or higher layer protocols (Padmavathi & Shanmugapriya, 2009).

- **Eavesdropping:** Capturing and decoding unprotected application traffic to obtain potentially sensitive information.
- **WEP Key Cracking:** Capturing data to recover a WEP key using passive or active methods.
- **Evil Twin AP:** Masquerading as an authorized AP by beaconing the WLAN's service set identifier (SSID) to lure users.
- **AP Phishing:** Running a phony portal or Web server on an evil twin AP to "phish" for user logins, credit card numbers.

- **Man in the Middle:** Running traditional man-in-the-middle attack tools on an evil twin AP to intercept TCP sessions or SSL/SSH tunnels.

Integrity Attacking Methods

These attacks send forged control, management or data frames over wireless to mislead the recipient or facilitate another type of attack (e.g., DoS) (Padmavathi & Shanmugapriya, 2009).

- **802.11 Frame Injection:** Crafting and sending forged 802.11 frames.
- **802.11 Data Replay:** Capturing 802.11 data frames for later (modified) replay.
- **802.1X EAP Replay:** Capturing 802.1X Extensible Authentication Protocols (e.g., EAP Identity, Success, Failure) for later replay.
- **802.1X RADIUS Replay:** Capturing RADIUS Access-Accept or Reject messages for later replay

Authentication Attacking Methods

Intruders use these attacks to steal legitimate user identities and credentials to access otherwise private networks and services (Agrawal & Sharma, 2011).

- **Shared Key Guessing:** Attempting 802.11 Shared Key Authentication with guessed, vendor default or cracked WEP keys.
- **Application Login Theft:** Capturing user credentials (e.g., e-mail address and password) from clear text application protocols.
- **Domain Login Cracking:** Recovering user credentials (e.g., Windows login and password) by cracking NetBIOS password hashes, using a brute-force or dictionary attack tool (Sreedhar & Kasiviswanath, 2010).

- **VPN Login Cracking:** Recovering user credentials (e.g., PPTP password or IPsec Pre-shared Secret Key) by running brute-force attacks on VPN authentication protocols.
- **802.1X Identity Theft:** Capturing user identities from cleartext 802.1X Identity Response packets.
- **802.1X Password Guessing:** Using a captured identity, repeatedly attempting 802.1X authentication to guess the user's password.
- **802.1X LEAP Cracking:** Recovering user credentials from captured 802.1X Lightweight EAP (LEAP) packets using a dictionary attack tool to crack the NT password hash.
- **802.1X EAP Downgrade:** Forcing an 802.1X server to offer a weaker type of authentication using forged EAP-Response/Nak packets.

Availability Attacking Methods

These attacks impede delivery of wireless services to legitimate users, either by denying them access to WLAN resources or by crippling those resources (Padmavathi & Shanmugapriya, 2009).

- **AP Theft:** Physically removing an AP from a public space.
- **Queensland DoS:** Exploiting the CSMA/CA Clear Channel Assessment (CCA) mechanism to make a channel appear busy.
- **802.11 Beacon Flood:** Generating thousands of counterfeit 802.11 beacons to make it hard for stations to find a legitimate AP.
- **802.11 Associate/Authenticate Flood:** Sending forged Authenticates or Associates from random MACs to fill a target AP's association table.
- **802.11 TKIP MIC Exploit:** Generating invalid TKIP data to exceed the target AP's

MIC error threshold, suspending WLAN service.

- **802.11 Deauthenticate Flood:** Flooding station(s) with forged Deauthenticates or Disassociates to disconnecting users from an AP.
- **802.1X EAP-Start Flood:** Flooding an AP with EAP-Start messages to consume resources or crash the target (Prttig & Davide, 2002).
- **802.1X EAP-Failure:** Observing a valid 802.1X EAP exchange, and then sending the station a forged EAP-Failure message.
- **802.1X EAP-of-Death:** Sending a malformed 802.1X EAP Identity response known to cause some APs to crash.
- **802.1X EAP Length Attacks:** Sending EAP type-specific messages with bad length fields to try to crash an AP or RADIUS server.

Bluetooth Attack

The cryptographic algorithms in Bluetooth are SAFER+ (Gehrmann & Smeets, 2004) for entity authentication and key establishment and the stream cipher E0 for data encryption. No weaknesses have been identified in SAFER+, but today more lightweight block ciphers are available that offer a similar security level. The stream cipher E0 is much less secure than anticipated: even if it has a 128-bit key. The protection is provided at the data link level, which means that all addresses are sent in the clear. By eavesdropping on a Bluetooth exchange, or by contacting a device that is in discoverable mode, an attacker can obtain the 48-bit Bluetooth address, and subsequently track the device. Even if a device is in non-discoverable mode, the 48-bit address may be discovered since it is known to be not random (24 bits are specific for the manufacturer, and some manufacturers preserve certain ranges for specific devices); depending on the information available to an attacker

and the number of devices used in the attack and being targeted simultaneously, recovering an address requires between a few hours to a few years. Moreover, passive attacks allow for the recovery of the PIN by exhaustive search; recovering a PIN up to 6 digits requires less than a second, while recovering an 8-digit PIN requires a few minutes.

Bluetooth enabled devices are potentially vulnerable to denial of service attacks. Rogue devices could repeatedly attempt connections, and in this way reduce the battery life of the victim (Anand, 2003). If a blacklisting system is implemented to reject future connections, a denial of service attack could be launched on the blacklisting mechanism itself, for example by initiating a large number of connections on behalf of another legitimate device without ever completing a successful authentication. The flaws in Bluetooth which have the most impact are related to implementation weaknesses. As an example the Bluesnarf attack allows to connect to some mobile phones and to gain access to the restricted portions of the data in the phone, including the entire phone book, calendar, IMEI (International Mobile Equipment Identity), etc. without the owner being alerted. The Bluejacking attack exploits the fact that up to 248 characters of the name of the other device is displayed during a pairing protocol to send advertisement to another device.

Attack WEP

In 2006, a large fraction of WLANs is still unprotected; among those that use security, more than 75% still use the WEP protocol (Padmavathi & Shanmugapriya, 2009). This observation motivated Bittau et al. to further optimize the existing attacks by exploiting fragmentation. Their attack requires less than a minute to allow an opponent to send and divert packets and requires fifteen minutes to recover 40-bit keys and two hours for 104-bit keys. Hence, because of the nature of wireless networks and the weaknesses of WEP, unauthorized access and spoofing are the most common threats to a wireless networks.

Figure 4 shows the block diagram of different attacking methods for the secure wireless communication systems.

SECURITY CHALLENGES OF WIRELESS COMMUNICATION NETWORKS

This Section wills summaries some of important challenges which discussed and treated with security and privacy and attacking methods of different wireless communication networks.

Figure 4. Block diagram of different attacks

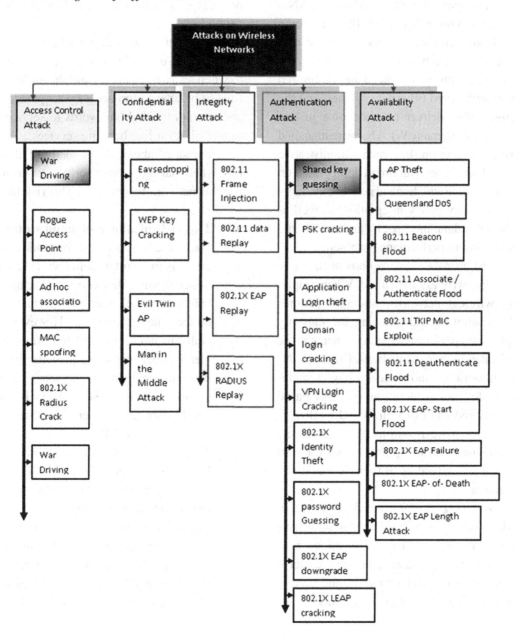

Examples of Different Challenges

Challenges of managing wireless security: When wireless LANs (WLANs) are deployed as mainstream enterprise network infrastructure, security and management become paramount concerns to corporations. Learning the key ways to integrate security and management strategies into your wireless networks (Laeeq, 2011).

The biggest wireless pain points challenging network managers: Wireless LANs (WLANs) have matured to the point where they are being integrated into corporate networks as mainstream infrastructure. That means that wireless APs and controllers must be managed and monitored consistent with wired Ethernet switches, and the connectivity they deliver must become just as reliable. In the past, many WLANs were managed as overlays, relying on their own administrative systems and processes. But broad deployment on a much larger scale will demand network management and security policy integration, as well as better tools for planning capacity and visualizing and responding to performance problems.

The worst mistake organizations make when implementing wireless networks: When implementing wireless networks, an organization's lack of attention to, and planning for, capacity and application performance requirements is the worst mistake. Many existing best-effort WLANs got by without this, and there's a huge temptation to deploy next-generation WLANs based on the same old rules of thumb and intelligent guesswork. Even organizations that conduct site surveys and use predictive planners may not start with a solid understanding of their own user and application needs.

New wireless security devices: Wireless security updates have slowed because standards have solidified. Wireless security innovations now revolve around making existing measures easier to see and apply on a much larger scale, and making them work well in tougher environments.

Open Wireless Networks security challenges: There are two main security challenges that emerge from a system of shared wireless. Both are essentially the result of not having a stable trust network between the owner of the wireless network node, and the user of the network (Sreedhar & Kasiviswanath, 2010).

The risk of someone abusing your network for unethical (or perhaps even illegal) activities, including access to unethical materials on-line or attempts to access personal data over the local network.

The risk induced by the need to trust the owner of whatever Access Point you happen to connect to when away from home, and the ability of that trust to be abused top access your personal data and attempt to steal passwords to services such as e-mail or on-line banking services.

The risk of abuse of connectivity, there is a risk, when sharing ones network, that users will not use this network responsibly. This risk includes:

- **The risk of abuse of bandwidth:** when you agree to share your network with others, it is most often done, with the implicit understanding that you are sharing excess bandwidth, i.e., that you probably won't notice the difference. However, especially in densely populated areas, a completely open network, may receive much more usage than the person sharing the network expects, thus adversely impacting his/her user experience (Sreedhar & Kasiviswanath, 2010).
- The risk of unethical (and sometimes illegal) use of network resources. This is a risk that receives a lot of attention from the media, (at least in Europe).
- The risk abuse of local network privileges. This is, perhaps, the biggest of the security challenges faced by average users sharing their bandwidth. Given the way many people share local resources amongst multiple

computers in the home, i.e. using windows file sharing or Apple Bonjour, and given the inherently insecure default configurations of most home computers, the trusted local network becomes an (unfortunately) critical part of home user security (Dong, & Nita-Rotaru, 2009).

- **VPN's and Tunneling:** For end-users without the skills or server access to setup SSH tunnels or their own VPN tunnel, using a VPN solution is not simple.

Challenges of Wireless Remote Monitoring: The financial benefits of using wireless for remote monitoring are compelling; yet, industry has been slow to adopt the technology. Security, reliability, integration, and power are all challenges that must be overcome before there is widespread adoption of wireless measurement systems.

Security and Reliability: Security is the number one concern for many engineers and scientists considering wireless. The reasoning behind this is due in large part to the failings of early wireless standards such as wired equivalent privacy (WEP), which did not prevent unauthorized access well. There are two main components of network security that must be addressed before wireless is widely adopted: authentication and encryption. Integration with Existing Systems: A common solution to wireless security vulnerabilities has been proprietary networking protocols. Many wireless sensor vendors use a proprietary network because its details are not publicly available. The problem with this solution is two-folds (Elminaam & Hadhoud, 2010):

- If the details of such a protocol are ever leaked, the entire system is compromised.
- Proprietary networks are difficult to integrate with existing wired systems. If you choose a proprietary protocol, you are locked into using network components from a specific vendor that may not be interoperable with your existing equipment.

This is also true of the software. Turnkey data-logging software is not typically open – modifications are difficult if not impossible.

Battery Life: A third potential challenge for wireless networks is power, though it is application specific. For most applications there is a tradeoff between power consumption and the amount of collect data. Wi-Fi, for example, requires more power than ZigBee, but can stream continuous waveform data. ZigBee and 802.15.4 on the other hand can run for years on batteries by limiting the amount of data they collect and the frequency with which they transmit it. Alternative energy sources are also in research, including solar panels and microgenerators that can convert vibrations into electrical energy.

Convergence Challenges: The wireless revolution is predicated on the convergence of a variety of information and communication technologies. Research focuses significantly on the associated problems. Historically, telecommunications systems have been relatively easy to operate. The move to more heterogeneous systems involves the integration of a variety of devices like computers, sensors, transmitters, radar, GPS and cameras, many of which require different amounts of bandwidth. This means that network management is becoming much more complex (Abu-Rgheff, 2007).

FUTURE RESEARCH DIRECTIONS

However, developing such a detection mechanism and making it efficient represents a great research challenge.

In future though the security mechanisms become well-established for each individual layer, combining all the mechanisms together for making them work in collaboration with each other will incur a hard research challenge. Even if holistic security could be ensured for wireless sensor networks, the cost-effectiveness and energy efficiency to employ such mechanisms could still pose great research challenge in the coming days (Agrawal & Sharma, 2011).

CONCLUSION

Generally, the ciphers use large arithmetic and algebraic modifications, which are not appropriate for hardware implementations. That is why cipher implementations allocate many of the system resources, in hardware terms, to be used as components. Therefore, in many cases, software applications have been developed to support the needs of security and cryptography. However, the software solution is not acceptable in the case of handheld devices and mobile communications with high-speed and low-power consumption requirements.

Research in COSIMA will not be limited to a theoretical and algorithmic levels but a heterogeneous multi-terminal hardware demonstrator will be constructed for the practical evaluation over realistic scenarios of the most promising developed cooperative and cognitive techniques. The hardware demonstrator will consist of a primary network made up of six high performance MIMO terminals (already available from previous projects granted by Plan Nacional I+D) and complemented with a secondary network made up of 20 low cost terminals constructed with GNU Radio technology.

The new wireless technologies are characterized by much greater interaction among the layers. Getting complex layered systems to communicate quickly enough is a major research challenge.

Convergence is all about the development of platforms and architectures that can be used for a wide variety of applications. The needs of specific sectors will nevertheless entail a certain amount of divergence in the context of the overarching trend towards convergence.

It can expect that in the next generation of smart phones users will install software with this capability, either directly for the 3GPP voice stream or in a VoIP protocol.

In spite of these security problems, GSM has been a massive commercial success, which suggests that attacks exploiting these weaknesses for financial gain can be kept under control. On the other hand, there should be no doubt that law enforcement; national security and organized crime have the ability to eavesdrop on GSM conversations.

One can conclude that the access security of 3GSM is more than adequate and that substantial progress has been made on network level security. On the other hand, it is also clear that if these networks move towards closer integration with the Internet, all network level attacks which are visible there (including viruses, worms, denial of service attacks, DNS level attacks) will need to be addressed on mobile networks as well.

REFERENCES

Abu-Rgheff. (2007). *Introduction to CDMA wireless communications*. London: Academic Press..

Agrawal, Jain, & Sharma. (2011). A survey of routing attacks and security measures in mobile ad-hoc networks. *Journal of Computing*, 3(1).

Ahmad. (2005). Wireless and mobile data. London: Wiley.

Al-Omari & Sumari. (2010). An overview of mobile ad hoc networks for the existing protocols and applications. *International Journal on Applications of Graph Theory and Ad Hoc Networks and Sensor Networks*, 2(1).

Anand. (2003). *Power aware public key authentication for Bluetooth*. (M.Sc. Thesis). University of Florida, Gainesville, FL.

Arslan, Chen, & Di Benedetto. (2006). Ultra wideband wireless communication. London: John Wiley & Sons..

Boncella. (2002). Wireless security: An overview. Communications of the Association for Information Systems, 9.

Çakıro, Bayilmi, Özcerit, & Çetin. (2010). Performance evaluation of scalable encryption algorithm for wireless sensor networks. *Scientific Research and Essays,* 5(9), 856–861.

Chen. (2007). The next generation CDMA technologies. London: Wiley..

Comaniciu, Mandayam, & Poor. (2005). *Wireless networks multiuser detection in cross – layer design*. Berlin: Springer Science.

Dong, Curtmola, & Nita-Rotaru. (2009). Secure network coding for wireless mesh networks: Threats, challenges, and directions. *Computer Communications, 32,* 1790–1801. doi:10.1016/j.comcom.2009.07.010.

Elminaam, Kader, & Hadhoud. (2009). Performance evaluation of symmetric encryption algorithms on power consumption for wireless devices. *International Journal of Computer Theory and Engineering, 1*(4), 1793–8201.

Elminaam, Kader, & Hadhoud. (2010). Evaluating the performance of symmetric encryption algorithms. *International Journal of Network Security, 10*(3), 216–222.

Gavrilovska & Prasad. (2006). *Ad hoc networking towards seamless communications*. Berlin: Springer..

Gehrmann, Persson, & Smeets. (2004). Bluetooth security. Boston: Artech House, Inc..

Gerkis. (2006). *A survey of wireless mesh networking security technology and threats*. SANS Institute.

Laeeq. (2011). Security challenges & preventions in wireless communications. International Journal of Scientific & Engineering Research, 2(5).

Lashkari, Danesh, & Samadi. (2009). A survey on wireless security protocols (WEP, WPA, and WPA2/802.11i). In *Proceedings of the 2nd IEEE International Conference on Computer Science and Information Technology*, (pp. 48-52). IEEE.

Mahmoud. (2007). Cognitive networks: Towards self- aware networks. London: John Wiley & Sons..

McCabe. (2007). *Network analysis, architedture, and design* (3rd ed.). London: Elsevier Inc.

Nicopplitidis, O. Papadimitrious, & Pomportsis. (2003). Wireless networks. Hoboken, NJ: John Wiley & Sons..

Olakanmi. (2012). RC4c: A secured way to view data transmission in wireless communication networks. International Journal of Computer Networks & Communications, 4(2).

Padmavathi & Shanmugapriya. (2009). A survey of attacks, security mechanisms and challenges in wireless sensor networks. *International Journal of Computer Science and Information Security, 4*(1).

Prttig, Szewczyk, Tygar, Wen, & Culler. (2002). SPINS: Security protocols for sensor networks, wireless networks. Dordrecht, The Netherlands: Kluwer Academic Publishers..

Schwartz. (2005). Mobile wireless communications. Cambridge, UK: Cambridge University Press..

Sen. (2009). A survey on wireless sensor network security. International Journal of Communication Networks and Information Security, 1(2), 55-78.

Sklavos & Xinmiao. (2007). *Wireless security and cryptography: Specification and implementation*. Boca Raton, FL: CRC Press..

Sreedhar, C., Verma, & Kasiviswanath. (2010). Potential security attacks on wireless networks and their countermeasure. *International Journal of Computer Science & Information Technology*, 2(5).

Tachikawa. (2002). *W-CDMA mobile communication systems*. London: Wiley and Maruzen.

Thurwachter. (2002). Wireless networking. Upper Saddle River, NJ: Prentice Hall..

Wang & Poor. (2003). *Wireless communication systems: Advanced techniques for signal reception*. Upper Saddle River, NJ: Prentice Hall..

Xiao, Chen, & Yang, Lin, & Du. (2009). Wireless network security. URASIP Journal on Wireless Communications and Networking.

Chapter 5
Security in Mobile Cloud Computing

Hero Modares
University of Malaya, Malaysia

Amirhossein Moravejosharieh
University of Canterbury, New Zealand

Jaime Lloret
Universidad Politecnica de Valencia, Spain

Rosli Salleh
University of Malaya, Malaysia

ABSTRACT

Cloud computing is a new and promising technology that is transforming the paradigm of traditional Internet computing and probably the whole IT industry. Cloud computing is predicted to expand in the mobile environment leveraging on the rapid advances in wireless access technologies. These mobile applications are built around mobile cloud computing techniques and models. In the Mobile Cloud environment, users can remotely store their data as well as enjoy high quality on-demand cloud applications without the limitations of having to purchase and maintain their own local hardware and software. However, data security is still a major concern and is the main obstacle preventing cloud computing from being more widely adopted. This concern originates from the fact that sensitive data stored in the public clouds is managed by commercial service providers who might not be totally trustworthy. As such, there are several security and privacy issues that need to be addressed. This chapter gives an overview on the cloud computing concept followed by a description on mobile cloud computing and the different security issues pertinent to the mobile cloud computing environment.

1. INTRODUCTION

Cloud computing has grown rapidly in the past few years in tandem with the increase in the network bandwidth, mature virtualization techniques, and emerging cloud-based business demands. Mobile devices will overtake the PCs as the most common web access entities worldwide by 2013. Thus, the future Internet work environment will be a mix of cloud computing with mobile technologies. Mobile Cloud Computing (MCC) refers to an infrastructure where both data storage and data processing are done outside of the mobile devices from which an application was launched. In addition, a mobile entity is limited not only to a mobile device, but more importantly; it encompasses

DOI: 10.4018/978-1-4666-4781-7.ch005

the cloud resources, infrastructure, services, and the users. In the same context, MCC is a cloud system where mobility involves the infrastructure, resources, services, user devices, and even people. Unlike standard computing, MCC has given rise to several issues which evoke reluctance and fear on the part of the users. Some of these issues include concerns privacy, data ownership, and security. Many of these concerns are highly relevant, especially, to mobile devices (Alizadeh, Hassan, Behboodian, & Karamizadeh, 2013; Khorshed, Ali, & Wasimi, 2012; Ko, Lee, & Kim, 2012; Popa, Cremene, Borda, & Boudaoud, 2013; Singh & Shrivastava, 2012). The primary focus of this work is an overview of security in MCC, but it is important to have a complete understanding of Cloud Computing in order to fully grasp the concept of MCC and security in MCC.

The rest of the chapter is organized as follows: Section 2 presents an overall look at the Cloud Computing, in the following section 3 we will focus on Mobile Cloud Computing. Section 4 includes the Mobile Cloud Computing Security. Section 5 will discuss about existing works in securing Mobile Cloud Computing. Finally we will conclude in section 6.

2. CLOUD COMPUTING

Cloud Computing has greatly facilitated the sharing of resources and common infrastructure. This had made it possible to provide on-demand services over the network to fulfil a wide range of today's business needs. In this type of dynamic business environment, the last user has no knowledge about the location of accessible physical resources and tools. Evolving, utilizing, and managing their applications 'on the cloud' involve virtualization of resources that keeps and directs itself are conducted by available facilities to users. The description of Cloud Computing by scientists at the U.S. National Institute of Standards and Technology (NIST) was influenced by an earlier guideline of the Cloud Security Alliance. Researchers have collaborated with the NIST to come out with the Working Definition of cloud computing, and generally, it has been well accepted. Thus, there was coherence and unanimity around a common language, and we can pinpoint on applicable cases rather than semantic nuance. As a result, organizations world-wide used and applied this guide. The NIST, however, is a US government organization, and the wide acceptance of this definition should not suggest that differing view's or views of other countries are ignored. The NIST definition of Cloud Computing comprised five essential qualities, three cloud service models, and four cloud deployment models. Table 1 shows a schematic representation of the definition, and further explained in the following subsections (Brunette & Mogull, 2009; Mell & Grance, 2011; Mirzaei, 2008; Subashini & Kavitha, 2011).

2.1. Service Models

Software as a Service (SaaS), sometimes introduced as a Service or Application Clouds, a particular cloud is responsible for a particular business function and business activities, that is,

Table 1. NIST visual model of cloud computing definition

Essential Characteristics	Broad Network Access	Rapid Elasticity	Measured Service	On-Demand Self-Service
	Resource Pooling			
Service Models	Software as a Service (SaaS)	Platform as a service (PaaS)	Infrastructure as a Service (IaaS)	
Deployment Models	Public	Private	Community	Hybrid

they provide applications/services through a cloud infrastructure or platform instead of providing cloud features to them. Also, a cloud is deemed to be a type of standard application software practicality, for examples, Google Docs, Salesforce CRM, SAP Business by Design.

In general, Cloud Computing is not limited to Infrastructure/Platform/Software as Service systems, even though it enhances the capabilities of these systems. I/P/SaaS can be regarded as specific "usage patterns" for cloud systems which refer to models already approached by Grid, Web Services, etc. Cloud systems offer great potential to implement these models and develop them further (Brunette & Mogull, 2009; Schubert, Jeffery, & Neidecker-Lutz, 2010; Srinivasa, Nageswara, & Kumari, 2009).

Platform as a Service (PaaS), a platform can prepare computational resources based on the developing and hosting characteristics of applications and services. Usually, dedicated APIs are used in PaaS to manage the behavior of a server hosting engine which performs and replicates the performance based on client demands. Each provider reveals his/her own API according to the respective core capabilities, thus, applications can be improved for one specific cloud provider but cannot be transferred to another cloud host – although there have been efforts to broaden common programming models with cloud abilities, for examples; Force.com, Google App Engine, and Windows Azure (Platform) (Brunette & Mogull, 2009; Schubert, et al., 2010; Srinivasa, et al., 2009).

Infrastructure as a Service (IaaS), also known as Resource Cloud, (controlled and scalable), provides services to the user. Basically, they provide improved virtualization abilities. Different resources may be provided through a service interface:

Data & Storage Clouds manage access to data of potentially dynamic size, compare resource operation with access requisites and/or quality definition, for examples; Amazon S3, SQL Azure.

Compute Clouds prepare access to computational resources, that is, the CPUs. Such low-level resources cannot be used on their own and are generally disclosed as part of a "virtualized environment" (not to be combined with PaaS). Thus, Compute Cloud Providers provide the access to typically virtualized computing resources (i.e. raw access to resources, unlike PaaS, which affords full software stacks to improve and create applications), to perform cloudified services and applications. IaaS gives extra abilities over a simple compute service, for examples, Amazon EC2, Zimory, and Elastichosts (Brunette & Mogull, 2009; Schubert, et al., 2010; Srinivasa, et al., 2009).

2.2. Cloud Deployment Models

Regardless of the service model used SaaS, PaaS, or IaaS, four deployment models are introduced for cloud services, with derivative changes that describe specific requirements (Brunette & Mogull, 2009; Group, 2009; Srinivasa, et al., 2009):

Public Cloud: The infrastructure of the public cloud is configured to be accessible to the general public or a large industry group, and is also owned by an organization selling cloud services. This environment can be used publicly, thus, it includes individuals, partnerships, and other types of organizations. Public clouds are generally managed by third parties or vendors over the Internet, and services are charged on a pay-per-use basis. Provider clouds also refer to this type. Business models like SaaS (Software-as-a-Service) and public clouds complement each other and qualify companies to enhance shared IT resources and services.

- **Advantages**
  - Development, deployment and management of business applications which are affordable and which can be extensively applied in Public clouds.

○ Organizations can quickly offer highly scalable and reliable applications which are more affordable.

- **Limitations**
    ○ It is crucial to offer tight security in public clouds and this is a great challenge.

Private Cloud: The private cloud infrastructure is adequate for a single organization. It is administered by the organization or a third-party, and could be set up as on-premise or off-premise implementation. This Cloud Computing set up is wholly proprietary to an organization and serves its own needs, thus, it is also referred to internal clouds. These internal clouds are usually established by the organisation's own IT department. Most organizations choose to optimize usage of their own infrastructure, and implement applications using the concepts of grid and virtualization (Brunette & Mogull, 2009; Group, 2009; Schubert, et al., 2010).

- **Advantages**
    ○ Average server utilization is improved and also low-cost servers and hardware are adequate to meet all computing needs, thus, cost will be greatly reduced.
    ○ High level of automation reduces the operating costs and managerial overheads.
- **Limitations**
    ○ High expenses are incurred for the IT team to maintain an independent cloud in the organization.

Community Clouds: Generally, the local infrastructure is adequate for the operation of the cloud systems, in other words, the public cloud providers recommend that clients have their own infrastructure. Although the provider could resell other provider's infrastructures, clouds do not collect infrastructures to establish larger,

cross-boundary structures. Community clouds are considered to be beneficial to specific small- and medium-sized enterprises (SMEs) in which several entities have their related (smaller) infrastructure. Public clouds or dedicated resource infrastructures can also be collected by Community clouds. In this way, private and public community clouds are determinable. For example, smaller organizations may cooperate just to share their resources through a private community cloud. The carrier grade cloud infrastructure management software from Zimory allows communication service providers (CSPs), enterprises, and cloud brokers to fully leverage the power and flexibility of cloud computing. It may share cloud resources from several providers and resell them. Community Clouds are still just an dream, although some of clouds such as Zimory (GmbH, 2011) and RightScale (RightScale Inc, 2009) are already available for such development. Community clouds and GRIDs technology have some common characteristics (Rochwerger et al., 2009; Schubert, et al., 2010).

- **Advantages**
    ○ It provides a secure and flexible platform for online exchange of file-based digital media contents.
    ○ Risks are mitigated when working with a single cloud vendor.
    ○ A diverse and robust platform and service is established by consolidating the efforts across the community.
- **Limitations**
    ○ It is crucial to offer tighter security in public clouds.

Hybrid Cloud: Combination of two or more clouds (private, community, or public clouds) makes the cloud infrastructure, but each cloud remains as a unique entity. Normalized or characteristic technology that authorizes information and application portability, however, attaches them to each other (e.g., cloud bursting for load-balancing between clouds). This is a combination of both private (internal) and public (external) Cloud Computing environments (Brunette & Mogull, 2009; Srinivasa, et al., 2009).

- **Advantages**
  - Hybrid clouds can operate from any part of the world and are accessible at any time.
  - This technology is available at a very reasonable cost.
- **Limitations**
  - Cloud adoption is the barrier to hybrid cloud for most enterprises.
  - Hybrid clouds have the largest 'surface' for attacks.

3. MOBILE CLOUD COMPUTING

There are various factors that can contribute to the decision to introduce of Mobile Cloud Computing (MCC). These include standard cloud computing, wireless communication, infrastructure, portable computing devices, location-based services, mobile internet, etc. MCC has made it possible for users to have both unlimited online computing power and storage. Mobile Cloud Computing has become a model for transparent elastic augmentation of the capabilities available in mobile devices using an ubiquitous wireless network access to cloud storage and computational resources along with context-aware dynamic adjusting offloading that changes according to the operating conditions. Unfortunately, mobile devices are batter operated, has limited processing power, low capacity, storage, few security features, problematic connectivity, and low energy. These will always pose problems for applications that require high computational capabilities and demand large storage capacity to run in a mobile environment. In order to augment the computing capability, storage capacity, and battery life of mobile devices, these high computational and large storage capacity demanding activities should be transferred to cloud.

More importantly, however, data security is still a concern and is the main obstacle to mobile cloud computing from being widely adopted (Fernando, Loke, & Rahayu, 2012; Huerta-Canepa & Lee, 2010; Kottari, Kamath, Saldanha, & Mohan, 2013; Rimal, Choi, & Lumb, 2009).

The general architecture of Mobile Cloud Computing is shown in Figure 1. By using the base stations (base transceiver stations or BTS, access points, satellites), mobile devices can connect to the mobile networks. These mobile base stations establish and control the connections or air link and the functional interfaces between both the mobile devices and the networks. The location and the ID of the mobile users are sent to the central processors connected to the servers that provide mobile network services. With such setup, the mobile network operators can give AAA (for authentication, authorization, and accounting) services to mobile users based on the home agent (HA) and subscribers information stored in the database. Subscribers request are sent to a cloud via the internet where the requests are processed by the cloud controller, thus, providing the users with the corresponding cloud services (Mane & Devadkar, 2013).

4. MOBILE CLOUD COMPUTING SECURITY

One of the key concerns of most cloud operators' is securing the mobile computing user's privacy and the data or application integrity. With both the mobile users and application developers benefiting from the large storage area the cloud, they must also be aware of the danger when dealing with data/application integrity, authentication, and digital rights. Mobile Cloud Computing is actually a combination of Cloud Computing and mobile networks, thus, issues relating to security can be divided into cloud security and mobile network user's security, respectively (Dinh, Lee, Niyato, & Wang, 2011; Huang, Zhou, Xu, Xing, & Zhong, 2011; Morrow, 2011; Preeti & Vineet, 2013).

Figure 1. Architecture of mobile cloud computing (MCC)

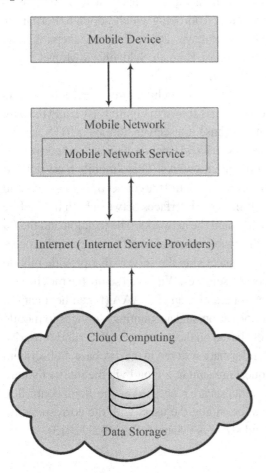

4.1. Mobile Network User's Security

There are many types of security vulnerabilities and threats to different mobile devices such as smart phones, PDAs, cellular phones, laptops, etc. Some applications can also cause security and privacy issues for mobile users (Dinh, et al., 2011). The four main problems concerning user or subscriber security are discussed below:

4.1.1. Security for Mobile Applications

One of the simplest ways to detect any security threats is to install and run security software or an antivirus programme on the mobile device.

However, because mobile devices have limited processing capabilities and power, it could be difficult to protect these devices against threats. Several approaches have been developed to transfer the security and threat detections mechanisms such as authentication, token management, authorization, and data encryption to the clouds. Applications will have to go through several levels of threat evaluation before it can be used by certain mobile subscribers. Verifications will be carried out to ensure that all contents sent to the mobile devices are not malicious in nature. Instead of running these anti-virus and threat detection software locally, mobile devices only need to perform lightweight functions such as executing trace transmitted to the cloud security servers.

4.1.2. Privacy

Private information such as the user's current location and other important data could compromise a user's, privacy. For example, the use of the global positioning system (GPS) for location based services (LBS). These threats to privacy can be minimised by selecting and analysing the nature of the applications, and what are the specific services that should be moved to the cloud. However, this gives rise to concerns that cloud providers or companies will use and the information or give this information to government agencies, etc., without the permission or knowledge of the users.

4.1.3. Data Ownership

Another issue relevant to Mobile Cloud Computing concerns ownership of the purchased digital media. With cloud computing, it is now possible to store media files such as audio, video, and e-books remotely. This raises the question of who actually owns these media. If a user bought the media through a certain service and the media is stored in a remote storage, there is the risk of losing access to the purchased media.

4.1.4. Data Access and Security

Issues relating to access and security are important to applications and programmes that rely on remote data storage and internet access to work. For example, the online calendar and contact applications are used by subscribers to store important dates and other user information, but should a power outage occur, then it would affect their daily function. Mobile Cloud Computing is vulnerable because it requires multiple points where access can be interrupted. High speed and strong signal reception can also adversely affect services to mobile devices users.

4.2. Securing Information on the Cloud

Both individuals and enterprises recognize the advantage of storing large amount of data and application on a cloud. As such, the issues of integrity, authentication, and digital rights must be addressed (Dinh, et al., 2011; Kanday, 2012; Khan, Mat Kiah, Khan, & Madani, 2012).

4.2.1. Integrity

Data integrity is one of the major concerns of mobile users when using the cloud. Several solutions have been proposed to address this issue (e.g. (Tanenbaum A & Van Steen M, 2007; W. Wang, Li, Owens, & Bhargava, 2009)). However, the energy consumption of mobile users has not been taken into consideration. Consideration for energy consumption was made in (Itani, Kayssi, & Chehab, 2010). There are three main components in this requirement: the mobile client, the cloud storage service, and a trusted third party. There are three phases in this scheme: the initialisation, the update and the verification phases. During the initialisation phase, a Message Authentication Code (MAC_{Fx}) will be assigned to files (F_x) to be sent to the cloud. The MAC_{Fx} is stored locally while the files to be sent will be stored in the cloud. In

the update phase, it considers a user's request to add data into the file (F_x). The clouds will send the file (F_x) to the user and at the same time send a requirement to the trusted crypto coprocessor (TCC) to create the MAC'_{Fx}. This is sent by the TCC to the client in order to verify F_x by comparing it together with the MAC_{Fx}. If everything has been authenticated and verified, the user can proceed with the editing or deleting of the data. Finally, the mobile device can request for file the integrity verification process, a collection of files, or the whole file system that is stored in the cloud. This process will start whenever the user sends a request to verify file integrity to the TCC. When the TCC receives the request, it produces a MAC'_{Fx} for the file that needs to be checked. The MAC'_{Fx} is sent back to the user where it will be compared with the locally stored MAC_{Fx} for integrity verification. This method not only verifies the integrity of the data, but it also saves energy for the mobile devices and the bandwidth for other communication functions. This is because all the checking and verification process are carried out on the TCC while the client only executes a simple comparison code. The results show that, almost 90% of processing requirements can be saved using this solution, and at the same time large amount of energy is stored for the mobile devices.

4.2.2. Authentication

Authors (Chow et al., 2010) proposed an authentication method using Cloud Computing as a mean to provide data security suitable for the mobile environments. This method combines TrustCube (Song et al., 2009) and implicit authentication (Jakobsson, Shi, Golle, & Chow, 2009; Shi, Niu, Jakobsson, & Chow, 2011) for mobile client authentication. TrustCube is a policy-based cloud authentication platform that uses open standards and supports the integration of other authentication methods. The developer had built an implicit authentication system that uses mobile data (calling logs, SMS messages, website accesses, and location) for the existing mobile environment. It faces input constraints and this makes it difficult for mobile users to use complex passwords. As a result, simple and short password or PIN is used. The system architecture and how the mobile user's access is made secure is shown in Figure 2. When the mobile client sends a request to the web server, it will redirect the request to the Integrated Authenticated (IA) Service together with the request details. The IA service then proceeds to retrieve the access request policy, extracts the enquiry information and then sends the inquiry to the IA Server via the trusted network connect (TNC) protocol. The IA Server will then generate a report and send it back to the IA Service, which will apply the authentication rule in the policy and check the authentication result to see whether the mobile client has been successfully authenticated for the request for access. The authentication result is then sent back to the web server. Depending on this result, the web server can either deny the request or provide the service to the mobile client.

4.2.3. Digital Rights Management

Most unstructured digital contents (videos, images, audios, and e-books) are often pirated and distributed illegally. Therefore, it is crucial for the content providers in MCC to protect these contents from any illegal access to Cloud Computing and peer-to-peer networks. (Zou, Wang, Liu, & Bao, 2010) proposed Phosphor, a mobile digital rights management (DRM) scheme based on cloud using a sim card in mobile phones as a way of improving flexibility while reducing vulnerability, at a lower cost. The developers designed the License State Word (LSW) that is located inside the sim card and the LSW protocol, which is based on the application protocol data unit (APDU) command. When an efficient unstructured data management service is added, it can meet the required performance with high elasticity. As such, when a mobile user receives encrypted data (e.g., video stream) from a content provider through the RTP protocol, the user decodes this data via the APDU command using the decryption key inside the sim

Figure 2. TrustCube architecture

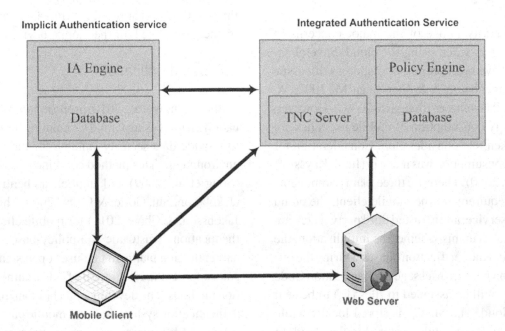

card. However, the drawback of such method is the reliance on the mobile phone sim card. It also cannot be accessed using a laptop with WIFI to access contents.

5. RELATED WORK IN SECURITY OF MOBILE CLOUD COMPUTING

The existing security issues in MCC can be divided into two categories:

- Security of data
- Security of application

5.1. Security of Data

The security of data deals with the protection of mobile user's files created and manipulated on a mobile device or the cloud server.

Itani et al. proposed an integrity verification method for mobile clients that are more energy efficient (Itani, et al., 2010). It uses an incremental message authentication code to verify the integrity of the files stored on a cloud server. It offloads most of the integrity verification tasks to the cloud service provider and the TTP, thus, minimising the processing requirements of the mobile devices. When the mobile client sends a request, the cloud service provider will redirect the stored files to the coprocessor, which will compute the incremental MAC for integrity verification. However, this proposed framework has overlooked the privacy of uploaded files. Also, the trusted coprocessors are installed on the cloud by the TTP in order to maintain integrity of the mobile users' file/data. The coprocessor has no problem in handling a certain number of mobile users but if the number of user increases beyond that, the performance of the coprocessor will degrade.

Jia et al. proposed a secure data service that outsources data and security management on cloud but not disclosing any user information (Jia, Zhu, Cao, Wei, & Lin, 2011). A proxy re-encryption

and an identity based encryption schemes are used for this purpose. Although the overhead and the responsibility of security management have been removed from the mobile users in this proposed data service, mobile devices still has to perform cryptographic operations before files can be uploaded to the cloud. These cryptographic operations involve extensive pairing evaluations and exponential calculations. These evaluation and calculation processes consume a high amount of energy, and this must be considered when designing a secure framework for the MCC. The cloud is also responsible for executing security management and re-encryption on behalf of the mobile users. This increases the utilisation of cloud resources which can result in the users being overcharged. It is important to make strong analyses of the tradeoff between cloud resource consumption and energy consumption of mobile devices when the secure data service is used.

A new scheme for smart phones that ensures the security, integrity, and authenticity of the user's data was proposed by Hsueh et al (Hsueh, Lin, & Lin, 2011). In this scheme, the mobile device will encrypt the files using the traditional asymmetric encryption techniques. These files will then be stored on the cloud servers together with the mobile user's name, signature, and password. However, these encrypted files with the user's credentials can also be stored on another cloud server belonging to an adversary, who might use the user's personal information to impersonate the user. Also, this proposed scheme ignores the processing and storing limitations of mobile devices. The mobile device has to perform the encryption, decryption, and even hash functions of an entire file by itself.

Yang et al. proposed another method that involves having a publicly provable data possession scheme to ensure privacy and confidentiality for mobile devices that has limited resources (Yang, Wang, Wang, Tan, & Yu, 2011). The TPP is responsible for encoding/decoding, encryption/ decryption, signature generation, and verification, on behalf of the mobile devices. This helps the mobile devices to conserve energy by offloading the user's tasks to the TPP, but this can result in performance degradation if the number of mobile devices increases.

The related works on security of data are compared in Table 2.

5.2. Security of Application

The security of applications deals with the protection of mobile applications or mobile application models, which use the cloud resources to provide better services for mobile users in the MCC environment.

A top, down spatial cloaking mechanism, with or without optimization, was proposed by Wang and Wang (S. Wang & Wang, 2010). It utilises the cloud resources to provide a more scalable, efficient and better privacy preservation framework for location-based services. The in-device spatial cloaking without optimisation requires communication with the cloud server to get the user count in different grid cells. This process of communication causes delay and incurs overhead as discussed in (S. Wang & Wang, 2010). A new technique was proposed to overcome this communication delay and overhead called the in-device spatial cloaking with optimisation. The effectiveness of this method depends on the historical lower bound of

Table 2. Comparison of the security of data category

	Data integrity	Authentication	Scalability
Itani et al.	√	X	√
Jia et al.	X	X	√
Hsueh et al.	√	√	√
Yang et al.	√	√	√

the number of users in each grid cell. This historical data is used to predict the number of user in each cell. If this is wrong, then user privacy can be compromised. The cloud is also responsible for maintaining and sharing each cell's historical information during start-up. This maintenance and processing of historical information imposes additional burden on the cloud, when compared to other techniques.

Huan et al. (Huang, Zhang, Kang, & Luo, 2010) proposed a MCC framework that provides conventional computation services. It also provides some improvement to the functionality of MANET pertaining to risk management, trust management, and secure routing. Despite the advantages available in MobiCloud over MANET, its framework does not consider the trustworthiness of the cloud nodes. There should be a mechanism to ensure that the mobile user information on the cloud servers is secure.

Chen and Wang (Chen & Wang, 2011) proposed a security framework for LBS and used a location-based group scheduling service called JOIN as a way for addressing the security concerns in LBS. The user's data such as ID, PWD and KA are revealed is visible to the cloud service provider if the JOIN server is hosted on a cloud. They did not suggest any method or mechanism to protect the user's personal information in the server. Also, the JOIN server uses the AES algorithm for encryption, and this makes it necessary for decryption to be done at the mobile device side. A lightweight encryption technique is required so that it is more beneficial for the mobile users to decrypt files at the same time, thus, preserving battery life and minimise processing. Finally, the most crucial part of the proposed security mechanism is the IMSI. If the IMSI information is leaked, then the whole security of the system will fail when attacked by an adversary.

The related works on security of application are compared in Table 3.

Table 3. Comparison of the security of application category

	Authentication	Trusted	Scalability
Wang and Wang	X	Semi trusted	√
Huan et al.	Risk management	X	√
Chen et al.	√	√	√

6. CONCLUSION

The long held view of computing as a function is becoming a reality. Cloud Computing is an example and it is becoming increasingly more popular. The cloud over the Internet provides the infrastructure for users to be served more effectively. IBM, Google, and Microsoft as leaders in the computing industry, have taken the lead in developing applications in support of cloud computing. However, research on Cloud Computing has yet to gain sufficient momentum. Many issues on cloud computing remain to be addressed, particularly, those pertaining to security. The outlook of Mobile Cloud Computing (MCC) involves work out with virtual representations without the physical existence of software or hardware. For example, programmers can design their applications using a web-based platform. Users can manage their businesses with simple-to-use online software. There are many benefits for switching over to MCC such as: capital expenditure costs are decreased as new systems and network and data security costs are largely reduced by way of pay-as-you-go methodology, developers of applications do not have to be concerned about interoperability. As Cloud Computing becomes more common, new challenges and regulatory issues will emerge, and therefore, useful polices on its usage and services will required to be addressed at both the local and international levels.

Mobile Cloud Computing may not be as simple as it seems, and it is fraught with challenges, but its potential benefits of offering new business models for outweigh the present challenges.

There are also many issues pertaining to compliance with standards, availability of bandwidth, global execution, IP violation, exploit of client data, location of client data, transparency, and legal considerations that need to be addressed. Businesses today require certainty and assurance of good service from the service providers; they also require the pliability to exploit services to meet their business requirements.

REFERENCES

Alizadeh, M., Hassan, W. H., Behboodian, N., & Karamizadeh, S. (2013). A brief review of mobile cloud computing opportunities. *Research Notes in Information Science, 12*, 155–159.

Brunette, G., & Mogull, R. (2009). Security guidance for critical areas of focus in cloud computing. *Cloud Security Alliance*, 1-76.

Chen, Y.-J., & Wang, L.-C. (2011). *A security framework of group location-based mobile applications in cloud computing*. Paper presented at the 40th International Conference on Parallel Processing Workshops (ICPPW). Taipei, Taiwan.

Chow, R., Jakobsson, M., Masuoka, R., Molina, J., Niu, Y., Shi, E., & Song, Z. (2010). *Authentication in the clouds: A framework and its application to mobile users*. Paper presented at the 2010 ACM Workshop on Cloud Computing Security Workshop. Chicago, IL.

Dinh, H. T., Lee, C., Niyato, D., & Wang, P. (2011). A survey of mobile cloud computing: architecture, applications, and approaches. *Wireless Communications and Mobile Computing*. London: Wiley. Retrieved from http://www.eecis.udel.edu/~cshen/859/papers/survey_MCC.pdf

Fernando, N., Loke, S. W., & Rahayu, W. (2012). Mobile cloud computing: A survey. *Future Generation Computer Systems, 29*, 84–106. doi:10.1016/j.future.2012.05.023.

Gmb, H. Z. (2011). *Zimory enterprise cloud.* Retrieved from http://www.zimory.de/index.php?id=75

Group, T. C. C. U. C. D. (2009). *Cloud computing use cases whitepaper.* Retrieved from http://www.scribd.com/doc/17929394/Cloud-Computing-Use-Cases-Whitepaper

Hsueh, S.-C., Lin, J.-Y., & Lin, M.-Y. (2011). *Secure cloud storage for convenient data archive of smart phones.* Paper presented at the 15th IEEE International Symposium on Consumer Electronics (ISCE). Singapore.

Huang, D., Zhang, X., Kang, M., & Luo, J. (2010). *MobiCloud: Building secure cloud framework for mobile computing and communication.* Paper presented at the Fifth IEEE International Symposium on Service Oriented System Engineering (SOSE). Nanjing, China.

Huang, D., Zhou, Z., Xu, L., Xing, T., & Zhong, Y. (2011). *Secure data processing framework for mobile cloud computing.* Paper presented at the IEEE Conference on Computer Communications Workshops (INFOCOM WKSHPS). Shanghai, China.

Huerta-Canepa, G., & Lee, D. (2010). *A virtual cloud computing provider for mobile devices.* Paper presented at the 1st ACM Workshop on Mobile Cloud Computing & Services Social Networks and Beyond. San Francisco, CA.

Itani, W., Kayssi, A., & Chehab, A. (2010). *Energy-efficient incremental integrity for securing storage in mobile cloud computing.* Paper presented at the Energy Aware Computing (ICEAC). Cairo, Egypt.

Jakobsson, M., Shi, E., Golle, P., & Chow, R. (2009). *Implicit authentication for mobile devices.* Paper presented at the 4th USENIX Conference on Hot Topics in Security. Montreal, Canada.

Jia, W., Zhu, H., Cao, Z., Wei, L., & Lin, X. (2011). *SDSM: A secure data service mechanism in mobile cloud computing.* Paper presented at the IEEE Conference on Computer Communications Workshops (INFOCOM WKSHPS). Shanghai, China.

Kanday, R. (2012). *A survey on cloud computing security.* Paper presented at the Computing Sciences (ICCS). Phagwara, India.

Khan, A. N., Mat Kiah, M., Khan, S. U., & Madani, S. A. (2012). Towards secure mobile cloud computing: A survey. *Future Generation Computer Systems, 5*(29), 22.

Khorshed, M. T., Ali, A., & Wasimi, S. A. (2012). A survey on gaps, threat remediation challenges and some thoughts for proactive attack detection in cloud computing. *Future Generation Computer Systems, 28*(6), 833–851. doi:10.1016/j.future.2012.01.006

Ko, S.-K. V., Lee, J.-H., & Kim, S. W. (2012). Mobile cloud computing security considerations. *Journal of Security Engineering, 9*(2), 143–150.

Kottari, V., Kamath, V., Saldanha, L. P., & Mohan, C. (2013). A survey on mobile cloud computing: Concept, applications and challenges. *International Journal of Academic Research, 2*(3), 487–492.

Mane, M. Y. D., & Devadkar, K. K. (2013). *Protection concern in mobile cloud computing-A survey.* Paper presented at the Second International Conference on Emerging Trends in Engineering. New Delhi, India.

Mell, P., & Grance, T. (2011). The NIST definition of cloud computing (draft). *NIST Special Publication, 800,* 145.

Mirzaei, N. (2008). *Cloud computing.* Bloomington, IN: Indiana University..

Morrow, S. (2011). Data security in the cloud. In *Cloud Computing: Principles and Paradigms*. London: Wiley. doi:10.1002/9780470940105.ch23.

Popa, D., Cremene, M., Borda, M., & Boudaoud, K. (2013). *A security framework for mobile cloud applications*. Paper presented at the 11th Roedunet International Conference (RoEduNet). Sinaia, Romania.

Preeti, G., & Vineet, S. (2013). Secure data storage in mobile cloud computing. *International Journal of Scientific & Engineering Research*, *4*(4).

RightScale Inc. (2009). *RightScale cloud management features*. Retrieved from http://www.rightscale. com/products/features/

Rimal, B. P., Choi, E., & Lumb, I. (2009). *A taxonomy and survey of cloud computing systems*. Paper presented at the 5th Int. Joint Conference of INC, IMS and IDC, NCM '09. Seoul, Korea.

Rochwerger, B., Breitgand, D., Levy, E., Galis, A., Nagin, K., & Llorente, I. M. et al. (2009). The reservoir model and architecture for open federated cloud computing. *IBM Journal of Research and Development*, *53*(4). doi:10.1147/JRD.2009.5429058.

Schubert, L., Jeffery, K. G., & Neidecker-Lutz, B. (2010). *The future of cloud computing: Opportunities for European cloud computing beyond 2010*. Brussels, Belgium: European Commission, Information Society and Media..

Shi, E., Niu, Y., Jakobsson, M., & Chow, R. (2011). Implicit authentication through learning user behavior. In *Proceedings of the 13th International Conference on Information Security (ISC 2010)*, (pp. 99-113). Berlin: Springer.

Singh, M. A., & Shrivastava, M. (2012). Overview of security issues in cloud computing. *International Journal of Advanced Computer Research*, *2*, 41–45.

Song, Z., Molina, J., Lee, S., Lee, H., Kotani, S., & Masuoka, R. (2009). Trustcube: An infrastructure that builds trust in client. In *Future of Trust in Computing*. Berlin: Springer. doi:10.1007/978-3-8348-9324-6_8.

Srinivasa, R., Nageswara, R., & Kumari, E. (2009). Cloud computing: An overview. *Journal of Theoretical and Applied Information Technology*, *9*(1), 71–76.

Subashini, S., & Kavitha, V. (2011). A survey on security issues in service delivery models of cloud computing. *Journal of Network and Computer Applications*, *34*(1), 1–11. doi:10.1016/j.jnca.2010.07.006.

Tanenbaum, A., & Van Steen, M. (2007). *Distributed systems: Principles and paradigms*. Englewood Cliffs, NJ: Pearson Prentice Hall..

Wang, S., & Wang, X. S. (2010). *In-device spatial cloaking for mobile user privacy assisted by the cloud*. Paper presented at the International Conference on Mobile Data Management (MDM). St. Louis, MO.

Wang, W., Li, Z., Owens, R., & Bhargava, B. (2009). *Secure and efficient access to outsourced data*. Paper presented at the 2009 ACM Workshop on Cloud Computing Security. Chicago, IL.

Yang, J., Wang, H., Wang, J., Tan, C., & Yu, D. (2011). Provable data possession of resource-constrained mobile devices in cloud computing. *Journal of Networks*, *6*(7), 1033–1040. doi:10.4304/jnw.6.7.1033-1040.

Zou, P., Wang, C., Liu, Z., & Bao, D. (2010). *Phosphor: A cloud based DRM scheme with sim card*. Paper presented at the 12th International Asia-Pacific Web Conference (APWEB). Busan, South Korea.

Chapter 6
A Cognitive Access Framework for Security and Privacy Protection in Mobile Cloud Computing

Gianmarco Baldini
Joint Research Centre – European Commission, Italy

Pasquale Stirparo
Joint Research Centre – European Commission, Italy

ABSTRACT

Information systems and wireless communications are becoming increasingly present in the everyday life of citizens both from a personal and business point of view. A recent development in this context is Mobile Cloud Computing (MCC), which is the combination of Cloud Computing and pervasive mobile networks. Ensuring the preservation of privacy can be difficult in MCC. Therefore, this chapter provides an overview of the main challenges in ensuring privacy in MCC and surveys the most significant contributions from the research community. The second objective of the chapter is to introduce and describe a new framework for privacy protection based on the concepts of Virtual Object (VO) and Composite Virtual Object (CVO), where data are encapsulated and protected using a sticky policy approach and a role-based access model. The proposed iCore framework is compared to the privacy challenges described in the first objective.

INTRODUCTION

Information systems and wireless communications are becoming increasingly present in the everyday life of citizens both from a personal and business point of view. This trend is supported by various drivers, which include greater business efficiency, improved quality of life, improved access to information and support for mobility. The recent emergence of cases of identity theft described by Ghosh (2010) has shown that the development and deployment of these technologies is still far from perfect and many challenges remain. A key challenge is to ensure that the same citizen's data,

DOI: 10.4018/978-1-4666-4781-7.ch006

which is used in business and personal transactions, is also not used by unauthorized parties or "reused" in contexts or applications that can bring harmful consequences to citizen and businesses.

There are various reasons for the "shortcomings" of the current pervasive information and communication technologies. Regulation and laws for these new issues have not been formulated yet, technologies to protect identity of citizens are still at the premature stage, and applications are often not designed considering privacy and security to be essential.. The Internet paradigm calls for "openness" but this should not mean that personal data is open to the world. In synthesis, there are various gaps and issues in the current regulatory and technology frameworks, which must be addressed.

Some issues are not easy to be resolved because they are part of a trade-off. Regulators, service providers and businesses do not want that the effort to ensure security and privacy is an obstacle to the development of new markets or integration of the old ones. There is a "tussle" between the need for openness to ensure efficient transactions among various applications and the need to restrict the access to data.

Another key element in this context is the evolution of wireless communications and support for mobility. Until a few years ago, wireless communication technology was used by the common citizen mostly for voice. Recent technological evolutions both from network and mobile devices has fostered the provision of data connectivity, which can be used to support new applications in a virtuous cycle: new applications and "hunger" for data support the deployment of networks, which can provide wireless broadband connectivity. At the same time, mobile devices have become increasingly powerful and reconfigurable. The gap between personal computers and mobile devices is now "blurred" in the sense that similar applications and services can be provided on both platforms.

A recent development in this context is MCC, which is the combination of Cloud Computing and mobile networks.

As described in Ghosh (2010) and Han, & Gani (2012), MCC can benefit mobile computing with increased capabilities and improved power efficiency. Mobile devices can rely on cloud computing to perform computationally intensive operations for various purposes such as multimedia or data processing. By offloading the execution of specific operations to the Cloud, mobile devices and networks can also improve power efficiency. The advantages of MCC for extending battery lifetime, improving data storage capacity and processing power are also described in Dinh, Lee, Niyato, and Wang (2011), where are also identified the outstanding issues for the integration of cloud computing and mobile networks. These issues include availability of the systems and their heterogeneity and that mobile networks may not provide the same bandwidth in all areas or time of the day due to different factors like traffic capacity, wireless coverage and propagation errors. The problems related to low bandwidth and high latency of cellular mobile networks are also mentioned in Bahl, Han, Li, and Satyanarayanan (2012), which proposes the seamless integration of cloudlet and public cloud, and infrastructure specialization for mobile applications. The cloudlet concept is described as a trusted cluster of computers mutually connected through a low latency, high bandwidth wireless network, which is well connected to the Internet and is available for use by nearby mobile devices.

From a security and privacy point of view, MCC may also create new issues. Mobile devices may provide users-related data to the Cloud applications to perform the computational intensive operations described above or just for outsourcing storage. Some Cloud applications such as remote healthcare may even process and store sensitive data related to the current health conditions of citizens. In most cases, the location of the mobile device and its user will be associated with any data transmitted from the mobile device.

As described in Chuang, Li, Huang & Kuo (2011), in comparison to other communication models, MCC has no explicit and defined boundaries. The Cloud applications are shared and they can be accessed by fixed and mobile terminals. The stored data collected from the mobile devices could theoretically be accessed and used by malicious parties. A potential scenario could involve a criminal who accesses the Cloud application to obtain the knowledge of the current location of a user, to predict that absence of the user at home and consequently attempt burglary. Even if the direct location is not directly available, it can be inferred by other data such as images or image meta-data taken with the user's mobile device and posted on the Web. Other scenarios can be envisaged, which can be even more harmful to businesses entities.

There is clearly a need to address these issues and guide the evolution of MCC to ensure the protection of the privacy of users without hampering the commercial development of MCC applications and the benefits for the society.

Various papers studies have proposed frameworks or access models with the objective to provide protect data protection of users' data. As mentioned in Chuang, Li, Huang & Kuo (2011), data protection frameworks in Cloud Computing or MCC may not provide adequate scalability for business users or they may introduce excessive overhead in terms of communication or processing resources. Another significant challenge is that MCC concepts and paradigms are usually derived from Cloud computing in the fixed communication domain where always-on and high quality connectivity is guaranteed. As described in Klein, Mannweiler, Schneider, & Schotten (2010), mobile computing is not always able to provide this type of connectivity and new access schemes may be needed. References Huang, Zhou, Xu, Xing & Zhong (2011) and Huang, Zhang, Kang,

Luo (2010) describe a secure mobile cloud data processing framework based on trust management and private data isolation, which may partly address these challenges. The mobile cloud data processing model is based on the following three components:

- The trust management function,
- Multi-tenant secure data management, and
- Extended Semi-Shadow Images (ESSI) data processing model.

Additional references on the current research activities are presented in section *Background*. However the research activities for security and privacy aspects in MCC are still limited and further work is needed.

The objectives of this book chapter are as follows:

1. The first objective is to provide an overview of the privacy challenges in MCC and to identify the most significant contributions from the research community.
2. The second objective is to introduce and describe a new framework for privacy protection based on a cognitive approach, where the information on the context such as level of access, connected systems, type of applications and type of users is used in a cognitive engine. This framework dynamically defines the most appropriate policies and rules for privacy protection.

The proposed cognitive framework is based on the concept that data of users can be represented as a Virtual Object (VO), where the level of access is regulated through a classic Role-Based Access Control (RBAC) approach complemented with a sticky policy approach Pearson & Mont (2011). The framework defines levels of access on the basis of the profile of the user or features of the data to be accessed. The level of access can change depending on the context or it can be delegated. For example, in an emergency crisis, the level of access of first-time responders can be enhanced to allow the access to the medical records of wounded citizens or it can be delegated to emergency medical operators belonging to another jurisdiction. The profile of the user is also represented as a VO, where one of the attributes is the current level of trust in the cognitive framework. The cognitive framework uses the information related to the context and of the users to dynamically define access rules and prevent malicious parties to access users' data. As a consequence, the concept of "cognitive" in this context is related to a cognitive cycle process, which starts from the observation of new real world "context" features (initial state) that are either triggered as "consequents" by sensor data processing tasks (i.e., event-condition based processing). The primary need for a cognitive cycle in the iCore framework is to allow domain experts to include their specific domain knowledge into the process (e.g., by means of expert systems, constraint based rules, and Bayesian graphical models, each coming with specific inductive bias) so that a degree of control can be influenced onto the iCore system and predictive behaviour developed, in order to generate relevant "real world knowledge" and actuation. More details on the cognitive capability is provided in the section *Cognitive Access Framework for Privacy Protection*.

BACKGROUND

Privacy in Mobile Cloud Computing: Concepts and Definitions

MCC is a new paradigm, which has many definitions from different sources.

A simple definition of MCC is the combination of Mobile Computing and Cloud Computing, where Cloud Computing is defined by Buyya, Yeo & Venugopal (2008) as a parallel and distributed computing system, which is combined by a group of virtual machines with internal links. Such systems dynamically offer computing resources from service providers to customers according to their Service level Agreement (SLA) computing system. Other authors pointed out that Cloud Computing is not entirely a new concept but it is a combination of various concepts such as distributed computing, Service Oriented Architecture (SOA) and virtualization. Youseff, Butrico, & Da Silva (2008) provides ontology of Cloud Computing, based on a stack of layers: application or services, software environment, software infrastructure, software kernel and hardware. These layers are then mapped to other definitions of the services offered by Cloud Computing as described in Figure 1.

The description of the Cloud Layers is as follows:

Figure 1. Cloud layers and Cloud services

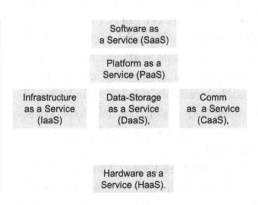

- **Cloud Application Layer:** The Cloud provides applications and the related services to the users. This is the upper layer of Cloud Computing. The advantage of hosting applications in the Cloud is to minimize the maintenance and related costs in comparison to a private computing facility. The Cloud Application layer is related to the model of Software as a Service (Saas), which is defined, as the capability to provide services to users by using the provider's applications running on a cloud infrastructure (Mell & Grance, 2011).

- **Cloud Software Infrastructure Layer:** The Cloud provides access of software infrastructures and frameworks or API to users. The users can use the Cloud to develop new applications. This layer is related to the model of Platform as a Service (PaaS), which is defined as the capability provided by the Cloud to the users to deploy applications created using programming languages, libraries, services, and tools hosted in the Cloud (Mell & Grance 2011).

- **Cloud Software Infrastructure Layer:** The Cloud provides resources to other high-level layers. The provided resources can be of the following different types: storage of data, communication, specific computing low-level services (e.g., encryption). This layer is related to the models of Infrastructure as a Service (IaaS), Data Storage as a Service (DaaS) and Communications as a Service (CaaS).

- **Cloud Software Kernel Layer:** This layer provides the basic software management for the physical servers that compose the cloud. For example, this layer can be based on operating system kernel, hypervisor, virtual machine monitor and/or clustering middleware.

- **Cloud Hardware Layer:** This layer represents the hardware components such as the physical networks, computers and storage hardware, which can be maintained by a Cloud provider. This layer is directly related to the model of Hardware as a Service (HaaS) proposed by Stanik, Hovestadt, & Kao (2012), where computing power is provided to users by the Cloud.

Mobile Computing also has many definitions. In this book chapter, we define Mobile Computing as the form of human-computer interaction where the computer itself can be mobile. In addition, the computer is able to connect to other computers and networks through wireless communications. From the user point of view, Mobile Computing offers the advantage of accessing services, while maintaining the mobility. It is obviously based on mobile communications, which provide connectivity between two or more mobile devices or a mobile device and a fixed communication infrastructure.

Mobile communications had a spectacular evolution in the last 20 years creating a significant market. Until recently, the main service offered by mobile communications was voice and limited messaging and data communications (e.g., narrowband data communications). The definition of new wireless communication standards (e.g., 3GPP (UMTS) and WiFi) for high speed communications and the increased capabilities of communication circuits according to Moore's law have fostered the development of wireless communication networks, which are able to support broadband wireless connectivity. In a similar fashion, because of technological progress, mobile devices have also increased their computing power, storage and autonomy related to power consumption.

Today, a consumer can access a wide range of services and applications from commercial mobile devices, which could only be accessed from fixed devices (e.g., Personal Computer) few years ago. Furthermore, mobile devices are now equipped with new sensors such as cameras, navigation sensors (e.g., GPS) and motion detectors, which can support new applications and services that are able to take advantage of the new information and data. Examples of these new services are the Location Based Services (LBS) where retailers use the location information to notify the potential consumers on available goods in the surrounding area. This trend is likely to continue in the future.

Still, the computing and connectivity capabilities of mobile devices are less powerful at present than fixed devices such as a personal computer connected with a high-speed fixed connection (e.g., ADSL or fiber optic) to the Internet.

Mobile Computing has the following disadvantages in comparison to "fixed computing":

- Even if telecom operators are rolling out new networks based on new standards, the coverage of broadband connectivity is not guaranteed everywhere but only where it is economically convenient for the operators.
- Wireless communication is vulnerable to unintentional threats such as buildings, landforms that block the propagation of electro-magnetic waves or it can be vulnerable to intentional threats such as jamming, where an attacker transmit in the same bands used by the consumer mobile device.
- Traffic capacity or provision of broadband connectivity is usually shared in a local environment (e.g., an UMTS cell) with the other users present in the cell. The overall capacity and available spectrum bands have limits imposed by the network deployed in the area or by spectrum regulators.
- Battery power imposes limits to the time for which the mobile devices can be used or their processing capabilities because power consumption is proportional to the computing complexity of the algorithms.

To conclude, while Mobile Computing offers to the consumer the important advantage of the mobility, the provided capabilities are still limited in comparison to fixed communications and computing.

MCC can address some of these challenges and provide additional services and capabilities to the consumer.

A description of MCC architecture is provided in Figure 2.

The main components of MCC are as follows:

- Client layer is composed of mobile devices such as tables, cellular phones, smartphones, and similar equipment, which run local client applications based on various operating systems (e.g., iOS, Android).
- The wireless access networks, which can have different features in terms of coverage, data rate, Quality of Service (QoS) and traffic capacity.
- The high-speed backbone networks that connect the wireless networks with the Cloud Infrastructures and the rest of Internet.
- The Cloud Infrastructures, which are structured according to Figure 2 as described above.

The implementation of MCC infrastructures can be very complex and can be vulnerable to various security and privacy threats.

In this book chapter, we will focus on the threats and related mitigation techniques to ensure protection of the privacy of users. A key concern by citizens and government is the proliferation of personal data including the identity data, through information systems outside the control of the citizen, and its use in contexts, that were not initially foreseen.

In Europe, there are several directives that aim at enforcing Privacy by Design in the EU regulation panorama. The main pillar is the Directive 95/46 described by Commission of the European Communities (1995), which regulates the process-

Figure 2. Overall architecture of mobile cloud computing

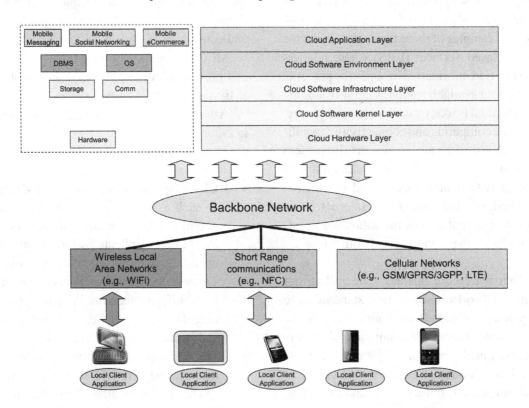

ing of personal data regardless of whether such processing is automated. Interesting points are the definitions of "personal data" (art. 2.a), which is described as information relating to an identified or identifiable natural person ('data subject'), the notion of "processing" (art. 2.b) described as any operation or set of operations performed upon personal data and the Article 17 "Security of processing," which requires data controllers to implement appropriate technical and organization measures to prevent unlawful data processing.

The R&TTE Directive described in Commission of the European Communities (1999) gives other interesting and important inputs. Article 3.3.c states that apparatus within certain equipment classes, or apparatus of particular types, shall be constructed so that it incorporates safeguards to ensure that the personal data and privacy of the users and subscribers are protected.

Finally, as indicated in Commission of the European Communities (2012), the European Commission proposed a comprehensive reform of the Data Protection Directive aiming to strengthen online privacy rights and boost Europe's digital economy, which includes the following items:

- It will enforce the rule of "Opt-in" as default when personal data may need to be treated,
- It will establish new privacy rights, including data subject's "right of portability," which will allow to transfer all data from one provider to another, and the "right to be forgotten," which will allow individuals to clear the history.

IDENTIFICATION OF MAIN ISSUES AND CHALLENGES

Various sources have identified potential security threats for Cloud Computing in general and more specifically for MCC. In this section, we will focus on the specific threats for MCC.

ENISA (2009) identified the most important security risks to cloud computing containing the violation of SLAs, the ability to risk assessment of cloud service providers, the protection of data privacy, virtualization, compliance etc.

Cloud Security Alliance (2010) identified the major security threats to Cloud Computing. Some of these threats also apply to MCC.

A detailed analysis of the security and privacy threats to MCC is out of the scope of this book chapter, where we focus only on specific privacy threats.

From the previous references, we can identify the following privacy threats.

Data breaches in the Cloud infrastructure: Because the connectivity to the Mobile Cloud is not always guaranteed at any time or place by the wireless access networks, mobile users may decide to trust sensitive data to the Mobile Cloud to facilitate operations or applications. For example, a mobile user may provide sensitive financial data to Mobile Cloud applications to automate financial transactions while he/she is not connected. Another example is where mobile users may upload images or videos to Mobile Cloud automatically while moving. In some cases, these images may contain private information, which can be exploited by malicious parties: an image taken by a user in a foreign city may give a hint that the personal belongings in the user's house can be stolen.

Data breaches in the Mobile Device: Mobile devices are becoming increasingly sophisticated with powerful computing and memory capabilities. Users are going to store more private and business data in their devices. These data can be stolen or tampered by malicious attackers through various ways, which include malware, eavesdropping or brute force attacks if the devices are stolen or lost. In addition, most applications still store and manage users data in an insecure manner, as shown in Stirparo & Kounelis (2012), which poses a serious potential threat for identity or financial theft whenever a lost/stolen smartphone falls into the wrong hands.

Confidentiality threats on the communication channel: A malicious attacker can intercept information communicated on the communication channel. The research activities and related mitigation techniques for communication systems are well documented in research literature, but the integration of MCC could generate new vulnerabilities, which could be exploited. For example, the same data available on the Cloud could be accessed from different communication systems with different levels of protection.

Incomplete data deletion: For Privacy reasons, it is very important that transitory data should be destroyed permanently. For example, in a business meeting executed with the support of MCC, participants probably exchange documents and data during the meeting. These data should be permanently removed from the Mobile Cloud infrastructure. Because data is often replicated in the infrastructure, this task can be relatively complex.

Isolation Failure: Mobile Cloud infrastructures are usually characterized by multi-tenancy and shared resources. Computing capacity, storage, and network are shared between multiple users. This class of risks includes the failure of mechanisms separating storage, memory, routing, and even reputation between different tenants of the shared infrastructure (e.g., so-called guest-hopping attacks, SQL injection attacks exposing multiple customers' data stored in the same table, and side channel attacks).

Integration of security and privacy functions: An important challenge is the integration of the security functions (e.g., authentication or authorization) of existing communication systems or applications with the Mobile Cloud Infrastructure. There are many open issues in this challenge: should the MCC Infrastructure use the security functions already implemented in the mobile communication systems or create a separate implementation? Both approaches have advantages and disadvantages. A similar issue is the integration of storage applications and services in the MCC infrastructure.

LITERATURE SURVEY

Mobile Cloud Computing systems have been proposed by various companies. Google App Engine cloud service described in Malawski, Kuźniar, Wójcik, and Bubak (2013) is an example of Platform-as-a-service (PaaS) cloud computing infrastructure because Web application developers can use it to create their applications using a set of Google tools. The cloud computing infrastructure is maintained by Google in a secure hosting environment. Google App Engine requires that application developers use only a limited set of supported programming languages together with a small set of APIs and frameworks that are mostly dedicated to Web applications. This can be a limitation for a potential deployment/integration of the framework presented in this book chapter.

Another well know cloud computing infrastructure is the Amazon Elastic Compute Cloud (EC2), which is part of a suite of cloud services called Amazon Web Services (AWS). AWS provide CaaS, IaaS, SaaS and PaaS via web-based APIs. EC2 allows users to deploy VM images with customized operating systems, libraries, and application code on virtual machines with a variety of pre-defined hardware configurations. Amazon EC2 can be integrated with framework defined in research activities like the one presented in this chapter. In Cong, Chow, Qian, Kui, Wenjing (2013), the authors proposes a privacy-preserving public auditing system for data storage security in

cloud computing, which is validated on Amazon EC2 from the performance point of view.

Cloud Security Alliance (2009) proposes a cloud security reference model based on the three-layer cloud service: Infrastructure as a Service (IaaS), Platform as a Service (PaaS), and Software as a Service (SaaS). The model maps the cloud service model to the security control model and highlights that the lower levels have more demanding security capabilities and management responsibilities than the upper layers in the Cloud Management infrastructure.

Huang, Zhang, Kang, Luo (2010) presented a secure MCC framework, called MobiCloud, which transforms traditional MANETs into a new service-oriented communication architecture, in which each mobile device is treated as a Service Node (SN), and it is mirrored to one or more Extended Semi- Shadow Images (ESSIs) in the cloud in order to address the communication and computation deficiencies of a mobile device.

Huang, Zhou, Xu, Xing & Zhong (2011) presented a mobile cloud data processing framework based on trust management and private data isolation. The objective of the framework is to protect the various types of data collected by the mobile devices and processed/stored in the Mobile Cloud Computing infrastructure. Collected information includes location coordinates, health related information, images, videos and others. The framework is based on the concept of Extended Semi- Shadow Images (ESSIs). Each mobile device is treated as a Service Node (SN), and it is mirrored to one or more Extended Semi- Shadow Images (ESSIs) in the secure mobile cloud called MobiCloud. In MobiCloud, a mobile device can outsource its computing and storage services to its corresponding ESSI and Secure Storage (SS). A trust management model is used to ensure that ESSIs are trustable and the transfer of information between mobile devices and MobiCloud is secure. The trust management model provides identity management, key management, and security policy enforcement functions and it is implemented with identity-based cryptography and attribute-based data access control.

As described in the introduction and section *Cognitive access framework for privacy protection*, the architecture framework proposed in this book chapter is based on a sticky policy approach coupled with a RBAC model.

The concept of sticky policy is introduced by Karjoth, Schunter, & Waidner (2002), and further described in Mont, Pearson, & Bramhall (2003), where sticky policies are defined as "conditions and constraints attached to data that describe how it should be treated." Personal and business data may be protected by unauthorized parties through encryption. Only users and applications satisfying specific policies and constraints (e.g., level of authorization) can decrypt and access the data. The original sticky policy approach specified that privacy preferences should be "embedded" with the data to ensure that they can always be enforced even across different organization boundaries. Pearson, Casassa, & Kounga (2011) describes how the sticky policy approach is applied in the context of the EnCoRe project. In EnCoRe, users disclose their personal data with privacy preferences. The EnCoRe framework encrypts the data and attaches sticky policies on the basis of the privacy preferences defined by the users. A data registry is used to track the use of the data across the system. Additional details on the sticky policy approach are provided in section *Cognitive access framework for privacy protection*.

The concept of RBAC has been extensively researched from the early 90' and in the seminal work of Ferraiolo & Kuhn (1992). The basic concept of RBAC is that access control decisions on data and services are often determined by the roles individual users take on as part of an organization. This includes the specification of duties, responsibilities, and qualifications, which are translated into formal specification in terms of:

- Role Assignment to a subject (e.g., user or application),
- Role Authorization to ensure that users can take on only roles for which they are authorized specific operations and
- Transaction authorization to ensure that a subject can execute a transaction only if the transaction is authorized for the subject's active role.

The RBAC concept has been translated to a standard as described in Sandhu, Ferraiolo, & Kuhn (2000). The standard defines the following four specific levels:

- Flat RBAC,
- Hierarchical RBAC,
- Constrained RBAC, and
- Symmetrical RBAC.

Each level is built upon the previous level and they are cumulative in the sense that each satisfies the requirement of the previous level. Hierarchical RBAC adds a requirement to support role hierarchies, Constrained RBAC adds a requirement to enforce the separation of duties and finally Constrained RBAC adds a requirement for the review of the permission roles.

The basic RBAC concept has been extended to more sophisticated frameworks. Ni, Bertino, Lobo, & Calo (2009) extends the RBAC model in order to provide full support for expressing highly complex privacy-related policies, taking into account features such as purposes and obligations.

In the context of cloud computing, various authors have investigated the application of different types of access control models for data protection in cloud computing. Zhiguo, June, Deng (2012) propose a hierarchical attribute-set-based encryption (HASBE) model which is based on the extension of ciphertext-policy attribute-set-based encryption (ASBE) with a hierarchical structure of users. The proposed model overcomes the limitations of the basic RBAC model, which requires that data owners and the service providers are within the same trusted domain. In addition, this model is more sophisticated than basic attribute-set-based encryption models, because it can provide support in dealing with multiple-levels of attribute authorities.

The ASBE model was introduced by Bobba, Khurana, and Prabhakaran (2009) to extend the classical attribute-set-based encryption (ABE) in enterprise environments where is required considerable flexibility and efficiency in specifying policies and managing user attributes. The ASBE model can be extended to protect outsource data in cloud computing infrastructure. In addition, ASBE can provide the capability of assigning multiple values to the same attribute, which can used to solve the user revocation problem by assigning different expiration times.

In Zhiguo, June, Deng (2012), the performance of the HASBE model is validated against various parameters like scalability, flexibility, fine-grained access control and efficient user revocation. HASBE is a very sophisticated model, which is conceptually close to traditional access control methods such as Role-Based Access Control (RBAC) used in the iCore framework presented in this book chapter. As mentioned in the conclusions and future developments, the iCore framework could be enriched with HASBE in future research.

The final element of the framework proposed in this book chapter is the cognitive capability. Langley, Laird, Rogers (2006) showed that research in true "cognitive" system in various domains is still open but commercial and government applications are increasingly required to exhibit intelligent behavior for various functions and tasks, which include: information collection, automatic composition of information in dynamic environment and decision support. The Soar cognitive architecture is one of the most developed cognitive architectures in literature. As described in Laird, Newell, & Rosenbloom (1987), procedural long-term knowledge in Soar takes the form

of production rules, which are in turn organized in terms of operators associated with problem spaces. Some operators describe simple, primitive actions that modify the agent's internal state or generate primitive external actions, whereas others describe more abstract activities. All tasks in Soar are formulated as attempts to achieve goals. Operators perform the basic deliberative acts of the system, with knowledge used to dynamically determine their selection and application.

A more recent cognitive architecture is ICARUS described in Langley, Cummings, & Shapiro (2004). ICARUS stores two distinct forms of knowledge. Concepts describe classes of environmental situations in terms of other concepts and percepts, whereas skills specify how to achieve goals by decomposing them into ordered subgoals. Both concepts and skills involve relations among objects, and both impose a hierarchical organization on long-term memory, with the former grounded in perceptions and the latter in executable actions.

The iCore cognitive framework proposed in this book chapter shares some similarities with the ICARUS framework in that it is more focused on the recognition and categorization of data (and its protection from unauthorized parties) rather than the decision-making process.

COGNITIVE ACCESS FRAMEWORK FOR PRIVACY PROTECTION

Description of the Cognitive Access Framework

Main Elements and Architecture

The iCore cognitive framework is based on the principle that any real world or digital object that is available, accessible, observable or controllable can have a virtual representation in the "Internet of Things," which is called Virtual Object (VO). The virtual objects (VOs) are primarily targeted to the abstraction of technological heterogeneity and include semantic description of functionality that enables situation-aware selection and use of objects. Composite virtual objects (CVOs) use the services of virtual objects. A CVO is a cognitive mash-up of semantically interoperable VOs that renders services in accordance with the user/stakeholder perspectives and application requirements.

The concept of VOs is not new. Object-oriented (OO) approaches have been used in computer programming for decades and distributed objects are used in Object-oriented middleware applications on the Web. The main idea of the iCore framework is to combine previous concepts with cognitive management mechanisms to create and maintain dynamic, intelligent virtual representation of real world/digital objects that can enhance the "Internet of Things."

As already introduced, the iCore framework comprises four layers of cognitive components, which are depicted in Figure 3.

The first cognitive management layer (VO level cognitive framework) is responsible for managing VOs throughout their lifecycle, ensuring reliability of the link to the real world object/entity (e.g., sensors, actuators, devices, etc.) that they represent, For example, in a logistic related scenario, tracking temperature controlled goods transport, individual goods boxes are represented by VOs the container transported by a truck is a VO as the truck itself. IoT-related applications can interface each of these VOs separately for different service reasons. The second cognitive management layer (CVO level cognitive framework) is responsible for composing VOs in a Composite VO. CVOs will be using the services of VOs to compose more sophisticated objects. In our example, the combination of the truck and the transported goods is represented in the framework as a CVO. The third level is the service layer, where services provided by different entities can be composed and used to address the user

Figure 3. Layers of cognitive management framework

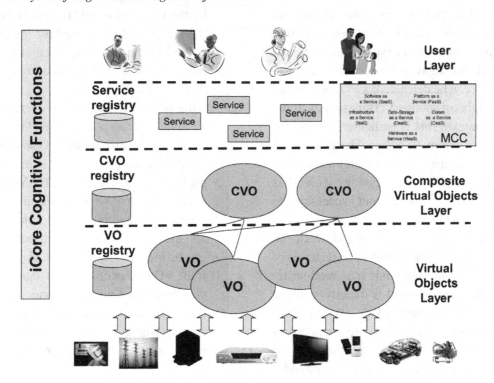

needs. Note that many MCC services provided by Cloud infrastructures are also mapped to this layer. The fourth level (User level cognitive framework) is responsible for interaction with User/stakeholders. The cognitive management frameworks will record the needs and requirements of users and will create/activate relevant VO/CVOs on behalf of the users. The iCore framework also manages the VO/CVO lifecycle: when a real object is recorded, the iCore framework creates the VO/CVO and records an entry in the VO registries with specific features.

Access Policy for Privacy

The iCore framework is based on the concept that access to VO/CVOs must be regulated through a sticky policy management approach similar to the concept described in Mont, Pearson, & Bramhall (2003). The underlying notion behind Sticky Policy is that the policy applicable to a piece of data (e.g., VO) travels with it and is enforceable at every point it is used. Therefore users will be able to declare privacy statements defining when, how and to what extent their personal information (also stored in a VO) can be disclosed. Note that there are different levels and types of access rights: create, read, and modify. Under specific rules, access rights can be delegated: a VO can acquire the access rights of another VO for a specific time, space, or context. This is particularly useful for the creation of automatic agents. The access level rights can also be used in the ontology and lookup mechanism in the CVO/VO registries: if a VO has higher access rights than the entity accessing the dictionary, the VO will not appear.

The VO is created by the user (which can be a person or an application) with specific levels of access for different operations (i.e., read-write-execute). Each access level is directly matched to a specific cryptographic key, which is used to ensure that only authorized parties can access the data and execute specific operations on the VO. The VO encapsulates the data and provides a public interface to access this data for the read-write-execute operations. A VO may provide different public interfaces depending on the levels of access. For example: it may provide the read and execute operation on the data for a specific level of access but not for the write operation, that requires a different level of access.

Figure 4 shows the lifecycle of a VO object from the creation by a user (i.e., User1) to the access from another user (i.e., User2).

The description of each step is as follows:

1. A user (e.g., a person or an application) identified as User1 in Figure 4 accesses the iCore web portal. The user is authenticated with a specific level of access. We consider a case in which the user would like to store sensitive data (e.g., financial data) in the iCore framework data or an executable (e.g., an analysis tool). In this case, the web portal requests the user what type of access should be defined on the data to be inserted in the system or if it can be modifiable or executable. Depending on the information provided by the user, the iCore framework requests the set of keys to be used for the creation of the VO and its encryption to the "Access function." The VO is created together with its set of sticky policies.

2. After the VO is created and encrypted, the VO object creator requests the VO registry to create a new entry for the VO so that it can be seen by any parties who are interested in the VO content or functions. The VO registry creates an entry with the specific level of access indicated by the VO object creator and user and with a set of attributes, which can be used by other parties. For example, if the VO is a set of financial data, the entry will be created with parameters/keywords "finance" and investment" and with the name/surname of User1. At this point the phase of VO creation is completed.

Figure 4. Access levels in the iCore framework

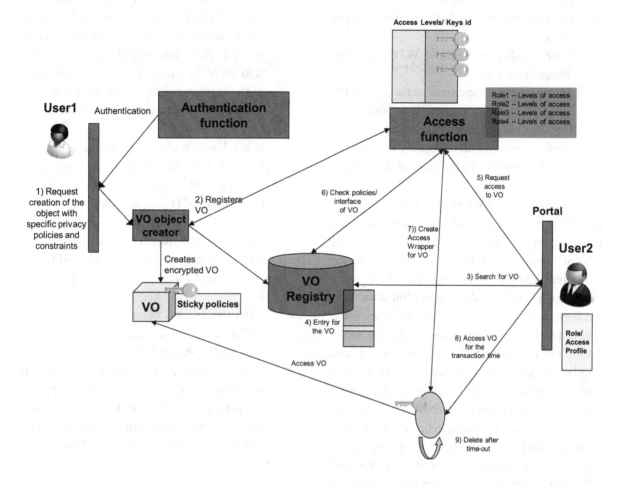

3. Another user, identified as User2 in the picture, would like to use the iCore framework to access specific information (e.g., the financial data) of User1. The user can be a real person (e.g., the personal financial accountant of User1) or an application (e.g., an automated investing application previously set up by User1). In the example, the user accesses the iCore web portal and search for information on financial data related to the name/surname of User1. A transaction is started by the iCore framework to track the requests by User2.

4. The VO registry identifies the VO created by User1 and matches the level of access of User2 with the VO. If User2 has an adequate

level of access, the VO registry confirms to User2 that the matching information exists. Note that the VO registry may not return a match to User2 if the level of access of User2 is not appropriate even if an entry is present in the registry

5. User2 then request the iCore framework to access the contents of the VO (i.e., read operation). The portal asks the Access function to provide access of the VO to the User2.

6. The Access function checks with the VO registry if User2 can perform a read operation on the VO. In this example, this operation is allowed.

7. The Access function creates a Wrapper object, which contains the key needed to

perform a read operation on the VO. User2 does not see the key but only the Wrapper object.

8. User2 reads the content of VO through the Wrapper object.

9. The Wrapper is destroyed at the end of the transaction or by a timeout if no activity by the User2 is detected. This operation is executed to remove all temporary data, which could jeopardize the privacy of the user.

The concept of a Wrapper object to interface the VO from the User is introduced to avoid the provision of the keys directly to the users. The keys are stored in the Wrapper object as private attributes and they are deleted when the transaction is completed. The direct provision of the keys the user can create security vulnerabilities if the role or level of access of such user changes in the future. For example, the level of access of User2 may be downgraded or removed (e.g., an employee leaving a company), but User2 could still access the VO even if it is not authorized. The following steps describe a bit more in detail what has been explained and shown in Figure 4, specifying the concept of Wrapped VO, how it is created and delivered, as well as the related cryptographic keys:

1. A VO is created every time a file (e.g. document, executable, etc.) is uploaded in the iCore framework. The file and related sticky policies compose the VO. Once created the VO is encrypted, with a secret key of the corresponding access level required, and stored. This first step is summarized in Figure 5.

2. When User2 will request access to the VO, the iCore framework will make a copy of the encrypted VO from the database and will decrypt the VO using the related secret key of the corresponding access level, which is defined when it has been created.

3. At this point, a one-time session key (OTSK) is generated and the VO is encrypted with it.

4. After the VO has been encrypted with the OTSK, the OTSK itself is encrypted with the User2's Public Key.

5. The Wrapper receives the VO, encrypted with the OTSK, and the OTSK, encrypted with the User2's Public Key, and "wraps" them together creating the Wrapped VO that will be delivered to User2 (see Figure 6).

Figure 5. Creation and encryption of a VO

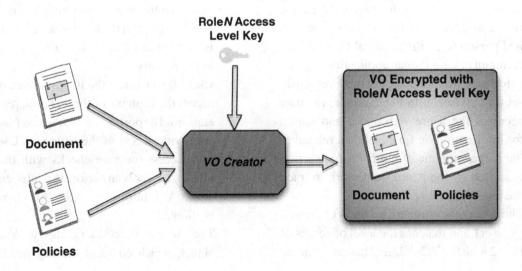

Figure 6. Generation, encryption and delivery of a wrapped VO

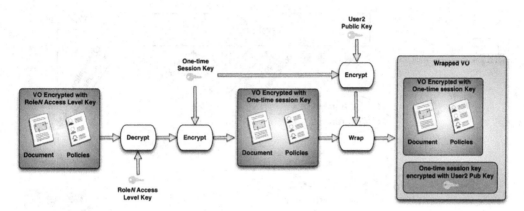

Following the example above, once User2 receives the Wrapped VO on his/her machine, the engine of the iCore framework will extract the original document from the Wrapper in a transparent way for User2. The advantages of delivering the contents with this mechanism are as follows:

- The original encryption key for a given Role - Access Level is never sent to the users,
- The VO is encrypted with an one-time session key that will never be used again so that, even if it is compromised or recovered somehow by User2, or if User2 would lose his right to access documents of that specific level due to downgrading or change of role, the secrecy and privacy of other VOs of the same access level is not compromised.

The architecture described until now does not identify the "cognitive" capabilities of the framework yet. In the following sections, we describe the cognitive capabilities of the iCore framework and how privacy features are embedded in it.

Cognitive Access

The Cognitive capability in the iCore framework is based on the following elements:

1. **Semantic proximity:** (Also called semantic similarity) VOs and CVOs can be more or less relatable depending on specific metrics and the value of their semantic attributes. For example: a type has an attribute of transportation and it can be related to a car, which has a similar attribute. The concept of semantic proximity is also presented in Lee & Pang (2009).
2. **Situation awareness:** The iCore framework can be connected to external sensors or applications, which provide dynamic information on the current context or situation. The sensor can be represented in the iCore Framework with a VO, whose attributes depend on the physical device.

An overview of the architecture for cognitive access and service composition, which complements what is described in the previous section, is provided in Figure 7.

A typical scenario can include both data stored in the iCore systems and external sensors and

Figure 7. Description of the cognitive capability

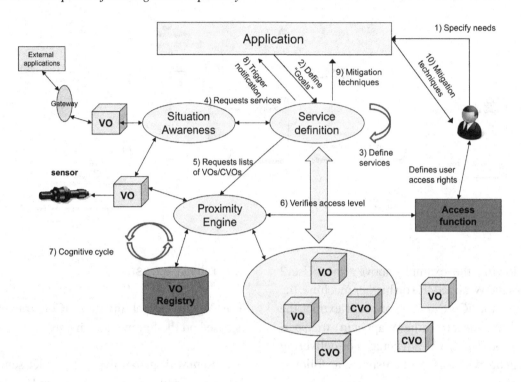

remote applications, which contribute to perform a specific goal.

The following main steps are identified:

1. A user specifies his/her preferences and needs to an application. For example, in an industrial application (e.g., a chemical plant) the user wants to be informed when the values of specific parameters such as temperature and pressure are above thresholds. In turn, the definitions of the values of the thresholds are based on the specific configurations of components of the systems. These configurations and the design of the overall system are stored as VOs and CVOs. An external application may also provide additional data in real-time (e.g., provision of water or energy from a utility). The user also requests the application to identify mitigation actions in case the thresholds are exceeded.

2. The application defines the "goals" to satisfy the requests of the user and translates

them into service specifications of the iCore *Service Definition* function, which can use the services available at the Service Layer including the MCC services. The application also sends information to the user such as the level and type of access and protocols (e.g., UMTS, Bluetooth). This information is needed by the iCore framework, as shown in the following steps.

3. On the basis of the required goals, the *Service Definition* function specifies and forwards requests to other functions in the iCore framework.

4. The *Situation Awareness* function is generally responsible for collecting and recording the status of the real sensors, devices, and external environment. The *Situation Awareness* function can also interface other applications that are external to the iCore framework through gateway mapped to VOs.

5. The *Proximity Engine* function provides a list of VOs and CVOs, which are semanti-

cally similar on the basis of specific criteria. The *Service Definition* function can specify the criteria and the *Proximity Engine* return the list of VOs and CVOs. For example, the *Proximity Engine* can provide the list of components in the system (i.e., VOs and CVOs), which can be impacted by an excessive increase in temperature through cascading effects.

6. Both the *Proximity Engine* and the *Situation Awareness* functions operate on the basis of the level of access of the user, which is passed as a parameter to the *Service Definition* function. For example, a user may not have the adequate level of access to a sensor or an external application. In addition, VOs or CVOs may not be accessible by the user. If the *Service Definition* function is not able to provide the requested services to the Application because of the access level or because of lack of available information, the user is notified that the needs cannot be satisfied.

7. Once the application has completed the requests to the iCore framework functions (either positively or negatively), the iCore framework is responsible for dynamically collecting information related to the status of the physical devices and external applications and raising a notification if a threshold is exceeded. The functions described in the iCore framework can also compensate changes in the components of the system. If a component, represented by a VO, has an internal failure, the Situational Awareness function requests the *Proximity Engine* to identify another VO or CVO, which can provide a similar service through the proximity concept. All these operations are executed by the functions of the iCore framework in an autonomous manner, without the need of user intervention.

8. Once a threshold is exceeded, the *Service Definition* function triggers a notification to the Application.

9. As requested by the user, the application collects information from the iCore framework to suggest mitigation techniques. The request of the information is still executed through the *Service Definition* and *Proximity Engine* functions, which identify the VOs/CVOs This can be useful to provide mitigation solutions to the user. As in the previous cases, access levels and sticky policies are still applied and the Application can only use the VOs/CVOs, that are adequate to the level of access of the user.

10. The application sends the mitigation solutions to the user in the form of data or potential actions. The features of the mobile device are used to mediate the type of information sent to the user. For example, if the user has a mobile device with poor capabilities or connectivity, the application will only send essential data and actions that are possible with limited capabilities.

The cognitive capability and situational awareness functions can be easily integrated in the MCC model. The services provided by the available Cloud systems at different layers (SaaS, PaaS, IaaS, DaaS, CaaS and Haas) can be basically mapped to the iCore framework service layer (see Figure 3), which can compose and use them on the basis of the requested needs and the context (e.g., connectivity). For example, the iCore framework may decide that a specific operation (e.g., execution of a pattern matching algorithm) is too computationally intensive to be executed on a mobile device and it decides to use a MCC service (e.g., SaaS). In another example, the identification of various failures in the overall system may point out to an impending system crash and the iCore framework may request a DaaS service to store the current status data.

SOLUTIONS AND RECOMMENDATIONS

The iCore framework presented in this book chapter can be applied to various contexts and domains, but it is particularly appropriate for MCC, where the Cloud Infrastructure is based on the iCore framework. A user, who accesses the system from a mobile device, can send data to the Cloud, which transforms it to VOs and CVOs. The limited capabilities of the mobile devices are stored in the iCore framework to profile the user and the mobile devices. The iCore framework is able to connect to various mobile devices directly or through gateways to access data or to collect information related to the environment.

Cloud applications are particularly adapt for mobile users, which may have limited or varying wireless data connectivity due to various factors such as limited coverage of high speed wireless data networks, limitations in traffic capacity and propagation errors and so on. The user can rely on mobile cloud applications for the execution of computing intensive tasks or to be informed by changes in domains, where the user has previously expressed interest.

The iCore framework applied to MCC is able to address the issues and challenges described in section *Identification of main issues and challenges*.

Data breaches in the Cloud infrastructure: The iCore framework protects the data through an access control model, where sensitive data is encapsulated in a VO or CVO and it can be accessed only with the right level of access. In this way, the iCore framework prevents data breaches. Even if a malicious attacker is able to break in a cloud datacenter, he or she would not be able to interpret the data because it is encrypted.

Data breaches in the Mobile Device: All sensitive data is stored in the Mobile Cloud based on the iCore framework. The user itself can access the Mobile Cloud.

Confidentiality threats on the communication channel: A malicious attacker can intercept infor-

mation passing on the communication channel. In the proposed approach, all the data distributed from the Mobile Cloud to mobile devices or other domains/applications is encrypted and embedded with sticky policies. Even if the communication channel is compromised, a malicious user cannot access the data.

Incomplete data deletion: The iCore framework functions are responsible to delete all replicas of VOs or CVOs, which are present in the iCore framework. Because the data is represented as VOs and CVOs tracked by the registries, the complete deletion of all the instances of the VOs and CVOs is easier to perform than in conventional mobile cloud infrastructures. Another feature of the iCore framework is to specify the lifetime of the VO and CVO, which can be removed by the iCore framework functions in the time specified by the user or related to the duration of the session where the user was involved.

Isolation Failure: This issue is not present in the iCore framework, because all the various tenants will use the iCore framework functions to manage the data or services represented by VO and CVOs.

Integration of security and privacy functions: As described in this book chapter, the security and privacy functions are embedded in the design of the iCore framework.

Overall, the design of the iCore framework provides the capabilities to address most of the issues and challenges currently present in MCC. The encapsulation of all data distributed and stored in the Mobile Cloud through VOs and CVOs provides improved data management and data protection of the user's data.

DEMONSTRATION AND PROTOTYPES

At the time of writing of this book chapter, the iCore project (where the iCore framework is defined) was still in the early stages and limited effort was dedicated to prototyping. Nevertheless, the implementation of prototypes and large scale demonstration systems is a very important part of the iCore project and this section describes more in detail this aspect.

An initial prototype of the iCore framework was presented at the Future Mobile Summit 2012 conference in Berlin (FUNEMS, 2012). The prototype showed a working implementation of how IoT and cognitive technologies can be used to empower ICT applications in a Smart Home environment for an elderly assistance use case. Sara is an elderly lady living at home. She has opted for an assisted living service. All necessary equipment (e.g., sensors, actuators, devices, everyday objects) is installed in Sara's home. A simulated medical center is connected to Sara's home and the equipment. The prototype showed what can be achieved virtualising sensing and actuating objects (iCore concept of Virtual Object), how VOs can be enriched with service

logic (iCore concept of Composite Virtual Object) and used in a personalised way fitting the user context. Moreover, the demo showed how the use of cognitive technologies supports the user in the selection of the most appropriate objects to fit the application requirements, reusing as necessary objects outside the purpose for which they were originally deployed. The prototype was able to respond to specific events and provide the necessary services to the simulated medical center. The derived solution (CVO composition) is recorded so that the next time a similar request is issued by the medical center knowledge on past CVO instantiations enables the direct deployment of the known CVO.

The overall diagram and pictures of the demo are presented in Figure 8. The physical sensors and actuators in the Elderly home are represented as VOs in the Medical Center. For a specific application like monitoring the status of the elderly patient and the conditions of the room (e.g., temperature,

Figure 8. Prototype of the iCore framework

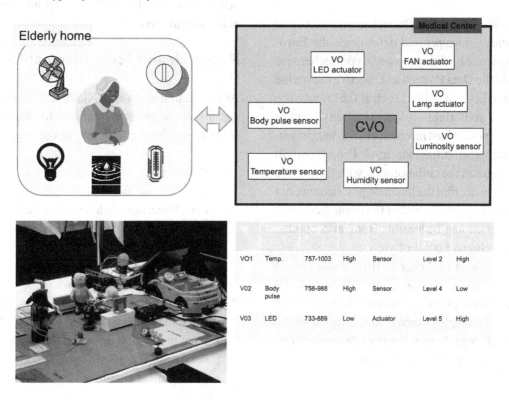

ID	Timestamp	LocalID	QoR	Type	Actual Scope	Proximity
VO1	Temp.	757-1003	High	Sensor	Level 2	High
V02	Body pulse	756-988	High	Sensor	Level 4	Low
V03	LED	733-889	Low	Actuator	Level 5	High

humidity), a CVO is created on the basis of the conceptual proximity of the VOs and their level of access (e.g., example the elderly patient may have not given consent to the Medical Center to use a specific sensor). If a sensor triggers a specific event (e.g., the temperature of the room is too high), the monitoring application checks the health of the elderly person or changes the conditions of the room through the actuators. The VOs needed for this task are retrieved on the basis of the available VOs, their functions and level of access.

This simple prototype is going to be expanded significantly to implement a scenario in the final part of the iCore project. The scenario will be based on an emergency crisis situation where applications based on the iCore framework can be used to support first time responders and citizens to respond more efficiently to the crisis.

FUTURE TRENDS

Regulatory Trends

As described in section *Privacy in Mobile Cloud Computing: concepts and definitions*, the European Commission has proposed a comprehensive reform of the Data Protection Directive to provide the citizen key capabilities such as the "right to be forgotten" and "right of data portability" and to introduce more robust mechanisms for data protection at European and national level. The reform will also strengthen the collaboration with the private sector to ensure that the business practices are not negatively impacted and that the implementation of regulations can be feasible from an economic and technological point of view.

As indicated in Weber (2010), this approach adopted by the European Commission could be the most appropriate: regulatory bodies define clear key principles centred to the rights of the individual, which can be complemented and implemented by the private sector in a more detailed way.

The challenge is that Internet of Things is really global regarding both the level of content and applications. As a consequence, an international framework would be preferable in this sense. The European Commission is working closely with other regulatory and standardization bodies to provide a common approach on privacy at the global level, but we must acknowledge that there are still significant differences between USA and Europe on privacy and data protection of the users. As described in King & Raja (2012), there is a comprehensive framework for data protection in the EU, which is currently under revision, while USA lacks a comprehensive regulatory framework for sensitive personal data, which gives the possibility to harm the privacy of consumers of large private business, particularly when they are operating on the Web, they use or manage cloud infrastructures.

While technical solutions such as the one proposed in this book chapter can mitigate privacy risks, the more appropriate approach would be the coordination of the regulatory and political process on privacy between USA and EU and other countries in the world to reach an agreement at the global level.

Research and Technological Trends

At the technical level, ENISA (2009) indicated the following potential actions to improve the security of Cloud computing in the near future:

1. Enhance system engineering of security services. Potential actions include standardization of interfaces to feed data to the cloud, and ensure scalability of security management solutions within cloud platforms. Adoption of resource isolation mechanisms for data, processing elements, services.
2. Improve the level of trust in the cloud by implementing end-to-end security solutions from the mobile device to the Cloud and by designing High Assurance functions in the Cloud Infrastructure.

3. Improve the level of Data Protection in the Cloud Infrastructure. Possible actions include design of better forensics, traceability tools, and improved infrastructure management applications.

Regarding item 1, the iCore framework presented in this book chapter addresses some of the identified actions as the VO/CVO concept allows the encapsulation of data, and it can be extended to processing elements (e.g., a computer can become a VO) and services. Besides, the iCore framework provides a uniform interface to users and applications to specify needs and to forward requests on data and services.

Regarding item 2, this is a significant challenge from the implementation point of view, because the Internet of Things is (and will be) a heterogeneous set of applications, devices and services. While the iCore framework can be used to implement an "Intranet" domain, it is more difficult to provide end-to-end security in IoT because it requires the secure interoperability of domains and applications, which may not be implemented on the iCore concepts. Gateways can be used to mediate the distribution of data among domains. Because data are encapsulated in VOs/ CVOs with sticky policies, the challenge is not really to validate the data protection requirements but to provide access to users, who are connected through remote applications or services. Future developments of this book chapter will investigate more in detail the provision of information assurance among different domains.

Finally, regarding item 3, the provision of forensics and traceability tools is not addressed in this specific book chapter. The iCore framework can be equipped with management functions to perform auditing functions on the internal data or services and with forensics tools to be used in case of a security breach.

Another important trend, already mentioned in the introduction, is the increasing computing and storage capabilities of mobile devices coupled with the pervasive broadband connectivity (at least in urban environments). In this context, it will be important not only for researchers to focus on new ideas for ensuring and assessing the privacy and security level of mobile applications but also for developers to apply current methodologies and techniques. The risk is that, by thinking that everything is in the Cloud, developers may pay less and less attention when writing their code. As underlined in the MobiLeak Project by Stirparo & Kounelis (2012), it is important to understand where data reside in order to be able to assess the privacy and security level properly. Starting from the three states in which data can exist: data at rest, data in use and data in transit, by moving towards the Cloud paradigm the data at rest state will basically not exist anymore on the mobile device, since all the data will reside in the Cloud. However, they will travel over the network (data in transit) and even if they are sent encrypted, they will have to be decrypted at a certain point on the device in order to be processed by the mobile applications (data in use). This means that, if not properly managed, data will be present unencrypted in the memory of the mobile device even after the application will be closed for a certain (although limited) amount of time.

Mobile cloud computing incorporates many elements, including consumer, enterprise, femtocells, transcoding, end-to-end security, home gateways, and mobile broadband-enabled services. Use of cloud services at home, in the workplace and in large enterprises has significantly increased. Now we are seeing a similar trend with mobile devices and cloud technology. It is only a matter of time until Cloud Computing technology becomes the central force to mobile applications. Work patterns and habits are also changing because of the mobile cloud. Experts surveyed by the Pew Internet Project think that by 2020, most people who use the Internet will work primarily through cyberspace-based applications on remote servers accessed through networked devices.

With all that being said, we believe that the future direction of research and development of MCC will go through the following four main pillars that represents both future risks and needs liked to the growth of MCC:

1. **Connection Availability:** The demand of compute intensive capabilities such as speech recognition, natural language processing, computer vision and graphics, machine learning, augmented reality, basic mobile cloud services such as presence services, memcache services, etc, by mobile applications is going to increase exponentially. All these services will require cloud infrastructure optimization for mobile applications but, as we also anticipated in the Introduction, the main challenge will be for the operators to be able to provide continuous, high-quality connection service to mobile devices.

2. **Security as a Service (SECaaS):** Increased access to company computing assets also brings an increased security risk. Companies are now starting to consider a variety of data user policies. For example, geolocation data available from a mobile platform might allow access to be declined if a mobile user is out of the country. However, with the paradigm of "everything as a service," the risk for the users is that also security will become a service offered by cloud providers instead of a built-in feature, as it should be.

3. **Lack of Standards:** Absence of standards is another barrier for mobile cloud computing and leads to problems like limited scalability, unreliable availability of service and service provider lock-in.

4. **Scalability and Fine-Grained Access Control:** As the quantity of data and mobile devices will increase, it is important to define access control model, which are both scalable and flexible to represent the reality with a reasonable level of detail to specify policies and managing VO/CVO attributes. The risk of using access control models, which are difficult to modify or have coarse granularity can obstacle the commercial deployment of frameworks like the one described in this book chapter or it can create vulnerability threats. Attribute-based encryption model could be used to address the identified challenges. In the iCore framework, attribute-based encryption model is easy to adapt because of the representations of digital and real-world information with VO and CVO with attributes already defined.

CONCLUSION

This book chapter has provided an overview of the iCore framework, which has the objective to facilitate and support Internet connected objects in a secure way. In particular, the iCore framework use the concepts of sticky policy associated to VOs and CVOs to protect the data and privacy of users. Further developments will focus on scalability, inter-domain interoperability and distributed role-based access control model of the iCore framework. In particular, the authors will explore the application of attribute-based encryption models to support flexibility and scalability of the iCore framework from a security and privacy point of view.

ACKNOWLEDGMENT

This work was funded by the EC through the FP7 project iCore (287708). The authors would like to thank everyone involved.

REFERENCES

Bahl, P., Han, R. Y., Li, E., & Satyanarayanan, M. (2012). Advancing the state of mobile cloud computing. In *Proceedings of the Third ACM Workshop on Mobile Cloud Computing and Services* (pp. 21—28). ACM.

Bobba, R., Khurana, H., & Prabhakaran, M. (2009). Attribute-sets: A practically motivated enhancement to attribute-based encryption. In *Proceedings of ESORICS*. Saint Malo, France: ESORICS.

Buyya, R., Yeo, C., & Venugopal, S. (2008). Market-oriented cloud computing: Vision, hype, and reality for delivering it services as computing utilities. In *Proceedings of the 10th IEEE International Conference on High Performance Computing and Communications, HPCC'08* (pp. 5–13). IEEE.

Calo, S., & Lobo, J. (2006). A basis for comparing characteristics of policy systems. In *Proceedings of Policies for Distributed Systems and Networks* (pp. 188–194). IEEE. doi:10.1109/POLICY.2006.1.

Chuang, I. H., Li, S. H., Huang, K. C., & Kuo, Y. H. (2011). An effective privacy protection scheme for cloud computing. In *Proceedings of the 13th International Conference on Advanced Communication Technology (ICACT)* (pp. 260-265). ICACT.

Cloud Security Alliance. (2009). *Security guidance for critical areas of focus in cloud computing V2.1*. Retrieved October 28, 2012, from http://www.cloudsecurityalliance.org/guidance/csaguide.v2.1.pdf

Cloud Security Alliance. (2010). *Top threats to cloud computing*. Retrieved October 28, 2012, from https://cloudsecurityalliance.org/topthreats/csathreats.v1.0.pdf

Commission of the European Communities. (1995). The protection of individuals with regard to the processing of personal data and on the free movement of such data. *Official Journal of the European Communities, 281*, 31–50.

Commission of the European Communities. (1999). Directive 1999/5/EC on radio equipment and telecommunications terminal (R&TTE). *Official Journal of the European Communities, 91*(10), 1–8.

Commission of the European Communities. (2012). *European data protection regulation*. Retrieved October 28, 2012 from http://ec.europa.eu/justice/newsroom/data-protection/news/120125_en.htm

Cong, W., Chow, S. S. M., Qian, W., Kui, R., & Wenjing, L. (2013). Privacy-preserving public auditing for secure cloud storage. *IEEE Transactions on Computers, 62*(2), 362–375. doi:10.1109/TC.2011.245.

Cong, W., Qian, W., Kui, R., Ning, C., & Wenjing, L. (2012). Toward secure and dependable storage services in cloud computing. *IEEE Transactions on Services Computing, 5*(2), 220–232. doi:10.1109/TSC.2011.24.

Dinh, H. T., Lee, C., Niyato, D., & Wang, P. (2011). A survey of mobile cloud computing: Architecture, applications, and approaches. In *Wireless Communications and Mobile Computing, 2011*. New York: Wiley Online Library. doi:10.1002/wcm.1203.

ENISA. (2009). *ENISA cloud computing risk assessment*. Retrieved October 28, 2012, from http://www.enisa.europa.eu/act/rm/les/deliverables/cloud-computingrisk-assessment

Ferraiolo, D. F., & Kuhn, D. R. (1992). Role-based access control. In *Proceedings of the 15th National Computer Security Conference* (pp. 554–563). IEEE.

FUNEMS. (2012). *iCore demo*. Retrieved from http://www.iot-icore.eu/latest-news/88-icore-project-demonstration-receives-the-runner-up-demonstration-award-at-funems-2012-berlin-germany

Ghosh, M. (2010). Mobile ID fraud: The downside of mobile growth. *Computer Fraud & Security*, (12): 8–13. doi:10.1016/S1361-3723(10)70155-X.

Guojun, W., Qin, L., & Jie, W. (2010). Hierarchical attribute-based encryption for fine-grained access control in cloud storage services. In *Proceedings of the 17th ACM Conference on Computer and Communications Security (CCS '10)* (pp. 735-737). ACM.

Han, Q., & Gani, A. (2012). Research on mobile cloud computing: Review, trend and perspectives. In *Proceedings of the Second International Conference on Digital Information and Communication Technology and its Applications (DICTAP)* (pp. 195-202). DICTAP.

Hitchens, M., & Varadharajan, V. (2000). Design and specification of role based access control policies. *Proceedings of IEEE Software*, *147*(4), 117–129. doi:10.1049/ip-sen:20000792.

Huang, D., Zhang, X., Kang, M., & Luo, J. (2010). MobiCloud: Building secure cloud framework for mobile computing and communication. In *Proceedings of the Fifth IEEE International Symposium on Service Oriented System Engineering (SOSE)* (pp. 27-34). IEEE.

Huang, D., Zhou, Z., Xu, L., Xing, T., & Zhong, Y. (2011). Secure data processing framework for mobile cloud computing. In *Proceedings of the 2011 IEEE Conference on Computer Communications* (pp. 614-618). IEEE.

Karjoth, G., Schunter, M., & Waidner, M. (2002). Platform for enterprise privacy practices: Privacy-enabled management of customer data. In *Proceedings of the 2nd Workshop Privacy Enhancing Technologies (PET 02)* (LNCS), (vol. 2482, pp. 69-84). Berlin: Springer.

King, N. J., & Raja, V. T. (2012). Protecting the privacy and security of sensitive customer data in the cloud. *Computer Law & Security Report*, *28*(3), 308–319. doi:10.1016/j.clsr.2012.03.003.

Klein, A., Mannweiler, C., Schneider, J., & Schotten, H. D. (2010). Access schemes for mobile cloud computing. In *Proceedings of the Eleventh International Conference on Mobile Data Management (MDM)* (pp. 387-392). MDM.

Kshetri, N., & Murugesan, S. (n.d.). Cloud computing and EU data privacy regulations. *Computer*, *46*(3), 86-89.

Laird, J. E., Newell, A., & Rosenbloom, P. S. (1987). SOAR: An architecture for general intelligence. *Artificial Intelligence*, *33*(1), 1–64. doi:10.1016/0004-3702(87)90050-6.

Langley, P., Cummings, K., & Shapiro, D. (2004). Hierarchical skills and cognitive architectures. In *Proceedings of the Twenty-Sixth Annual Conference of the Cognitive Science Society* (pp. 779–784). CSS.

Langley, P., Laird, J. E., & Rogers, S. (2006). Cognitive architectures: Research issues and challenges. *Cognitive Systems Research*, *10*(2), 141–160. doi:10.1016/j.cogsys.2006.07.004.

Lee, W. H., & Pang, C. T. (2009). An extension of semantic proximity for fuzzy functional dependencies. In *Proceedings of the Annual Meeting of the North American Fuzzy Information Processing Society* (pp.1-6). IEEE.

Malawski, M., Kuźniar, M., Wójcik, P., & Bubak, M. (2013). How to use Google app. engine for free computing. *IEEE Internet Computing*, *17*(1), 50–59. doi:10.1109/MIC.2011.143.

Mell, P., & Grance, T. (2011). The NIST definition of cloud computing. NIST Special Publication, 800(145).

Mont, M. C., Pearson, S., & Bramhall, P. (2003). Towards accountable management of identity and privacy: Sticky policies and enforceable tracing services. In *Proceedings of the 14th International Workshop on Database and Expert Systems Applications* (pp. 377- 382). IEEE.

Morshed, M. S. J., Islam, M. M., Huq, M. K., Hossain, M. S., & Basher, M. A. (2011). Integration of wireless hand-held devices with the cloud architecture: Security and privacy issues. In *Proceedings of 2011 International Conference on P2P, Parallel, Grid, Cloud and Internet Computing (3PGCIC)* (pp. 83-88). 3PGCIC.

Ni, Q., Bertino, E., Lobo, J., & Calo, S. B. (2009). Privacy-aware role-based access control. *IEEE Security & Privacy*, *7*(4), 35–43. doi:10.1109/MSP.2009.102.

Pearson, S., Casassa, M. M., & Kounga, G. (2011). Enhancing accountability in the cloud via sticky policies. *Secure and Trust Computing. Data Management and Applications*, *187*, 146–155.

Pearson, S., & Mont, M. C. (2011). Sticky policies: An approach for managing privacy across multiple parties. *Computer*, *44*(9), 60–68. doi:10.1109/MC.2011.225.

Sandhu, R., Ferraiolo, D., & Kuhn, R. (2000). The NIST model for role-based access control: Towards a unified standard. In *Proceedings of the 5th ACM Workshop on Role-Based Access Control* (pp. 47–63). ACM.

Sohr, K., Drouineaud, M., Ahn, G.-J., & Gogolla, M. (2008). Analyzing and managing role-based access control policies. *IEEE Transactions on Knowledge and Data Engineering*, *20*(7), 924–939. doi:10.1109/TKDE.2008.28.

Song, W., & Su, X. (2011). Review of mobile cloud computing. In *Proceedings of the 2011 IEEE 3rd International Conference on Communication Software and Networks (ICCSN)* (pp. 27-29). IEEE.

Stanik, A., Hovestadt, M., & Kao, O. (2012). Hardware as a service (HaaS), the completion of the cloud stack. In *Proceedings of the 8th International Conference on Computing Technology and Information Management (ICCM)* (pp. 830-835). ICCM.

Stirparo, P., & Kounelis, I. (2012). The MobiLeak project: Forensics methodology for mobile application privacy assessment. In *Proceedings of the International Conference for Internet Technology and Secured Transactions (ICITST 2012)*. ICITST.

Weber, R. H. (2010). Internet of things – New security and privacy challenges. *Computer Law & Security Report*, *26*(1), 23–30. doi:10.1016/j.clsr.2009.11.008.

Yang, T., Lee, P. P. C., Lui, J. C. S., & Perlman, R. (2012). Secure overlay cloud storage with access control and assured deletion. *IEEE Transactions on Dependable and Secure Computing*, *9*(6), 903–916. doi:10.1109/TDSC.2012.49.

Youseff, L., Butrico, M., & Da Silva, D. (2008). Toward a unified ontology of cloud computing. In *Proceedings of Grid Computing Environments Workshop, 2008* (pp. 1–10). GCE.

Zhiguo, W., June, L., & Deng, R. H. (2012). HASBE: A hierarchical attribute-based solution for flexible and scalable access control in cloud computing. *IEEE Transactions on Information Forensics and Security*, *7*(2), 743–754. doi:10.1109/TIFS.2011.2172209.

Chapter 7
Agent–Based Resource Management for Mobile Cloud

Zhili Sun
University of Surrey, UK

Yanbo Zhou
University of Surrey, UK

Yichao Yang
University of Surrey, UK

Haitham Cruickshank
University of Surrey, UK

ABSTRACT

Mobile cloud computing is a new computing paradigm to integrate cloud computing technology into the mobile environment. It takes full advantages of cloud computing with great potential to transform a large part of the IT industry. The objectives of mobile cloud computing are to meet user demand, efficiently utilize a pool of resources, including mobile network, storage, and computation resources, and optimize energy on mobile devices. Here, the authors review the current mobile cloud computing technologies, highlight the main issues and challenges for the future development, and focus on resource management. Then, combining the current agent architectures and resource optimization strategies, they present an agent-based resource management to deal with multiple data and computation intensive applications of user demand. The chapter offers a promising solution of selecting the best service provider and efficiently utilizing mobile network resources given the user's request constraint.

INTRODUCTION

Mobile cloud computing (MCC) provides on-demand service to mobile users through different mobile cloud service providers (MCSP) (Wei-guang & Xiaolong, 2011). As increasing of user demand and mobile applications, MCC allows to integrate mobile network technology into the cloud computing. It takes advantages of typical cloud computing characteristics such as non-front investment, lower operating cost, highly scalable and easy access (Vaquero, Rodero-Merino, Caceres, & Lindner, January 2009). It also brings new types of services to mobile users and utilizes cloud computing to provide ubiquitous mobile service access. Cloud computing is a new computing paradigm that aims to provide reliable service and elastic scalable on demand of applications (Buyya, Yeo, & Venugopal, 2008). It has emerged

DOI: 10.4018/978-1-4666-4781-7.ch007

to utilize the Internet resources (e.g., computation, storage) conveniently and ubiquitously.

As cloud computing, MCC delivers new computing service to mobile users that including infrastructure-as-a-service (IaaS), platform-as-a-Service (PaaS), and software-as-a-Service (SaaS), in which users' applications are deployed and perform in the cloud(Vaquero, et al., January 2009). From the perspective of the cloud service providers, cloud computing is often viewed as a pool of resources in stationary machines for service delivery. These service providers manage a global network of datacenters, with each networked to combine the computing power of tens of thousands of commodity servers.

Cloud computing promises the availability of virtualized infinite resources. These elastic resources for mobile applications in a mobile environment, called mobile cloud computing (Gupta & Gupta, 2012). On the other hand, mobile computing technology played as an important role in the Internet. Today, mobile devices (e.g., tablet PC, Pad, smartphone, etc.), have become an essential part of human life. These devices need to be used "anywhere at anytime." In the mean times, we have also seen the rapid growth of mobile applications due to the mobile device popularity and ubiquity of mobile access. Many of mobile applications such as email, real-time multimedia, data and computation intensive applications can be performed on these mobile devices.

The mobile devices can sense the environment and e-health parameters to enhance the quality of life, remote monitor and gather relevant information. However, these devices still cannot execute multiple data and computing-intensive applications with large-scale data management and data mining. These applications often hit a performance wall because the mobile devices have limited storage, processing capability, scarce mobile network and energy resources comparing to a desktop PC. Unlimited resources offered by cloud computing

can help break through this wall and turn the problem into a vast opportunity for the growth of mobile computing. As increasing the number of mobile applications, it demands great resources and needs improving interactivity for better service provisioning. This underlines the importance of cloud computing for mobile services.

Mobile technology enters cloud computing domain by trying to access the shared pool of resources in data centres. Mobile technologies are drawing the attention to the clouds due to the demand of the applications requirement in terms of more computation capability, larger storage space and more processing power. By 2015, more than 240 million business customers will be leveraging cloud computing services through mobile devices according to the ABI Research (Narain), and the Juniper Research reports the market for cloud-based mobile applications is also expected to grow 88% annually by 2014 (Juniper Research). There are already some well-known cloud-based mobile applications; for example, Google's Gmail for iPhone (Google App Engine) and Cisco's WebEx on iPad. Cloud computing can broaden the range of applications available to mobile users beyond conventional office by supporting applications, such as 3D virtual environments, large storage capacity, or 3D medical imaging (Meir & Rubinsky, 2009). Mobile cloud provides new types of services and facilities for mobile users to gain full advantages of cloud computing.

A general view of mobile cloud computing scenario is shown in Figure 1. These applications are then accessed over the mobile network based on a thin native client or web browser on the mobile devices. In the other word, the mobile network and end-system resources can be allocated dynamically. Data and computation intensive mobileapplications benefiting from a mobile Cloud are related to various domains such as social networks, location based services, context-aware systems etc.

Figure 1. A general scenario of mobile cloud computing

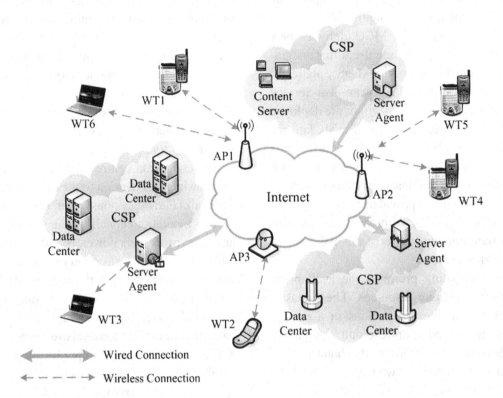

Challenges and Motivations

MCC is still in its infancy, but it has presented new opportunities to mobile users and developers to benefit from economics of scales, commoditization of assets and conformance to programming standards. Its attributes such as scalability, elasticity, flexibility, reliability, efficiency, seamless coverage and a utility type of delivery make this new paradigm to deliver service for satisfying many users' request over mobile network. MCC aims to enable mobile users to utilize resources in an on-demand fashion. Mobile users will expect to perform data and computing intensive application through cloud service provider. However, mobile cloud computing is a combination of two different fields: cloud computing and mobile computing. Therefore, there are many issues need to be addressed including the following paragraphs.

Resource heterogeneity in mobile cloud environment: Currently, many different mobile applications have been applied in mobile cloud environment. MCC technology will allow different mobile network and end-system resources to provide "always-on" connectivity. When users access many different mobile clouds, they would like to select the mobile cloud service providers (MCSP) with the best services, which depending on different radio accesses technologies such as WLAN, 3G/4G and available end-system resources ability. For instance, if the MCSP only provides the best of mobile network service, but cannot support efficient data service from end-system resources, or the other way round, the users' request cannot be served satisfactorily. As the result, the issue of selecting the best combined mobile network and end-system resources to provide mobile user always best connected from service provider is becoming a challenge work. Therefore, they will need to address the heterogeneity issue.

Energy optimization in mobile device: Mobile devices have limited power supply. It is important to achieve energy optimization in mobile devices. Power consumption of mobile applications relates to energy consumption of data transfer and execution. However, limited resources such as storage space, computation capability are intrinsic characteristics of the mobile device. MCC allows mobile users to access to leverage unlimited computing power and storage space, thus the space of storage and computation capability can be easily extended to save energy in mobile devices. Therefore, how to optimize energy, furthermore, extending battery lifetime of mobile device for performing applications in MCC is an important issue.

Meta-job scheduling in service provider: In mobile cloud environment, the MCSP need to efficiently utilize different virtual machines in order to minimize the meta-job execution time over the Internet. This meta-job execution time can be related to the idle power of the mobile device. Furthermore, the idle power of the mobile device can be saved.

Delivering multimedia content to mobile users: In MCC, mobile users need to access to content servers in the cloud. However, mobile users have to face some problems due to the limitation of mobile network capacity, disruptions, and users' mobility. The bandwidth is an important issue when delivering multimedia contents since the radio resources for mobile network is much scarce as compared with the traditional wired network.

These issues bring great challenges in the area of mobile cloud computing. This research offers a promising solution by a combination of the mobile communication and cloud computing using agent-based resource management architecture. This architecture will enable users to discover suitable service according to demand of application to select the required resources from different cloud service providers. From the user's perspective,

the MCC is to satisfy more users' request, utilize limited resources on mobile device and provide reliable service in mobile environment. From the MCSP's perspective, the MCC aims to optimize the scheduling schemes to provide services and improve resource utilization.

Objectives and Techniques

The objectives to study agent-based resource management related to wireless cloud computing are explained in the following paragraphs.

Agent-based resource management architecture: We present agent-based resource management architecture. This architecture helps users to make decision to select the best service from MCSPs. It aims to support on demand service for users. It is also responsible for satisfying more users' request, selecting MCSP, meta-job scheduling and efficiently utilizing wireless cloud resources such as wireless network and content servers.

An analytic hierarchy process (AHP) and grey relational analysis (GRA) methods for selecting MCSP in wireless clouds: We introduce AHP and GRA method to solve the problem of selecting MCSP in wireless cloud environment. These methods provide wireless users with best connection to MCSP. The AHP decides the relative weights of evaluative criteria set according to the user preference and various wireless cloud applications. The GRA method ranks the service providers with considered status of wireless network and end-system resource information.

An adaptive offloading strategy for saving energy for wireless computation-intensive applications: We present adaptive offloading strategy (AOS) to extend the utility of storage space and computation capability as well as the battery power can be sufficiently saved on wireless device. The core of the AOS is the fuzzy control model that presented for making jobs offloading decision. This model is applied to perform a number of fine-gained multiple computation applications on wireless device. The AOS also addresses the scheduling problem of meta-jobs execution on remote virtual machines (VM) belonging to MCSP.

A convex optimization approach for wireless resource selection: We present convex optimization algorithm to solve the problem of low wireless network for delivering multimedia content in MCC environment. The wireless network resources are always scarce among a range of wireless real-time applications. In this regard, on one hand correct access point (AP) should be nominated for the user; on the other hand the user should be overloaded by excessive data traffic. In that case, Lagrange duality model is used to model the wireless network optimization problem to utilize efficiently wireless network resources in order to support the users' request.

BACKGROUND

A cloud service is able to supply scalability solutions according to the demand, to provide functionality without dealing with the underlying technologies, and to leverage the distributed physical infrastructure for using the cloud as a virtual pool of resources. Therefore, MCC has the potential to provide great performance benefits to mobile users as well as mobile cloud service provider. The current MCC aims to provide reliable service for mobile users in on-demand fashion. That is, from the user's perspective, applications may be executed on a cloud without the need to know which servers is being used, or where they are physically located.

Aepona (White Paper, November 2010) describes MCC as a new paradigm for mobile applications whereby the data processing and storage are moved from the mobile device to powerful and centralized computing platforms located in clouds. These centralized applications are then accessed over the mobile connection based on a thin native client or web browser on the mobile devices. MCC can also be considered as a combination of mobile terminal and cloud computing, which is the most popular tool for mobile users to access applications and services on the Internet. Briefly, MCC provides mobile users with the data processing and storage services in clouds.

Mobile Cloud Resource Management System

The idea of the mobile cloud resource management come from existing grid resource management which provides an enabling technology for a grid to coordinate the sharing, scheduling, and collaborative utilization of distributed and geographically dispersed computing resources (Nabrzyski, Jennifer, & Weglarz, 2003). Grid computing is often requires the concurrent allocation a wide range of heterogeneous, loosely coupled multiple resources in a consistent manner. These computing resources in the grid are usually a multiprocessor or cluster of machines, which are distributed geographically, connected with physical network, and administrated within the same organization. The main function of this resource management system is to identify user's requirement, match and allocate resource, schedule and monitor resource, so as to make resource usage as efficiently as possible (Nabrzyski, et al., 2003). Grid resource management system (RMS) focuses on controlling grid resource to provide capacity and available service to other users. The greatest feature is the coordinated use of distributed and heterogeneous resource.

Resource management is also an important aspect of MCC. Mobile clouds are systems that involve coordinated mobile resource sharing in heterogeneous dynamic environments to meet the different users' demands. Nonetheless several of the grids oriented resource management system could be extended for mobile clouds. Due to the existing features in mobile cloud such as heterogeneous, unstable and dynamic, making resource management on mobile environment is more complex. Therefore, it is very necessary to establish a resource management system model adapts to mobile cloud, and research its features and functions for to achieve specific mobile cloud resource management system.

In this MCC paradigm, the main objective of resource management system is maximizing the mobile applications performance and providing on-demand service with the dynamic resource provisioning. These resources can be dynamically changed over the time, including mobile network, storage, memory and CPU, etc. The resource selection and allocation process has to be dynamic in order to ensure that the system performance is optimised at all times. Optimal resource allocation is often a complex problem. The following are some of the key points.

Firstly, in MCC, there are many service providers that provide its own service to global users via mobile network connection. The capability of resource management need to be enhanced with the emergence of the service oriented architecture and virtualized technology.

Secondly, the ability of mobile cloud to federate many heterogeneous distributed resources enables collaborations and supports applications. Mobile clouds are being deployed in enterprise environment to achieve cost-effective, on-demand service of resource provisioning to applications. Therefore, effective management of resources is crucial for fully realizing the promise of the computing paradigms.

Thirdly, the mobile cloud resource manager has the following runtime functions:

- The request for new deployments for a specific type of service and the release of a resource after its use ended;
- It is responsible for provisioning, releasing, and checking the status of virtualized resources;
- Control and manage the mobile network resource according to user's request; and

- The limited resources of mobile terminal will be efficiently utilized with improved the application performance.

Finally, resource management in MCC is often interactive and as a result. User demand can vary highly over time. This means that the allocation of resources needs to be recomputed frequently.

Mobile cloud computing is to make scalable end-system resources available to users. It offers a deal of utilizing mobile resources and providing on-demand service for users. In traditional computing system, an end user submits its request to the resource management for job executing on resources. These users' requirements such as job execution deadline, the maximum cost of execution are constraint for processing jobs. The main function of the resource management is to take the job specification and estimate the resource requirements such as the number of processors, data file size required, the execution, and memory required. After estimating the resource requirements, RMS is responsible for discovering available resource and selecting appropriate resources for job execution. The RMS is also responsible for monitoring and reporting the job as well as resource status and resource usage.

Agent Technology in Resource Management

In MCC, RMS provides reliable and on-demand service to mobile users. Agent technology is an emerging technology in the area of resource management to support flexible and adaptable distributed environments. The agent system is implemented in resource management to bridge the gap between mobile cloud users and service providers in order to efficiently utilized resource for mobile user's request (Singh & Malhotra, 2012). The mobile cloud agent system is created based on existing agents system such as mobile agents, single agent or multi-agent systems. Mobile cloud agent needs to reduce the time of resource discovery, mobile network load, overcome latency, resource scheduling, execute asynchronously and autonomously, and adapt dynamically to the environment.

Agent technologies have been developed for over recent years. They are becoming common solutions to address the problems of distributed applications such as resource discovery and resource allocation, network management, load balance, and fault tolerance in mobile computing. Agents can be treated as a high-level abstraction from physical resources for the modelling of complex software system. This technology provides a flexible, scalable, and efficient resource discovery, broking, and allocation service.

In an agent-base system, a hierarchy of homogeneous software agents can provide a scalable and adaptable abstraction of the system architecture. Therefore, using agents can improve the efficiency of the resource management and scheduling system. Agents can interact with the local or remote resources of the specified host. A large number of individual agents can also work and interact with each other forms a multi-agent system (MAS) (Ray-Yuan, Michael, Martin, & Greg, 2009). In a cooperative MAS, the agents work in unison towards achieving a common global goal, while each agent continues to pursue its own goal autonomously; there is no centralized control. Multi-agent systems (MAS) have been advocated as the natural solution to real-world problems that necessitate some form of decentralized control within dynamic and uncertain environments. There are several different agent systems for resource management as shown in the following paragraphs.

A4 (Agile Architecture and Autonomous Agents): The A4 project (Cao et al., 2002) developed a framework for agent-based resource management. This technique is used for service discovery as well as monitoring of the key performance metrics of the agent-based grid system.

ADELE (An Agent for Distance Learning Environments): The ADELE (Capera, Picard, & Gleizes, 2004) guides the development of adaptive multi-agent systems. The ADELE methodology is based on some well-known tools and notations coming from the object-oriented software engineering.

AOMG (Agent-Oriented Modelling based on Grid): The AOMG (Liu, Liu, & Shi, 2005) environment helps to analyze and design the Grid system at the agent-level. AOMG is an agent oriented analysis and design modelling method based on OGSA grid architecture.

MAGE (Multi-Agent Environment): MAGE (Shi et al., 2003) is an agent-oriented environment for software design, integration and execution. MAGE provides the facility for agent mental state representation, planning, reasoning, communication, cooperation and negotiation. It allows facilitates negotiation and cooperation design to enable agent-based computing.

From the survey of existing agent-based resource managements, we can see that the resources are managed via different agent architectures. These agents have addressed some issues related to dynamic resource scheduling and monitoring. However, according to characteristics of mobile environments, mobile devices have many considerations, such as disconnection operation, mobility management, device heterogeneity, service discovery, resource sharing, and so on. Obviously, such needs cannot be directly achieved with the highly demanding mobile applications. Therefore, as increasing the number of users' request, mobile cloud service performance will be surely impacted by the limited resources.

Mobile cloud resource management must address the ability for selecting best service from different MCSPs to guarantee the service performance, deal with computation-intensive applications, support real-time multimedia mobile application, and provide the ability to efficiently utilize mobile network resource via mobile cloud technology.

Agent-based resource management architecture includes mobile user agent (WUA) on different mobile devices and service provider agent (SPA) on mobile cloud. The WUA manages the user (mobility, profile, etc.), resource on mobile device and the issues related with heterogeneity of the mobile devices. The SPA will be present in the mobile cloud service providers for managing cloud resources to obtain all the information needed.

Different scheduling algorithms have been applied in the framework in order to address the issue of both satisfying more user's demand, efficiently utilizing potential physical resources and handling dynamic situations of virtual machines. Therefore, agent-based resource management can provide benefit for mobile users and mobile cloud service provider.

Agent-Based Resource Management Architecture

Resource selection is a main function in traditional distributed systems. In our scenario, the computing resources are homogeneous for computing-intensive applications. The mobile cloud computing not only enables the different agents of a service provider to provide service to many users, but also makes users easy access to a mobile cloud environment to access their data and obtain the computation services at any time anywhere.

However, the mobile network resources are highly unpredictable and changing over time, which may provide mobile network connection and disconnection from the service provider at any time. In addition, the selection of the mobile network and computation resources among multiple agent servers that made it difficult for user to choice.

Here, we proposed an agent-based resource management architecture that is shown in Figure 2. The selection of mobile cloud resources takes into consideration the characteristic of mobile network resources and end resources.

Figure 2. Agent-based resource management architecture for MCC

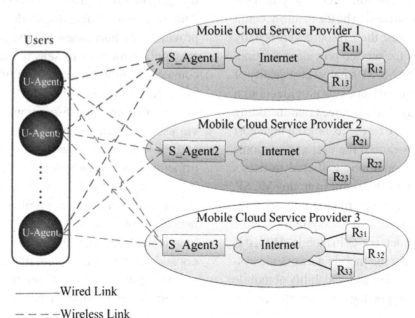

RESOURCE MANAGEMENT IN MOBILE CLOUD COMPUTING

Selection of Mobile Cloud Service Providers

As increasing numbers of mobile applications along with the numerous mobile devices, more and more different cloud service providers (CSP) provide a variety of services for mobile users. Consequently, mobile cloud computing (MCC) technology is employed to satisfy these mobile applications. In fact, MCC is an emerging type of service model and facilities for mobile users to take full advantages from cloud computing (Dinh, Lee, Niyato, & Wang, 2011). However, this technology has been used in highly heterogeneous networks in terms of mobile network access point through different radio access technologies such as 3G/4G networks and WLAN, etc (Larosa, Jiann-Liang, Der-Jiunn, & Han-Chieh, 2011). Since mobile users may access application and data of the "cloud" from anywhere at any time, it is difficult for the users to select the adequate mobile network and end-system resource from various mobile cloud service providers (MCSP).

Both of mobile network and end-system resources information need to be taken into account in each MCSP, because these resources are equally important factors for service provider selection. For example, if one MCSP support best quality of mobile connection, but it does not provide enough capacity of end-system resources that including computing or storage resource, or even high cost of these resources exceed the user expectations, then under such conditions will lead to user's requested service unsuccessful from this MCSP. Due to the heterogeneous mobile networks uncontrollable behaviour and end-system resource with different characteristics in mobile cloud, it is difficult to maintain the mobile network always-on connectivity, on-demand scalability of mobile connectivity and support the service performance.

A hierarchical radio resource management framework which was designed to support a seamless handoff between a cellular network and WLAN is presented in (Karetsos, Kyriazakos, Groustiotis, Giandomenico, & Mura, 2005). In (Ormond, Murphy, & Muntean, 2006), an admission control scheme is applied in an integrated WLAN and code-division multiple access (CDMA) cellular network for a vertical handoff. In this scheme, the objective of an optimization problem is to minimize call blocking probability while packet delay performances and throughput are maintained at the certain level. Also in (Park et al., 2003) which is aims to maximize throughput for non-real-time services through deciding optimal handoff instance and minimizes handoff delay for real-time services. From (Buyya, Pandey, & Vecchiola, 2009), it presented a market-based mechanism to allocation resources in a cloud environment, where the resources are virtualized and delivered to users as services. However, these traditional mobile network selection strategies are only presented for the improvement of system performance with status of access point or conditional of mobile users (Jarek, Jennifer, & Jan, 2004).

Agent-based resource management architecture provides on-demand services of user access data from the different mobile cloud service providers. In this framework, the AHP and GRA are applied for user to selects the best mobile connection from different agent which provided by different MCSP. The AHP consists of the construction of pair-wise comparison matrices via user preferences and different applications, and the extraction of weights by means of the principle right eigenvector (R. W. Saaty, 1987; T. L. Saaty, 1990). In fact, it is mainly applied to the decision making problem with evaluation criterions and uncertainty condition. After hierarchical decomposition from different layers and through the quantitative judgment with seeking relations among them, the AHP is made a synthetic evaluation. It can provide that the user as a decision-maker has full mobile channel information to choose a suitable plan. The mobile cloud resources are selected for the user demand according to the weight of each mobile channel determined by reciprocal pair-wise comparison matrix of agent preference.

There are different mobile channels which could have conflicting preferences. GRA is a quantitative technique of selecting the best option among the comparative choices through building grey relationships with the ideal option (Ng, 1994). It can describe and explain the relationship between the referential sequence and the compared sequence under a grey system.

The rest parts of this chapter are organized as follows. The next section briefly describes the agent-based resource management architecture in mobile cloud environment and problem formulation of this work.

Offloading Technology for Computing-Intensive Applications

Mobile devices still cannot execute a large number of computation-intensive applications such as complex image processing, large-scale data management and data mining. MCC technology allows shift of computing-intensive applications from mobile devices to the cloud to extending or augment the limited storage space, computation capacity by leveraging cloud distributed resources, thereby reducing their limitations (Forman & Zahorjan, 1994). This can improve both the user experience or application performance as well as battery lifetime which is limited on mobile devices. Furthermore, capacity of battery grows by only 5% annually, which cannot support the trend of the explosive development of mobile computation-intensive applications and services (Cui, Ma, Wang, Stojmenovic, & Liu, 2012).

Mobile cloud computing allows users to share resources and execute multiple computation–intensive applications without capital expenditure on hardware and software resources. It provides mobile users with on-demand service from cloud service provider which can provide unlimited pool of diverse resources. It also allows many of cloud computation applications to be carried out in mobile devices with limited computation and storage resources. These can reduce the cost and utilize resources of mobile computing to the end users. Therefore, the performance of multiple applications performing on a mobile device will be enhanced due to the applied mobile cloud computing. At the same time, it also has benefit for developers which is accessible to wider audience of many mobile users from mobile cloud computing. There are many use case for applications in mobile cloud environment (Goatman, Amanda, Laura, & Nussey, 2011; Rao, Sasidhar, & Kumar, 2010).

The offloading technology which is employed in mobile cloud computing to address these issues is shown in Figure 3. The basic concept of this technology aims to transfer application or application code execution from mobile a device to surrogate (Kumar & Yung-Hsiang, 2010). Furthermore, heavy data processing and store a large amount of data will be alleviated within resource-constrained mobile devices. Different approaches have been presented to solve this problem by using different offloading strategies (Kumar, Liu, Lu, & Bhargava, 2012). These approaches often applied for dynamic partitioning the single application and offloading part of application code execution to a powerful nearby surrogate.

According to these application requirements, we need employ offloading technology to extend or argument storage space and computation capability. The main idea of this offloading concept is to dynamically partition the multiple computation applications during runtime, and migrate some of the applications to a mobile cloud service provider for data processing. This offloading technique has been proved to be an effective way to improve data performance and energy saving on mobile devices (Kumar & Yung-Hsiang, 2010; Kun, Shumao, & Hsiao-Hwa, 2008; Li, Wang, &

Figure 3. Offloading scenario in mobile cloud computing

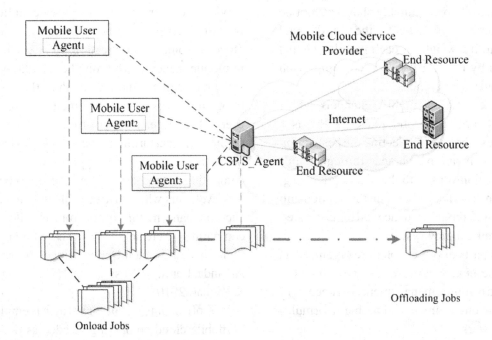

Xu, 2001). Optimal multi-jobs partitioning for resources offloading depends on the tradeoff between the storage space and the energy consumption in the mobile devices. The storage space and computation workload may change with different applications. Thus, optimal decision on multiples jobs partitioning must be executed at run time when sufficient resource information in terms of CPU workload and storage space requirement becomes available.

This agent-based resource management architecture is presented for offloading applications in mobile cloud computing. The adaptive offloading strategy is applied in this architecture for meta-job offloading processing. This strategy performs partitioning and offloading algorithm on a mobile device, and also meta-job scheduling on the service provider.

It is an automatic distributed partitioning system that provides automatically partitions of distributed applications into client and server components (Hunt & Scott, 1999). These applications must be constructed to use Microsoft's

Component Object Model (COM) components to reduce the network communication cost of partitioning components. The relevant CPU-intensive part of an application can be offloaded to cloud server for data processing (Cuervo et al., 2010).

The other ideas of offloading application enable moving an entire OS and all its running applications. Both CloudLets (Satyanarayanan, Bahl, Caceres, & Davies, 2009) and CloneCloud (Byung-Gon, Sunghwan, Petros, & Mayur, 2010) system are presented by employing this technique to mobile device environments. CloneCloud (Chun, Ihm, Maniatis, Naik, & Patti, 2011) uses a combination of dynamic profiling and static analysis to automatically partition an application so that it migrates and executes in the cloud. The meta-jobs offloading strategy can efficiently save the energy of mobile device. In this paper, we presented the agent-based resource management architecture to design, implementation and evaluation of our offloading applications.

Our offloading strategy considers a combination of multiple mobile resources including CPU, storage, battery lifetime and communication cost (i.e., mobile bandwidth resource). This approach aims to minimize cost of total energy consumption for executing meta-jobs on the mobile device, furthermore, efficiently utilize these resources as much as possible. Thus, the multiple requirements of users will be satisfied.

The agent-based resource management architecture for offloading service makes intelligent offloading decisions to deliver partitioned jobs from resource-constrained mobile device to cloud with minimum cost. In order to ensure efficiently executing multiple computation applications via runtime offloading service on mobile device, three key decision making problems must be addressed:

1. How to partition multiple applications which is meta-jobs,
2. Which offloading decision strategy will be used to select applications to offload, and
3. How to minimize the meta-jobs processing time within mobile cloud service provider.

To solve the first problem, grouped jobs strategy in meta-job partition analyzer decides which jobs should be executed on mobile device, which jobs have to be offloaded to cloud and which jobs should be direct for offloading decision engine to further jobs partitioning.

To solve the second problem, the offloading decision engine can provide adaptive offloading strategy to efficiently utilize storage space and energy consumption. To achieve both scalability and stability, this decision engine employs the fuzzy control model for making offloading decisions (Lee, 1990). This model can be applied to fine-gained multiple applications adaption via runtime offloading.

The final problem can be solved by a service provider agent which employ network-aware suffrage heuristic algorithm to minimize the meta-jobs execution on multiple virtual machine in mobile cloud (Yang, Zhou, Sun, & Cruickshank,

2012). Furthermore, the idle power of the mobile device can be saved via cloud. The critical resource constraints of mobile device are its strict storage, computation and energy limitation. This agent-based resource management architecture will allow multiple computation applications to be performed on a mobile device by employing offloading technology.

Multimedia Content Delivery for Mobile Application

Mobile cloud computing technology can also be used to deliver multimedia content to mobile device. This technology can provide on-demand service of mobile users and helps to overcome the limitation of mobile resource utilization. It needs to drive the deployment of service provisioning for user access mobile cloud and efficiency of physical resource management in mobile cloud environment.

Figure 4 shows the overview of mobile cloud computing system with an agent-based architecture for supporting service of mobile users. This architecture includes mobile connection which connects mobile user agents to Access Point (APs) and wire connection which connects service provider agent between APs and data servers. Eventually, users will get content service through this architecture.

In mobile area, APs allow the users to connect the mobile cloud service provider via mobile connections. These users are free to move their locations without any restriction, while retaining their connection to the services. Here, the mobile network resources are always limited. When mobile network infrastructures are under a rapid extension to include more and more APs to accommodate the increasing user demands, a user can be reached by several routes through different APs. A major concern is to develop a way of achieving efficient and fair share of network resources, which is built of various APs and shared

Figure 4. Overview of mobile cloud scenario for multimedia content applications

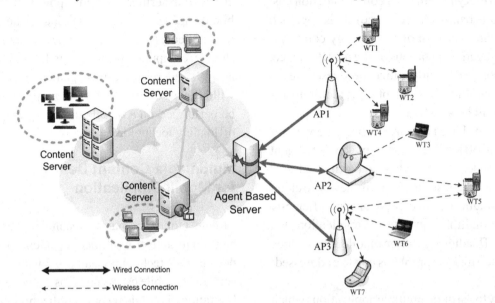

among multiple users. In this regards, two important issues for users to efficiently access those mobile network infrastructures are

1. How to bind with an appropriate AP among a succession of available APs in the mobile network; and
2. How to limit sending rate to avoid overloading the network.

These can be answered by finding a distributed manner for AP selections and flow controls, which optimises the performance of mobile networks.

In the existing systems, each user independently and autonomously selects its AP based upon Received Signal Strength (RSS) and send data in a rate controlled by transport layer protocols, e.g. TCP. However, such a selection strategy could cause a concentration of users at specific APs because the distributions of APs are normally uneven depending on physical conditions. Consequently, the traffic load is very likely to be concentrated at a part of APs, thus degrading the efficiency of the network and lowering achievable throughput and fairness of each user.

Traditionally, the AP selection keeps in the stage of static setting and RSS driven, and no special congestion control mechanism against the wired Internet (Gwon, Funato, & Takeshita, 2002).Improvement can be made by introducing decision metrics and decision policy in the context of vertical handover for a single mobile user running multiple communication sessions (Park, et al., 2003). For examples, it can let users to choose a pricing plan based on their data delay considerations, described by a user utility function (Das, Lin, & Chatterjee, 2004), such as an Always Cheapest Network Selection strategy (Ylitalo, Jokikyyny, Kauppinen, Tuominen, & Laine, 2003), an auction based pricing scheme (Bodic, Girma, Irvine, & Dunlop, 2000), or user preference for networks with a good reputation(Roveri et al., 2003). It optimises the cost function-based algorithm by separating cost function factors into three different categories:

- QoS factors,
- Weighting factors, and
- Network priority factors.

The (Akan & Akyildiz, 2006) proposed an adaptive transport layer for heterogeneous mobile networks with the capabilities of adaptive congestion control, multimedia support, and providing fairness of transmission. The (Niyato & Hossain, 2008) proposed a non-cooperative game-theoretic framework for radio resource distribution in mobile networks. The limitation for the previous mobile network resource management methods include:

- They mostly consider the user-centric AP selection, however in the asymmetric mobile channels, it does not give an optimised solution for traffics. Selfish AP selection at local point cannot maximise global utility.
- Congestion control mechanism has not been integrated into the network optimisation strategy, which affects the resource optimisation.

Constrained optimisation methods have become computational tool of central importance in engineering. Lagrange duality is a widely used convex optimisation method that takes constrains into account by augmenting the objective function with a weighted sum of the constrained function. It has the ability to solve very large, practical, and distributed problems reliably and efficiently in (Freund, 2004; Low, 2003).

The function of service provider agent provides content service from end-system resources to mobile users via different APs. In fact, once the user reached the AP, the service provider agent will discover the available content from the content server for user's request. The crucial aspect of satisfying more users' request and guaranteed the data transfer is implemented by the server provisioning algorithm. The capacity of a connection server is usually constrained by total number of active connections and throughput on the server. If the numbers of servers are under provisioned, the many of user request will be rejected or users receive errors of "server not available." Sharing

of content servers can be achieved by Round Robin approach, or weighed server provisioning algorithm for balancing load of servers and satisfy different user's requirements. The service provider agent also provides reservation mechanism to guarantee the application performance.

CONCLUSION

This chapter presents an overview of mobile cloud computing systems. We present agent-based resource management architecture to address the challenges for data access and computation in mobile cloud environment. Three different types of resource management are considered, including AHP, GRA and their combination for selecting best service provider; the architecture can be applied for partitioning and offloading meta-job and network-aware heuristic scheduling for minimizing the idle power on mobile device, and convex optimization for efficiently utilizing wireless network resource to satisfy more users' requirements.

REFERENCES

Akan, O. B., & Akyildiz, I. F. (2006). ATL: An adaptive transport layer suite for next-generation wireless internet. *IEEE Journal on Selected Areas in Communications, 22*(5), 802–817. doi:10.1109/JSAC.2004.826919.

Bodic, G. L., Girma, D., Irvine, J., & Dunlop, J. (2000). *Dynamic 3G network selection for increasing the competition in the mobile communications market.* Paper presented at the IEEE Vehicular Technology Conference. New York, NY.

Buyya, R., Pandey, S., & Vecchiola, C. (2009). *Cloudbus toolkit for market-oriented cloud computing.* Paper presented at the 1st International Conference on Cloud Computing. Beijing, China.

Buyya, R., Yeo, C. S., & Venugopal, S. (2008). *Market-oriented cloud computing: Vision, hype, and reality for delivering IT services as computing utilities.* Paper presented at the 10th IEEE International Conference on High Performance Computing and Communications (HPCC '08). New York, NY.

Byung-Gon, C., Sunghwan, I., Petros, M., & Mayur, N. (2010). CloneCloud: Boosting mobile device applications through cloud clone execution. *Journal of CoRR.*

Cao, J., Spooner, D., Turner, J. D., Jarvis, S., Kerbyson, D. J., Saini, S., et al. (2002). *Agent-based resource management for grid computing.* Paper presented at the 2nd IEEE/ACM International Symposium on Cluster Computing and the Grid. New York, NY.

Capera, D., Picard, G., & Gleizes, M.-P. (2004). *Applying ADELFE methodology to a mechanism design problem.* Paper presented at the 3rd International Joint Conference on Autonomous Agents and Multiagent Systems. New York, NY.

Chun, B.-G., Ihm, S., Maniatis, P., Naik, M., & Patti, A. (2011). *CloneCloud: Elastic execution between mobile device and cloud.* Paper presented at the 6th Conference on Computer Systems. Salzburg, Austria.

Cuervo, E., Balasubramanian, A., Cho, D.-K., Wolman, A., Saroiu, S., Chandra, R., et al. (2010). *MAUI: Making smartphones last longer with code offload.* Paper presented at the 8th International Conference on Mobile Systems, Applications, and Services. San Francisco, CA.

Cui, Y., Ma, X., Wang, H., Stojmenovic, I., & Liu, J. (2012). A survey of energy efficient wireless transmission and modeling in mobile cloud computing. *Mobile Networks and Applications, 1–8.*

Das, S. K., Lin, H., & Chatterjee, M. (2004). An econometric model for resource management in competitive wireless data networks. *Journal Network: The Magazine of Global Internetworking, 18*(6), 20–26. doi:10.1109/MNET.2004.1355031.

Dinh, H. T., Lee, C., Niyato, D., & Wang, P. (2011). A survey of mobile cloud computing: Architecture, applications, and approaches. *Journal of Wireless Communications and Mobile Computing.*

Forman, G. H., & Zahorjan, J. (1994). The challenges of mobile computing. *Journal of Computer, 27*(4), 38–47. doi:10.1109/2.274999.

Freund, R. M. (2004). Applied lagrange duality for constrained optimisation. *Lecture notes of Massachusetts Institute of Technology.*

Goatman, K., Amanda, C., Laura, W., & Nussey, S. (2011). Assessment of automated disease detection in diabetic retinopathy screening using two-field photography. *PLoS ONE, 6.* PMID:22174741.

Google App. Engine. (n.d.). Retrieved July, 2008, from http://appengine.google.com

Gupta, P., & Gupta, S. (2012). Mobile cloud computing: the future of cloud. *International Journal of Advanced Research in Electrical, Electronics and Instrumentation Engineering, 1*(3).

Gwon, Y., Funato, D., & Takeshita, A. (2002). *Adaptive approach for locally optimized IP handoffs across heterogeneous wireless networks.* Paper presented at the 4th International Workshop on Mobile and Wireless Communications Network. New York, NY.

Hunt, G. C., & Scott, M. L. (1999). *The coign automatic distributed partitioning system.* Paper presented at the 3rd Symposium on Operating Systems Design and Implementation. New Orleans, LA.

Jarek, N., Jennifer, M. S., & Jan, W. (2004). Grid resource management: State of the art and future trends. In *Grid resource management* (pp. 507–566). Boston: Kluwer Academic Publishers..

Juniper Research. (n.d.). Retrieved June, 2010, from http://www.juniperresearch.com/index.php

Karetsos, G. T., Kyriazakos, S. A., Groustiotis, E., Giandomenico, F. D., & Mura, I. (2005). A hierarchical radio resource management framework for integrating WLANs in cellular networking environments. *Journal of IEEE Wireless Communications*, *12*(6), 11–17. doi:10.1109/MWC.2005.1561940.

Kumar, K., Liu, J., Lu, Y. H., & Bhargava, B. (2012). A survey of computation offloading for mobile systems. *Journal of Mobile Networks and Applications*, 1-12.

Kumar, K., & Yung-Hsiang, L. (2010). Cloud computing for mobile users: Can offloading computation save energy? *Journal of Computer*, *43*(4), 51–56. doi:10.1109/MC.2010.98.

Kun, Y., Shumao, O., & Hsiao-Hwa, C. (2008). On effective offloading services for resource-constrained mobile devices running heavier mobile internet applications. *IEEE Communications Magazine*, *46*(1), 56–63. doi:10.1109/MCOM.2008.4427231.

Larosa, Y. T., Jiann-Liang, C., Der-Jiunn, D., & Han-Chieh, C. (2011). *Mobile cloud computing service based on heterogeneous wireless and mobile P2P networks*. Paper presented at the 7th International Wireless Communications and Mobile Computing Conference (IWCMC). New York, NY.

Lee, C. C. (1990). Fuzzy logic in control systems: Fuzzy logic controller II. *IEEE Transactions on Systems, Man, and Cybernetics*, *20*(2), 419–435. doi:10.1109/21.52552.

Li, Z., Wang, C., & Xu, R. (2001). *Computation offloading to save energy on handheld devices: A partition scheme*. Paper presented at the International Conference on Compilers, Architecture, and Synthesis for Embedded Systems. Atlanta, GA.

Liu, W., Liu, Z.-T., & Shi, B.-S. (2005). *AOMG environment: An environment for agent-oriented analysis and design modeling based on grid*. Paper presented at the IEEE International Conference on Software - Science, Technology and Engineering. New York, NY.

Low, S. H. (2003). A duality model of TCP and queue management algorithms. *IEEE/ACM Transactions on Networking*, *11*(4), 525–536. doi:10.1109/TNET.2003.815297.

Meir, A., & Rubinsky, B. (2009). Distributed network, wireless and cloud computing enabled 3-D ultrasound, a new medical technology paradigm. *Journal of PLoS ONE*, *4*(11), e7974. doi:10.1371/journal.pone.0007974 PMID:19936236.

Nabrzyski, J., Jennifer, M. S., & Weglarz, J. (2003). *Grid resource management: State of the art and future trends*. Berlin: Springer..

Narain, D. (n.d.). Mobile cloud computing the next big thing. *ABI Research* Retrieved July, 2010, from http://ipcommunications.tmcnet.com/topics/ip-communications/articles/59519-abi-research-mobile-cloud-computing-next-big-thing.htm

Ng, D. K. W. (1994). Grey system and grey relational model. *SIGICE Bull*, *20*(2), 2–9. doi:10.1145/190690.190691.

Niyato, D., & Hossain, E. (2008). A noncooperative game-theoretic framework for radio resource management in 4G heterogeneous wireless access networks. *IEEE Transactions on Mobile Computing*, *7*(3), 332–345. doi:10.1109/TMC.2007.70727.

Ormond, O., Murphy, J., & Muntean, G. M. (2006). *Utility-based intelligent network selection in beyond 3G systems.* Paper presented at the IEEE International Conference on Communications (ICC '06). New York, NY.

Park, H. S., Yoon, S. H., Kim, T. H., Park, J. S., Do, M. S., & Lee, J. Y. (2003). *Vertical handoff procedure and algorithm between IEEE802.11 WLAN and CDMA cellular network.* Paper presented at the 7th CDMA International Conference on Mobile Communications. Seoul, Korea.

Rao, N. M., Sasidhar, C., & Kumar, V. S. (2010). Cloud computing through mobile-learning. *International Journal of Advanced Computer Science and Applications, 1*(6).

Ray-Yuan, S., Michael, C., Martin, O. H., & Greg, S. (2009). *Multiagent-based adaptive pervasive service architecture (MAPS).* Paper presented at the 3rd workshop on Agent-oriented Software Engineering Challenges for Ubiquitous and Pervasive Computing. London, UK.

Roveri, A., Chiasserini, C. F., Femminella, M., Melodia, T., Morabito, G., Rossi, M., et al. (2003). *The RAMON module: Architecture framework and performance results.* Paper presented at the Second International Workshop on Quality of Service in Multiservice IP Networks. New York, NY.

Saaty, R. W. (1987). The analytic hierarchy process—What it is and how it is used. *Mathematical Modelling, 9*(3–5), 161–176. doi:10.1016/0270-0255(87)90473-8.

Saaty, T. L. (1990). How to make a decision: The analytic hierarchy process. *European Journal of Operational Research, 48*(1), 9–26. doi:10.1016/0377-2217(90)90057-I.

Satyanarayanan, M., Bahl, P., Caceres, R., & Davies, N. (2009). The case for VM-based cloudlets in mobile computing. *IEEE Pervasive Computing/IEEE Computer Society [and] IEEE Communications Society, 8*(4), 14–23. doi:10.1109/MPRV.2009.82.

Shi, Z., Zhang, H., Dong, M., Zhao, Z., Sheng, Q., Jiang, Y., et al. (2003). *MAGE: Multi-agent environment.* Paper presented at the International Conference on Computer Networks and Mobile Computing. New York, NY.

Singh, A., & Malhotra, M. (2012). Agent based framework for scalability in cloud computing. *International Journal of Computer Science & Engineering Technology, 3*(4).

Vaquero, L. M., Rodero-Merino, L., Caceres, J., & Lindner, M. (2009). A break in the clouds: Towards a cloud definition. *ACM SIGCOMM Computer Communication Review,* 50-55.

Weiguang, S., & Xiaolong, S. (2011). *Review of mobile cloud computing.* Paper presented at the 3rd International Conference on Communication Software and Networks (ICCSN). New York, NY.

White Paper. (2010). *Mobile cloud computing solution brief.* AEPONA.

Yang, Y., Zhou, Y., Sun, Z., & Cruickshank, H. (2012). Heuristic scheduling algorithms for allocation of virtualized network and computing resources. *Journal of Software Engineering and Applications, 6*(1).

Ylitalo, J., Jokikyyny, T., Kauppinen, T., Tuominen, A. J., & Laine, J. (2003). *Dynamic network interface selection in multihomed mobile hosts.* Paper presented at the 36th Annual Hawaii International Conference on System Sciences (HICSS'03). Hawaii, HI.

Chapter 8
Transporting the Cloud

Claudio Estevez
Universidad de Chile, Chile

ABSTRACT

Cloud computing is consistently proving to be the dominant architecture of the future, and mobile tech-nology is the catalyst. By having the processing power and storage remotely accessible, the main focus of the terminal is now related to connectivity and user-interface. The success of cloud-based applica-tions greatly depends on the throughput experienced by the end user, which is why transport protocols play a key role in mobile cloud computing. This chapter discusses the main issues encountered in cloud networks that affect connection-oriented transport protocols. These issues include, but are not limited to, large delay connections, bandwidth variations, power consumption, and high segment loss rates. To reduce these adverse effects, a set of proposed solutions are presented; furthermore, the advantages and disadvantages are discussed. Finally, suggestions are made for future mobile cloud computing transport-layer designs that address different aspects of the network, such as transparency, congestion-intensity estimation, and quality-of-service integration.

INTRODUCTION

Mobile Cloud Computing is a large-scale network architecture in which computing power, software, storage services, and platforms are delivered on demand to end users. This new concept brings a whole new set of applications to the Internet. There is a large amount of cloud-computing ap-plications, and this figure is growing at a rapid pace. With the appropriate software, also referred

in cloud computing as middleware, a mobile cloud-computing system could execute any program that a high-end computer can. These programs can range anywhere from a simple word processor to an advanced grid-computing simulator software. The cloud could even perform the functions of an advanced graphics card, returning the processed display information assuming it is aware of the users display configuration, eliminating even fur-ther complexity and cost from the mobile device.

DOI: 10.4018/978-1-4666-4781-7.ch008

There are several advantages of deploying mobile cloud computing on a particular network. A few general advantages of launching a cloud network include:

- End-users can access data and applications from any location and at any time, through any link to the Internet. Data and applications will not be confined to one location (e.g. university, enterprise or home) allowing a ubiquitous access.
- Client hardware cost will drop drastically, and the need for upgrades will become less frequent.
- Corporations running licensed software can have a centralized processing grid that allows access to its employers reducing licensing costs.
- Organizations with server and massive storage needs can save physical space, energy consumption and managing costs, by hiring these cloud-computing services. By utilizing cloud-computing services, consumer organizations will save money on support, as streamlined equipment, in general, have fewer problems than fully integrated systems.
- Finally, if the service provider has a grid computing system, then the client can take advantage of the network's parallel processing power.

The advantages mentioned earlier will depend greatly on the performance of the backbone network that is linking the client and the cloud service provider (CSP). If the exchange of information is unsatisfactory, mainly determined by the throughput of the connection, the client will be discouraged from employing cloud-based services. For this reason the transport layer plays a critical role in mobile cloud computing, particularly connection-oriented transport protocols such as the Transmission Control Protocol (TCP). For self-containment reasons a brief explanation

of the term connection-oriented is found in the Background section of this chapter. The most significant TCP parameters that determine the quality of a connection are throughput, delay, timeout, and segment loss rate. As it will be discussed further ahead, these parameters are correlated and changing one of them affects the rest. By intelligently managing these factors the TCP performance can be improved, hence improving mobile cloud services.

This chapter is organized as follows. The background section discusses the traditional transport control protocols and modeling techniques. The models subsection discusses the two most common throughput models, both based on renewal-reward theory. A quick mention of other types of models is made. It is a great basis for undergraduate students and it serves as a review for graduate students, professors and other professionals. The remaining sections are aimed to complement the knowledge of professionals, which include models, drawbacks, solutions and future work. The *Research in Mobile Cloud Computing Issues* section has drawbacks of TCP transmissions interlaced with the proposed solutions. This order facilitates the reading of a particular issue and some suggested solutions, may this be bandwidth-delay product solutions, wireless edge issues, service level agreement benefits, etc. The chapter concludes with future work suggestions.

BACKGROUND

Transport-layer connection-oriented protocols are mostly composed of TCP-based protocols. In the lexicon of this chapter, a TCP-based protocol (or simply TCP) is any protocol that employs the TCP segment format, regardless of the congestion-control algorithms implemented. A connection-oriented transmission, in short, is a virtual link between the end users. More precisely, this indicates there is an initial exchange of control messages (three-way handshake) with the purpose of allocating resources destined for this particular connection. Once the handshake is completed the data transmission initiates. To guarantee the correct order each segment is assigned a sequence number (SEQ), in units of bytes, to which the receiver replies with an acknowledgement number (ACK). The ACK corresponds to the next expected SEQ, which is simply computed by adding the SEQ to the data length (LEN). After the data is completely received, there is a final exchange of control messages to close the connection and release the reserved resources. In contrast, a connectionless transmission sends out data with no type of confirmation mechanism. This is the case for the User Datagram Protocol (UDP). The sender is not aware if the information is been received, is in order, or if the integrity is compromised. The integrity is a requisite for data file transmissions. If the data were altered in transit, it would be corrupted and most likely unusable. For this reason, there are many applications that require the use of TCP-based protocols.

Most of the traffic that flows through the Internet is composed of TCP transmissions. Many sources claim percentages that range between 85% and 95%, where 90% seems to be the most predominant figure (Thompson, Miller, & Wilder, 1997) (Williamson, 2001) (Fraleigh, et al., 2003). In some enterprises, measurements indicate that TCP can even reach 98% of the traffic (Lee, Carpenter, & Brownlee, 2010). The exact proportion depends highly on the specific network and time the samples are taken, but it is incontrovertible that TCP is the predominant transport layer protocol. This portrays the impact that TCP has on data transfer; a key aspect of cloud computing networks. Therefore, improving the performance of TCP-based transmissions will improve the performance of the cloud network.

To design future transport protocols it is essential to study its evolution. Traditional TCP is a term used to denominate all versions of TCP that utilize some or all, but not additional, of the four basic congestion control algorithms. The four congestion control algorithms are defined in the original TCP and subsequent modifications (Jacobson, 1988) (Stevens, 1997). Fast Recovery has three versions and it is what distinguishes TCP Reno (Allman, Paxson, & Stevens, 1999), New Reno (Floyd & Henderson, 1999), and SACK (Mathis, Mahdavi, Floyd, & Romanow, 1996) (Floyd, Mahdavi, Mathis, & Podolsky, 2000) (Blanton, Allman, Fall, & Wang, 2003) as each have their own method of recovery. In summary, Traditional TCP encompasses all the protocols that lead to the design of TCP SACK. For this reason, occasionally the term Traditional TCP and TCP SACK are interchanged.

The most fundamental variable used by TCP to regulate the flow of traffic through the network is the congestion window size (*cwnd*). The *cwnd* determines the amount of segments that can be released by the sender at any point in time. The *cwnd* is managed by the four basic congestion control algorithms: slow start, congestion avoidance, fast retransmit, and fast recovery. Each state plays a fundamental role. Slow start is an algorithm that increases the size by one segment each time an ACK arrives. If the transmission is just initiating or a timeout (no packets arrive before an expiration time) is detected, TCP sets the *cwnd* to its minimum value, which is typically two to four segments, and initiates the slow-start process. While in the slow-start state it can be observed that over time the *cwnd* increases exponentially, more specifically, at each round-trip time the *cwnd* will double its size. This continues until the *cwnd* exceeds the slow-start threshold or a loss is detected. If the slow-start threshold is reached then TCP switches states, from slow start to congestion avoidance. Congestion avoidance has a more conservative *cwnd* increase algorithm than the slow start; this avoids saturating the network unnecessarily. Congestion avoidance, in theory, consists of increasing the congestion window by $1/cwnd$ (i.e. $cwnd_{n+1} = cwnd_n + 1/cwnd_n$) upon an ACK arrival, but in practice there is an ACK counter that resets itself each time it reaches the current *cwnd*, at which point the *cwnd* increases its value by one. This is also known as the additive increase. It is part of TCP's additive-increase multiplicative-decrease (AIMD) algorithm that describes the iterative mechanism use to converge at the available throughput. Congestion avoidance has a linear growth with respect to time. Slow start and congestion avoidance are algorithms that execute while no segments are lost; if a segment loss is detected, there are various methods of handling the recovery process.

The recovery process depends on the versions of TCP implemented. All traditional versions have a timeout (TO) mechanism; the TO is a retransmission timer computed based on the round trip time (*RTT*) and the delay jitter. The main difference between Tahoe, Reno, New Reno and SACK is the mechanisms use to recover from a loss (see Figure 1). TCP Tahoe uses fast retransmit (but not fast recovery), which implements the monitoring of duplicate ACKs. An ACK has two functions, to acknowledge arrived segments and to indicate the next expected segment, acknowledging all previous segments (even out-of-order segments). A duplicate ACK means the expected segment did not arrive (but one that is after did). A duplicate ACK can occur for at least three different reasons: in the event that a segment is lost, duplicated, or arrives in a different order. If a triple-duplicate ACK (four continuous segments with the same ACK, i.e., one expected plus three duplicates) is detected it is assumed the expected segment is lost and the slow-start mode is initiated without waiting for a TO. TCP Reno implements fast recovery, besides the other basic congestion control

algorithms. After a triple-duplicate ACK, the Reno fast recovery algorithm computes the new slow-start threshold by taking the flight size (all segments that are not acknowledged) and dividing it by two, also known as the multiplicative-decrease process. Under normal circumstances the Reno fast recovery does not enter the slow-start mode, as in Tahoe. The New Reno fast recovery is a small modification of Reno. It differs from Reno in the way it handles a burst of losses (more than one loss in less than a *RTT*). TCP Reno has difficulties handling multiple losses; once it recovers from the first loss, if the non-duplicate ACK does not acknowledge all the intermediate segments (called a partial ACK) it means there was another loss. The sender has enough information to infer this, but it is programmed to go through the triple-duplicate ACK and reducing the *cwnd* by half again. New Reno stores the value of the last SEQ when a triple-duplicate ACK is triggered and when the non-duplicate ACK is received it is compared with the value stored and if it is lower it means it is a partial ACK. In this case, the SEQ that corresponds to the partial ACK is retransmitted without waiting for a triple-duplicate ACK or reducing the *cwnd* again. Finally, the SACK fast recovery is built over Reno, as it leaves New Reno obsolete. To work, both end users must support the SACK option, which has reserved fields in the segment header. If a loss occurs, a triple-duplicate ACK is imminent and the ACKs are built and interpreted as in Reno. In the case of multiple losses within the same *RTT*, the second and subsequent losses will have the SACK option set to on by the receiver and the options data field

Figure 1. Flow diagram of the behavior of TCP Tahoe, Reno, New Reno, and SACK

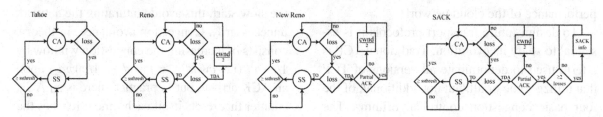

will contain the information about the missing segments in a single acknowledgement segment. This way the sender can be aware prematurely (does not wait for non-duplicate ACK) of all the losses and it can retransmit all the missing segments within a single *RTT*.

These are the fundamental mechanisms of traditional TCP and it will help to understand the drawbacks of these protocols and the differences with the newer protocol versions. The performance comparison of all these implementations of TCP: Tahoe, Reno, New Reno, and SACK can be found in (Fall & Floyd, 1996).

MODELING OF TCP

Modeling is an essential research tool. The models presented here are generic in the sense that these are not network specific. The input parameters will determine what type of network is modeled (i.e., core network, mobile network, etc.). There are various methods of modeling transport control protocols. The two most common models are based on renewal-reward theory. One model is referred here as the segment-time area model (Padhye, Firoiu, Towsley, & Kurose, 1998), and the second is the Markov process model (Misra & Ott, 1999). The details of these models can be found in the respective papers, but a summary is provided below.

Before introducing the derivation of these stochastic models it is important to establish the assumptions made:

- The slow-start mechanism of TCP is neglected and the model only considers the steady-state region of the *cwnd*.
- The probability of losing a segment has a Bernoulli distribution and is i.i.d.
- When the *cwnd* is halved, during the multiplicative decrease algorithm in the event of a segment loss; the result is converted to an integer using the ceiling function.

This prevents the model from entering a non-existing state. It also becomes more realistic because TCP does not send partial or incomplete segments.

Segment-Time Area Model

The segment-time area model derived here is a simplified version of the derivation presented in the original paper. The steady-state throughput is defined as:

$$T = \lim_{t \to \infty} \frac{N_t}{t} = \frac{E[Y]}{E[A]} \qquad (1)$$

N_t is the number of segments sent in the interval $[0, t]$. This definition is extended to the renewal-reward theory case, where the evolution of the congestion window is analyzed in a per-cycle basis, i.e., analyzed in terms of Y_i and A_i, which are objects of the set Y and A, respectively. Y_i corresponds to the amount of segments sent during time A_i in cycle i. The period is chosen to be the triple-duplicate-ACK period (*TDAP*), i.e., the time interval between two segment losses (see Figure 2). This is a convenient choice because the congestion window increases consistently during this interval. W_i is defined as the congestion window at the end of the cycle. p is the segment loss rate. To compute the average value of $\{Y_i\}$, i.e., $E[Y]$, the number of successfully transmitted segments, $1/p$, is added to the number of in-flight segments, $E[W]$, at the moment of the loss occurrence:

Figure 2. Example of triple-duplicate-ACK periods

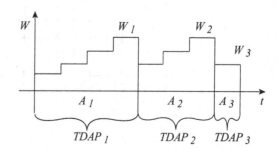

$$E[Y] = \frac{1}{p} + E[W] \qquad (2)$$

Computing the average *TDAP* time given $E[X]$ is straight-forward assuming the round-trip time (*RTT*) is known. X_i is the round-trip in which the loss occurs (ass seen in Figure 3), hence $X_i + 1$ is the total amount of round-trips in $TDAP_i$. *RTT* is the round trip time. Therefore,

$$E[A] = (E[X] + 1)\, RTT \qquad (3)$$

The relation between $E[X]$ and $E[W]$ can be found from the growth pattern of W_i dependent on X_i, as seen in Figure 3, which is:

$$E[W] = \frac{2}{b} E[X] \qquad (4)$$

where b is the number of segments that are acknowledged by a received ACK (Stevens, 1994), which is typically 2.

Finally, a fourth equation can be obtained from the "area" under the *cwnd* curve within a cycle. This can be split into two areas, the rectangle formed by $E[W]/2$ times $E[X]$ and the triangle with the same segment differential (height) and duration (width). Therefore,

$$E[Y] = \frac{E[W]}{2} E[X] + \frac{1}{2} \frac{E[W]}{2} E[X] + E[\xi]$$
$$= \frac{E[X]}{2}\left(E[W] + \frac{E[W]}{2}\right) + \frac{E[W]}{2} \qquad (5)$$

The term ξ_i is the amount of segments in round trip X_{i+1} that remain in-flight. Because ξ_i can take any value between $[0, W_i]$ hence it can be approximated by assuming it is uniformly distributed within this range yielding $E[\xi] = E[W]/2$. Because there are two equations containing $E[X]$ and $E[W]$, the values can be obtained. To reduce the expression obtained for $E[X]$ and $E[W]$ it can be assumed that $p << 1$ yielding:

$$E[W] = \sqrt{\frac{8}{3bp}} \qquad (6)$$

and

$$E[X] = \sqrt{\frac{2b}{3p}} \qquad (7)$$

Finally, substituting (6) and (7) in (2) and (3), respectively, gives us $E[Y]$ and $E[A]$, which can

Figure 3. Segments sent during a TDAP

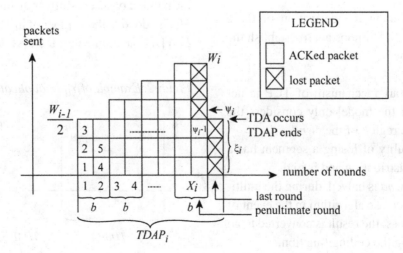

be substituted in the original expression of (1). This gives us the same throughput expression from the work of (Padhye, Firoiu, Towsley, & Kurose, 1998). This expression is in units of segments per second. To obtain the throughput in different units multiply this expression by the segment size (bytes or bits).

$$T = \frac{E[Y]}{E[A]} \cong \frac{1}{RTT} \sqrt{\frac{3}{2bp}} \qquad (8)$$

This expression serves as a basis for research work. It can be used to check simulation models and experimental testbeds. It is a fundamental equation for any researcher in the field of connection-oriented transport protocols. This equation reflects the behavior of long-lived connections, which is particularly useful for backup and other similar cloud applications. If short-lived connections are to be modeled (e.g. email), then the effects of slow-start cannot be neglected and a more appropriate model is the one described in (Zhou, Yeung, & Li, 2005).

Markovian Process Model

The other renewal-reward theory model is the one derived from a Markov process. It is used in (Misra & Ott, 1999) and (Kumar, 1998). The version presented here is far more simplified than the model presented in these references. Through this model the estimated *cwnd* is obtained, to be comparable with the previous model the *RTT* must be known.

The size of a congestion window evolves according to the following expression:

$$cwnd_n = \begin{cases} cwnd_{n-1} + \dfrac{1}{cwnd_{n-1}} & \text{no segment loss} \\[2ex] \left\lceil \dfrac{cwnd_{n-1}}{2} \right\rceil & \text{segment loss} \end{cases}$$

$$(9)$$

The value of n corresponds to the chronological position. The positions are spaced by *RTT* (i.e., the time elapsed between n and $n + 1$ is *RTT*). If the probability of losing a segment at any given time is fixed and equal to p, then the probabilities of incrementing in 1 or halving the size of the congestion window at any given time are given by:

$$\Pr\{cwnd_n = k + 1 \mid cwnd_{n-1} = k\} = (1 - p)^k \quad (10)$$

$$\Pr\{cwnd_n = \lceil k/2 \rceil \mid cwnd_{n-1} = k\} = 1 - \Pr\{cwnd_n = k + 1 \mid cwnd_{n-1} = k\} = 1 - (1 - p)^k \quad (11)$$

Note that this formulation satisfies the Markovian property in the sense that $\Pr\{cwnd_{n+1} \mid cwnd_n, \ldots, cwnd_1\} = \Pr\{cwnd_{n+1} \mid cwnd_n\}$, based on recursion (9).

Figure 4 depicts the Markov chain state diagram induced by $\{cwnd_n\}$. State transitions are rather "sparse", in the sense that the kth state is only connected to the states $\lceil k/2 \rceil$ and $k + 1$. All these connections are summarized in the matrix of states transitions **P**, shown in Equation (12) (see Box 1). The matrix is filled by zeroes except for two elements per row:

Figure 4. Markov chain state diagram induced by {cwnd$_n$}

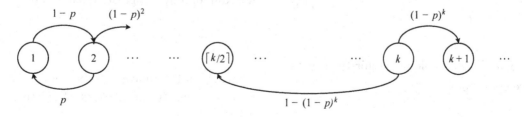

Box 1. Equation 12

$$\mathbf{P} = \begin{bmatrix} p & 1-p & 0 & 0 & 0 & 0 & 0 & \cdots \\ 1-(1-p)^2 & 0 & (1-p)^2 & 0 & 0 & 0 & 0 & \cdots \\ 0 & 1-(1-p)^3 & 0 & (1-p)^3 & 0 & 0 & 0 & \cdots \\ 0 & 1-(1-p)^4 & 0 & 0 & (1-p)^4 & 0 & 0 & \cdots \\ 0 & 0 & 1-(1-p)^5 & 0 & 0 & (1-p)^5 & 0 & \cdots \\ 0 & 0 & 1-(1-p)^6 & 0 & 0 & 0 & (1-p)^6 & \cdots \\ \vdots & \vdots & \vdots & \vdots & \vdots & \vdots & \vdots & \ddots \end{bmatrix}$$

If k is even: $P_{k,k/2} = 1 - (1-p)^k$ and $P_{k,k+1} = (1-p)^k$.

If k is odd: $P_{k,(k+1)/2} = 1 - (1-p)^k$ and $P_{k,k+1} = (1-p)^k$.

To characterize the distributions of congestion window lengths we need to compute the equilibrium distribution π of the Markov chain characterized by $\mathbf{P}$. If (12) is an irreducible Markov chain with matrix of state transitions $\mathbf{P}$, then there exists a non-negative, summing up to 1, solution $\pi = [\pi_1 \, \pi_2 \, \ldots]$ to the linear set of equations $\pi = \pi \mathbf{P}$ in which case π is exactly the unique stationary distribution for the Markov chain. This result provides a way to compute such limiting distribution if we can prove that the Markov chain defined by $\mathbf{P}$ is irreducible, i.e., that all states communicate. We are going to proceed assuming that this result holds, and solve (12). First, note that the matrix $\mathbf{P}$ has a recursive structure that can be exploited to compute this solution. We are going to define a sequence of block matrices of the following form:

$$\mathbf{A}_{k+1} = \begin{bmatrix} \mathbf{A}_k & \mathbf{B}_k \\ \mathbf{C}_k & 0 \end{bmatrix} \tag{13}$$

where $\mathbf{B}_k \in \mathbb{R}^k$ is a column vector filled with zeros except for position k:

$$\mathbf{B}_k = [\, 0 \, \ldots \, 0 \, (1-p)^k \,]^T \tag{14}$$

and $\mathbf{C}_k \in \mathbb{R}^k$ is a row vector filled with zeros except for position $\lceil (k+1)/2 \rceil$:

$$\mathbf{C}_k = [\, 0 \, \ldots \, 0 \, 1 - (1-p)^{k+1} \, 0 \, \ldots \, 0 \,]. \tag{15}$$

Therefore,

$$\mathbf{P} = \lim_{k \to \infty} \mathbf{A}_k.$$

The question is, if the sequence of probability distributions k that satisfies $\pi_k = \pi_k \mathbf{A}_k$ converges to π such that $\pi = \pi \mathbf{P}$. To compute the estimated *cwnd* it is necessary to define a finite space. If each $\mathbf{A}_k$ defines a Markov chain on the state space $S_k = \{1, \ldots, k\}$ and the result holds this will be a practical algorithm for computing π. Numerically computing π with the truncated version of the original Markov chain, considering a k large enough so that it contains most of the mass of the probability distribution, will indicate where the center of mass is located. This corresponds to the average *cwnd*. This can be computed using the Kolmogorov-Chapman equations of the form:

$$\pi_{n+1}^{(k)} = \pi_n^{(k)} A_k, \tag{16}$$

where $\pi_n^{(k)}$ is the truncated probability mass function over the reduced state space S_k. Considering a large computational range will ensure that the limiting distribution converged. Alternatively, one can use a precision criterion based, for example, in a metric between $\pi_{n-1}^{(k)} - \pi_n^{(k)}$, such as the Kullback Leibler discriminant, to introduce a stopping condition in the upper bound computation.

To find the center of mass just perform a summation over π to find the value of k that splits the left and right hand regions in equal masses, i.e., the average value of *cwnd*.

$$\sum_{i=1}^{\breve{k}} \pi_i \leq \frac{1}{2}, \qquad (17)$$

The value of $\breve{k} = \lceil E[cwnd] \rceil$, this means that

$$T \approx \breve{k} \,/\, RTT. \qquad (18)$$

This model applies to long-lived transmissions. For short-lived transmissions, where the slow-start effect plays a significant role, a Markov model can be found in (Fortin-Parisi & Sericola, 2004).

Additional Modeling Techniques

Other types of models exist. These are less common, but depending on the subject in matter these could provide an interesting and more accurate model, for this reason they are briefly described and references are included. These less common models include: fluid models (Misra, Gong, & Towsley, 2000), and control theoretic (Hollot, Misra, Towsley, & Gong, 2001). The fluid model consists on treating data traffic as a fluid by using a stochastic differential equation. The equation from the provided reference is:

$$dW_i(t) = \frac{dt}{R_i\big(q(t)\big)} - \frac{W_i(t)}{2} dN_i(t), \qquad (19)$$

where i is a particular flow, W_i is the *cwnd*, R_i is the *RTT*, q is the amount of segments queued, N_i is the number of losses, and t is the time. A series

of equations derive from (19) that can be solved numerically because the amount of equations will always be the same as the amount of unknown parameters. Finally, the control theoretic model of TCP, as described in the reference provided, is composed of three control systems: TCP window control, TCP load factor, and queue. TCP window control is a closed-loop system while the rest are open. Balancing the system yields the control model.

RESEARCH IN CLOUD COMPUTING ISSUES

As mentioned in the introduction, mobile cloud computing architecture has many advantages. As a technology in the innovation stages of the technological S-curve model, mobile computing over the cloud has and will encounter several difficulties that need to be addressed before it moves into a more stable stage. Some of these issues are directly or indirectly related to the transport layer, so the synergy between the transport layer and the system as a whole needs to be improved. Some known issues, that will be discussed in more detail ahead, are related to: Quality of Experience (QoE), Quality of Service (QoS), Service Level Agreement (SLA), mobile networks, privacy, and architectural. All these issues affect the design of the transport protocol. Before discussing the problems and solutions of TCP performance in specific environments it is important to review what is the purpose of TCP.

Purpose

So far some basic mechanisms, congestion control algorithms, and various traditional TCP versions have been discussed. At this point the reader probably wonders what is the purpose or goal of having all these techniques and congestion window management schemes. There are several answers that converge to one. A possible answer could be to deliver reliable and ordered delivery of data, but this was achieved in the first version. Another objective is to manage the amount of traffic flow without saturating the network, but this was also achieved in the early versions. One key answer is found in the throughput: TCP-based protocols attempt to probe the network in search of the throughput capacity to be able to transmit at the highest rate possible without overcoming other transmissions that are sharing the same pipeline. There may be other goals, but it is important to define the problem before discussing the solution.

Drawbacks/Solutions

High Bandwidth-Delay-Product Networks

One of the fundamental issues of TCP-based protocol is overcoming the problems caused by networks with large *RTT*s. This is a determinant factor in the QoE of the user. TCP manages a *cwnd* parameter that controls the traffic flow. The ideal *cwnd* value is the bandwidth-delay product (BDP), more precisely the product of the available bandwidth and the *RTT*. Cloud-based services have network characteristics that complicate the task of TCP-based protocols. Any service that is available worldwide will inherently have a significant delay. With fiber optic networks improvements, now reaching 10 Tb/s transmissions over a single superchannel (Yu, et al., 2011), the core networks can now support much greater bandwidths. This combination of high bandwidth-delay networks can cause serious problems to the transport-layer performance. This issue is known for many years (Jacobson & Braden, 1988), but in the past this effect was not detrimental to the system. Today, the available bandwidth is becoming difficult to attain and maintain. The dominance of wireless technology at the edge of the network only aggravates this situation, because segment loss rates increase in this domain. One of the reasons the protocol exhibits poor performance under these conditions is related

to the *cwnd* increase and decrease algorithm. Many versions of TCP, including modern versions, have an AIMD *cwnd* management. This means that the *cwnd* increases conservatively (additive) but decreases aggressively (multiplicative). If there is a considerable amount of loss and long delays in the network it is extremely difficult for the congestion control mechanism to reach the throughput capacity. From the model obtained in (Padhye, Firoiu, Towsley, & Kurose, 1998) the dependence on these variables can be noted. When all segment losses are indicated by triple-duplicate ACKs, the TCP throughput B can be expressed as in (8). TCP cannot fully utilize the reserved bandwidth when *RTT* is large, because TCP throughput is inversely proportional to *RTT*. This problem can be relieved temporally by using jumbo frames or parallel TCP connections. But the inverse proportional decay of TCP throughput is a fundamental constraint. TCP was designed for best-effort segment switching networks without previous knowledge about available bandwidth. The TCP sender has to probe the available bandwidth using the acknowledgement feedback from the receiver. As *RTT* increases, TCP estimates available bandwidth less accurate and responds to congestion slower.

The limitations of high bandwidth-delay-product networks have been a topic of discussion for over two decades (Jacobson & Braden, 1988). One of the first proposed solutions was a protocol called HighSpeed TCP (Floyd, 2003). In this work Table 1 is presented. The values used to obtain this table are: packet size = 1500 bytes, *RTT* = 0.1 seconds, and $b = 1$ substituted in (8). The RTTs between losses can be obtained directly from (7). The values indicate that for standard sized packets and typical *RTT*s the user requires a loss rate of 0.0002 to be able to reach a theoretical throughput of 10 Mb/s. It is difficult to guarantee this loss rate in a high bandwidth-delay product network, and the scenario is aggravated if the end user is on a wireless network, where the traffic is exposed to further loss. The situation gets more complex if higher throughputs are desired.

Table 1. Required values to obtain the specified throughput for traditional TCP

TCP Throughput [Mb/s]	RTTs Between Losses	*cwnd* [segment]	Segment Loss Rate *p*
1	5.5	8	2E-2
10	55	83	2E-4
100	555	833	2E-6
1,000	5,555	8,333	2E-8
10,000	55,555	83,333	2E-10

The solution proposed is to alter the AIMD behavior based on the *cwnd*. The behavior is described by the following expressions.

$$cwnd_{n+1} = cwnd_n + a(cwnd_n)/cwnd_n \qquad (20)$$

$$cwnd_{n+1} = (1 - b(cwnd_n)) \, cwnd_n \qquad (21)$$

a(*cwnd*) = 1 and b(*cwnd*) = 1/2 for *cwnd* < 38, where 38 segment correspond to a loss of 10^{-3}. In the case that *cwnd* > 38, then a(*cwnd*) takes values higher than 1 and b(*cwnd*) takes values lower than 1/2 (but greater than 0). There is a suggested relation for a(*cwnd*) and b(*cwnd*), obviously as a function of *cwnd*, and a table provided in the referenced work (table is in the Appendix). Because *cwnd* is only dependent on the network parameter *p* (*b* is a protocol design parameter), this is an indirect measure to accelerate the *cwnd* growth when the loss rate is lower than 10^{-3}. To prove that *cwnd* only depends on the variable *p*, substitute the expression *cwnd* = *T·RTT* in (8). The result of having more aggressive AIMD values when the *cwnd* exceeds 38 (loss rate is lower than 10^{-3}) is better performance in high bandwidth-delay networks, where high *cwnd* is needed. By aggressive it should be understood that the a(*cwnd*) and b(*cwnd*) parameters are modified to increase growth acceleration, while a lenient behavior would imply that these parameters cause a slow growth of the *cwnd*. One drawback from this method is that is it not fair. Because the next protocol discusses fairness, this term will be discussed in the following.

Differentiated Services

Differentiated services are a form of QoS. Having this at the transport layer level can assist the QoS mechanisms provided at other levels. A proposal that resembles a lot the mechanisms employed by HighSpeed TCP is presented in (Yang & Lam, 2000). This work presents a General AIMD (GAIMD) congestion control and it is shown that the proposed protocol can provide differentiated services. The AIMD behavior is described by:

$$cwnd_{n+1} = cwnd_n + \alpha/cwnd_n \qquad (22)$$

$$cwnd_{n+1} = \beta \, cwnd_n \qquad (23)$$

In this work the α and β values are chosen such that the protocol is fair. Fair means that no protocol is overcoming the rest of the protocols sharing the same link and is usually measured by *cwnd* dominance by plotting the proposed protocol versus Traditional TCP in orthogonal axes; if the trace remains in the *x* = *y* plane the proposed protocol is considered fair. To ensure fairness the throughput equations of Traditional TCP and the GAIMD protocol are equaled and the relation between α and β is derived. Using a similar technique than the one used in (Padhye, Firoiu, Towsley, & Kurose, 1998) the throughput model of GAIMD is obtained and yields

$$T = \frac{1}{RTT} \sqrt{\frac{\alpha(1 + \beta)}{2b(1 - \beta)p}} \qquad (24)$$

where the throughput expression due to timeout is omitted in both (8) and (24) because its effect on the throughput is limited to high loss rate cases. Nevertheless, to expressions relating α and β are derived, one from the throughput model based of triple-duplicate ACKs, as those described by (8) and (24), and from the throughputs obtained from timeout portion of the models. Because the relation of the AIMD parameters α and β should be valid for the whole range of segment loss rate p it was determined that the relation

$$\alpha = \frac{4(1 - \beta^2)}{3} \qquad (25)$$

works best for a larger range of p. The claim that this protocol can provide differentiated services comes from the expression (Equation 5 in the referenced paper):

$$T_{GAIMD} = d\, T_{TCP}$$

or

$$\sqrt{\frac{1 - \beta^2}{\alpha}} = \frac{1}{d}\sqrt{1 - (1/2)^2}$$

or

$$\alpha = d^2 \frac{4\left(1 - \beta^2\right)}{3}. \qquad (26)$$

If $d = 1$, the protocols are fair. It can be observed that substituting $d = 1$ in (26), yields (25). From (26) it can be inferred that increasing (or decreasing) the throughput ratio by d, will increase the additive factor α by d^2. As an example: if the differentiated service is setup such that the flow of traffic from GAIMD is twice as much as the competing flow (assuming it is a fair protocol), the value of α will increase by four. An interesting exercise can be to study the stability of the protocol for values that are near the usable limit, i.e. $\alpha \approx 0$ and $\beta \approx 1$.

Traffic Policing

In most, if not all, networks have some level of traffic policing. The policy is usually described in the service level agreement (SLA). This agreement usually specifies information about the restrictions applied to the customer's traffic. Two common specifications are the committed information rate (CIR) and the excess information rate (EIR). If the protocol is aware of these specifications it can incorporate it into the congestion control algorithm to further optimize the usable range of the *cwnd*. Work that has incorporated SLA information into the protocol is found in (Estevez, Angulo, Abujatum, Ellinas, Liu, & Chang, 2012), study that originated in (Xiao, Estevez, Ellinas, & Chang, 2007). By incorporating SLA information the proposed protocol, called Ethernet Services Transport Protocol (ESTP), can improve its throughput performance. The congestion avoidance algorithm is the same as the Traditional, but the fast retransmit/recovery will set the *cwnd* to a minimum value that corresponds to the CIR traffic rate, i.e., $cwnd_{MIN} = CIR \cdot RTT$. Using this value, the *cwnd* expression can be lower bounded as shown:

$$cwnd_{n+1} = \frac{cwnd_n - cwnd_{MIN}}{2} + cwnd_{MIN} \qquad (27)$$

This technique takes full advantage of the bandwidth provided to the provider, such as a CSP, by maintaining the throughput above the CIR. The throughput can be further improved by utilizing the EIR information. $cwnd_{MAX}$ can be obtained similarly to $cwnd_{MIN}$ but using EIR rather than CIR: $cwnd_{MAX} = EIR \cdot RTT$. With this value, the upper bound of the congestion window can be controlled. An upper bound is set because once the *cwnd* exceeds $cwnd_{MAX}$, the throughput will exceed EIR and the traffic policing enforced at the lower layers will discard excess packets. Once that happens, the TCP will initiate its congestion control mechanism and decrease the congestion window. This is unnecessary because there is no congestion in the network. By maintaining the *cwnd* at its maximum value, the throughput will not be reduced by the protocol's congestion control and the subscriber will get maximum throughput until a random loss (e.g. link loss) or congestion loss occurs. The additive increase properties of AIMD of the proposed protocol will then be expressed as:

$$cwnd_{n+1} = \min\left(cwnd_n + \frac{1}{cwnd_n}, cwnd_{MAX}\right)$$

(28)

Traditional TCP is then a special case when $cwnd_{MIN} = 0$ and $cwnd_{MAX} = \infty$. The traffic-loss profile matching and the *cwnd* boundary mechanism implemented by the additive-increase multiplicative-decrease (AIMD) techniques distinguishes ESTP from other transport protocols and makes its implementation desirable for CSPs.

Mobile Communication

Mobile communication has changed the way society interacts with each other. Today almost every person has a mobile device. How does this affect the transport layer? TCP suffers significant throughput degradation if the end-to-end connection includes mobile technology (Balakrishnan, Padmanabhan, Seshan, Stemm, & Katz, 1997). The impact of bandwidth variation due to wireless links on the performance of TCP is studied in (Moon & Lee, 2006) and (Yavuz & Khafizov, 2002). It is well known that bandwidth oscillations occur in mobile networks, such as UMTS and CDMA2000. This is due to signal fading and other radio phenomenon in cellular networks. High Speed Downlink Segment Access (HSDPA) technology is introduced for high speed data access, HSDPA augmented the bandwidth variation.

In addition, dynamic resource sharing among concurrent data users, the channel-state-based scheduling mechanisms also result in variations of the bandwidth available for TCP connections in the transport layer. Available bandwidth oscillation and spurious timeout are identified as some of the most important factors of TCP throughput degradation (Chan & Ramjee, 2004) (Khafizov & Yavuz, 2002) (Ren & Lin, 2011). Bandwidth variations will cause *RTT* predictions to fluctuate triggering more frequent timeout retransmissions than those considered in a constant bandwidth model.

Modeling Throughput with Mobile Edge Network

The throughput model of TCP over the wireless link can be obtained from extending the model presented in (Lakshman & Madhow, 1997), where the throughput of TCP is analyzed in an environment with fixed link capacity, fixed round trip time, and loss only due to buffer overflow. The model consists of three epoch regions: congestion avoidance (epoch A), fast retransmit/recovery (epoch B), and slow start (epoch C). t_X represents the duration of epoch X and n_X represents the amount of segments transmitted during epoch X. The variable $T = RTT + 1/b_W$, where b_W is the fixed link bandwidth. $cwnd_0$ is the initial congestion window size and $cwnd_{max}$ is the maximum.

$$t_A = T(b_W T - cwnd_0),$$

(29)

$$n_A = \frac{cwnd_0 \, t_A + \dfrac{t_A^2}{2T}}{T},$$

(30)

$$t_B = \frac{cwnd_{max}^2 - (b_W T)^2}{2b_W},$$

(31)

$$n_B = b_W t_B.$$

(32)

TCP has an additional epoch C where the congestion window grows exponentially from 1 to $cwnd_0$, whose value is half of the window size when the last segment loss. Thus, the TCP throughput is calculated by $(n_A+n_B+n_C)/(t_A+t_B+t_C)$, where

$$t_C = [\log_2(cwnd_0 + 1)]T, \qquad (33)$$

$$n_C = cwnd_0. \qquad (34)$$

In fact, the congestion window evolutions of TCP correspond to a typical slow start and fast retransmission. The slow start phase is always initiated by a fast retransmission, which implies that $cwnd_0 = cwnd_{max}/2$. To capture the highly variable congestion window behavior under bandwidth variation, we make definitions as follows:

$$p_1 = \frac{N_{TO}}{N_D} \qquad (35)$$

$$T_h = \frac{p_1(n_C + n_A) + (1 - p_1)n_A + n_B}{p_1(t_C + t_A) + (1 - p_1)t_A + t_B}. \qquad (36)$$

where N_{TO} is the number of retransmissions and N_D is the number of lost segments, hence p_1 is the ratio of $N_{TO}:N_D$. The work referenced presents a method to estimate p_1 and therefore increasing the accuracy of the throughput model under mobile networks (bandwidth variation environment).

Privacy Issues

One of the biggest concerns in cloud computing are the privacy issues. Privacy issues can arise in almost any layer. At the transport layer it affects in the sense that TCP-based transport protocols can be sorted into two categories: transparent and opaque. Transparent is used here in the same context as the lexicon of Metro Ethernet Networks (MENs), where transparent means that the network is not aware of what type of traffic flows through it; the traffic is "invisible" to the core network.

Privacy could imply that the underlying network supports virtual connections and do not exchange transport layer (or higher) information. Ethernet Virtual Connections (EVC), for example, use Multiprotocol Label Switching (MPLS), which route from node to node using short path labels, and do not even require the use of routing tables or to read any address information. It also prevents data from crossing one EVC link to another EVC, protecting the integrity of the information. This does not mean that Carrier Ethernet Network will become the future backhaul network of cloud computing services, but it is certainly an attractive option.

In contrast, some transport layer designs, with the goal of improving the congestion control, interact with routers. This allows the router to view (and even alter) the information contained in the segment. Protocols running Explicit Congestion Notification (ECN), described in (Ramakrishnan, Floyd, & Black, 2001), are probably discouraged in cloud networks; in Carrier Ethernet Networks (CENs) these are prohibited because of transparency issues. ECN is a congestion feedback tool that allows queuing schemes to label certain segments with a congestion warning, rather than drop the segment. These will inform the end user that the network is congested without having to discard the segment sent. An example of a protocol that uses ECN is the eXplicit Control Protocol (XCP) (Zhang & Henderson, 2005). XCP has been proposed as a multi-level network feedback mechanism for congestion control of Internet transport protocols.

Flexible Scalability

One innate advantage of transport layer protocols is that two completely different protocols can interact with each other without knowing the specific methodology implemented. As long as the basic receiving mechanisms are the same (triple-duplicate ACK, SACK, etc.) the receiver does not need to know how the sender administers the flow. Because the server manages the *cwnd*, all downstream traffic flow will be controlled by the server. If the server is upgraded rather than the whole network, then all downstream traffic will experience the benefits of the new upgraded protocol. This avoids forklift upgrades, which can be expensive.

Power Consumption

Power consumption has also been addressed at the transport layer. This is a relevant topic in wireless communications, where it is desirable to extend the battery life of portable/mobile devices. It has been suggested (Haas & Agrawal, 1997) that the intelligence, related to the transmission, be shifted toward the gateway. The gateway initiates two TCP sessions, one with the mobile device and another with the corresponding host. The TCP session between the mobile device and the gateway should flow fairly smooth, as it is a one-hop system, and the gateway handles the flow control. The authors argue this will decrease the power consumed in the processing and packet handling.

Latency Issues

As mentioned in the *High Bandwidth-delay-product Networks* section, high RTTs cause a detrimental performance drop in TCP transmissions. One alternative, that is probably underutilized, is the use of performance enhancing proxies, as described in section 5 of (Caini, et al., 2006). This consists in having a TCP proxy in between the sender and receiver. The proxy will queue the data packets and send fake ACKs to the server, hence cutting the feedback time, potentially in half. If the proxy is located exactly in the middle (in terms of time) of the sender and receiver, then by the time the first data packet arrives at the receiver, the sender will receive the first ACK cutting the perceived RTT in half. In the general case, the perceived RTT can be computed as:

$$RTT_{perc} = \max(RTT_{i,j}) \qquad (37)$$

where $RTT_{i,j}$ is the round trip time between two adjacent nodes (proxy server, sender or receiver). Because RTT_{perc} will always be lower or equal than the total RTT, it can be observed that substituting RTT_{perc} for RTT in (9) will increase the performance of TCP. This technique is commonly used in satellite communication, but it is not widely used in the Internet. One reason is that the proxies require a vast amount of memory to queued packets and also needs to keep track of every single connection that flows through it. Both of these tasks require a large amount of resources.

Additional Transport Layer Protocol Designs

There are many TCP-based protocols not mentioned in this section, mainly to maintain this infusion of information brief. But the reader is encouraged to examine these additional protocols: BIC (Xu, Harfoush, & Rhee, 2004), CUBIC (Ha, Rhee, & Xu, 2008), Hamilton TCP (HTCP) (Shorten & Leith, 2004), Scalable TCP (Kelly, 2003), and FAST (Jin, Wei, & Low, 2004). These protocols perform well and most can be found in the Linux OS, which allows for accessible testing.

LATEST TECHNIQUES

There have been many interesting topics in the later years, but one that has awaken some interest in the field of transport layer design is congestion intensity estimation. In particular, two techniques have been suggested. The first is a metric of Φ = goodput – throughput and the second is the separation between two packet losses. In both cases, the information is fed back to the increase and decrease algorithms to improve the congestion control mechanism.

Congestion Estimation based on Goodput-Throughput (G–T)

The work discussed here is from (Jung, Kim, Yeom, Kang, & Libman, 2011), but the G–T concept was first suggested in (Jung, Kim, Yeom, & Kang, 2010). The former, work done in 2011, is discussed because of the interesting criteria involved in its design. The proposed protocol is called Adaptive end-to-end Congestion control Protocol (ACP). There are various aspects of the protocol working consecutively. As mentioned earlier, one interesting aspect is the congestion intensity estimation. The protocol measures the goodput and throughput rates. The goodput is the amount of data received successfully within a range of time. The throughput is all the data sent independent of its success to reach the destination. A metric, defined as Φ = goodput – throughput, is used to determine the congestion intensity of the network. If $\Phi > 0$ it means that the amount of data acknowledged is greater than the data sent out for the same range of time and therefore there is a high probability that the network is not congested. Inversely, if $\Phi < 0$ it means that the data acknowledged is lower than the amount that is been sent out for the same range of time; therefore it is more likely that the network is congested. Needless to say, this information is very valuable to the congestion control algorithm.

Alongside with congestion intensity estimation there is a fairness measure. The fairness requires the estimation of a few parameters to be computed using the channel capacity of the bottleneck link divided by the number of connections actively flowing through this link. So the fair share of link capacity per connection is given by C/n. Additionally, the occupied throughput flow is computed by taking $w_i(t) = cwnd_i(t)/RTT$. Once these values are obtained the fairness metric is given by the expression:

$$F_i = \frac{w_i(t)\,n}{C} \tag{38}$$

Because these are parameters that are not available at the transport layer, the protocol needs to estimate it when the available information. The estimation of F, denoted by $\dot{F}$, is approximated using an estimate of the queue growth (Q^{RTT}), divided by the *cwnd* difference in during the time *RTT*. The queue growth is computed as shown in (40). $\Delta cwnd$ means the amount of change that *cwnd* had during the time *RTT*, and ΔRTT is how much did *RTT* change in one *RTT*.

$$\dot{F}_i = \frac{Q^{RTT}}{\Delta cwnd} \tag{39}$$

$$Q^{RTT} = \frac{cwnd + \Delta cwnd}{RTT + \Delta RTT}\,\Delta RTT \tag{40}$$

Similarly to the previous metric, there are two regions of interest. When $\dot{F} > 1$ it means that the flow is occupying more than its fair share of bandwidth. Inversely, if $\dot{F} < 1$ it means that the flow is underutilizing its fair share of bandwidth (see Table 2).

There are many more interesting details surrounding this work, including the adaptive increase and adaptive decrease algorithms. The information presented is an introduction to this work.

Table 2. Flow states and control policy of ACP

Flow States			Policy
Congestion State	**Fairness State**	**Loss Event**	
$\Phi \geq 0$	N/A	No	Adaptive Increase
$\Phi < 0$	$\dot{F} \geq 1$		
	$\dot{F} < 1$		
	$Q \geq$ threshold		Adaptive Decrease
N/A		Yes	

Congestion Estimation based on the Distance between Two Segment Losses

The final mechanism discussed in this chapter is the congestion intensity estimation based on the distance between two segment losses. This work is presented in (Estevez, Angulo, Abujatum, Ellinas, Liu, & Chang, 2012). Congestion intensity estimation is one of the most important characteristics of the protocol proposed, and it should not be confused with congestion detection (single segment loss event). The level of congestion is related to the amount of segments successfully delivered between two segment losses, plus one to be exact. The instantaneous amount of segments delivered between two segment losses plus one is defined here with the parameter α (see Figure 5). The value of α is mapped into an exponential profile to determine a less strenuous multiplicative-decrease factor defined as $1/map(\alpha)$. The purpose of choosing an exponential profile is to match the exponential probability distribution exhibited by the interval between two segment losses. In reality the distribution is not exactly exponential, but this approximation works very well for the typical values of α. By having the congestion window dependent on the network congestion level, the size of the congestion window can be controlled more efficiently and with higher granularity.

The distance between two lost segments is the amount of successfully delivered segments found in-between these two losses plus one (the lost segment). The value of α will range from 1 to ∞, which implies that the extreme cases are two consecutive losses and a lossless transmission. The value of α is mapped to the value of $map(\alpha)$, which is the denominator of the multiplicative-decrease factor and ranges from 2 to 1. This means that the proposed protocol can divide the congestion window size by a factor no greater than two (inclusive), and no smaller than one (exclusive). Because a factor of 1 is selected for $\alpha = \infty$ (lossless transmission), it is obvious that the protocol will never choose the exact factor of $map(\alpha) = 1$. This mapping scheme is desirable because if α takes a small value, it is assumed to be the result of a highly congested network and therefore the congestion window size is reduced more aggressively (similar to Traditional TCP). Inversely, if the value of α is large, it is assumed that the network is not experiencing high levels of congestion and the congestion window is only slightly reduced in size. To achieve this mapping and at the same time match the traffic loss probability distribution, an exponential function is chosen. The details of how to obtain the mapping function are found in the referenced work, but a brief explanation is that the segment loss is assumed to have a Bernoulli distribution, so segment loss "arrival" has a Poisson distribution and by definition the difference between two variables that exhibit a Poisson distribution will have an exponential distribution. With this approach the distribution of α is matched by the mapping function.

Figure 5. Value of α is the amount of successfully transmitted segments in-between two segment losses plus one

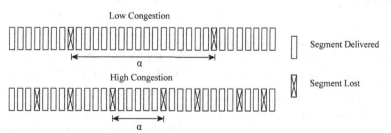

$$\frac{1}{map(\alpha)} = \left(e^{-\frac{\alpha-1}{\tau}} + 1 \right)^{-1} \tag{41}$$

The exact mapping function can be altered, even though for stability it is probably best to choose a monotonically decrease function. The main purpose is to give greater granularity to the congestion mechanism. The value of τ is a design parameter. Decreasing this value will result in a more aggressive behavior. It is recommended to set it at $\tau = 1/p_{max}$, where p_{max} is the highest loss rate that the system can handle. If there is a SLA guarantee for maximum segment loss rate, this value is should be used. The resulting multiplicative-decrease algorithm is then:

$$cwnd_{n+1} = \frac{cwnd_n}{map(\alpha)} = cwnd_n \left(e^{-\frac{\alpha-1}{\tau}} + 1 \right)^{-1} \tag{42}$$

One interesting characteristic of this protocol is that when the connection is relatively unused the protocol will not decrease its *cwnd* aggressively, so it is excellent for high BDP networks. If the link is been shared and the bandwidth decreases the protocol will have more consecutive losses therefore decreasing the *cwnd* more aggressively. Nevertheless, if the *RTT*s between losses are large (and the same) for both Traditional TCP and the proposed protocol, the proposed protocol will reduce its *cwnd* less. To maintain fairness the additive-increase function needs to be scaled accordingly using the relation discuss previously in (25).

TCP Reconfigurability

The final topic is reserved for a novel technique called reconfigurable TCP (Oguchi & Abe, 2011). It is specifically oriented to mobile cloud services, particularly to the inherent susceptibility to changing conditions. In mobile cloud computing not only the wireless nature of the network can cause abrupt network changes (throughput, RTT, loss rate, etc.) but also a technique called live migration used by data centers. This technology enables virtual machine images to be moved from one physical machine to another while the current session is active. The concept of reconfigurable TCP assumes that no one protocol is the optimal choice for all network conditions. By creating a selection of congestion control techniques based on known transport protocols an optimal method can be selected given the network conditions. The assortment is not limited to whole protocol functionality but can be a combination of specific congestion avoidance techniques implemented by different existing protocols. A protocol tuning plane is constantly supervising the throughput, RTT, loss rate, jitter, and other parameters and dynamically choosing the optimal methods based on the characteristics of the link.

CONCLUSION

Mobile cloud computing offer a wide range of advantages, including: remote access of data and applications, lower cost of mobile devices, centralized licensing options, space and resource savings, and access to grid computing to satisfy high processing needs. The transport layer connection-oriented protocols play a big role in the success of cloud computing because the user experience depends highly on the timely manner in with the information is delivered to the end user. It was shown that TCP has slowly evolved satisfying issues that rose in the past. To help evolve several models were created and the optimizations made to these models lead to further improvements.

There are many issues been research related to disadvantages that TCP-based protocol have in cloud computing network environment. Proposed protocols are designed to solve each of these aspects. These aspects include subjects like: achieving transmission rates that match or get close to the available throughput in high BDP networks, creating differentiated services support at the transport layer, incorporating traffic policing issues into the congestion control algorithm to further increase its performance, overcome the bandwidth variation problems cause by wireless networks, reducing issues related to privacy by better selection of transport protocols, and reduce the need of forklift upgrades to increase scalability.

Finally, some recent techniques were discussed, including a very important issue in mobile cloud computing, which is congestion intensity estimation. This will reduce many of the adverse effects discussed in the previous sections particularly the reduction of the limitations imposed by high BDP networks. Two techniques are discussed: Goodput-Throughput (G–T) and the distance between two segment losses method. Both techniques offer interesting and proven-effective approaches. Both protocols prove that congestion intensity estimation provides feedback that is utilized to efficiently adjust the traffic flow and, along with the reconfigurable support discussed, may set a new era in transport-layer design.

REFERENCES

Allman, M., Paxson, V., & Stevens, W. (1999). *TCP congestion control. RFC 2581*. Internet Engineering Task Force..

Balakrishnan, H., Padmanabhan, V., Seshan, S., Stemm, M., & Katz, R. (1997). A comparison of mechanisms for improving TCP performance over wireless links. *IEEE/ACM Transactions on Networking, 5*(6), 756–769. doi:10.1109/90.650137.

Blanton, E., Allman, M., Fall, K., & Wang, L. (2003). *A conservative selective acknowledgment (SACK)-based loss recovery algorithm for TCP. RFC 3517*. Internet Engineering Task Force..

Caini, C., Firrincieli, R., Marchese, M., de Cola, T., Luglio, M., & Roseti, C. etal. (2006). Transport layer protocols and architectures for satelite networks. *International Journal of Satellite Communications and Networking, 25*(1), 1–26. doi:10.1002/sat.855.

Chan, M., & Ramjee, R. (2004). Improving TCP/IP performance over third generation wireless networks. In *Proceedings of IEEE Infocom*. Hong Kong, China: IEEE.

Estevez, C., Angulo, S., Abujatum, A., Ellinas, G., Liu, C., & Chang, G.-K. (2012). A carrier-ethernet oriented transport protocol with a novel congestion control and QoS integration: Analytical, simulated and experimental validation. In *Proceedings of the IEEE International Conference on Communications (ICC)* (pp. 2673-2678). Ottawa, Canada: IEEE.

Fall, K., & Floyd, S. (1996). Simulation-based comparisons of Tahoe, Reno and SACK TCP. *ACM SIGCOMM Computer Communication Review, 26*(3), 5–21. doi:10.1145/235160.235162.

Floyd, S. (2003). *HighSpeed TCP for large congestion windows. RFC 3649*. IETF..

Floyd, S., & Henderson, T. (1999). *The NewReno modification to TCP's fast recovery algorithm. RFC 2582*. Internet Engineering Task Force..

Floyd, S., Mahdavi, J., Mathis, M., & Podolsky, M. (2000). *An extension to the selective acknowledgement (SACK) option for TCP. RFC 2883*. Internet Engineering Task Force..

Fortin-Parisi, S., & Sericola, B. (2004). A Markov model of TCP throughput, goodput and slow start. *Performance Evaluation, 58*, 89–108. doi:10.1016/j.peva.2004.07.016.

Fraleigh, C., Moon, S., Lyles, B., Cotton, C., Khan, M., & Moll, D. etal. (2003). Packet-level tra c measurements from the sprint IP backbone. *IEEE Network, 17*(6), 6–16. doi:10.1109/MNET.2003.1248656.

Ha, S., Rhee, I., & Xu, L. (2008). CUBIC: A new TCP-friendly high-speed TCP variant. *ACM SIGOPS Operating Systems Review*, *42*(5), 64–74. doi:10.1145/1400097.1400105.

Haas, Z., & Agrawal, P. (1997). Mobile-TCP: An asymmetric transport protocol design for mobile systems. In *Proceedings of the International Conference on Communications* (pp. 1054-1058). Montreal, Canada: IEEE.

Hollot, C., Misra, V., Towsley, D., & Gong, W.-B. (2001). A control theoretic analysis of RED. *Infocom*, *3*, 1510–1519.

Jacobson, V. (1988). Congestion avoidance and control. *Computer Communication Review*, *18*(4), 157–173. doi:10.1145/52325.52356.

Jacobson, V., & Braden, R. (1988). *TCP extensions for long-delay paths. RFC 1072*. Internet Engineering Task Force..

Jin, C., Wei, D., & Low, S. (2004). FAST TCP: Motivation, architecture, algorithms, performance. In *Proceedings of IEEE Infocom*. Hong Kong, China: IEEE.

Jung, H., Kim, S., Yeom, H., & Kang, S. (2010). TCP-GT: A new approach to congestion control based on goodput and throughput. *Journal of Communications and Networks*, *12*(5), 499–509. doi:10.1109/JCN.2010.6388496.

Jung, H., Kim, S., Yeom, H., Kang, S., & Libman, L. (2011). Adaptive delay-based congestion control for high bandwidth-delay product networks. In *Proceedings of IEEE Infocom*. Turin, Italy: IEEE.

Kelly, T. (2003). Scalable TCP: Improving performance in highspeed wide area networks. *ACM SIGCOMM Computer Communication Review*, *33*(2), 83–91. doi:10.1145/956981.956989.

Khafizov, F., & Yavuz, M. (2002). Running TCP over IS-2000. In *Proceedings of the International Conference on Communications*. New York, NY: IEEE.

Kumar, A. (1998). Comparative performance analysis of versions of TCP in a local network with a lossy link. *IEEE/ACM Transactions on Networking*, *6*(4), 485–498. doi:10.1109/90.720921.

Lakshman, T., & Madhow, U. (1997). The performance of networks with high bandwidth-delay products and random loss. *IEEE/ACM Transactions on Networking*, *3*(4), 336–350. doi:10.1109/90.611099.

Lee, D., Carpenter, B., & Brownlee, N. (2010). Observations of UDP and TCP ratio and port numbers. In *Proceedings of the Fifth International Conference of Internet Monitoring and Protection (ICIMP)*. Barcelona, Spain: ICIMP.

Mathis, M., Mahdavi, J., Floyd, S., & Romanow, A. (1996). *TCP selective acknowledgment options. RFC 2018*. Internet Engineering Task Force..

Misra, A., & Ott, T. (1999). The window distribution of idealized TCP congestion avoidance with variable packet loss. *Infocom*, *3*, 1564–1572.

Misra, V., Gong, W., & Towsley, D. (2000). A fluid-based analysis of a network of AQM routers supporting TCP flows with an application to RED. In *Proceedings of Sigcomm*. Stockholm, Sweden: ACM. doi:10.1145/347059.347421.

Moon, J., & Lee, B. (2006). Rate-adaptive snoop: A TCP enhancement scheme over rate-controlled lossy links. *IEEE/ACM Transactions on Networking*, *13*(3), 603–615. doi:10.1109/TNET.2006.876154.

Oguchi, N., & Abe, S. (2011). Reconfigurable TCP: An architecture for enhanced communication performance in mobile cloud services. In *Proceedings of the International Symposium on Applications and the Internet* (pp. 242-245). Munich, Germany: IEEE/IPSJ.

Padhye, J., Firoiu, V., Towsley, D., & Kurose, J. (1998). Modeling TCP throughput: A simple model and its empirical validation. *ACM SIGCOMM Computer Communication Review, 28*(4), 303–314. doi:10.1145/285243.285291.

Ramakrishnan, K., Floyd, S., & Black, D. (2001). *The addition of explicit congestion notification (ECN) to IP. RFC 3168*. IETF..

Ren, F., & Lin, C. (2011). Modeling and improving TCP performance over cellular link with variable bandwidth. *IEEE Transactions on Mobile Computing, 10*(8), 1057–1070. doi:10.1109/TMC.2010.234.

Shorten, R., & Leith, D. (2004). H-TCP: TCP for high-speed and long-distance networks. In *Proceedings of PFLDNet Workshop*. Argonne, IL: PFLDNet.

Stevens, W. (1994). TCP/IP illustrated: Vol. 1. *The protocols*. Boston: Addison-Wesley..

Stevens, W. (1997). *TCP slow start, congestion avoidance, fast retransmit, and fast recovery algorithms. RFC 2001*. Internet Engineering Task Force..

Thompson, K., Miller, G., & Wilder, R. (1997). Wide-area internet traffic patterns and characteristics. *IEEE Network, 11*(6), 10–23. doi:10.1109/65.642356.

Williamson, C. (2001). Internet traffic measurement. *IEEE Internet Computing, 5*(6), 70–74. doi:10.1109/4236.968834.

Xiao, C., Estevez, C., Ellinas, G., & Chang, G.-K. (2007). A resilient transport control scheme for metro ethernet services based on hypothesis test. In *Proceedings of the IEEE Global Telecommunications Conference (Globecom)* (pp. 2461-2466). Washington, DC: IEEE.

Xu, L., Harfoush, K., & Rhee, I. (2004). Binary increase congestion control for fast long-distance networks. In *Proceedings of IEEE Infocom*. Hong Kong, China: IEEE.

Yang, Y., & Lam, S. (2000). General AIMD congestion control. In *Proceedings of International Conference on Network Protocols (ICNP)* (pp. 187-198). Osaka, Japan: ICNP.

Yavuz, M., & Khafizov, F. (2002). TCP over wireless links with variable bandwidth. In *Proceedings of the IEEE Vehicular Technology Conference*. Birmingham, AL: IEEE.

Yu, J., Dong, Z., Xiao, X., Xia, Y., Shi, S., Ge, C., et al. (2011). Generation, transmission and coherent detection of 11.2 Tb/s (112x100 Gb/s) single source optical OFDM superchannel. In *Proceedings of the OSA/OFC/NFOEC National Fiber Optic Engineers Conference*. Los Angeles, CA: OSA/OFC/NFOEC.

Zhang, Y., & Henderson, T. (2005). An implementation and experimental study of the explicit control protocol (XCP). In *Proceedings of IEEE Infocom* (pp. 1037–1048). Miami, FL: IEEE..

Zhou, K., Yeung, K., & Li, V. (2005). Throughput modeling of TCP with slow-start and fast recovery. In *Proceedings of the Global Telecommunications Conference (Globecom)*. St. Louis, MO: IEEE.

KEY TERMS AND DEFINITIONS

ACK: Acknowledgement number of a TCP packet.

AIMD: Additive increase multiplicative decrease.

Application Level Throughput (Goodput): Only the data portion of the successfully delivered packets is considered; this excludes lost traffic, packet headers, control packets, etc. It can be computed by dividing the file size by the total transmission time.

BDP: Bandwidth-delay product.

Committed Information Rate (CIR): Transmission rate reserved for a particular customer.

Congestion Window Size (*cwnd*): It is the size of the sliding window managed by TCP.

CSP: Cloud service provider.

ECN: Explicit congestion notification.

Epoch Regions: Intervals of time in which TCP is running a particular congestion avoidance algorithm.

EVC: Ethernet virtual connection.

Excess Information Rate (EIR): Maximum transmission rate allowed to a particular customer. Packets that exceed this rate will be discarded.

Fairness: Metric used to determine whether users or applications receive a fair share of system resources.

In-Flight Segments: Segments that were sent to the destination host that have not been acknowledged.

LEN: Data field size (length) of a TCP packet.

MEN: Metro Ethernet network.

MPLS: Multi-protocol label switching.

QoE: Quality of experience.

QoS: Quality of service.

Round Trip Time (RTT): It is the time taken for a packet to travel from the source to the destination plus the time taken to return from the destination to the source.

SEQ: Sequence number of a TCP packet.

Service Level Agreement (SLA): It is an agreement or contract, between the service provider and the customer, which specifies the service parameters of the purchased link.

TCP: Transmission control protocol.

Triple Duplicate ACK Period (TDAP): The time interval between two segment losses that do not occur within a RTT.

UDP: User datagram protocol.

Chapter 9
Mobile Video Cloud Networks

Qi Wang
University of the West of Scotland, UK

Christos Grecos
University of the West of Scotland, UK

James Nightingale
University of the West of Scotland, UK

Xinheng Wang
University of the West of Scotland, UK

Runpeng Wang
Beijing Foreign Studies University, China

Abbes Amira
University of the West of Scotland, UK

Naeem Ramzan
University of the West of Scotland, UK

Chunbo Luo
University of the West of Scotland, UK

ABSTRACT

Mobile multimedia computing has become ubiquitous in everyday life. However, mobile device users involved in resource-demanding visual applications such as video streaming often encounter performance degradations due to their mobile devices' intrinsic constraints in processing power, storage, and battery capacity. Cloud computing can be explored to circumvent such problems thanks to the vast resources available in the cloud. Mobile video cloud computing has thus emerged as an important research and development topic to achieve high-performance, innovative networked video applications. This chapter discusses the recent advances in mobile video cloud technologies and applications. The authors investigate mobile video cloud systems starting with the various mobile cloud paradigms and then present challenges and solutions of mobile video cloud management for mobility, context, and security. Furthermore, the authors examine the latest video coding standards and explore methods based on parallelisation and scalability for their optimised application over mobile clouds, followed by three highlighted mobile cloud video applications including streaming, transcoding, and gaming. Finally, future directions in this area are envisioned.

INTRODUCTION

Video content has become a ubiquitous presence with ever-growing demands for higher quality at any time, any location and an expanding variety of user equipment such as laptops, tablet PCs and smart phones equipped with increasing media signal processing and networking capabilities. According to (Gartner, 2011; 2012), worldwide mobile device sales reached 1.6 billion in 2010, and the sales of smart devices (smartphones and tablets) alone will rise to 1.2 billion in 2013. Consequently, recent years have witnessed that video applications such as broadcasting, videocon-

DOI: 10.4018/978-1-4666-4781-7.ch009

ferencing, video on demand, peer-to-peer streaming, and Internet Protocol (IP) TV are becoming a majority of network traffic worldwide in both wired and wireless/mobile networks. According to the yearly report from Cisco (2013), global mobile data traffic grew 70% in 2012, of which mobile video traffic account for 51%. It is the first time in history that mobile video traffic exceeded 50%. It is predicted that mobile video traffic will increase 16 fold between 2012 and 2017 and 2/3 of the world's mobile data traffic will be mobile video by 2017.

Meanwhile, despite the remarkable advances in technical specifications, smart mobile devices are struggling in handling the escalating computation and storage workload imposed by multimedia (especially video) applications of increasing complexity and quality. Because mobile devices have intrinsic constraints in storage, processing and battery capacity, mobile applications especially visual applications often hit a performance barrier. The vast computing and storage resources offered by cloud computing can be utilised to break through this barrier and convert the challenges into opportunities for the sustainable growth of mobile multimedia computing (Dey, 2012; Lawton, 2012). Therefore, recent years have been experiencing a major paradigm shift from conventional mobile computing to mobile cloud computing (Fernando, Loke & Rahayu, 2013), which combines the mobility convenience in mobile computing and the extraordinarily powerful capacity in existing and emerging Internet-based cloud infrastructure and beyond. Mobile cloud computing is thus gaining increasing global momentum. According to Juniper Research (Holden, 2010), the market for cloud-based mobile applications is expected to grow from $400 million in 2009 to reach $9.5 billion by 2014, yielding an average 88% phenomenal annual increase.

A mobile cloud offers on-demand, cost-effective (pay-as-you-go or sometimes almost free) computing utilities analogous to electricity or gas utilities and mobile users can receive services from a cloud on the move as if they were employing a portable super computer. Mobile cloud networking promotes innovation in distributed, parallel, and pervasive mobile computing and applications, and creates new pathways between mobile devices and the wireless Internet. Resource-demanding, computation-intensive applications such as video networking are launched at mobile devices whilst the enormous volume of application data is stored and the tremendous intensity of the processing tasks is handled in the cloud, transparent to the mobile users. For instance, cloud-based video processing and networking can bridge the gap between mobile users' demanding application requirements and the limited resources in their mobile terminals. A number of applications can benefit from mobile cloud computing, including mobile commerce, mobile learning, mobile healthcare, mobile gaming, and other practical applications e.g. for tourists such as various searching services and for social networking users such as mobile experience sharing (Dinh et al., in press).

In this book chapter, the authors focus on video applications over mobile cloud networks. The building blocks in mobile cloud video systems are illustrated in Figure 1. In the bottom layer, various mobile cloud paradigms are constructed to provide physical cloud computing and networking platforms for mobile users. In the middle layer, both mobile cloud management schemes (mobility support, context awareness and management, and security) and video coding standards are implemented over the mobile cloud paradigms to support mobile cloud applications. In the top layer, mobile cloud video applications and services are deployed to deliver cloud-based video applications such as streaming, transcoding and gaming.

The reminder of the chapter is organised as follows. The Background summarises the evolution of video coding standards, mobile networking and cloud computing. The subsequent four sections discuss the involved building blocks in details

Figure 1. Building blocks in mobile video cloud systems

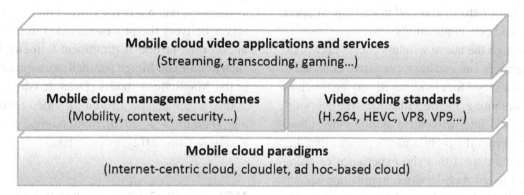

following a bottom-up approach of Figure 1. The Future Trends section then presents the future research and development topics and directions in this area. Finally, concluding remarks are provided.

BACKGROUND

Video applications over mobile cloud networks is a multidisciplinary, cross-layer topic, covering video signal processing standards and techniques, mobile networking standards and mobility support protocols, cloud networking paradigms and service/resource management, the operation and quality of service of the applications and the system, and users' experience. It is noted that both video coding/compression standards and mobile networking standards have been developing rapidly in the last two decades to meet the demands for high-quality, pervasive and innovative mobile video applications (Grecos & Wang, 2011).

From the video coding perspective, built upon the success of the H.261, H.262/MPEG-2 and H.263 standards, the latest generation in increasingly dominant use is the H.264/MPEG-4 Advanced Video Coding (AVC) standard (ITU-T & ISO/IEC, 2010). Further functionality extensions such as Scalable Video Coding (SVC) and Multi-View Coding (MVC) to H.264/AVC have

also been proposed. As the latest standardisation effort by ITU-T Video Coding Experts Group (VCEG) and the ISO/IEC Moving Picture Experts Group (MPEG), through the Joint Collaborative Team on Video Coding (JCT-VC), has led to the definition of the next-generation video coding standard, namely High Efficiency Video Coding (HEVC, anticipated to be H.265 in the ITU-T H series). HEVC has recently received ITU-T first stage approval and become an MPEG Final Draft International Standard (ISO/IEC, 2013a).

From the wireless/mobile networking perspective, the globally successful second-generation (2G) GSM/GPRS cellular system standardised in 1990s has gradually evolved to the third-generation (3G) networks and beyond (such as the Long Term Evolution or LTE), having been standardised and updated by 3GPP since around 2000. Currently, the fourth generation (4G) systems that can achieve 1 Gbps peak data rate, represented by LTE-Advanced and WiMAX 2, have also emerged. In addition to the wide-area cellular systems and the metropolitan-area WiMAX networks, WiFi wireless local-area networks have been standardised in the IEEE 802.11 series such as the recent 802.11n-2009 (802.11-2012), 802.11ac and 802.11ad. It is widely envisioned that these existing and emerging wireless/mobile networks would complement each other e.g., in coverage and capacity, and thus they would coexist and converge into a common IP-based (packet-switched) integrated platform and collaboratively support legacy and new applications.

Through the above wireless access networks, mobile users can establish pervasive connectivity with a cloud for cloud-based services such as video streaming. Figure 2 illustrates the overview of a typical Internet-centric mobile video cloud system. From the mobile user's perspective, he/she would expect that the experience of using a cloud-based mobile video application should be ideally comparable to that of a native mobile video application installed and run in their mobile devices. Therefore, the overall quality of experience (QoE) of the mobile user has to be acceptable, which is related to the quality of service (QoS) of the system such as throughput, delay and jitter, mobility support experience, as well as the perceived visual quality of the application. At the cloud side, a video processing task (either offloaded by the mobile user or created as a cloud service) is typically distributed by a Splitter among a number of processing entities (in terms of physical servers, virtual machines or VMs, etc.) for parallelised processing. A Merger then collects all the processed video slices from the

processing entities and integrates them to obtain a complete, reconstructed video. Finally, a video server delivers the processed video to the user, in real time or not. A prominent framework for such a Split and Merge parallelisation procedure is the MapReduce model (Dean & Ghemawat, 2008), which can be utilised for video encoding e.g., (Pereira et al., 2010), transcoding e.g., (Lao, Zhang & Guo, 2012), or other tasks.

MOBILE CLOUD NETWORKING PARADIGMS

Internet-Centric Cloud for Mobile Users

With the tremendous popularity in both mobile devices and Internet cloud services, it is a natural evolution to extend wired cloud to support mobile consumers. Therefore, the first mobile cloud paradigm is simply a mobile extension to Internet cloud infrastructure, as shown in Figure 2. In this paradigm, mobile subscribers access remote cloud servers through various wireless access networks (Abdallah-Saleh et al., 2012).

Figure 2. Overview of a typical mobile video cloud system

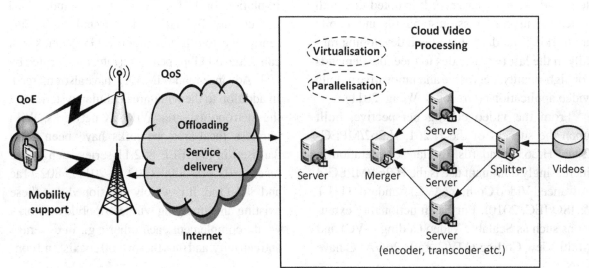

Currently, such Internet-centric mobile cloud model is the dominant mobile cloud networking paradigm, where most cloud-based applications so far are proposed and deployed, and thus is the focus of this chapter.

Offloading and HTML5 are the two major drivers for Internet-centric mobile clouds (Holden, 2010). Among other attractive new features, HTML5 has built-in support to tackle poor connectivity, which is commonplace in mobile cloud networking. Offloading relieves resource-constrained mobile devices from computation/ storage-intensive, battery-consuming processing tasks by transferring these tasks to the cloud and only running a thin client locally, as proved in numerous studies such as MAUI (Cuervo et al., 2010) and CloneCloud (Chun et al., 2011). ThinkAir (Kosta & Mortier, 2012) further addressed the scalability and elasticity of the cloud by creating smartphone virtualisation in the cloud and adopting an online method-level offloading. In addition, efficient on-demand cloud resource allocation was considered, and cloud parallelism was exploited to reduce execution time and energy consumption by dynamically managing the VMs based on mobile users' workloads and task deadlines. Meanwhile, it has to be noted that offloading may not always achieve the desired results such as energy saving (even for video applications). Therefore, algorithms should be in place to determine if it would worth transferring the workload to cloud at all. For instance, the GreenSpot algorithm (Namboodiri & Ghose, 2012) considered the trade-off between application features and energy efficiency for offloading decision making. Finally, the choice of which wireless access networks to be utilised for traffic transmission is also important when the mobile user can access multiple, usually heterogeneous wireless networks. Typically, WiFi and femtocell are preferred due to cost and performance considerations (Mohiuddin et al., 2012).

Cloudlet for Nomadic Users

For interactive and other real-time video services, Internet-centric clouds may not be able to meet the time constraints due to the high, sometimes intolerable round-trip time or end-to-end delay. To address this challenge, an alternative paradigm called cloudlet has been proposed by Satyanarayanan et al. (2009). Such a paradigm, as shown in Figure 3, can explore the benefits of deploying distributed mini-clouds to bring cloud resources and capabilities much closer to end users for time-sensitive services. Simulation results by Fesehaye et al. (2012) indicated that cloudlet of up to two hops always outperformed remote, conventional cloud in terms of reduced transfer delay and increased throughput for video streaming, collaborative chatting and file editing. Experimental results by Clinch et al. (2012) have also confirmed the advantage of cloudlets. This paradigm would appeal to cloud service providers for hotspots such as café, restaurants, airports, hospitals and other public (or private) venues. To deploy instant wireless provision to nomadic consumers in hotspots, the wireless mesh networking technology can be integrated with the cloudlet paradigm (Khan, Wang & Grecos, 2012).

Ad Hoc-Based Mobile Cloud

Unlike the above two paradigms, an ad hoc-based mobile cloud attempts to form a purposely built or spontaneous collaborative communication group that explores the cloud computing concept by sharing resources, as illustrated in Figure 4. Among other scenarios, this paradigm can enhance the travelling experience of a group of smart mobile device users. It is noted that although infrastructure is not relied upon, ad hoc-based mobile clouds can be complemented by interworking with the Internet or the other two mobile cloud paradigms aforementioned. An ad hoc-based mobile cloud

Figure 3. Distributed cloudlets for mobile users

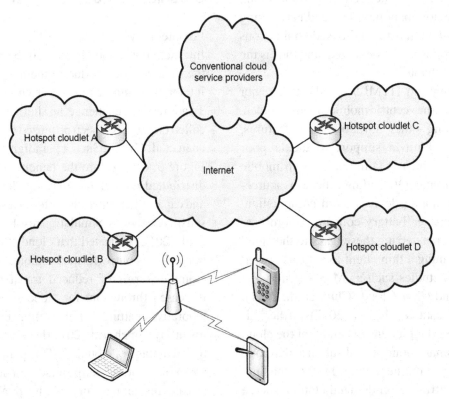

Figure 4. Ad hoc-based mobile cloud

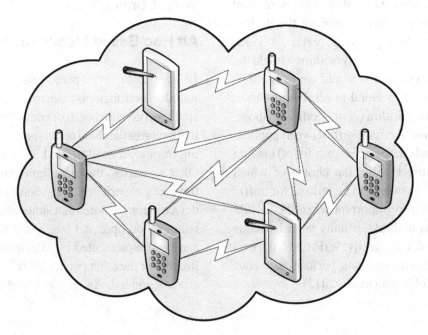

can establish its physical connectivity through short-range wireless networking technologies, among which the WiFi ad hoc mode would be the most popular, ready-to-use choice.

There are a number of challenges in this innovative mobile cloud approach, e.g., service discovery, service resilience against dynamic network topology and service availability, trust management, user privacy protection, and business models. Nguyen, Senac & Ramiro (2011) assessed the impact of mobility on performances of distributed computation in such mobile cloud networks, and their simulation results demonstrate that user movement could actually enhance the processing capacity and resilience significantly by introducing a small percentage of highly mobile nodes in a highly localised mobile cloud network. Pederson & Fitzek (2012) argued that network coding and social networking would be the key technologies to enable media content distribution with energy saving, privacy, security, data protection, and fast content (and potentially

other resources) sharing. It is noted that a proof-of-concept testbed had been implemented by Vingelmann et al. (2011) to demonstrate network coding-based video streaming from one mobile device to 16 other handheld terminals connected to an ad hoc network created using a mobile phone, whilst user cooperation and multi-hop ad hoc networking support were planned as future work.

Comparison of Mobile Cloud Paradigms

The above three mobile cloud paradigms are further compared in Table 1, partially based on (Satyanarayanan et al., 2009) and (Nguyen, Senac & Ramiro, 2011). Most of the differences among them originate from the different network architecture employed and the services targeted. Each of them also has major challenges as listed to cope with, some of which have not been sufficiently investigated in the literature. Apart from the challenges specific to each paradigm,

Table 1. Comparison of mobile cloud paradigms

	Internet-centric cloud	Cloudlet	Ad hoc-based cloud
Architecture	Infrastructure mode	Infrastructure mode	Ad hoc mode (infrastructureless)
Network	Internet (wide area network)	Local area network	Ad hoc network
Location	Dedicated, specialised data centres	Local business premises	Omnipresence (wherever appropriate)
Ownership	Centralized ownership by big companies	Decentralized ownership by local business	Decentralized ownership by end users
Management	Professional administration	Self-management	Self-management
Deployment and maintenance cost	High	Low to medium	Low
Capacity and availability	High	Medium	Low
Server	Large scale, clusters of servers	Cloud in a box	Distributed, any member node can be a server (as well as a client)
Client	Thin client	Thin client	Smart user device
Services	Offloading services	Time-constrained services	Spontaneous, opportunistic, peer-to-peer services
Scale	Large number of users	On-site users	On-site users
Challenges	Cost-effective, scalable cloud operation; optimal offloading	Cloud service customisation to business	Connectivity; service discovery and access; business model

there are common essential management issues that have to be addressed in all the paradigms, including mobility support, context awareness and management, and security, to be discussed in the subsequent section.

MOBILE CLOUD MANAGEMENT SCHEMES

Mobility Support

Mobility support is fundamental to enable mobile cloud applications. The various mobility types envisioned by Wang & Abu-Rgheff (2003) for next-generation wireless networks are largely applicable to mobile cloud networking scenarios. With enriched context taken into account, Figure 5 illustrates the multiple dimensions of mobility challenges (and opportunities) for a mobile cloud user, who has access to a variety of mobile devices, various pervasive wireless access networks, available subscribed cloud services (in formats of different cloud service providers or domains administrated by the same provider), and a number of mobile cloud paradigms (infrastructure- or ad hoc-based clouds or cloudlets).

Imagine the following application scenario. Jane is a businesswoman boarding a train whilst receiving a cloud-based video service via her smartphone. Once she is seated, she instructs her smartphone to hand the ongoing video session over to the in-seat bigger-sized screen (referred to as *session mobility*, between user terminals) for better video quality and saving the battery of her smartphone. The video service in the cloud detects this handover and switches to video content delivery of higher resolution. The train passes the urban area (covered by WiFi hotspots in the train station and then 3G/4G cellular sys-

Figure 5. Multi-dimensional mobility for mobile cloud users

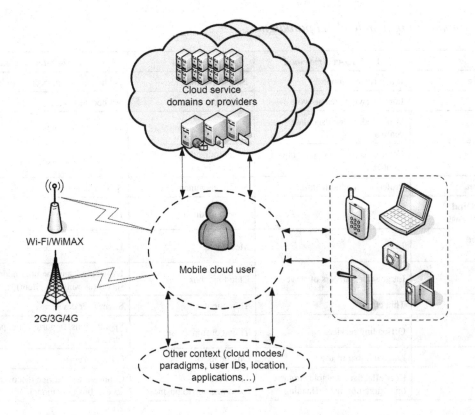

tems), the rural areas (e.g., WiMAX networks), and finally arrives at the destination city (another cellular system). The video session accordingly experiences a number of handovers between base stations of the same or different radio access technologies (referred to as homogeneous or heterogeneous *terminal mobility* respectively) without being dropped. During the course, the video service in the cloud continuously monitors the diverse networks' transmission conditions, adapts the video quality on the fly, and dynamically organises resources in the cloud especially when transitions between service provisioning domains take place (i.e., cloud *service mobility*). Once Jane arrives at the conference room, she then joins the ad hoc mobile cloud formed by the participants' smart devices (cloud *mode mobility*, from infrastructure mobile cloud to ad hoc mobile cloud). In addition, Jane should be able to be contacted through a user-level identifier (ID) regardless of her locations and devices being used (known as *personal mobility*).

Clearly, to enable such complex, multi-dimensional mobility capabilities especially for resource-demanding (and often time-constrained) video applications, innovative, advanced mobility management schemes and architectures have to be in place, taking into account a greater context awareness including not only user movement, terminal handover and heterogeneous wireless/mobile access networks but also dynamic cloud resource allocation, inter-cloud cooperation and so on. Since mobile cloud networks are based on the Internet, existing IP-based mobility management schemes such as the IETF Mobile IP standards (Perkins, 2010; Perkins, Johnson, & Arkko, 2011) and its variants are largely applicable to mobile cloud networks. These schemes can support terminal mobility, network mobility (movement of a whole mobile network) e.g., via the IETF NEMO standard (Devarapalli et al., 2005), generic mode mobility (between ad hoc and infrastructure wireless networks) and potentially even more mobility

types such as personal mobility (one user ID for multiple locations) and service mobility when combined with other application-level schemes such as the Session Initiation Protocol (SIP) (Rosenberg et al., 2002) and its extensions, e.g., as shown in (Wang & Abu-Rgheff, 2006).

Moreover, due to the richer context brought about by the mobile cloud computing paradigms and cloud-specific management and application challenges, cloud-aware mobility support schemes are essentially required to enable cloud-specific operations such as inter-cloud service mobility, or highly desirable to enhance system performance and user experience. Such schemes are highlighted as follows. Kim, Lee & Congdon (2012) shared the multi-dimensional mobility view, and proposed a cloud-centric architecture for rich mobile experience networking. In the proposed architecture, the mobile device's networking protocol stack, the wireless access networks, and the cloud jointly monitor and analyse the mobile context, manage the virtualised resources, and support the mobile connectivity of a set of mobile devices belonging to the same user, referred to as a mobile personal grid (MPG). The cloud maintains the connectivity states of the MPG and performs computation-intensive tasks for the MPG through a personal connectivity assistant (Avatar).

To meet the growing demand for ubiquitous service mobility across clouds, there is a rising trend to deploy Internet-wide, large-scale federated cloud paradigms. Shan et al. (2012) highlighted the lack of widely accepted standard or application programming interfaces (APIs) for inter-cloud operations despite several industry projects on the standardisation of cloud interoperation, and proposed an architecture for inter-cloud operations based on the next generation service overlay network (NGSON), defined in the IEEE P1903 standard. It is noted that related standardisation work is underway in a number of standardisation bodies such as ETSI, IEEE, IETF, ITU-T and ISO/IEC, and the IEEE ICWG-2301 and -2302 are two notable examples. In addition, mechanisms (e.g., Liang et al., 2012; Niyato et al., 2012) to promote economic gains are also critical for sustainable cloud federation in supporting service mobility.

Context Awareness and Management

Mobility in various dimensions aforementioned brings about significant, dynamic changes to the operation context of cloud applications in terms of terminal capacities, locations, service providers, available resources, security and privacy etc., and thus poses great challenges to cloud applications, especially resource-demanding, real-time applications such as video streaming. Apart from the mobility management schemes described, a promising approach towards further resolving these challenges is to introduce context awareness in the cloud application system and explore such awareness to enhance mobile users' QoE.

In most recent years, a number of context-aware frameworks have been proposed for mobile cloud users. A context management framework was proposed by Klein et al. (2010) to enhance mobile users' access to clouds across heterogeneous wireless networks. Both dynamic context (mobility model, environmental model, traffic model, and link model) and static context (user profile, device capabilities, deployment model, and policy model) were taken into account. Nevertheless, the focus on the work was at the access network layer with an overall aim to optimise network utilisation and network selection. La and Kim (2010) considered device context, user preference, situational context (the user's location, time etc.) and service context (current service's QoS attributes) in a context-concerned hierarchy, which consisted of a context monitoring and service adaptation chain.

Whilst the above architectures explore context awareness in infrastructure-based cloud computing platform for mobile users, relevant research has also emerged regarding context utilisation in ad hoc mobile clouds. Huerta-Canepa and Lee

(2010) described a framework to create virtual ad hoc cloud service providers by applying the cloud computing concept into mobile devices in a neighbourhood. A context manager was proposed to extract and handle context information with the location and status of nearby devices highlighted. Mechanisms in ad hoc networks such as neighbour discovery can be used to monitor the status. Only neighbours in a stable location (or following the same movement pattern) may be explored for the formulation of the ad hoc mobile cloud. A prototype based on Hadoop was outlined with results reported on comparing local execution and offloading.

Security

One of the top concerns for adopting mobile clouds is security, which includes data protection, privacy, trust/identity management, authentication/authorisation/accounting in a cloud and inter-clouds etc. In infrastructure-based public mobile clouds and cloudlets, typically user data and/or applications have to reside in a shared, public platform and thus data protection/confidentiality is indispensable. Meanwhile, protection for video content often leads to significant processing and storage overhead in the system. Therefore, cloud-based security schemes are desired to explore a cloud's resources to secure itself. For instance, Diaz-Sanchez et al. (2012) proposed a distributed video content encoding and protection architecture by utilising the MapReduce model (Dean & Ghemawat, 2008) in clouds. Distributed encryption and flexible key management were also designed. Although the schemes were described in the context of the H.264/SVC video coding standard, the design principles are largely applicable to other advanced codecs.

Privacy management in mobile video clouds is also essential for protecting sensitive user data. Troncoso-Pastoriza and Pérez-González (2013) discussed the enabling technologies, theories (including privacy measures) as well as practical solutions for privacy-preserving multimedia cloud processing. Non-interactive solutions based on homomorphic computation (operation in the encrypted domain without needing decryption) appear to be most promising for mobile clouds. Such solutions can utilise the capacity of the cloud part for unattended, computation-intensive privacy management operations that can be conducted homomorphically whilst avoiding extra communication needs over the typically bandwidth-constrained mobile network part.

In ad hoc-based mobile clouds, a major concern is malicious users if the cloud is formed spontaneously with unknown users. MobiCloud (Huang et al., 2010) considered trust management including attribute-based identity management and data access control by using either cryptography or explicit access control lists. Secure routing and risk management were also proposed based on the awareness of context information such as device sensing values, location, and neighbouring device status.

Furthermore, security concern becomes even more pronounced in the inter-cloud, multi-provider service mobility context. Towards addressing this issue, Kretzschmar and Grolling (2011) described a security management framework to assist cloud providers to analyse inter-cloud security issues, and identify, integrate, and manage different security technologies for secure inter-cloud operability. The Trusted Computing technology can be leveraged to encourage cloud federation and increase inter-cloud security, especially when VM migration takes place between cloud providers for service mobility (Celesti et al., 2011).

Despite all the above advances, further exploration is needed in the joint design and optimisation of system security and other essential management tasks such as context awareness and mobility support in a more holistic manner over mobile clouds.

VIDEO CODING STANDARDS

We focus on the mainstream state-of-the-art H series video coding standards defined by ITU-T and ISO/IEC, whilst it is noted that other open standards such as VP8 and its successor VP9 are competitive alternatives (Bankoski et al., 2013).

H.264/AVC

H.264/AVC (ITU-T & ISO/IEC, 2010; Wiegand et al., 2003) is an international standard for video compression first introduced in 2003. It is the most widely used video codec today and is deployed in broadcasting, storage and streaming solutions across the whole spectrum of consumer products and services. Codecs are available as both software and hardware implementations, with recent versions of Intel processors having built-in high definition H.264/AVC encoding capabilities and almost all modern mobile phones having H.264/AVC decoding functionality. Popular cloud-based streaming platforms such as Adobe Media Server (AMS) and Wowza use H.264/AVC compression as do streaming providers like YouTube and Vimeo. High definition digital television broadcasting is also based on H.264/AVC compression.

The H.264/AVC encoder is split into two layers. The Video Coding Layer (VCL) provides all of the compression algorithms, including motion compensation, entropy encoding and discrete cosine transform mechanisms that are applied to the video content to create the encoded video content. At the VCL layer, a range of frame types are supported. Intra-frame (I) macroblocks (the basic coding unit in H.264) are only predicted from other macroblocks of the same frame, independently from the previous or the following frames. The first frame of a Group of Pictures (GOP) is coded as an I frame. An Instantaneous Decoding Refresh (IDR) frame is an I frame that guarantees a random access entry point of a coded video stream. Macroblocks of Inter-frame (P) frames are encoded by predicting them from other macroblocks belonging to a previous frame using a motion compensation algorithm. Bidirectional-frame or *B* frames can be predicted from the previous or the following frame, or even from both by using interpolation.

The Network Abstraction Layer (NAL) presents the VCL representation of the video content in a format suitable for storage or transmission over a range of transport protocols e.g., the Real-Time Transport Protocol (RTP) in IP networks (Wang et al., 2011). Figure 6 illustrates the H.264/AVC encoding and IP networking process: the VCL representation of the video stream is partitioned and formatted (with accompanying control data) into NAL units, which in turn are packetised into packets (with transport protocol stack-specific headers) for transmission over IP networks. This process, in principle, is also applicable to H.264/AVC's scalable extension (H.264/SVC) and its successor (HEVC).

Figure 6. H.264/AVC encoding and IP networking

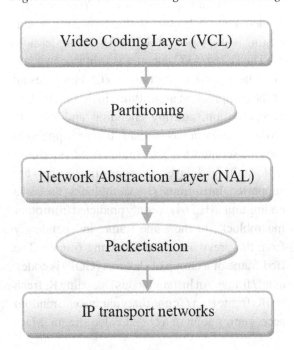

H.264/SVC

The ability to match the bandwidth required to transmit a video stream to what is available within the transmission path(s) is a very desirable feature in any video streaming system. Also, in order to conserve bandwidth and prevent the transmission of data that cannot be used by the receiving client, it is preferred that only video streams that the client is capable of decoding and playing back should be transmitted. H.264/SVC (Shwarz, Marpe & Wiegand, 2007) allows the encoding of a video stream as a number of sub-streams. In H.264/SVC, a stream consists of an AVC-compliant base layer, providing a minimum quality of video, and a number of enhancement layers, each of which improves the quality of the received stream.

There are three possible scalable enhancement dimensions (spatial, temporal and quality) in H.264/SVC. *Spatial scalability* is used to produce scalable H.264/SVC layers at different spatial resolutions. An example may be that the base layer is encoded at QCIF (176 × 144) with the first enhancement layer increasing the spatial resolution to CIF (352 × 288) resolution and the second enhancement layer carrying the additional data required to produce a stream at 4CIF (704 × 576). With *temporal scalability* the frame rate of a video sequence is increased by each enhancement layer. A video sequence with an original frame rate of 30 fps may be encoded with a base layer of 7.5 fps, a first enhancement layer that increases the frame rate to 15 fps and a second enhancement layer increasing the frame rate to 30 fps. Temporal scalability is achieved using a hierarchical prediction structure. *Quality* or *SNR (Signal to Noise Ratio) scalability* is achieved by firstly encoding the base layer in H.264/AVC format. Enhancement layers are encoded at a lower quantisation parameter and employ inter-layer prediction to exploit redundancy between successive layers, and thus the quality increases at every enhancement layer.

HEVC

HEVC is the next-generation international video compression standard (ISO/IEC, 2013a; Sullivan et al., 2012). HEVC employs a hybrid codec design similar to H.264/AVC, and also has the VCL and NAL layers. Compared with H.264/AVC, HEVC employs a much more flexible coding structure within a picture, which facilitates more powerful prediction, transform or quantisation. Thanks to this and other new encoding innovations and enhancements, HEVC has been proven to be able to deliver the same visual quality at only approximately half of the required storage space or network bandwidth, compared with H.264/AVC. Therefore, HEVC is destined to revolutionise the world of video applications, especially for mobile users in wireless networks such as mobile clouds, featured with limited storage at the mobile devices and constrained bandwidth in the mobile network part.

HEVC can essentially support all existing H.264/AVC applications such as broadcasting, Internet streaming and storage, although it particularly focuses on greater video resolution (beyond high definition, e.g., 8k × 4k) and parallel processing capacity. The integration of HEVC into IP networks and other systems are discussed by Schierl et al. (2012). In particular, HEVC over RTP transportation largely reuses most of the packetisation methods defined for H.264 over RTP (Wang et al., 2011). HEVC also has built-in temporal scalability, similar to that in H.264/SVC, which can be explored for adaptive HEVC video delivery in the temporal domain. In addition, HEVC has further improved H.264/AVC in high-level syntax by introducing additional parameter sets, the new Clean Random Access (CRA) and Broken Link Access (BLA) picture syntax for improved random access, more robust reference picture management, and so on (Sullivan et al., 2012). Although the commercialisation of HEVC is still at the early stage, its widespread adoption is expected to take place in the near future.

Exploring Video Coding Standards for Mobile Video Clouds

In conventional mobile video networks, media/codec-aware networking solutions mainly concentrate on adaptive video delivery in response to dynamic transmission conditions over wireless/mobile networks. A Media-Aware Network Entity (MANE) can be deployed to perform video stream adaptation to a network constraint such as bandwidth. In particular, the NAL unit header in the above H series standards can be accessed by MANEs along the end-to-end route for video stream adaptation or other intelligent manipulation. In mobile video clouds, the above media/codec-aware networking schemes are still largely applicable to the transmission of the cloud-processed video over the mobile network part of the system. However, more functionalities in the video coding standards can be explored to take advantage of the cloud part. In conventional video networks, video is typically processed in a serial fashion. In contrast, a cloud video network is empowered by parallelised video signal processing (Figure 2), significantly speeding up this resource-demanding, computation-intensive and thus time-consuming task.

First of all, typical (closed) GOPs are self-contained, independent segments in a video sequence, and thus they can be distributed over multiple processing entities in a cloud and be processed independently in parallel. GOP-based parallelisation schemes are applicable to all the above H series video coding standards in principle. In such schemes (e.g., Pereira et al., 2010; Diaz-Sanchez et al., 2012), a video sequence is first analysed to determine the markers of independent segments. If some form of temporal compression exists in the video to be processed (especially to be transcoded), the key frames (*I* or IDR frames) are identified and then the corresponding segmentation is performed. For a video with open GOPs, where inter-GOP dependency exists, special handling is required, e.g., through duplicating one

GOP after the segmentation point (Lao, Zhang & Guo, 2012). In addition, through CRA/BLA pictures, HEVC has enhanced support of open GOPs compared with H.264/AVC (Schierl et al., 2012), and thus can be explored to parallelise open GOPs processing more efficiently. Moreover, in HEVC, the different encoding modes should be further taken into account. Guang, Tao & Wen (2012) proposed the following scheme: for the Intra mode, each picture, which is an IDR, can be processed in parallel; for the Low-Delay mode, a GOP-based parallelisation can be applied; for the Random-Access mode, a GOP and an extra *I* frame can be processed in parallel. The experiments indicate that the speedup ratio is linear to the degree of parallelism.

Furthermore, finer granularity of segmentation and thus parallelisation is also feasible. Most notably, HEVC has built-in support for parallelisation with the Tiles (rectangular regions of a picture), Wavefront Parallel Processing (WPP) and Dependent Slice Segments tools (Sullivan et al., 2012). This unique new feature, in contrast to H.264 and other conventional codecs, enables HEVC to be more ready to be deployed in systems that support parallelisation. Therefore, an HEVC encoder or transcoder based on a mobile cloud paradigm can designate its multiple cores, processors, Graphics Processing Units (GPUs) etc. to process parts of a picture in parallel using the tools. For loss-prone wireless/mobile networking environments such as mobile clouds, the Tiles tool would be a good choice thanks to the fact that the Tiles approach disregards the coding dependencies and thus is robust to errors. Chi et al (2012) discussed the scalability and efficiency of HEVC parallelisation in more details.

Finally, the rich scalability offered by H.264/SVC can be exploited in different ways in mobile cloud networks. Firstly, in addition to slice or macroblock level parallelisation, scalable layer-based parallelised video processing can be achieved in H.264/SVC in a mobile cloud (Huang et al., 2011). Secondly, to conserve mobile network resources, only those layers that the client device is capable of handling are extracted from the stream at the cloud to produce a scalable sub-stream. Extraction is made at given spatial, temporal or quality levels or at a given bandwidth suitable for the mobile network. Thirdly, if there is insufficient bandwidth to deliver the entire stream, network-based adaptation may be employed. Higher enhancement layers are dropped at a MANE, reducing the bandwidth requirement and thus ensuring delivery of the base layer and lower enhancement layers. To facilitate stream adaptation, scalability information is carried in an extended NAL unit header. Although H.264/SVC has not yet been widely adopted in commercial products other than video conferencing, recent proposals (Huang et al., 2011; Wang et al., in press; Zhu, Li & Chen, in press) have suggested that it may be valuable in cloud-based video applications.

MOBILE CLOUD VIDEO APPLICATIONS AND TECHNOLOGIES

The mobile cloud computing paradigms can be leveraged to provide cost-effective support of various video applications including but not limited to video streaming, interactive services such as video on demand (VoD), video rendering for gaming etc., virtual reality, augmented reality e.g., (Taylor & Pasquale, 2010), video analytics e.g., (Lee et al., 2012), video encoding e.g., (Pereira et al., 2010), video storage and sharing, video authoring e.g., (Zhu et al., 2011). Highlighted here are video streaming, transcoding and gaming over mobile clouds which are promising yet challenging cloud applications.

Mobile Cloud Streaming

Scalable Cloud Video Streaming with Network Mobility

Nomadic users increasingly expect to have ubiquitous access to streamed multimedia content. Supporting such expectations can be challenging for network operators, particularly when the users are passengers on public transport systems such as buses or trains. The successful delivery of multimedia content is reliant upon high-bandwidth, low-delay communication channels that provide universal coverage for the duration of a passenger's journey. The IETF network mobility or NEMO protocol (Devarapalli et al., 2005) addresses the needs of groups of users moving together. A mobile router, handling the external connectivity and mobility of all users, is deployed within the mobile network (on the bus or train). In order to overcome the lack of universal coverage from any one single service provider, the NEMO protocol has been extended to permit the mobile router

(and hence all users in the mobile network) to simultaneously connect to and make use of the multiple network paths based on user-defined policies (Wang et al, 2009). These paths may be from different service providers and be heterogeneous in nature, employing a range of communication technologies such as WiFi, WiMax, 3G or 4G. Although making concurrent use of several network paths can overcome bandwidth limitations and the lack of universal coverage by a single provider, additional complexity in the form of path selection and packet scheduling is introduced.

In Figure 7, multiple instances of both video streaming servers and MANEs are located with the cloud domain where the co-ordination of their allocation and use is performed by the cloud controller. MANEs are commonly proposed in conjunction with using the scalable extension (H.264/SVC) to the H.264/AVC standard (ITU-T, 2010). Doing so provides a means of intelligently adapting the video stream to meet the limitations imposed by network conditions in a way that has the least impact on the quality of received

Figure 7. Mobile cloud streaming system (with network mobility support)

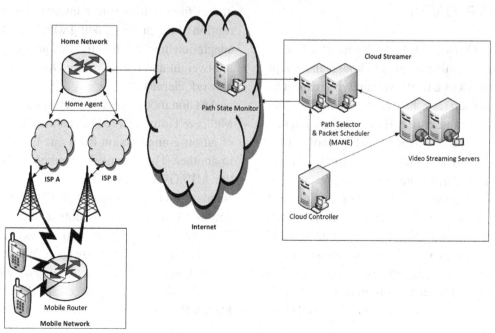

171

video. The use of H.264/SVC has recently been explored in the context of both delivering video streams over the aggregated bandwidth of multiple paths in mobile networks (Nightingale, Wang & Grecos, 2012) and providing cloud-based video content delivery (Wang et al, in press; Zhu, Li & Chen, in press).

The framework for H.264/SVC based streaming over RTP with NEMO, described by Nightingale, Wang & Grecos (2012), made use of information on network path states to inform the path selection and packet scheduling process. Streams were adapted in response to network path conditions and distributed over the aggregated bandwidth of multiple paths. The scheduling agent was co-located with the video streaming server. Moving both of these components into the cloud domain, as shown in Figure 7, would improve the scalability of the solution by providing multiple instances of both entities, each of which could be intelligently located in a cloud cluster geographically or logically close to the home agent which directs traffic from all external sources to the mobile network.

Dynamic Adaptive Streaming over HTTP (DASH)

DASH (ISO/IEC, 2011; Sodagar, 2012) empowers a streaming client to choose and adapt characteristics of a media stream with respect to resolution, frame rate, bit rate etc. on the fly while benefitting from existing HTTP infrastructures. Main stages include creating and uploading user generated content (UGC) by a content provider to a DASH server, generating media presentation description and multimedia chunks, and playing back the received video at the client. To watch the programme, the customer selects the desired content through a URL. While watching a program the client can personalise the stream by selecting a live channel or on-demand program and use intelligent functions e.g., PAUSE, PLAY and STOP.

The server side provides the functions to prepare the media to be encoded and indexed for the distribution, which can take advantage of cloud computing. The partitioner system segments the original encoded video file into video chunks that can be played independently. This feature is the basis for the support of live video streaming, as it turns independent of the media timeline the moment when a user joins the stream (a user can join at any moment of the timeline and immediately begin watching the stream). Take H.264/AVC as an example. The segmentation is conducted by cutting the video data over Supplemental Enhancement Information (SEI) NAL units. Each chunk starts when a SEI NAL unit appears in the encoded file and ends in the NAL unit that precedes the next SEI NAL unit.

The ability to dynamically adapt to different network conditions is implemented in the client media player by a QoS monitoring module. This module collects network statistics data (e.g., latency, packet loss, and jitter) during the session, allowing the client to react to network conditions by setting the adequate attributes for maximising the QoE. The adaptation method by QoS monitoring and session updates is performed automatically in real time, without user intervention or interruption of the program being watched. This QoS adaptation method has the advantage of being lightweight and not requiring QoS support from network elements.

Session mobility for DASH was addressed by Müller & Timmerer (2011), enabling the handover of an on-going session from one mobile device to another. The proposed scheme was based on the MPEG-21 Digital Item Adaptation (DIA) standard, and the Content Digital Item (CDI) was employed to contain all context information in XML and was transferred to the target device for the reconstruction of the session. Work towards integrating DASH and cloud computing has also emerged. For instance, AngelCast (Sweha, Ishakian, & Bestavros, 2012) allows a content provider to have access to extra resources ("Angels") on demand from the cloud to maintain the quality of HTTP-based peer-to-peer streaming in terms of a desirable bit rate. Extending the protocol to conform more closely to DASH was planned.

Mobile Cloud Transcoding

In mobile video cloud networks, the heterogeneity and constraints in mobile users' devices and wireless access network bandwidth often entail transcoding, which convert the original video files or streams, either offline or online, to another format that is playable by the mobile devices and is typically a scaled-down version to meet the network bandwidth limits and the mobile devices' screen sizes.

A Cloud Transcoder (CT) was proposed by Li & Wang (2012) to offloading video transcoding processing and storage from mobile devices to the transcoding facility in a cloud. In this architecture, a user sends a request for transcoding to the cloud with the URL link to the original video file on the Internet, together with the desired transcoding parameter defined by the user. Upon receiving the request, the cloud downloads the original video, and dispatches the task to a transcoder, which transcodes the video to the user specific parameters. Finally, the transcoded video is delivered back

to the user. Cloud cache is employed to mitigate the downloading and transcoding workload in the cloud at the cost of storage. Figure 8 illustrates the generic architecture of such a cloud-based transcoding system.

It is noted that the CT system has been implemented in a production environment, and receives nearly 8,600 transcoding requests every day. On average, it takes 33 minutes for a mobile user to retrieve a transcoded video of 466 MB. The view-as-download function for transcoded video is enabled thanks to the average downloading date rate of 1.9 Mbps. Another commercial implementation of cloud-based transcoding application is Cloudcoder (Zhu et al., 2011), which has demonstrated the benefits of such an approach in terms of scalability, cost efficiency, and time to market.

The successful deployment of CT and Cloudcoder has demonstrated the potential of cloud-based transcoding for mobile users. However, real-time transcoding has not been achieved to support interactive services such as VoD or real-time services like IPTV. Towards realising real-time, high-quality transcoding e.g., for streaming, CloudStream (Huang et al., 2011) employed an H.264/SVC-based transcoding proxy, which first converts the original format video to H.264/SVC and then utilises H.264/SVC for scalable video streaming adaptive to network conditions. To

Figure 8. Mobile cloud video transcoding system

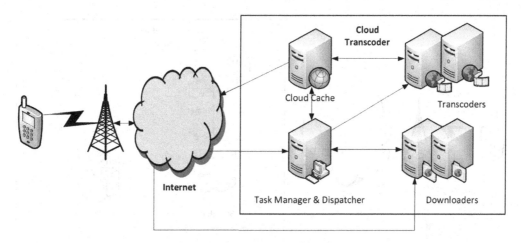

achieve fast transcoding and reduce transcoding jitters, a multi-level encoding parallelisation framework was proposed taking into account both inter-node and intra-node parallelism, together with an optimisation algorithm to minimise transcoding jitters and the number of computer nodes for inter-node parallelism. The transcoding performance of CloudStream was evaluated on a campus cloud testbed, whilst large-scale implementation and testing are yet to be conducted.

Mobile Cloud Gaming

Recent years have witnessed that the online games' requirements have been increasingly outpacing the progress in the capacities of mobile devices, especially for 3D games. For instance, as compared in (Wang & Dey, in press), the recommended GPU requirements of Call of Duty 7 (2010) and Battlefield 3 (2012) are 14.2 GPixels/s and 25.9 GPixels/s respectively, whereas the GPU capacities of iPhone 4 and iPhone 5 are just 0.5 GPixels/s and 4.9 GPixels/s respectively. In addition, 3~4 GB memory is typically recommend for the above games, whilst only 0.5~1 GB memory is available in the iPhones.

Cloud-based video rendering offers a feasible approach to allow mobile gamers to enjoy multiview, immersive experience that is previously only available to desktop PC gamers. The Cloud Mobile Gaming (CMG) framework (Wang & Dey, in press; Wang, Liu & Dey, 2012) aimed to enable rich multiplayer Internet-centric cloud games on mobile devices. In this framework, cloud servers are employed to fulfil computing-intensive tasks like graphic rendering in response to gaming commands from a mobile device, and the rendered video is then streamed back to the mobile device in near real time. To achieve scalable rendering and fast video return, a rendering adaptation scheme, analogous to transcoding, was proposed to adapt the complexity and richness of the rendering to the cloud server utilisation and network bandwidth by dynamically varying the computation loads on the cloud servers and the encoding bit rate of the rendered video. Experimental results demonstrated the effectiveness of the proposed scheme in improving gamers' experience and the system's scalability. Figure 9 summarises the typical setting of a cloud-based video rendering system for mobile gaming.

Furthermore, dynamic resource allocation is essential in cloud-based gaming, especially in the context of a Massively Multiplayer Online Game (MMOG), where numerous online players are engaged in a game simultaneously. Weng & Wang (2012) employed virtual machine servers to replace traditional physical game servers in their cloud

Figure 9. Mobile cloud video gaming/rendering system

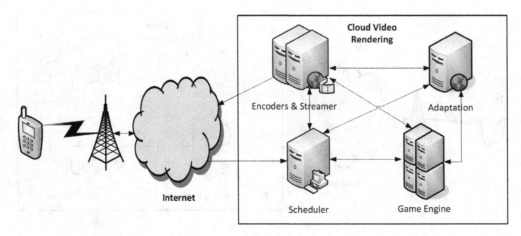

gaming architecture, and proposed an adaptive neural fuzzy inference system to predict the load of each game world zone based on historical game data. The prediction was then coupled with resource allocation policies executed by virtual machine servers. Simulation results demonstrated the cost-effectiveness of the proposed scheme. In addition, efficient management of cloud resources across multiple cloud domains is required for mobile gamers to achieve gaming service mobility and for the cloud service provider(s) to balance the loads among the multiple domains (Liang et al., 2012).

Finally, an open source architecture for mobile cloud gaming is highly desired to promote the development of this challenging application. It is noted that most existing cloud-gaming systems are closed-source and employ proprietary protocols. GamingAnywhere (Huag et al., 2013) is however a notable open source, cross-platform system, whose implementation is based on a range of publicly available libraries. Thanks to its open and modular design approach, customised, new cloud gaming systems can be readily developed, e.g., by changing the default H.264/AVC codec to more powerful alternatives. Empirical evaluation has also demonstrated that GamingAnywhere outperforms two commercial cloud gaming systems.

FUTURE RESEARCH DIRECTIONS

Scalable HEVC and Beyond

Whilst HEVC has reached the Final Draft International Standard status in January 2013, further work has been underway to enhance the capacity of HEVC with three extensions, among which the scalability extension is of high interest to mobile cloud video applications. Through the scalability extension to HEVC, also known as the Scalable HEVC (SHVC), flexible adaptation will be enabled in response to dynamic cloud service provision, user context, and multi-dimensional

mobility scenarios. The same HEVC coded video content can be extracted in different versions suitable for different transmission conditions. In July 2012 the JCT-VC released a call for proposals to develop SHVC (ITU-T & ISO/IEC, 2012). Proposals were sought for spatial and SNR extensions that when, combined with the temporal scalability already present in HEVC, would permit a three dimensional scalability for HEVC that would be conceptually similar to H.264/SVC. Four categories of scalable extension were specified. In each case, the proposals were for a two-layer system of a base layer and one enhancement layer. This lower level of granularity, than can be achieved in H.264/SVC, is likely to have some impact on the viability of directly applying adaptation schemes proposed for H.264/SVC to SHVC.

The first version of the SHVC reference software was released in February 2013, and it does not include either SNR or coding standard scalability (the use of an AVC-compliant base layer), although the latter will be added to the next version of the software. The other two extensions include the multiview video coding for 3D applications, and application range extensions for higher-resolution colour representation and higher-precision for video processing applications. Development of these extensions is currently at a very early stage and is scheduled to be completed in early 2014 (ISO/IEC, 2013b).

Advanced, Intelligent Mobile Video Cloud Platforms and Applications

To promote and facilitate mobile cloud multimedia applications, mobility- and multimedia-ready cloud platforms are highly desired in the future. We envision that more powerful, built-in mobility and multimedia support by design would be introduced to future versions of cloud platforms in various mobile cloud paradigms. Such designs would go beyond the cloud-aware multimedia and multimedia-aware cloud vision (Zhu et al., 2011), and would greatly simplify multimedia service creation and accelerate deployment. We would also expect more innovative designs and implementations to promote the cloudlet and the ad hoc-based mobile cloud paradigms and applications. The OSGi-based mobile cloud service model called MCC-OSGi (Houacine et al., 2013) can run on both infrastructure-based and ad hoc-based mobile cloud computing paradigms, and is a useful pilot in this direction. More convenient, purposely-built APIs for creating cloud-based video services beyond the MapReduce architecture (Dean & Ghemawat, 2008) are in great demand by cloud video application developers and thus is another area requiring further development.

Moreover, innovative QoS- and QoE-aware cloud video services and architectures are of increasing importance to fulfil mobile user's overall experience. There are a number of challenges in cloud QoE management to be addressed, as highlighted by Hobfeld et al. (2012), although some initial studies have been underway. Such work includes modelling and measuring QoE in the mobile cloud gaming context (Wang & Dey, 2012) and the InSite scheme proposed towards QoE-aware cloud-based video delivery (Gabale et al., 2012). Cloud-specific subjective or objective QoE metrics may be required for more relevant evaluation and adaptation.

Regarding QoS, real-time cloud video processing and networking performances for mobile users need to be further addressed, especially in the emergence of the next-generation video coding standard HEVC. For instance, more work needs to be conducted for fast transcoding between existing formats and HEVC, as the recent work on H.264/AVC to HEVC transcoding by Zhang et al. (2012) did. Cloud delay and response time management should be deployed (Dey, 2012), e.g., through transport-layer protocol optimisation and in the DASH streaming case potentially integrated with HTTP or TCP mobility management protocols for improved mobility support. In addition, we would expect more standards in mobile cloud computing to emerge.

Finally, the seemingly unlimited power of the cloud could promote artificial intelligence-based innovative applications e.g., for smart living to an unbelievable level. For instance, when looking into the future of cloud-based entertainment, Hughes (2012) imagined a cloud-enabled personal agent who was able to serve as a personal expert consultant, secretary and carer for personalised, context-aware augmented reality in Sci-Fi style scenarios. Such a personal agent would be able to fully explore cloud-resident intelligence to take care of a person's social life and beyond with learning, searching and other versatile capabilities, far more advanced than the personal connectivity assistant ("Avatar") proposed by Kim, Lee & Congdon (2012), which is nevertheless a promising first step. Such fantastic smart living and working scenarios may be in our imagination now, but they may appear sooner than we think in the future.

CONCLUSION

With the evolution in particular the latest advances in cloud computing, mobile networking, and video processing technologies, mobile cloud video networking and applications are gaining increasing popularity. Mobile users can offload their computation-intensive tasks such as video rendering to the cloud, and the cloud in its own right can create or support a range of resource-demanding video applications such as streaming and transcoding. This phenomenal shift of paradigm is driven by the integration of these cutting-edge technologies and the mobile users' ever-growing expectation to enjoy high-quality, real-time, media-rich experiences regardless of locations, devices, service providers and other personal context. Key technology enablers include cloud and video coding parallelisation, multi-dimensional mobility support, pervasive context awareness, inter-cloud operation and security management. With further development in these areas, future years will expect more personalised, intelligent mobile multimedia cloud platforms and applications.

ACKNOWLEDGMENT

This work has been partially supported by the UK Engineering and Physical Sciences Research Council (EPSRC) under grant number EP/J014729/1: Enabler for Next-Generation Mobile Video Applications.

REFERENCES

Abdallah-Saleh, S., Wang, Q., Grecos, C., & Thomson, D. (2012). Handover evaluation for mobile video streaming in heterogeneous wireless networks. In *Proceedings of the 16th IEEE Mediterranean Electrotechnical Conference (MELECON)* (pp. 23-26).

Bankoski, J., Bultje, R., Grange, A., Gu, Q., Han, J., Koleszar, J., et al. (2013). Towards a next generation open-source video codec. In *Proceedings of the SPIE Conference on Visual Information Processing and Communication IV.*

Celesti, A., Salici, A., Villari, M., & Puliafito, A. (2011). A remote attestation approach for a secure virtual machine migration in federated cloud environments. In *Proceedings of the IEEE 1st International Symposium on Network Cloud Computing and Applications (NCCA)* (pp. 99-106).

Chi, C., Alvarez-Mesa, M., Juurlink, B., Clare, G., Henry, F., Pateux, S., & Schierl, T. (2012). Parallel scalability and efficiency of HEVC parallelization approaches. *IEEE Transactions on Circuits and Systems for Video Technology, 22*(12), 1827–1838. doi:10.1109/TCSVT.2012.2223056.

Chun, B., Ihm, S., Maniatis, P., Naik, M., & Patti, A. (2011). Clonecloud: Elastic execution between mobile device and cloud. In *Proceedings of ACM EuroSys'11* (pp. 301-314).

Cisco. (2013). *Cisco visual networking index: Global mobile data traffic forecast update, 2012-2017.* Retrieved May 30, 2013, from http://www.cisco.com/en/US/solutions/collateral/ns341/ns525/ns537/ns705/ns827/white_paper_c11-520862.html

Clinch, S., Harkes, J., Friday, A., Davies, N., & Satyanarayanan, M. (2012). How close is close enough? Understanding the role of cloudlets in supporting display appropriation by mobile users. In *Proceedings of the 2012 IEEE International Conference on Pervasive Computing and Communications (PerCom)* (pp. 122-127).

Cuervo, E., Balasubramanian, A., Cho, D., Wolman, A., Saroiu, S., Chandra, R., & Bahl, P. (2010). MAUI: Making smartphones last longer with code offload. In *Proceedings of ACM MobiSys'10* (pp. 49-62).

Dean, J., & Ghemawat, S. (2008). MapReduce: Simplified data processing on large clusters. *Communications of the ACM, 51*(1), 107–113. doi:10.1145/1327452.1327492.

Devarapalli, V., Wakikawa, R., Petrescu, A., & Thubert, P. (2005). Network mobility (NEMO) basic support protocol. *IETF RFC, 3963.*

Dey, S. (2012). Cloud mobile media: Opportunities, challenges, and directions. In *Proceedings of International Conference on Computing, Networking and Communications (ICNC)* (pp. 929-933). IEEE.

Diaz-Sanchez, D., Sanchez Guerrero, R., Marin Lopez, A., Almenares, F., & Arias, P. (2012). A H.264 SVC distributed content protection system with flexible key stream generation. In *Proceedings of the 2012 IEEE International Conference on Consumer Electronics - Berlin (ICCE-Berlin)* (pp.66-70).

Dinh, H. T., Lee, C., Niyato, D., & Wang, P. (2013). *A survey of mobile cloud computing: Architecture, applications, and approaches*. Wireless Communications and Mobile Computing.

Fernando, N., Loke, S. W., & Rahayu, W. (2013). Mobile cloud computing: A survey. *Future Generation Computer Systems*, 29(1), 84–106. doi:10.1016/j.future.2012.05.023.

Fesehaye, D., Gao, Y., Nahrstedt, K., & Wang, G. (2012). Impact of cloudlets on interactive mobile cloud applications. In *Proceedings of 2012 IEEE 16th International Enterprise Distributed Object Computing Conference* (pp. 123-132).

Gabale, V., Dutta, P., Kokku, R., & Kalyanaraman, S. (2012). InSite: QoE-aware video delivery from cloud data centers. In *Proceedings of 20th IEEE International Workshop on Quality of Service(IWQoS)*.

Gartner. (2011). *Gartner says worldwide mobile device sales to end users reached 1.6 billion units in 2010, smartphone sales grew 72 percent in 2010*. Retrieved March 18, 2012, from http://www.gartner.com/newsroom/id/1543014

Gartner. (2012). *Gartner says 821 million smart devices will be purchased worldwide in 2012, sales to rise to 1.2 billion in 2013*. Retrieved February 9, 2013, from http://www.gartner.com/newsroom/id/2227215

Grecos, C., & Wang, Q. (2011). Advances in video networking: standards and applications. *International Journal of Pervasive Computing and Communications*, 7(1), 22–43. doi:10.1108/17427371111123676.

Guang, Tao, & Wen. (2012). Parallelise encoder of HM reference software for multi-core/cluster environment. *Input Document to JCT-VC*. JCTVC-K0137.

Hobfeld, T., Schatz, R., Varela, M., & Timmerer, C. (2012). Challenges of QoE management for cloud applications. *IEEE Communications Magazine*, 50(4), 28–36. doi:10.1109/MCOM.2012.6178831.

Holden, W. (2010). Mobile ~ ahead in the cloud. *Juniper Research*. Retrieved February 9, 2013, from http://www.juniperresearch.com/shop/products/whitepaper/pdf/Juniper%20Research%20Cloud%20WhitepaperS.pdf

Houacine, F., Bouzefrane, S., Li, L., & Huang, D. (2013). MCC-OSGi: A OSGi-based mobile cloud service model. In *Proceedings of the IEEE 11th International Symposium on Autonomous Decentralized Systems (ISADS)*.

Huang, C., Hsu, C., Chang, Y., & Chen, K. (2013). GamingAnywhere: An open cloud gaming system. In *Proceedings of ACM Multimedia Systems 2013*.

Huang, D., Zhang, X., Kang, M., & Luo, J. (2010). Mobicloud: Building secure cloud framework for mobile computing and communication. In *Proceedings of the 5th IEEE International Symposium on Service Oriented System Engineering* (pp. 27-34).

Huang, Z., Mei, C., Li, L. E., & Woo, T. (2011). CloudStream: Delivering high-quality streaming videos through a cloud-based SVC proxy. In *Proceedings of IEEE INFOCOM*, 11, 201–205. doi:10.1109/INFCOM.2011.5935009.

Huerta-Canepa, G., & Lee, D. (2010). A virtual cloud computing provider for mobile devices. In *Proceedings of 1st ACM Workshop on Mobile Cloud Computing & Services: Social Networks and Beyond* (pp. 6:1-6:5).

Hughes, K. (2012). The future of cloud-based entertainment. *Proceedings of the IEEE, 100,* 1391–1394. doi:10.1109/JPROC.2012.2189790.

ISO/IEC. (2011). Dynamic adaptive streaming over HTTP (DASH). *ISO/IEC FCD 23001 -6.*

ISO/IEC. (2013a). High efficiency video coding. *ISO/IEC 23008-2.*

ISO/IEC. (2013b). MPEG HEVC – The next major milestone in MPEG video history is achieved. *ISO/IEC JTC 1/SC 29/WG 11 N13253.*

ITU-T & ISO/IEC. (2010). Advanced video coding. *ITU-T Rec. H.264 and ISO/IEC 14496-10.*

ITU-T & ISO/IEC. (2012). Joint call for proposals on scalable video coding extensions of high efficiency video coding (HEVC). *ITU-T SG16/ Q6 and ISO/IEC JTC 1/SC 29/WG 11 document VCEG-AS90 and WG 11 N12957.*

Khan, K., Wang, Q., & Grecos, C. (2012). Experimental framework of integrated cloudlets and wireless mesh networks. In *Proceedings of the 20th Telecommunications Forum (TELFOR)* (pp. 190-193). IEEE.

Kim, K., Lee, S., & Congdon, P. (2012). On cloud-centric network architecture for multi-dimensional mobility. *Computer Communication Review, 4*(42), 509–514. doi:10.1145/2377677.2377776.

Klein, A., Mannweiler, C., Schneider, J., & Schotten, H. D. (2010). Access schemes for mobile cloud computing. In *Proceedings of 11th International Conference on Mobile Data Management* (pp. 387-392). IEEE.

Kosta, S., & Mortier, R. (2012). ThinkAir: Dynamic resource allocation and parallel execution in the cloud for mobile code offloading. In *Proceedings of IEEE INFOCOM 2012* (pp. 945-953).

Kretzschmar, M., & Golling, M. (2011). Security management spectrum in future multi-provider Inter-Cloud environments — Method to highlight necessary further development. In *Proceedings of 5th International DMTF Academic Alliance Workshop on Systems and Virtualization Management (SVM)* (pp.1-8). IEEE.

La, H. J., & Kim, S. D. (2010). A conceptual framework for provisioning context-aware mobile cloud services. In *Proceedings of IEEE 3rd International Conference on Cloud Computing* (pp. 466-473).

Lao, F., Zhang, X., & Guo, Z. (2012). Parallelizing video transcoding using map-reduce-based cloud computing. In *Proceedings of the 2012 IEEE International Symposium on Circuits and Systems (ISCAS)* (pp.2905-2908).

Lawton, G. (2012). Cloud streaming brings video to mobile devices. *IEEE Computer, 45*(2), 14–16. doi:10.1109/MC.2012.47.

Lee, J., Feng, T., Shi, W., Bedagkar-Gala, A., Shah, S. K., & Yoshida, H. (2012). Towards quality aware collaborative video analytic cloud. In *Proceedings of IEEE 5th International Conference on Cloud Computing (CLOUD)* (pp.147-154).

Li, Z., & Wang, F. (2012). Cloud transcoder: Bridging the format and resolution gap between Internet videos and mobile devices. In *Proceedings of ACM NOSSDAV'12.*

Liang, H., Cai, L. X., Huang, D., Shen, X., & Peng, D. (2012). An SMDP-based service model for interdomain resource allocation in mobile cloud networks. *IEEE Transactions on Vehicular Technology, 61*(5), 2222–2232. doi:10.1109/ TVT.2012.2194748.

Mohiuddin, K., Mohammad, R., Raja, A., & Begum, S. (2012). Mobile-cloud-mobile: Is shifting of load intelligently possible when barriers encounter? In *Proceedings of the 2012 International Conference on Computing, Networking and Communications (ICNC)* (pp. 326-332). IEEE.

Müller, C., & Timmerer, C. (2011). A test-bed for the dynamic adaptive streaming over HTTP featuring session mobility. In *Proceedings of the 2011 ACM Multimedia Systems (MMSys)*.

Namboodiri, V., & Ghose, T. (2012). To cloud or not to cloud: A mobile device perspective on energy consumption of applications. In *Proceedings of the 2012 IEEE International Symposium on a World of Wireless, Mobile and Multimedia Networks (WoWMoM)* (pp. 1-9).

Nguyen, A., Senac, P., & Ramiro, V. (2011). How mobility increases mobile cloud computing processing capacity. In *Proceedings of the 2011 First International Symposium on Network Cloud Computing and Applications (NCCA)* (pp. 50-55). IEEE.

Nightingale, J., Wang, Q., & Grecos, C. (2012). Removing path-switching cost in video delivery over multiple paths in mobile networks. *IEEE Transactions on Consumer Electronics, 58*(1), 38–46. doi:10.1109/TCE.2012.6170053.

Niyato, D., Wang, P., Hossain, E., Saad, W., & Han, Z. (2012). Game theoretic modeling of cooperation among service providers in mobile cloud computing environments. In *Proceedings of IEEE WCNC, 2012*, 3128–3133.

Pedersen, M. V., & Fitzek, F. H. P. (2012). Mobile clouds: The new content distribution platform. *Proceedings of the IEEE, 100*, 1400–1403. doi:10.1109/JPROC.2012.2189806.

Pereira, R., Azambuja, M., Breitman, K., & Endler, M. (2010). An architecture for distributed high performance video processing in the cloud. In *Proceedings of 2010 3rd IEEE Third International Conference on Cloud Computing (CLOUD)* (pp. 482-489).

Perkins, C. (Ed.). (2010). IP mobility support for IPv4, revised. IETF RFC 5944.

Perkins, C., Johnson, D., & Arkko, J. (Eds.). (2011). Mobility support in IPv6. IETF RFC 6275.

Rosenberg, J., Schulzrinne, H., Camarillo, G., Johnston, A., Peterson, J., Sparks, R., Handley, M., & Schooler, E. (2002). SIP: Session initiation protocol. *IETF RFC 3261*.

Satyanarayanan, M., Bahl, P., Caceres, R., & Davies, N. (2009). The case for VM-based cloudlets in mobile computing. *IEEE Pervasive Computing, 8*(4), 14–23. doi:10.1109/MPRV.2009.82.

Schierl, T., Hannuksela, M. M., Wang, Y., Wenger, S., & Member, S. (2012). System layer integration of high efficiency video coding. *IEEE Transactions on Circuits and Systems for Video Technology, 22*(12), 1871–1884. doi:10.1109/TCSVT.2012.2223054.

Schwarz, H., Marpe, D., & Wiegand, T. (2007). Overview of the scalable video coding extension of the H.264/AVC standard. *IEEE Transactions on Circuits and Systems for Video Technology, 17*(9), 1103–1120. doi:10.1109/TCSVT.2007.905532.

Shan, C., Heng, C., Xianjun, Z., & Co, H. T. (2012). Inter-cloud operations via NGSON. *IEEE Communications Magazine, 50*(1), 82–89. doi:10.1109/MCOM.2012.6122536.

Sodagar, I. (2012). The MPEG-DASH standard for multimedia streaming over the internet. *IEEE MultiMedia, 18*(4), 62–67. doi:10.1109/MMUL.2011.71.

Sullivan, G. J., Ohm, J., Han, W.-J., & Wiegand, T. (2012). Overview of the high efficiency video coding (HEVC) standard. *IEEE Transactions on Circuits and Systems for Video Technology, 22*(12), 1649–1668. doi:10.1109/TCSVT.2012.2221191.

Sweha, R., Ishakian, V., & Bestavros, A. (2012). AngelCast: Cloud-based peer-assisted live streaming using optimized multi-tree construction. In *Proceedings of 2012 ACM Multimedia Systems* (MMSys).

Taylor, C., & Pasquale, J. (2010). Towards a proximal resource-based architecture to support augmented reality applications. In *Proceedings of 2010 Cloud-Mobile Convergence for Virtual Reality Workshop (CMCVR)* (pp. 5-9). IEEE.

Troncoso-Pastoriza, J. R., & Perez-Gonzalez, F. (2013). Secure signal processing in the cloud: Enabling technologies for privacy-preserving multimedia cloud processing. *IEEE Signal Processing Magazine, 30*(2), 29–41. doi:10.1109/MSP.2012.2228533.

Vingelmann, P., Fitzek, F. H. P., Pedersen, M. V., Heide, J., & Charaf, H. (2011). Synchronized multimedia streaming on the iphone platform with network coding. *IEEE Communications Magazine, 49*(6), 126–132. doi:10.1109/MCOM.2011.5783997.

Wang, Q., & Abu-Rgheff, M. (2003). Next-generation mobility support. *IEEE Communication Engineer, 1*(1), 16–19. doi:10.1049/ce:20030104.

Wang, Q., & Abu-Rgheff, M. (2006). Mobility management architectures based on joint mobile IP and sip protocols. *IEEE Wireless Communications, 13*(6), 68–76. doi:10.1109/MWC.2006.275201.

Wang, Q., Hof, T., Filali, F., Atkinson, R., Dunlop, J., Robert, E., & Aginako, L. (2009). QoS-aware network-controlled architecture to distribute application flows over multiple network interfaces. *Wireless Personal Communications, 48*(1), 113–140. doi:10.1007/s11277-007-9424-7.

Wang, S., & Dey, S. (2012). Cloud mobile gaming: modelling and measuring user experience in mobile wireless networks. *Mobile Computing and Communications Review, 16*(1), 10–21. doi:10.1145/2331675.2331679.

Wang, S., & Dey, S. (2013). Adaptive mobile cloud computing to enable rich mobile Multimedia applications. *IEEE Transactions on Multimedia*. doi:10.1109/TMM.2013.2240674.

Wang, S., Liu, Y., & Dey, S. (2012). Wireless network aware cloud scheduler for scalable cloud mobile gaming. In *Proceedings of IEEE ICC 2012* (pp. 2081-2086).

Wang, X., Chen, M., Kwon, T., Yang, L., & Leung, V. (2013). AMES-cloud: A framework of adaptive mobile video streaming and efficient social video sharing in the clouds. *IEEE Transactions on Multimedia*. doi:10.1109/TMM.2013.2239630.

Wang, Y., Even, R., Kristensen, T., & Jesup, R. (2011). RTP payload format for H.264 video. *IETF RFC 6184*.

Weng, C., & Wang, K. (2012). Dynamic resource allocation for MMOGs in cloud computing environments. In *Proceedings of the International Wireless Communications and Mobile Computing Conference (IWCMC)* [IEEE]. 2012.

Wiegand, T., Sullivan, G., Bjontegaard, G., & Luthra, A. (2003). Overview of the H.264/AVC video coding standard. *IEEE Transactions on Circuits and Systems for Video Technology, 13*(7), 560–576. doi:10.1109/TCSVT.2003.815165.

Zhang, D., Li, B., Xu, J., & Li, H. (2012). Fast transcoding from H.264 AVC to high efficiency video coding. In *Proceedings of 2012 IEEE International Conference on Multimedia & Expo (ICME)* (pp. 651-656).

Zhu, W., Luo, C., Wang, J., & Li, S. (2011). Multimedia cloud computing. *IEEE Signal Processing Magazine*, *28*(3), 59–69. doi:10.1109/MSP.2011.940269.

Zhu, Z., Li, S., & Chen, X. (2013). Design QoS-aware multi-path provisioning strategies for efficient cloud-assisted svc video streaming to heterogeneous clients. *IEEE Transactions on Multimedia*. doi:10.1109/TMM.2013.2238908.

KEY TERMS AND DEFINITIONS

Cloud-Based Video Applications: Video applications that utilise the resources provided by a cloud.

Cloud Context Awareness: Awareness of context parameters/information related to the cloud.

Cloud Mobility Management: Location and handover management for mobile cloud users in various dimensions.

Cloud Security: Cloud security issues such as data protection, privacy, trust/identity management, authentication/authorisation/accounting in a cloud and inter-clouds.

Mobile Cloud Computing: Cloud computing for mobile users.

Mobile Cloud Paradigm: The networking model/architecture of a mobile cloud.

Video Coding Standards: Standards for video compression.

Chapter 10
Cloud-Based Service Delivery Architecture with Service-Populating and Mobility-Aware Mechanisms

Fragkiskos Sardis
Middlesex University, UK

Glenford Mapp
Middlesex University, UK

Jonathan Loo
Middlesex University, UK

ABSTRACT

Advances in Mobile and Cloud technologies have redefined the way we perceive and use computers. Mobile devices now rely on Cloud technology for storage and applications. Furthermore, recent advances in network technology ensure that mobile devices in the future will have high-bandwidth connectivity at all times. This drives the incentive of doing all the processing and storage in the Cloud and using mobile devices to access the services. In this chapter, the authors argue that always-on connectivity along with increased demand of Cloud services will contest the Internet backbone and create problems in the management of Cloud resources. Client mobility is also a factor that should be taken into account when providing Cloud services to mobile devices. The authors therefore propose a new service delivery architecture that takes into account client mobility as well as the distance between clients and services in order to manage Cloud and network resources more efficiently and provide a better Quality of Experience for the user.

DOI: 10.4018/978-1-4666-4781-7.ch010

1. INTRODUCTION

In recent years, Cloud computing has taken the front line in terms of service provisioning. The ability to provide affordable services on-demand along with its elastic nature in terms of resource management and billing has made it a very popular technology for individual users and enterprises alike. Cloud technology, like other distributed architectures, is highly scalable and gives its owners the ability to add resources easily in order to increase performance and enhance the offered services. These characteristics made Cloud computing a lucrative business that has brought many service providers into the marketplace, all competing with their own unique set of services.

Meanwhile, High-Definition (HD) content has now become more easily accessible than ever. What we define as HD content is typically high resolution images and videos as well as multi-channel audio recordings. This type of multimedia content requires high storage capacity and when viewed online, generates a high volume of traffic. As a result, until a few years ago, it was almost impossible to stream such content directly from the Internet. Bandwidth limitations made it prohibitive to watch HD movies online, while at the same time, content providers would have increased storage costs in order to host such content. However, Cloud technology and the evolution of networks, now allows us to store and access this content on the Internet and even watch live events via HD streaming.

However, HD content streaming is not the only thing that Clouds have made possible. Among the latest service offerings, Cloud gaming is becoming increasingly popular in recent years with many providers already on the market. This type of Service-On-Demand performs all the intensive game computations on the Cloud and streams the rendered images to the user, effectively transforming the player's node into a thin gaming client. Since the processing is done on the Cloud, one advantage of this technology is that it makes

cross-platform gaming possible without having to programme a game for multiple platforms. Naturally, in order to make a game playable on the Cloud, we have to provide a low latency connection. As a consequence, this technology can potentially generate a large amount of traffic that is also very sensitive to latency and jitter.

As we will see in the following sections, the increasing popularity of real-time entertainment services is putting a very high traffic load on the Internet and the evolution of network technologies is not as fast-paced as it used to be, leaving us with constantly increasing demand for high-bandwidth and low-latency but without the infrastructure to support it. This however is not a new problem and the use of caches brought the solution in an era when most of the content on the Internet was static. However, this is not applicable to real-time services and a new solution is needed for this type of content. Furthermore, as mobile devices are becoming more popular and increasingly make more extensive use of Cloud resources, we are faced with the second aspect of the problem which is the provision of consistent connection characteristics to mobile users. This is particularly challenging since it is often impossible to predict user mobility patterns and compensate for the changes in their connections. As a result, a mobile node, switching between networks may experience largely varying conditions to their connections and consequently, the user's Quality of Experience for real-time entertainment may deteriorate. Therefore, if in the future we are to provide QoS-sensitive Cloud services to mobile devices, we must first guarantee that the connection between the mobile node and the Cloud is reliable and meets certain criteria.

To provide a potential solution to the above problems, in this chapter, the authors investigate a new service-delivery framework that makes use of Cloud Interoperability mechanisms in order to move Cloud services closer to their clients. This approach can minimise the distance that data has to travel between a Cloud and its clients and therefore reduce global traffic congestion while increasing the Quality of Service delivered to the users. Section 2 will review current Cloud technologies and the on-going research in the field of Cloud computing, as well as the present state of the Internet in terms of network technology and traffic demands. Section 3 will present the investigated framework and look at some of the underlying mechanisms that can be used to implement it. Section 4 presents the future trends and gives proof as to why the proposed solution can be beneficial for the future. Finally, Section 5 contains the summary and conclusions and presents some of the open research topics.

2. BACKGROUND

From the author's perspective, Cloud technology will be the predominant platform for delivering real-time services to mobile clients in the foreseeable future. Cloud's elasticity and scalability is what makes it the best solution for efficiently providing services to users that do not have powerful local computing resources. Mobile devices inherently lack local resources and therefore constitute possible the biggest "client" to Cloud services in terms of providing content to the end-user. In this section we will review some of the Cloud-related research in the fields of resource-management and QoS provisioning as well as the existing trends in wireless and wired networking that will form a platform for future mobile devices. We will begin by giving an overview of Cloud services in the following subsection.

Cloud Services

Clouds can be divided into public and private deployments. A private Cloud belongs to an organisation and is used for its internal needs without giving open access to the public. If a private implementation is used by multiple entities that share the same mission, then we call it a community Cloud. A public Cloud implementation as the name suggests allows the general public to access its resources via the Internet. Furthermore, it is possible to join multiple distinct Clouds in order to form a hybrid implementation that allows its clients to move data and services across the participating Clouds.

Clouds can provide services in three different ways which are presented in Figure 1. In Software as a Service (SaaS), users access software on-demand via a web-browser or a thin client. The second type is Platform as a Service (PaaS) and it provides end-users with a computing platform including software development packages and APIs. This service makes it easy for developers to create and deploy applications without having to worry about maintaining the underlying software and hardware. Finally, the third type is Infrastructure as a Service (IaaS) which provides users with raw computing resources such as a complete virtual network of machines, where software can be installed and used according to the client's needs.

Figure 1. Cloud service layers

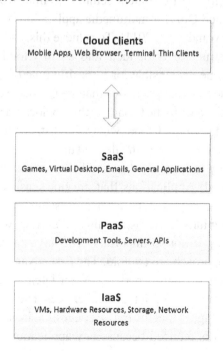

Based on these three main categories of Cloud services, we have a more fine-grained division of them based on the actual service delivered to the end-user. Such services can include storage, security and desktop. In recent years, however, we now see a new type of service emerge aimed at mobile devices. Mobile Application as a Service (MAaaS) is a new trend aimed at providing platform agnostic applications to mobile devices (Rosenberg, 2009). This approach removes current limitations in the way applications are made available in different types of smartphones and tablet computers.

Due to the vast range of services that can be delivered using Clouds, there are many areas of research open for investigation focusing on Cloud resources' management and QoS optimisation. In the following subsections, we will present some research topics that are relevant to the framework we are investigating in this chapter.

Media-Edge Cloud

Media-Edge Cloud (MEC) is an architecture aimed at improving the performance of Clouds. The main focus of this architecture is to improve the QoS and QoE for multimedia applications (Zhu, Luo, Wand & Li, 2011). To achieve this, a Cloud infrastructure is divided into small Cloudlets, each one responsible for a specific type of task. Services and applications that are QoS-sensitive are allocated to the Cloudlets that are located near the edge of the Cloud, where the distance to the public interfaces is smaller and thus, any internal latency induced by the Cloud's infrastructure is reduced. Applications that are not sensitive to QoS or require long-term processing are sent further into the infrastructure of the Cloud where latency is not so important. The advantages of this approach are twofold. The first advantage is that clients will experience lower latency to the Cloud when using interactive services. The second advantage is that the traffic congestion inside the Cloud is reduced because any applications that

generate a high number of real-time data over the network are located very close to the public interfaces and do not have to travel through the network hierarchy of the Cloud in order to reach the public interface.

The proposed project and research presented in this chapter shares the same two objectives with the MEC and uses similar methods to achieve results. The first objective is to minimise the distance that data has to travel in order to improve the QoS and the second objective is to reduce the congestion on the Internet, also by minimising this distance.

Cloud Interoperability Groups

We see how within a Cloud, researchers are attempting to minimise the distance between virtual machines that exchange information in order to reduce the network congestion, make more efficient use of resources and finally, improve the performance. We believe that this approach is also applicable on a global scale at an Inter-Cloud level. We also believe that we can use these techniques to create regional caches of Cloud services that replicate automatically according to user demand. To achieve such a complex task, however, we must first ensure that there is a level of interoperability between different Cloud platforms that will allow Clouds to co-operate even if they belong to different entities.

In April 2011, IEEE announced two Cloud Interoperability groups. The first group was tasked with creating a draft standard for workload portability. The main aim of the project is to establish a portability roadmap that will define the steps into developing APIs, management interfaces, file formats and operation conventions in such a way that will allow tasks assigned to a Cloud to be moved to another without the need to rewrite the code (IEEE-SA, 2013).

The second group's task is to create a set of standards that will allow a system within one Cloud to work with a system in another. The term used for this functionality is Intercloud Interoperability and it will enable Cloud vendors to form federations with each other even if they use heterogeneous platforms. This is done in hopes that Cloud federations will be formed and in the future we will have an Internet of Clouds where resources are shared with everyone and a larger economy of scale is created that will reduce the prices of computing and storage resources while being completely transparent to the user (IEEE-SA, 2013).

The work of these groups focuses on mechanisms and standards that can be used in order to bring interoperability across different Cloud technologies. However, for our purposes, we will also need a framework that will enable us to perform the migration of services automatically in response to user mobility and QoS characteristics.

Bandwidth Limitation and Traffic Management

In recent years, we have seen a rapid growth of multimedia services available on the Internet. Cloud computing is what has made possible the centralised storage and processing of such a vast amount of content. Because of this, on-demand, real-time entertainment is now something that many people use daily. In fact, these services are now becoming so accessible to the general public that 58% of the total Internet traffic in North America is generated by real-time entertainment such as Netflix and Youtube. Meanwhile, the Internet Exchange Point (IXP) bandwidth growth has stagnated since the mid-2000s and since IXPs form the core of the Internet we may eventually experience limited bandwidth supply in an era where people always demand for more (Weller, D., Woodcock, B., 2013).

Heterogeneous Networking and the Future of Mobility

Mobile devices currently use Cloud technology as a means to store user data and make it available online. This eliminates the inherent limitation in storage that comes with such devices while it also makes it possible to synchronise user data between them.

A lot of research in the area of wireless communications is now taking place with the aim to address mobility problems. The area of vertical handovers is popular because it gives us the ability to seamlessly switch between different networking technologies while maintaining active data streams. An example of network architecture that addresses mobility for the future is the Y-Comm ("Middlesex University, Y-Comm Research," n.d.). It is a new architecture that addresses mobile heterogeneous networking based on observations about how the Internet is currently evolving. The constant deployment of new wireless networks and the widespread use of wireless technologies are the two main factors that drive the development of Y-Comm. At the Core of the Internet, where no wireless networks are used, the Y-Comm assumes fast connections. On Peripheral networks where wireless technologies are deployed, the Y-Comm assumes slower connections that are prone to vertical handovers due to client mobility. The architectural layers of the Core and Peripheral networks join at the bottom and form a Y, hence the name Y-Comm. Figure 2 shows the layers of the architecture.

In the future, we expect all devices to be able to switch connections seamlessly between different network technologies and in the case of mobile devices; this will pave a future where they will have always-on connectivity and as a result the connection between them and Cloud services will be available at all times.

3. RESEARCH PERSPECTIVE AND PROPOSED SOLUTION

Because mobile devices inherently possess a small amount of local processing and storage resources, they will slowly become more dependent on Clouds for storage and services. Furthermore,

Figure 2. The Y-Comm framework

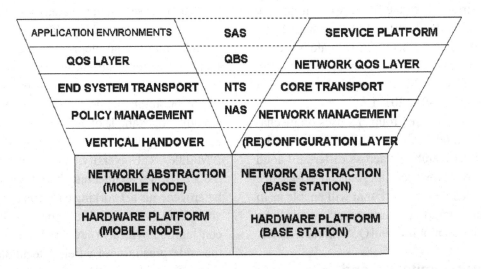

mobile users will expect to access on-demand, real-time content, whether that is for entertainment or for work. The trends show increasing demand for such services and a lack of bandwidth growth to support the traffic generated by them. Furthermore, there are no QoS guarantees on the Internet since there is no global agreement between providers to prioritise packets in the same manner. Therefore, accessing Cloud services from a remote location often means that data has to cross multiple networks. This increases the chances of QoS deterioration.

We are therefore proposing that the distance between a service and its clients should be minimised if that service is sensitive to QoS parameters and if it generates a large amount of traffic that could potentially cause problems on the Internet's backbone connections. In essence, the concept is similar to regional Internet caches for static content but applied to active content that cannot be cached and therefore, the entire service has to be cached. In the following section we will present the framework we are investigating at Middlesex University which will enable the migration of services across Clouds in different administrative domains.

Service Migration Framework

The service delivery framework we are proposing and currently investigating is service-centric with its main focus on maintaining a high QoS by means of moving instances of services across Cloud boundaries. The framework can be applied to any underlying networking technology using different mechanisms and it can also be applied to individual hosts that do not use Cloud technology. However, virtual machine migration technologies are already implemented and offer a solid platform to our framework in the context of Cloud computing.

It is important to note at this point that the presented framework does not provide a Cloud interoperability solution but rather uses Cloud interoperability as the basis of migrating services freely on the Internet, independently of who the service provider and who the Cloud owner is. The motivation behind this is that if we are going to advocate regional replication of services based on demand, we cannot expect that every Cloud should be using the same platform. Therefore, Cloud Interoperability is a key requirement in this as is the ability for Clouds and Service providers to use a standard framework for allocating resources to the migrating services. Another aspect of this framework covers billing between clients, service providers and Cloud owners. It may also be argued that the framework presented is also new service delivery architecture since it deals with how services are allocated resources, how the clients may access these services, how the billing is processed between the different entities and how the service is delivered to the client.

The architecture we are proposing has six layers which are explained in the following paragraphs (see also Figure 3).

The *Service Management Layer (SML)* is the top layer in the framework. It contains a Service and Security Level Agreement (SaSLA) which deals with how services are registered in a Cloud. The SaSLA contains the unique Service ID as well as parameters that define the minimum amount of resources the service will need in order to run in the Cloud. In this layer, we also process billing information between service providers and Cloud hosts. Essentially in this layer we are declaring a minimum set of requirements that the service provider considers adequate in order to run the service in a Cloud. We can also define here, the maximum resources that we wish to be allocated to the service in order to maintain costs within an acceptable range. Therefore, the SaSLA is not a rigid set of instructions given by the service providers but rather a range of requirements

Figure 3. Cloud-based service delivery framework

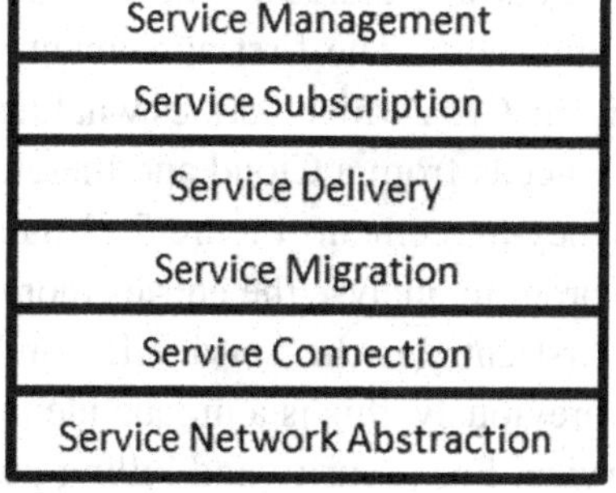

Service Management
Service Subscription
Service Delivery
Service Migration
Service Connection
Service Network Abstraction

that will guarantee that a service will operate within a Cloud in a satisfactory manner. This SaSLA is always reported by the service when it makes a request to populate a Cloud. If the requirements do not match, then the service is not allowed to populate. Similarly, Cloud administrators can set up rules to reject specific services for security reasons or in order to maintain a level of performance in their Cloud.

The *Service Subscription Layer (SSL)* holds information that handles the subscription of the clients to a service. The subscription of clients at this layer does not involve a contract but rather a list of preferences that the client has in terms of QoS. So in this layer, we are matching the User ID, with a Service ID and we hold Service Level Agreement (SLA) information for each subscription. The SLA at this layer allows us to define client-specific QoS requirements such as higher quality video streams, elevated security, higher storage capacity and increased priority over other clients. This is supplementary to the SaSLA at the layer above and also defines how each client will be billed by the service provider.

The *Service Delivery Layer (SDL)* is responsible for delivering services to clients. This layer sends instructions to the layers below it regarding the connections of individual clients as well as populating Clouds. The mechanisms in the SDL receive QoS information from the mobile devices either by means of a separate process that reports this information periodically or as part of a QoS-aware transport protocol such as The Simple Protocol (SP) (Padiy, Riley & Mapp, 2012).

The *Service Migration Layer (SMiL)* is responsible for populating Clouds. It deals with the negotiation and allocation of resources between a migrating service and the hosting Cloud. The mechanisms in this layer will also perform a service-level handover for the active client connections between the two Clouds after a migration occurs. In other words, this will transfer contextual information of the service such as cached user files. We are assuming that Clouds are able to report whether or not they can meet the SaSLA agreement at the current state. It is up to the SMiL to report the SaSLA to the Cloud and then based on the response, either instruct the service that it can move or report to the SDL that the Cloud cannot accept the service.

The *Service Connection layer (SCL)* is responsible for monitoring the connections between clients and services. It is the mechanisms at this layer that send information to the SDL regarding the status of connections and the location and movement of the clients. This information is then processed at the SDL and it may trigger service migrations in order to compensate for network conditions. Because we are dealing with future mobile devices and we expect vertical handovers to be commonplace, events such as changes in bandwidth and latency or complete change of network technology such as going from Wi-Fi to GSM will be reported. The last task of this layer is to handle the connection handover between the clients and the service. This should not be confused with a network-level handover where the connection endpoints remain the same and the underlying network interfaces change. In this handover we are dealing with the transfer of active client connections from one service instance to another and it happens after the client-specific data held by the service has been transferred by the SMiL.

The *Service Network Abstraction Layer (SNAL)* is the last layer in the framework and its function is to make the underlying network technology invisible to the upper layers in order to simplify and unify the process of migration. As the name suggests, the SNAL will interface between the service delivery framework and the underlying network technology such as IP or new technologies such as the Y-Comm.

Mechanisms

In order to implement the proposed framework we will need mechanisms that perform the func-

tions that each layer calls for. In order to gather QoS information from the clients, we use a QoS Agent. The agent is part of the SCL and it can function either as a separate process or as part of a transport layer protocol. We consider this mechanism to be passive in the sense that it does not actively influence connections or services but it simply reports statistics.

At the SDL we need a mechanism that will resolve human-friendly names to the unique Service IDs. This mechanism will have two modes of operation. It will allow users, either to directly access a particular service from a specific provider or it will allow users to request for an abstract service such as weather or news and then pick the best available provider for them. We call this mechanism Service Tracking and Resolution server (STAR) and it functions similarly to a DNS. It keeps a record of Service IDs available globally and in which locations they have running instances. It uses location data given by the QoS Agent in order to locate users and connect them to the closest instance of a service. Once STAR has decided on which service the client should connect to, the name of the service can be forwarded to a DNS in order to send the client the appropriate network address. An example of this process is shown in Figure 4. The SDL is also responsible for the processing of data sent by the QoS Agent.

Messaging Protocols

As mentioned previously, in order to facilitate automatic migrations we need a method for introducing services to Clouds and clients to services. This is handled in the two top layers of the framework. The first agreement we will look at is the CLA which defines what resources a service needs from a Cloud and therefore acts as a tenancy-agreement. Figure 5 visualises the CLA in order to analyse the entries more easily.

The first entry is the Service ID, and as explained previously, this is a unique identifier for each service. For security and billing purposes,

Figure 4. Service ID resolution

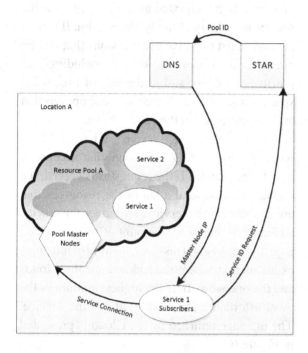

each service is tied to a particular provider ID which is reflected in the second field of the agreement. This will allow Cloud vendors to identify who the service belongs to and charge them accordingly for the resources used. The Instance ID field identifies a particular instance of a service when multiple services are running globally for load balancing. Since we assume each Cloud to only run one of each service instance, this field

may be redundant because the combination of Service ID and Cloud ID can also be used to identify a particular instance. However, in order to accommodate unforeseen scenarios, this field is included. The next field is used for authentication and security purposes. This may be presented in the form of a passphrase that further authenticates a service. Where possible, any identified security concerns about the framework will be addressed, however it is outside the scope of this project to provide a complete security solution for migrations. The next two fields define if a service can be migrated and what level of security is required to perform a migration. This gives service providers the ability to lock their services to a particular cloud and forbid replications. Furthermore, it allows providers the request of a certain level of encryption to be used for the transfer of a service between Clouds. This can be very useful when sensitive services have to be migrated over an untrusted network. Finally, before we define the resources that a service requires, we define the performance to cost priority in order to give service providers the flexibility of choosing between low costs and minimum resource allocation (including bandwidth for migrations) or high cost and maximum resource allocation. Following this, we define the minimum requirements needed in terms of storage, memory and processing resources. We also define

Figure 5. Cloud level agreement structure

Service ID	Provider ID	Instance ID	Authentication
Migration Flag	Migration Security Level	Performance/Cost Priority	
Min. CPUs	Min. RAM	Min. Storage	Cache Security
Target Cloud ID	Source Cloud ID	Requested Client B/W	
Max. Internal Cloud Latency		Max. Latency to Target Network	
Min. Client Security		Estimated Transfer Time	
Service Dependency IDs			
Session ID's and Service-Specific Options and Preferences			

whether or not the cache should be encrypted in order to prevent other services from reading service data that are stored on the Cloud.

After declaring the above information, the following fields are used for service migration. Target and source Cloud IDs define where the service is coming from and where it is replicating to. We are also requesting a certain amount of network bandwidth to be reserved for the clients of the service. The Maximum Internal Latency field specifies the internal network latency of a Cloud. This is useful for Clouds to perform internal configuration in order to accommodate for the service as described in the Media Edge Cloud project. The next field specifies the maximum latency that the target Cloud should have to a specific public network (usually where a group of clients is located) in order to provide a good QoS to its clients. The Min. Client Security field defines the level of security required in the connections to the clients. This can be used by the Cloud in order to secure the connections so that the service does not have to be responsible for that. If the Cloud does not offer this option, it is up to the service to secure the connections. The Estimated Transfer Time field presents an estimate of how long it will take for the service to complete the migration. This can be calculated by measuring the available connection bandwidth between the source and destination Clouds. In the next field, we list the service's dependencies to other services that may or may not reside on the target Cloud. Some

of them may be reached remotely, while others may have to be migrated as well in order for the service to function. Finally, the Session IDs field contains a list of active user sessions that will be migrated along with the service (including user profiles and data), and at the end of this, some space is reserved for service-specific options that are not addressed in the fields above.

Upon receiving a service's CLA, a Cloud will reply by sending a message that accepts or rejects the request. If the request is accepted, the Cloud will also send a list of the resources that are allocated to the service. This gives the service a chance to review the amount of resources and adjust accordingly. This mechanism also functions as an auction where the bidders are the Clouds and the one who offers the highest amount or the most affordable resources will get the service. The message returned by the Cloud is presented in Figure 6.

Following this message, the service will respond with an acknowledgement of the provided resources and parameters and will then proceed with the migration. The message structure is shown in Figure 7.

The CLA and message structures presented above are a draft of the specification and their structures are not well defined yet, however, as the various aspects of the framework are becoming clearer, this will be optimised and the various fields will be structured into a complete messaging protocol.

Figure 6. Cloud response to migration request

Cloud ID	Service ID	Authentication	Response
Migration Security Level		Client Connection Security Level	
Alloc. CPUs	Alloc. RAM	Alloc. Storage	Cache Security
Reported Internal Cloud Latency		Available Client B/W	
Latency to Target Location		Estimated Transfer Time	
Available Cloud Service IDs			
Service-Specific Optional Response			

Figure 7. Service acknowledgement for migration

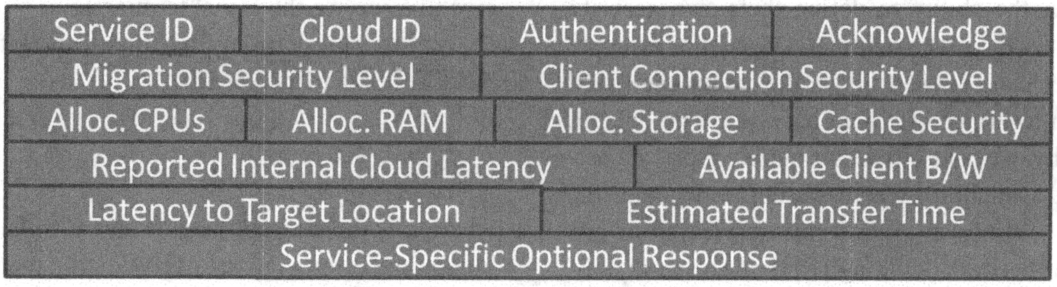

Service ID	Cloud ID	Authentication	Acknowledge
Migration Security Level		Client Connection Security Level	
Alloc. CPUs	Alloc. RAM	Alloc. Storage	Cache Security
Reported Internal Cloud Latency		Available Client B/W	
Latency to Target Location		Estimated Transfer Time	
Service-Specific Optional Response			

The next second agreement developed is the SLA. This represents the functionality of the second layer of the framework and defines what resources a user is requesting from a service. A better way to think of it is to consider it as a registration certificate for a client. It contains a list of client-specific preferences as well as ways to identify the client for billing purposes where applicable. The agreement structure is visualised in Figure 8.

The first two fields are used to identify the service and its provider. The third field represents a unique client ID that is used to identify the client for billing purposes and in order to access a personalised service profile where applicable. The device ID is also given as this allows clients to access different personalised profiles based on what device they are using to access the service. Finally, a client authentication field is included

to prevent impersonation attacks to the service. If it is applicable to a service, the processing, memory and storage resources are defined here along with a request for bandwidth reservation and a requested latency. This allows per-client customisation of QoS parameters and gives more flexibility in terms of billing and resource consumption. Similar to the performance to cost priority field in the CLA, in this agreement, it defines whether the client wishes more resources allocated to them when available and at extra cost. If not, the service will always provide the minimum requested without attempting to scale upwards. The connection security field defines customisation of security parameters for the connection. At the CLA it is already defined what the minimum connection security should be but here we are able to define per client for anyone who wishes to use higher levels of security. Similarly, to the

Figure 8. Service level agreement

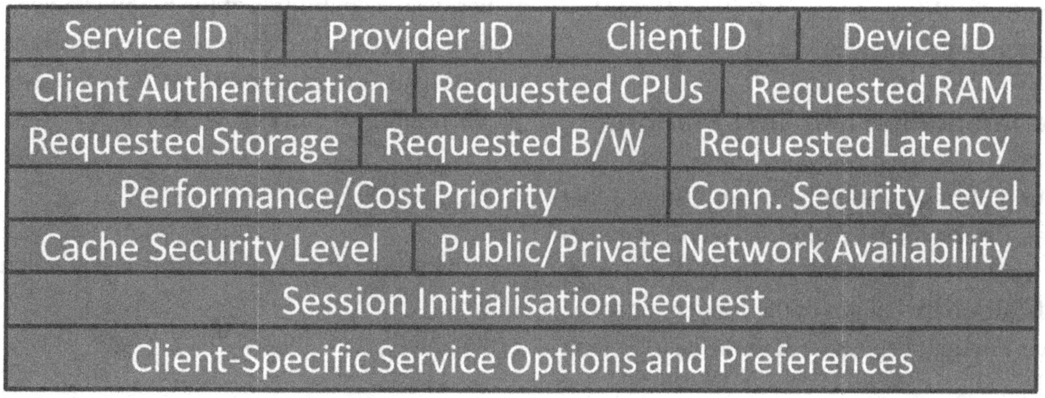

Service ID	Provider ID	Client ID	Device ID
Client Authentication		Requested CPUs	Requested RAM
Requested Storage	Requested B/W		Requested Latency
Performance/Cost Priority		Conn. Security Level	
Cache Security Level		Public/Private Network Availability	
Session Initialisation Request			
Client-Specific Service Options and Preferences			

connection security, the cache security also gives a user the ability to define their own security level for their data within a service. For example a user can choose to have their data encrypted when a service offers no encryption by default. Finally, we have a field for public or private network availability where we define whether the client wishes to access this service from any public network or through a private network only. The session initialisation request is used when a client wishes to start a session with the service. This is only used when the user wishes to start or terminate a session and therefore be charged for the resources used. Terminating a session does not delete the user's profile from a service and therefore this agreement is always in effect between services and clients until one of them chooses to terminate it completely. The last field in the CLA is reserved for client-specific options and preferences and gives us the ability to define options that are particular to a service type and do not fall under any of the above categories.

The two agreements presented here are currently in a draft format. There is further analysis to be made before their fields are finalised and once this is done, they will be used as the basis for messaging protocols that implement the functionality of the top two layers of the framework. The fields within each agreement are not presented in any particular order that is crucial to their functionality. The order chosen is simply for presentation purposes. As part of the development of messaging protocols using these agreements, some message structures for the reporting of QoS and mobility are currently investigated.

Experimentation and Test Platform

For our preliminary testing we had assumed that a user's geographical location and physical movement would be a major factor in the QoS and more specifically in the latency of the connection to the service. For this purpose we devised the following

QoS monitoring mechanism that could be used to give to a service the signal to migrate.

We start by defining the time to prefetch p blocks of data (Thakker, 2010):

$$T_{prefetch} = L + C \times p,$$

where L is the network latency and C is the per-block time of moving data between the memory cache and the network buffers. We want p to be at least equal to the number of blocks required to display an entire video frame. If we look at a lightly loaded network we can consider these values constant. In the case of a mobile environment however, L changes as the client moves farther away from the service which is the direct result of the data having to travel a greater distance and therefore network links. In this case we calculate L as follows:

$$L = F_{n,s,\theta} + F_{cloud} + F_{protocol},$$

where $F_{n,s,\theta}$ is the latency incurred by the number of links (n) between service and client, the network bandwidth of each link (s_i) and the network load on each link (θ_i). The latency incurred by the network topology and hierarchy within the Cloud is represented as F_{cloud} and $F_{protocol}$ is the latency caused by the transport protocol.

We define T_{cpu} as the times it takes for a device to display a number of blocks in the form of audio and video frames. Therefore, T_{cpu} is dependent upon the type of video being displayed and the hardware capabilities of the mobile device. If the time it takes to prefect p blocks is larger than the time it takes to consume them, then we have jitter. Therefore, we can express this as:

$$T_{prefetch}(p) \leq T_{cpu} \times p.$$

Considering the above, this is equivalent to

$$F_{n,s,\theta+} Fp_{rotocol} + Fc_{loud} \leq (Tc_{pu} - C) \times p.$$

For each link we have transmission delay and queuing delay D_i and Q_i respectively. Therefore we can express the total latency as the sum of latencies for each link between the client and the service.

$$F_{n,s,\theta} = \sum_{i=1}^{n} \left(D_i + Q_i \right)$$

We denote the block size as b. Therefore we calculate that the time to transmit p blocks over a link is equal to the number of blocks multiplied by the block size and divided by the bandwidth of each link. Thus, the transmission delay for p blocks over a link I is $\dfrac{p \times b}{S_i}$ where S_i is the bandwidth of the link and therefore

$$F_{n,s,\theta} = \sum_{i=1}^{n} \left(\frac{p \times b}{S_i} + Q_i \right)$$

By combining all the above equations we get:

$$F_{cloud} + F_{protocol} + \sum_{i=1}^{n} \left(\frac{p \times b}{S_i} + Q_i \right) \leq \left(T_{cpu} - C \right) \times p$$

On a lightly loaded system we consider $F_{protocol}$, F_{cloud} and Q_i to be negligible. So a simplified version of the above becomes:

$$\sum_{i=1}^{n} \left(\frac{b}{S_i} \right) \leq T_{cpu} - C.$$

However, in order for this equation to work in the real world, the physical movement of a user away from the service should result in an increasing number of routers between the user and the service.

In our testing we found that this is not the case because a user connected to a 3G network for example, will always be a constant number of routers away from a fixed target (the service). This occurs because the network topology of Internet providers typically places users within a specific layer inside their network hierarchy, and no matter their physical location, the user's device will always be at the same layer within that hierarchy and therefore, will always have a constant hop distance to the target. We are presenting in Figures 9, 10, and 11, some of our traceroute results using mobile devices connected to the Wi-Fi network in London's tube stations. We are also presenting a traceroute using a static ADSL connection. The network provider in both cases is Virgin Media. We must also add at this point, that the target server we are using is located at Middlesex University in London and we welcome anyone who wishes to participate in our experiments to contact the authors.

Figure 9. Bellsize Park: London tube

```
Tracing route to netlag.mdx.ac.uk [158.94.0.56]
over a maximum of 30 hops:

  1     2 ms     2 ms     2 ms  10.108.0.1
  2     4 ms     3 ms     3 ms  brnt-core-2b-xe-030-666.network.virginmedia.net [82.13.111.252]
  3    20 ms     3 ms     3 ms  brnt-bb-1c-ae12-0.network.virginmedia.net [62.253.174.57]
  4     5 ms     4 ms     5 ms  brnt-bb-1b-ae7-0.network.virginmedia.net [62.253.174.33]
  5    21 ms     3 ms     3 ms  brnt-tmr-1-ae5-0.network.virginmedia.net [213.105.159.50]
  6     6 ms     4 ms     4 ms  telc-ic-1-as0-0.network.virginmedia.net [62.253.185.74]
  7     5 ms     4 ms     4 ms  linx-gw2.ja.net [195.66.236.15]
  8     4 ms     4 ms     3 ms  ae1.lond-sbr3.ja.net [146.97.35.173]
  9     6 ms     5 ms     5 ms  ae13.read-sbr1.ja.net [146.97.33.145]
 10     9 ms     7 ms     7 ms  be1.londic-rbr1.ja.net [146.97.35.150]
 11     9 ms     7 ms     7 ms  middlesex-university.ja.net [146.97.136.182]
 12     8 ms     7 ms     7 ms  netlag.mdx.ac.uk [158.94.0.56]

Trace complete.
```

Figure 10. Elephant and castle: London tube

```
Tracing route to netlag.mdx.ac.uk [158.94.0.56]
over a maximum of 30 hops:

  1     4 ms     3 ms     4 ms   10.109.0.1
  2    29 ms     5 ms     5 ms   brnt-core-2b-xe-030-666.network.virginmedia.net [82.13.111.252]
  3    30 ms     8 ms     5 ms   brnt-bb-1c-ae12-0.network.virginmedia.net [62.253.174.57]
  4     8 ms     5 ms     5 ms   brnt-bb-1b-ae7-0.network.virginmedia.net [62.253.174.33]
  5     5 ms     5 ms     5 ms   brnt-tmr-1-ae5-0.network.virginmedia.net [213.105.159.50]
  6     5 ms     5 ms     6 ms   telc-ic-1-as0-0.network.virginmedia.net [62.253.185.74]
  7     6 ms     6 ms     7 ms   linx-gw2.ja.net [195.66.236.15]
  8     6 ms     6 ms     6 ms   ae1.lond-sbr3.ja.net [146.97.35.173]
  9     7 ms     7 ms     7 ms   ae13.read-sbr1.ja.net [146.97.33.145]
 10    10 ms     9 ms     8 ms   be1.londic-rbr1.ja.net [146.97.35.150]
 11     9 ms     9 ms     8 ms   middlesex-university.ja.net [146.97.136.182]
 12     9 ms     9 ms     9 ms   netlag.mdx.ac.uk [158.94.0.56]

Trace complete.
```

Figure 11. Home Internet connection: London, Tuffnel Park

```
Tracing route to netlag.mdx.ac.uk [158.94.0.56]
over a maximum of 30 hops:

  1    11 ms    14 ms    13 ms   cpc4-dals17-2-0-gw.hari.cable.virginmedia.com [94.173.125.1]
  2    28 ms    17 ms     8 ms   hari-core-2a-ae4-621.network.virginmedia.net [81.96.17.109]
  3    13 ms    13 ms    11 ms   brnt-bb-1a-ae8-0.network.virginmedia.net [81.96.16.201]
  4    11 ms    11 ms    10 ms   brnt-bb-1b-ae0-0.network.virginmedia.net [213.105.174.226]
  5    18 ms    11 ms    11 ms   brnt-tmr-1-ae5-0.network.virginmedia.net [213.105.159.50]
  6    20 ms    14 ms    18 ms   telc-ic-1-as0-0.network.virginmedia.net [62.253.185.74]
  7    13 ms    12 ms    14 ms   linx-gw2.ja.net [195.66.236.15]
  8    46 ms    21 ms     9 ms   ae1.lond-sbr3.ja.net [146.97.35.173]
  9    14 ms    20 ms    13 ms   ae13.read-sbr1.ja.net [146.97.33.145]
 10    15 ms    15 ms    23 ms   be1.londic-rbr1.ja.net [146.97.35.150]
 11    16 ms    14 ms    18 ms   middlesex-university.ja.net [146.97.136.182]
 12    17 ms    18 ms    17 ms   netlag.mdx.ac.uk [158.94.0.56]

Trace complete.
```

From our findings, we see that the location of the user does not affect the hop count to the service. Therefore, it is of no benefit to consider a user's geographical location but instead what is important is the user's "network" location and latency. We repeated our experiments in various locations in London using 3G connections on mobile phones and we had similar results.

The conclusion of these experiments was that mobility does not affect the hop count as long as the user remains within the same network. However, if we consider a static user who is changing networks then the hop count does change as the device becomes part of a different network. We confirmed this by using mobile phones and switching between local Wi-Fi and 3G by different providers and we found that even though we were not moving, the hop count could vary greatly.

It is possible that our results are affected by modern QoS routing protocols such as Multiprotocol Label Switching (CISCO, 2013) that results in hiding some of the routers in the data's path but overall the conclusion is that we should not be monitoring a user's mobility but rather the probability of switching network providers as they move. For our next step in experimentation we are planning to use latency as the input to trigger a service migration. We are currently in the process of building a small Cloud at Middlesex University which we will customise with a mechanism that receives the reported latency from a client node and automatically moves a virtual machine when a user-specified threshold is exceeded. In our initial implementation we are using virtual machines because it is easy to migrate them to different Cloud nodes. We will connect the different nodes in the Cloud to different interfaces that provide varying levels of bandwidth and QoS and we will investigate how we can position the service optimally based on where the client is connected. The initial aim is to give the client a good quality of experience and to investigate in such a scenario how much time it will realistically take for the VM to migrate without causing further QoS degradation. The second step is to integrate a mechanism that predicts how likely the mobile client is to remain within a network. To do this we need information on the coverage of wireless networks in an area and we have to calculate how long the client is likely to remain connected to a specific network given his mobility patterns. We call this the Network Dwell Time and its calculation has already been solved in a research paper (Mapp et al., 2012). With this information we can predict whether or not it is worth moving a service to a new location based on how long we expect the user to remain in a specific network.

The testing we are planning does not represent a full implementation of the framework and mechanisms (we are simply moving a machine to another node instead of a Cloud) but rather a simplified scenario that can be used as guidance.

Security

The migration of services could potentially include the transfer of sensitive user data. The proposed solution is mutual authentication for services and Clouds with a trusted authority. Services are required to register with the Service Registry (SR) on order to operate within a region. On registration, a service submits its CLA to the SR and upon storing it the SR responds with a security key and a randomly generated nonce which is the token

for registration. These two parameters are known only by the SR and the service.

The Registration Protocol uses Public Key Encryption (PKE) as Pub(Reg) and Priv(Reg) are the Public and Private Keys of the SR. Pub(Ser) and Priv(Ser) are the Public and Private Keys of a particular service. So the sequence for service registration is as follows:

- **Service to Registry**: [Service_ID, Provider_ID, Pub(Ser), N{A}] Pub(Reg)
- **Registry to Service**: [Service_ID, Provider_ID, N{A}, N{B}, SK] Pub (Ser)
- **Service to Registry**: [(N{B}) SK] Pub (Reg)
- **Registry stores**: [Service_ID, Provider_ID, N{B}] SK
- **Service stores**: (N{B}) SK

To perform a service migration, we use the following sequence:

- **Service to New Cloud**: [Service_ID, Provider_ID, CLA, ((N{B}) SK)] Pub(Cloud)
- **New Cloud to Registry**: (Service_ID, Provider_ID, ((N{B})SK)) Pub(Reg)
- **Registry to New_Cloud**: (Yes/No)
- **New Cloud to Service**: (Cloud_ID, Cloud Provider_ID, ((N{B(cloud)})SK(cloud)) Pub(Service)
- **Service to Registry**: (Cloud_ID, Cloud Provide_ID, ((N{B(cloud)})SK(cloud)) Pub(Reg)
- **Registry to Service**: (Yes/No)

The security mechanism we are presenting in this section is quite basic and it does not cover all of the security requirements called for by this framework. We are simply presenting this mechanism as the most basic security we can provide and we are currently investigating various security mechanisms that can be used for our purposes.

4. FUTURE TRENDS: MORE HD CONTENT, CLOUD GAMING AND EMERGING MARKETS

In recent years we saw the popularity of video-on-demand and other Cloud services rise. We also saw HD content become available online with the option of live streaming. As presented in previous sections this popularity is growing so fast that we now have a very large amount of Internet traffic generated only by such content. Furthermore, on-demand Cloud gaming is now also offered to mobile devices. Application developers for mobile devices often use Clouds to store user data and make it accessible from other devices. With time, these applications started using Clouds for more than just storage. Instead of processing content locally, all content is processed and stored on the Cloud and simply displayed on the mobile device in order to reduce energy consumption. Mobile gaming is taking a similar turn and we now see Cloud solutions that offer games for mobile platforms with all the processing and rendering done on the Cloud. One example of this technology is OnLive and it is available for the two most popular mobile platforms (OnLive, 2013). The important thing to note about this type of service is that we cannot use precaching methods to compensate for high latency since the users are expected to interact in real-time. Therefore we need to eliminate latency inducing factors between the service and the client.

Combining the above two trends with the emerging markets in Asia, where smartphones are now slowly being adopted and smartphone manufacturers are planning affordable devices targeted at those markets (Worstall, T., 2013), we see that in the future we will most likely see a vast amount of traffic on the backbone of the Internet as data has to cross continents in order to be fetched from remote Clouds. We can only assume that when this happens, Internet providers will compensate by deploying faster connections on the backbone, however using available technology to constantly overprovision for the user's needs is not a sustainable solution. As we have seen, the available network bandwidth is not increasing as rapidly as it used to and as new technologies and as new content beyond HD becomes available, a point will eventually be reached where we will have to compromise on the user experience or the availability of content.

5. CONCLUSION

Recent technological developments have changed the way we perceive computing. Mobile devices have revolutionised the way we use computers and access online resources. Furthermore, modern hardware makes it possible to create and distribute high-definition content over the Internet. Cloud technology has provided a solution to the problem of the ever-growing demand for storage and processing resources that are required in order to store this content. At the same time, mobile devices are becoming smaller and lighter and with every new generation more functionality is expected. This is made possible using Cloud resources and accessing them via wireless connections to the Internet.

Despite the high dependency of mobile devices on the Internet and Clouds, there is no framework in place that will optimise Cloud services for mobile users. Mobility can affect QoS in unpredictable ways and one way to tackle this problem is by reducing the distance between a service and its clients and thus minimising the number of networks that data has to cross. This eliminates the number of factors that can affect a good QoS. The proposed framework takes into account user mobility and participates in the development of Cloud interoperability techniques that will enable services to migrate automatically across Clouds.

REFERENCES

CISCO. (2013). *MPLS whitepaper*. Retrieved May 20, 2013 from http://www.cisco.com/en/US/tech/tk436/tk428/technologies_white_paper09186a00800a4455.shtml#wp15329

IEEE-SA. (2013). *Guide for cloud portability and interoperability profiles*. Retrieved 8 March, 2013 from http://standards.ieee.org/develop/project/2301.html

IEEE-SA. (2013). *Standard for intercloud interoperability and federation*. Retrieved 8 March, 2013from http://standards.ieee.org/develop/project/2302.html

Mapp, G., Katsriku, F., Aiash, M., Chinnam, N., Lopes, R., Moreira, E.,... Augusto, M. (2012). Exploiting location and contextual information to develop a comprehensive framework for proactive handover in heterogeneous environments. *Journal of Computer Networks and Communications*, 1-17.

Middlesex University. (2013). *The y-comm research*. Retrieved 8 March, 2013 from http://www.mdx.ac.uk/research/areas/software/ycomm_research.aspx

OnLive. (2013). *Mobile platforms*. Retrieved 8 March, 2013from http://www.onlive.co.uk/mobile

Padiy, A., Riley, L., & Mapp, G. (2012). *yRFC: The simple protocol specification*. Retrieved October 30, 2012, from http://ebookbrowse.com/yrfc2-sp-protocol-v2-doc-d357544954

Rosenberg, D. (2009). Why mobile applications need cloud services. *Cnet*. Retrieved October 20, 2012, from http://news.cnet.com/8301-13846_3-10300564-62.html

Thakker, D. N. (2010). *Prefetching and clustering techniques for network based storage*. (Doctoral Thesis). Middlesex University, London, UK.

Weller, D., & Woodcock, B. (2013, January). Bandwidth bottleneck. *IEEE Spectrum Magazine*.

Wenwu, Z., Chong, L., Jianfeng, W., & Shipeng, L. (2011). Multimedia cloud computing: An emerging technology for providing multimedia services and applications. *IEEE Signal Processing Magazine*.

Worstall, T. (2013). Rumours of two new apple phones this year: iPhone 5S and a cheap iPhone for emerging markets. *Forbes Online Article*. Retrieved May 20, 2013, from http://www.forbes.com/sites/timworstall/2013/04/04/rumours-of-two-new-apple-phones-this-year-iphone-5s-and-a-cheap-iphone-for-emerging-markets/

Chapter 11
QoS in the Mobile Cloud Computing Environment

Zhefu Shi
University of Missouri – Kansas City, USA

Cory Beard
University of Missouri – Kansas City, USA

ABSTRACT

Mobile Cloud Computing (MCC) integrates cloud computing into the mobile environment and overcomes obstacles related to performance (e.g., bandwidth, throughput) and environment (e.g., heterogeneity, scalability, and availability). Quality of Service (QoS), such as end-to-end delay, packet loss ratio, etc., is vital for MCC applications. In this chapter, several important approaches for performance evaluation in MCC are introduced. These approaches, such as Markov Processes, Scheduling, and Game Theory, are the most popular methodologies in current research about performance evaluation in MCC. QoS is special in MCC compared to other environments. Important QoS problems with details in MCC and corresponding designs and solutions are explained. This chapter covers the most important research problems and current status related to performance evaluation and QoS in MCC.

1. INTRODUCTION

Cloud computing is considered as the next generation's computing infrastructure. Cloud computing provides services such as Infrastructure as a Service (IaaS), Platform as a Service (PaaS), Software as a Service (SaaS). Cloud providers, such as Google, Amazon, and Microsoft, are providing more and more applications, including mobile applications. Cloud computing is a large scale economic and business computing paradigm. The cloud computing system provides various QoS guaranteed services such as hardware, infrastructure, platform, software and storage to

DOI: 10.4018/978-1-4666-4781-7.ch011

Figure 1. Cloud service model

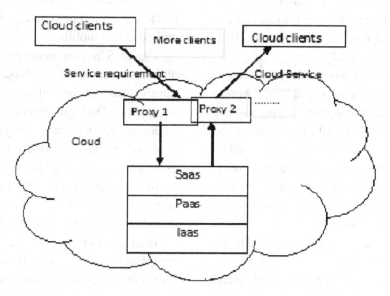

different Internet applications and users. Cloud computing includes resources of computing and storage. It includes infrastructure layer, platform layer, and application layer (Figure 1).

Mobile Computing is a form of human-computer interaction. Mobile computing is based on a collection of three major concepts: hardware, software and communication. Hardware is mobile devices, such as smartphone and laptop, or their mobile components. Software of mobile computing is the numerous mobile applications, such as the mobile browser, and games. The communication issue includes the infrastructure of mobile networks, protocols and data delivery.

The features of mobile computing include:

- **Mobility:** Mobile nodes can establish connections with others or with fixed nodes through a Mobile Support Station (MSS) as they are moving.
- **Diversity of Network Conditions:** Networks used by mobile nodes are not unique; such networks can be a wired network with high-bandwidth, or a wireless Wide Area Network (WWAN) with low-bandwidth.

- **Frequent Disconnection and Consistency:** Mobile nodes will not always keep the connection, but disconnect and are consistent with the wireless network passively or actively.
- **Low Reliability:** A mobile computing system needs to be considered from networks, database platforms, and applications development to address the security issue.

MCC is an integration of cloud computing into mobile network. From MCC Forum, MCC is defined as:

MCC at its simplest refers to an infrastructure where both the data storage and the data processing happen outside of the mobile device. Mobile cloud applications move the computing power and data storage away from mobile phones and into the cloud, bringing applications and mobile computing to not just smartphone users but a much broader range of mobile subscribers.

Because mobile applications can be quickly released and minimally managed, MCC brings new types of services and facilities. Mobile applications include mobile commerce, mobile learning, and mobile healthcare (Doukas, Pliakas, Maglogiannis, 2010; Rao, Sasidhar, Kumar, 2010; Prasad, Gyani, Murti, 2012).

The development of mobile devices in these years has dramatically changed the wireless landscape for both wireless providers and handset users. For providers, the popularity of iPhone and Android-based phones has been accompanied by an explosion in mobile data use. For users, emerging mobile applications such as Email, Twitter, Facebook, video/photo uploading are essentially cloud-based services. (Qi, Gani, 2012)

In MCC, mobile devices are connected to the mobile networks via base stations, such as base transceiver station, access point, to establish and control the connections. Mobile users' requests are transmitted to servers. At server side, mobile network operators provide authentication, authorization, and accounting services. Then users' requests are transmitted to the cloud by Internet. Cloud computing providers to provide corresponding services and transmit related information back to users' mobile devices.

In MCC, mobile users need access to servers located in a cloud when requesting services and resources in the cloud. However, the mobile users may face some problems such as congestion due to the limitation of wireless bandwidths, network disconnection, and the signal attenuation caused by mobile users' mobility. They cause delays when users want to communicate with the cloud, so QoS is reduced significantly (Marinescu, 2012).

Several research papers proposed an optimal solution addressing problem of limitation of wireless bandwidths (Shi, Beard, Mitchell, 2011; Shi, Beard, Mitchell, 2012b). We will explain in details in section 4. Another solution is 4G network. 4G network is a technology significantly increases bandwidth capacity. 4G network can provide up to 100 Mbit/s (for "LTE Advanced" standard) and 128 Mbit/s (for "Wireless MAN-Advanced" standard) for mobile users. Moreover, 4G network

provides wide mobile coverage and smooth quicker handoff to overcome signal attenuation caused by mobile users' mobility.

The QoS requirements are different among different types of mobile cloud applications. File transfer, one of best-effort applications, does not require QoS guarantees. Audio and video streaming applications, one type of multimedia applications, have soft real-time constraints such as maximum delay and throughput.

In this chapter, first the most popular QoS approaches in Mobile Cloud Computing are introduced. At the beginning, emergency management is presented. In a natural disaster, battle field, or terrorism attack, high priority mobile users need to satisfy their requests, such as low end to end delay or minimum end to end throughput. It requires high priority service provision and important data backup. In an MCC system, users' requests come from all over the world. A geographically distributed cloud system is applicable to connect to cloud resources that are geographically "close" to their mobile devices. Some design, such as "WhereStore" is presented (Stuedi, Mohomed, & Terry, 2010). The third problem is service selection. The fourth design is QoS Monitoring. QoS monitoring in MCC is very important for a company's success.

In the next chapter, the most popular Performance Evaluation approaches are introduced. At the beginning the Markov Process is introduced. The Markov Chain is widely used in performance evaluation in many topics, such as networking protocols, cloud computing system, etc. The carrier sense multiple access (CSMA) protocol is one of the most popular protocols; it is also being used in the cloud computing system. In this chapter, a Markov process model for the CSMA protocol is introduced. Using this model, Performance Evaluation can be precisely calculated. A Markov Decision Process is also applied in analysis of collected user profile. Based on these profiles, applications can help other users' applications based on available resources. A game theoretical approach is useful in resource allocation. We analyze Competition and Cooperation of resources, such as network bandwidth allocation, among MCC applications.

The organization is as follows: In Section 2, QoS in the Mobile Cloud is introduced. In Section 3, we presented current research problems and designs about QoS for the Mobile Cloud. In Section 4, we introduce the most popular Performance Evaluation methodologies of QoS in the Mobile Cloud. For Section 5 we conclude this chapter and discuss future work.

2. QUALITY OF SERVICE IN THE MOBILE CLOUD

MCC is a novel computing mode consisting of mobile computing and cloud computing. MCC is a development of mobile computing, and an extension to cloud computing. MCC applications offer several advantages:

- Applications are provided on demand, so cost could be reduced;
- Applications have high scalability; and
- Applications can be accessed from everywhere at any time.

Cloud computing is regarded as the future of mobile computing. However, cloud computing still has QoS challenges. A service provider needs to ensure QoS of its cloud services, especially for mobile users (Zhang, Yan, 2011).

QoS comprises requirements on all the aspects of a connection, such as service response time, loss. It also comprises aspects of a connection relating to capacity and coverage of a network, for example guaranteed maximum blocking probability and outage probability.

In packet-switched networks, QoS refers to resource reservation control mechanisms. QoS is the ability to provide different priority to different applications, users, or data flows, or to guarantee a certain level of performance to a data flow. In packet-switched networks, QoS is affected by "human" and "technical" factors. Human factors include: stability of service, availability of service, delays, user information. Technical factors include reliability, scalability, effectiveness, maintainability, grade of service, etc. Table 1 lists some metrics.

MCC has several classes of applications: Mobile Commerce, Mobile Learning, Mobile Healthcare, and other practical applications (Doukas, Pliakas, Maglogiannis, 2010; Rao, Sasidhar, Kumar, 2010; Prasad, Gyani, Murti, 2012).

Mobile commerce applications are for commercial usage. The mobile commerce applications, such as mobile payments and mobile stock market messaging transmission, provide commercial services with mobility. The mobile commerce applications need to satisfy high QoS requirements, low error rate, low packet loss ratio, high security level (Prasad, Gyani, Murti, 2012).

Mobile learning applications are designed for electronic learning with mobility. Mobile learning applications need to provide users services with large data volume, fast process speed, and longer battery life. For example, students can use mobile

Table 1. QoS metrics

Throughput	Due to varying traffic loads, the maximum throughput that can be provided may be too low for MCC real time multimedia services.
End to end delay	Due to long waiting queues in routing paths, non-optimal routing paths. End to end delay may vary time by time.
Jitter	A packet's delay varies between source and destination and its value can vary unpredictably. This variation in delay is known as jitter and can seriously affect the quality of streaming audio and/or video.
Dropped packets	The routers might fail to deliver some packets if their data is corrupted or receivers' buffers are already full.
Errors	Packets sometimes are corrupted due to bit errors caused by noise and interference, especially in wireless communications.

applications built on a smartphone apps engine to communicate with their teachers. Teachers need to receive students' questions and answer these questions within some time limitation (Rao, Sasidhar, Kumar, 2010).

Mobile healthcare applications help to improve limitations of traditional medical treatment. Mobile healthcare applications help doctors and mobile users to access patient's healthcare resources, such as patient health records, with convenience. Health monitoring services enable patients to be monitored at anytime and anywhere. Patient's health metrics, such as pulse-rate, blood pressure can be detected and transmitted to healthcare monitoring systems. Healthcare applications need to protect patient's privacy (Doukas, Pliakas, Maglogiannis, 2010).

There are other types of applications which could help users to share interests on Facebook and Twitter. Users could also use mobile cloud applications to plan their travel, check itinerary, and check shopping and restaurant information.

Because there are so many emerging applications in MCC, and they share MCC resources, QoS is becoming more and more important. There are several types of QoS mechanisms:

- **Admission Control:** This control accepts and rejects mobile client requests. It depends on available resources and mobile client's profile and policies. These policies include Game Theory approaches. We will explain more details about Game Theoretical approaches in a later section.
- **QoS Monitoring and Service Discovery:** QoS metrics, such as end to end delay, can be monitored by a sampling mechanism. Also it discovers new available MCC services.
- **QoS Analysis:** By observing these QoS values, QoS analyzer can observe which MCC service is in good status, and give feedback to scheduling algorithms for new coming MCC service requests.

- **Mobile Profile Monitoring:** This process monitors mobile profiles such as calling profile, signal strength profile, and power profile.
- **Mobile Profile Analyzer:** This process analyzes mobile profiles specially power level, signal strength profile, location pattern. These analysis results will be used for scheduling and optimization.
- **Scheduling:** Service requests from MCC become traffic to the cloud. At some places, e.g., MCC proxies, they form a service requests queue. Based on policies and priority, scheduling algorithms decide which request gets MCC service first.

3. QoS IN MOBILE CLOUD APPLICATIONS

The rapid growth of MCC and Internet services has triggered the emergence of mobile cloud services. QoS management is one of the crucial issues for MCC applications.

There are more and more MCC applications are developed. Special applications have special QoS constrains. In emergency situations, such as natural disaster and battle field, high priority users have special QoS requirements. For example, healthcare MCC applications need quick response and high security data. Also MCC users are all over the world. So distributed MCC services need to have extensive research. The third problem is service selection. The fourth design is QoS Monitoring. QoS monitoring in MCC is very important for a company's success. In this section, MCC QoS problems and solutions are introduced.

3.1. Emergency Management

The MCC provides great opportunities for emergency management, since data and services can reside in the cloud and not be subject to network and hardware failures due to disasters or traffic overloads. In a battle field or terrorism attack, high priority mobile users need to satisfy their requests, such as low end to end delay, minimum end to end throughput. These service requests must be satisfied before other type of service requests. Recent emergency situations in the world show the tendency that the frequency of occurrence of natural disasters is expected to increase in future. A natural disaster is severe and may cause damage of billions of dollars. After the disasters the destruction continues with outbreak of epidemic diseases, undernourishment, sickness and other diseases (Alazawi, Altowaijri, Mehmood, Abdl-jabar, 2011; Velev, Zlateva, 2011; Zhou, Beard, 2009).

In cloud computing data is hosted externally, backed up frequently, and stored in multiple redundant locations. The key elements are:

- **Data Storage:** A cloud computing vendor hosts data in a remote location, and this location should provide secure access to your data;
- **Data Backups:** In planning for disaster recovery, data backups should be frequent; and
- **Application Availability:** MCC applications should be highly available.

The above elements make sure that users have access to MCC applications and data at all times, even in a natural disaster. Many organizations are looking at cloud computing as a new form of emergency management which will keep business continuity.

After a disaster, cell phone and wired networks are frequently overused. SMS messaging is a reliable tool. However, it does not connect multiple response personnel who are affected. Therefore, using social networking such as Facebook and Twitter is reliable. The Department of Health and Human Services (HHS) had sponsored a challenge for software application developers to design a Facebook application to help people prepare for emergencies and to obtain support from friends and families during its aftermath. Lockheed Martin had responded to this challenge by creating a cloud and mobile based Facebook application called the Personal Emergency Preparedness Plan (PEPP). PEPP applications reside in hosting services which are on Facebook platform. PEPP apps integrate features that provide critical information for emergency responders as found in Google Person Finder and Lockheed Martin's Open911.

In a cloud computing based disaster management system, users could access information, communicate, and collaborate from all types of computing devices, including mobile handheld devices, such as smart phones, PDAs and iPads. With the development of Web 2.0 technologies and more and more popular of mobile wireless devices, these facilitate most population's involvement in the generation, propagation, and consumption of information from anywhere and anytime. Therefore government, army, police, and individuals could interact with each other to achieve massive collaboration.

In a disaster environment, network disconnection is not unusual. Zhang et al. propose a multi-hop WiFi system called MoNet, and a distributed content sharing protocol for a network without an infrastructure (Zhang, Ding, Wan, Gu, Li, 2010). Each node periodically broadcasts control messages about its status (e.g., connectivity). Each node has a neighbor node list and each node's role. The nodes with the shortest path and correct role are selected as the next nodes to receive contents.

3.2. Distributed Services in Geographic Locations

The MCC system is not only aimed at providing fixed services for users in certain areas, but also to establish connections among mobile users all over the world. Because of the MCC mobility, a geographically distributed cloud system is applicable to connect to cloud resources that are geographically "close" to their mobile devices.

This design leads to less round trip delay (Bahl, Han, Li, Satyanarayanan, 2012). Also MAP Cloud, a hybrid, tiered cloud architecture consisting of local and public clouds, is proposed to increase both performance and scalability of mobile applications (Rahimi, Venkatasubramanian, Mehrotra, Vasilakos, 2011).

Many companies and organizations distribute business data is in multiple data systems across many different servers in different locations. In cloud computing, multiple copies of a data set should be created and kept in sync. Data availability, backups and redundancy are crucial to emergency management because it is possible to lose data in a natural disaster. Data should be frequently backed up and stored in multiple locations. A key feature of cloud computing is that information of the users is stored in multiple, geographically dispersed data centers that provide extensive backup, data archive and failover capabilities.

This geographic separation introduces several big problems:

- Long distance leads to higher bandwidth costs;
- Synchronous replication is feasible only if data centers are within a limited distance from each other. Asynchronous techniques can lead to greater data loss during a disaster. So it introduces cost; and
- Long distance leads to huge network latency. Increasing round trip time increases application response time.

Based on the above problems, distance can be a challenge (Jian, Hu, Zhao, Zhang, 2009).

Replicating data across multiple sites is one solution. Caching the data into the cloud decreases the overall data access latency. Also it reduces the probability of when data is unavailable. "Where-Store" is presented (Stuedi, Mohomed, & Terry, 2010). "WhereStore" is a location-based data store for Smartphones interacting with the cloud.

WhereStore borrows some ideas from Filtered replication systems. Filtered replication systems allow applications to select only a subset of information to be stored in the cloud. The basic idea is to find out a pattern to filter out the subset of information. This subset of information is likely to be accessed in the near future, based on the user's current and predicted location.

But how do we find out a pattern as a filter? There are two key indications:

1. One key property is to uses the mobile device location history. A person's past and current location is a good indication of where the user is next.
2. Another key property is the data usage history. What data a user needed before is also a clear indication and hence his future information needs.

Replication systems are commonly used to keep data synchronized between a set of peers. The fundamental data structure of any replication system is a collection. A collection consists of a set of items. Replicas are local copies of a subset of a collection. In a filtered replication system, a filter is used to describe which subset of a collection should be stored in a given replica.

WhereStore is layered on top of a filtered replication system and a location service. The replication layer maintains a collection per application and creates replicas both on phones and in the cloud. The data managed by WhereStore is stored directly within the replicas location. WhereStore operates on data items, groups and regions. Examples of groups are "movies," "work related documents," "text_les," and "reviews." Examples of regions are "@home," "@work," "shopping," and so on. WhereStore creates and updates a set of filters, one for each possible future location, including the current location. WhereStore makes use of the location prediction service to determine the set of future locations.

It is important to propose a cloud provisioning platform by considering mobile users and experimenters to solve the problems raised by the emergence of the popular geo-distributed cloud systems. MobiCloud, a geo-distributed MCC resource provisioning system, is proposed (Xing, Huang, Ata, Medhi, 2012).

In MobiCloud, the system is divided into different types of components which are listed in Table 2.

The major contributions of the MobiCloud platform are:

- The MobiCloud framework is designed, and a novel extension model CaaS is proposed. Components are implemented and a geo-distributed infrastructure is established.
- MobiCloud is a geo-distributed MCC service provisioning platform including elastic computing, secure storage, and layer-2 and above networking capabilities.

Table 2. MobiCloud components

Name	Definition
Computing Component	The computing component is the entity that provides computing resources, i.e., cloud hosts. Cloud resources are grouped into a resource pool that always has at least one master node. Other physical nodes are described as slave nodes.
Storage Component	Storage contains all resource images and users' data. Resource is prepared to store data in the storage repository.
Administrative Component	Dedicated physical servers are for administrating resources and monitoring network traffic within and across domains.
Networking Component	The control plane and the data plane are isolated. There are four networks in each cluster. The data network switch is a managed switch with supper for VLAN that enables VMs from different physical servers.

3.3. MCC Selective Service System

The MCC selective service is a recent problem in research and practice. QoS aware service selection aims at efficiently finding the best combination of web service candidates that satisfies a set of end-to-end QoS constraints in order to fulfill a given SLA.

It is more and more important to satisfy QoS from the perspective of the customer's service requests in the MCC. A proper service selection system is one of the critical steps to solve this problem. The service selection is a procedure of client select service from the cloud. When the client service request reaches to a proxy, the proxy selects a service from the available service list. A proxy needs to consider the QoS of a client's request, such as maximum end to end throughput, minimum end to end delay, etc. If the selected service provider doesn't respond to the client's request, the proxy will select a second optimum cloud service. The number of retrial can be configured. At the end the proxy forwards a cloud service response back to the client.

Service requests are delayed from queuing and retrials. Therefore, a performance and resource allocation model should understand these effects. The process can be modeled in several ways, but a very helpful approach is given in Figure 2. It shows a Markov Chain for a single proxy server, and the Markov chain models a retrial process. Markov chains assume each request arrives without memory of previous requests and the solutions are tractable.

Each state signifies the number of requests that are queued at the servers and the backoff process that is used if requests collide so client can try again. States down each column correspond to the retrial process, and each column represents the number of requests that are queued. For example in Table 3, service requests arrive for a

Figure 2. Markov chain model for service selection process

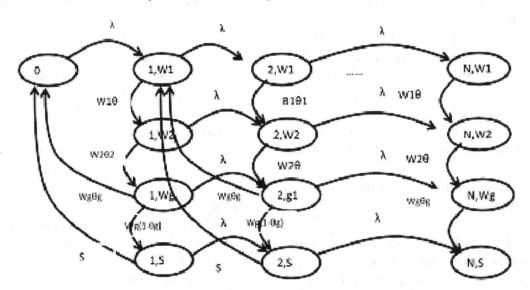

Table 3. Markov chain notation and description

Notation	Description
(n, W_1)	Queue occupancy is n, and in the first stage
(0)	Steady state probability at the proxy when it is idle
(n, g)	Steady state probability at the proxy when queue occupancy is n, and in gth stage
Λ	Service request arrival rate to the proxy
W_g	Backoff retrial rate at stage g
θ_g	Probability that a request failed to receive service at stage g

proxy from State (0); then a try is made in state (1, W1). A failed service request occurs there with probability θ_1, after which the system state goes to state (1, w2) and takes on a random backoff wait time, then tries again, with probability of success θ_2. If a service request is successful, the system state goes to (1,S) where the request is served. These models can be applied to systems not necessarily following a binary exponential retrial rule.

Solutions to this system are provided in Shi, Beard, Mitchell, (2009) and Shi, Beard, Mitchell, (2012a).

It is also feasible to model the selection for service request in the proxy as an M/G/1/N process. The service request arrival rate is assumed to follow an exponential distribution, which is expressed as "M." The service process can follow any general distribution, which is expressed as "G." "1" stands for only one service is selected at one time. "N" is the length of the queue in the proxy for this type of service application. This model can be used to evaluate performance of the service selection process. Similar models can be referred to in reference papers Shi, Beard, Mitchell (2009), Shi, Beard, Mitchell (2012a) and Shi, Beard, Mitchell (2012b).

3.4. QoS Monitoring

QoS monitoring in the MCC is very important for a company's success. Evaluation of actual service quality is a mission-critical business practice requirement (Romano, De Mari, Jerzak, Fetzer, 2011).

Top management challenges are as follows (ZOHO Corporation, White Paper from Manage Engine):

- Inability to identify applications that could be seamlessly moved to the cloud;
- Inability to make educated decisions about adding or terminating cloud resources;
- Inability to monitor performance of applications that are being "pulled" from different resources; and
- Improving scalability of the infrastructure creates heterogeneous environments that are more difficult to manage.

As a design of QoS monitoring, it must be able to track the evolution of services and must be able to provide continuous QoS monitoring, even while there are any changes taking place, such as cloud infrastructure changes and networking changes are taking place. QoS monitoring scenarios can exist such as:

- Run-time monitoring of the hosting environment in order to detect possible deviations of the delivered QoS from that specified in the SLA; and
- Requesting application hosting environment reconfiguration, if delivered QoS deviates from SLA.

QoS monitoring includes retrieving QoS parameters from the SLA between service provider and requester. QoS monitoring is a discrete process with determined intervals. Since the QoS monitoring module periodically performs checking, if the QoS levels of service are lower than an accepted level of the request, a service request module will be notified to launch a new request to discover a new service satisfying the new requirements. QoS monitoring needs to monitor performance of direct applications, but also the different computing resources on which these applications depend. Normally it is easier to monitor the performance of applications that are hosted at a single server as opposed to the performance of composite applications that using computing resources from different sources. Notice QoS monitoring traffic consumes some bandwidth, so it needs to keep the balance of regular traffic and QoS monitoring traffic.

QoS-MonaaS (QoS Monitoring as a Service) is a QoS monitoring facility. The reliable and timely QoS monitoring service allows a business process to monitor any failure caused by the cloud service provider, the network infrastructure.

4. A MODELING METHOD FOR QoS IN THE MCC

The MCC environment is very dynamic. System load and the computing resource utilization exhibit a rapidly changing characteristic over time. Cloud service providers' over-provision the computing resources to accommodate the peak service requests and system resources but these are under-utilized when service requests are not overloaded. The often significantly under-utilized cloud resources lead to the potential of exploiting surplus resources for jobs in cloud systems.

The MCC has many advantages for mobile users and service providers. By using the MCC, both the data storage and the data processing happen outside of the mobile device. MCC applications move the computing power and data storage away from mobile phones and into the cloud.

However, because of the integration of cloud computing and mobile networks, which are two different areas, MCC has many technical challenges. This section presents research progress in MCC QoS methodologies. Then, the available solutions to address these issues are reviewed.

Generally, a Markov Chain can be applied to build a QoS model at each single node in an MCC. Then a game approach can be applied to analyze competition and cooperation among MCC nodes. And scheduling algorithms can be applied to schedule workload among MCC nodes.

4.1. Markov Process

There is a sequence of random variables X_1, X_2, X_n. Starting from one of these states, transition happens successively from one state to an adjacent state. Each move is called a step.

Given the present state, the future and past states are independent. It is expressed in formula as:

$$\Pr(X_{n+1} = x_{n+1} \mid X_1 = x_1, X_i = x_i, X_n = x_n)$$
$$= \Pr(X_{n+1} = x_{n+1} \mid X_n = x_n)$$

Markov chain can be described as a directed graph. Each edge is labeled by the probabilities when a state changes to another state. If the current state is x_i, it moves to state x_j with a probability p_{ij}. The probabilities p_{ij} are called transition probabilities.

The Markov property refers to the memoryless property of a stochastic process. The Markov property means the conditional probability of the future states depends only upon the present state, not on the sequence of events that happened before the current state. Of course, in real applications such properties are not always true, but in many cases this is a fair approximation and allows for tractable analytic analysis.

The Markov process is also useful in performance evaluation of networking protocols. CSMA protocols are some of the most widely used networking protocols in WiFi and LTE. MCC applications heavily depend on this type of protocols random access is much more practical in many situations instead of centralized control. CSMA relies on the random deferment of frame transmissions, e.g., binary exponential backoff, in a shared wireless channel network. These types of MAC protocols are widely used and are being proposed in many new protocols, such as 4G wireless systems, ad hoc networks, etc. Generally, it is assumed that all nodes obey the protocol rules but there is no centralized controller.

A new set of models in CSMA systems is provided, which is accurate over all ranges of potential offered loads (Shi, Beard, Mitchell, 2009; Shi, Beard, Mitchell, 2007). Matrix exponential distributions are used to model performance.

In section 3.3, a Markov Chain is applied to the service selection process in the MCC. Using the model in Figure 2 of a Markov chain model for service selection process, performance metrics of service request, such as delay and throughput, could be evaluated at an MCC proxy server. The Markov Chain model can also be applied to an MCC server from which MCC services are provided.

This author has been performing Performance Evaluation Modeling using Markov Chain for years, especially more advanced approaches using Matrix Exponential distributions that allow close approximations to General distributions. The Markov chain has been intensively used in operating system, databases, networks, and system design. The Markov Chain is a very useful tool for mathematical modeling.

There are different types of Markov Chains, which generally can be divided into M/M, M/G, G/M, G/G systems. Here M stands for the Markov memoryless property, which means it is an exponential process. G stands for general; i.e., it can be a process with any distribution (Lipsky, 2006). Depending on the system to be modeled, a researcher could choose one of the four types above.

Real world systems are complicated. An exact model could have millions of states. Mathematically even if it is still possible to be expressed in formulas, this still introduces a very expensive computational cost. So model approximation is a feasible methodology. One type of approximation is changing from a G/G model to M/G or M/M model (Shi, Beard, Mitchell, 2012a). The second approach is to decompose a complicated model into several simpler models (Shi, Beard, Mitchell,

2012b; Shi, Beard, Mitchell, 2008). Using approximation, models could be much simpler and model calculation requires much less resources.

One disadvantage is that approximation will introduce inaccuracy. However, depending on model requirement, the disadvantage will be offset by the benefits. In Shi, Beard, Mitchell, (2012a) and Shi, Beard, Mitchell, (2012b), the number of states in the model is reduced from millions to thousands and accuracy is only affected very little. But one big problem is that model approximation has no formal steps to follow. It heavily depends on system characteristics and researcher's experience. Once the performance model is built, researchers can easily adjust formula parameters to satisfy QoS constraints.

4.2. Scheduling Algorithms

Job scheduling is one of the major activities performed in cloud computing. To efficiently increase the working of cloud computing environments, job scheduling is one the tasks performed to gain maximum profit.

A scheduling algorithm decides which threads, processes or data flows are given access to system resources (e.g. network bandwidth). A scheduling algorithm is used to load balance a system effectively and satisfy a QoS requirement.

The main concerns of a scheduling algorithm in the MCC are listed in Table 4.

Table 4. A scheduling algorithm main concerns

Throughput Latency	The Total Number of Processes that Complete their Execution per Time Unit
Turnaround time	Total time between submission of a process and its completion
Response time	Amount of time it takes from when a request was submitted until the first response is produced.
Fairness/ Waiting Time	Equal CPU time to each process (or more generally appropriate times according to each process' priority). It is the time for which the process remains in the ready queue.

In practice, these goals often conflict (e.g. throughput vs. latency), thus a scheduler will implement a suitable compromise. Preference is given to any one of the above mentioned concerns depending upon the user's needs and objectives.

Job scheduling problems are of paramount importance relating to the efficiency of cloud computing facilities. Scheduling algorithms usually spread workload on processors and maximizing their utilization and minimizing the total task execution time. Scheduling algorithm plays the key role. The target is to schedule jobs to minimum resources in a proper sequence under service request constraints (Li, Qiu, Ming, Quan, Qin, Gu, 2012; Yamauchi, Kurihara, Otomo, Teranishi, Suzuki, Yamashita, 2012; Zhou & Beard, 2007).

However, there are not many research papers dealing with cloud computing service providers to meet cloud computing task QoS requirement.

By analysis the differentiated QoS requirements of cloud computing jobs, a non-preemptive priority M/G/1 queuing model is built (Li, 2009). The target is to gain the maximum profits. A system cost function is built for this queuing model. Based on the queuing model and system cost function, the corresponding strategy and algorithm are given to get the approximate optimistic value of service for each job. It is proved that this approach not only can guarantee the QoS requirements of the users' jobs, but also can make the maximum profits for the cloud computing service providers.

Scheduling algorithms are widely used in QoS research problems. Different scheduling algorithms are applied to applications based on different constraints. How to use scheduler depends on QoS constraints.

Preemptive scheduling algorithms are used to satisfy emergency QoS constraints. It is capable of forcibly removing non-emergency tasks from queue, so emergency task can use resource. The key idea in preemptive scheduling is to set strict criteria between emergency and non-emergency task.

In Priority scheduling there exist multiple queues. Each queue has different priority based on QoS requirements, and each task in a queue has the same priority. Scheduler allocates resources to task with comparatively higher priority. For example, in the selective service process we introduced in section 3.3, there could be more than one service request queue in proxy. By using priority scheduling, proxy can decide from which priority queue a service request needs to be pulled out and send to cloud service. The multiple-queue system is shown in Figure 3.

Round robin scheduling algorithm is the most popular scheduler in industry. The advantage is its stable performance and easy implementation. The disadvantage is that standard round robin cannot differentiate task priority. So weighted round robin scheduler is developed.

4.3. Game Theory Methodology

Game Theory is designed to address situations in which the outcome of a person's decision depends not just on how they choose among several options, but also on the choices made by the people they are interacting with. Game theory is mainly used in economics, political science, psychology, and logic (Nash, 1950).

A game consists of a set of players, a set of strategies, and a specification of payoffs for each combination of strategies. A game could be divided into two categories: cooperative games and non-cooperative games. A cooperative game is a game where groups of players ("coalitions") may enforce cooperative behavior; hence the game is a competition between coalitions of players. A non-cooperative game is a game where players make decisions independently. Because of that, even though players could cooperate, it must be self-dependent. A game theoretical approach is useful in resource allocation. Game theoretical approaches can help to resolve the problem of limitation of wireless bandwidth.

A new method was presented for the study of the competition and cooperation relationships among nodes in a network using a CSMA protocol in Shi, Beard, Mitchell (2011) and Shi, Beard, Mitchell (2012b). A QoS model is obtained after applying a Markov Chain. The QoS models developed with a Markov Chain can be applied with Particle Swarm Optimization (PSO) and Game Theory to find optimal solutions. Other heuristic algorithms can also be applied based on our model. Optimal results applying PSO are presented in the referenced paper Shi, Beard, Mitchell (2012a). The choice of which one to use would depend on differences in their implementation complexity, desired modeling accuracy, and computation time. Meanwhile, these models have strong extensibility because more variables, such as power and cost, can be included.

Assume this scenario: There are four proxies, numbered 1, 2, 3, 4. Proxy 1 can access cloud resource set 1; Proxy 2 can access cloud resource set 2; Proxy 3 has set 3; Proxy 4 has set 4. Set 1 and set 2 have intersections. Due to some reason, e.g., policy or location, set 1 and set 3 have no intersection, which means proxy 1 and 3 cannot access the same resources in the cloud. Based on the same logic, set 2 and 3 have intersection, and set 2 and 4 have no intersection. Set 3 and 4 have intersection. These relationships are described in Table 5.

Given our equations, Table 6 was developed. It shows how π_i, the probability of a successful service request, changes with respect to changes in w_i, the backoff rate that is used when service

Figure 3. Multiple queues with different priority

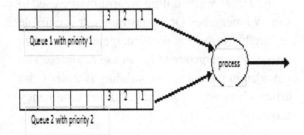

Table 5. Resource set intersection relationship

	Set 1	Set 2	Set 3	Set 4
Set 1	N.A.	Y	N	N
Set 2	Y	N.A.	Y	N
Set 3	N	Y	N.A.	Y
Set 4	N	N	Y	N.A.

Table 6. $\pi_{i,s}$ first derivative with respect to b_j

	π_1	π_2	π_3	π_4
$w_1 \uparrow$	↑	↓	↓	↓
$w_2 \uparrow$	↓	↑	↓	↓
$w_3 \uparrow$	↓	↓	↑	↓
$w_4 \uparrow$	↓	↓	↓	↑

requests use random backoff to avoid collisions. Again, π_i is probability that a service request is successful to provide throughput at proxy "i." Consider if proxy 1 increases its backoff rate w_1, which means it backs off more often per time unit or backs off less time per backoff. If proxy 1 increases w_1 to make $w_1 >> w_2$, because set 1 and set 2 have intersection, then service requests from proxy 1 has more chance to get cloud service than proxy 2 requests because they try more often. This makes π_1 increase, signified by "↑" and $\pi_2 \downarrow$. If $\pi_2 \downarrow$, proxy 2 will try to get service from resources in set 2, but mostly not in the part of set 1 and set 2 intersection. This makes proxy 2 compete for resources with proxy 3 and makes $\pi_3 \downarrow$. Proxy 3 makes the same effort. This introduces the same effect to proxy 4, which makes $\pi_4 \downarrow$. This is a domino effect. In consequence, proxy 2, 3, 4 will increase w_2, w_3 and w_4. If this process keeps on going, then it will be an avalanche. In an avalanche situation, no proxy can benefit. It is a "lose-lose" game. So the question is: if proxy 1 wants to increase π_1, how much to change to w_1? This change should be in the acceptable range to affect changes to π_2, π_3, and π_4. And if proxy 2, 3, and 4 want to do corresponding change to w_2, w_3, and w_4,

how much should the change be? If every proxy increases w_i infinitely, then no one get resources. It becomes a "lose-lose" situation (Shi, Beard, Mitchell, 2012a).

Here we could use the models derived from Markov theory we introduced in section 3.3 and 4.3. Markov models provide a set of formulas for performance evaluation. Combining these formulas and the game approach analysis introduced in this section provides a new understanding of performance effects from competition and cooperation relationships among proxies in an MCC environment. Furthermore, analysis shows there exists self-organized behavior in proxies' competition and cooperation. This type of game approach analysis could be used in MCC to optimize service QoS. Each application acts like a person and these applications can group themselves. So competition and cooperation exists among all applications. That's why concepts "friend," "enemy" are proposed (Shi, Beard, Mitchell, 2012b; Shi, Beard, Mitchell, 2011).

Cloud computing providers can cooperate to establish a resource pool to support and offer services to mobile cloud users. The cooperative behavior of multiple cloud providers is studied (Niyato, Vasilakos, Kun, 2011). A hierarchical cooperative game model is presented. A performance evaluation is presented to investigate the decision making of cloud providers. This performance evaluation proves cooperation that can lead to the higher profit. All applications are competing for resources. Meanwhile, currently applications are programmable, which means applications can intelligently select strategies to maximize their QoS benefits. That's why Game Theory is more and more attractive to researchers.

Game theory is useful to identify competition and cooperation relationships. It is even more powerful when combined with mathematical performance models. This combination introduces quantitative analysis. Researchers could use formulas to analyze individual competition and cooperation, and group behavior. Not only this, optimization solutions can be further developed. Artificial intelligence algorithms, such as particle swarm and simulated annealing optimizations, are developed based on quantitative probability models (Kennedy, Eberhart, 1995; Bertsimas, Tsitsiklis, 1993). QoS metrics can be calculated based on these models.

5. CONCLUSION AND FUTURE WORK

There are several classes of MCC applications: Mobile Commerce, Mobile Learning, Mobile Healthcare, and other practical applications. Each class of application has its own QoS constraints. Mobile commerce applications are used for commercial usage. Mobile commerce applications need to satisfy high QoS requirements, low error rate, low packet loss ratio, high security level. Mobile learning applications are designed for electronic learning with mobility. Mobile learning applications need to provide users services with large data volume, fast process speed, and longer battery life. Mobile healthcare applications help to improve limitations of traditional medical treatment. Healthcare applications need to protect patient's privacy. Other types of applications also need to satisfy QoS constraints low packet loss rate, low end to end delay, etc.

As more and more MCC applications are developed, there are two main problems:

1. More MCC applications will have more complicated combinations of QoS constrains, and
2. Cloud computing resources will be shared by more users.

These problems raise demands for optimal solutions about how to manage and allocate cloud computing resources.

The QoS-aware service selection problem is by given the user service mashup requirements and QoS constraints, how to

*   Select the required service instances,
*   Route the data flows through these instances, and
*   Satisfy QoS requirements.

One challenging problem is finding service paths. The difficulty is to find a route path to the correct service provider meanwhile still satisfying applications' QoS constraints and resource requirements. A Markov chain can be applied to build a QoS model at each node in the MCC. Then QoS models can be used to study QoS along each service routing path. A game theory approach can also be used to analyze competition and cooperation among each service routing path in MCC.

Now, cloud service is an application programming platform where developers can create new applications and mashup the functionality offered by others. Services mashup provides a method to build distributed and dynamical large-scale Internet applications. A large number of services can be found for realizing a small piece of a big task. So how to schedule workload to participate in the composition is important. Distributed parallel scheduling methodologies need to be well designed for this problem.

Due to energy constraints on a mobile device, it is important to improve performance of applications. Since many applications are using XML, it has been shown that a significant fraction of the performance overhead is incurred by XML parsing. Related topics are combining bus bandwidth utilization, hardware cost, and energy consumption. Study in this area could help to improve performance of MCC applications, furthermore, to satisfy QoS requirements (Tang, Thanarungroj, Liu, Liu, Gu & Gaudiot, 2013; Tang, Liu, Liu, Gu & Gaudiot, 2012).

Mobile Cloud Computing (MCC) integrates cloud computing into the mobile environment and overcomes obstacles related to performance (e.g., bandwidth, throughput) and environment (e.g., heterogeneity, scalability, and availability). This chapter has covered the most important research problems and current status related to performance evaluation and QoS in MCC.

REFERENCES

Alazawi, Z., Altowaijri, S., Mehmood, R., & Abdljabar, M. B. (2011). Intelligent disaster management system based on cloud-enabled vehicular networks. In *Proceedings of ITS Telecommunications* (ITST), (pp. 361 – 368). ITST.

Ambike, S., Bhansali, D., Kshirsagar, J., & Bansiwal, J. (2012). An optimistic differentiated job scheduling system for cloud computing. *International Journal of Engineering Research and Applications*, 2(2), 1212–1214.

Bahl, P., Han, R. Y., Li, L. E., & Satyanarayanan, M. (2012). Advancing the state of MCC. In *Proceedings of MCS"12*. MCS.

Bertsimas, D., & Tsitsiklis, J. (1993). Simulated annealing. *Statistical Science*, 8(1), 10–15. doi:10.1214/ss/1177011077.

Chun, B. G., Ihm, S., Maniatis, P., Naik, M., & Patti, A. (2011). CloneCloud: Elastic execution between mobile device and cloud. In *Proceedings of the 6th Conference on Computer Systems* (EuroSys), (pp. 301-314). EuroSys.

Dinh, H. T., Lee, Ch., Niyato, D., & Wang, P. (2011). *A survey of MCC: Architecture, applications, and approaches*. Hoboken, NJ: Wiley Online Library..

Doukas, C., Pliakas, T., & Maglogiannis, I. (2010). Mobile healthcare information management utilizing cloud computing and Android OS. In Proceedings of Engineering in Medicine and Biology Society (EMBC), (pp. 1037 - 1040). IEEE..

Hwang, J., & Wood, T. (2012). Adaptive dynamic priority scheduling for virtual desktop infrastructures. In *Proceedings of 2012 IEEE 20th International Workshop on Quality of Service* (IWQoS). Coimbra, Portugal: IEEE.

Jian, X., Hu, J., Zhao, H., & Zhang, S. (2009). An optimized solution for mobile environment using MCC. In Proceedings of Wireless Communications, Networking and Mobile Computing, 2009. WiCom..

Kennedy, J., & Eberhart, R. (1995). Particle swarm optimization. In *Proceedings of Neural Networks, 1995* (Vol. 4, pp. 1942–1948). IEEE..

Lee, Z., Wang, Y., & Wen, Z. (2011). A dynamic priority scheduling algorithm on service request scheduling in cloud computing. In *Proceedings of Electronic and Mechanical Engineering and Information Technology (EMEIT)*. Harbin, China: EMEIT. doi:10.1109/EMEIT.2011.6024076.

Li, J., Qiu, M., Ming, Z., Quan, G., Qin, X., & Gu, Z. (2012). Online optimization for scheduling preemptable tasks on IaaS cloud systems. *Journal of Parallel and Distributed Computing*, 72(5), 666–677. doi:10.1016/j.jpdc.2012.02.002.

Li, L. (2009). An optimistic differentiated service job scheduling system for cloud computing service users and providers. In *Proceedings of Multimedia and Ubiquitous Engineering*. Qingdao, China: MUE. doi:10.1201/9781420093391.

Lipsky, L. R. (2006). *Queuing theory: A linear algebraic approach*. Berlin: Springer.

Marinescu, D. C. (2012). Cloud computing: Theory and practice. ISBN: 9780124046276.

Nash, J. (1950). Equilibrium points in n-person games. *Proceedings of the National Academy of Sciences of the United States of America*, *36*(1), 48–49. doi:10.1073/pnas.36.1.48 PMID:16588946.

Niyato, D., Vasilakos, A. V., & Kun, Z. (2011). Resource and revenue sharing with coalition formation of cloud providers: Game theoretic approach. In Proceedings of Cluster, Cloud and Grid Computing (CCGrid). Newport Beach, CA: CCGrid..

Prasad, M. R., Gyani, J., & Murti, P. R. K. (2012). MCC: Implications and challenges. *Journal of Information Engineering and Applications*, *2*(7).

Qi, H., & Gani, A. (2012). Research on MCC: Review, trend and perspectives. In Proceedings of Digital Information and Communication Technology and it"s Applications (DICTAP). DICTAP..

Rahimi, M. R., Venkatasubramanian, N., Mehrotra, S., & Vasilakos, A. V. (2011). MAPCloud: Mobile applications on an elastic and scalable 2-tier cloud architecture. In *Proceedings of Utility and Cloud Computing (UCC)*. IEEE..

Rao, N. M., Sasidhar, C., & Kumar, V. S. (2010). Cloud computing through mobile-learning. *International Journal of Advanced Computer Science and Applications*, *1*(6).

Romano, L. De Mari, D., Jerzak, Z., & Fetzer, C. (2011). A novel approach to QoS monitoring in the cloud. In Proceedings of Data Compression, Communications and Processing (CCP), (pp. 45 – 51). CCP..

Shi, Z., Beard, C., & Mitchell, K. (2007). Misbehavior and MAC friendliness in CSMA networks. In *Proceedings of Wireless Communications and Networking Conference, 2007*. Hong Kong, China: IEEE.

Shi, Z., Beard, C., & Mitchell, K. (2008). Tunable traffic control for multihop CSMA networks. In *Proceedings of Military Communications Conference*. San Diego, CA: IEEE.

Shi, Z., Beard, C., & Mitchell, K. (2009). Analytical models for understanding misbehavior and MAC friendliness in CSMA networks. *Journal Performance Evaluation*, *66*(9-10), 469–487. doi:10.1016/j.peva.2009.02.002.

Shi, Z., Beard, C., & Mitchell, K. (2011). Competition, cooperation, and optimization in Multi-Hop CSMA networks. In *Proceedings of the 8th ACM Symposium on Performance Evaluation of Wireless Ad Hoc, Sensor, and Ubiquitous Networks*. ACM.

Shi, Z., Beard, C., & Mitchell, K. (2012a). *Analytical models for understanding space, backoff, and flow correlation in CSMA wireless networks*. Journal Wireless Networks. doi:10.1007/s11276-012-0474-8.

Shi, Z., Beard, C., & Mitchell, K. (2012b). Competition, cooperation, and optimization in multi-hop CSMA networks with correlated traffic. *International Journal of Next-Generation Computing*, *3*(3).

Stuedi, P., Mohomed, I., & Terry, D. (2010). WhereStore: Location-based data storage for mobile devices interacting with the cloud. In *Proceedings of the 1st ACM Workshop on MCC & Services: Social Networks and Beyond*. San Francisco, CA: ACM.

Tang, J., Liu, S., Liu, C., Gu, Z., & Gaudiot, J.-L. (2012). Acceleration of XML parsing through prefetching link. *IEEE Transactions on Computers*.

Tang, J., Thanarungroj, P., Liu, C., Liu, S., Gu, Z., & Gaudiot, J.-L. (2013). Pinned OS/services: A case study of XML parsing on Intel SCC. *Journal of Computer Science and Technology*, *28*(1), 3–13. doi:10.1007/s11390-013-1308-6.

Velev, D., & Zlateva, P. (2011). Principles of cloud computing application in emergency management. In *Proceedings of 2011 International Conference on E-business, Management and Economics*. IPEDR.

Xing, T., Huang, D., Ata, S., & Medhi, D. (2012). MobiCloud: A geo-distributed MCC platform. In *Proceedings of Network and Service Management (CNSM)*. Las Vegas, NV: CNSM..

Yamauchi, H., Kurihara, K., Otomo, T., Teranishi, Y., Suzuki, T., & Yamashita, K. (2012). Effective distributed parallel scheduling methodology for MCC. In *Proceedings of SASIMI*. SASIMI.

Zhang, L., Ding, X., Wan, Z., Gu, M., & Li, X. Y. (2010). WiFace: A secure geosocial networking system using WiFi-based multi-hop MANET. In *Proceedings of the 1st ACM Workshop on Mobile Cloud Computing & Services: Social Networks and Beyond* (MSC). ACM.

Zhang, P., & Yan, Z. (2011). A QoS-aware system for MCC. In Proceedings of Cloud Computing and Intelligence Systems (CCIS), (pp. 518 - 522). CCIS..

Zhou, J., & Beard, C. C. (2007). Adaptive probabilistic scheduling for a cellular emergency network. In *Proceedings of IPCCC 2007*. IPCCC.

Zhou, J., & Beard, C. C. (2009). A controlled preemption scheme for emergency applications in cellular networks. *IEEE Transactions on Vehicular Technology, 58*.

Chapter 12

The New Paradigms of the Internet Combined with Energy Management:
New Models and Tools to Aid the Integration of Data

Joel G. Oliveira
Center of Information Technology Renato Archer – Santa Maria, Brazil

ABSTRACT

Earlier this century there was a crisis among the major Web companies. Berners-Lee started the concept of semantics for the Web. The large academic centers began to create tools to support the dissemination and research associated with their work; the collaborative networks emerged. Taking advantage of this new concept and seeking to attract new users to the Web, social networks began to emerge with a single purpose: to enable new users to customize data. Startups represent this new concept of the Web of the 21st century. In this sense, cloud computing, as well as energy efficiency should represent the biggest advances of this decade, enabling the growth of new market niches. This, along with the need for integration and mobility, is the object of study in this chapter.

INTRODUCTION

There is no more space for virtual environments without discussion, debate rages as an inclusion of groups and individuals. This new paradigm is the new challenge of the digital world. This new concept has been developed since the 2000s. Earlier, only the Semantic Web, however, this paradigm evolved into a closer concept of reality in the society. In everything or almost everything is passive debate, without interaction. This new model of knowledge or knowledge management is supported by rules. These rules need to follow certain models that consider not only the result, but the construction of the dialogue.

Accordingly since 2009 I have been working in a management model that incorporates knowledge from the description of information

DOI: 10.4018/978-1-4666-4781-7.ch012

to the end result. This model aims to manage the entire lifecycle of information. It was divided into three major items. The first, the formal description of a model of knowledge management, which was based on this model can work on the treatment of the data produced. The amount of data produced every day is a challenge to any mechanism of knowledge management, mainly due to the fact that much of this material is low technical quality.

Thus, the current models of knowledge management should manifest the quality of information, one of the elements of the Semantic Web. However, to choose what represents a quality material amidst dozens of other content associated with the same theme is a complex task. Accordingly formal models help building a more affordable model construction and elaboration of reputation mechanisms. This model includes elements that lists the degree of credibility of the source of information, covering concepts related to society, such as reputation.

The second temporal model includes the description of the data, this is the time it takes to translate information from the time when this was posted to the result of the search. In this case it is necessary to consider that many other data will be similar and that one should attempt to list in order of importance and the subject person or entity. The third model includes the description of reuse that gave the battery ecological principle, awarded by Siemens. This model allows to work with the management of data, power and energy management platform based on the consumption of each type of data from processing to the share, thus helping to build a model of battery smarter and therefore more durable.

The three models are described below. The first of them is described in the architecture. This architecture was developed over two years in which several tests in order to produce a model of reuse systems were made. An architecture three entities which later proven effective for

the production of a three cells feed system, one graphene.

The second model is described in a temporal, with mathematical elements in high-level language. The third is in the process patent and thus there is only a symbolic description of its functionality.

Behind all these concepts need of union in which language communication is no barrier or production. The increasing international competition, while creating new opportunities, opening markets that were previously distant, whether due to culture or language. The location becomes the lowest barrier in this new digital world.

BACKGROUND

This section presents the key concepts behind the changes present in new applications, and communication systems on the web.

Globalization has given a new model for the business, the language does not represent a significant barrier, the website follows this growth and modernization rather than just a production environment to aggregate multimedia text, allowing a new market niche and diversified in full transformation. The competition requires business entities such strategies conquests, and customizing a technique facilitating this process.

In this new paradigm of society, where many options and services are provided (Reategui &Lorenzatti, 2005, p.1) for the sake of convenience or momentum needed to keep up the fast pace of everyday life, the recommendation systems emerge as a mean to restrict these options to a small number and therefore, easily accepted (Reategui & Lorenzatti 2005, p.2). In a typical system people provide information as inputs, the system adds value and directs individuals.

The e-commerce is currently a major focus for the use of recommender systems (Reategui & Lorenzatti, 2005, p.3), employing different techniques to find the most suitable products for their customers and increase profits. It is necessary to capture and store their personal data and related behavioral (Reategui & Lorenzatti 2005, p.3). Such data collection can be done implicitly or explicitly identifying the user on the server, for example, through cookies.

These systems work based on characteristics of the user or group, the recommendation in this regard may be sent by a software agent or directly by another user. The initial bottleneck of such a system is in need of personal details (date of birth, name, city) that characterize each user. Whether for lack of time or fear of disclosing personal information on newly discovered services, the initial information provided does not contribute to such systems make use of personalization strategies.

This strategy consists of maintaining lists of items organized by types of interests (Reategui & Lorenzatti, 2005, p.5). There is no detailed analysis of user data to create these lists, only the observation of the most popular types of items, and sorting these groups. Another strategy is to associate a specific content to the user to enable the recommendation requires that associations are a narrower scope, such as books by the same author or the same category or content-based (Reategui & Lorenzatti, 2005, p.5).

To Haythornthwaite (2009, p.1) two forms of organization for collaboration dominate the debate on free participation and production on the Internet: a clustering model based on micro participation of many unrelated individuals, and a virtual community model, based on strong connections among a group of dedicated members interrelated. Therefore, we describe the e-commerce and social networking.

Haythornthwaite (2009, p.2) questions some points, among them the contribution models governing these new mechanisms of production, economic and personal? And as the social and technical systems should be designed to promote collaboration and participation? It is in this sense

that the Semantic Web designed by Berners-Lee, Hendler, Lassila (2001) is more active role in order to maximize new mechanisms for the Web.

To Haythornthwaite (2009, p.2-3) the idea of clusters (crowdsourcing) and provides the basis for communities to identify two contrasting models of peer production processes. They are, lightweight peer production (CPPs) - A PPL is based on a large number of employees, each of which providing minimal additions to the product as a whole, according to pre-established rules. The second would be heavy peer production (PPP) - The heavy model doesn't only involves contributions to the product, but also attention to the actions and contributions of others and a commitment to maintain and support the direction and viability of the community.

The PPP model defined by Haythornthwaite (2009, p.3) reflects the commitment to the enterprise as a whole, including products, internal processes, social and emotional experience of community and continuity of its existence. According to Haythornthwaite (2009, p.3) heavy ventures depend on a critical mass of employees who contribute significant portions of their time and energy to set and maintain the rules of operation, this concept presented by Costa et. al. (2009) in its collaborative network, the A.M.I.G.O.S.

Costa proposed (2009) for Haythornthwaite (2009, p.3) requires engagement with others, encouraging the contribution of all members of the group, collective and collaborative construction of structures and internal rules. Learning the rules of interaction, conversation and participation is very important to signal membership, while the absence of proper behavior characterizes the employee as a stranger or as an apprentice in the community.

In this context social networks emerge as a promoter element of new horizons, opening a market opportunity. The development of these new research and production has enabled the emergence of a new concept of collaborative networks, where the need of user groups lead to production of specific applications. This new digital approach, distributed requires little resources for its creation and development, despite it doesn't provide limits to attract consumers.

This new business paradigm, where small groups produce applications with specific purposes and at the same time is called distributed startups, a term in use for at least two decades, but in the last five years has grown globally. All continents are sources of ideas that turned into products, valuable brands, such as Facebook and Instagram. Born focused on disclosure of circles of friends and posting photos.

The current scenario of technology applications adds random elements, conveying the idea of participation in shaping the content, which approximates the users of the tools and thus begin to recommend it, popularizing it quickly. In this new business environment, the recommendation of the users are the key to success or failure of new products. Add value has been the goal of many developers, entrepreneurs and young professionals.

Recommendation Systems

To minimize the doubts and needs we face the choice between alternatives (Reategui & Lorenzatti, 2005, p.3), usually rely on recommendations that are passed by others, which can reach directly (word of mouth) (Maes & Shardanand, 1995), recommendation letters, opinions of reviewers of movies and books, printed newspapers, among others.

The recommendation systems help to increase the capacity and effectiveness of this nomination process already well known in the social relationship between humans (Resnick & Varian, 1997). Proponents of the first recommendation system called Tapestry (Goldberg et al., 1992) (Resnick & Varian 1997), created the term "collaborative filtering", to designate a specific type of system in which the information filtering was performed with the aid human, ie the collabora-

tion between stakeholder groups (Reategui & Lorenzatti, 2005).

For Reategui & Lorenzatti (2005) one of the oldest techniques used in these systems is known as collaborative filtering (Herlocker et al., 2000). This technique provides the preferences of a user based on the preferences of others with similar behavior.

The collaborative filtering technique has been successfully used in several research projects. The project Tapestry (Goldberg et al., 1992), an early work in collaborative filtering recommender systems, used opinions of people in a small community (eg office or workgroup) to find recommendations.

Already the GroupLens project at the University of Minnesota (Sarwar et al., 1998), Reategui & Lorenzatti (2005) helps the users to find movies on their interests. Nowadays, however, the recommendation systems have already migrated from research labs to the marketplace of the Internet, and can be found in large websites like Amazon.com bookstore or record shop CDNow. com (Schafer, Konstan, & Riedl, 1999).

The authors (Reategui & Lorenzatti, 2005; Haythornthwaite, 2009) prefer to use the term recommender systems (instead of collaborative filters), as a generic term and hold this position for two reasons: first because it cannot explain who recommends their collaboration because members are generally unknown, and ultimately may suggest items of particular interest, including those that could be disregarded.

To Jorge et al. (2010) recommendation systems are designed to assist in obtaining information relevant to the user, for Cazella et al. (2013) obtain this information may be done by the use of your profile or the profile of the group to which it is registered. The Recommender Systems using the filtering technique called, filtering based on content, performing a filtering of items to be recommended based on analysis of the content item already consumed in the past by the user.

It carried a cross between the item to be recommended (eg a scientific paper) and user profile in order to check whether the item is or is not relevant to the target user of the recommendation (Adomavicius & Tuzhilin 2005). At this cross necessary elements appear for customization of data.

To Jorge et al. (2010) in Recommender Systems are used in one of three general techniques for filtering information cited below: content-based filtering (CBF), collaborative filtering (CF), also known as social filtering and hybrid filtering (FH). A web server makes requests to the recommendation system, which returns recommendations, content, services and offers customized (Cazella et al., 2013).

According to Jorge et al. (2010) so that a recommendation system can appropriately recommend items to users, the system must constantly gather data about users. These data refer to behaviors (eg navigation and purchase) and possibly demographic.

This collection is often done implicitly, ie, without the user necessarily notices that there is information being stored in the system. This practice brings some privacy issues. One of the challenges of this type of system is the difficulty to estimate the similarity between users, giving way to techniques that seek to infer user preferences through their implicit statements of interest with respect to a given artifact.

The great advantage of this technique is that the expressions of interest to users are silently left as a natural result of the manipulation of the artifacts, rather than being explicitly requested users. This leads on solving a major problem faced by collaborative filtering techniques, which is a "cold start" (cold-start problem), i.e., the system loses efficiency estimates until a sufficient number of reviews are performed (Reategui & Lorenzatti, 2005).

In the case of technique implicit evaluations are implied the data generated by users and are collected primarily through the use of heuristic

(Bagheri, Zafarani, & Ebrahimi, 2009), for example, in the system PHOAKS, a first programming technique (Reategui & Lorenzatti, 2005). To Reategui & Lorenzatti (2005) the system recommends URLs (Uniform Resource Locators) based on the inclusion of these addresses in messages sent between users of Usenet. Using this heuristic, two users are deemed similar if the same URL was exchanged between them in a message.

A weight is given to the link that is implicitly formed between users based on the number of users who recommend the same URL, which generates a ranking of reputation, studied by Bagheri, Zafarani, & Ebrahimi (2009). This metric was then extended, formalized and named as "weight of authority". Another aspect concerns the context in which the user is involved, to find a relationship between two people is certainly a problem that can be investigated with heuristics, structural analysis and graph theory.

Extract some meaning from the relationship between two people is certainly a semantic problem that leads us to ask: "In what context are the two people related?" In fact, the issue of context reappears at various times throughout the history of the area of Human Computer Interaction (HCI). To Bagheri, Zafarani, & Ebrahimi (2009), the context influence in establishing reputation in the relations between users.

Set the context between two users from the social interaction between them is a compatible task with the paradigm of the tools that compose the social web today. Interaction situations that promote a bond between two people abound in these environments and awaken therefore great interest for research in recommender systems.

The A.M.I.G.O.S (Multimedia Environments for Integration Groups and Social Organizations) is an environment for web-based social networks (Web-Based Social Network - WBSN) (Costa et. al., 2009), whose purpose is to promote communication, cooperation and interaction between employees that form.

According to Costa et. al. (2009) This environment promotes knowledge sharing among its users through the creation of communities, user profiles, quizzes and polls, classification (folksonomy), and recommendation of stories people use to chat, and the addition of several association media and discuss topics through stories, forums, threads and comments.

Besides these, second (Costa et. al., 2009), the A.M.I.G.O.S offers several features to facilitate access to and retrieval of information. Examples of these are search engines, creating clouds of keywords (tag clouds), the availability of web-feeds in RSS and tracking updates by email communities.

This preliminary study on the current models, techniques and tools available have led to the creation of an architectural model itself, focused communication platform and multi-entity. Where the same user can be connected through different devices such as mobile phones, tablets or laptops. Whatever device used, the system must be able to recognize the user's profile as he logged in or not.

Another factor taken into account in the development of this architectural model was the response time for each request processed by the system, and associated consumption at this time. Consumption by the user and the system. This study enabled the creation of a temporal model of three cells. Communication and functionality of each cell was tested in the distance of nearly three years. In this period, more than eighty tests were done.

The tests were intended to establish the chaos to the system, then it was possible to predict the maximum connections and consumption associated with this capability, avoiding in this way the system working unexpectedly when there are many connections. This was only possible with the construction of the ecological system battery. The system was done in software, with the property management and balancing feature so that no task occupies more energy than needed or that such use was undefined. For this,

the proposed architecture model includes an approach to reuse data, this approach allows to filter temporal samples of data which reduces the process of new quests and increases the quality of the data entered.

This quality can be perceived through the return speed reduced each new iteration. Another model is that the first interaction of the user and the system does not require many user information, since the system feeds the results of research and inserts user data. This system adds value to each new search, which allows the creation of user profiles from searches, data entry and reading the data submitted through the system.

The timing of the data is synchronized with a system in clouds. The timer allows you to optimize the search for new data, so the user profile is built. Since the profile is constructed by crossing data and the recommendation of the data through the intersections of information between various users with profiels similar search, in this new model of building profile, it is not initially necessary to initially populate a list of information with personal data but only summarized data. This crossing time, made each new interaction allows the creation of a bank's reputation.

The architectural model was proposed using the formal language Full Lotos, xml and java implementation of the reuse system. The timing proved to be effective in the management of energetic components, leading to the creation of an integrated battery of self-feeding. The hardware was developed in part, made using verilog.

Figure 1 describes the proposed model. In this model the client is connected to multiple devices, logged or not. The entity recognizes a mediator by id registered in the first access. This way the user profile is updated and requests are routed to their service, always trying to reduce the turnaround time. The user satisfaction is measured by the number of recommendations that he suggested to other members or the number of invitations sent with suggestions for use. A reputation is measured

Figure 1. Architectural model of the system

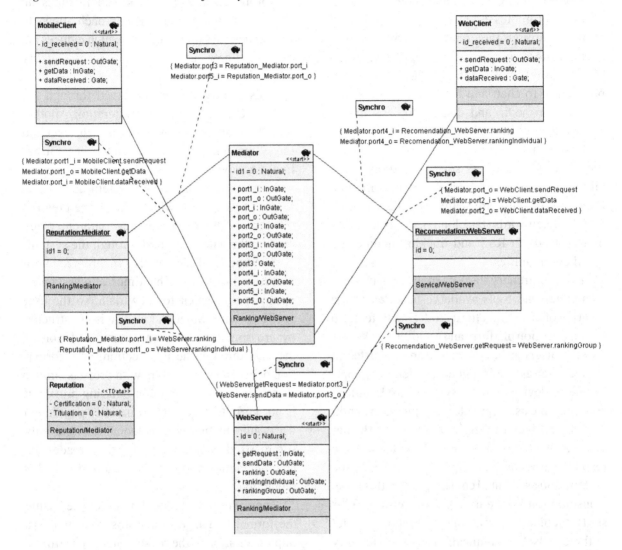

based on the return of those requests from other members of the system. With particular concern about the timing of the data, avoiding outdated information being transferred.

A particularly rule is that the temporal response time should never be more than forty percent of the time of last request or the last search. To achieve this time the mediator makes use of three services. The first is responsible for the recommendation data, in which lists items that have recently been recommended and have resemblance to the item sought by users. This first list can be omitted if the user is not interested. The second listing database is made based on the history of the users, ie, the mediator makes a search for searched items on pages already accessed and potentially arouse the interest of the user. The third list uses new data, and cross-check which information were relevant to that user or group. Thus the response time of the requests users can be reduced without generating harm to the quality of the provided information.

The time pattern is shown in Figure 2. This model allows to systematize from the more

Figure 2. Temporal model of the system

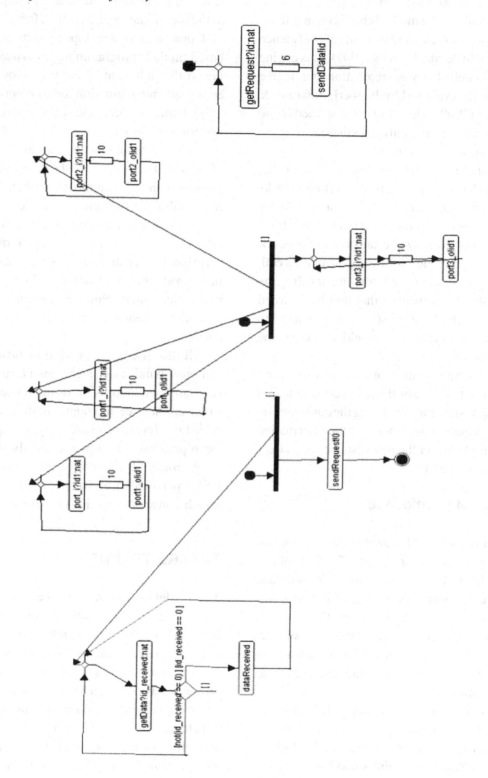

complex scenarios to the simplest. The proposal of this architectural model is based on including quality requirements and the mills of confidence presented by Kovač & Trcek (2009). This engine includes control of your reputation and degree of influence evaluated by Bagheri, Zafarani, & Ebrahimi (2009). The numbers described in the model represent temporal cycles that each request consumes up to be completed.

At this time pattern of three separate cells, each one having a function. The leftmost works with each user's profile. It is responsible for sending requests to the mediating entity. Each of this entity prioritize certain users at times of heavy flow of requests. Already the middle cell, the entity mediator must worry about filling the three lists of information that will be returned to users, each of these lists can consume up to 10 processing cycles, but should not exceed the maximum time.

The maximum time for a request to be answered is established by the cell over the right, it is also responsible for calculating the consumption of each request. Come out of it the information necessary to power the processing cycle battery system ecological.

Models of Confidence

Recognition of visible counts include computational cycles (Holohan & Garg, 2009) weblinks (Park, 2003; Thelwall & Vaughn, 2004), page hits, citation statistics or lists of publications. Reputation is gained or lost by the attention given to these acknowledgments by members of the community, it is a sufficient indicator of compliance with production standards and norms of the community.

Reputation is a network effect. It is a form of social capital that emerges from the actions of members of a social network (Lin, 2001; White et al., 2004). Rather than being something owned by an individual that makes up the network. Rewards

result of reputation and benefits are passed on to the individual, such as status, fame or wealth.

Open source developers earn reputation based on their programming expertise, according to the judgment of other employees; they earn academic reputation for comment on their publication, as well as the successful navigation system of opinions.

Those reputable receive reward in the form of status: the peer of Slashdot are vetted and promoted, in a community of teachers known as MirandaNet, participants become "companions" (fellows) as their contribution increases (Preston, 2008), and academics earn higher ranks. Not surprisingly, Twitter is so successful around the world, this application follows the same academic, which reinforces the importance of combining theoretical concepts with living in society.

All this discussion about trust turned to the web are to build object inferences, i.e. rules. These rules are used in mills (mills inference) in order to ensure service providers, particularly those with high levels of availability, a requirement for reputation. Startups are mostly developed in environments that easily allow their users to build a personal scenario, stimulating the recommendation and promotion of these applications.

FUTURE TRENDS

The model timing data allowed to work with based on energy consumption of each request, from a simple address search on the web, even the more complex as the location of a service to control airline where a system failure can generate emission over a ticket for the same seat, causing inconvenience to thousands of passengers. Whatever the request needed, it is necessary some time to be processed. During it, thousands of new requests were made and all must be met.

The temporal approach is to establishes a maximum time to meet the first and last received request. This time is calculated for each request, which allows a variation in time, but this variation must not exceed forty percent of the time rate calculated for this to be feasible because there is a list of three processes in which the idea is to allow the user to choose the best service available. However, this procedure still requires a high energy consumption on the mobile devices, primarily. To resolve this issue one battery model was proposed.

The concept of ecological battery is first: to establish a system of balancing tasks, so that a request for high consumption doesn't take account of all the energy resource of the device. Second, once connected, the system must allow a minimum visual comfort to the user, even in conditions where there is a risk of downloading and once downloaded the device must maintain the integrity of all data stored and processed, hence the connection with the cloud computing. The timing data allows saving everything that was being done in the instant before the device was turned off by power outages.

As proved to be advantageous to create a system of three levels, was also feasible to create a battery with three cells. The challenge of this project was what would be the types used in the model and what each unit would be responsible for processing. Saw that it was necessary that one of the three cells have the power of high throughput communication. Because it is an integrated project, the best option would be an integrated circuit.

This circuit has the capacity for data processing, while we could manage its own resources, in order to prevent the system was interrupted every low energy of the system. Thus, the first cell was built with the purpose of preparing and analyzing the particles of atoms present in the air, aiming mainly to trigger the operation of the battery. Because it is a digital circuit, the battery would be integrated to the equipment, or the equipment would serve as the power source.

This silicon cell allows to manage the process of battery power.

The battery can be recharged directly into an outlet in the home user or feed solar energy. It was noted that the battery could have a duration greater if she fed constantly, e.g. heat or atoms, such as CO_2 that although inefficient is widely available in major cities and the goal is not just load, but keep the battery charged.

This feeding process of the device is done through the second cell responsible for ensuring that the battery works and receive energy of the whole device. The third cell in graphene allows data and communication between cells occur quickly. Thus, it is a prototype battery environmentally friendly. The problem with this would be the size of the battery. With technology and financial resources available today, its size would be only compatible to notebook and tablet. The miniaturization process is a little more costly, and will require more research time.

Despite its size, the battery ecological proved to be an innovative and promising for the near future, proof of this was to have been a finalist in the innovation competition sponsored by Siemens in Brazil in 2011. Surpassing more than three thousand papers, has been one of fifteen finalists in the Siemens Student Award.

The major innovative element of this new system concept, where software and hardware are connected, and are designed to self-sufficiency that is request for mobility today, as hours are lost in route home from work. This new model of management and energy efficiency is a prototype that has been developed since August 2009. From beginning to conclude the first truly functional version, which was only possible in 2011, numerous tests were made. These tests aimed at the integration of data between the mobile and the cloud, and between the device itself, so that he himself was a functioning system.

Initial results were unsatisfactory leading to revision of the model, that review was possible to understand that the battery should also be provided with three cells, as well as the system and that one of them should be responsible for the communication between them and the system. This communication should be fast, so it was introduced in the graphene unit. After this review, the model of temporalization worked within the stipulated limit, the rate of forty percent of the time between the first and the last request received in a time slot dynamically calculated. After it was done I had the opportunity to submit it to the Siemens Award, surpassing where thousands of jobs in different areas, established itself as one of the winners at a ceremony held at the Football Museum in April 2012 in the city of São Paulo, SP, Brazil.

CONCLUSION

The customization of the data acts as an agent developer of new digital tools, tools that aim to assist the social integration of various communities without the language barrier, making use of universal languages of communication, such as photography, music, micro-stories. Following this line, in this chapter describes topics that are described common elements of digital communication and mobile devices. After all, mobility has been the major focus of the technological world market in recent years. It does not mean there are not challenges to be overcome.

What distinguishes this work from the approach of many others is that besides the architectural model or the system itself, there is an energy management geared to meet the demands of users. It is at this point that there is a great development and in relation to all work related reference sources for this in other works not the link between hardware and software. As much as the battery is still a prototype, it has been playing great relevance and gaining more space inside Brazil.

However, part of this work is to spread the concept of a unified system where hardware and software are designed in a way to increase revenue without increased energy consumption. For this it is necessary to think about strategies for monitoring consumption, such strategies are played by the temporal model.

Thus, this system developed in three levels. Where the first one is composed of architecture and system developed in java. The second one works exclusively about data and cross-checks in order to manage it and build models of recommendation and trust these data. The third level builds on hardware cells capable of feeding on particles, this feeding process is managed by a microcontroller analog signal mixel.

REFERENCES

Adomavicius, G., & Tuzhilin, A. (2005). Toward the next generation of recommender systems: A survey of the state of-the-art and possible extensions. *IEEE Transactions on Knowledge and Data Engineering*, 17, 734–749. doi:10.1109/TKDE.2005.99.

Bagheri, E., Zafarani, R., & Ebrahimi, M. B. (2009). Can reputation migrate? On the propagation of retation in multi-context communities. *Knowledge-Based Systems*, 22, 410–420. doi:10.1016/j.knosys.2009.05.007.

Baum, J. A. C., Calabrese, T., & Silverman, B. S. (2000). Don't go it alone: Alliance network composition and startups' performance in Canadian biotechnology. *Strategic Management Journal*, 21, 267–294. doi:10.1002/(SICI)1097-0266(200003)21:3<267::AID-SMJ89>3.0.CO;2-8.

Berners-Lee, T., Hendler, J., & Lassila, O. (2001). The semantic web. *Scientific American*. doi:10.1038/scientificamerican0501-34.

Blois, A. P. T. B. (2006). *Uma abordagem de projeto arquitetural baseado em componentes no contexto de engenharia de domínio.* (Unpublished doctoral dissertation). Universidade Federal Do Rio De Janeiro, Rio de Janeiro, Brazil.

Bosma, N., Mirjam, V. P., Roy, T., & de Wit, G. (2002). *The value of human and social capital investiments for the business performance of startups.* Tinbergen, The Netherlands: Tinbergen Institute..

Cazella, S. C., Nunes, M. A., & Reategui, E. (2013). *A ciência da opinião: Estado da arte em sistemas de recomendação.*

Costa, R. A., Oliveira, R. Y. S., Silva, E. M., & Meira, S. R. L. (2009). A.M.I.G.O.S: knowledge management and social networks. In *Proceedings of Sigdoc'08.* Lisbon, Portugal: ACM..

Falub, C. V., von Käne, H., Isa, F., Bergamaschin, R., Marzegalli, A., & Chrastina, D. et al. (2012). Scaing hetero-epitaxy from layers to three-dimensional crystals. *Science, 335*(6074), 1330–1334. doi:10.1126/science.1217666 PMID:22422978.

Fillipo, D., Raposo, A., Markus, E., & Hugo, F. (2007). Ambientes colaborativos de realidade virtual e aumentada. In SBC–Sociedade Brasileira De Computação (Ed.), Porto Alegre, (pp. 168-191). Press..

Fuks, H., Raposo, A., & Gerosa, M. A. (2002). *Engenharia de groupware: Desenvolvimento de aplicações colaborativas.* XXI Jornada De Atualização Em Informática, Anais Do XXII 188. [Projeto E Aplicações Congresso Da Sociedade Brasileira De Computação.]. *Realidade Virtual E Aumentada: Conceitos, 2,* 89–128.

Goldberg, D., Nichols, D., Oki, B. M., & Terry, D. (1992). Using collaborative filtering to weave an information tapestry. *Communications of the ACM, 35*(12), 61–70. doi:10.1145/138859.138867.

Haythornthwaite, C. (2009). Agrupamentos e comunidades: Modelos de produção colaborativa leve e pesada. *Estudos Midiáticos, 11*(3), 161–175. doi:10.4013/fem.2009.113.01.

Herlocker, J., Konstan, J., & Riedl, J. (2000). Explaining collaborative filtering recommendations. In *Proceedings of ACM 2000 Conference on Computer Supported Cooperative Work.* ACM.

Holohan, A., & Garg, A. (2009). Collaboration online: The example of distributed computing. *JCMC, 10*(4).

Jacob, R. L., & Alan, J. S. (1997). *Software strategies for portable computer energy management* (Report No. UCB/CSD-97-949). Berkeley, CA: Computer Science Division, University of California.

Jorge, V. D., Silvio, C., & Jonas, L. V. B. (2010). Um serviço para recomendação de artigos científicos baseado em filtragem de conteúdo aplicado a dispositivos móveis. *Cinted-Ufrgs, 8*(3).

Kovač, D., & Trcek, D. (2009). Qualitative trust modeling in SOA. *Journal of Systems Architecture, 55*(4), 255–263. doi:10.1016/j.sysarc.2009.01.002.

Lin, N. (2001). *Social capital: A theory of social structure and action.* Cambridge, UK: Cambridge University Press. doi:10.1017/CBO9780511815447.

Maes, P., & Shardanand, U. (1995). Social information filtering: Algorithms for automating word of mouth. In *Proceedings of Human Factors In Computing Systems* (pp. 210–217). IEEE..

Nonaka, I. (1991). The knowledge-creating company. *Harvard Business Review,* 96–104.

Okamura, H. (2007). A laser motor directly transforms light energy into mechanical energy. *SPIE.* Retrieved November 17, 2007 from http://Spie.Org/X8435.Xml

Park, H. (2003). What is hyperlink network analysis? A new method for the study of social structure on the web. *Connections*, *25*(1), 49–61.

Preston, C. (2008). Braided learning: An emerging practice observed in e-communities of practice. *International Journal of Web Based Communities*, *4*(2), 220–243. doi:10.1504/IJWBC.2008.017674.

Raposo, A., & Fuks, H. (2002). Defining task interdependencies and coordination mechanisms for collaborative systems. *Frontiers in Artificial Intelligence and Applications*, *74*, 88–103.

Reategui, E., & Lorenzatti, A. (2005). Um assistente virtual para resolução de dúvidas e recomendação de conteúdo. In *Proceedings of XXV CSBC*. CSBC.

Resnick, P. E., & Varian, H. R. (1997). Recommender systems. *Communications of the ACM*, *40*(3), 55–58. doi:10.1145/245108.245121.

Reynolds, P. D. (2000). National panel study of U.S. business startups: background and methodology. *Databases for the Study of Entrepreneurship*, *4*, 153–227. doi:10.1016/S1074-7540(00)04006-X.

Sarwar, B., Konstan, J., Borchers, A., Herlocker, J., Miller, B., & Riedl, J. (1998). Using filtering agents to improve prediction quality in the grouplens research collaborative filtering system. In *Proceedings of the 1998 Conference on Computer Supported Cooperative Work*. New York: CSCW.

Schafer, J., Konstan, J., & Riedl, J. (1999). Recommender systems in e-commerce. In *Proceedings of ACM E-Commerce*. ACM.

Thelwall, M., & Vaughn, L. (2004). Webmetrics. *JASIST, 55*(14).

White, H. D., Wellman, B., & Nazer, N. (2004). Does citation reflect social structure? *JASIST, 55*(2), 111–126. doi:10.1002/asi.10369.

KEY TERMS AND DEFINITIONS

Applications Mobility: Applications developed for mobile devices.

Cooperation/Collaborative Systems: Systems made with the purpose of sharing experience and broaden the interaction between individuals in related fields.

Personalization Data: Characterization of a tool based on the user profile.

Power Management: Energy management, made by measuring consumption by active device.

Recommendation Systems: Display systems developed for applications according to the needs of each customer.

Semantic Web: Adds semantic searches for data or images on the internet.

Trust Model: Metric that calculates the level of credibility of information.

Chapter 13
A2Cloud:
The Anytime Anywhere Cloud

João Nuno Silva
INESC-ID, Instituto Superior Técnico, Universidade de Lisboa, Portugal

Luís Veiga
INESC-ID, Instituto Superior Técnico, Universidade de Lisboa, Portugal

ABSTRACT

This book chapter presents the integration of widely available technologies to bridge the gap between mobile devices and their computational rich surrounding environments. Taking as common glue Cloud Storage systems, new interaction between devices becomes more natural. The processing of files can be transparently executed on nearby computers, taking advantage of better hardware and saving mobile devices power. In this chapter, the authors present a novel resource evaluation mechanism, which allows a finer evaluation and more precise comparison of remote resources, leading to fewer wasted resources and better use of those resources. The use of remote resources can be performed by means of processing offloading, executing complete application on remote devices or by relocation of mobile classes. Both methods resort to the presented resource evaluation mechanism. Monolithic applications are transformed (with information from a configuration file) into distributed application, where some components execute on remote devices: nearby computers (to take advantage of existing human-computer interaction devices) or on the cloud (to speed processing). Processing offloading is accomplished by executing on nearby computers applications compatible with the one on the mobile device. This speeds that processing task (better CPU, better interaction devices), reducing the mobile device's power consumption.

INTRODUCTION

In his seminal paper, Mark Weiser (1991) predicts the disappearing of the computer as it was known and its transformation on transparent ubiquitous devices. Although not fully realized, the current

personal computing environment is much different from what it was 30 years ago: users move freely with close to complete connectivity and carry along a myriad of mobile devices (smart phones, laptops on even computing tabs). In a keynote at the UIST '94 Symposium on User Interface Software and Technology (Weiser, 1994), Weiser presented a graph depicting the evolution

DOI: 10.4018/978-1-4666-4781-7.ch013

of the various computing paradigms, showing the obvious decline of the mainframe. Again, the computing environment has changed from the 90s but has not evolved as predicted.

Today the computing environment ranges from the old desktop computer, to the mobile tablet or smart-phone, to the centralized (from the user point of view) cloud provider, but with close to continuous connectivity. Wireless 3G coverage is close to total, free or public wireless networks exist, and most homes have wireless routers, all providing the necessary network access to the full integration of the available resources.

Although cloud resources (storage and processing power) have become widely available, and personal computers have become mobile devices (still with limited battery power and computing capacity), applications for such devices are still developed as if for fixed desktop PCs. Neither connectivity, nor battery capacity are taken into account, nor available resources are used to offload computations.

Previous work has been developed in the area of ubiquity, but it was not completely successful at easing the access to cloud resources from a mobile device, unable to transparently (with respect to programming) offload computations from the mobile device.

In this work, we investigate and develop a suite of methods that, combined, aim to allow an easy development of mobile applications (those that execute in mobile devices) that can take advantage of cloud resources (storage and processing power) along with others available in the surroundings of the device (idle computers or large displays).

We address this gap, by allowing programmers to develop centralized applications, to be executed on mobile devices, and at run-time split them and execute parts of it (UI, or processing intensive classes) on remote resources. The resulting infrastructure resorts to a mobile code execution platform in order to allow the execution of, otherwise centralized, code on remote devices.

The same platform is used for the offloading of user interfaces (for instance, to larger displays) to nearby devices, and for the offloading of more intensive processing to the cloud.

These applications should be adapted transparently by middleware that helps to decide where to process data or present user interfaces and results taking into account the following:

- Available battery power,
- Wireless connection availability,
- Available neighboring resources, and
- Remote cloud resources.

These factors impact greatly the way data can be processed: if, for instance, the mobile device has network connectivity, but not enough battery, the data can be processed in the cloud (close to where it was stored) and, if a large display is available, results can be made available on a close-by display.

Due to the different nature of the involved devices (resource constrained mobile devices, desktop PCs, set-top boxes, or cloud servers), a mobile code platform should also allow the replacement of the classes to be remotely executed by others with the same functionality and interface, but optimized to the target architecture. This enables the presentation of different UIs for the same application (taking into account the display size or input methods) and the execution of optimized code for a particular target.

The work in *A2Cloud* described here follows up, enhances, and integrates the previous work that allowed the automatic and transparent offloading of class objects to remote hosts without user intervention and program modification (Silva, 2004; Silva, 2009) and an algebra for precise evaluation of resources (Silva, 2010).

It also applies the resource evaluation mechanisms to optimize processing offloading. This document also shows how to improve user experience when handling cloud stored data from mobile devices.

Document Organization

The next section presents and overview of work related to A2Cloud, presenting work on the area of pervasiveness, mobile Cloud, and underling supporting technologies (Application and UI adaptation, and resource discovery. The following section presents A2Cloud, along with its three main modules. This document concludes with the evaluation and validation of A2Cloud and the conclusion.

BACKGROUND

In this Section, we address and discuss the related work relevant to *A2Cloud* which falls into the following main areas regarding current mobile, pervasive and cloud computing integration:

1. Application Pervasiveness,
2. Mobile Cloud,
3. Application Adaptation,
4. User Interface Adaptability, and
5. Resource Discovery.

Application Pervasiveness

Application pervasiveness refers to the ability of applications to execute in a seamless way, while in fact code, data, and execution flows may be crossing different environment and device boundaries. The seminal Pervasive Computing Systems (Román, 2002; Ponnekanti, 2003), all address this key issue by providing a middleware to connect devices and a set of programming APIs to develop the applications to take advantage of the integrated environment: an Active Space. In GAIA (Román, 2002) applications are composed of CORBA components that are connected by means of LUA scripts. GAIA applications can be dynamically partitioned and efficiently executed on available resources. IROS (Ponnekanti, 2003) allows the development interactive workspaces,

where distributed applications execute. Both systems require the development of special applications to take advantage of the environment.

Other research initiatives have adopted the OSGi framework as application execution platform (Rellermeyer, 2007; Preuveneers, 2010). Concierge (Rellermeyer, 2007) presents the use of OSGi as service platform for constrained devices. In this approach most of the processing code is installed as bundles in a server, which is then contacted by the mobile device when such services are needed. The work by Preuveneers (2010) further enhances this client-server architecture allowing the migration of services between servers. Although allowing transparent integration of localized resources, these systems impose programming requirements that are different from the traditional centralized (executed in the mobile device) application development method. The use of remote services may also not be practical when connectivity is not possible.

Earlier work related to what we are aiming includes some migratory applications systems. The work done by Krishna Bharat (1995) allowed the development of graphical applications that could roam between several computers, but in a monolithic way. In the work of Harter (2002), by using a VNC server, the interface of an application could be moved from a display to another, but the code remained running in the same server.

The use of the Remote Evaluation Paradigm (Fuggetta, 1998) overcomes the deficiencies of the previous systems by allowing the development of reconfigurable applications (Raatikainen, 2002) with code mobility. There is no need to program where and when the objects should move to. The programmer must only develop the code taking into account that it will be mobile and state which requirements the remote host should satisfy. For instance, in Fargo (Holder, 1999) the programmer must develop a special kind of component: the complete. While developing these special components, the developer must program how the objects will roam among the computers:

environment requirements, object aggregation. After the development of these components the application must be compiled so that the mobile code is inserted in the application.

Our work also relates to projects such as JavaParty (Philippsen, 1997) or Pangaea (Spiegel, 2000), in the sense that the distribution of the objects and the decision on where they should run is hidden from the programmer. In JavaParty the system hides the remote creation of objects and its mobility, but the programmer must tag these with a special keyword. A separate compiler is needed. In Pangaea, a special compiler analyzes the source code and transforms it so that some objects are created on remote hosts.

Mobile Cloud

With recent increasing adoption of cloud technology, integration of Cloud and mobile devices tries to use exiting Cloud infrastructures as target of some mobile computation. Giurgiu (2009) develops applications as a set of OSGi components and parts of them are executed on the remote device. Mobile OGSI.NET (Chu, 2004) also integrates OSGI services with mobile devices UbiCloud (Chen, 2010) and VM-based Cloudlets (Satyanarayanan, 2009) also allows the execution of predetermined components on the cloud. The work in (Zhang, 2011) splits the application into UI (running in the mobile device) and a core that executes in the cloud. Both systems require the previous application implementation as a predetermined set of components or services.

CloneCloud (Chun, 2011) is a system that automatically transforms mobile applications to benefit from the cloud, by optimizing the execution time and the energy used in the mobile device. The system solves problems such as bringing a demanding mobile application to needed cloud resources. It tends to be inflexible since an application is either written as a monolithic process, or it is split in the traditional client-server paradigm,

pushing most computation to the remote server, or can be tailored to match an expected environment.

Jupiter (Guo, 2011) is a system to augment the capabilities of smart-phones transparently with the support of cloud computing. One or more cloud servers can be employed as the extension of the storage and computing capabilities of smart-phones. The cloud provides storage of applications and user data, and also provides virtual machines to execute large applications that cannot be on smart-phones due to resource constraints. Jupiter aims to achieve three primary goals:

- Transparent mobile application management to be transparent to the user.
- Transparent data storage
- Desktop application execution.

Jupiter does task based optimization and offloading, by either selecting the best local application or a remote service to be used when performing a task (e.g. PDF generation or presentation) and requires those application to be specially developed.

The Cuckoo framework (Kemp, 2012) simplifies the development of smart-phone applications that benefit from computation offloading and provides a dynamic run-time system that decides, at run-time, if a part of an application is going to be executed locally or remotely. This framework can be used to easily write and efficiently run applications that can offload computation. Cuckoo offers a very simple programming model that is prepared for mobile environments. This programming model offers the developers an interface of the system, so it should be easy to use and understand. It must support both local and remote execution since when the mobile devices are not connected to the Internet, the cloud resources are unreachable. It must also allow the remote method implementation to be different from the local implementation. For example, the remote method could be parallelized in order to get full performance from the remote resources.

With respect to Cloud and mobile integration, the work done does it at the expense of the specific applications. These applications, although capable of taking into account remote resources, are limited when connectivity is not available.

Application Adaptation

Application adaptation and adaptability are fundamental characteristics of modern pervasive computing system, since to ease development only a single version of the applications should be used. One of the first adaptive offloading systems (Gu, 2004) required a modified java virtual machine in order to allow the execution of classes on remote surrogates. Furthermore, only battery was taken into consideration and no selection of an alternative and more appropriate class was possible. João Sousa (2006) presents a higher level adaptation; the minimal execution unit is not a class, but a task. Each task is composed of activities and its data, and is tagged with its requirements and service qualities. The underlying system should optimize task assignment to available systems. With respect to systems or applications implemented as composition of services, Murarasu, (2009) presents architecture for a middleware for automatic reconfiguration of applications. In this work the only reconfiguration performed is the selection of one of the available services (local or remote) and the migration of services between different providers. This approach, as well as others based on service or component composition (Rellermeyer, 2007; Preuveneers, 2010), require programmers to develop their application using such frameworks and require a complete service or component infrastructure.

An early approach to the adaptation of applications in mobile environments was to adapt the data transmitted to and from remote computers. The solutions proposed range from the development of specific proxies to the use of distributed middleware that handles the adaptation of the data transmitted. The proxy solution was first applied to the web contents (Han, 1998; Fox, 1996) and allowed the transformation of the contents so that its download time is reduced. In the other edge we find systems that allow the development of mobile application that interact with a data source. In the work done by T. Kunz (1999) the communication is done by a series of objects: some local to the mobile device and others in the data source that adapts the information transmitted according to the resources available. These solutions have the drawback that only the data is adapted to the device's environment. Another approach to the adaptation of the application execution is the development of middleware platforms that are environment aware. These systems range from the generic system discovery such as Satin (Zachariadis, 2003) or Icrafter (Ponnekanti, 2001) to the more specific work done by Nakajima (1997) with a middleware for graphical and multimedia applications. These solutions are valid but solve the problem of constrained resources by invoking services on remote computer but not executing the applications original code on a more suited host.

Some systems use reflection (Capra, 2003; Zachariadis, 2003; Grace, 2003) to accomplish the transparent adaptation of the applications but its scope is the same as the systems described previously. Only logic mobility is performed, a task is executed in a remote host, but no application code moved to the remote computer, the service performed should be already present there.

On a lower level, adaptation of application components requires some transformation code, that can be inserted by various means: modification of the virtual machine (Gu, 2004), explicitly programmatically by means of an API (Ponnekanti, 2003), and implicitly by means of aspect weaving (Truyen, 2008), intermediate compiling (Marques 2008), or meta-classes (Silva, 2004).

User Interface Adaptability

Earlier works on the adaptability of user interfaces include Plastic User interfaces (Calvary, 2001), which allowed the development of applications whose user interface (UI) depended on the device running the application. In Icrafter (Ponnekanti, 2001) the various devices could be handled in various ways (HTTP or applets) by means of multiple UIs. Other works on plastic UIs try to adapt the concrete UI at run-time taking into account, for instance, the display size.

The 4C (Demeure, 2008; Vanderdonckt, 2010) reference model presents various distributed user interfaces scenarios: single device/multiple displays and multiple device/multiple displays. 4C works at the pixel level, transforming (with rotation and scaling) the UI elements in order to present them in the multiple available displays. Donatien (Grolaux, 2005; Vanderdonckt, 2010) proposes detachable UIs, where part of the UI (for instance, canvas or set of buttons) can be detached and even sent to another device. Although usable on the envisioned environment, some shortcomings are present: the work of Icrafter is tailored to a client/server approach, where users access services on remote servers. The other approaches do not take into account the variation in input methods present in the available devices.

The Fluid Computing Middleware (Bourges-Waldegg, 2005) allows the distribution of the UI on remote devices, as long as the application follows the Model-View-Controller design pattern in its implementation. The work in (Melchior, 2011) proposes a model-based approach to the distribution of UIs, composed of various descriptions: a distribution graph (that states how the various components can be distributed) and a distribution language (that states when the various components can be distributed). After the construction of the User Interface, the programmer must define how and/or when that User interface is to be distributed to another host. The work by Manca (2011) offers a similar solution. None of these approaches allows the selection of various UI elements, taking into account the available resources at each situation and context, they only allow their distribution.

Resource Discovery

Ultimately, due to the limited battery power and reduced computing power and aggregate bandwidth of mobile devices, mobile solutions usually rely on large-scale backbone infrastructures such as server farms, data centers, or telecommunication companies operated cloud infrastructures. In such infrastructures, that may have do attend to numerous requests from a multitude of mobile devices, two issues are of key importance to most work done in this area: discovery (of services or resources) and management. The previous aims at ensuring functionality are encountered, while the latter tries to preserve its availability for all users and in balanced manner as possible. They provide the invisible support to mobile solutions. We address from higher to lower level of abstraction: service discovery, grid resource management, related cycle-sharing systems, and network related protocols.

Service Discovery Protocols

Service discovery protocols, such as SSDP (Goland, 1999) and SLP (Guttman, 1999), allow a client computer to search and discover other computers that are service providers. These protocols allow a service provider to advertise its presence. In this advertisement the service provider sends a description of the exported service. A client that receives such a message compares the service description with the desired service requirement. If the requirements match the service description, the client can start using the service. The discovery of the services can also be initiated by the client, by broadcasting a message with the requirements the service provider must comply to. Every service provider that has a service that matches the requirements answers with its identification. SLP (Guttman, 1999) also allows the existence of Directory Agents, central servers that are contacted by the client when looking for services and by the

Service Providers to publicize its services. Even if it is possible to find devices and hosts that have a certain service, it is not possible to easily evaluate the available resources given that these protocols were designed to ease the discovery (i.e., mere presence) of services. The requirements are tested against the static characteristics of the service, not allowing the evaluation of the computer available resources. Whenever several versions of the same service could be used by the client, these protocols still do not allow the association of utility depreciation to outdated versions (i.e., accepting some outdated versions while preferring current one), therefore being inflexible.

Grid Resource Management

In order to optimize the use of grid resources it is necessary to choose the hosts that best fulfills the application's needs. Both Condor (Litzkow, 1988) and Legion (Grimshaw, 1996) provide mechanisms to state what requirements must be meet in order to execute efficiently some code. The Legion system has Collections (Chapin, 1999) that are repositories of information describing the resources of the system. These repositories are queried to find the hosts that have the required resources. The Collection queries are built with the usual relational and logical operators.

Condor uses Classad (Raman, 1999) objects in order to describe computing nodes resources (provider) and define requirements and characteristics of programs (customer). A Classad is a dictionary where each attribute has a corresponding expression. These attributes describe the owner of the Classad. Matchmaking of requirements and resources is accomplished by comparing customers and providers Classads. The rank attribute allows the ordering of the customers and providers that have matching attributes. These systems allow the description of the requirements of a program, as well as the discovery of a computer that allows its efficient execution. However, if a host does not completely satisfy a requirement, it is considered

as not-usable. Besides this problem, these systems require a central server and the set of possible resources is fixed and hard coded.

Current Globus GRAM (Globus, 2012) implementations, as described by Czajkowski (1998), suffer from these same problems: a fixed infrastructure is needed and the set of resources to state and evaluate is fixed. This makes Grid Resource Management systems unusable in dynamic environments, where there is no centralized infrastructure and the resources to evaluate are highly variable.

In the work described by Huedo (2004), clients are able to select host based on user-provided ranking expressions, in order to evaluate resources considering peak and off-peak periods, sustained availability over a period of time, time of day. Othman (2003) describes an adaptive resource broker that estimates job completion time based on periodically sampling available resources (CPU) in order to trigger job migration. However, both systems are designed to speed up execution and trigger job migration, bearing no information on how multiple resource requirements (besides CPU) and their partial fulfillment could be described and evaluated.

Cycle Sharing Systems

Currently available cycle sharing systems allow the development of parallel applications that execute in remote computers. Projects like BOINC (Anderson, 2006) provide a centralized infrastructure for code distribution and result gathering, while systems such as that described by Mason (2003) or CCOF (Zhou, 2004) provide a truly P2P access to computing cycles available remotely, employing advertisement propagation, expanding ring search, and rendezvous supernodes.

In either set of systems the processing power or other relevant resources are not taken into consideration. In projects such as BOINC or CCOF, only the processor state is relevant when selecting the remote host that will execute the code. This solution is easy to implement, fair to the owner of the remote computer, but may slow the overall application, while being restrictive not considering other resources and partial fulfillment.

Network Management Protocols

Network management protocols can be used to query remote computers about its resources, thus allowing the evaluation of the surrounding environment. Currently two major standards exist: SNMP and WBEM/CIM. SNMP, Simple Network Management System, is a protocol used in remote management of computer networks. The original RFC (Case, 2006) defines the architecture, the representation of the information managed and the operations supported on the managed information. Subsequent RFCs define the managed information base (MIB). For instance, the MIB−II (Rose, 1990) specification defines the data that an agent (i.e., a resource provider) must export to management applications. Other MIB defines what information related to storage, processes, or memory usage is exported through this protocol.

The Distributed Management Task Force is developing several standards related to the management of computing resources. These standards range from the definition of APIs the hardware should comply with, to the development of protocols of remote network management. The CIM (DTMF, 2005) specification defines a management information conceptual model and the set of operations to manage the information. The Web Based Enterprise Management (DTMF, 2009) has three main components: CIM, that defines the structure of the managed data, the XML encoding specification for the representation of CIM classes and instances, and a protocol of CIM operations over HTTP, enabling the management of remote computers using the CIM exported information.

All these protocols allow the query of the resources available in a remote computer, but all the network communication and resource com-parison must be explicitly coded by the application programmer. Even-though, these protocols may help define what computer resources should be evaluated and provide an interface to locally access the state of the resources.

A2CLOUD

None of the available solutions are of practical use for the common user neither takes into account the actual mobile environment. Users use mobile devices like regular desktop computers, using commodity application to view and edit regular documents. Furthermore, data is replicated and synchronized among not only multiple devices, but also on the cloud.

Although the work on pervasiveness allows the use of remote resources, most systems require the special development of the pervasive application. These applications become distributed independently of the available resources, always requiring network access to the remote resources. The integration of the cloud with the mobile devices suffers the same problems, applications must be specially developed, and do not take into account the fact that mobile devices, sometimes must act as full feature computers. Adaptive User Interfaces, only allow the adaptation or mobility of the UI, requiring the processing code to always remain on the same host. Ideas from this field can be taken into consideration, but currently adaptive user interfaces do not help optimize the mobile experience.

A2Cloud presents architecture and solutions to take advantage on the new mobile environment and to tackle new uses given to mobile devices.

Its architecture maps (presented in Figure 1) on the various offered functionality:

- Offloading of computation to remote computers
- Partition and distribution of application
- Evaluation of the surrounding environment

Figure 1. A2Cloud overall architecture

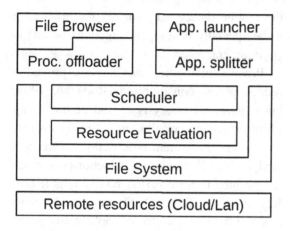

The Cloud Storage glues all components and allows an efficient data transmission between participating computers.

In the remaining of this book chapter we present how the seamless integration of cloud storage with mobile code execution can be accomplished, allowing a transparent access to files and remote resources. We also present how a more expressive resource evaluation mechanism is fundamental to optimized resource usage. The work here presented shows a possible integration of our previous independent work (Silva, 2004; Silva 2010) and further enhances it with the presentation of ST-SPADE

Each of the developed modules tries to address current systems limitations with respect to various factors.

- The Application Splitting (App_Splitter) module allows the automatic distribution of applications into remote computers. This distribution can be of User Interface components to nearby computers or computing intensive code to servers on the cloud.
- The Processing Offloading (ST-SPADE) module allow the execution of complete application on a nearby computer, taking advantage of larger display, higher processing speed, and reducing the mobile device power consumption.

- The Resource Evaluation (STARC) module, depending on the provided requirement (display, clock speed, libraries, and installed applications) finds, evaluates, and chooses the more appropriate nearby computer.

One of the requirements for A2Cloud is its ubiquity with respect to target devices. In order to reduce development burden, the underlying infrastructure should be common to all target systems: Windows, Linux, Mac OS X, and, more recently, Android.

From initial observations, the only programming language and application execution environment that would allow the execution of a single application on these targets without modification was Python (Rossum 1997). Pyhton interpreters are available on most operating systems, offers a consistent execution environment (all libraries are available on all Python implementations) and allow the execution of a full featured application without modification.

Although presented in different sub-sections, the Resource Evaluation Module is fully integrated with both the application splitting module (to find the best place to execute mobile code) and with the processing offloading module (to find the best host where to offload computations).

Shortcoming of Current Solutions

When developing mobile applications, the solution that may seem optimal is to write specific code to handle distribution, using special APIs and explicitly code all communication.

This requires all behavior to be hard coded into the application, and requires the programmer must also know in advance how all objects will interact when deployed in remote computer. Even if using specialized mobile deployment libraries, it is necessary to change the original code and take into account all possible execution scenarios (available remote resources, available communication links).

By performing code transformation, the application can be automatically modified to handle new execution environments and scenarios, but guaranteeing the existence of a single code base. These transformation tools read the source code (or a binary version) and, taking into account configuration files or environment characteristics, modify or extend the original code. The code to handle the environment awareness and application transformation is inserted in a latter phase of the development, closer to the execution step.

If the transformation is done at compile time, several binary versions will exist. Although better that the development of multiple code versions, still has some drawbacks: the new binary versions may to take into account all characteristics of the environment and in some way a selection of the proper binary application must be made.

To overcome these problems run-time code transformation is better, since all transformation is performed taking into account the real characteristics of the environment.

None of the currently existing systems support for a transparent development of mobile applications: programmers are required do have a different code base for the mobile version of the application and another for the serial one.

Mobile grids may be a solution to the problem of offloading lengthy tasks from mobile devices. Recent work on mobile grids, such as Mobile OGSI.NET (Chu, 2004) or Concierge (Rellermeyer, 2007), has been centered on the integration of services with mobile devices. Their aim is to develop infrastructures to help the deployment of distributed applications running on mobile devices and accessing remote services.

The approach used to develop mobile computing systems, consisted on splitting the application on components, e.g. ICrafter (Ponnekanti, 2001). The user interface runs on the mobile device and the computing intensive parts running on a remote computer. This approach reduces the burden on the mobile device but requires the application to be specially developed targeting the mobile environment.

Process offloading has already proved to reduce power consumption (Rudenko, 1998), but required the analysis and adaptation of application source code as proposed by Zhiyuan Li (2001). The system proposed performs code analysis in order to discover functions that would be executed faster if offloaded to a remote host. Rajesh Krishna Balan (2007) presents a language to simplify the adaptation of applications, so that they can be easily offloaded from mobile devices, to allow cyber foraging. The presented solution is composed of: i) a language to define how the application should be split; ii) a middleware for management of every distributed application; and iii) stub generators for the modules that should be offloaded. With these modules, programmers can modify any application so that part of it can be executed on a remote host. In summary, even though such code offloading solutions provides good results, they all require modifications at the application source code level. Presently, no tool allows the efficient execution of unmodified commodity applications from mobile devices, taking advantage of remote devices, to speed them, ease user iteration and reduce power consumption.

Today, there are many systems supporting the discovery of resources; e.g., grid infrastructure schedulers (Chapin, 1999; Raman, 1999) and service discovery protocols (Goland, 1999; Guttman, 1999). These systems were designed with certain architecture in mind. Grid infrastructure schedulers require a fixed centralized infrastructure, which is impractical in a volunteer P2P computing environment. Furthermore these classes of systems only return a binary answer stating if the remote computer fulfills the requirements. Besides this, none of these solutions solve the extensibility problem, as it is impossible to define new resources to be evaluated or new ways to evaluate them.

Network management protocols (DTMF, 2009; Case, 2006) allow a fine grained resources query and search, but the programmer must deal with all low level issues. The client programmer must use a network management programming API in its applications, not allowing the separation between the resource location and evaluation issues and its application logic. Web Services discovery protocols allow the discovery and evaluation of a fixed, predefined set of resources. If a programmer has a different requirement that remote hosts must fulfill, service discovery protocols are of no use. As the requirements cannot be matched to the services available, the shipping of the resource evaluation code is the only solution to these cases.

Application Splitting (App_Splitter)

Today, most mobile devices (e.g. smartphones, tablets, PDAs) are in some way associated to a fixed personal computer or server. In general this relation is only taken into account for synchronization purposes.

This is rather restrictive since, while away from these fixed computers, such mobile devices may require resources that are not available (e.g. network bandwidth, processing power or storage space). This lack of resources prevents the user from doing what he wants when he wants.

We propose a system in which, by enabling automatic remote code execution on a remote computer, these limitations are subdued. At run time it is decided whether some application code should run locally or on a remote computer. This is achieved using runtime meta-programming and reflection: we transform a centralized Python application so that some part of its code is run on another computer, where the needed resource is known to be available. This is accomplished without any manual code change. The performance results obtained so far, i.e. with no optimizations, are very encouraging.

With the advent of mobile communication technologies, the resources available to mobile devices are no longer constant. In a certain instant, the connectivity and bandwidth can be low and in the next instant these resources can be widely available. This variation on the environment and how the application must react poses a challenge to the development of environment aware applications. Adding to the mobility of these devices we now have a large number of personal computers with highly available resources (disk, bandwidth, screen...); when the user is roaming with its mobile device such resources are available but not used.

One kind of module that behave independently of the environment resources are the video player plugging in web browsers. In a portable device, while browsing a site, if the user wants to see a downloaded movie, this action is always performed in the device. The browsing application isn't aware of nearby computers that may have a larger display or better connectivity. If these computers could be used in a transparent and automatic way, the user would benefit from it, in terms of speed and ease of usage. If the network bandwidth is limited or the storage space is insufficient, a better approach would be to execute the download to a remote computer.

For example, a web browser application that displays HTML pages or stores downloaded files can benefit from the resources available in the remote computers. If a nearby device has a larger display or better network link, all work should be accomplished by this more apt computer. This computer should be able to execute some code on the background (for instance the code that is to download a file) or even show some UI components on its larger display.

Such environments poses new challenge, how to develop and adapt mobile computer applications to its environment but also how to evaluate the useful surrounding resources, In the remaining of this section we address the problem of how to split a monolithic application so that it can run and take advantage of nearby devices.

App_Splitter

Since the initial prototypes where developed in python, in order to modify the binary application, metaclasses (that intercept code loading) where used. Depending on the configuration files and the characteristics of the environment, the code gets modified.

With this approach only one binary file exists and depending on the transformation metaclasses and environment characteristics, different final versions can be generated.

By using metaclass programming we manage to intercept the class loading in an easy and straightforward way. We implemented a metaclass, defined in the constructor of all loaded classes and made it responsible for the adaptation of the code being loaded.

App_Splitter Architecture

In order to distribute a centralized application, the following steps must be accomplished:

1. Load the application requirements,
2. Transform the mobile classes,
3. Select the suitable remote host to execute the code, and
4. Allow the remote execution and mobility of the code.

Steps (1) and (3) are handled by the STARC resource evaluation module.

The application splitting module is made by two different components (presented in Figure 2): the Code Transformer and the Remote Execution engine. The format of the class requirements and the resource evaluation mechanisms are described in the Resource Evaluation section.

A configuration file that states what classes are mobile and what their requirements are is required and is loaded before any code transformation. This file also contains the requirements that will be later evaluated

The Code Transformer module contains all transformation code and modifies classes that can run remotely (those referred in the configuration file) into mobile classes. This module changes the class code and attaches it the requirements that are to be evaluated when creating objects.

The Remote Execution module is distributed between the mobile device and on the remote computer and is responsible for the creation of the remote objects and the communication between the mobile device and the remote computer. This module transparently handles code upload the code into the remote computer

Application Transforming and Execution

When executing applications the App_Splitter module performs the following steps:

- Check for class mobility
- Transform class code

It is the application programmer that is responsible for tagging classes that can be executed remotely. A configuration file stores the name of all those classes. These classes must have a well-defined interface only exposing methods. Furthermore the programmer must also provide the class requirements that will later be used to decide what hosts are fitter to execute it.

Several mechanisms exist to transform classes, either before the application execution (resorting to code transformation or special compilers) or during execution (by means of metaclasses).

Figure 2. App_Splitter architecture

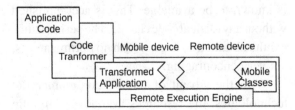

After the bootstrap of the transformed application, it is necessary to decide whether a class is to be executed locally (if no nearby resource exist) or select the more apt neighbor. This is accomplished by the resource Evaluation sub-system.

If, due the environment characteristics, it is better for the object to run locally, a normal local object is created. Otherwise, the Remote Execution module creates an instance of the class on the remote computer and a proxy on the local device. This proxy will replace the object, intercept all method calls and redirect them to the remote object.

App_Splitter Implementation

In the prototypical implementation of our system we used the Python language. We took advantage of its portability and dynamic nature and the presence of introspection and reflection mechanisms on all tested platforms. There are fully functional Python interpreters to most desktop and server platforms and to most portable devices (Windows, Android and Linux). In order to transform in run time the application we used the python reflection built-in mechanisms and to make communication between computers possible we used the Pyro (Jong, 2012) package.

The Code Transformation module intercepts all code loading and on a first step decides whether the class should run created unmodified or not. If a requirement file to that class exists, the class is transformed. The class loading interception is accomplished using a customized metaclass.

The classCreator metaclass (Listing 1) is responsible for the interception of the program's classes loading: whenever a class is loaded from disk the buildClass method is executed.

This code checks if the class being built was referred in the configuration file (Line 3) by verifying if its name was previously inserted into the at the remClass hash-table. This hash-table contains the names of the classes within the configuration files. If its name is not present in the hash-table, this class is built normally by the system default metaclass type (Line 10).

If the class being built was referred in the configuration file, the original class must replace by a proxy class (Lines 4-8 in Listing 1). The original class (Lines 4 and 6) is stored in an attribute of the proxy class, so that later it can be accessed to create local or remote objects. The remoteCodeCreator will act as a proxy class; it is built on Line 5 and configured with the original class (Line 6) and the execution requirements (Line 7).

The returned class (a proxy to the original one) intercepts object creation calls, contains the code needed to evaluate the requirements and creates remote objects. Its code is shown in Listing 2. The code that handles object creation is not the one in the original class but the one present in the remoteCodeCreator.

Listing 1. Class loading interception

```
class classCreator(type):
    def buildClass(ClassName):
        if (name in classCreator.remClss):
            oldclass = type.buildClass(name+"old")
            replaceClass = type.buildClass(name, remoteCodeCreator)
            replaceClass.originalClass = oldclass
            replaceClass.server = classCreator.remClss[name]
            return replaceClass
        else:
            return type.builtClass(name)
```

Listing 2. RemoteCodeCreator replacement class

```
class remoteCodeCreator (object):
    def buildObject(this, *args):
        host = this.find_device()
        if decision == 'local':
            obj = this.originalClass.createObject()
        else:
            URI=genURI(host)
            proxy = getAttrProxyForURI(URI)
            cdURI = proxy.createObject(this.originalName,args)
            obj = getProxyForURI(cdURI)
        return obj
```

Line 3 evaluates the requirement on several hosts discovering the more apt. If the local device is the one with more resources to satisfy the rule, a local object is created (Lines 4 and 5). In the opposite case a remote object must be created in a remote computer.

To create the new object in the remote computer, the Remote Execution module contacts the remote computer (Lines 7 and 8) and creates an instance of the original class on the remote computer (Line 9) and its proxy locally (Line 10).

This method can either return (Line 11) a local object or a proxy to a remote object. This proxy transparently implements and exports the same interface as the original class. From this point forward the original application transparently interacts with a remote object by calling methods from the proxy.

The Remote Execution module is distributed between the mobile device (client side) and the fixed computer where the remote code will execute (server side). The server side contains a service that receives requests from the clients to create new objects, creates and makes them made available to be remotely called.

When creating a remote object (described in Listing 2), first a proxy to the server is obtained and the calls are forwarded to the located object. When requesting the creation of a remote object (Line 9 of Listing 2), if its code is not present in the remote computer, the server automatically downloads the necessary code to create and execute the objects.

After the code is loaded and the object is created, this new object is registered as a new server in order to receive the call made in the original application. On the original application side, after the remote object creation, the URI returned is used to create a new proxy to the remote object. From this point forward the call made supposedly to a local object is redirected by the Pyro proxy to the remote object stored and available in the server.

In order to use this system and allow the automatic remote execution of the code, there isn't any need to change the original code, nor the Python code interpreter. Instead of calling the application the usual way (python app.py) one only needs to add an argument to the command line: python codetrans.py app.py. One can also configure python so that our system is always loaded whenever a python program runs.

This codetrans.py file is responsible for bootstrapping our system by loading the configuration file associated with the python program and registering the classCreator metaclass (Listing 1) as the default metaclass. After these initial steps the original python file is loaded, transformed as described in a previous section and the application starts executing.

In order to create objects in remote computers, the server responsible for it must be running on those computers.

The selection of the remote host to create objects is performed by means of STARC module.

Processing Offloading (ST-SPADE)

The previous section presented mechanisms to take advantage of nearby remote devices to execute parts of a mobile application.

Another possibility to take advantage of such resources, is to execute complete applications on those more apt (bigger screens, better bandwidth) computers.

Since these mobile devices are becoming more and more connected it would be good to allow the transparent execution of ordinary productivity applications on the available computers, thus, taking advantage of, for instance,

With ST-SPADE, we present a tool that allows the remote execution of common computing tasks on several remote computers, otherwise executed on mobile devices. Users should be able to speed the execution of tasks such as image manipulation by taking advantage of remote idle computers, releasing the mobile device to other tasks and reducing power consumption. We propose the application of processing offloading (in part, similar to the ones used in Grid and Cluster computing), while taking into account the particularities of mobile users.

On the area of scientific computing the offloading of computations to more powerful remote computers is a good solution to speed lengthy jobs, but users are required to use specific tools to start its remote jobs. On mobile devices, if a user wished to run applications with desktop speed, he would have to initiate the computation on the remote computer using, for instance, VNC. In this case, the data should be, not in the mobile device, but already on the remote desktop computer, furthermore the display would still be the one of the mobile device.

The offloading of computations to remote hosts has been proposed earlier, but involved the evaluation and adaptation of application source code. Remote execution of generic software packages may seem impractical and without standard use, but from the moment data and files are shared among devices (using cloud bases storage systems), mobile devices are replicating desktop computers (allowing the editing of, for instance spreadsheet, and text files) and mobile devices connectivity are close to total, there are a class of applications that can be offloaded from these mobile devices to nearby computers.

Here we present ST-SPADE, a system that facilitates the execution of commodity software on nearby computers in order to reduce battery consumption and increase usability.

From the moment it gets installed on the mobile device, when a user opens (for reading or editing) a file, it becomes possible for that file to be transparently opened on a nearby computer. If the file is stored in the cloud (and accessible from a fixed PC), if the fixed PC has a compatible application installed, the user can start using the larger display to edit or view that file.

ST-SPADE will be responsible for discovering a nearby computer, contact it with the file identifier, and order it to open. After editing, the fixed PC will store the new file version on the cloud, which will later be synchronized to the mobile device.

ST-SPADE

As a tool to offload computations from mobile devices to remote computers, ST-SPADE is most useful to those tasks that can take advantage of the better input devices on a fixed PC (larger display and keyboard). All tasks requiring the usual productivity suits fit nicely into the target of ST-SPADE.

Since common users (with low computing knowledge) should be able to use such system, its installation and use should be simple. No complex configuration should be performed, and, in order to start a remote application, a single click should be enough.

One of the most relevant factors for the success of a system like ST-SPADE is the amount of applications that can be executed in it. Such class of application should exist both in mobile devices and fixed computers, and range from the office suits (word processor, spreadsheet) to the image manipulation applications. Any other class of applications that read and process files with a predetermined type (extension of content-type) can be used within ST-SPADE. Scripts of interpreted languages (Java, python, R) can also take advantage of remote computers.

ST-SPADE should allow a simple interaction: the user clicks on a file, and if a nearby computer exists that files opens there. Intermediate authorization steps can occur.

ST-SPADE Architecture

In order to allow the opening of files on remote computers, a ST-SPADE daemon must be running in each cycle provider (desktop computer), while the mobile device only needs a client. Its architecture is presented in Figure 3.

Each ST-SPADE client is composed of a File Explorer Extension, in order intercept file access, and by an Execution Redirection module. The daemon is only composed of a module responsible for receiving requests from the client and executes the adequate application.

The Client only needs to intercept file open events from the installed file explorer. Depending

Figure 3. ST-SPADE overall architecture

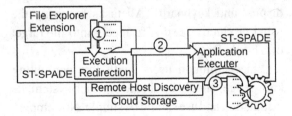

on the installed operating system, this step can be performed in various ways: interception of the file open event or use of context menu.

The client also needs to get a unique file identifier, so that the ST-SPADE daemon can access the corresponding file. This identifier must be supplied by the underling Cloud storage systems.

Inside the ST-SPADE daemon, after receiving the identifier, the Application Executer is responsible for finding a suitable application and executes it.

The Remote Host Discovery module is responsible for finding a suitable computer: one that is near, has better characteristics than the client (larger screen, or better bandwidth), and has an appropriate application installed. The Cloud Storage host the files (cached on multiple devices) that are to be edited, viewed or processed on the more apt computer available.

ST-SPADE Execution Overview

The ordinary execution of ST-SPADE can be split in three main steps.

The first step corresponds to the opening of a file on a mobile device using the available file explorer. After the file opening is intercepted (step 1 in Figure 3) ST-SPADE verifies that the requested file is stored in a Cloud Storage platform and contacts the Remote Host Discovery module.

The remote host discovery module, not only discovers nearby computers, but also evaluates them for their characteristics (for instance, display size). Next, the ST-SPADE daemon obtains (using the Cloud Storage programming API) a unique identifier for the accessed file and sends it to the potential target for the execution (step 2).

The ST-SPADE daemon looks for an appropriate application to process the requested file and executes it (step 3).

Any result produced by the remote processing will be stored on the Cloud and later transferred to the mobile device.

Since the ST-SPADE is to be executed on a local area network, on an initial phase, security can be relaxed.

ST-SPADE Implementation

The ST-SPADE client was developed in Python and creates a unique identifier for that file (the path inside the DropBox mounting point) using the available DropBox programming API.

The communication between the client and the daemon is performed using a python based Pyro (Jong, 2012) remote object infrastructure.

The daemon was also developed in Python and implements a simple Pyro server, also using the available DropBox API. To experiment with heterogeneity the ST-SPADE daemon runs in Linux with the KDE graphical environment.

The next section (Resource Evaluation) describes how resources are evaluated and hosts selected.

Resource Evaluation (STARC)

The efficient use of the surrounding resources relies on an efficient network link, but, also from an adequate and precise evaluation of such resources. Furthermore this evaluation is of greater importance since there are an increasing number of resources a mobile device can use to increase its efficiency, ranging from nearby devices, which can for instance lend its display or network link, to cloud servers where complex computations can take place or data is stored.

Currently available service discovery and matchmaking solutions are unsuited to highly mobile and heterogeneous environment as they are limited to predefined sets of characteristics. Applications with highly specific previously unforeseen resource requirements cannot take advantage of the surrounding environment.

In the remaining of this chapter we present an extensible, expressive, and flexible resource discovery middleware, and resource requirement specification language. Besides standard resources (memory, network bandwidth), application developers may define new resources requirements and new ways to evaluate them. Small custom functions may be developed that, once uploaded to the remote computer, are executed returning values representing host capacity to fulfill each requirement.

Application programmers can write complex requirements (that evaluate several resources) using the fuzzy logic operators. Each resource evaluation (either standard or specially coded) returns a value between 0.0 and 1.0. This value states the capacity to (partially) fulfill the requirement, considering client-specific utility depreciation. By comparing the values obtained from the various hosts, it is possible to precisely know which one best fulfills a client's needs, regarding a set of required resources.

STARC

Taking into account the characteristics and limitations of currently available resource discovery and evaluation systems we designed STARC to make resource discovery more adaptive via extensibility (ability to incorporate new resources) and flexibility (expressiveness in requirement description, utility function depreciation on partial fulfillment, and employing fuzzy-logic to combine multiple requirements).

Thus, STARC rates the neighbor hosts indicating which one is more capable. Its extensibility allows not only the evaluation of most usual resources (memory, display characteristics,...) but also the dynamic inclusion of new characteristics (presence of specific libraries or hardware, processing speed,...) to be evaluated. Furthermore, each host can define how the requirements are evaluated against its resources.

In order to know what requirements remote computers must fulfill, the STARC middleware requires a file stating client's resource requirements. Thus, the application programmer must associate a file to the modules, classes or applications that have such execution requirements. The requirements file states, using logic operators, the relation between the several resource characteristics that are relevant, with associated value ranges, and utility depreciation in the case of only partial fulfillment being possible (i.e., sets of utility ranges).

When an application needs to find a host that best answers to a set of requirements, the local STARC middleware is contacted. The application provides the STARC middleware with the requirements with utility ranges that will be transmitted to the available remote hosts. Each remote host compares its resources with the requirement utility ranges stated in the file and returns a numeric value stating how its resources fit the client's requirements.

If the requirements are completely fulfilled, the evaluation returns 1.0 and, when there are absolutely no resources (or a minimum cannot be satisfied) to meet the requirements, the 0.0 value is returned. Hosts that partially meet the requirements will return a value between 0.0 and 1.0, taking into account the partial fulfillment ranges and associated utility depreciation (not necessarily strict linear mappings), provided by the client. The values returned by remote hosts are compared by the client that triggered the resource discovery; the host with the greatest value is the one whose resource best matches the client's requirements.

STARC provides means to perform resource discovery and evaluation without an explicit intervention of the application programmer. All low level issues, such as communication and resource querying, are transparently handled by STARC.

The STARC middleware allows an application to discover and evaluate the resources present in remote computers. In addition, it eases the comparison of computers that have suitable resources.

The STARC middleware is an assemblage of components named STARC daemons, which execute both in clients and in resource providers. In order to use the STARC middleware, a programmer must write a XML file stating its application requirements and feed it to a locally running STARC daemon. This daemon is responsible for the discovery of remote hosts and the evaluation of the requirements on those computers. The application will receive a list identifying the available hosts and how capable they are of fulfilling the requirements. These requirements can range from available memory or processor speed to certain libraries of helping applications.

Listing 3 presents a possible requirement for an application that requires a large display (larger than 800x600) and one of two possible graphical libraries.

This class of requirements should and can be handled by STARC, allowing an efficient and precise evaluation of the resources available on a

Listing 3. Application Requirement example

```
• Application requires a large display
  o a 1280x1024 pixel display is required
  o a 1024x768 pixel display is second best
  o a 800x600 pixel display is inadmissible
• System should provide a graphical Library
  o Either Qt Library
    ▪ at least version 4
    ▪ version 2 second best
  o Or any version of WxLibrary
```

single computer, but also the ordering of different of the various providers.

Listing 4 presents a formal representation of the requirements presented in Listing 3. A requirement can refer a simple resource (display in Listing 4) or it can be a complex composition of other requirements using logical operators. The composition of requirements is accomplished by using usual logical operators: and, or, not.

In order to precisely define a required resource, it is necessary to state its name and, if necessary, the ranges of resource values and associated utility depreciation. These elements (e.g. displayResolution and version in Listing 4) will be used during the corresponding resource evaluation. From the evaluation of each resource, taking into account, each range and associated depreciation, it is possible to precisely know if a computer is adequate

or not, and on a set of computer which one satisfies best the user requirements.

Listing 5 presents the DTD for the requirement XML files. The previous example would not be verified by this dtd, because all <or>, <and> and <resource> tags should be enclosed on a requirement, furthermore, the configuration of each resource evaluation should also be enclosed in a <config> tag.

With this syntax it is possible to write complex requirements with the conjunction or disjunction of the characteristics of the resources. For instance, it is possible to state that a program needs a display with a minimum size and either one of two libraries as illustrated in Listings 3 and 4. In this example we want to know if a certain computer has a display, preferably larger than 1280 × 1024 pixels, and has either the Qt (an updated version) or the Wx library installed.

Listing 4. simplified XML requirement example (note the nonlinear depreciation of utility values in displayResolution and version number for partial fulfillment ranges).

```
<and>
    <resource>    <name>display</name>
        <displayResolution>
            <range> <minx>1280</minx> <miny>1024</miny> <util>1.0</util>
            </range>
            <range> <minx>1024</minx> <miny>768</miny> <util>0.5</util>
            </range>
            <range> <minx>640</minx> <miny>480</miny> <util>0</util>
            </range>
        </displayResolution>
    </resource>
    <or>
        <resource>   <name>QtLybrary</name>
            <version>
                <range> <minnumber>4</minnumber> <util>1.0</util> </range>
                <range> <minnumber>2</minnumber> <util>0.5</util> </range>
            </version>
        </resource>
        <resource>   <name>WxLibrary</name>   </resource>
    </or>
</and>
```

Listing 5. Requirement DTD

```
<!ELEMENT requirement (resource| and|
or| not)>
<!ELEMENT and (requirement+)>
<!ELEMENT or (requirement+)>
<!ELEMENT not (requirement)>
<!ELEMENT resource (name, config?)>
<!ELEMENT config (#PCDATA)>
<!ELEMENT name (#PCDATA)>
```

To state this information we use the <or> and the <and> logical operators and three different resources. Inside the display resource element we state what the required size is: we use the displayResolution, range, minx and miny XML elements to specify that information. As will be seen later, this evaluation configuration XML will be handled by the code responsible for the evaluation of each resource.

A requirement can refer a simple resource (for instance display in Listing 4) or it can be a complex composition of other requirements using logical operators. The composition of requirements is accomplished by using usual logical operators: and, or, not. In order to precisely define a required resource, it is necessary to state its name and, if necessary, the ranges of resource values and associated utility depreciation, in the config element. This config element will be used during that resource evaluation. From this expression it is possible to know if the computer is adequate or not.

Figure 4. STARC architecture

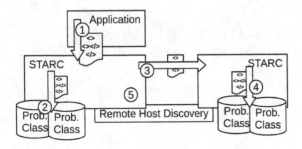

STARC Architecture

The architecture of the STARC middleware is presented in Figure 4. The STARC middleware is composed of STARC Daemons, which execute in the various devices, either clients or resource providers. Each daemon handles all requirement evaluation requests: those generated from a local application and remote requests generated by another remote daemon.

To use the STARC middleware, an application, must provide to the local STARC daemon a XML Requirement File containing a description of the hardware or software requirements (Step 1 in Figure 4). The STARC daemon reads the requirement and executes locally the relevant Environment Probing Classes (Step 2) in order to know how the resources fulfill the requirements. The logical expressions are evaluated using the values returned by the Environment Probing Classes.

The evaluation of each resource is performed by a specific Environment Probing Classes. The name of these classes is obtained from the XML name element. With this name, it is possible to dynamically load the correct class. After local resource evaluation, the STARC daemon contacts the remote daemons (Steps 3). Each contacted daemon evaluates the requirements (Step 4) and returns the resulting value (Step 5).

The Remote Host Discovery module finds the hosts that have a STARC daemon running and stores them in a list. This module is independent, of the resource evaluation steps, and multiple discovery protocols can be simultaneously used.

In the XML Requirement File, by means of the resource elements, the application programmer states the resource that must be probed and evaluated. Its required characteristics are stated in the config element. When it is necessary to check a resource state or configuration, the STARC middleware executes the corresponding Environment Probing Class. In the example in Listing 4 the necessary Environment Probing Classes are: QtLybrary, WxLibrary and display.

Every Environment Probing Class must have a predefined interface composed of a constructor with no arguments and a method called evalResource.

This evalResource method is invoked by the STARC middleware and receives as a parameter the config XML snippet presented earlier.

For instance, the display Environment Probing Class receives a XML snippet stating the desired display sizes by means of the displayResolution element (shown in Listing 4). Other Environment Probing Classes receive different config XML snippets.

The evalResource method returns a value between 0.0 and 1.0 that states how the computer meets the requirement stated in the XML Requirement File. This fuzzy boo lean value represents the total fulfillment of the requirement (1.0), the total lack of resources (0.0) and also the partial fulfillment of the stated requirement. In the example in Listing 4, the Environment Probing Classes PQtLybrary and WxLibrary return 0.0 if the requested library is not installed or 1.0 if an updated version is available. In the case of Wx-Library, a value in between is returned if only an outdated version of that library is available.

The display resource (evaluated with the XML presented in Listing 4) turns a fuzzy set similar to the one shown in Figure 5. From the XML code

we know that 1280×1024 is the desired display size: if the device's display is larger than that, the Environment Probing Class returns 1.0. If the display is smaller, the resource evaluation returns a value in the interval [0.0, 1.0[. For instance, if a host only has a 1024 × 768 pixel display, the eval-Resource calculates a value of 0.6 (code presented in Listing 6). This value will be subject to an utility depreciation factor specified in the requirement XML file provided by the client, representing how (un-)willing the client is to accept lower resolutions (it defaults to 1.0). Thus, the same host resolution and the same code will produce different partial fulfillment levels of resource availability, adapted to each client's specifications.

If a host returns the highest value, we are sure that it is the one with the display that best fits the requirement. This way we solve the problem of binary answers to the evaluation of requirements: if a host does not fulfill a requirement it does not necessarily returns 0.0. The returned value states its partial capacity to meet the requirement, further

Listing 6. Display evalResource function

```
requiredPixel = minY*minY
actualPixel = realX * realY
return min(actualPixel/requiredPixel, 1.0)
```

Figure 5. Display evalResource value return set

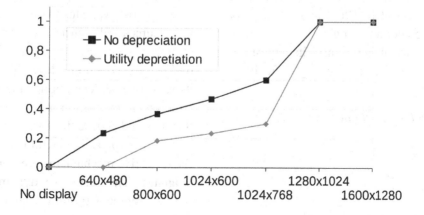

attenuated with client-specific utility depreciation, hence its adaptability.

The use of Environment Probing Classes for probing the resources allows the correct evaluation of resources whose characteristics change with time. Every time this code is executed, its answer reflects the actual state of the resource. The use of these classes also eliminates the need to persistently store the information describing the resources.

The set of standard Environment Probing Classes (display, memory. network connectivity, etc.) is present in every host running the STARC middleware and is located in the STARC daemon installation directory. If not present in the remote host, the Resource Probing Classes can be transferred from the local computer that initiated the requirement evaluation and executed in a restricted safe environment, allowing the evaluation of specific user requirements.

If for some reason the Environment Probing Class associated to a resource cannot be executed, the evaluation of that resource requirement will return 0.0, meaning the computer does not have the resources to meet that requirement.

Systems with requirement representations similar to STARC's XML Requirement Files evaluate these expressions using ordinary Boolean operator, leading only to a binary answer, thus, not being able to provide and ordered metric of partial requirement fulfillment.

In the STARC middleware the evaluation of these logical expression is accomplished using the fuzzy logic (Zadeh, 1965) and, or and not operators presented in Listing 7.

The or operator always returns its largest operand. This means that the capacity to fulfill an

Listing 7. Zadeh Logical operators

```
and (A, B) = min{A, B}
or(A, B) = max{A, B}
not(A) = (1 - A)
```

or requirement is the capacity to fulfill one of its composing requirements. With the and operator we want to guarantee that all requirements are meet, the returned value is the lowest of the operands.

In the same manner as the Environment Probing Classes return values between 0.0 and 1.0, these logical operators return values in the same range, indicating how capable a host is to satisfy the requirements. Using these operators and comparing the value returned from the evaluation of a requirement on different computers, it is possible to find the one more capable: the one with the highest requirement evaluation value.

STARC Implementation

STARC is implemented in Python (Rossum 1997). The Python standard XML processing library is used to parse the requirement files and generate an internal representation of the logical expressions. The Communication module uses the Pyro (Jong, 2012) remote object invocation library. To simplify our system, the interaction between any application and its local STARC daemon is also made by means of a Pyro invocation.

Due to the target environment of this work (home environments and access to cloud computing infrastructures), in its implementation, the Remote Host Discovery module only maintains an updated list of devices on a LAN. Any other computer discovery protocols could have been used (e.g., Jini, UPnP, Pastry).

Each host evaluates the requirements against its resources and returns a fuzzy value. After the remote evaluations, the local STARC daemon builds a list containing hosts identification and its return value. The application requesting the requirement evaluation is responsible to handle this data and choose the host more apt.

In order to easily extend our system we use the reflective mechanisms present in the Python language. The reflective dynamic loading of the Environment Probing Classes supports the addition of new resources to be evaluated. Any programmer can define new proprietary resources to be evaluated by developing a new Environment Probing Class. This new class should be placed in either the STARC daemon or application directories, from where it will be later loaded. Although we used the Python programming language, any other language that supports dynamic code loading, remote method invocation, and remote code loading could have been used.

We have developed a set of probing classes that allow the evaluation of a series of resources in computers running Windows or Linux: CPU frequency, cache size, memory size, available memory, display size (in pixels and inches), network link speed. In the implementation of these classes we used the WBEM capabilities provided by Windows and the /proc/ file system in Linux.

In order to use the STARC middleware, the client or application programmer must only write the XML file stating the necessary resources and call a single method. The way these XML files are evaluated is transparent to the programmer.

VALIDATION AND EVALUATION

All described modules were developed and integration between STARC and the other modules (App_Splitter and ST-SPADE) was performed. With these integrations it was possible to define the requirements classes (App_Splitter) or applications (ST-SPADE) had, and select the more apt host to execute them. The prototypes are able to execute on all the available desktop operating systems available (Windows, Linux, Mac OS X and Android).

The quantitative tests were executed using a Net-book as mobile device. The computer runs Windows XP and has one 1.6GHz Intel(R) Atom(TM) processor and 2 GB of memory.

With respect to qualitative evaluation, we managed to integrate STARC with App_Splitter and STARC with ST-SPADE, in order to optimize

neighbor devices. With respect to App_Splitter and ST-SPADE, the usage experiments described use as resource evaluation the STARC module.

App_Splitter

In order to evaluate the possible uses of our system, we developed two test applications. One application reads a URL from the keyboard and downloads that file to the hard disk. The second one receives also read a URL, downloads the correspondent text file and shows it in a graphical window.

By using our system we managed to execute part of the applications in mobile phones (executing Android and Windows) and execute the other part in a remote computer. In the first test the code responsible for the download of the file runs in the remote computer. In the second test we managed to run the download code and open a new graphical window on a remote computer. These distributed applications were executed without any change to the original code.

In order to evaluate the overhead incurred by our system, we developed a series of micro-benchmarks that allows to measure the time spend in each stage of execution. Next is the description of the potential overheads and the applications used to measure them:

- **Bootstrap:** In this test we measure the time to execute a simple application that only prints a message on the display. We managed to measure the bootstrap of our systems without loading any XML configuration file.
- **Class Loading:** The test program used to evaluate the time spent in the class loading, loads 100 classes that don't have any rule associated.
- **Class Transforming:** This test is similar to the previous one, but the loaded classes have a rule associated, allowing us to measure the time to transform a class.

These test applications were run on Net-book with a 1.6GHz Intel(R) Atom(TM) processor and running Windows(R) XP. The results are presented in Table 1.

From the values shown in Table 1 we conclude that our system overhead mostly comes from the bootstrap (about 0.12s).

All the other tasks have a minimal impact on the execution time. The loading of 100 unmodified classes takes 0.60s, instead of taking 0.22s. The transformation of a class is slower: loading and transformation of the same 100 classes takes 1.14s.

ST-SPADE

The evaluation of ST-SPADE is twofold: qualitative and quantitative. With respect to qualitative evaluation, the initial prototypes prove that it is possible to transparently to the user offload processing to a more apt computer. The only requirements are the installation of the client and daemons, and the configuration of the DropBox folder on each computer, tasks easily done by any computer user. On the mobile device, the user selects a video to be played, but after contacting nearby hosts and deciding the most apt host, the video gets played on a remote computer.

Since there is no file transmission between client and daemons, after the discovery of the daemon to contact, the initialization of any remote execution take constant time. With respect to the evaluation of ST-SPADE, the measured time is only dependent on the processing of the file name, and communication of the request. The

value was always around 40ms, measured on the 1.6GHz Net-book.

In order to prove energy efficiency gains, we measured the power consumption when playing the video locally on the mobile device and remotely by means of ST-SPADE. Initial evaluation shows that for a 9 minute video, there is a 33% efficiency gain when using ST-SPADE to offload the video visualization to a remote computer. This evaluation compared to different scenarios:

- Movie playing on the mobile device (with network off, but display on)
- Movie playing on the remote computer (with network on and display off)

Longer tasks will provide better results since communication will be farther apart.

STARC

With respect to performance, only the evaluation of the requirements has some impact on the usability of the STARC middleware. The discovery of the remote hosts is made in the background, so it is not relevant to the evaluation times.

The client computer, where all remote evaluations were initiated is an the 1.6GHz Net-book, while the remote computer (where resources are evaluated) is a 3.2 GHz Pentium 4 personal computer running Windows. These computers were connected by a 54Mbs wireless network link.

In order to measure a requirement evaluation time we wrote a simple requirement, stating a minimum necessary amount of memory. We also wrote a complex requirement which is a conjunction of 20 simple requirements.

In Table 2 we present the performance results obtained by evaluating memory resources. In the WBEM line we present the time to measure the locally available memory, using the WBEM protocol. In the following experiments we evaluated the simple and complex requirements. We evaluated them locally (without the intervention

Table 1. Application Splitting execution times (sec)

	Unaltered	Adaptation System	Overhead
bootstrap	0.12	0.50	0.38
100 class loading	0.22	0.60	0.38
100 class transformation	0.22	1.14	0.92

of the STARC middleware and directly calling the Environment Probing Classes), using the STARC daemon and programmatically (using the SNMP GetRequest and GetBulkRequest methods).

The local evaluation were performed and initiated on the Pentium 4 computer, while the remote evaluations were initiated on the net-book computer.

In the experiments whose results are on the upload column, the code necessary to perform memory evaluation was not yet available in the Pentium 4 computer.

From the results in Table 2 we conclude that the STARC middleware scales well with respect to the size of the requirement (simple vs. complex) and with respect to the location of the evaluation local vs. remote).

The remote evaluation is slightly slower (a few milliseconds) than the equivalent local evaluation. This is due to the communication overhead. The memory evaluation code upload time is only 80 milliseconds. Other Environment Probing Classes will take a different time to upload.

When evaluating simple requirements, the STARC middleware is comparable to WBEM and better that SNMP. In the case of the complex requirement, the use of the SNMP API is better than the STARC middleware, but the evaluation of the logical operators must be explicitly programmed. If the evaluation is performed from a

Table 2. STARC performance and comparison (in milliseconds)

		Remote	
	Local	No Upload	Upload
WBEM	21		
Local (simple)	23		
Local (complex)	587		
STARC (simple)	30	32	90
STARC (complex)	605	610	713
SNMP (simple)	60	250	
SNMP (complex)	107	550	

remote computer the timing difference between STARC and SNMP is smaller.

Since the answers are fuzzy values, they represent with better details the fitness of the resource to fulfill the requirements.

CONCLUSION

On ever evolving environment, the evaluation of surrounding resources is fundamental. STARC goes a step forward from other exiting resource evaluation mechanism. STARC is capable of evaluating and comparing different resource providers with respect to client specific resource requirements, considering ranges of partial fulfillment and utility depreciation.

With the proposed XML DTD it is possible to define any kind of requirement a module or a complete application can have and that a resource provider must satisfy. The use of fuzzy logic operators eases the comparison of different hosts. Their results clearly states how the requirements are totally or partially fulfilled. When evaluating multiple hosts, the values returned by each evaluation can be compared to find the one that best fit the client requests, with respect to all required resources and perceived utility depreciation. This way, resource discovery is more effective (and will result in fewer resource discovery failures) than a simple matching approach.

The splitting of application, transforming them in distributed ones, allows applications to take advantage of surrounding resources. These applications can execute, part on the mobile device, part on a remote hosts, more fit to execute the mobile modules. The programmer does not have to use complex API, only being required to follow a few programming patterns and define what classes can be mobile on a configuration file. The experiments performed shown that the incurred overhead is minimal, allowing the use of nearby computers or hosts on the cloud.

In a different fashion, ST-SPADE also allows the use of nearby computers (present in the same home network. The order to open a file is made on the mobile device, but the application that will process it is executed on a remote computer, taking advantage of desktop applications and better hardware.

With the presented components, it is possible to take advantage of the Cloud based storage systems that gives data transmission layer between devices.

Both computing offloading and code mobility take advantage of a more precise resource evaluation mechanism (STARC) in order to use more efficiently surrounding resources. Experiments show that these three components can be used in regular mobile device usage, and allow power consumption gains.

REFERENCES

Anderson, D. P., & Fedak, G. (2006). The computational and storage potential of volunteer computing. In *Proceedings of the Sixth IEEE International Symposium on Cluster Computing and the Grid* (CCGRID '06) (pp. 73-80). IEEE Computer Society.

Balan, R. K., Gergle, D., Satyanarayanan, M., & Herbsleb, J. (2007). Simplifying cyber foraging for mobile devices. In *Proceedings of the 5th International Conference on Mobile Systems, Applications and Services* (MobiSys '07) (pp. 272-285). ACM.

Bharat, K. A., & Cardelli, L. (1995). Migratory applications. In *Proceedings of the 8th Annual ACM Symposium on User Interface and Software Technology* (UIST '95) (pp. 132-142). ACM.

Bourges-Waldegg, D., Duponchel, Y., Graf, M., & Moser, M. (2005). The fluid computing middleware: Bringing application fluidity to the mobile internet. In *Proceedings of the The 2005 Symposium on Applications and the Internet* (SAINT '05), (pp. 54-63). IEEE Computer Society.

Calvary, G., Coutaz, J., & Thevenin, D. (2001). Supporting context changes for plastic user interfaces: A process and a mechanism. In *Proceedings of AFIHM-BCS Conference on Human-Computer Interaction IHM-HCI* (pp. 349-363). Springer-Verlag.

Capra, L., Emmerich, W., & Mascolo, C. (2003). Carisma: Context-aware reflective middleware system for mobile applications. *IEEE Transactions on Software Engineering*, 29(10), 929–945. doi:10.1109/TSE.2003.1237173.

Case, J., Fedor, M., Schoffstall, M., & Davin, J. (1990). *RFC 1157: The simple network management protocol*. Internet Activities Board..

Chapin, S. J., Katramatos, D., Karpovich, J., Karpovich, A. G., & Grimshaw, A. (1999). Resource management in legion. *Future Generation Computer Systems*, 15(5-6), 583–594. doi:10.1016/S0167-739X(99)00011-4.

Chen, Y., Zhu, Z., Zeng, Y., & He, Z. (2010). UbiCloud: A cloud computing system for ubiquitous terminals based on end user virtualization. In *Proceedings of the 2010 IEEE/IFIP International Conference on Embedded and Ubiquitous Computing* (EUC '10) (pp. 363-367). IEEE Computer Society.

Chu, D., & Humphrey, M. (2004). Mobile ogsi.net: Grid computing on mobile devices. In *Proceedings of the Fifth IEEE/ACM International Workshop on Grid Computing* (pp. 182-191). IEEE Computer Society.

Chun, B. G., Ihm, S., & Maniatis, P. M. Naik, & Patti, A. (2011). CloneCloud: Elastic execution between mobile device and cloud. In *Proceedings of the Sixth Conference on Computer Systems* (EuroSys'11) (pp. 301-314). New York: EuroSys.

Czajkowski, K., Foster, I., Karonis, N., Kesselman, C., Martin, S., Smith, W., & Tuecke, S. (1998). A resource management architecture for metacomputing systems. In *Proceedings of IPPS/SPDP '98 Workshop on Job Scheduling Strategies for Parallel Processing* (IPPS/SPDP '98) (pp. 62-82). Springer-Verlag.

de Jong, I. (n.d.). *PYRO - Python remote objects.* Retrieved 1 October 2012, from http://pypi.python.org/pypi/Pyro

Demeure, A., Sottet, J., Calvary, G., Coutaz, J., Ganneau, V., & Vanderdonckt, J. (2008). The 4C reference model for distributed user interfaces. In *Proceedings of the Fourth International Conference on Autonomic and Autonomous Systems* (ICAS '08) (pp. 61-69). IEEE Computer Society.

Distributed Management Task Force, Inc. (2005). *DMTF CIM specification.* Author..

Distributed Management Task Force, Inc. (2009). *DMTF CIM operations over HTTP.* Author..

Fox, A., Gribble, S. D., Brewer, E. A., & Amir, E. (1996). Adapting to network and client variability via on-demand dynamic distillation. In *Proceedings of the Seventh International Conference on Architectural Support for Programming Languages and Operating Systems* (ASPLOS-VII) (pp. 160-170). ACM.

Fuggetta, A., Picco, G. P., & Vigna, G. (1998). Understanding code mobility. *IEEE Transactions on Software Engineering, 24*(5), 342–361. doi:10.1109/32.685258.

Giurgiu, I., Riva, O., Juric, D., Krivulev, I., & Alonso, G. (2009). Calling the cloud: Enabling mobile phones as interfaces to cloud applications. In *Proceedings of the 10th ACM/IFIP/USENIX International Conference on Middleware* (Middleware '09). Springer-Verlag.

Globus Alliance Resource Management (GRAM). (n.d.). Retrieved 1 October 2012, from http://www.globus.org/toolkit/docs/2.4/gram/

Goland, Y., Cai, T., Leach, P., & Gu, Y. (1999). *Simple service discovery protocol/1.0 operating without an arbiter.* Internet Engineering Task Force..

Grace, P., Blair, G. S., & Samuel, S. (2003). Remmoc: A reflective middleware to support mobile client interoperability. In *On the Move to Meaningful Internet Systems 2003: CoopIS, DOA, and ODBASE* (pp. 1170–1187). Berlin: Springer. doi:10.1007/978-3-540-39964-3_75.

Grimshaw, A. S., & Wulf, W. A. (1996). Legion - A view from 50, 000 feet. In *Proceedings of the 5th IEEE International Symposium on High Performance Distributed Computing* (HPDC'96). IEEE Computer Society.

Grolaux, D., Vanderdonckt, J., & Van Roy, P. (2005). Attach me, detach me, Assemble me like you work. In *Proceedings of the 2005 IFIP TC13 International Conference on Human-Computer Interaction* (INTER-ACT'05) (pp. 198-212). Berlin: Springer-Verlag.

Gu, X., Messer, A., Greenberg, I., Milojidc, D., & Nahrstedt, K. (2004). Adaptive offloading for pervasive computing. *IEEE Pervasive Computing Magazine, 3*(3), 66–73. doi:10.1109/MPRV.2004.1321031.

Guo, Y., Zhang, L., Kong, J., Sun, J., Feng, T., & Chen, X. (2011). Jupiter: Transparent augmentation of smartphone capabilities through cloud computing. In *Proceedings of the 3rd ACM SOSP Workshop on Networking, Systems, and Applications on Mobile Handhelds* (MobiHeld '11). ACM.

Guttman, E. (1999). Service location protocol: Automatic discovery of ip network services. *IEEE Internet Computing, 3*(4), 71–80. doi:10.1109/4236.780963.

Han, R., Bhagwat, P., LaMaire, R., Mummert, T., Perret, V., & Rubas, J. (1998). Dynamic adaptation in an image transcoding proxy for mobile web browsing. *IEEE Personal Communications Magazine, 5*(6), 8–17. doi:10.1109/98.736473.

Harter, A., Hopper, A., Steggles, P., Ward, A., & Webster, P. (2002). The anatomy of a context-aware application. *Wireless Networks, 8*(2-3), 187–197. doi:10.1023/A:1013767926256.

Holder, O., Ben-Shaul, I., & Gazit, H. (1999). Dynamic layout of distributed applications in fargo. In *Proceedings of the 21st International Conference on Software Engineering* (CSE '99), (pp. 163-173). ACM.

Huedo, E., Montero, R. S., & Llorente, I. M. (2004). Experiences on adaptive grid scheduling of parameter sweep applications. In *Proceedings of 12th Euromicro Conference on Parallel, Distributed and Network Based Processing* (PDP'04). IEEE Computer Society.

Kemp, R., Palmer, N., Kielmann, T., & Bal, H. (2012). Cuckoo: A computation offloading framework for smartphones mobile computing, applications, and services. [LNCS]. *Proceedings of Social Informatics and Telecommunications Engineering, 76*, 59–79.

Kunz, T., & Black, J. (1999). An architecture for adaptive mobile applications. In *Proceedings of the 11th International Conference on Wireless Communications* (Wireless 99) (pp. 27-38). IEEE.

Li, Z., Wang, C., & Xu, R. (2001). Computation offloading to save energy on handheld devices: A partition scheme. In *Proceedings of the 2001 International Conference on Compilers, Architecture, and Synthesis for Embedded Systems* (CASES '01) (pp. 238-246). ACM.

Litzkow, M., Livny, M., & Mutka, M. (1988). Condor - A hunter of idle workstations. In *Proceedings of the 8th Intl. Conf. of Distributed Computing Systems* (pp. 104-111). IEEE.

Manca, M., & Paternò, F. (2011). Flexible support for distributing user interfaces across multiple devices. In *Proceedings of the 9th ACM SIGCHI Italian Chapter International Conference on Computer-Human Interaction: Facing Complexity* (CHItaly) (pp. 191-195). ACM.

Marques, E., Veiga, L., & Ferreira, P. (2008). Transparent mobile middleware integration for java and. net development environments. In *Proceedings of the 14th International Euro-Par Conference on Parallel Processing* (Euro-Par '08) (pp. 47 – 57). Berlin: Springer-Verlag.

Mason, R., & Kelly, W. (2003). Peer-to-peer cycle sharing via.net remoting. In *Proceedings of AusWeb 2003 - The Ninth Australian World Wide Web Conference.* Retrieved 23 April 2013, from http://ausweb.scu.edu.au/aw03/papers/mason/paper.html

Melchior, J., Vanderdonckt, J., & Roy, P. V. (2011). A model-based approach for distributed user interfaces. In *Proceedings of the 3rd ACM SIGCHI Symposium on Engineering Interactive Computing Systems* (EICS '11) (pp. 11-20). ACM.

Morais, J., Silva, J. N., Ferreira, P., & Veiga, L. (2011). Transparent adaptation of e-science applications for parallel and cycle-sharing infrastructures. In *Proceedings of the 11th IFIP WG 6.1 International Conference on Distributed Applications and Interoperable Systems* (DAIS' 11) (pp. 292-300). Berlin: Springer-Verlag.

Murarasu, A. F., & Magedanz, T. (2009). Mobile middleware solution for automatic reconfiguration of applications. In *Proceedings of the 2009 Sixth International Conference on Information Technology: New Generations* (ITNG '09) (pp. 1049-1055). IEEE Computer Society.

Nakajima, T., & Hokimoto, A. (1997). Adaptive continuous media applications in mobile computing environment. In *Proceedings of the 1997 International Conference on Multimedia Computing and Systems* (ICMCS '97). IEEE Computer Society.

Othman, A., Dew, P., Djemame, K., & Gourlay, I. (2003). Adaptive grid resource brokering. In *Proceedings of Fifth IEEE International Conference on Cluster Computing* (CLUSTER'03). IEEE.

Philippsen, M., & Zenger, M. (1997). JavaParty - Transparent remote objects in Java. *Concurrency (Chichester, England)*, 9(11), 1225–1242. doi:10.1002/(SICI)1096-9128(199711)9:11<1225::AID-CPE332>3.0.CO;2-F.

Ponnekanti, S., Johanson, B., Kiciman, E., & Fox, A. (2003). Portability, extensibility and robustness in iROS. In *Proceedings of the First IEEE International Conference on Pervasive Computing and Communications* (Percom 2003). IEEE Computer Society.

Ponnekanti, S., Lee, B., Fox, A., Hanrahan, P., & Winograd, T. (2001). ICrafter: A service framework for ubiquitous computing environments. In *Proceedings of the 3rd International Conference on Ubiquitous Computing* (UbiComp '01) (pp. 56-75). Berlin: Springer-Verlag.

Preuveneers, D., & Berbers, Y. (2010). Context-driven migration and diffusion of pervasive services on the OSGi framework. *International Journal on Autonomous and Adaptive Communications Systems*, 3(1), 3–22. doi:10.1504/IJAACS.2010.030309.

Raatikainen, K., Christensen, H. B., & Nakajima, T. (2002). Application requirements for middleware for mobile and pervasive systems. *ACM SIGMOBILE Mobile Computing and Communications Review*, 6(4), 16–24. doi:10.1145/643550.643551.

Raman, R., Livny, M., & Solomon, M. H. (1999). Matchmaking: An extensible framework for distributed resource management. *Cluster Computing*, 2(2), 129–138. doi:10.1023/A:1019022624119.

Rellermeyer, J. S., & Alonso, G. (2007). Concierge: A service platform for resource-constrained devices. In *Proceedings of the 2nd ACM SIGOPS/EuroSys European Conference on Computer Systems 2007* (EuroSys '07) (pp. 245-258). ACM.

Román, M., Hess, C., Cerqueira, R., Ranganathan, A., Campbell, R. H., & Nahrstedt, K. (2002). A middleware infrastructure for active spaces. *IEEE Pervasive Computing/IEEE Computer Society [and] IEEE Communications Society*, 1(4), 74–83. doi:10.1109/MPRV.2002.1158281.

Rose, J. (1990). *RFC 1158: Management information base for network management of TCP/IP-based internets: MIB-II*. Internet Activities Board..

Rudenko, A., Reiher, P., Popek, G. J., & Kuenning, G. H. (1998). Saving portable computer battery power through remote process execution. *ACM SIGMOBILE Mobile Computing and Communications*, 2(1), 19–26. doi:10.1145/584007.584008.

Sampaio, P., Ferreira, P., & Veiga, L. (2011). Transparent scalability with clustering for Java e-science applications. In *Proceedings of the 11th IFIP WG 6.1 International Conference on Distributed Applications and Interoperable Systems* (DAIS'11) (pp. 270-277). Berlin: Springer-Verlag.

Satyanarayanan, M., Bahl, P., Caceres, R., & Davies, N. (2009). The case for VM-based cloudlets in mobile computing. *IEEE Pervasive Computing/IEEE Computer Society [and] IEEE Communications Society*, 8(4), 14–23. doi:10.1109/MPRV.2009.82.

Silva, J., & Ferreira, F. (2004). Remote code execution on ubiquitous mobile applications. In *Proceedings of the Second European Symposium on Ambient Intelligence* (EUSAI 2004) (pp. 172-183). Berlin: Springer.

Silva, J. N., Ferreira, P., & Veiga, L. (2010). Service and resource discovery in cycle-sharing environments with a utility algebra. In *Proceedings of 2010 IEEE International Symposium on Parallel & Distributed Processing* (IPDPS). IEEE.

Silva, J. N., Veiga, L., & Ferreira, P. (2009). Mercury: A reflective middleware for automatic parallelization of bags-of-tasks. In *Proceedings of the 8th International Workshop on Adaptive and Reflective Middleware* (ARM'09). ACM.

Sousa, J. P., Poladian, V., Garlan, D., Schmerl, B., & Shaw, M. (2006). Task-based adaptation for ubiquitous computing. *IEEE Transactions on Systems, Man and Cybernetics. Part C, Applications and Reviews, 36*(3), 328–340. doi:10.1109/TSMCC.2006.871588.

Spiegel, A. (2000). Automatic distribution in pangaea. In *Proceeding of the 3rd International Workshop on Communication-Based Systems* (CBS 2000) (pp. 119-129). Berlin: Springer.

Truyen, E., & Joosen, W. (2008). Towards an aspect-oriented architecture for self-adaptive frameworks. In *Proceedings of the 2008 AOSD Workshop on Aspects, Components, and Patterns for Infrastructure Software* (ACP4IS '08). ACM.

van Rossum, G. (1997). *Python programming language*. Retrieved 1 October 2012, from http://www.python.org

Vanderdonckt, J. (2010). Distributed user interfaces: How to distribute user interface elements across users, platforms, and environments. In *Proceedings of XIth Congreso Internacional de Interacción Persona-Ordenador* (Interacción' 2010). Retrieved 23 April 2013, from http://lilab.isys.ucl.ac.be/BCHI/publications/2010/Vanderdonckt-Interaccion2010.pdf

Weiser, M. (1991, September). The computer for the twenty-first century. *Scientific American*, 94–100. doi:10.1038/scientificamerican0991-94 PMID:1675486.

Weiser, M. (1994). *Building the invisible interface*. Paper presented at UIST '94 Symposium on User Interface Software and Technology. Marina del Rey, CA. Retrieved 23 April 2013, from http://www.ubiq.com/hypertext/weiser/UIST94_4up.ps

Zachariadis, S., Mascolo, C., & Emmerich, W. (2003). Adaptable mobile applications: Exploiting logical mobility in mobile computing. In *Proceedings of 5th Int. Workshop on Mobile Agents for Telecommunication Applications* (MATA03) (pp. 170 – 179). Berlin: Springer-Verlag.

Zadeh, L. (1965). Fuzzy sets. *Information and Control, 8*(3), 338–353. doi:10.1016/S0019-9958(65)90241-X.

Zhang, X., Kunjithapatham, A., Jeong, S., & Gibbs, S. (2011). Towards an elastic application model for augmenting the computing capabilities of mobile devices with cloud computing. *Mobile Networks and Applications, 16*(3), 270–284. doi:10.1007/s11036-011-0305-7.

Zhou, D., & Lo, V. (2004). Cluster computing on the fly: Resource discovery in a cycle sharing peer-to-peer system. In *Proceedings of the 2004 IEEE International Symposium on Cluster Computing and the Grid* (CCGRID '04). (pp. 66-73). IEEE Computer Society.

KEY TERMS AND DEFINITIONS

Code Mobility: The ability to execute code on remote computers taking into account the available resources and without requiring the remote execution to be hardcoded.

Processing Offloading: Mechanism to execute lengthy tasks on remote computer, in order to speed such tasks or reduce power usage.

Reflective Adaptability: The ability an application has to observe the environment and own characteristics and adapt (runtime change of the executed code) taking into account the available resources.

Resource Discovery: Mechanisms to discover remote resources available remotely and useful to the completion of a task.

Resource Evaluation: Mechanisms to evaluate the usefulness of discovered resources, so that they can be ordered and a better QoS is attained.

Utility Depreciation: Mechanisms to allow a nonlinear depreciation of a given resource, allowing the user to state different levels of satisfiability.

Utility Function: Resource evaluation mechanism that states the usefulness of a given resource. The retuned value depends on the characteristics of the resource, but also on the user requirements.

Chapter 14
Vehicular Cloud Computing:
Trends and Challenges

Kayhan Zrar Ghafoor
Koya University, Iraq

Kamalrulnizam Abu Bakar
Universiti Teknologi Malaysia, Malaysia

Marwan Aziz Mohammed
Koya University, Iraq

Ali Safa Sadiq
Universiti Teknologi Malaysia, Malaysia

Jaime Lloret
Universidad Politecnica de Valencia, Spain

ABSTRACT

Recently, Vehicular Ad Hoc Networks (VANET) have attracted the attention of research communities, leading car manufacturers, and governments due to their potential applications and specific character-istics. Their research outcome was started with awareness between vehicles for collision avoidance and Internet access and then expanded to vehicular multimedia communications. Moreover, vehicles' high computation, communication, and storage resources set a ground for vehicular networks to deploy these applications in the near future. Nevertheless, on-board resources in vehicles are mostly underutilized. Vehicular Cloud Computing (VCC) is developed to utilize the VANET resources efficiently and provide subscribers safe infotainment services. In this chapter, the authors perform a survey of state-of-the-art vehicular cloud computing as well as the existing techniques that utilize cloud computing for perfor-mance improvements in VANET. The authors then classify the VCC based on the applications, service types, and vehicular cloud organization. They present the detail for each VCC application and formation. Lastly, the authors discuss the open issues and research directions related to VANET cloud computing.

INTRODUCTION

Recently, the growth in the number of vehicles on the road has put great stress on transportation systems. This abrupt growth of vehicles has made driving unsafe and hazardous. Thus, existing trans-portation infrastructure requires improvements in

traffic safety and efficiency. To accomplish this, Intelligent Transportation Systems (ITS) have been considered to enable such diverse traffic applications as traffic safety, cooperative traffic monitoring and control of traffic flow. These traffic applications would become realities through the emergence of VANET because it is considered as a network environment of ITS. The increasing necessity of this network is an impetus for vehicle

DOI: 10.4018/978-1-4666-4781-7.ch014

manufacturers, research communities and government agencies to increase their efforts toward creating a standardized platform for vehicular communications (for instance, Vehicle Safety Communication Consortium, Network-on-Wheels and Honda's Advances Safety Vehicle Program (Olariu, 2009). In particular, the 5.9 GHz spectrum band has been allocated for licensed Short Range Communication (DSRC) between vehicles. In addition, in the near future, more vehicles will be embedded with devices that facilitate communication between vehicles, such as Wireless Access in Vehicular Environment (WAVE) (ITS-Standards, 1996). When vehicles are equipped with WAVE, they can communicate with nearby cars and access points within their coverage area.

In addition, car manufactures have advanced and hence fitted out better storage, computation and communication devices in the vehicles. These advances are all for the sake of improving traffic safety and efficiency (Ghafoor, 2013a), (Sommer, 2010), (Ghafoor, 2013b). A long with this development, vehicles can also access internet services and thereby various benefits will be offered to the drivers and passengers (Hussain, 2012). Thus, these advancements in vehicular

technology and communication will provide wide potential applications to meet safety and comfort requirements for driver. However, the phenomenal on-board resources are remaining under-utilized by the aforementioned applications (Li, 2007).

In an attempt to address the problem of resource under-utilizing, the authors in (Eltoweissy, 2010) have proposed the concept of vehicular cloud. VCC is defined as paradigm shift from conventional VANET to vehicular cloud in which vehicles use their on-board resources and cloud resources as well (Olariu, Khalil, & Abuelela, 2011; Abid, 2011). The motivation of merging mobile cloud computing with VCC is the dynamic accessibility of resources. In other words, the VCC follows the concept of pay as you go model instead of buying resources and infrastructure. With this technology, vehicle's communication, computing and storage capabilities can be combined with those of other drivers or rented to the participated cars. This concept is similar to the traditional cloud computing but sensing nodes in VANET are vehicles and they travelling with high speed. VCC is still in its infancy stage of researching and need to be explored more (Arif, 2012). Figure1 shows the number of articles published in the last years.

Figure 1. Number of publications in the last years

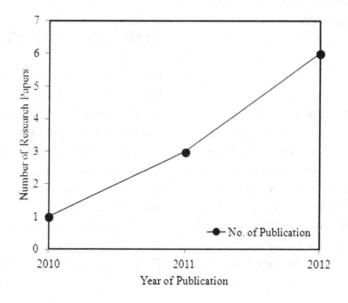

In this Chapter, we surveyed the state-of-arts of vehicular clouds, which is considered as a development of traditional cloud computing with novel features. More precisely, the aims of this Chapter are to introduce the concepts of vehicular clouds and highlight the prospective applications for sake of improving the efficiency of vehicular networks. We explained the existing techniques that utilize cloud computing for performance improvements in VANET. We then classified the VCC based on the applications, services types and vehicular cloud organization. Moreover, we explained the communication paradigm and organization of vehicular clouds. Based on this though study on VCC, we discussed the open issues and research directions related to VANET cloud computing. To the best of our knowledge, this research paper is the first attempt in thoroughly reviewing state-of-arts of VCC and highlighting its challenges.

The rest of the Chapter is organized as follows: introduction section provides an overview of the current state of the arts of VANET. The cloud computing taxonomy and its illustration are discussed in CC section, followed by the discussion on vehicular cloud computing and its architecture, where we also highlight the applications of vehicular clouds and the layers of the vehicular clouds. Finally, conclusion section concludes the paper and discusses future directions.

VANET

The number of vehicles contending for space in existing transportation systems is growing rapidly. This abrupt growth of vehicles has made driving unsafe and hazardous. Thus, existing transportation infrastructure requires improvements in traffic safety and efficiency. To achieve this requirement, Intelligent Transportation Systems (ITS) have been considered to enable diverse traffic applications such as traffic safety, cooperative traffic monitor-

ing and control of traffic flow. Vehicular networks are considered as a network environment for ITS.

Over the past decade, the employing of vehicular communications to support traffic safety and comfort related services have earned much attention in both industry and academia. A divergent number of wireless technologies have been used such as Infrared (infrared) (Kwak, 2004), Bluetooth (Sugiura, 2005) and cellular (Santa, 2008). However, IEEE 802.11 based solutions has witnessed to be the popular and appropriate solution. This advancement is continued as the IEEE 802.11p (Jiang, 2008; Uzcategui & Acossta-Marun, 2009) amendment to the standard is attracting increasing interest. A range of flourish applications are required to aim the uptake of vehicular communications and massive numbers of solutions have already been proposed, with safety applications being the most prominent (Yang, 2009; Yang, 2008) These traffic safety applications are relying on Inter-vehicle Communications (IVC) and the formation of VANET. In addition to the traffic safety services, VANET offers prosperous services like internet on the wheel, high-speed tolling, information infotainment and video on demand (Anda, 2005; Karagiannis, 2011). Due to high mobility of vehicles, however, many research challenges still need to be addressed.

CLOUD COMPUTING

Cloud computing is a style of a new computing paradigm that enables on-demand service to consumers through various cloud service providers. These cloud computing services can be accessed through internet from configured and shared resources like computing storage and applications in a virtual manner. Some of the services are provided for free while others are based on 'pay as you go' model from hardware and system software in remote datacenters (Rodrigues, 2012), (Wlodarczyk, 2011), (Song, 2011). The cloud service providers manage a network infrastructure of datacenters in order to combine the computing power of massive number of servers. Moreover, the 'pay as you go' characteristics of cloud computing enable many advantages such as non-front investment, lower operating cost, highly scalable and easy access. Example of cloud computing are Amazon S3, Google Drive and Microsoft Sky-Drive and they could provide virtualized infinite amount of resources.

With the existence of a pool of resources in mobile environment, a new computing field is emerged called Mobile Cloud Computing (MCC) (Gupta, 2012). In this environment, every mobile device can act as mobile client or service provider. It is witnessed that the popularity of mobile devices (e.g., tablet computer, iPad, and Smartphone) for internet access are increasing day-by-day as compared to stationary personal computers. This

is because significant improvements of mobile devices have shown in terms of hardware, operating system and transmission capability. Recently many mobile applications like real time services, instant email checking, social networking can be performed ubiquity through mobile device. These mobile devices effectively form mobile cloud to access internet cloud ubiquity. For instance, a mobile device interested in downloading an application from nearby mobile node. This information is stored and propagated in the mobile cloud (Gerla, 2012). Moreover, there are many services of MCC such as Google Gmail, Maps and Navigation systems for mobile, Voice Search, and some applications on an Android platform, that offers great applications to the end users. The general architecture of MCC is illustrated in Figure 2 (Gupta, 2012).

Figure 2. Mobile cloud computing communication paradigm

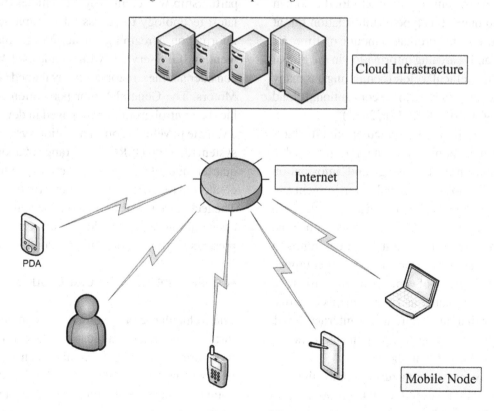

Vehicular Cloud Computing

A massive number of resource-rich vehicles that are travelling on the highways and urban areas possess internet access services, on-board storage, high computation and sensing capabilities. In our daily life, many vehicles spend a substantial time in malls, parking garages and drive ways. With these features, vehicles can be utilized as a cloud node within neighborhood cars that are involved in the cloud formation. Indeed, the drivers may rent their vehicle's on-board resources to the cars that are demanding specific service for stipulated time period (Eltoweissy, 2010). In such situations, vehicles have the capability to cooperate for the sake of solving problems that would happen in centralized system. For instance, a driver raises the question to vehicular cloud regarding the cause of traffic jam in the next road segment. In response to this query, the vehicular cloud creates, maintain and propagate this information to the relevant vehicles. Internet cloud also can be used to query this type of information but at the expensed of inordinate amount of time for querying and searching information in the global cloud. Thus, vehicular cloud computing has many advantages as compared to the conventional cloud computing (Gerla, 2012; Lin, 2011).

More significantly, vehicular clouds have various crucial applications ranging from traffic safety, environment sensing, and information distribution to the commercial advertisement and traffic infotainment. For instance, vehicles will capture information like traffic condition, road condition, cars in the vicinity, and environment condition and surveillance videos via equipped sensors. This group of vehicles in a specific road segment can exchange and maintain this information rather than uploading to the internet cloud. Among group of vehicles, participated cars can excess the cloud data in the VC.

Recently, car manufacturing companies and governments of several countries attempt to promote the cloud computing in the vehicular networking. For example, in the USA, the Federal Communications Commission's allocated Dedicated Short Range Communications (DSRC) with a range of 75 MHz of the spectrum (5.850 to 5.925 GHz) in support of vehicular networking (Ghafoor, 2013a; Ghafoor, 2012; Ghafoor, 2010). Moreover, roadside infrastructures such as inductive loop detectors, video cameras, acoustic tracking systems, microwave radar sensors, and access points are also helpful for VCC. As part of a project, Ford motor company combines social networks, GPS location awareness, and real-time vehicle data in ways that help drivers go where they want efficiently by using the cloud (2012). Ford is equipped with cloud features called Ford SYNC, which connects customers to real time traffic updates, information, turn-by-turn driving directions, business, sports, weather, and news through voice commands. Recently, Toyota and Microsoft announced a new, 12 million partnership to bring cloud computing to Toyota vehicles. The partnership will equip Toyota vehicles with the latest technology to access telecommunications information, streaming music, energy management, and GPS services, while on the road. We also consider another motor company named General Motors. The General Motor perception and vehicular control groups are engaged in developing a vehicle to vehicle communication system. This system relies on DSRC with a range of about one-quarter mile (400 m) in all directions, with radios connected to traffic lights or construction zones. The technology will provide viable solutions for essential safety information for drivers. Figure 3 presents a taxonomy of vehicular cloud computing.

Architecture of Vehicular Clouds

The vehicular cloud computing composed of three layers of communication. As can be seen in Figure 4, the three communication layers are on-board layer, communication layer and cloud computing layer. In the on-board layer, a vehicle could sense the environment condition, road

Figure 3. Taxonomy of the literature on vehicular cloud computing

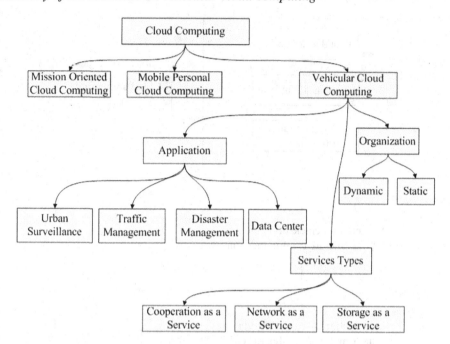

condition or other parameters and these collected data will be shared with neighborhood vehicles in the vicinity. Perhaps beacon frame is used to synchronize and handshake among vehicles and hence sharing operational data. The second layer enables communication between vehicles and vehicular clouds. As vehicles are equipped with IEEE 802.11p transceivers, they can exchange information either vehicle-to-vehicle (V2V) or vehicle-to-infrastructure (V2I) by using Wi-Fi, IEEE 802.11p, WiMAX or 3G cellular communications.

In V2V architecture, cars communicate with each other in the vicinity in order to enable traffic safety for the drivers and passengers as well as comfort related applications. As it was witnessed in the past decade, this communication has important role in reducing number of crashes, collisions in vehicular scenarios. VCC also can be formed among V2V communication scenarios, in case of abnormal road condition or driver behaviour, a vehicle that observed this traffic abnormality will send an event-driven emergency message to the formed vehicular cloud storage and hence all vehicles that are registered within this VC will receive the emergency message. Event-driven emergency message contains the positional information of the location where abnormal situation occurs (Chen, 2009; Yang, 2008; Yang, 2009; Xu, 2004). Moreover, VANET utilizes fixed gateways such as WLAN access points, WiMAX base stations or 3G networks in order to exchange packets among vehicles and internet. The V2I is complementary to V2V architecture and can raise driver safety and reduce traffic deaths and injuries by implementing collision avoidance and warning systems (Bordley, 2012). As V2I requires high cost of infrastructure installation, V2V is considered more feasible (Huang, 2010). It is worth mentioning that traditional vehicular networks consist of the lower two layers: on-board and communication layers. Moreover, the cloud computing layer provides communication at the cloud level through roadside unit or mobile gateways.

Figure 4. Vehicular cloud computing architecture

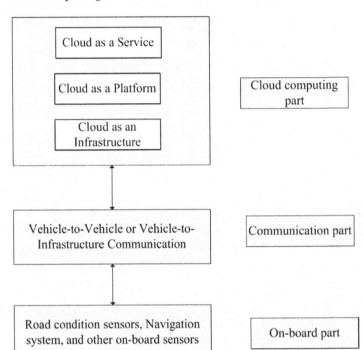

The cloud computing layer of vehicular cloud consists of three sub-layers (i.e. cloud as an infrastructure, cloud as a platform and cloud as service). Cloud as an infrastructure provides Computation and storage capabilities for vehicles. The sensed data is classified based upon the type of information and then stored in the storage unit of a vehicle. Then, vehicles use their computation capability to analyze the data that is stored in the storage unit. Cloud as a platform consists of development tools that are hosted in the cloud and accessed via a group of vehicles within the same cloud. Moreover, the cloud as a service offers network as service, cooperation as a service and storage as a service (Eltoweissy, 2010). Some vehicles have internet access while they are moving. Those vehicles can share this luxury with neighbor vehicles within the same vehicular cloud. In the same way, some vehicles have sufficient amount of storage while others need extra storage. Storage as a service can offer storage to the vehicles which need extra

storage. Cooperation as a service also is used to provide various services to the drivers via V2V communication.

Organization of Vehicular Cloud Computing

The vehicular cloud is formed as the following.

Static VC

In our daily life we spend a substantial amount of time on the street and parking lot. On the roads, the traffic situation is dynamic and is varied from normal to abnormal scenarios such as traffic congestion and accidents. In such abnormal traffic conditions, VC is mimic to the traditional cloud computing services. This similarity between VC and traditional cloud computing is also true when vehicles remain static in malls or parking garages. Consider an information technology company that offers IT services and solutions to its customers. In such company many vehicles of staff members remain idle in the parking lot and their computational resources also remain un-utilized. The companies' top management may request the formation of static vehicular cloud by providing rewards to those employees who want to rent the on-board resources of their vehicles. As a result, the formed static VC will take benefit from the cooperation of on-board resources of vehicles that are participating in the cloud formation. Figure 5 shows the static formation of vehicular cloud. As can be seen in Figure 5, vehicles are parked in front of the company and this company offers incentive to the drivers who will rent on-board resources of their vehicles. This kind of VC formation is called stationery VC since all vehicles are static.

Dynamic VC

Advances in vehicular networks in one hand and cloud computing in the other motivate the necessity of dynamic formation of VC. As vehicles are travelling with high mobility and the network changes rapidly, the mobility parameter plays an important role in VC formation. Mobile vehicular cloud would be formed among vehicles with similar mobility. The reason is that among similar velocity vehicles the relative velocity will be reduced and the cloud will long last. Thus, moving vehicles can make a cloud of storage and

computation resources autonomously. The process of dynamic VC formation is mimic to the dynamic cluster formation in VANET.

Dynamic VC is formed by first electing a vehicle that has smallest value of relative mobility to the nearby cars. The elected vehicle is known as cloud head and will form the VC by inviting the neighbor vehicles to join its VC. The invited neighbor vehicles should response back the request from the cloud head. If the number of vehicles is sufficient, the cloud head will declares the cloud formation. Thus, VC enables a seamless integration and pooling of resources of the vehicles that are registered in the VC. With this capability, the VC provides a large computer cluster and a huge distributed data storage facility (Olariu, Khalil, & Abuelela, 2011). In contrast to stationary formation of VC, Figure 6 illustrates that the neighbor vehicles are involved in formation of dynamic vehicular cloud. This is called dynamic VC since all vehicles within the VC are travelling on the roads.

Applications of Vehicular Cloud Computing

In this section several possible implementation scenarios and the application outcome of VCC are discussed (Olariu, Khalil, & Abuelela, 2011; Abid, 2011; Gerla, 2012; Alazawi, 2011).

Figure 5. Static vehicular cloud formation

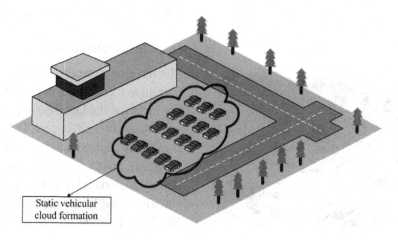

Static vehicular cloud formation

Figure 6. Dynamic vehicular cloud formation

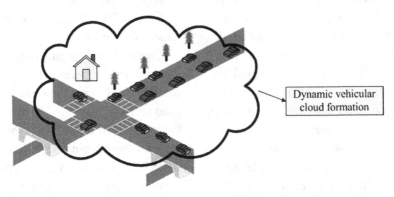

Datacenter Formation

In our daily life, people are spending hours in malls for shopping purpose in holidays or weekends. As illustrated in Figure 7, many cars are parked in the parking garage and their owners spend substantial amount of time for shopping. During the time of shopping, these cars remain idle with under-utilized computation resources. These on-board resources can shared/rented to the interested customers with permission of the cars owners. This process can be handled by the mall IT management department. For instance, each vehicle has Ethernet interface and in each parking spot the mall management should provide Ethernet cable. If a driver intends to rent the resources of its car, he needs to connect the Ethernet cable to

Figure 7. Datacenter formation in VC

vehicle's Ethernet interface. In this case, the mall management should reward drivers who rented the on-board resources of their vehicles for the sake of static VC formation.

Some people are travelling from a country to the other one. When they travel, they left their vehicles in the parking lot of an airport. It is a great opportunity to exploit the resources of these vehicles in order to form a VC in a parking spot. For instance, the airport management section can offer power source, storage or Ethernet connection to the vehicles that are interested to rent those resources for a stipulated time period. The participated vehicles in a VC will reveal their arrival and departure times. This information helps the airport management to schedule the shared on-board resources. Thus, long-term parking lot and sharing travel plan by participated cars will provide plentiful, stable and long-term resources (Olariu, Khalil, & Abuelela, 2011).

Disaster Management

The reaction to emergency situations is very important as its consequences are very catastrophic. For instance, the Japan earthquake, 11 September in USA and other disasters. The total cost of Japan tsunami is approximately about 300 billion USD (Alazawi, 2011). Certainly, communication technology has crucial role in responding emergency situations and hence reducing human death toll. VCC can be used to manage disaster events by forming vehicular clouds that are participating in the evacuation operation. The evacuation system should provide a safe area for the people when a disaster situation occurs in a city. For instance, evacuation zones should be chosen based on the low travelling time and availability of resources such as medicine, food and water. The authors in (Alazawi, 2011) proposed intelligent disaster management system for Ramadi city in Iraq. The proposed work leverage vehicular networks and MCC for the evacuation procedure in case of unpredicted disaster.

Traffic Management

Nowadays the on-board navigator can estimate the traffic fluidity and patterns from MC and forwards the optimal route to the vehicles. The navigator service enables traffic management through the communication between on-board and server navigator. The on-board navigators send time, position and position of destination in a fixed rate to a server navigator in internet. The server responses back the best route based on the estimated load and delay on the incremental route to the destination. This cooperation is considered as an interaction between VC and internet cloud. More precisely, the VC through on-board navigator senses the traffic congestion of road segments whereas the internet cloud through server navigator

estimates the traffic flow on those roads. With the help of such applications, vehicles can compute local traffic of roads and determine the reasons of traffic jam in order to address the traffic deadlock and react accordingly (Gerla, 2012).

Urban Surveillance

Vehicles in VANET are equipped with sensors and they communicate with each other for mobile surveillance and environment monitoring. Traditional urban surveillance systems for monitoring security attacks rely on the fixed roadside infrastructure. This method is not efficient as compared to the mobile surveillance via vehicles. With cooperation of VCC video surveillance can be done on-demand via vehicles that are travelling on the urban roads and highways. For urban surveillance, self-organized vehicles participating in surveillance system will form a vehicular cloud and they can report any suspected activity such as terrorist attack to a specific zone. Mobile surveillance can also be used in investigations after the event has occurred. For instance, after any event the video file exist in the storage of a vehicle and it can be used in forensic investigation (investigation of a platoon of crashes in the urban area) (Gerla, 2012). Figure 8 shows an example of urban surveillance system integrated with VC. As can be seen, the blue vehicles are considered

Figure 8. Urban surveillance system in VC

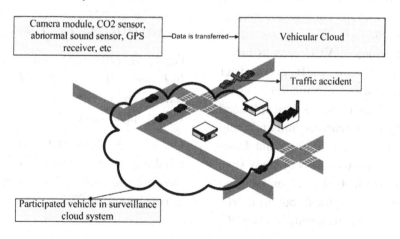

as self-organized cars and they formed vehicular cloud for surveillance activities. For instance, the on-board video surveillance that is stored in the VC can be used to investigation on the traffic accident between red vehicles.

CONCLUSION

Vehicles have powerful source of computing and sensing on-board resources that are useful for traffic safety and comfort-related applications. These underutilized resources can be pooled among all vehicles in the vicinity. Vehicular clouds has emerged due to high vehicle's computation and storage resources, sensing capabilities and traditional cloud computing. The VCC is considered as a complementary of traditional cloud computing but with more services and applications. Participated vehicles can share/rent their on-board resources such as computation, storage and internet access, to the VC subscribers. When the VC is fully deployed, many applications would be realized such as urban surveillance, environment monitoring, reducing traffic accidents, traffic and disaster managements. The outcome of these applications will impact the drivers and the community.

In this Chapter, We presented the classification of VCC based on the applications, services types and vehicular cloud organization. We then highlighted the communication paradigm of VCC that consists of three layers: car level, communication layer and cloud layer. We also pointed out the crucial applications of VCC such as urban surveillance and monitoring, traffic and disaster management, and datacenter formation in VC.

VCC is new and exciting topic and still need to be explored by the research community and academia. The research opportunities and directions are falls in the various areas of study such as security issues in formation of VC and sharing information in VC, geographical routing in VC, and algorithms for disaster management using VC.

REFERENCES

Abid, H. A. (2011). V-cloud: Vehicular cyber-physical systems and cloud computing. In *Proceedings of the 4th International Symposium on Applied Sciences* (pp. 165-170). San Francisco, CA: ACM.

Alazawi, Z. A. (2011). Intelligent disaster management system based on cloud-enabled vehicular. In *Proceedings of the 11th International Conference on ITS Telecommunications* (pp. 361-368). London: ITST.

Anda, J. A.-N. (2005). VGrid: Vehicular adhoc networking and computing grid for intelligent. In *Proceedings of the 61st IEEE Vehicular Technology Conference* (pp. 2905--2909). Madrid: IEEE.

Arif, S. A. (2012). Datacenter at the airport: Reasoning about time-dependent parking. *IEEE Transactions on Parallel and Distributed Systems*, 23(11), 2067–2080. doi:10.1109/TPDS.2012.47.

Bordley, L. A. (2012). Commercial motor vehicle wireless roadside inspection pilot test. In *Proceedings of the 91st Annual Meeting on Transportation Research* (pp. 6-12). IEEE.

Chen, C. A. (2009). Fairness and QoS guarantees of WiMAX OFDMA scheduling with fuzzy. *EURASIP Journal on Wireless Communications and Networking*, 1–14. doi:10.1155/2009/512507.

Eltoweissy, M. A. (2010). Towards autonomous vehicular clouds. *Ad Hoc Networks*, 49, 1–16. doi:10.1007/978-3-642-17994-5_1.

Gerla, M. (2012). Vehicular cloud computing. In *Proceedings of the The 11th Annual Mediterranean on Ad Hoc Networking* (pp. 152-155). Philadelphia: IEEE.

Ghafoor, K. Z. (2010). A novel delay-and reliability-aware inter-vehicle routing protocol. *Network Protocols and Algorithms*, 2(2), 66–88. doi:10.5296/npa.v2i2.427.

Ghafoor, K. Z. (2012). Fuzzy logic-assisted geographical routing over vehicular ad hoc networks. *International Journal of Innovative Computing, Information, & Control*, 8(7B), 1–26.

Ghafoor, K. Z. (2013a). A fuzzy logic approach to beaconing for vehicular ad hoc networks. *Telecommunication Systems Journal.*, 52(1), 139–149. doi:10.1007/s11235-011-9466-8.

Ghafoor, K. Z. (2013b). Intelligent beaconless geographical forwarding for urban vehicular. *Wireless Networks*, 19(3), 345–362. doi:10.1007/s11276-012-0470-z.

Gupta, P. A. (2012). Mobile cloud computing: The future of cloud. *International Journal of Advanced Research in Electrical. Electronics*, 1(3), 134–145.

Huang, C. A. (2010). Adaptive intervehicle communication control for cooperative safety. *IEEE Network*, 24(1), 6–13. doi:10.1109/MNET.2010.5395777.

Hussain, R. A. (2012). Rethinking vehicular communications: Merging VANET with cloud computing. In *Proceedings of the IEEE 4th International Conference on Cloud* (pp. 606-609). New Orleans, LA: IEEE.

ITS-Standards. (1996). *Research and innovative technology administration (RITA)*. Retrieved January 10, 2013, from http://www.standards.its.dot.gov/about.asp

Jiang, D. A. (2008). IEEE 802.11 p: Towards an international standard for wireless access. In *Proceedings of the Vehicular Technology Conference* (pp. 2036-2040). IEEE.

Karagiannis, G. A. (2011). Vehicular networking: A survey and tutorial on requirements, architectures. *IEEE Communications Surveys & Tutorials*, 13(4), 584–616. doi:10.1109/SURV.2011.061411.00019.

Kwak, J. S. (2004). Infrared transmission for intervehicle ranging and vehicle-to-roadside. *IEEE Transactions on Intelligent Transportation Systems*, 5(1), 12–19. doi:10.1109/TITS.2004.825082.

Li, F. A. (2007). Routing in vehicular ad hoc networks: A survey. *IEEE Vehicular Technology Magazine*, 2(2), 12–22. doi:10.1109/MVT.2007.912927.

Lin, Y.-W. A.-M.-J. (2011). Cloud-assisted gateway discovery for vehicular ad hoc networks. In *Proceedings of the 5th International Conference on New Trends* (pp. 237-240). IEEE.

Olariu, S. A., Weigle, M. C. (2009). Vehicular networks: From theory to practice. London: Chapman and Hall/CRC. doi:doi:10.1201/9781420085891 doi:10.1201/9781420085891.

Olariu, S. A., Khalil, I., & Abuelela, M. (2011). Taking VANET to the clouds. *International Journal of Pervasive Computing and Communications*, 7(1), 7–21. doi:10.1108/17427371111123577.

Rodrigues, J. J., Zhou, L., Medes, L. D. P., Lin, K., Lloret, J. (2012). Distributed media-aware flow scheduling in cloud computing environment. *Computer Communications*, 35(15), 1819–1827. doi:10.1016/j.comcom.2012.03.004.

Santa, J., Gómez-Skarmeta, A. F., Sánchez-Artigas, M. (2008). Architecture and evaluation of a unified V2V and V2I communication. *Computer Communications*, 31(12), 2850–2861. doi:10.1016/j.comcom.2007.12.008.

Sommer, C. A. (2010). Adaptive beaconing for delay-sensitive and congestion-aware traffic. In *Proceedings of the IEEE International Vehicular Networking Conference* (pp. 1 - 8). IEEE.

Song, W. A. (2011). Review of mobile cloud computing. In *Proceedings of the 3rd International Conference on Communication* (pp. 1-4). IEEE.

Sugiura, A. A., Dermawan, C. (2005). In traffic jam IVC-RVC system for ITS using Bluetooth. *IEEE Transactions on Intelligent Transportation Systems*, 6(3), 302–313. doi:10.1109/TITS.2005.853704.

Uzcategui, R., & Acossta-Marun, G. (2009). Wave: A tutorial. *IEEE Transactions on Communications Magazine*, 47(5), 126–133. doi:10.1109/MCOM.2009.4939288.

Wlodarczyk, T. W. (2011). An initial survey on integration and application of cloud computing. In *Proceedings of the Third International Conference on Cloud* (pp. 612-617). IEEE.

Xu, Q. A. (2004). Vehicle-to-vehicle safety messaging in DSRC. In *Proceedings of the International Workshop on Vehicular Ad* (pp. 28-38). Philadelphia, PA: ACM.

Yang, L. A. (2008). Congestion control for safety messages in VANETs: Concepts and framework. In *Proceeding of the 8th International Conference on ITS Telecommunications* (pp. 199-203). IEEE.

Yang, L. A. (2009). Piggyback cooperative repetition for reliable broadcasting of safety. In *Proceeding of the Consumer Communications and Networking Conference* (pp. 1-5). Anchorage, AK: IEEE.

Chapter 15
Mobile Healthcare Computing in the Cloud

Tae-Gyu Lee
Korea Institute of Industrial Technology, Korea

ABSTRACT

Previous medical services for humans provided healthcare information using the static-based computing of space-constrained hospitals or healthcare centers. In contrast, current mobile health information management computing and services are being provided so that they utilize both the mobility of mobile computing and the scalability of cloud computing to monitor in real-time the health status of patients who are moving. In addition, data capacity has sharply increased with the expansion of the principal data generation cycle from the traditional static computing environment to the dynamic computing environment. This chapter presents mobile cloud healthcare computing systems that simultaneously leverage the portability and scalability of healthcare services. This chapter also presents the wearable computing system as an application of mobile healthcare.

INTRODUCTION

This chapter describes system structure, information flow and application or service scenario in order to build a cloud computing based on mobile healthcare system. In order to implement this system, one must satisfactorily accommodate the characteristics of mobile healthcare device, client, or the special advantages of information system on the mobile computing, ubiquitous computing, wearable computing and cloud computing, etc (Barry, 2006; Gunther, 2006; Monique, 2010).

First, mobile healthcare is rising as an important concept to implement real-time remote medical treatment service. The mobile healthcare is increasing usage of portable devices such as PDA or Smartphones/Smartpads while guaranteeing mobility of patients, for their free activity. It also

DOI: 10.4018/978-1-4666-4781-7.ch015

identifies the condition of patients on a real-time basis, in other words in order to provide healthcare information service immediately without delay of time. HL7 establishes a standard of supporting messaging interwork and compatibility between existing information system and health & medical treatment information service based on the standard layer of OSI. This can support the scalability of mobile health care (Jim, 2007; Daniel, 1999; Vietanh, 2000; Deborah, 2001; Ian, 2002; Malik, 2003).

Second, mobile computing implements multilateral healthcare services through gathering and analyzing various types of healthcare information without setting limitations on the specific medical treatment of mobile users. And it extends the static computing based on wire as a dynamic and flexible computing environment.

Third, ubiquitous computing supports a sensing network, which recognizes user status (place, time, weather and temperature, etc) without limitation of place and time. It also supports freedom of user connection and seamless connectivity.

Fourth, wearable computing is an item which is steadily being studied in various business fields because of its advantages such as clothing-based wearability, portability, and lightness. This is attracting people's interest as a next generation computing item with a composition that has combined the advantages of mobile computing and ubiquitous computing (Rehman, 2012; Polly, 2000; Sungmee, 2003; Peter, 2007; Franz, 2004; Shirley, 2009). Especially, it shows strength as a form of important critical mission applications from the emergence of the cases of applying wearable computing to the field of healthcare (Peter, 2007; Franz, 2004; Shirley, 2009).

Fifth, cloud computing has been proposed based on the distribution of the system in order to consolidate the economic efficiency of existing computing or system flexibility and scalability aspects (Bhaskar, 2009; Hoang, 2011; Sanjit, 2010). The implementation of healthcare-cloud

information system based on such cloud system can effectively support large-scale healthcare client as a background computing system located in the back of mobile healthcare user.

Healthcare clients would want to identify their own health condition on a real-time basis at a free daily living environment and receive medical services instantly in case abnormal symptoms are discovered. In order to implement such real-time mobile client healthcare, the following requirements must be supported. First, the body information of mobile user must be gathered on a real-time basis. Second, a seamless wireless mobile network infrastructure must be supported for the satisfactory transmission of health information continuously.

In order to satisfy these requirements, wearable computing and clouding computing must be combined based on the mobile healthcare client, mobile computing and ubiquitous computing as it is described above. Through such various integrated configuration of computing, the mobile healthcare service for mobile client shown as Figure 1 should be implemented.

Mobile healthcare can provide a mobile healthcare solution that makes information available to users (Wikipedia, 2012). Recently, mobile healthcare has been an increasingly important topic because it employs bio-sensing and mobile user information to provide real-time monitoring of a customer's body. The flow of information in embedded bio-sensing systems from the standpoint of the user of mobile healthcare is a series of forwarding processes, which collect sensing data from bio-sensing nodes. First, the sensing node senses the state of the user's body, and collects analogue or digital bio-signal data. Next, it delivers the collected data over wired or wireless communication links. Finally, a backbone-computing node in the Internet receives the filtered data as a relay or a final node. When executed in reverse, a healthcare process may be executed that

Figure 1. Healthcare services in mobile computing

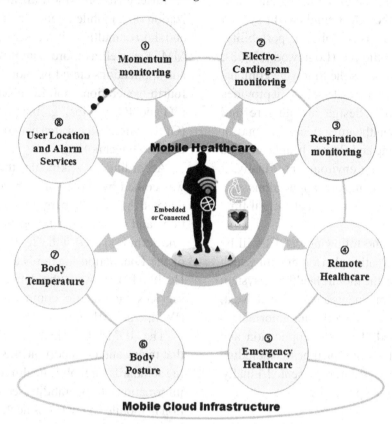

will control or monitor the bio-sensing nodes on the user's body.

Figure 1 depicts services that monitor the momentum, the electrocardiogram, and the respiration, which are mobile healthcare services. These services check the user's health as the user changes location. Furthermore, the remote healthcare service makes doctor-patient consultation possible, and the emergency healthcare service supports emergency calls and emergency medical services. In addition, the body posture service monitors the body shape in order to observe the acute syncope patients such as the elderly. The body temperature service checks the mobile user's body temperature and provides notification when it is abnormal. Finally, the user location and alarm services provide the appropriate medical information and notification via alarm about a hazardous area as required depending on the location of the user.

In order to build a mobile healthcare service, the mobile cloud infrastructure is provided various computing to mobile users at the rear including bio-information sensing, transfer, storage, analysis, evaluation, and feedback. The mobile cloud enhances the features of mobile computing such as scalability, portability, compatibility, etc of system resources including the user.

Mobile healthcare is recognized as the best alternative to monitor and to guide the health status of the mobile user. Mobile cloud is recognized as the best alternative to support mobile computing services of mobile or wireless devices, and is recognized as a means to differentiate economy, flexibility and lightweight in the mobile healthcare system (Pat, 2013; Zachary, 2013).

For providing the fast and accurate healthcare of mobile user, the mobile healthcare devices located on the front need lightweight and real-time characteristics. At the same time, the mobile cloud system located on the rear strengthens the system characteristics such as scalability, portability, safety, security, mobility, etc (Logicworks, 2013).

This chapter proposes the following computing service objectives to readers. First, it provides a mobile computing design architecture and organization for healthcare services. Second, it shows the processing and flow of healthcare data in a mobile computing environment. Finally, it provides versatile healthcare applications and healthcare-information services that use real-time cloud computing.

In this chapter, the following details will be described as an alternative plan for reflecting such requirements. First, the mobile healthcare system architecture and components are presented. Next, the mobile healthcare networks and information flows are described. Then the application and service sectors of mobile healthcare including wearable healthcare system are presented. Finally, the conclusion will be presented.

BACKGROUND

Mobile healthcare stands for all healthcare services provided to the user moving freely based on the mobile healthcare information system including mobile devices and remote medical devices. The definition of such mobile healthcare has been defined in the following various fields.

The definition of mHealth of the Global Observatory for eHealth (GOe) of the WHO (World Health Organization) is as follows:

mHealth is a component of eHealth. mHealth or mobile health is the realization of medical and public health supported by mobile devices, such as mobile phones, patient monitoring devices, personal digital assistants (PDAs), and other wireless devices (Misha, 2011, p.6; Guido, 2007).

mHealth involves the utilization of and capitalization on a mobile phone's core utility of voice and short or multimedia messaging service (SMS/MMS) as well as more complex functionalities and applications including mobile web, third and fourth generation mobile telecommunications (3G and 4G systems), global positioning system (GPS), wireless local area network (WLAN), and Bluetooth technology.

According to Wikipedia, the term mHealth was coined by Professor Robert Istepanian and denoted the use of "emerging mobile communications and network technologies for healthcare." The definition used at the 2010 mHealth Summit of the Foundation for the National Institutes of Health (FNIH) was "the delivery of healthcare services via mobile communication devices" (Wikipedia, 2012).

The HL7 Mobile Health Workgroup declared that they want to support the mission of developing standards for mobile health services, data and information interoperability, security and integration in mobile and wireless healthcare and public health systems to reduce costs, improve quality and delivery, guide informed-decisions and promote individual and population health (HL7, 2012).

The existing definition on mobile healthcare or special features, advantages and disadvantages on access are in the following (Misha, 2011; Panagiotis, 2005; Khamish, 2005; Daniela, 2007; Guido, 2007).

As the initial information service of mobile healthcare, simple text, emergency call and voice information are exchanged while providing healthcare services such as medical examination reservation, specialized counseling and treatment management, etc. But it has many shortcomings in disease prevention, real-time health monitoring and implementing diagnostic services. Also, the situation is that latest smart devices and wearable medical services are almost nonexistent.

IT medical information technology supports remote counseling between doctor and patients through remote information exchange. However, this has limitations on new healthcare market of health monitoring, sports guide and healthy life guide, etc. This does not have latest smart device and wearable computing components. Especially, since the healthcare sensing is single module or functional approach products and services, a balanced aspect based on overall healthcare information system is absent.

HL7 supports messaging interwork and compatibility between existing information system and healthcare system based on the standard layer of OSI. But it has structural limitations in real-time, mobility and scalability aspects. This also gets limitations in the interwork of recent smart technology and cloud system technology (Bhaskar, 2009; Hoang, 2011; Sanjit, 2010). This gets restricted as a medical information system limited to application layer such as SaaS in order to building up a cloud medical information system. This becomes difficult to build up platform and infrastructure of medical information system with lower cloud systems such as PaaS or IaaS.

Previous mobile health service remains at a simple medical supplemented information services such as message, emergency call and voice counseling, etc. In order to expand as healthcare real-time monitoring and healthcare diagnosis service, the installation of wireless transmission system for sending medical information such as photo image or video, etc and the installation of cloud information transmission environment for implementing economical large scale real-time information transmission service are required as well as the client device technology.

In order to build up a cloud based mobile healthcare service, the following issues must be solved. First, the mobile client must support lightweight and mobility support for mobile healthcare. Also, it must support seamless healthcare information flows and heterogeneous network integration for mobile healthcare. The components and applications of mobile healthcare (variety/diversification) must support modules and apply products that in-

terwork with existing e-health/health center while providing an exclusive handheld mobile device, supporting interwork module with commercial smart phones and must support new personal healthcare devices such as wearable products.

The features of mobile cloud such as scalability, portability, safety, security, mobility, etc enhances the mobile healthcare service of mobile users. Scalability should ensure the continued scalability of the system resources, due to the increase in the number of users of mobile healthcare. Portability is to support the user's devices replacement, the program transplant, etc using the mobile agent technique. For safe information transmission, the safety enforces the safe network and information system by the fault-tolerant network configuration. Mobile cloud security supports the security cloud configuration, which is required for supporting dynamic security based on context-awareness. Mobility cloud supports to ensure a seamless user-mobility. Mobile cloud computing can improve the performance of healthcare organization, but mobile cloud infrastructures require a highly secure and auditable computing platform to meet statutory and regulatory requirements governing the handling of protected health information (Chris, 2013; Shams, 2013).

HEALTHCARE APPLICATION SCENARIOS AND SERVICES

In this section, we present mobile healthcare scenarios and describe the issues related to mobile computing components working in real-time.

Mobile healthcare applications include applications related to health/medicine, social network/life, and human-to-human services. These mobile healthcare applications may be applied to all aspects of our lives.

In mobile healthcare services, information scenarios are provided to optimize computing performance and resource efficiency. Especially event scenarios that occur in mobile healthcare can be divided according to the logic of the components that make up the network topology of mobile computing. This study generally assumes that the following stepped (or partial) processes are present, across the entire process from the bio-sensing node to the application servers as shown in Figure 2. Moreover, these scenarios can be used to evaluate the optimal methods for processing real-time event-scenarios for the entire process.

It first monitors the patent's status and detects the abnormal states of the patient. It captures the developing state of a patient's body. Finally, it informs a patient about dangerous environmental information.

It provides the sensed information to a home medical station or doctor. It analyzes the details of the patient's healthcare information and it also delivers the doctor's instructions. It can provide selective medical knowledge using the healthcare expert system, which accumulates the know-how of physicians and healthcare professionals. It can deliver the healthcare information and treatment methods such as the type of workout for a patient.

The applications that take advantage of mobile healthcare services are as follows.

A *health-related sport information system* can provide the knowledge services using an intelligent database. Such a system can be applied to monitoring the health and conducting sports training. The health management system including diet is implemented. A health management cycle including amount of food, amount of exercise and resting time, etc is established in order to improve stamina and physical strength, etc. This system can

Figure 2. Mobile healthcare application scenarios

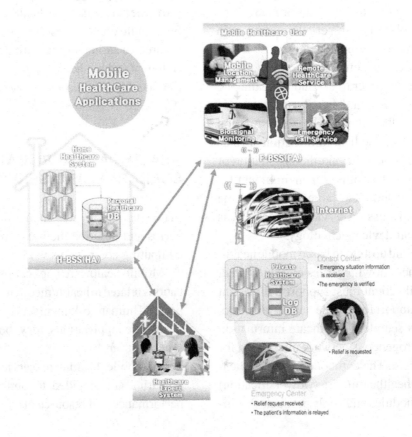

be applied to health management of an ordinary person and record management of sports players.

The *cloud expert system* can provide medical knowledge services using an intelligent database. Such a system continuously constructs medical knowledge using intelligent logic and verified knowledge patterns. The cloud system expands the coverage of the medical knowledge system to a virtual and large database present in the space of the Internet. This space created for the virtual knowledge can integrate or interconnect with the distributed knowledge resources of medical experts via the Internet.

A *mobile healthcare information* system can be used in the field of health and medical forensics applications. Forensics applications require a forensics information guide and healthcare data logging as countermeasures against medical accidents. For example, forensics logging collects the data about the user context and constructs an indexing structure that can be used to search for specific data. The forensics data structure consists of a user id, a user location, a user health state (ECG, respiration, body-temperature, etc.), a dosage, etc. on the path of a mobile user. The forensics logic involves the use of event-based logging and the processing of checkpoints using registered events. The system operators can register the specific events into a dataset that can be stored in a health/medical forensics database.

Emergency relief services support applications that process events of interest to a user. It provides a health medical service whereby a user monitors and detects the status of one's own body. The service then informs by means of an emergency alarm, which alerts to an abnormal health state or other dangerous environmental information. An emergency call is placed to the doctor on call and to a home station. In response, critical analysis and the instructions of the doctor are passed onto the user. Normally, a user's health status and the response thereto are provided to the user in the form of the amount of exercise, an exercise class, etc.

As *military, police, and firefighting services, the biorhythm and survival status information, etc* of mobile user are identified in order to support the performance of public mission-critical applications of military, policy and fire fighting, etc. Therefore, the optimum mission performance information environment will be established. This guides various strategic activities including placement, role and method of mission performer.

THE ARCHITECTURE AND COMPONENTS OF MOBILE HEALTHCARE

The architecture and components of mobile healthcare are shown in Figure 3. It is based on three cloud systems, each of which interacts with the mobile healthcare client, the closed intranet background computing, and Internet open services, respectively.

The first mobile healthcare client layer in the top level imports the sensing event-data from a mobile user or an environmental sensor and exports the data for reporting using the mobile cloud with mobile healthcare agents. The human health-related data and the data about device internals are collected by the mobile embedded station (MES or attached mobile terminal) of each mobile user. The collected data is transferred into the next layer, which is a closed layer taking place in the background, by a base support station (BSS or namely Sync center), which is interconnected with the Intranet infrastructure (namely, an Infra-Network). The mobile networks support external wireless networking (namely Ex-Network) based on an infrastructure network (namely, Internet-working) which is ad-hoc networks that provide direct communication among mobile users. The Ex-Network can include such wireless local networks as BAN/PAN. It dynamically supports user's status sensing network environments based on the location, dangerous event, contact user, etc. of mobile users. The mobile healthcare users

Figure 3. Mobile cloud healthcare architecture

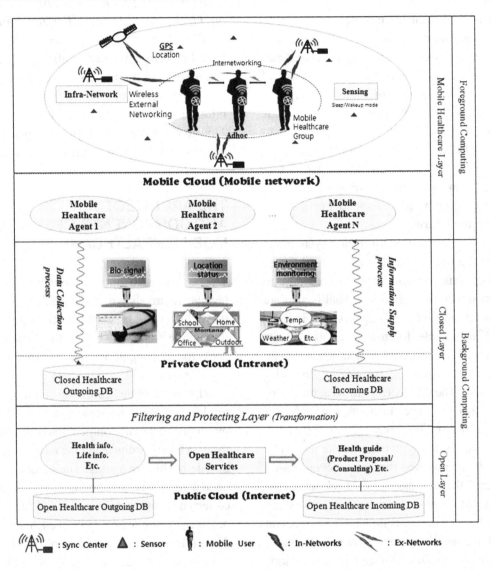

can dynamically form a mobile healthcare group over such wireless networks. Such a mobile healthcare client layer should take into account user mobility and sensing data; hence, the *mobility issue* applies to this phase.

Mobile cloud operates the mobile agents on MES terminal for information transfer of an individual mobile healthcare use. It can support user mobility, wireless transmission of bio-information sensing data, and seamless transmission.

Secondly, a closed layer manages the closed healthcare database and the log data of mobile-healthcare-users by providing background-support infrastructure, which is provided by an operating company or hospital. This closed layer receives the healthcare data collected by mobile users from the upper mobile-healthcare-client layer, analyzes real-time event data or non-real-time planning data, and reports information to the mobile user. Also, it provides filtering and transformation services between the mobile healthcare client layer and the Internet open service layer. This closed layer should offer support for personal information protection and security services in order to provide safe mobile healthcare client computing; this is the *security issue*. A private cloud running on the intranet executes user's device backup, data analysis, control and feedback, location management, etc as the server and center in the rear of the mobile healthcare users.

Finally, an Internet-open-service layer provides, based on the Internet, the available non-security data about human-life related healthcare information service. Also, this layer provides each mobile user's interesting healthcare information as feedback to a mobile healthcare client layer at the top level. This open layer should have high transfer speed and provide convenient user access so that information can be provided rapidly, so that the issue present in this layer is *performance*. Private cloud support a variety of valuable health information services such as health guide, health information sharing, health life-cycle management for supporting mobile healthcare on the Internet.

Overall, the raw data that originated with a mobile user in the first mobile healthcare client layer is collected after passing through the second closed layer into a third open layer in a downward data collection process which is shown in Figure 3. Figure 3 also shows how the collected data is analyzed, filtered, and stored in both the second and the third layers. The service information produced by the third service layer is delivered to the mobile user in the top layer, which is the mobile healthcare client layer, by an upward-oriented healthcare information support process. The download data collection process collects information about healthcare and living from a mobile user. The upload information support process provides a health guide and other guidance for a mobile user.

In order to maximize the portability and mobility of mobile healthcare user, implementing embedded client of healthcare device depends on the implementation of lightweight, thin, small,

and flexible devices. Such mobile healthcare client devices are classified into input devices, output devices, computing devices, and network device. The individual devices develop implementation characteristics independently while two or more device modules can be integrated as single device module. An integrated single module configuration lowers the probability of being exposed to defects because of its concise structure and economical because the production cost is lowered. Also, the dual configuration of client device consolidates system stability as it consolidates the restoration ability followed by defect and failure.

User mobility supports user location recognition and location tracing. Such attribute supports various healthcare services based on user location. For example, it supports emergency call and rescue service of acute patients.

Data mobility supports connectivity and synchronization between healthcare client and data backup center. Data connectivity means supporting the path where the data gathered at the client gets sent to the server and the data at the backup server gets sent to the client. Data synchronization means the data store at the client and the same data stored at the server must be identical.

Service mobility supports disconnected operations and service migration using checkpoint and log in order to guarantee performance and stability of the healthcare and application service which is being executed. Disconnected operations means the fact that the performing service should be recovered and performed continuously when the client gets disconnected. Service migration is the process of moving the location of BSS (Background Support Station) depending on the movement of healthcare user by organizing the mobile agent that supports the client. The relationship between mobile health client and mobile agent is composed of 1:1 mapping structure. This structure can be extended as 1: n or n: 1 relation. For the recovery during client or service disconnection, checkpoint or log is stored periodically or non-periodically during the normal healthcare information service.

Background cloud computing components support real-time mobile healthcare. In mobile healthcare computing, it is an important issue to provide real-time cloud computing model using integrated wireless and wired network environments. The components of real-time healthcare are a *mobile embedding component* and a *background support component*.

The internal component can be virtualized in order to support the optimal real-time mobile communication and computing. From the sensing node to the embedded mobile station, the embedded components are unified by the virtualization of resources within a mobile embedded device, and they can be selectively used to provide optimal real-time computing.

The computing component can be virtualized to create a background computing system including the second closed layer and the third open layer that can support the real-time mobility of

a mobile healthcare user. In the external system of mobile healthcare service, the virtualization of components requires not only that the wireless base stations, user location be virtualized, the Internet and network be virtualized, but also that the servers be virtualized, and that there be the virtualization of healthcare applications and interfaces. In particular, a system optimizing real-time mobility can be configured by identifying and selecting the factors influencing real-time processing. Also, virtualization can provide a virtual API and libraries so that versatile healthcare information services can be easily developed.

Figure 3 shows the cloud computing structure for mobile healthcare. The one showing network configuration of transmitting the healthcare information of mobile user and mobility model of mobile client is Figure 4. In Figure 4, the wearable healthcare user attaching MES device transmits body signal through Foreign BSS. At the Home BSS of home or hospital where the background computing center of wearable user is located, the

Figure 4. Wearable mobility model and computing components in mobile healthcare

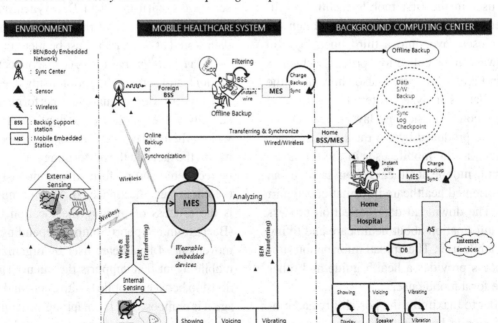

synchronization with offline backup of mobile healthcare client is supported.

The wearable computing system can be provided as a mobile healthcare platform as shown in Figure 4. Each device component is interconnected via a wired or wireless transmission network. In the instance depicted, the following components are present.

MES (Mobile Embedded Station): An MES is an embedded or connected to digital garment, which is interconnected with internal sensors by means of a wireless connection or wired conduction fibers. The MES is also connected with external sensors by a wireless local network. It supports applications that deal with events of interest to the user. The status of an MES can be assigned that of My MES, to invoke a user, or Friend MES, which is connected to a garment friend by P2P communications as shown in Figure 4.

Sensors: Sensors detect the origination of events that have occurred in the human body or the external environment in real time. The internal sensors can sense the body temperature, respiration, ECG, etc. whereas external sensors detect the temperature, weather, location, etc.

BSS (Background Support Station): A BSS is located on a wired link and supports data transfer and the processing of MES in the background. It provides background application services that enable background knowledge monitoring, knowledge information analysis, etc. It can support data exchange with other BSSs. A BSS provides the functions of power charging, data synchronization or backup with an MES (Mobile Support Station). It transfers data over wired/wireless global foreign networks to a home BSS or Monitoring and Syncing Center (MSC). It can also support a monitoring service using peer-to-peer communication over a wireless local network. BSSs may be classified into a Home BSS and a Foreign BSS as Figure 4. The Home BSS originates and registers an MES with itself. Here, a Home BSS is a computing system that creates and registers a wearable host, and manages the home address

of the host. It manages the mobile position and open Internet services of a wearable healthcare host using a background-computing center (Figure 4). Secondly, the Foreign BSS is a BSS that is visited by a foreign MES. A "Foreign BSS" is a computing system that registers a visiting wearable host, and manages the foreign address of the visiting wearable host.

DB (database): The DB stores the information about running applications and the resource information of a wearable healthcare user.

AS (application server): An application server is connected to a gateway system to provide Internet open services. The gateway system is located between the Internet and Internet provides information about security, data filtering, firewall operations, etc. An open user accesses various community services using an application server accessed over the Internet. The BSS interconnects with Internet by means of an application server (AS) as shown in Figure 4.

The issues and requirements related to mobile healthcare architecture and components are as follows. As the mobile cloud architecture of Figure 3 is interworked with three cloud systems, the healthcare data transmission interface must be supported. The transmission network must provide effective and high performance transmission ability in the infrastructure aspect. And the wire network healthcare information transmission path configuration must be changed depending on the mobile network environment of mobile healthcare client. For example, the transmission performance and transmission cost vary depending on the information transmission path of the instance where mobile user connects to wide area mobile network (3G/4G) and local wireless network (WLAN). The migration technique for location synchronization of mobile agent that effectively supports information transmission depending on the moving position of mobile client is required. To improve information protection between the 2rd closed layer and the 3rd open layer or efficiency of information access, the configuration of computing system supporting filtering logic and semantic information selection logic (for example, expert system) is required. To support information gathering and information interaction of the mobile healthcare users in Figure 3 and Figure 4, the integrated mobile cloud network configuration is required for supporting the virtualized access of ad-hoc and infrastructure wireless network. In order to provide warning and health guide services satisfactorily for the user by analyzing the body signal information gathered by mobile healthcare client MES of Figure 4, the output device to feedback information to the mobile client such as display, speaker and vibration is required.

MOBILE HEALTHCARE INFORMATION FLOWS

For the satisfactory information transmission of mobile healthcare, seamless data transfer must be supported. To construct the seamless data flow, the heterogeneous network integration, the disconnected operations, and the communication link redundancy are important issues.

To configure heterogeneous cloud system as single information transmission flow, a compatible interface for information security and information transmission of bio-signal must be supported. Also in order to configure by integrating the mobile healthcare cloud system, the components for minimum basic standard configuration and open interface specification must be proposed (*Heterogeneous network integration*).

The disconnected operation in mobile healthcare is a method for minimizing the side effect of disconnecting healthcare data transmission followed by cutoff of network resources or failure of transmission node. The methods of backing up the body signal at the transmission terminal of the part where transmission cutoff has occurred or evading by predicting transmission cutoff re required (*Disconnected operations*).

The transmission stability and transmission performance are maximized by overlapping two or more transmission links between nodes to guarantee transmission stability. Therefore, the method of configuration by overlapping the link of part with high transmission failure rate and low transmission performance as priority is required (*Link redundancy*).

Figure 5 shows the system process chain that analyzes the mobile healthcare information flow based on a linear model. The components chained

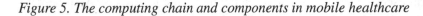

Figure 5. The computing chain and components in mobile healthcare

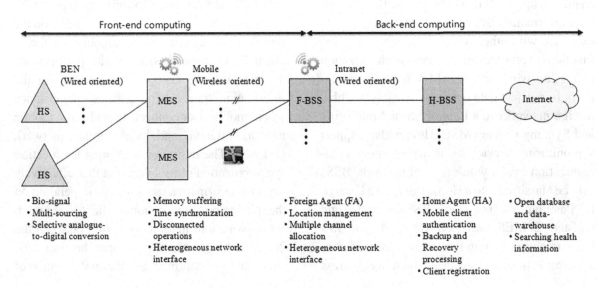

together include a healthcare sensor (HS), a mobile embedded station (MES), a foreign agent (FA) or foreign background support station (F-BSS), a home agent (HA) or home background support station (H-BSS), and the Internet.

The system process chain provides information service flow. This process chain embodies the entire service platform of mobile healthcare computing system from the body sensor to the application server in the sequence shown in Figure 5. The computing and communication components of the mobile healthcare system chain are present in the following sequence.

HS transmits the gathered body signal based on the body embedded network (BEN) configured as wire link. When the information gathered at many HS's are gathered at the MES, the data must be synchronized depending on the time.

MES supports memory buffering in order to solve the transmission speed gap between HS and F-BSS. And MES supports disconnected operations in order to overcome the cutoff of vulnerable wireless link while transmitting data to F-BSS through wireless link.

For monitoring the internal and external interacting environments of the moving MESs, a short-distance network configuration is required as BAN/PAN. It can dynamically transmit the mobility status-sensing events related to the location, dangerous event, contact user, etc. of mobile users.

F-BSS transmits the data transmitted from many mobile clients as the base station of AP or 3G/4G of wireless LAN. Therefore, an independent multiple channel allocation for each client. To support data transmission of mobile client, the foreign agent is supported. And management is required for the seamless data transmission of mobile client. F-BSS transmits the bio-signal gathered from each mobile client to the H-BSS where the corresponding mobile client is registered through private intranet.

H-BSS supports the authentication service to check whether the mobile client registered to one's own. H-BSS registers the newly created

mobile healthcare client and operates home agent in order to support the transmission of mobile client. In order to minimize the data loss of mobile client registered to them, the backup and recovery process are supported. Then this gets redefined as shared database for the open service of health information of mobile healthcare client accumulated at many H-BSS. The internet based health information service users access after searching the information they desire by connecting to the database.

In Figure 5, the heterogeneous network interface is an important factor for MES and F-BSS. In H-BSS, data filtering and security of heterogeneous network are important factors. Especially, link redundancy and disconnected operation are important in a wireless link connecting MES and F-BSS.

In order to maximize system flexibility and scalability in the mobile healthcare computing chain, the installation of cloud system is required. In the front-end computing part of Figure 5, mobile personal cloud system is the main foundation for supporting mobility and various terminal interface of mobile healthcare client. And the back-end computing part is classified as private cloud and public cloud as two sub-parts. F-BSS and H-BSS are configured as private cloud while Internet part is configured as public cloud.

However, such cloud system configuration is configured independently from the applied service and can be flexibly and selectively configured depending on installation cost, system scale and required performance, etc. Figure 6 shows the information flow in the mobile healthcare client aspect. These mobile client based data flows create their own bio-signal information and form the following cycles after wearing the wearable embedded devices. The healthcare information of mobile client is mainly classified into two types. They are forward direction information flow sending by gathering information collected from the user and the feedback information flow such as guide information, etc according to setup info or

Figure 6. Mobile healthcare client and information flows

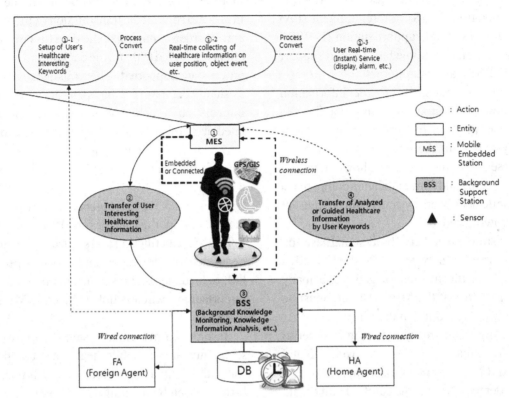

analysis result for data gathering of user. Process convert can internally switch each unit process of MES in Figure 6.

In the forward information flow, the embedded MES of mobile user gathers digital bio-signal data, user location and environment information, etc. next the gathered information is periodically or non-periodically transmitted to BSS. In the feedback information flow on the contrary, the command of BSS or healthcare guide information are transmitted to the MES of mobile user to change the settings of mobile user. Also, the necessary healthcare information is designated by setting up the interested health information of mobile user to the MES. The following service process provides the logic sequences to mobile healthcare computing system.

First, the MES goes through three sub-processing steps as shown in Figure 6. In the first sub-process (1 of Figure 6), a mobile user selects an interesting keyword for each life sector. In the second sub-process (2 of Figure 6), mobile information including the user position, object event, etc. related to the data of interest to the user given in the previous step is often gathered into MES. In the third sub-process (3 of Figure 6), it performs real-time health monitoring services for the information of interest to the user and the mobile resources including clothing-attached sensors, MES, etc. For mobile healthcare applications, the messages including ECG, body temperature, respiration, etc. containing health-related information are displayed or are presented in the form of an alarm.

Next, it transfers information analyzed or guided by the keywords of interest to the user between the MES and the BSS. The real-time event information collected by the MES is transferred to the BSS, or the application information analyzed by the BSS is fed back or provided to the MES.

Finally, the guided information is transmitted to the MES of a mobile user from the BSS. The information is analyzed or guided according to the keywords of interest to the user and the knowledge in the DB on the BSS.

The mobile healthcare client of Figure 6 can be applied as wearable client model. The wearable computing requires methods such as synchronization, high real-time and emergency network, etc. It requires step by step synchronization method to guarantee integrity of information transmitted as stepped from the wearable healthcare client to the server. And a high real-time support method is necessary in order to improve low real-time due to long transmission distance of data transmission path. Finally, a new emergency networking method is necessary in order to safely transmit the emergency information of wearable user.

The information flow processes for mobile healthcare users may be generally represented by the seven processes shown in Figure 7, which depicts the detailed flow of information for a mobile healthcare computing system from the body sensor to the application server using a forward sequence of events. The forward sequence can be applied in reverse to create a backward sequence,

which would indicate the flow of data from the application server to the sensor.

First, the healthcare-data generation process detects its sensing information using a body textile or an environmental sensor. If necessary, the key-in process is performed by a mobile user. Environmental events or unexpected bio-signal events are randomly generated on the MES of a mobile healthcare user. The raw sensory data is transferred to the MES over a wired digital yarn or wireless medium on a user body. Data generation using the digital garment system is divided into data about the internal resources of the digital clothing and data about the external environmental resources. The internal resources as biosensors, key-in, etc. occurs the internal events. Biosensors detect the human health-related events in a body-embedded sensor network. Using key-in devices, the user will enter the user events. The external environmental resources occurs the external events as follows. Environmental sensors detect the environment around the mobile users using natural resources such as the temperature and weather. Event messages are occurred by an emergency caused by an artifact around the mobile users.

Figure 7. The detailed information flow process for mobile healthcare

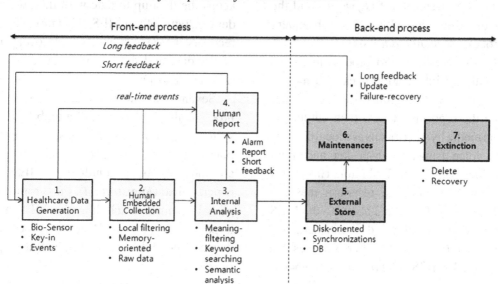

289

Second, the human embedded collection process collects the raw data or local filtered data and sends it to the memory of the MES. Data collection is performed by the MES embedded on a mobile client. The MES locally receives raw physical data over wired or wireless links from the internal or external resources of its mobile client. Data that has been buffered, filtered, and locally collected on the MES can be stored by performing a manual offline backup. The MES executes the following operations. Periodic or non-periodic filtering is supported (*Local filtering*). Memory buffering supports real-time transfers, which relay the filtered data from the MES to the BSS, or vice versa (*Memory buffering*). The received raw data is transformed into the formatted standard-format of thee BSS on the Intranet (*Raw-data formatting*).

Third, the collected data in the MES is quickly analyzed using the keywords of interest to the mobile user. Also, the data is filtered by using the semantic meanings. Local analysis is promptly performed by MESs such as smart phones. Keywords of interest to a user are searched, sorted, and evaluated. The keywords are found and sorted (*Searching keywords*). The event messages related to the keywords of user interest are accepted; otherwise, they are discarded (*Filtering meanings*). The meaning of the filtered event-message is compared with that of the user-interest keywords, and the analysis results are passed onto the subsequent report process (*Semantic analysis*).

Fourth, the human report process feeds the quickly analyzed information back to a mobile healthcare user over a digital yarn/wireless network, and the reporting data is then output via embedded media by such means as a local display, creating a voice using a local speaker, and creating vibrations using a local vibrator. This report process passes a real-time response message received from step 1 to step 3 above to the MES user. An MES user is informed by an emergency alarm (*Alarm*). Local-based report services can be supported by BSS (*Report*). The response

messages corresponding to real-time events can be reported (*User short feedback*).

Fifth, the fast filtered data of the third process can be stored externally on disk storage. Local data can be transferred over wireless external networks to the BSS (Monitoring and Syncing Center) to be monitored and synchronized. The stored data requires synchronization to ensure the integrity of the bio-signal data. All MES data is accumulated onto a disk-based database (DB) and is statistically analyzed by a BSS such as a server computer. The operations of this process take place on the medium of storage (*Disk-oriented storage*). Data and status of each MES should be continuously synchronized with BSS storage (*Synchronizations*). The forecasting services are mainly provided by statistical analysis (*Long feedback*). Managing the DB has the privileges to perform creation, update, and deletion on a database (*DB management*).

Sixth, for the healthcare data maintenance, an update strategy and a failure-recovery process are activated for each MES. The transferring and synchronizing of global information takes place between friendly users over wired/wireless global home networks. Data to be filtered and globally collected on the BSS can be stored by performing a backup manually offline. The update process is keeps the data up to date with the program and device status of the MES (*Update*). The failure-recovery process supports a recovery process of the data and the program for a failed MES (*Failure-recovery*).

Seventh, in the registration and extinction process, all the resources of a mobile healthcare system can be removed or destroyed in this extinction process. Initial setup and registration of all global resources including the MES and BSS is performed (*Registration*). Final removal of all global resources including the MES and BSS is performed (*Delete*) Recovery processes of a device-failed MES and a failed BSS are supported (*Recovery*)

The processes of steps 1 to 4 occur on the MES and are called *front-end processes*. The cycle processes of steps 5 to 7 take place on the BSS and are referred to as *back-end processes*. All of these steps require real-time or non real-time feedback to their routines.

FUTURE RESEARCH DIRECTIONS

In this section, the issues that mobile healthcare will be faced with in the future are presented.

The current healthcare information system and service status show the following characteristics. First, the hospital or healthcare center oriented medical information system is consolidated. Second, the private medical information system within the wire and wireless intranet based limited range (security system oriented) must be consolidated. Third, the gathering (group and classification) oriented medical information system installation, in other words the symptom oriented medical information or treatment information system must be continuously developed. In order to develop the healthcare information system currently established based on hospital or healthcare support center, the following requirements must be improved.

First, the shift of medical information paradigm for the proposal of new preventive healthcare information system is required. It is necessary to build up healthcare information service of preventing disorders targeting healthy people from being patient treatment oriented medical service. This provides personal disease history prediction service as an implementation of healthcare expert system based on building up personal disease history DB, family disease history DB and group disease history DB.

Second, it must be expanded and built as a daily healthcare information production system producing healthcare information out of patient's or ordinary person's daily information from the medical information center oriented medical information production system.

Third, the buildup of individual oriented customized healthcare information system from being gathering (group) centered is required: Personal medical information device (personal health and medical information analysis indicator role is necessary), personal healthcare self-treatment information device, digital healthcare garment, personal healthcare sensing module and building up network are necessary.

Fourth, the alternative toward compatibility and convergence with the existing medical information system is required.

Fifth, the buildup of new personal or group medical information life cycle system is required. This would be building up the life cycle system of healthcare information production, storage, distribution and extinction, etc.

Sixth, preparing opportunity for popularization of existing high priced healthcare devices: The disease free health service of human race is implemented by extending healthcare service accessibility of general public through implementation of economic value according to lighter healthcare devices, implementation of mass production system and popularization of information healthcare technology followed by application of information technology.

There are many issues and problems to using mobile healthcare computing and these should be accordingly addressed. The following is a list that the author has compiled.

Embedded sensing networking: Conductive fibers are required to collect or deliver the sensory information in real-time and to deliver it safely. Also, a Personal Area Network (PAN) or a Body Embedded Network (BEN) is required in order for the installation of additional sensory devices to be rendered convenient

Dynamic binding and tuning of mobile healthcare device: This binding requires garment binding or user binding by means of changing a personal garment or the user of a garment, respectively.

Also, creating this binding requires that the tuning of a real-time garment system be dependent on the status of every garment user.

Cost effectiveness: The procurement of new digital garments entails the increased expense of the new garments. The price of the new garments can be from several fold higher to dozens of times more expensive. Therefore, there is a need for the production of digital garments to use standardized production methods and standardized components in order to realize low cost when placed on the market.

Backup-support services: This is related to real-time user state analysis, database construction, and intelligent system construction. Real-time user state analysis provides instant and powerful analysis of a garment user. This real-time analysis is performed using a background system like BSS, which supports the real-time monitoring of user events. Secondly, database construction is associated with the continuous compilation of a database to perform statistical analysis of garment users and their environments. Finally, intelligent system construction is helpful because to make the response of a digital garment user successful, the interaction and guidance of application services for the garment user are required. Otherwise, the user instructions are updated or changed dependent on the intelligent logic and statistical data.

More enhanced personal security: The central location of the personal information is the closed layer consisting of the Intranet on which the BSS is located. Because the privacy of individuals becomes more concentrated on the BSS on the closed layer than on the existing desktop or a centralized server, the importance of security should receive more emphasis. Mobile cloud security supports the security cloud configuration, which is required for supporting dynamic security based on context-awareness.

Lightweight mobile device: Mobile healthcare devices still heavy. It needs continuously to make the mobile devices lightweight.

Side-effects: Some mobile devices can consist of a lot of wiring and can cause irritation in heat and headaches. Such side-effects should be avoided or prevented using the advanced technologies and methods.

Privacy and Security: Mobile healthcare devices can invade privacy because of being tracked wherever you go. And they can be used to gain an unfair advantage over others such as hacking.

Safety and QoS: For safe information transmission, it needs the fault-recovery processes that can immediately recover its connections *when a m*obile healthcare device is disconnected. Also, the differential performance quality should be supported for different healthcare applications.

Scalability and Portability: Scalability should ensure the continued scalability of the system resources, due to the increase in the number of users of mobile healthcare. Portability is to support the user's devices replacement, the program transplant, etc using the mobile agent technique. Mobility cloud should be supported to ensure a seamless user-mobility.

CONCLUSION

This chapter firstly described the mobile healthcare system architecture and components, which emphasized the lightweight mobile client and devices and the flexibility and scalability of background healthcare supporting components. Secondly, it presented the information data flows and cycles for supporting mobile healthcare computing. Finally, it described various applications and health-medical issues and characteristics. The following objectives will be presented in order to build up the mobile healthcare information system described in this chapter.

Firstly, a medical service that can be accessed at any time and place will be implemented by discovering various mobile healthcare services continuously and developing the mobile healthcare information lifecycle.

Secondly, a universal economic medical information system will be implemented by spreading low cost individual healthcare information devices in order to implement the personal healthcare service.

Thirdly, a healthcare information expert system will be built in order to switch the healthcare service from background healthcare service to prevention-oriented forefront healthcare service.

Lastly, the subject of healthcare service must be extended from patient-oriented to medical staff such as doctors or nurses. A convenient and safe healthcare information system should be established for monitoring and caring for the health status of medical staff which is not building up healthcare information devices and system as a tool for medical activity (such as treatment).

Through accomplishment of such goals, a harmonious and cooperative healthcare information system between the patient, the family, the doctor and the hospital can be achieved.

Also, the mobile cloud, the private cloud and the public cloud must configure the overall system by combining the following characteristics of their own in order to build up a mobile healthcare cloud system.

Firstly, a mobile healthcare cloud must satisfactorily support the synchronization between various mobile devices, as well as having easy interface design and user mobility.

Next, a private cloud must consolidate the performance of elements such as the cloud system, system safety and information security.

The public cloud must support system scalability in order to consolidate usability through the development of various applications, and consolidate economic efficiency by lowering service cost and support large-scale users.

REFERENCES

Akyildiz, I. F., Su, W., Sankarasubramaniam, Y., & Cayirci, E. (2002). A survey on sensor network. *IEEE Communications Magazine*, 102–114. doi:10.1109/MCOM.2002.1024422.

Barbará, D. (1999). Mobile computing and databases-A survey. *IEEE Transactions on Knowledge and Data Engineering*, *11*(1). doi:10.1109/69.755619.

Bertucci, G. (2007). Compendium of ICT applications on electronic government: Vol. 1. *Mobile applications on health and learning*. New York: Department of Economic and Social Affairs, United Nations..

Bujnoch, Z. (2013). Enabling collaborative workflows: Shaping the future of mobile healthcare. *Frost & Sullivan*. Retrieved from http://www.frost.com

Coyle, S. (2009). *BIOTEX–Bio-sensing textiles for healthcare*. Paper presented at Smart Textiles Salon. Ghent, Belgium.

Dash, S. K., Mohapatra, S., & Pattnaik, P. K. (2010). A survey on applications of wireless sensor network using cloud computing. *International Journal of Computer Science & Emerging Technologies*, *50*(1).

Dinh, H. T., Lee, C., Niyato, D., & Wang, P. (2011). A survey of mobile cloud computing: Architecture, applications, and approaches. In *Wireless Communications and Mobile Computing*. Hoboken, NJ: Wiley. Retrieved from http://onlinelibrary.wiley.com/doi/10.1002/wcm.1203/abstract

Estrin, D. (2001). Comm'n sense: Research challenges in embedded networked sensing. *UCLA Computer Science Department Research Review*. Retrieved from http://lecs.cs.ucla.edu

Geier, J. (2007). *Wireless network industry report*. Wireless-Nets, Ltd.

Germanakos, P., Mourlas, C., & Samaras, G. (2005). A mobile agent approach for ubiquitous and personalized ehealth information systems. In *Proceedings of the Workshop on 'Personalization for e-Health' of the 10th International Conference on User Modeling (UM'05)*, (pp. 67–70). eHealth.

Gough, C. (2009). *Industry brief: Healthcare cloud security*. Intel IT Center..

HL7. (2012). Retrieved from http://www.hl7.org/Special/committees/mobile/index.cfm

Harold, P. (2007). MyHeart - Fighting cardiovascular diseases through prevention and early diagnosis. *Philips Research Password*, *29*, 12–15.

Huang, P. (2000). *Promoting wearable computing: A survey and future agenda*. Academic Press..

Hyek, P. (2013). mHealth: Mobile technology poised to enable a new era in health care. *Ernst & Young*. Retrieved from http://www.ey.com/Publication/

Kay, M., Santos, J., & Takane, M. (2011). mHealth new horizons for health through mobile technologies. In Global Observatory for eHealth. Geneva: WHO Press.

Logicworks. (2013). *Logicworks healthcare cloud*. Retrieved from http://www.logicworks.net

Malhotr, K., Gardner, S., & Rees, D. (2005). Evaluation of GPRS enabled secure remote patient monitoring system. [Riga, Latvia: ASMTA.]. *Proceedings of ASMTA*, *2005*, 41–48.

mHealth. (2012). *Wikipedia*. Retrieved from http://en.wikipedia.org/wiki/MHealth#Definitions

Miller, F. (2004). Wearables–Clothing with a sixth sense. *Fraunhofer magazine*, 38-39.

Nguyen, V. (2000). *Mobile computing & disconnected operation: A survey of recent advances*. Retrieved from http://www.cis.ohio-state.edu/~jain/cis788-95/mobile_comp/index.html

Park, S., & Jayaraman, S. (2003). Enhancing the quality of life through wearable technology. *IEEE Engineering in Medicine and Biology Magazine*. PMID:12845818.

Pfaltz, M. C., Grossman, P., Michael, T., Margraf, J., & Wilhelm, F. H. (2010). Physical activity and respiratory behavior in daily life of patients with panic disorder and healthy controls. *International Journal of Psychophysiology*, *78*, 42–49. doi:10.1016/j.ijpsycho.2010.05.001 PMID:20472006.

Rehman, A., Mustafa, M., Javaid, N., Qasim, U., & Khan, Z. A. (2012). Analytical survey of wearable sensors. In *Proceedings of BioSPAN with 7th IEEE International Conference on Broadband and Wireless Computing, Communication and Applications (BWCCA)*. Victoria, Canada: IEEE.

Rimal, B. P., Choi, E., & Lumb, I. (2009). A taxonomy and survey of cloud computing systems. In *Proceedings of Fifth International Joint Conference on INC, IMS and IDC*. IEEE.

Schadow, G., Mean, C. N., & Walker, D. M. (2006). The HL7 reference information model under scrutiny. *Master of Industrial Engineering*, *124*, 151–156. PMID:17108519.

Sloninsky, D., & Mechael, P. N. (2008). *Towards the development of a mhealth strategy: A literature review*. Geneva: World Health Organization..

Smith, B., & Ceusters, W. (2006). HL7 RIM: An incoherent standard. *Studies in Health Technology and Informatics*, *124*, 133–138. PMID:17108516.

Tubaishat, M., & Madria, S. (2003). Sensor networks: An overview. *IEEE Potentials*, *22*(2), 20–23. doi:10.1109/MP.2003.1197877.

Zawoad, S., & Hasan, R. (2013). *Cloud forensics: A meta-study of challenges, approaches, and open problems*. Retrieved from http://arxiv.org/abs/1302.6312

Chapter 16
A Proposal for Multidisciplinary Software for People with Autism

Eraldo Guerra
Center of Advanced Studies and Systems of Recife, Brazil

Felipe Furtado
Federal University of Pernambuco (UFPE), Brazil

ABSTRACT

This chapter is about the study of treatments for autistic children and interventions of entertainment games with the purpose of developing a technological solution in order to promote a better adaptation between the autistic children and treatment, consequently showing better results in a shorter period of time. The multidisciplinary software for Autism treatment is being developed. It is based on PECs, ABA, and TEACCH methods, and it uses ludic games and activity interventions. Before applying technology to autism treatment, a deep study about autistic children is made. This way, concepts such as customization and the use of Kinect, Mobile (WP7), and Cloud Computer technologies take part as a stimulator system, since they are responsible for intensifying cognitive development and reducing the patient's excitement, aggressiveness, and irritability.

1. INTRODUCTION

The term autism was first argued by Bleuler (1911) to designate the disorder of the loss of contact with reality, which makes the communication very difficult or even impossible. Kanner (1943) argued the same term to describe 11 children who had a quite unique behavior in common.

He suggested that this had to do with an innate inability to establish affective and interpersonal contact and was a very rare syndrome, but one for which, probably, cases had been more frequently diagnosed than hitherto supposed (Lazzeri, 2008).

According to Thais Lazzeri (2011), in her article "Autism: Universe Around Me," because of the lack of accurate clinical diagnosis, is difficult to quantify how many autistic people there are in the world. In Brazil, for example, some say

DOI: 10.4018/978-1-4666-4781-7.ch016

170,000 people suffer from this disorder. But the numbers are underestimated. An estimative says one million Brazilians have any degree of autism, which has dozens of subtypes. The degree of the disorder determines what skills an autistic person, when stimulated, can develop.

For this disease, according to the Autistic Friends Association (AMA in Portuguese), the treatment consists in psycho-educational intervention, family counseling and developing language and/or communication. These take place under three main strategies, and at the same time, the patient takes medication (AMA, 2008).

TEACCH (Treatment and Education of Autistic and Related Communication Handicapped Children): An educational program and clinical practice with a predominantly psych pedagogical created from a research project that sought to deeply observe the behaviors of autistic children in different situations and against different stimuli.

PEC'S (Picture Exchange Communication System): Communication is one of the many areas affected by autism. PEC'S is a process and assists in the development of language and proposes to implement a "way" communication between the autistic and the environment that surrounds it. The PEC'S is this fundamental instrument to assess and understand the autistic routine. Created more than 12 years the Delaware Autistic Program, this method is based on ABA (Applied Behavior Analysis) and teaches the autistic to exchange a picture for something you want.

ABA (Applied Behavior Analysis): A psychological approach that uses the theory of behaviorism to modify human behaviors as part of a learning or treatment process. By functionality, it assesses the relationship between a targeted behavior and the environment, the methods of ABA can be used to change that behavior. Research in applied behavior analysis ranges from behavioral intervention methods to basic research which investigates the rules by which humans adapt and maintain behavior.

Thus it is observed that in the majority of treatment for autism, proceeds from isolated form of each strategies, physical form and always needing follow-up of a specialist. Consequently development or treatment of the child is conditioned to the unique moments and isolates with the specialist and with a single method of treatment. Suppose that this procedure is to intensify the cognitive and social problem, once taken into consideration as an example. For a child that makes use of the treatment by means of the PEC's, in a social conviviality may need the letters to randomly place them in public spaces. What can be expected to create some discomfort or embarrassment, that is not a practice that stimulates the social conviviality.

In addition he said it is perceived that the activities related to treatment, independent of the strategy used PEC's, ABA or TEACCH, Occur, by the fact of being a learning moment, a realization of activity. In which they occur, by means of a situation of playful banter that comes to captivate the child and stimulate to it. Being an important fact, because it serves to one of the characteristics of autistic child that is the resistance to traditional methodologies of teaching.

Based on these arguments, we developed a multidisciplinary software for the treatment of children with autism, in which presents a structure of games, as the same and an artifact attraction is common in life and great part of the children. The act of playing, the child will develop the activities of learning, observing the characteristic of resistance to traditional teaching methods. It may be intensified the treatment by the motivation of the child to want to play with the software. The World Health Organization (OMS in Portuguese) estimates that reduce the learning time. According to Novaes (1992, p. 28)

The teaching, absorbed in a playful, is acquiring an important aspect in developing effective and permanent of the intelligence of the child.

Because it is a virtual game, can be used in different environments and any time of day without any social constraint, the game comes out to be a socializing agent among the children, young people and adults. This fact has proven its importance for the words of Ronca (1989):

The play allows the child to explore the body's relationship to space, causes and possibilities of shifting gears, or creates mental condition to get out of trouble, and then she will assimilate and spend so much, that this movement seeks and lives different fundamental activities, not only in the development of his personality and his icon as well as along the cognitive construction of your body (p.27).

We understand that the structure of the software and a game, in which through the act and game will promote the learning and socialization of autistic child of playful way. Thus, enabling a greater motivation of the same for the realization of the activities related to the treatment in a way that will reduce the amount of time to learning, promote social interaction and other factors that will be perspectives more forward.

2. JUSTIFICATIVE

The need for multidisciplinary treatment is essential for the change in the behavior of the child. Under the gaze of treatment and according to Carlos A. Gadia (2004) the search, deal with the autistic patients requires a multidisciplinary approach. The base treatment involves behavioral changes, technical, educational or work programs and language/communication therapy. According to the Aman MG (2005) the treatment planning must be structured according to the phases of the life of the patient. Therefore, the priority with small children and the language and social interaction therapy/language, special education and family support. Speaking on adolescents, the targets

would be the social skills groups, occupational therapy and sexuality. With adults, issues such as the options for housing and protection should be focused. Unfortunately, there are no options for housing in Brazil, as well as treatment planning, areas widely neglected, bringing concerns for the parents of the patient.

Through such information, the software features in addition to the multidisciplinary environment. A structure and customizable interface that comes to help in treatment, since the professional responsible for treatment or even by the child can modify the same. In a way that will meet, the specific needs of the patient, by the need to develop some skills, or according to the phases of the life of the patient. This perception will be clearer in overview of the software.

It is a fact that information technology is being used as a tool facilitator on the process of treatment of children with autism. According to Cleonice Alves Bosa (2002) article, communication devices computerized are being specially designed for autistic children. In general, the focus is on engaging the public and encourages the interaction. Keyboards interchangeable, of increasing complexity, allow the advancing children gradually from a keyboard with only a symbol for the use of independent multi-symbol, which are adjusted in a personalized manner to the current environment, the needs or interests of the individual. Another factor in favor of the use of computers is that the visual material is more understood and accepted than the verbal. However, it is important to note that the common computers without a customization for the patient can lead to hostility.

On the current scenario of treatment of children with autism (2012), we can infer that if presents various researches. Guillermo Sapiro (2012) presents a research on the Kinect[1] in which uses the tool as behavioral assessment instrument to the autistic child (ABA). To this end, this research could have another purpose. Discover the existence of some type of obsessive-compulsive behavior (for example: figures, action, cartoons) for the same, they were encouraged by parents and relatives, as a facilitator in the treatment. Of course, one must be a caution, because it should not be too encouraged, since it can interfere with the learning process, if there is not a control, such as generating an eternal dependence.

The kinect is a device that has motion capture and audio, is the same used for interaction with various games and applications. With this in mind the choice of the same device for integration of software with the autistic child is due to the fact the device follow some of the main features of the autistic children between them:

- Facilitator agent and your use, is contextualized under the autistic characteristics such as: intolerance to touch (avoid using controls or mouse).

- Capture of audio which comes to contribute to diagnosis and treatment phonological. Since it is a common problem in autistic children the communication and perceived problems with repetition of words, diction and others.

- Motor difficulties what comes to be corrected and encouraged since the child will feel need to play. As soon as more and more it will need precise movements.

- The autistic child if uses of information by gesture to express what you want. It is through these gestures recognized by kinect and answers your request for the software.

- Hyperactivity can be focused on the use of the software, in which by means of kinect will reduce the same by physical effort.

- Fixation for an icon (customizable interface) social interactions issues (portability and mobility), and others. This way, the studies indicate the use of Kinect, Cloud Computer and Mobile technology.

In addition to these characteristics, others were considered so that this whole scenario developed provides new learning experience the autistic child.

As mentioned, the game he is customizable. In addition to the factors already mentioned the same you can modify the color and icon, which will interact with the child. This is in addition to understanding the fact that every child has a mounting for an icon and use the same as stimulus. There is concern in reducing the rate of attention deficit, and this a great challenge. The customization is happening, the same are maintained for all software. Given another characteristic which is resistance to change of routine, the choice of icon comes also break a little the characteristic of the autistic child, as to not want to mix with other children. Once that besides the icon interacts with the child the same interacts with other icon.

And these are some of the characteristics and reasons that led to the study and development of this project.

3. GOAL

Develop a multidisciplinary software for autism, having its development based on the main autism characteristic, which is the identification of an icon. The icon is used to intensify the cognitive development, etiological, and mainly, reduce the excitement, aggressiveness and irritability.

4. PROJECT METHODOLOGY

In order to establish a comparison among different autistic needs, by the usability view, customization, ludic games, cognition and teaching methodology, which can affect directly and indirectly the autistic treatment, was developed a bibliographical research that approaches these same topics, so it can justify and complement this research.

4.1. Working Planning

For this research execution, many activities are needed. They involve the bibliographic work in related areas, the proposal elaboration and implementation, among others.

4.1.1. Literature Revision

The literature review was at the beginning of 2012. The reading of books and articles about Software of health, ludic games, autism, Cognitive interface, Kinect Technology, Mobile Technology, Systems of cloud of computer education and usability were made. The review will last for the entire period of the research, in order to continue to monitor the improvements to the area and, perhaps, adding new works that were not mentioned at the beginning of the review. It will be completed by the end of 2013.

4.2. Data Collection and Analysis

The questionnaires were applied in an order of objective and subjective, in July 2012, in order to understand the needs autistic, individually and as a group. Participated in the research were health professionals, education and treatment (caregivers), in addition to the patient's family. Material collected, can be used as a research tool to find the specificities and needs of autism, so that contributed to the development of a virtual prototype. All the information, were analyzed in a way that was drawn up a mapping so that was done an elicitation of main requirements being these functional and non-functional (quality). In order to not only prioritize the important requirement, but also understand the needs major, for which they had been answered in this project. Soon, you will notice that the data collection should happen during every project, whether during the use of the game, as in the use of your smartphone. This way such information is useful to identify various problems, such as usability, learning and others. Thus, within one of the requirements if you have set as a priority the traceability. Is it done by amount of clicks on the screen of the smartphone (usability), or by the absence of clicks. In which in this situation by means of a Short Message Service (SMS), will be reported to the Father and Doctor, the end of which it has knowledge and can ascertain whether everything is well with the child. The same proceeds with the Kinect in order to evaluate the behavioral issue (ABA), having its storage of data on a server in the cloud available to all. Among all forms of data collection, the Survey Monkey[2] was the most used as a tool for data collection, such as the profile of the children, needs of the same parents, and doctors, in relation to the system. The use of this system has facilitated the process once that this technology does not require that all are all in the same physical location.

4.3. Proposed Game Scenario Design

The design of the game is the main factor to win the user (autistic child). The design has to be adapted and understandable, so that the children can develop their interest in the game and therefore intensify its use. The interfaces were developed using the ludical digital artifacts (LDA), which are organized in four main axs: human interaction, ludicity, information and human relationship with the computer. This relation maintains a system of interrelationships and interdependencies that are articulated according to the child's active participation, which streamlines the system in the pragmatics of human communication.

The ludical communication potentiates the transmission of information and knowledge. This way, the technological interaction lucidity reinforces this transmission, since the concept of information and the learning process is in the message, issued by the game. Thus, the game features scenarios with greater identification of icon and recreational activities proposed. Thus the design of the scenario the functionalities of the software, to the use of physical movement used by Kinect technology and voice commands by customizable Microsoft Speech[3]. It is one of the strategies adopted; motivate the interactions between the patient and the environment of the game. In addition to the choice of the icon and the color made by the child which will customize the interface.

4.4. Development of Game Proposed Scenario

In accordance with the concept of the ABA, the icon will act as tutors in the activities that are carried out. If the child are unsure of how to perform the same, the icon show what should be done, as the answer, the kinect capture video by the behavior of the child. To subsequently be evaluated by doctors, from the viewpoint of PEC's whole scenario is well illustrated with images, similar to that used in the treatment. This concern was due to the fact that does not generate a change or a lack of understanding of the activity.

If that's not enough the character and images for understanding of the activity, will be prepared texts which will simulate rules, known as TEACCH. Another important factor was the ransom cultural, some traditional games, bringing the games of trays, riddles and other to the virtual world. Where were adapted to the learning process and development of patients, each scenario should propose some indices of evaluations time of execution of the activities, errors, hits and interest. These data will be used for evolutionary follow the treatment, as well as improvement of the software.

Among the activities developed we have: activities related to speech therapy, social organization, mathematics among others. In accordance with the development of the project, new activities can be implemented, allowing the scalability of the project and meet the demand or need of the user. For this service these Plug-ins are arranged in cloud services being accessed by the physician or professional responsible.

4.5. Cognitive Treatment Development

Thinking of two main problems in the life of the autistic child, learning and social interaction, it was conceived and developed, a mobile application, in which was taken as a starting point the windows phone seven (WP7), in order to allow independence for autistic children. In which was noticeable, during some collections of data, and that children who use the form of treatment, through the PEC's, has throughout its development by means of letters that represent activities, being the same arranged in various places. An example is the act of taking a shower, where there are letters (Pictures/Image) in the bathroom with the step-by-step procedure. By this, it becomes clear that such a practice would be complicated, in the midst of public places. Being able to set up a situation of embarrassment for the child, which does not come to facilitate or promote a practice of social inclusion. Thus, the use of mobile technology comes to propose these activities, without the need to modify the environment through the PEC's, or through TEACCH by rules.

The same proceeds with the kinect, since this is a virtual game being common good to any child and being factor of social integration. Thus, it was found that each segment of the cognitive process concerns the manipulation of information active, involving the act of thinking. This choice is because the approach of Vygotsky (1989) contrasts with that of Piaget (1975), since its focus is on the role of the environment for the intellectual development of the child. Vygotsky (1989.p 84) says that this development is specifically held outside to inside, through internalization.

The knowledge and the context, states that the social influences are more important than the biological aspect. For Vygotsky's (1989) theory, therefore, the social factors play a fundamental role in the development intellectual. They learn, and the result has been the development of the psychological processes, through action. We know that, today, technology and the media bring the information, the knowledge.

The current society is known by the information society, where the libraries are no longer the only source used for information, being replaced by other technological means.

4.6. 3D or 2D Modeling and Prototyping

The scenario model of interaction both in the game and on your smartphone, initially was prioritized the modeling development in 2D. Since the images used in PEC's are static and do not have effects of third dimension (shadow, light, depth). But realizing the technological advance and the market shift from 2D to 3D, are also studying the possibility of creating this scenario. The main objective is to promote a better understanding of the autistic child in relation to the image she sees in the software with the object in the real world. Thus, the creation of more detailed scenarios and to promote this closer contact between the virtual and the real, needs further study. Therefore, you can understand what profile of child that will make good use and not reject such a change. A priori tests to be performed in children with autism low level and that they have used or tested the software makes it possible to obtain good results. The goal is that the 3D facilitates understanding and contributes to the educational process.

4.7. Cloud Services

The choice of service in the cloud is due to the fact of being a tool facilitator under the various looks, a time that will be available all the services required for the software meets its objective. Some of these services are the use of the software without having to have anything installed, what comes to facilitate mobility within clinics, schools and in the house of children. Thus, allowing them to be done at any time of day, anywhere and reducing

investments in expanding infrastructure, which could be a disturbing factor, requiring only the Kinect and WP7 in addition to the computer.

Another costs important factor become viable because the applications are on-demand, which means that many users make the costs to go up, and few users reduce costs. Thirdly, the hardware infrastructure can be trusted, because the companies that operate the cloud services are concerned to maintain its excellence in addition to the database in the cloud, which is a security and huge storage capacity on servers, because they are important data that need to be accessible and maintain their integrity. Being these significant advantages over the alternatives of role, in addition to the professionals responsible for treatment. Parents can access the files and become more involved in their education, learning process and evolution of the treatment.

4.8. Rehearsals and Virtual Tests

The game has the purpose to simulate the conditions of treatment activities for autistic children in a virtual world, so that he can use this learning to the real world. To do this at this stage were granted several tests and tests with the purpose of knowing if the software meets the expectations, which had been developed. Thus, the tests occurred under different character, such as usability, learning, and attention deficit among others being accompanied by the medical team and authorized by family members. Such concern is overlooked by the fact questions internal generated, as well as:

- If the child will interact with the game or with wp7, by who knows what the activity represents or why was conditional on this?
- If the child has learned the meaning of virtual activity, will she be able to take the decision and carry out in the real world?
- What are the possible risks that the child may suffer from using the software?

- The software will actually promote a greater freedom of autonomy to carry out activities in your home?
- Will reduce the time and learning?

In addition to these other issues were requiring this phase of the project were well studied and well carried out in a manner that will allow the final prototype successfully meet their expectations.

4.9. Refinement of the Proposed Approach

The proposed process must be refined while the initial prototype goes through tests cause as the evaluation results are obtained, new changes can be applied. The activities described in the previous sections must be reformulated if necessary, and described in a higher level of detail, knowing that the methodology may change according to the requirements requested by the responsible professional or requirements raised by requiring a new plan.

5. LITERARY REFERENCES

Baron Cohen, Leslie e Frith (1985) emphasized the relation between social and communication loss and cognitive failure present in patients with infantile autism. These patients showed severe disability in the symbolical capacity, which prevents them from establishing a reciprocal social skill. The mental representation is fundamental in the construction of the language, and it is essential even for the acquisition of words. Therefore, this study aimed to evaluate the play of children with autism and the use of images that contribute to this mental representation.

As soon as provide a playful space by means of digital medium different from school, inspire children to create and interact through activities such as storytelling, games with music adapted and sport. Children have a natural pleasure and spontaneous play, in the game of make-believe, the child manages the mastery of the situation, create and live a fantasy and reality itself. This ability brings the spontaneity of ludic activity the meaning of freedom, which reinforces the motivation for the game (Monteiro, 1994).

For Winnicott (1975) the act of play can be understood as meaning shift, as movement, has a language and it is a project in action. While playing, the human being subjectivity is worked, the reality is wedged and time/space is established. Playing is create a non-conventional way of utilize objects, material, ideas and imagine.

These references are arguments that instigate the practice of this project as a mean to promote good social practice.

6. OVERVIEW OF MANAGEMENT OF TREATMENT

Knowing that currently the technology is increasingly present in the daily life of all, especially in children, by insertion into virtual games, use of social networks, applications and by the technological question. The same has committed an important role for the development, for the construction of social relations, through the diversity and accessibility to information, stimulating communication that comes to configure each of the main phases of social inclusion. In this way these factors, conditionates the other to include some of the issues found in the daily life of autistic children.

The system consists of a game (software), an application (smartphone) and a website. The web site entitled "Can Game" allows the father, the family doctor, and others, to make the account of the child and download the application to your Smartphone. Upon registration the responsible makes use of a virtual agenda with the activities required for the learning and social interaction in an independent manner.

The activities can be scheduled per day or per hour in accordance with the rhythm of life of each child. Such concern is given to the fact that the autistic child is not very tolerable to changes. As well as the fact that the insertion of a smartphone in their routine, comes to be a change that may not be well accepted in some cases. After the adaptation of the child with your smartphone and accept its use, which by suggestion of this research the same is being used in an arm support thus avoiding loss of the appliance. Beginning the process of learning the system, where the father or doctor, shows the relationship of the images displayed on the screen of your smartphone, with the activities carried out in their day by day.

At the ceremony in which the father is the record of the smartphone of the child, the same should be done for your smartphone, your e-mail address and email of the doctor because the whole process is traceable, allowing monitor the achievement or not of the activities. The site also comes to allow the creation of a folder that is conditional on the profile of the register (Figure 1), which will store all the information and learning difficulties generated by the child in application usage. This being done in character of usability, by the amount of click's, by response time and non-execution of

the activities in this way by means of a generated report, the application makes the upload of such information being available for knowledge of the Father and of the professionals responsible for monitoring of treatment. For such, is only login, and set your user profile because it is necessary to differentiate access permissions. Once a father can only have access to the folder of your Son, but the doctor can have access to the quantity of folders which is responsible for processing and still have access to a collaborative folder where all the doctors use the system to share information.

On the perspective of the application, which is represented in Figure 2, the same follows the process by means of a loop in three attempts, the first that configures the image displayed. If it is not running the activity (doing the touch screen confirming that he did or will do), in the second attempt, below the image appears a word or informational text that will strengthen the understanding of the image. If the child still continue without interacting with the application in their last attempt to image, along with the text emit a song in order to draw the attention of the child. If it still does not have an interaction inform the application by means of an SMS text message to

Figure 1. Login screen of the user profile

Figure 2. Table of activities present on site with time and day

Monday, 29 October 2012.

	Sunday	Monday	Tuesday	Wednesday	Thursday	Friday	Saturday
7:00							
9:00							
11:00							
13:00							
15:00							
17:00							

your smartphone from the parent or guardian, acting as a security monitor.

The images that will represent the activities will be prepared on site and may be updated in accordance with the needs of children. To this end the update comes through new packages which can be downloaded by the Father for your profile, after this procedure, the use of the agenda of the site comes be well simple. Just click and drag the image that refers to the desired activity, for the day and time you want.

The software features a playful game format being based on basic principles for the treatment of autism, the identification of the icon and the customization of the interface of the game (Figure

3), and used the technology Kinect, as a facilitator instrument. The end of that whole process can also be tracked and done a login and password by the doctor or father that will identify the child who will use the game and thus be able to identify the evolution of its treatment. At the end the physician or parent has access to the report and files generated by the use, in which through the site can upload the same. Provide the material for studies and diagnoses in the clouds. Following the concepts of the ABA, the character chosen acts as a tutor virtual, in which he explains the implementation of the activities, in such a way that will motivate the child to perform them in their daily life, as well as rules of social coexistence

Figure 3. Personalization screen of the game

and etc. In addition to this factor the act of the child interacting with the icon chosen, comes to be a facilitator in the process of social inclusion, which may be artifacts of stimuli or examples.

After the choice of icon (Figure 4) and presented the activity menu found in the game, which can be accessed by the child or directed by a physician or responsible parent, depends on the degree of autism, the treatment time or learning that the child is receiving, this screen displays four menus, which will be better presented to the front.

A description of the game features and scenarios are presented in the following paragraphs.

Home Screen: This scenario uses as a reference the board game, where the icon chosen must arrive at their destination, usually is going back home. During the course of the game the character is faced with various animals and objects, chosen by the speech pathologist. This process is similar to the process of scheduling activity, present on the site. The choice can be made upon the need to intensify vocal exercises, which the child find more difficulty or as examination of the issue of speech. As the icon moves by scenario, upon the moves made with given. That defined the quantity steps that the icon should give the same you will find with such characters or selected objects. To find the same will communicate with the character chosen by the child, by issuing so sound that

represents. The sound is repeated three times to ensure that the child understands, and can be repeated again if the speech pathologist wishes (by voice command Repeat). Past this process the child repeats the sound. This is a practice common good in treating speech pathologist fricatives[4] and Onomatopoeia[5]. After a repetition of the sound made by the child, the character back to keep on the board game. Meanwhile with the use of the Kinect, by means of a SDK Microsoft Speech, the sound emitted by the child is captured and stored. In a way that contributes to diagnosis and correction of vocal problems, as well as the speech (Figure 5).

Screen School: The scenario consists of educational activities, which will stimulate and promote the basic learning linked to knowledge: science, mathematics and writing. Taking as an example the game of science, the child, through the act of coloring (being a joke well pleasing to every child) she will learn concepts of human body by painting parties requested (Figure 6). After learning what are upper limbs, lower limbs, body and head. The game goes to a new phase, which corresponds to the understanding of the senses (sight, touch, smell, taste and hearing). The child organizes by means of a break virtual head, understanding and learning what these are and what purpose they serve. With examples and simple to use, by means of images that portray

Figure 4. Custom menu screen with the character of the dog and the color blue

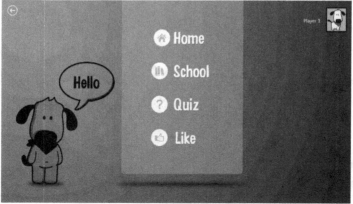

Figure 5. Screen activity in which the child plays the sound of animals beside or icons chosen by the physician during the activity, which is captured in all the sound emitted by the autistic child

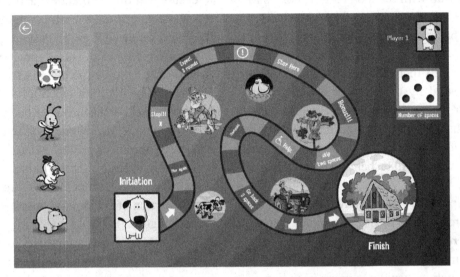

this, nose, smell being displayed by an image of the character chosen smelling a flower. In This game is not allowed to relate the parts of the body with the wrong way, if it happens the game restarts for the child, sets and registers your entire movement between right and wrong. Already in mathematics through a living history character, chosen, the child will learn basic operations to add, divide, multiply and subtract. The correct realization of mathematical operations allows us to help the character, with the implementation of their activities. Which are described by means of questions. Finally in the logbook, a kind of virtual book, the child exercises the practice of communication, by means of voice command recognized by Microsoft Speech, in which he will write these words in his diary. Simulating an essay, this scenario has content free where children may report the matter to your interest or suggested by the physician. The aim of this scenario is to know a little more of the child so that she comes to speak as also stimulate speaks to reduce communication problems (Figure 6).

Figure 6. Screen of sciences, with activity of coloring part of the human body

Screen Quiz: This scenario comes to simulate the game of hangman. Where by means of images, the child identifies what it refers, done the same spell the letters that will compose the name that identifies the image. Initially were chosen objects and animals that are common to the child's environment, thus promoting the integration of the virtual environment with the real world. To illustrate the scenario, the image of a bird was used if the child identifies in a given period and complete the name, the Image emits a sound of bird singing, estimating that every time the child listen or view a bird she can identify it. In addition the child begins to learn the letters, being important for the educational development and their

learning. It was also thought that the letters are only accepted in the right order, so that the child should learn to build words (Figure 7).

Like Screen: Acts as a strengthening of the activities performed by the smartphone (WP7), presenting an agenda of interaction of the day's activities. Initially the child or father or doctor suggests an activity to be carried out (Go to the bathroom, Taking a shower, brushing your teeth). This choice must be synchronized with the clock or with what she needs to do at that time. Thus the choice of what to do in the game, you will be associated with what must be done in their day by day activities (Figure 8).

Figure 7. Academic Activities, spelling for voice use

Figure 8. Screen of activities that simulates a day in the life of a child

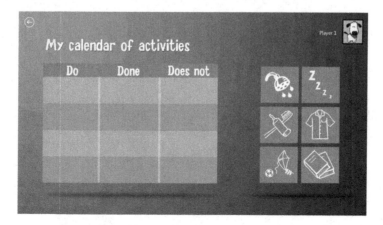

Done to choose a new screen will appear with the chosen activity, being necessary now performs it step by step. Thus the choice of what to do in the game, you will be associated with what must be done in their day by day activities (Figure 9). Done to choose a new screen will appear with the chosen activity, being necessary now performs it step by step. For this reason the child needs to arrange the order of correct actions, putting in spaces that define this priority. After the completion of the same properly, the game returns to the previous screen which will request that the child choose a new activity. For that same build step by step of your process, but before that is allowed a time so that the child can make the activity that was held game. It is important to know if the child has learned the process to perform the activity. Each activity carried out the agenda and completed simulates the actions of a day. If the child feels difficulty, the icon will help the child in the implementation!

Compatibility with Cloud Services: with the service offered you can add other services that may provide specific services to the level of autism or the needs that children could use thus, generating a catalog of services that could include services that are specific to education, such as an e-assessment to manage the assessments of the child's development, less of an educational point of view or the point of view of the development of the treatment. For the construction of this service, in addition to the measurement by means of the Attention Deficit Disorder with Hyperactivity (ADHD), should be put other measurement points and have all your architecture elaborated by the participation of professionals who deal with the child. In order that the estimates generated may be near or inside the reality of medical assessment.

A content management services that teachers use to designate the content to be taught to the child, with a focus on their difficulties in such a way that even a child using the software in addition to the even send information for analysis and diagnosis that the same can be remotely custom and a service of online community where teachers, doctors and parents can interact with their views and experiences, sharing of knowledge and information that can contribute to the treatment of the child, being a service common good in environments of distance education but with a greater interaction and with the provision of various services. Could be interesting in this environment the father have access to the service of e-assessment.

It may accompany and know how the evolutionary process of learning of their autistic son goes.

Figure 9. Activities organizational personnel

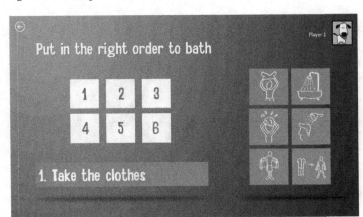

7. MODEL AND SERVICE

The process of developing the software "Can Game" under aspect of cloud computing has evolutionary way which, its main objective is to capture and make available the information of greatest interest in an environment of treatment of autistic children through technology. The software must have the ability to allow remote access to videos, audios and reports generated in a direct way (point-to-point), evade the need to send these to a third party outside (e.g., an Internet data center). In the way, the stored data comes to be, secretive being restricted to health professionals that begat/acquired such data, as the method of treatment and the parents or guardians with the prior written consent of access.

The process is carried out in a simple way for the health care professional, which by means of a scenario proposed within the Game can have a unified view of the environment. In which shows the locations where are the files that are generated, identified by the name of the patient if setting within the model of service platform to the Service (PaaS)[6]. For such a choice of service was the Windows Azure[7], because it has an infrastructure that meets the needs of the project. What will allow a scalability of services offered by the Can Game in applications for your smartphone (wp7) or for the Kinect.

A good example of needs met by Windows Azure services are incorporated. Windows Azure platform AppFabric and SQL Azure. The AppFabric becomes more simple connect applications on-premises (installed in the clinic or at home) with the cloud. The AppFabric provides identity management is a messaging bus friendly and safe to protect your files, allowing a connectivity and secure exchange of messages between the applications on-premises and cloud-based services. Thus by means of an Application Programming Interface (API)[8] public REST based on calls Hypertext Transfer Protocol (HTTP), communication protocol, is to facilitate the connection between other parts of the cloud with the external environment.

This service is located in service bus[9] Azure platform AppFabric that acts to circumvent some existing barriers in the communication network, such as firewall and NAT[10] devices. Already the authentication service is performed by Access Control[11] that integrates authentication providers, such as Windows Live[12], facebook[13], which comes to facilitate at the time of registration. The flow of information is very simple and is taken as an example (Figure 10), the communication by the use of the service in desktop with the Kinect.

1. To carry out the activities proposed by the game, the clinical treatment of autism. All information is captured (audio, video, and recorded the hits and errors), through the activities performed;

2. The responsible professional, logs your login to perform the sending of information. The push model is done by means of the protocol of standard information for medical use, Digital Imaging and Communications in Medicine (DICOM), all captured files are forwarded to the local server;

3. The collected material becomes available for which the responsible physician can set parameters for the identification of this material collected (DICOM), as also define which doctors are authorized to access and include new information or material, among other desirable parameters;

4. The metadata of the treatment are sent to a server to external reference. With the purpose of data recovery, and accessibility of such information by means of an electronic record;

5. The application can Game (Customer), used by health professionals, performs the synchronization at regular time intervals, when searched for new updates, available on the external server (cloud).

Figure 10. Scenario of sending information by service in the cloud

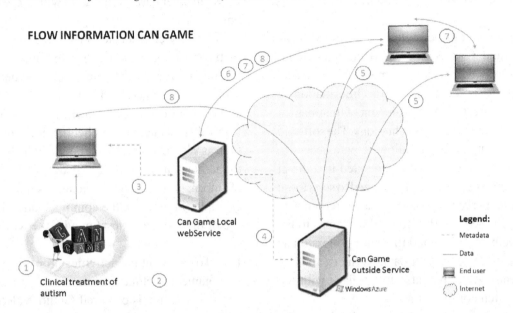

6. Health professionals may, from this point, show the result of the treatment. By means of information included in the metadata;

7. Diagnostics and other documents may be submitted and attached to the exam, making themselves available, collaboratively, to professionals who also have authorization to the aforementioned diagnosis;

8. The diagnosis, as well as the type of treatment, the evaluation of the evolutionary process of the treatment, if it becomes available for all physicians may also for the parents of the child.

The complexity of the information mentioned above and abstracted away from the end user, a time that the process has come to facilitate the communication and thus improve the diagnosis and medical intervention on the treatment of children with autism. In addition, the application itself is installed and automatically logged in user computer, by editing the file ServiceDefinition.csdef in eXtensible Markup Language (XML)[14]. For this the same interacts with an environment by means of a script of the Structured Query Lan-

guage (SQL)[15] Server Management Studio, which set the appropriate options for export.

Next step is to run the script to create a schema to SQL database of Windows Azure. The SQL Azure and SQL server hosted on cloud, where has the characteristic of a relational database. But with an additional function in a high-availability platform, scalable and with control of load balancing. Another advantage of choice and there is no need to purchase hardware to host the database, nor even to install the software infrastructure for the database management system (DBMS). The SQL Azure, is also responsible for replicating data, deal with hardware failures and climb the database for more or less depending on the need.

Upon what was mentioned above, next step and mitigate problems of communication between the local server and the SQL database, so used the Sync Framework[16] to perform the synchronization. The process is simple, running on the local computer which uses the SqlSyncProvider[17] to connect to SQL Azure database as with any other SQL Server database. After synchronizing the database creates the tables of metadata necessary storage and the procedures that the Sync Framework requires to perform synchronization.

The storage in Windows Azure, and done in a redundant fashion, thus protects in case of failure of hardware and software. An important point is the presence of semi-structured tables, which allows the manipulation of data CRUD (Create, Read, Update, and Delete), for any type of data that the user may require.

On the optical layers was developed a model in three logical layers (Figure 11):

Layer 1: Storage service, as mentioned will be storing information (video, audio, report of hits and errors, guest diagnostics). That can be deployed at each clinic, NGO's or school that deals with autism, using these technologies: DICOM and the local SQL Server. The services running on the Windows platform is implemented and operationalized in a semi-automatic by means of a configuration module.

Layer 2: Integration service controls and offers the services of the layer 1 for the distributed clients. Thus the thy as an intermediate layer, providing a security service and promoting a HTTP access.

Layer 3: Distribution service, whose main function is to maintain a mirror of unified metadata of information collected during the treatment. In addition to the configurations already mentioned of access and security, which are locally defined and replicated to the external server (this layer).

Which is promoting a more flexible architecture, updates, new plug-ins or even substitutions of specific technologies. Thus the replacement can occur without causing impact on other layers, since that suit the interfaces. The separation also facilitates the display service and presentation of information collected during the treatment.

The model has been tested, evaluated and improved with the intervention of doctors, psycholo-

Figure 11. Abstraction layer logic of communication can game

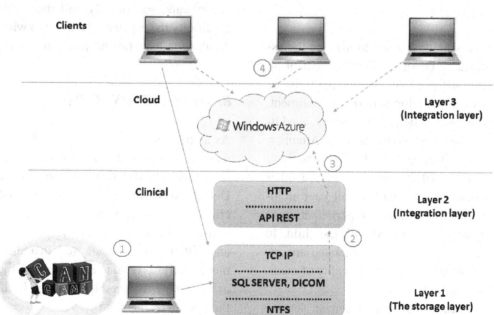

gists and speech therapists in the city of Recife Pernambuco, present in clinical partner of this project which obtains the results of treatment for autistic children being carried out by the software can Game. Knowing that the communication and the exchange of information has to be something impactful new studies will occur including the possibility of interoperability between systems free. In order to encompass all who wish to use the software and be able to reduce costs. In this way the software can Game has a final vision provide to the community a service robust, adaptable and that meets the specificities which was developed. For such a series of tests in character of software, were performed. Being discussed more in front.

7.1. Scalability with Cloud Service

The choice of cloud service, related to the project is due to the fact that adding other services that can add value to the treatment of children with autism. Thus, the elaboration of a service catalog, which would be available for Plug-ins, which can be defined for each level of autism or that may include specific services for education, treatment and other:

- **E-Assessment:** Service to manage the assessment of children's development of an educational point of view or the point of view of the development of the treatment. For the construction of this service, in addition to the measured by means of Attention Deficit Disorder with Hyperactivity Disorder (ADHD), must be placed other measuring points and have all your architecture drawn up with the participation of professionals who deal with the child. In order that the estimates generated are approaching or are within the reality of medical assessment;

- **E-Content:** Content management service that teachers or health professionals. Can use to designate the content to be taught to

children, with a focus on their difficulties, reported by data collection made by the system. The intention is that even a child using the software, in your home or in a non-governmental organization (NGO's) and other places. Thus remotely the doctor/professor determines the software to provide the requested activity;

- **E-Community:** A service of online community where teachers, doctors and parents can interact by exchanging information and experiences. The sharing of such knowledge and information has been to contribute to the treatment of the child. Being a service common good in environments of distance education (EAD), but presents a greater interaction and with the provision of various services. Could be interesting in this environment the father have access to the service of E-assessment. Thus, the same may accompany and how will the evolutionary process of learning of their autistic son.

Such services have been set up a scalability of software, so not only will meet with better specificity the treatment of children with autism. As also graduate this project as a Star Up.

8. TEST AND HYPOTHESIS

As a strategy for the validation of the software were performed initial test of icon for usability, performance and learning, by means of Attention Deficit Disorder with Hyperactivity (ADHD) in a clinic X, which allowed the test in fifty children, with ages between 4 and 18 years, of both sexes and with the autism diagnosed. In addition to the mentioned tests conducted a risk assessment, such as in Table 1, which might happen in the use of the system by the child.

The tests occurred as a recreational activity, offering no risk to physical integrity, psycho-

Table 1. Risk assessment in potential, so that can be neutralized

Risk	Trigger	Impact	Likely	Action	Solution
R001	Miss the Smartphone	Too high***	Medium**	Compromising the treatment, cause irritation and insecurity.	Use of a bracket for your smartphone
R002	Broken the Smartphone	Too high***	Medium**	Compromising the treatment, cause irritation and insecurity.	Use of a bracket for your smartphone.
R003	Physical Accidents	Low*	Low*	Not configured according to tests performed.	Not present.
R004	Ergonomic Accidents	Medium**	Too high***	The excessive use of Kinect could cause muscular discomfort.	Set hours of use and duration of use, by parents or guardians.
R005	Misuse of the System	Too high***	Low*	Compromise the treatment of the child.	Training and orientation to the father or responsible about the system.

* low to medium; ** medium to high; ***too high

logical of the child, the change in his routine of activity and not lasting more than 5 minutes with each child during a period of six weeks. Respected the fact that the child does not want to do the test, so that did not generate any embarrassment or discomfort, to any participant. Being recorded all the information as given in the research. It was considered in the test of usability that the adaptation of the child's treatment is not always simple, because it is something new, that causes new behaviors, knowing that the autistic child is resistant to change. As the test progressed, was conducted a survey of requirements, with the purpose to build a better understanding of the specific needs of children with autism. Contributing to the improvement of the system. The tests took place by means of the following interventions.

Test with Your Smartphone no. 1: This test used images similar to the framework of activity (PEC's) of usual clinical X, following the sequence of routine of learning with the use of the images. This way, it was hoped that the child performs the same activity, present in the table, making use of the information provided by your Smartphone. For this the doctor has helped and guided the children, in the use of the same and how it should act. This test was added to the evaluation of usability with clinical evaluation as shown in Table 2;

Test with Your Smartphone no. 2: This test was a repetition of the test 1, with the same children, and was not allowed the participation of the doctor in order to view the understanding and response of the child. Such test generated a questioning if the child would execute the process of touch on the screen for which I had to touch (something mechanical) and those that do not have touched it because. Being assessed in both cases the ADHD, presented in Table 3. In order to know whether the same comprehended what was to be held in an autonomous manner. This being the initial proposal of the system;

Test with Your Smartphone no. 3: This phase of the test, was compared to what the child or thereabouts in image (PEC's) supplied by smartphone was understood as an activity to be performed in their routine. This concern was due to the fact that the questioning generated in test no. 2. This was allowed a time so that the child identifies the image, it compares to the framework of activity of the Clinic X, and finally executes the activity and it is confirmed that held on the smartphone. We compared the time of this test with the time of the completion using the framework of activities of usual clinical X and behavioral issue;

Test with Game (kinect) no 1: The process repeated the same sequence of the test with your smartphone. In which were carried out educational activities (mathematics, Portuguese language,

Table 2. Result of sampling in a group of 10 children of fifty under the aspect of usability of the system, with medical guidance and understanding

Child	Age	Doctor	Application	Stress	R001/R002	Result	Percentage
Bela 1	5 years	Yes	*Smartphone*	A	0	Positive	97%
André 2	8 years	Yes	*Smartphone*	A	0	Positive	78%
André 3	10 years	Yes	*Smartphone*	A	0	Positive	80%
André 4	8 years	Yes	*Smartphone*	A	0	Positive	75%
André 5	11 years	Yes	*Smartphone*	B	0	Positive	82%
Bela 6	4 years	Yes	*Smartphone*	E	0	Negative	0%
André 7	9 years	Yes	*Smartphone*	C	0	Negative	37%
André 8	7 years	Yes	*Smartphone*	C	0	Positive	90%
André 9	12 years	Yes	*Smartphone*	B	0	Positive	82%
André 10	18 years	Yes	*Smartphone*	B	0	Negative	100%

Table 3. Result of sampling in a group of 10 children of fifty under the aspect of a deficit of learning (ADHD), the system without guidance of a physician. The ADHD was analyzed by the amount of occurrence of the tests.

Child	Age	Doctor	Application	Stress	R001/R002	ADHD	Description
Bela 1	5 years	No	*Smartphone*	A	1	2	Difficulty to pay attention and to keep with your smartphone. However when requested attention performed the activity.
André 2	8 years	No	*Smartphone*	B	2	3	Problem in maintaining attention in situations of routine. However when requested attention performed the activity, but soon lost the attention.
André 3	10 years	No	*Smartphone*	B	2	3	Difficulty of attention, understanding of the activity and activities performed with request. Without total autonomy.
André 4	8 years	No	*Smartphone*	C	3	4	Difficulty in hearing, maintain the attention, it lost the attention very easily. Performing the activities only when requested.
André 5	11 years	No	*Smartphone*	C	3	4	Difficulty of learning motivated by the high level of distraction.
Bela 6	4 years	No	*Smartphone*	E	5	4	Did not want to perform the activity, several difficulties presented.
André 7	9 years	No	*Smartphone*	C	4	3	Inability to pay attention, little skill, apathy or lack of motivation and high level of distraction. Not held activity.
André 8	7 years	No	*Smartphone*	C	3	4	Inability to complete the activity, by losing the attention very easily. It's necessary to request frequent attention.
André 9	12 years	No	*Smartphone*	A	0	1	Held the activity, but lost your smartphone.
André 10	18 years	No	*Smartphone*	A	0	0	Held the activity, without any difficulty.

Legend ADHD: 0 = never; 1 = rarely; 2 = occasionally; 3 = frequently; 4 = very often
Legend of the probability of risks: 0 = never; 1 = low; 2 = moderate; 3 = high; 4 = often; 5 = very often

sciences and social practices), test of usability, performance of the system and behavioral analysis (ADHD);

Test with Game (kinect) no. 2: The process was repeated without the participation of the doctor, being made an interaction by means of a dialog or questioning of the activities, motivating the social life of the child.

Such tests have provided a new insight on the software developed, as it was based on a theoretical framework. As soon as he felt the need to change the sensitivity of the game, in system response time, in the capture of the movements and the child's attention. Conceiving as well the need of a change to the interface, so that attach more attention of the child being adopted some sounds that can contribute to this, such as animated images.

The medical corps who accompanied the project has made a positive assessment of the system, with a strong potential to meet the need of the child and the completion of treatment. This conclusion is given to the fact that the period of adaptation by children was short. But that presented significant results in relation to the completion of the activities and interests of the same in return to using the game. Being such a strong point that will facilitate the treatment of children with autism where the same evaluated the importance of services in the cloud for analysis of collected material, to form collaborative and interdisciplinary as a large differential. Since the perspective of each professional connected to the child's treatment may include the treatment. At the end of the testing stage, all points were considered: response time, difficulty or ease of interaction, understanding and change of

mood (and the level of stress, as shown in Figure 12), so that involve a new version of the system. But this new version requires a greater study and deepening in autism, once which was discarded the fact that the system was used by children who already carry out the treatment for a period of time in the Clinic X. Knowing that the autistic person learns in an evolving, slow for a whole life, as mentioned at the beginning of this article, the system must submit versions of according to age of autism. Because there are different needs in terms of treatment, thus needed new data to be collected, compared and analyzed in a period longer than six weeks and with a new user profile.

From the perspective of the services in the clouds, suggested a new assessment of resources through suggestions of the medical staff. Being considered the creation of a communication channel where parents or family members can participate, so that will contribute to the child's treatment. And it is commonly known as a service of community online. The doctor can manage the content of the game of form online (remotely), offering a customizable game for each specific child so that the game may have a better applicability outside the medical environment. These include houses, schools and other places, i.e. the same procedure that happens with the activities of smartphone happen with the activities of kinect. And finally develop a database that allows the customization with other icons, with more color options, with Plug-in or new services. As for example the doctor prepare the activity, creating new scenarios or adjusting scenarios already existing, in the clouds by allowing this action will

Figure 12. Representative picture of emotional behavior of the child during the testing process

A   B   C   D   E

motivate increasingly the child to use the system and that it must be more specific for each need and thus contribute to the treatment. Such services are in a study or test for the viability of the system, in order to further contribute to the treatment of autism.

9. CONCLUSION

This chapter discusses treatments for autistic children and interventions that use educational games and sets out the author´s on-going research on developing a technological solution that aids children to adapt better to treatment with a view to achieving more results that are significant in shorter intervals. It is concluded that, by means of ludic games by means of a pleasant process, the system is expected to promote the use of software by autistic child, making this motivation is essential for the construction of learning, the development of multidisciplinary autonomously. Providing a greater awareness of what is happening in their environment, making the environment they live in becomes an agent dialer, socialization and learning.

It is noticed that through the tests performed, the attention deficit of the child in the absence of a common person in his daily life (medical or family), increases significantly. Generating questions about the learning, through the realization of the activities. However, as known, it is known that the autism treatment it occurs gradually and for an indefinite period, in which a longer interval of time, this problem can be mitigated. This way, through this project the intervention can happen in several units for the treatment of autistic patients, as well as in homes and schools, allowing above all the social inclusion of children in common environments in their lives on a daily basis. Once that because it is a virtual game there will be no changes in the environment or the creation of scenarios for special processing. Both being different from the reality of a real society, which does not prejudge a social practice.

The virtual games and applications for your smartphone, are tools and common in children, adolescents and adults. That many times, that same technology are an instrument for social interaction. Allowing a child might make to your treatment, without any restrictions or perceptions of other people on what is happening avoiding any embarrassment. Thus, new studies through the some of the changes will be started so that this possibility has become a common practice.

Therefore, the project concludes with a phrase from Gilberto Freyre (1996):

Without a social goal, knowledge is the greatest of trifles.

REFERENCES

Ajuriahuerra, J. (1977). Las psicosis infantiles. In Manual de Psiquiatría Infantil (4ªed.). Barcelona: Toray-Masson..

AMA. (n.d.). *Treatment*. Retrieved June 29, 2012 from http://www.ama.org.br

Aman, M. G. (2005). Treatment planning for patients with autism spectrum disorders. *The Journal of Clinical Psychiatry*, 66(10), 38–45. PMID:16401149.

Bonk, C. J., Olson, T., Wisher, R., & Orvis, K. L. (2002). Learning from focus groups: An examination of blended learning. *Journal of Distance Education*, 17(3), 97–118.

Bosa, C. (n.d.). *Shared care and early identification of autism*. Retrieved March 14, 2012 from http://www.scielo.br/pdf/prc/v15n1/a10v15n1.pdf.

Chirigati, F. S. (n.d.). *Cloud computer*. Retrieved June 30, 2012 from http://www.gta.ufrj.br/ensino/eel879/trabalhos_vf_2009_2/seabra/index.html

Cohen, S. B., & Frith, L. A. (1985). Does the autistic child have a theory of mind? *Cognition*, *21*, 37–46. doi:10.1016/0010-0277(85)90022-8 PMID:2934210.

da Autonomia, F. P. P. (1996). *Saberes necessários a prática educativa*. São Paulo, Brazil: Paz e Terra..

Downer, S. R., Meara, J. G., & Costa, A. C. (2005). Use of SMS text messaging to improve outpatient attendance. *Med J Aust.*, *183*(7), 366-368. Retrieved March 14, 2012 from http://www.ncbi.nlm.nih.gov/pubmed/16201955

Francisco, K. C. (n.d.). *News about phones: The approaches of newspapers*. Retrieved August 30, 2012 from http://sbpjor.kamotini.kinghost.net/sbpjor/admjor/arquivos/9encontro/CL_87.pdf

Gadia, A. (n.d.). *Autism and pervasive development disorders*. Retrieved March 14, 2012 from http://www.scielo.br/pdf/jped/v80n2s0/v80n2Sa10.pdf

Gomes, P. (n.d.). *Kinect helps diagnose and treat autism review*. Retrieved August 30, 2012 from http://porvir.org/porcriar/kinect-ajuda-diagnosticar-tratar-autismo/20120612

Guilhermo, Sapiro, & Firth, N. (n.d.). *Kinect cameras watch for autism*. Retrieved August 28, 2012 from http://www.newscientist.com/article/mg21428636.400-kinect-cameras-watch-for-autism.html

Júnior, P. (n.d.). *Brazil is featured on world autism*. Retrieved August 14, 2012 from http://www.revistaautismo.com.br/diamundial2011

Lazzeri, T. (n.d.). *Autism: The universe around me*. Retrieved August 30, 2012 from http://m.parc.terra.com.br/efamilynet/dev/generic/interna.php?id_cat=25&article_id=557

Lim, M. S., Hoking, J. S., Hellard, M. E., & Aitiken, C. K. (n.d.). SMS STI: A review of the uses of mobile phone text messaging in sexual health. *Int JSTD AIDS*, *19*(5), 287-290. Retrieved August 30, 2012 from http://www.ncbi.nlm.nih.gov/pubmed/18482956

Lopes, M. C. (2004a). *Communication*. Aveiro, Portugal: Edição Universidade de Aveiro..

Lopes, M. C. (2004b). *Playfulness*. Aveiro, Portugal: Edição Universidade de Aveiro..

Monteiro, R. F. (1994). Jogos dramáticos (3ª ed.). São Paulo, Brazil: Agora..

Nitz, J. C. et al. (2010). Is the Wii fit a new-generation tool for improving balance, health and wellbeing? A pilot study. *Climacteric: The Journal of the International Menopause Society*, *13*(5), 487–491. doi:10.3109/13697130903395193 PMID:19905991.

Nogueira, a.j. (2000). methodology of scientific work. *Impresso no Brasil, 21*(1).

Novaes, J. C. (1992). *Play wheel*. Rio de Janeiro, Brazil: Agir..

Tamanaha, A. C. (n.d.). *The play activity in infantile autism*. Retrieved April 14, 2012 from http://www.pucsp.br/revistadisturbios/artigos/Artigo_490.pdf

Vitorino, A. J. (n.d.). *Mobile technology applied in health care and support*. Retrieved March 14, 2012 from https://docs.google.com/viewer?a=v&q=cache:mwR9kk1xCGkJ:www.faculdadeflamingo.com.br/ojs/index.php/rit/article/download/5/15+&hl=pt-BR&gl=br&pid=bl&srcid=ADGEESi1qWzMCFVrYfqykdZb7dgRmw1aoS-d0D_k7hCeJahO0a3Fdc8k-iC4Z_nw17Gzgbh8Ch63v-yhSYL6EG-oLm1UzTOQejOwZ_ejmN9_nXdagq6d_SFsHZjO__3Bsj0XCM7MU6fU-&sig=AHIEtbQwnVYJiM1UP7pETAuTxocudXGoGw

Winnicott, D., & Autismo, W. (1997). *Thinking about children*. Porto Alegre, Brazil: Artes Médicas..

Winnicott, W. D. (1975). *Playing and reality*. Rio de Janeiro, Brazil: Imago..

KEY TERMS AND DEFINITIONS

Attention Deficit Disorder with Hyperactivity (ADHD): Is a neurobiological disorder, genetic causes, which appears in childhood and frequently accompanies the person throughout his life.

Cloud Computer: Refers to the use of memory and storage capacities and calculation of shared computers and servers and interconnected via the Internet, following the principle of grid computing.

Digital Imaging and Communications in Medicine (DICOM): Is a set of standards for treatment, storage and transmission of medical information (medical imaging) in an electronic format, structured protocol.

Kinect: Is a motion sensor developed for the Xbox 360 and Xbox One, along with the company Prime Sense.

Microsoft Speech: SAPI is an API developed by Microsoft to allow the use of speech recognition and speech synthesis within Windows applications.

Multidisciplinary: Is a set of disciplines to be worked on simultaneously, without making appear the relations that may exist between them, and is designed for a system of one level and unique objectives, without any cooperation.

Smartphone: Is a mobile phone with advanced features that can be extended through programs run by your operating system.

WP7: Is a mobile operating system developed by Microsoft, successor to the Windows Mobile platform.

ENDNOTES

[1] Technology capable of letting players to interact with electronic game without the need of having in hands a joystick, innovating in the field of gameplay.

[2] Allows you to create quizzes online for free. http://www.surveymonkey.com/s/rvlqggj

[3] Applications of speech recognition allows a computer respond to commands to speak or write text in response to the spoken words.

[4] Has unique importance in the speech-language practice, because they are the target of interest and studies, both in the areas of hearing, language (oral and written), oral motricity, and in the area of voice.

[5] Is imitating a sound with a phoneme or word. Noises, screams, corner of animals, sounds of nature, the noise of machinery, contributing to formation of words.

[6] Offers an environment of high level to create, test, and deliver custom applications.

[7] It is a special platform for running applications and services, based on the concepts of cloud computing.

[8] It is a set of routines and standards established by a software for the use of its features for applications that do not wish to become involved in implementation details of the software, but only use their services.

[9] It is a service that provides connectivity options for Windows Communication Foundation (WCF) and other service endpoints - including end points REST - that would otherwise be difficult or impossible to achieve.

[10] In this case considered network address translation.

[11] Access Control Service.

[12] It is an email address and password with your profile, provided by Microsoft.

13 It is a social network that unites people.

14 In this case it is a language that creates a single infrastructure for several languages.

15 It is the language of search default declarative for relational database

16 Sync Framework is a comprehensive synchronization platform that enables collaboration and offline scenarios for applications, services and devices.

17 Represents a provider of synchronization that communicates with a SQL Server database and shields of other components of the Sync Framework from the specific implementation of the database.

Chapter 17
Application of Mobile Cloud–Based Technologies in News Reporting:
Current Trends and Future Perspectives

Charalampos Dimoulas
Aristotle University of Thessaloniki, Greece

Andreas Veglis
Aristotle University of Thessaloniki, Greece

George Kalliris
Aristotle University of Thessaloniki, Greece

ABSTRACT

Cloud Computing is one of the most rapidly evolving technologies available today that offers the possibility of multimedia content exploitation with rich media experience. Cloud computing users have the flexibility to enjoy media content independently of time and space. Multimedia cloud computing encompasses technology, multimedia data, and community contribution, offering augmented multimodal interaction and advanced processing services to the users. Mobile multimedia resources can now be accessed through the cloud practically at anytime and from anywhere, facing contemporary demands for information access and process, thus perfectly matching to the nature of news media. Such features are very favorable in online journalism and specifically in news reporting services. This chapter presents technological and application-oriented trends in cloud-based mobile news reporting both at journalists' (news producers) and users' (news consumers) sides. Future and emerging perspectives, such as ubiquitous and pervasive computing, incorporating context and location-aware services in semantic interaction modes, are also described from the news-reporting point of view.

DOI: 10.4018/978-1-4666-4781-7.ch017

INTRODUCTION

The rapid evolution of Information and Communication Technologies (ICTs) has affected almost all aspects of human activities. The digitalization of the work process, along with the introduction of the Internet and its services has had a major influence in the journalism profession (Erdal, 2007; Veglis, 2009). Digital technology has revolutionized newspaper production, whereas computers and computerized editorial systems are utilized while writing texts, processing images, reporting on news events, etc. (Sabelström, 2001; Veglis, Tsourvakas, Pomportsis, & Avraam, 2005). Radio, television and their contemporary ICT counterparts have expanded their influence and also created new opportunities in receiving and consuming, but also in creating and disseminating news (Chung, Kim, Trammell, & Porter, 2007; Geoghegan & Klass, 2007; Simpson, 2008). Audiovisual streaming technologies and user generated content (UGC) approaches have become very popular in breaking news and generally timely news coverage (Dimoulas, Tsourvakas, Kalliris, & Papakis, 2012; Geoghegan & Klass, 2007; Kotsakis, Kalliris, & Dimoulas, 2012; Simpson, 2008). Nowadays, the journalist is expected to have the ability to exploit many tools, services and platforms in order to be informed, but also to produce and deliver news (Spyridou, Matsiola, Veglis, Kalliris, & Dimoulas, 2013). The 24-hour cycle of producing news does not exist anymore. The news is produced 24 hours per day and it is made available at once in many alternative publishing channels (Sabelström, 2001; Veglis, 2012). It is also updated continuously in order to include all the latest developments (Veglis, 2010). This is closely related to the vision of "information access (and process) at any time and place," which has been inspiring for the Cloud Computing (CC) and the Mobile Cloud Computing (MCC) initiatives in the mid-90s (Khan & Ahirwar, 2011; Satyanarayanan, Bahl, Caceres, & Davies, 2009).

CC and MCC models enable the delivery of data-storage, services, software, and processing capacity from the Internet. It is about offloading data, applications and computing from the client side into the "cloud," trading-off storage and processing demands with networking bandwidth resources. In this context, cloud approaches offer convenient and on demand access to remote computing resources, minimizing management efforts and expertise in the client side (Kovachev, Cao, & Klamma, 2011). The difference between CC and MCC lays on the fact that in the MCC model the client's access terminal is a mobile device, supporting also the "information at my fingertip" vision (Satyanarayanan et al., 2009). In this context, MCC attempts to further extend flexibility and mobility, incorporating also increased interaction and functional capabilities, so that, besides storage and download services, more powerful applications can be deployed, anticipating more significant growth (Dey, 2012; Dinh, Lee, Niyato, & Wang, 2011; Kovalick, 2011). The use of CC/MCC has many benefits in terms of management, ease of operation and upgrading for the average user, as well as in security issues, although new threats and security difficulties arise.

Among the various fields and disciplines that CC and MCC services are massively deployed in, infotainment and media-related applications are very common (Dey, 2012; Khan & Ahirwar, 2011; Kovalick, 2011; Raj & Mala, 2012). The present chapter focuses on the current trends and the future perspectives of the MCC-based news reporting services. The rest of the chapter is organized as follows. In the next section, the technological and operational background of MCC is briefly provided, with emphasis on media-related cloud application and services. CC and MCC advantages and disadvantages are also discussed with regard to the news reporting paradigm. In the main thrust of chapter the MCC-based news reporting challenges are described, while related characteristic examples are listed. News acquisition and dissemination diagrams are presented, along with MCC-adapted dataflow, news content types and interaction concepts, both at the producer and consumer sites. Advanced and future trends are then discussed, with emphasis on pervasive computing and augmented interaction approaches that can be employed in media and news reporting MCC. Summary and concluding remarks are provided in the last section.

BACKGROUND

Underlying Technology and Basic Definitions

The mobile cloud concept was necessary in order to overcome difficulties in providing rich media experience to the mobile users, considering that mobile and generally portable devices are resource-limited, both in computing power and storage capabilities. Hence, MCC approach allows users to run demanding services, trading off computational power with higher speed network access (Fernando, Loke & Rahayu, 2013; Kovachev et al., 2011; Ling, Chen, Zhang, & Tian, 2011). In this context, substantial resources management improvements are viable, including also the deployment of centralized security and privacy policies, increasing trust and reliability. All these features have a great impact on running-cost savings and new market opportunities, further strengthening the potentials of "on demand computing," "utility computing" or "pay as you go computing" strategies that define the cloud approach (Dinh et al., 2011; Fernando et al., 2013). MCC applications are delivered as services with the help of hardware and software resources located in remote data centers (i.e. grids, content delivery networks, server-based computing and peer to peer (P2P) networks, Wi-Fi, cellular networks, etc.). Thus, large networks of heterogeneous wireless/mobile terminals with different clients/server architectures are involved (Kesavan, Anand, &

Jayakumar, 2012; Lin, Ge, Wang, Zhu, & Ryu, 2012; Rodrigues, Zhou, Mendes, Lin, & Lloret, 2012; Silva, Neves, Denko, & Rodrigues, 2009; Vassilaras & Yovanof, 2011; Zhu, Luo, Wang, & Li, 2011).

CC services are usually deployed in three different modes: hardware resources, development platforms and end-applications. Hence, there are three major different models regularly used in the literature: Infrastructure as a Service (IaaS), Platform as a Service (PaaS) and Software as a Service (SaaS). IaaS refers to the availability of the necessary hardware resources that are needed to be used by cloud users. PaaS is a development platform that offers the necessary programming tools and environments to the cloud-developers in order to implement and deploy their own software services. SaaS is a model of remote application access and generally on demand provision of utilities (Dinh et al., 2011; Fernando et al., 2013; Zhu et al., 2011). These three basic modes are graphically presented in Figure 1, along with the media related services that are discussed in the next subsection.

Media-Related Cloud Services

Media as a Service (MaaS) is a sub-case of SaaS, whereas multimedia applications are involved. The importance of studying separately such a model is two-folded. Firstly, the nature of multimedia content and interaction is very close to the mechanisms of news-content production, editing and dissemination. Secondly, multimedia content and applications are affined with increased computational load and storage demands, as well as with minimum delay and latency tolerance. The positive trade-off for these requirements lays on the fact that multimedia content provides rich media experience to the user. This is also related to the inherent multimodal interaction, considering that different complementary content modalities are involved. Especially in the case of mobile computing, the multimodal aspect is extended in the

Figure 1. Relationship between infrastructure (IaaS), platform (PaaS) and software as a service (SaaS) models with (multi)media as a service (MaaS) cloud computing

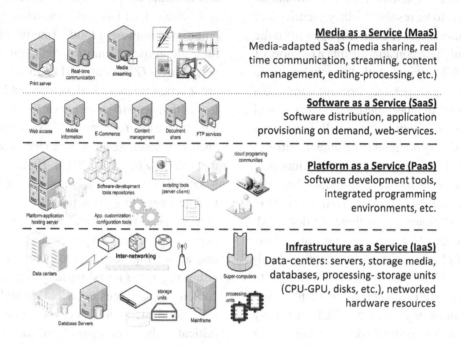

diversity of the mobile terminals and its interfacing modes, that attempt to augment human-machine interaction. Hence, MaaS is placed at the top of the remaining SaaS services, as one of the most demanding cases that requires special treatment.

As it is depicted in Figure 1, media content can be in the form of text, photos and images, audio and video, or as multimedia structures containing all the previous entities at various multimodal interaction relationships. Hence, MaaS can have the form of a simple utility for storing and sharing multimedia content, but it can also feature more advanced functional characteristics, such as audiovisual streaming-based real-time communication, media content processing, description and management, offering of media analytics tools, as well as customizable options (Dey, 2012; Khan & Ahirwar, 2011). All these features are nowadays very popular and closely related with the development of Web 2.0, whereas Internet multimedia is emerging as a service. In the mobile MaaS paradigm, end users, administrators,

content producers and distributors can initiate any transaction accessing a database system independently of time and space (Khan & Ahirwar, 2011). Users can now run multimedia processing services in a distributed manner, thus eliminating full media installation, software maintenance and upgrade needs, without requiring exaggerated computational power and energy consumption in their mobile terminals (Zhu et al., 2011).

Current Challenges and Expectations

There are many advantages that can be exploited by adopting CC and MCC, including the rapid and continuous evolution of smart phones, tablets and mobile devices in general. However, there are also certain limitations and difficulties that have to be faced. Hence, offloading to the cloud is not always a solution. In particular in MCC, besides poor performance of the mobile terminals, limited communication bandwidth, limitations of the mobile database models, data consistency and synchronization demands are some additional issues that need to be resolved. Many security and interoperability issues remain still open from the client point of view, considering that a plethora of different mobile devices, with different hardware characteristics and operating systems compose a very complex "mobile landscape." Unaccepted delays and network latencies are usually introduced making MCC very difficult to be implemented in computational intensive and critical applications, such as real-time media communication and MaaS in general. New sophisticated networking processing techniques are continuously deployed, such as cloudlets (that move the execution of the applications closer to the client than the cloud) and intelligent cloudlet-agents that attempt to optimally manage cloudlets and available computing resources in general. Similarly, a variety of sensors and sensor-networks are tested along with energy-efficient and secure routing algorithms, as well as media-aware flow scheduling techniques (Lin et al., 2012; Rodrigues et al., 2012). In the same context, data securing and cryptography techniques are implemented along with digital rights management (DRM), media content integrity, authentication and identification strategies (Dinh et al., 2011; Gayathri, Thomas, & Jayasudha, 2012; Lin et al., 2012).

Indeed, there are still many unresolved technical issues that are related to packet losses, delays and delay variations that determine network quality of service (QoS) (Dinh et al., 2011; Hakkani-Tür, Tur, & Heck, 2011; Khan & Ahirwar, 2011; Satyanarayanan et al., 2009; Verbelen, Simoens, De Turck, & Dhoedt, 2012). In practice, every communication system has issues regarding QoS and Quality of Experience (QoE), with the later to be important in media related applications (Kalliris, Dimoulas, Veglis, & Matsiola, 2011; Ries & Gardlo, 2010; Vegiris, Avdelidis, Dimoulas, & Papanikolaou, 2008). Many researchers focus on QoS adaptation in order to achieve high and acceptable QoE in various media-related ap-

plications (i.e. storage and sharing, authoring and mashup, adaptation and delivery, rendering and retrieval and others), examining both the "multimedia-aware cloud" (media cloud) and the "cloud-aware multimedia" (cloud media) perspectives (Zhu et al., 2011). In addition, there are several research and development MaaS challenges that need to be faced, such as "multimedia and service heterogeneity," "QoS heterogeneity," "network heterogeneity," "device heterogeneity and others (Zhu et al., 2011). Hence, examining MaaS news reporting scenarios is not only an up to date interesting issue, but also a very useful case study to further analyze MCC limitations, expected progress and perspectives. Among others, answering society acceptance and market issues regarding users' participation and billing, content and services contribution and generally user-cloud interaction seems very interesting and critical at the same time (Fernando et al., 2013; Satyanarayanan et al., 2009; Zhu et al., 2011).

MOBILE CLOUD-BASED TECHNOLOGIES IN NEWS REPORTING

Modeling News Reporting Workflow

ICT progress has favored news reporting techniques and practices from the journalist's point of view. At the same time, UGC approaches have become very popular in breaking news and generally timely news coverage that are posted in all applicable content types in news reports (Kalliris & Dimoulas, 2009; Kotsakis et al., 2012; Raj & Mala, 2012). In both cases, news articles need to have some minimum desired characteristics, like having few or no mistakes as they have been written by professionals, containing rich information about the involved parties in the story (people, locations, etc.), posing compactness but also easy linkage to other small articles that could be coupled together into larger news stories (Raj &

Mala, 2012). Furthermore, in most cases online news seem to have similar structural characteristics, favoring users in recognizing and identifying news pages, thus offering easy access with "confident" news-browsing and consumption (Wu et al., 2010). To meet the above demands, besides news collection and dissemination, the phases of information validation, processing, shaping and presentation are very important in the news reporting process (Kalliris & Dimoulas, 2009; Veglis & Pomportsis, 2012; Zhu et al., 2011), as depicted in Figure 2. The "cloud-processes" that are presented in Figure 2 denote that the various phases of news production and dissemination flow are usually conducted in distributed locations, both in terms of content processing and storing, as well as users' and reporters' actions. For instance, even in the early days of press, reporters were collect-

ing information at the "news scenes," while news processing and presentation were conducted in the premises of the news organization, whereas content was archived prior to its final distribution to the news consumers. The same applies in today's news reporting scenarios, with the valuable help of ICT that has a major impact in the whole process, minimizing time and distances from news collection to news consumption sites.

A very positive consequence of the ICT domination is the fact that meta-processing might be applied, offering elegant content documentation and archiving. Also useful user feedback can be proven valuable towards content annotation and semantic interaction concepts. Obviously, this has a positive impact on media life-cycle expansion, considering that archived material can be further exploited in various content re-use scenarios at

Figure 2. News reporting diagram: news processing flow, content types and media life-cycle

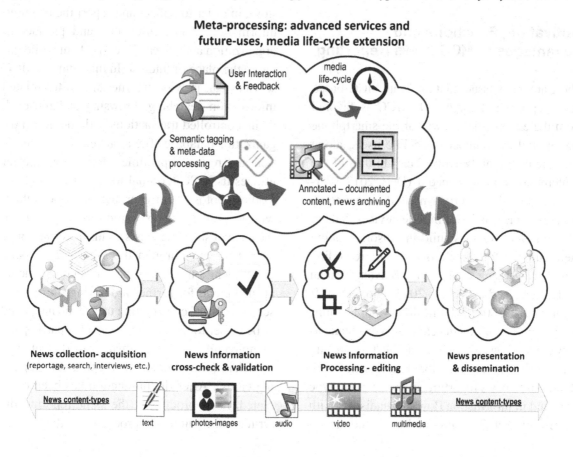

the producer domain, but also in demanding user-adaptive content searching and retrieval services (Dimoulas et al., 2012; Kalliris & Dimoulas, 2009; Kotsakis et al., 2012). It is also clear that the diagram of Figure 2 is generic and applies to most, if not all, news reporting scenarios, regardless to news topic-coverage, while it perfectly suits to the cases of CC- and MCC-based news reporting. In this context, the clouds might represent intranet nodes within media agency facilities, or correspond to public or virtual private network Internet sites. Similarly, news producer and consumer sites are not really distinguishable, meaning that each end can belong to any node of the cloud process. Hence, the role of professional journalists and ordinary users can now be fully interchanged, considering that the former consumes news as part of his everyday personal and professional habits in order to be constantly informed, while the latter can contribute content in the context of UGC models.

Motivation, Functions and Advantages of MCC News Reporting

There are many issues that motivate MCC-based news reporting. First of all, MCC is favored from the exponential growth of the smartphone market and the number of mobile users, along with the new rapidly evolved capabilities of the contemporary mobile media (Dey, 2012; Verbelen et al., 2012). Furthermore, there are some unique characteristics of mobile devices that are related to their various build-in sensors, making them suitable for mobile multimedia recording and sharing (Ling et al., 2011; Satyanarayanan et al., 2009; Verbelen et al., 2012; Zhou, Dun, & Billinghurst, 2008). Mobile MaaS applications and generally multimedia cloud services stand as very demanding cases in CC and MCC, featuring many technical and functional similarities with cloud-based news reporting, both at content type level and in information flow mechanisms. With the rise of Web 2.0, news and media content is

easily produced and disseminated through the Internet, as the huge success of YouTube[1] and similar services imply (Zhu et al., 2011). Hence, multimodal news information can be acquired, processed and transmitted entirely from the mobile terminal, as the flow diagram of Figure 3 suggests. Indeed, most of the ICT-skilled journalists and reporters prefer nowadays to use their personal smartphone or tablet in their daily news reporting tasks. In addition, portable computers can be further exploited for more demanding editing, presentation and meta-processing applications.

Figure 3 depicts an end-to-end flow diagram, presenting the functional processes that are encountered in a typical use case of MCC-based news. First of all, a reporter (a professional journalist who is employed in a media organization, or a free launcher, or even a UGC contributing user) who is employed in a media organization (or a free launcher, or even a UGC contributing user) has to visit the natural place of the news story, in order to collect and report the acquired information. Topic informing and production organization actions can be carried out while going to the place of interest. In this context, MCC services can provide Internet access for related information searching, browsing and retrieval, while controlled transactions with the media organization database offer archived content selection and re-use capabilities. Next, the reporter utilizes its MCC terminal for capturing and uploading photos, audio recordings and videos along with accompanying text compositions (usually in the form of short messages). This material can be shared directly through the Web and/or social media, while it can also be sent into the media agency cloud for further processing. In the first scenario, UGC contributing users who happened to be closer to the incidents can also participate, by uploading their own amateur media captures (which is quite common in breaking news reporting cases). After the production has been completed, news producers (the same reporter, the writer or the editor) can proceed with the remain-

Figure 3. Flow diagram of typical MCC news reporting use case

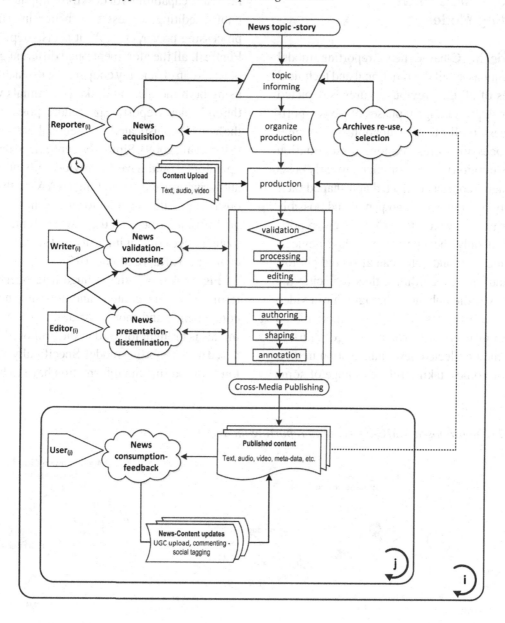

ing validation, processing and editing phases. Similarly, news shaping, presentation and content description strategies can be applied along with cross media publishing dissemination under the editor's supervision. CC and MCC-based services can be still engaged in all of the above phases, allowing for remote collaboration between all the involved parties. Finally, published content can be accessed from both ordinary users and others involved in the journalism profession, allowing them to be informed but also to contribute via UGC uploads and/or feedback comments. These processes can be repeated several times in a news story or in broader topics of related stories, as the loop diagrams of Figure 3 imply.

A Generic MCC News Reporting Model

A generic MCC-based news reporting model that encompasses all the functional and technical attributes of all the previous figures is depicted in Figure 4, presenting all phases of news reporting process (collection, validation, processing/meta-processing, presentation, dissemination and consumption). Hence, similarly to early press years where reporters collected and shaped their information using paper and pencil and possibly a typewriter afterwards, today MCC-news reporters exploit only their personal mobile devices, that besides text and notes can also hold photos, sound and video recordings, thus replacing the need for extra dictaphones, photographic or video camera. Nevertheless, journalists, reporters and participating users still have the change to further process their collected news information in their offices or homes, taking full advantage of some

favorable capabilities of desktop computers in the publish-editing process (i.e. better interfacing, processing power, etc.). As it is also depicted in Figure 4, all the aforementioned different groups of users can efficiently cooperate with each other, using both mobile and desktop terminals within the entire news reporting procedure, possibly with the help of sophisticated mobile collaboration tools (Silva et al., 2009). Similarly, centralized network operators would have to provide authentication, authorization and accounting (AAA) to the various user profiles, in order to ensure the minimum quality requirements of the news content, but also to guarantee content integrity and security (Dinh et al., 2011; Raj & Mala, 2012).

Figure 4 shows that a huge heterogeneity in terms of media content and formats, network components, and mobile or desktop access terminals is brought forward in the proposed MCC-based news reporting model. Specifically, various kinds of multimedia information have to be cap-

Figure 4. The proposed MMC-based news reporting model

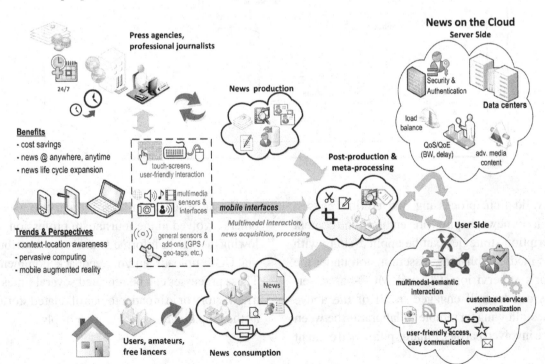

tured, processed and complemented, requiring similar cloud services for distributed parallel multimedia processing and/or authoring. QoS and QoE parameters, besides their impact on the quality of the transmitted content, they also influence the applicability of different publishing channels. Hence, according to the users' skills and preferences, news can be disseminated through Internet, digital audio and video broadcasting platforms and in wireless entry points that can be accessed through office, in-vehicle infotainment or even in more demanding work and physical exercising actions that require hand-free operations (Kalliris et al., 2011; Kesavan et al., 2012; Vegiris et al., 2008; Zhu et al., 2011). In the following paragraphs, we will focus on each content type since they require different treatment but also feature dissimilar advantages and disadvantages for all the news production, post-production and consumption processes.

It is well known that text is appropriate for in-depth presentation and comprehensive understanding of a topic, thus it is the main content type that knowledge is imprinted and imparted by. On the other hand, in the absence of accompanying images, photos or any other multimedia element, plain text is very poor and indirect in terms of presentation and communication. These two characteristics form the exact opposite condition that a mobile terminal would favor. It is obvious that neither the creation of elongated text is easy using the mobile keyboard during news production, nor the presentation of extended plain text is convenient in mobile news consumption. However, small messaging service (SMS) -based communication is dominant in mobile devices, while similar abstracting textual messaging and micro-blogging tools (i.e. RSS) are very popular, not only in personalized services and communication, but also in public domains and in the case of social networking messaging (Montalvo, Palomo, & Laguna, 2010). For instance, Twitter[2] enables users to send and read short messages (the so-called "tweets"), serving online social networking and micro-blogging. Thus, it is very helpful in composing small news-headlines as well as breaking news alerts (Li et al., 2011) that can be easily handled from the mobile user, both acting as reporter and as news reader. Similarly, the role of keywords is very important and significant in timely news coverage and news-articles post-browsing, while keyword composition can be easily conducted from the mobile user during news collection, processing and meta-processing. Mobile text processing seems to be more important from the MCC news consumption point of view, where various corpora abstraction techniques are currently deployed aiming at facilitating easier browsing with summarization automation.

Along with the development and spread of Web 2.0, the use of multiple content types that are combined together, rather than single content entities, seems to emerge. This approach of multimodal information processing and presentation is closely related to the multimedia nature of news content, but also to most of the media related services. Internet services and applications tend to be dominated by audio and audiovisual media content. Much of this content includes amateur or semi-professionally produced recordings, although in many cases such material is very important and sometimes unique. A professional audio or audiovisual production deploys, all appropriate recording, processing, editing and mastering techniques in order to achieve the best possible result (Dimoulas et al., 2012; Geoghegan & Klass, 2007; Kotsakis et al., 2012; Simpson, 2008). On the other hand, amateur or semi-professional productions often suffer from various quality degradation and noise issues in both audio and video content. Restoration, aesthetical treatment and processing require both expertise and dedicated toolkit repositories that also have to be available online during content production. MCC seems to be the right answer to the above issues, combining mobile devices technology with CC trends.

In the case of MCC-based audio news reporting, both professional journalists and participating users can contribute via audio news collecting and online sharing (podcasting), taking advantage of mobile networking along with sound recording capabilities (Geoghegan & Klass, 2007; Kotsakis et al., 2012). The same applies also to the case of video news collection and sharing (vodcasting, iReport, iCaught, uReport, etc.), using photo capturing and video recording utilities that mobile devices offer (Dimoulas et al., 2012; Satyanarayanan et al., 2009; Simpson, 2008; Zhou et al., 2008). Particularly in the news reporting scenario, access to dedicated online environments is necessary for the demanded audiovisual processing tasks (i.e. audiovisual editing and authoring, subtitling, content annotation, access to "podsafe" and properly-licensed music and audiovisual effects, etc.). From a journalism point of view, content description and management is really interwoven to the information validation, documentation and archiving tasks of the news reporting process and of the journalistic profession in general. Hence, CC-available multimedia annotation tools can be easily utilized from the news producers in all the discussed MCC aspects (Dinh et al., 2011; Hopfgartner & Jose, 2009; 2010; Kovalick, 2011). User interaction and content labeling provide very useful feedback toward user-customization and profiling for personalized communication and services (Hopfgartner & Jose, 2009; 2010). Hence, user preferences can be processed in terms of news categorization/classification, topics selection and general infotainment interests, providing user-adaptive news-access interfaces. Further adaptation in terms of location-awareness can also be served (Dinh et al., 2011; Hakkani-Tür et al., 2011; Hopfgartner & Jose, 2010; Satyanarayanan et al., 2009; Silva et al., 2009). A characteristic example of location-awareness is the case of news.google[3] and similar web services, where the order of the presented news is related to each user's location and its customized preferences. Similarly, professional news reporters may collaborate within the staff of the news organization that they are employed (or even they can register and subscribe on similar informing services that are offered from third parties), in order to receive customizable news alerts, according to the topics that cover, the places that are located each time and other aspects of their surrounding context (Silva et al., 2009). Another example is location-aware advertising opportunities (Satyanarayanan et al., 2009) that have been very popular recently, but also very significant to the news reporting work, which is traditionally financed from the advertising market.

Technical Solutions and Recommendations: Pilot Applications and Related Research

A complete repository of multimedia processing and authoring cloud services is necessary in order to confront with the demands of the generic MCC news reporting model of Figure 4. Multimodal content and services interaction and collaboration are also demanded towards the materialization of interoperable solutions that offer appropriate content organization and management mechanisms (Dinh et al., 2011; Hopfgartner & Jose, 2009; 2010; Kovalick, 2011). Nowadays there is a plethora of cloud tools that besides text can also support demanding audio and audiovisual productions, with each of them featuring certain advantages and difficulties. Although most of these services have not been exclusively developed to support MCC news reporting, they seem to be very helpful in all phases of information acquisition, validation, processing and dissemination. In addition, there are many research projects aiming at optimal information acquisition, processing and management, taking advantage of state of the art ICT and CC solutions. Indeed, these approaches suit perfectly to the functional necessities and the technical requirements of the discussed problem, so that they can stand as applicable utilities in demanding MCC news reporting scenarios. At the same time, integration projects are also deployed by assembling individual tools in larger scale frameworks, in order to support specific information processing needs, including on demand publishing and news reporting CC examples[4].

Starting with related generic tools and pilot applications, there are many cloud-adapted digital audio workstations (DAW) that can be easily exploited from the mobile user in the news reporting process. As example we may refer Soundstation[5], Indabamusic[6], Scratchaudio[7], Audiotool[8], DropVox[9], SoundCloud[10], Audioboo[11] Evoca[12] and others, that more or less offer sound and music production capabilities, multichannel mixing, editing and generally post-production processing, as well as podcasting, audio file storage and sharing utilities. Similarly, cloud-based photo and video sharing and/or processing can also apply for MCC-based collaboration and news reporting dissemination, using popular utilities and social networks, such as Shozu[13], Flickr[14], Aviary[15], Facebook[16], etc. Furthermore, Youtube[1], besides storage and video on demand services, since 2010 offers additional audiovisual editing, transcoding and processing, but also tagging and time annotation concepts, similarly to videotoolbox[17], filelab[18], wevideo[19], stupeflix[20], vimeo[21] and others, while Ustream[22] supports online media streaming. Although such services might still exhibit market instability, at the same time, professional audiovisual production and media assets management products already release their cloud-counterparts (i.e. Adobe-creative-cloud[23], Avid-viewpoint[24] cloud service, etc.). Along with all these, textual tools are also included or they are separately available for content subtitling, commenting and abstracting, offering also additional text processing capabilities. For instance, both news producers and consumers can take full advantage of the translation tools that are currently available on the cloud (such as the translate.google[3] service), in order to release multilingual news content and/or to access foreign language news articles (Vasiljevs, Skadiņš, & Samite, 2012).

Extending the above, more sophisticated text and audiovisual processing systems are currently deployed in research level and as pilot projects, aiming at increasing automation. Hence, textual natural language processing services can be employed to provide web news recognition, news topic classification, keyword extraction, news filtering, abstraction, visualization and summarization (Hopfgartner & Jose, 2009; Li et al., 2011; Raj & Mala, 2012; Turcu, Foster, & Nestorov, 2010; Wu et al., 2010). Similarly, cloud-tag extraction techniques are used to provide semiotic visualization of the key words, indicating the most important and frequent terms that appear within text corpora (Papapetrou, Papadakis, Ioannou, & Skoutas, 2010; Raj & Mala, 2012; Wu et al., 2010). In addition, applicable video indexing can be deployed taking advantage of motion and/or color features, while the interaction with audio parameters is very powerful towards multimodal event detection, segmentation, summarization and highlighting (Dimoulas, Avdelidis, Kalliris and Papanikolaou, 2008). This is also fuelled by the evolution of machine learning algorithms and hybrid expert systems (i.e. mixtures of intelligent processing modules) that facilitate many interdisciplinary research topics and knowledge management application areas (Dimoulas, Papanikolaou & Petridis, 2011). Although there are still many supervised learning difficulties that are related to the need for annotated "ground-truth" content and classification rules, these works have promoted the overall progress of multimodal audiovisual analysis automation, especially in prolonged duration multichannel recordings (Dimoulas et al., 2011; Dimoulas et al., 2008; Kotsakis et al., 2012; Symeonidis & Mitkas, 2005). Along with supervised learning, cluster and association analysis techniques are also deployed in order to summarize, group, associate and match data in large databases of various forms of content. Especially, text and web-mining algorithms elaborate with the inclusion of additional audiovisual features, thus promoting multimodal data mining in multimedia databases (Khan & Ahirwar, 2011; Kotsakis et al., 2012; Symeonidis & Mitkas, 2005).

For instance, intelligent multimodal content processing can serve efficient news browsing, documentation and archiving, by providing events-indexing and abstraction utilities in large media databases (Figure 5). Similarly, cloud-tag extraction techniques can be extended to "audio-keywords" and "visual snapshots" providing multimedia visualization of the news-content attributes (Katayama, Mo, & Satoh, 2011; Papapetrou et al., 2010; Raj & Mala, 2012; Wu et al., 2010). Although we are still far from the deployment of such sophisticated analysis tools in real world practical scenarios, still, intelligent multimodal content processing is already deployed in equally demanding and meaningful tasks, such as content-based searching and retrieval (i.e. "Search by image" and "Voice Search" services offered by Google[3] and similar service providers), TV news ranking and indexing (Katayama et al., 2011), news-topic recognition (Raj & Mala, 2012), audio-news events detection and classification in radio broadcasting (Kotsakis et al., 2012), or even more demanding voice-searching, language identification and speech recognition tasks (Avdelidis, 2012; Hakkani-Tür et al., 2011). As already stated, the above approaches attempt to provide applicable solutions to the global requirement for efficient content description and management, due to the huge paces that new content is produced (Dimoulas et al., 2012; Kalliris & Dimoulas, 2009; Kotsakis et al., 2012). In this context, semantic content annotation and tagging is not only necessary in terms of content documentation, archiving and personal preferences, but also in order to produce ground truth databases for the training of intelligent processing and management systems. The above functionalities are depicted in the use case diagram of Figure 5.

FUTURE RESEARCH DIRECTIONS

Critical Issues: Technology Adoption, Anticipated Progress, and Solutions

The intense and continuous market competition has brought tremendous evolution in the mobile computing performance, and is expected to further progress MCC. Considering storage, processing and power capabilities in the first generation of mobile cellular phones, it is obvious that there is nothing to compare with today's smartphones and tablets. On the other hand, no matter how much the mobile computing performance will further increase, still "resource-rich mobile computing" seems rather oxymoron, considering that mobile hardware will always be resource poor relative to desktop computing (Satyanarayanan et al., 2009). Hence, CC and MCC services will always be desired for further increasing mobile computing capabilities. Especially in the media landscape, portable computing experience and mobile Internet access seem to have high penetration to the journalism community and equally high adoption by the professional journalists, as recent research revealed (Spyridou et al., 2013). Hence, it is quite easy to conclude that MCC-based news reporting can be considered still immature, and anticipate that a lot of progress is expected to occur in the following years. Current ICT trends, such as performance improvements, better storage exploitation, cost and even energy savings, under the "Green IT" context, seem to favor CC and MCC related applications, offloading computational intensive tasks in powerful and energy efficient environments (Dinh et al., 2011; Fernando et al., 2013; Khan & Ahirwar, 2011). A lot of researchers and market analysts predict that the current models of software development, distribution, installation and maintenance will radically change

Figure 5. Flow diagram of intelligent content processing in multimodal news reporting use case

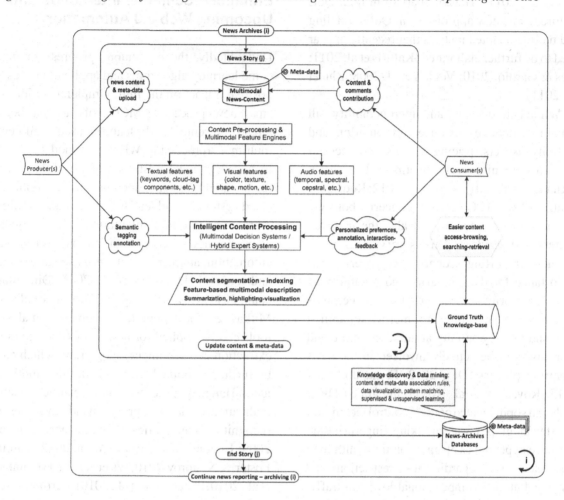

in the near future, whereas access to SaaS services will dominate (Khan & Ahirwar, 2011; Zhu et al., 2011). These new models are also favored by the software development companies that foresee an opportunity to reduce software piracy by deploying user personalized software distribution models (Khan & Ahirwar, 2011; Kovachev et al., 2011). In the same context, open source software developing communities have also found CC very suitable for contribution, testing and dissemination of their implemented code.

Except from the aforementioned positive expectations, it is also undeniable that CC and MCC have certain implementation limitations and operation difficulties that have to be faced. First

of all, delay and jitter issues seem to be one of the major problems, especially in demanding rich media application that require high QoE. Considering that WAN-latency is unlikely to be drastically improved, cloudlets have already presented as a promising solution (Dey, 2012; Khan & Ahirwar, 2011; Ling et al., 2011; Satyanarayanan et al., 2009; Verbelen et al., 2012). Besides bandwidth and QoS limitations, other network-related issues include network access management and traffic balancing. Because of the vast time varying attributes of the wireless and especially the mobile communication channels, QoS requirements are even more demanding in order to avoid turning MCC in disruptive technology (Ling et al., 2011;

Zhu et al., 2011). Hence, apart from high QoE requirements, new approaches in QoE modeling and mobile-adapted metrics that recently appear need to be further elaborated (Kalliris et al. 2011; Ries & Gardlo, 2010; Vegiris et al. 2008; Zhu et al., 2011).

While heterogeneity and interoperability still remain critical, experience, presentation and usability aspects, pricing models and security issues also require careful treatment (Dey, 2012; Fernando et al., 2013; Lin et al., 2012; Rodrigues et al., 2012). MCC security concerns both users and cloud resources, but also the involved content and services. This is very sensitive in the news reporting scenarios, considering the importance for data integrity and reliability of the news information. Hence, effective measures have to be taken in order to improve reliability, trust and privacy, aiming at attracting more and more users to be actively involved in the news reporting process (Dey, 2012; Fernando et al., 2013; Kovachev et al., 2011). Integrated DRM tools and sophisticated content control techniques like steganography, watermarking, fingerprinting, etc. have appeared as elegant solutions, although new issues arise regarding user restrictions and privacy, but also computational load and traffic increase (Dinh et al., 2011; Gayathri et al., 2012; Lin et al., 2012). As already implied, future trends on mobile authentication, authorization and accounting are expected to play a significant role towards content rights and royalties, encouraging meta-processing and user feedback actions along with content re-use scenarios (Dinh et al., 2011; Raj & Mala, 2012). Appropriately documented news articles can ensure proper referencing to the news producers. Among the emerging research fields where innovative applications and services have begun to be massively deployed, enhanced semantic interaction and mobile augmented reality (MAR) technologies are considered to be very important, so that they are further analyzed in the following subsections.

Enhanced Semantic Interaction and Upcoming Web 3.0 Automations

Undoubtedly, the continuous progress in machine learning algorithms and applications has a positive impact on the future implementation of smart news processing MCC tools, as it has been already presented for the feature-based intelligent multimedia processing. While multimodal content management mechanisms are very useful in news media archiving and documentation, sophisticated systems could lead to semantic knowledge extraction and implementation of intelligent agents for news media classification, processing automation, augmented content-based searching and retrieval (Dimoulas et al., 2008; Dimoulas et al., 2011; Kotsakis et al., 2012; Symeonidis & Mitkas, 2005). Among these, semantic analysis tools can be applied for news indexing, opinion extraction and sentiment recognition, which can be further combined with web and text mining, natural language processing and semantic conceptualization modalities, providing advanced news recognition capabilities (Hopfgartner & Jose, 2009; Li et al., 2011; Raj & Mala, 2012; Turcu, Foster, & Nestorov, 2010; Wu et al., 2010Montalvo et al., 2010; Papapetrou et al., 2010). Furthermore, multilingualism and translation automation tools are welcomed, along with related subtitling textual entries, voice over and audio dubbing utilities. Speech-to-speech translation under unlimited vocabulary dialogues, real-time constrains and/ or other natural multimodal communication conditions are also considered among the trends, whose future implementation will significantly propel semantic interaction and media processing automation (Avdelidis, 2012; Hakkani-Tür et al., 2011). Likewise, virtual graphic tools and digital characters can be used in collaboration with audiovisual content in order to confront the video storage and bandwidth demands, as well as to provide enhanced multimodal interaction with the mobile terminal, promoting user profiling, customization and personalization (Avdelidis et al., 2001; Avdelidis, 2012)

The fact that mobile terminals offer explicit feedback channels is very positive toward registration of personalized annotation that could support individualization, but also gradual construction of generic knowledge bases (Hakkani-Tür et al., 2011; Hopfgartner & Jose, 2009, 2010). In this context, adaptive processing and/or automated recognition of processing demands can face content deficiencies due to the lack of expertise and/ or high end equipment in the UGC cases. Semi-automated tools may enable "cloud-experts" to supervise the above processes, offering at the same time useful semantic feedback and control over ground-truth knowledge acquisition extending systems intelligence. Automated transcoding and smart content profiling could also be elaborated, fulfilling the needs of different thematic content and topics, but also offering customization with respect to the MCC requirements of various user groups. Agent technology can provide intelligent analysis perspectives, not only from the content point of view, but also in resource virtualization and optimal exploitation of the CC components, by dynamically adjusting offloading with respect to the mobile-user operating conditions (Kim, Yoon, & Lee, 2011; Kovachev et al., 2011; Symeonidis & Mitkas, 2005). For instance, internetworked mobile and desktop terminals can be adaptively selected and configured with respect to the available news content, in order to provide advanced cross-publishing utilities (Erdal 2007; Hakkani-Tür et al., 2011; Veglis, 2009; 2012).

Augmented Interfacing and Ubiquitous Computing

As already mentioned, smartphones and mobile devices offer a variety of sensors (mic, camera, gyroscope, GPS, etc.), facilitating the implementation of enhanced news reporting services and cloud interfaces. In this framework, context-aware properties can be utilized in ubiquitous computing services, taking under consideration three important aspects: the user's location, the presence of other users nearby and the user's environment (Fernando et al., 2013; Satyanarayanan et al., 2009). For instance, issues like day time, weather and lighting conditions, ambient noise presence and attributes, networking capabilities, communication channels availability and costs, form the contextual information around a participating user (Fernando et al., 2013). Hence, most of the already discussed news production, processing and dissemination modalities can be adaptively customized according to the conditions (contexts) and the preferences of the involved producers, contributors and consumers. Augmented reality (AR) merges the physical with the virtual world, offering augmented information views and interaction in the favor of mobile users (Fernando et al., 2013; Raj & Mala, 2012; Zhou et al., 2008). Indeed, most AR applications are designed to be executed on mobile terminals, so that they would be able to run anywhere (Ling et al., 2011). Thus, it is obvious that MAR services are going to overwhelm the new enterprise desktop of MCC and generally mobile IT, affecting all aspects of human computing, networking and ICT usage in general, including MCC infotainment services. In this context, MCC-based weather news reporting is a typical case that MAR services could be very helpful. In addition, sport related news are very expedient for MAR services to be deployed in, whereas the exploitation of multiple content uploads would offer very favorable and innovative multi-view content selection and projection services (Dey, 2012; Khan & Ahirwar, 2011; Satyanarayanan et al., 2009).

In fact, some of the above MAR scenarios have been already deployed in various daily habits, such as map information gathering, traffic navigation, culture and tourism guidance (Dey, 2012; Hakkani-Tür et al., 2011; Zhou et al., 2008). It is clear that all kinds of the involved users in MCC news reporting can be beneficiated from such MAR services, throughout all the phases of the news production-consumption chain. For instance, a reporter or a UGC-contributor may have various alerting and guidance facilities during its news covering activities. In addition, such MCC/MAR services further expand the media life cycle duration and use of the news content (as Figures 2 and 4 imply). Hence, properly documented breaking news and archived collections could be optimally exploited in alternative uses, such as training, or guidance on specific areas of human activity like public administration, history, culture, tourism and others. Extending further the end user point of view, multiple and various content types covering the same story (object, place, etc.) can be combined together, increasing user experience via multi-view selection and augmented projection services that could also offer time-lapse navigation and/or 360° panorama views (Dey, 2012; Hakkani-Tür et al., 2011; Khan & Ahirwar, 2011; Montalvo et al., 2010; Satyanarayanan et al., 2009; Zhou et al., 2008; Zhu et al.; 2011). Clearly, such kinds of future services are very favorable in sports coverage and general infotainment stories, while they can be even further productive toward ubiquitous advertising services in accompanying MCC news reporting scenarios.

Location-aware pervasive computing services are expected to be further enhanced taking advantage of the constant context monitoring of the mobile user. Although such kind of surveillance may raise privacy and uncomforting issues, still there are many location-based MAR services that could be positively deployed in the favor of users (Dey, 2012; Silva et al., 2009). For instance, geo-tags, GPS, Wi-Fi positioning and Radio-Frequency Identification (RFID) technologies can be exploited for object recognition services, providing useful information for the surrounding environment, or even gaining authorized entrance to controlled areas using RFID-based digital passports (Dey, 2012; Silva et al., 2009; Zhou et al., 2008). Hence, journalists and UGC participating users may request and gain granted access to specific scenes, but also to valuable information

through databases related to the place and the topic of their news covering. Similarly, end users, while visiting a location of a news story, they are able to obtain further information, searching and retrieving articles from linked databases through MAR services.

These kinds of tools, in combination with headmost speech recognition, natural language understanding and dialog management components, could further extend the potentials of user-machine interaction in mobile terminals, overcoming current interfacing limitations and offering advanced multimodal augmented communication capabilities (Hakkani-Tür et al., 2011; Satyanarayanan et al., 2009; Zhou et al., 2008). According to recent research reports, content-based searching and retrieval services will also dominate the MAR landscape (Raj & Mala 2012; Zhou et al.; 2008), offering the change for deploying innovative news reporting assisting services. For instance, a picture that has been taken with a mobile terminal could be the only and entirely adequate input feature to look for further associated information, without the necessity for geo-tags or other RF-signals and signatures in the surrounding area. Content-based information retrieval (CBIR) modules can search inside linked databases and return related images and general information, in the way that Google[3] and other CBIR services[23, 24] work (Raj & Mala 2012; Satyanarayanan et al., 2009; Zhou et al., 2008; Zhu et al.; 2011). Extending the above, smart multimodal CBIR while are rapidly evolving, they also massively migrate as services in the "mobile world" (Avdelidis, 2012; Dimoulas et al., 2008; Dimoulas et al., 2011; Hakkani-Tür et al., 2011; Zhou et al., 2008; Zhu et al.; 2011). Such kinds of future technologies are expected to diminish presentation and usability issues in the "mobile environment," offering enhanced user-machine interaction that will imitate many attributes of the natural human communication features. Along with these advances, MCC news reporting and generally multimedia mobile cloud computing services will continue to evolve.

CONCLUSION

In the current chapter, emerging mobile cloud computing news reporting technologies, services and applications were examined. Current status of news coverage strategies, models and practices were presented, along with the technological and functional background of cloud and mobile multimedia computing. Operational and technological attributes of the cloud paradigm were modeled with respect to the news reporting process, bringing forward advantages and drawbacks, both at news production and consumption sides. Already launched cloud services that are being utilized in journalism and infotainment, but also in more general application areas, were also discussed. Media-related cloud computing services were then presented, redrawing their relationship to basic cloud models, while news reporting processing flow was adapted to the cloud computing paradigm. A generic MCC news reporting model was carefully designed and presented, along with exemplary use case scenarios, constituting the major research contribution of the chapter. Based on this, the roles of professional journalists, ordinary and/or contributing users can be fully interchanged, blurring the boundaries between news production and consumption, while enhancing cross publishing and versatile news updating. Overall, the model encompasses current technological trends but also future perspectives, foreseeing the role of all end users, content contributors and professional journalists. In this context, news classification and semantic conceptualization approaches are considered to be very important for efficient content description and management of news databases, providing sophisticated content re-use mechanisms and allowing for more reliable, objective and diverse informing services. Along with these, augmented human-machine interaction, mobile augmented reality and ubiquitous computing services are expected to further enrich media experience, offering innovative push and pull services in the news reporting process. Based on the presented arguments, it can be easily concluded that MCC services are expected to flourish and dominate, thus radically changing the news reporting landscape.

REFERENCES

Avdelidis, K., Dimoulas, C., Kalliris, G., Bliatsiou, C., Passias, T., Stoitsis, J., & Papanikolaou, G. (2001). *Multilingual automated digital talking character.* Paper presented at the International Broadcasting Convention. Amsterdam, The Netherlands.

Avdelidis, K. A. (2012). *Synchronous voice and speech analysis and synthesis techniques using visual and auditory information. (Unpublished Ph.D.).* Thessaloniki, Greece: Dept. of Electrical and Computer Engineering, Aristotle University of Thessaloniki..

Chung, D. S., Kim, E., Trammell, K. D., & Porter, L. V. (2007). Uses and perceptions of blogs: A report on professional journalists and journalism educators. *Journalism & Mass Communication Educator, 62*(3), 305–322. doi:10.1177/107769580706200306.

Dey, S. (2012). *Cloud mobile media: Opportunities, challenges, and directions.* Paper presented at the 2012 International Conference on Computing, Networking and Communications. New York, NY.

Dimoulas, C., Avdelidis, A., Kalliris, G., & Papanikolaou, G. (2008). Joint wavelet video denoising and motion activity detection in multimodal human activity analysis: Application to video–Assisted bioacoustic/psycho-physiological monitoring. *EURASIP Journal on Advances in Signal Processing.* doi:10.1155/2008/792028.

Dimoulas, C., Papanikolaou, G., & Petridis, V. (2011). Pattern classification and audiovisual content management techniques using hybrid expert systems: A video-assisted bioacoustics application in abdominal sounds pattern analysis. *Expert Systems with Applications, 38*(10), 13082–13093. doi:10.1016/j.eswa.2011.04.115.

Dimoulas, C., Tsourvakas, G., Kalliris, G., & Papakis, N. (2012). Audiovisual content management for the new media environment and economic aspects. Paper presented at the *10th World Media Economics and Management Conference*. Thessaloniki, Greece.

Dinh, H. T., Lee, C., Niyato, D., & Wang, P. (2011). *A survey of mobile cloud computing: Architecture, applications, and approaches*. Wireless Communications and Mobile Computing. doi:10.1002/wcm.1203.

Erdal, I. (2007). Researching media convergence and crossmedia news production mapping the field. *Nordicom Review, 28*(2), 51–61.

Fernando, N., Loke, S. W., & Rahayu, W. (2013). Mobile cloud computing: A survey. *Future Generation Computer Systems, 29*(1), 84–106. doi:10.1016/j.future.2012.05.023.

Gayathri, K. S., Thomas, T., & Jayasudha, J. (2012). Security issues of media sharing in social cloud. *Procedia Engineering, 38*, 3806–3815. doi:10.1016/j.proeng.2012.06.436.

Geoghegan, M., & Klass, D. (2007). Podcast solutions: The complete guide to audio and video podcasting (2nd ed.). New York: Frieds of ED..

Hakkani-Tür, D., Tur, G., & Heck, L. (2011). Research challenges and opportunities in mobile applications. *IEEE Signal Processing Magazine, 28*(4), 108–110. doi:10.1109/MSP.2011.941132.

Hopfgartner, F., & Jose, J. M. (2009). Semantic user modelling for personal news video retrieval. *Lecture Notes in Computer Science, 5916*, 336–346. doi:10.1007/978-3-642-11301-7_35.

Hopfgartner, F., & Jose, J. M. (2010). Semantic user profiling techniques for personalised multimedia recommendation. *Multimedia Systems, 16*(4-5), 255–274. doi:10.1007/s00530-010-0189-6.

Kalliris, G., & Dimoulas, C. (2009). *Audiovisual content management issues for the new media environment*. Paper presented at the International Conference on New Media and Information: Convergences and Divergences. Athens, Greece.

Kalliris, G., Dimoulas, C. A., Veglis, A., & Matsiola, M. (2011). Investigating quality of experience and learning (QoE & QoL) of audiovisual content broadcasting to learners over IP networks. In *Proceedings of IEEE Symposium on Computers and Communications*. New York, NY.

Katayama, N., Mo, H., & Satoh, S. (2011). News shot cloud: Ranking TV news shots by cross TV-channel filtering for efficient browsing of large-scale news video archives. *Lecture Notes in Computer Science, 6523*, 284–295. doi:10.1007/978-3-642-17832-0_27.

Kesavan, S., Anand, J., & Jayakumar, D. J. (2012). Controlled multimedia cloud architecture and advantaged. *Advanced Computing: An International Journal, 3*(2), 29–40. doi:10.5121/acij.2012.3204.

Khan, A., & Ahirwar, K. (2011). Mobile cloud computing as a future of mobile multimedia database. *International Journal of Computer Science and Communication, 2*(1), 219–221.

Kim, M. J., Yoon, H. G., & Lee, H. K. (2011). An intelligent multi-agent model for resource virtualization: Supporting social media service in cloud computing. *Studies in Computational Intelligence, 365*, 99–111. doi:10.1007/978-3-642-21375-5_9.

Kotsakis, R., Kalliris, G., & Dimoulas, C. (2012). Investigation of broadcast-audio semantic analysis scenarios employing radio-programme-adaptive pattern classification. *Speech Communication, 54*(6), 743–762. doi:10.1016/j.specom.2012.01.004.

Kovachev, D., Cao, Y., & Klamma, R. (2011). Mobile cloud computing: A comparison of application models. *Computing Research Repository, 1009*(3088).

Kovalick, A. (2011). Cloud computing for the media facility: Concepts and applications. *SMPTE Motion Imaging Journal, 120*(2), 20–29.

Li, L. T., Yang, S., Kavanaugh, A., Fox, E. A., Sheetz, S. D., Shoemaker, D., & Srinivasan, V. (2011). *Twitter use during an emergency event: The case of the UT Austin shooting.* Paper presented at the ACM International Conference. New York, NY.

Lin, K., Ge, X., Wang, X., Zhu, C., & Ryu, H.-G. (2012). Research on secure data collection in wireless multimedia sensor networks. *Computer Communications, 35*(15), 1902–1909. doi:10.1016/j.comcom.2012.03.010.

Ling, C., Chen, M., Zhang, W., Tian, F. (2011). AR cloudlets for mobile computing. *International Journal of Digital Content Technology and its Applications, 5*(12), 162-169.

Montalvo, S., Palomo, J., & Laguna, P. (2010). *Bridging the gap between teaching and breaking news: A new approach based on ESHE and ICT.* Paper presented at the Procedia - Social and Behavioral Sciences. New York, NY.

Papapetrou, O., Papadakis, G., Ioannou, E., & Skoutas, D. (2010). Efficient term cloud generation for streaming web content. *Lecture Notes in Computer Science, 6189,* 385–399. doi:10.1007/978-3-642-13911-6_26.

Raj, D. A. A., & Mala, T. (2012). *Cloud press: A next generation news retrieval system on the cloud.* Paper presented at the 2012 International Conference on Recent Advances in Computing and Software Systems, RACSS 2012. New York, NY.

Ries, M., & Gardlo, B. (2010). Audiovisual quality estimation for mobile video services. *IEEE Journal on Selected Areas in Communications, 28*(3), 501–509. doi:10.1109/JSAC.2010.100420.

Rodrigues, J. J. P. C., Zhou, L., Mendes, L. D. P., Lin, K., & Lloret, J. (2012). Distributed media-aware flow scheduling in cloud computing environment. *Computer Communications, 35*(15), 1819–1827. doi:10.1016/j.comcom.2012.03.004.

Sabelström, K. (2001). *Information categories and editorial process in multiple channel publishing. (Unpublished Ph.D.).* Stockholm, Sweden: Royal Institute of Technology, Department of NADA, Division of Media Technology and Graphics Arts..

Satyanarayanan, M., Bahl, P., Caceres, R., & Davies, N. (2009). The case for VM-based cloudlets in mobile computing. *IEEE Pervasive Computing/IEEE Computer Society [and] IEEE Communications Society, 8*(4), 14–23. doi:10.1109/MPRV.2009.82.

Silva, B. M. C., Neves, P. A. C. S., Denko, M. K., & Rodrigues, J. J. P. C. (2009). *MP-collaborator: A mobile collaboration tool in pervasive environment.* Paper presented at the WiMob 2009 - 5th IEEE International Conference on Wireless and Mobile Computing Networking and Communication. New York, NY.

Simpson, W. (2008). Video over IP: IPTV, internet video, H.264, P2P, web TV, and streaming: A complete guide to understanding the technology. Oxford, UK: Focal Press, Elsevier..

Spyridou, L.-P., Matsiola, M., Veglis, A., Kalliris, G., & Dimoulas, C. (2013). Journalism in a state of flux: Changing journalistic practices in the Greek newsroom. *International Communication Gazette, 75*(1).

Symeonidis, A. L., & Mitkas, P. A. (2005). Agent intelligence through data mining. In *Multiagent systems, artificial societies, and simulated organizations series* (Vol. 14). Berlin: Springer..

Turcu, G., Foster, I., & Nestorov, S. (2010). Reshaping text data for efficient processing on amazon EC2. In *Proceedings of the 19th ACM International Symposium on High Performance Distributed Computing,* (pp. 435-444). ACM.

Vasiljevs, A., Skadiņš, R., & Samite, I. (2012). Enabling users to create their own web-based machine translation engine. In *Proceedings of the 21st Annual Conference on World Wide Web Companion,* (pp. 295-298). IEEE.

Vassilaras, S., & Yovanof, G. S. (2011). Wireless going in the cloud: A promising concept or just marketing hype? *Wireless Personal Communications, 58*(1), 5–16. doi:10.1007/s11277-011-0284-9.

Vegiris, C., Avdelidis, K., Dimoulas, C., & Papanikolaou, G. (2008). Live broadcasting of high definition audiovisual content using HDTV over broadband IP networks. *International Journal of Digital Multimedia Broadcasting.* doi:10.1155/2008/250654.

Veglis, A. (2009). *Cross media communication in newspaper organizations.* Paper presented at the MCIS 2009. New York, NY.

Veglis, A. (2010). *Modeling cross media publishing in radio and TV stations.* Paper presented at the 2nd International Conference on Advances in Multimedia, MMEDIA 2010. New York, NY.

Veglis, A. (2012). Journalism and cross media publishing: The case of Greece. In A. Veglis, & E. Siapera (Eds.), *The Wiley-Blackwell handbook of global online journalism.* Oxford, UK: Blackwell Publishing. doi:10.1002/9781118313978.ch12.

Veglis, A., & Pomportsis, A. (2012). *Journalists in the age of ICTs: Work demands and educational needs.* Unpublished.

Veglis, A., Tsourvakas, G., Pomportsis, A., & Avraam, E. (2005). The exploitation of information technology by Greek journalists. *1st Monday, 10*(8).

Verbelen, T., Simoens, P., De Turck, F., & Dhoedt, B. (2012). Cloudlets: Bringing the cloud to the mobile user. –In *Proceedings of the 3rd ACM Workshop on Mobile Cloud Computing and Services,* (pp. 29-35). ACM.

Wu, X., Wu, G.-Q., Xie, F., Zhu, Z., Hu, X.-G., Lu, H., & Li, H. (2010). News filtering and summarization on the web. *IEEE Intelligent Systems, 25*(5), 68–76. doi:10.1109/MIS.2010.11.

Zhou, F., Dun, H. B.-L., & Billinghurst, M. (2008). Trends in augmented reality tracking, interaction and display: A review of ten years of ISMAR. In *Proceedings - 7th IEEE International Symposium on Mixed and Augmented Reality 2008, ISMAR 2008,* (pp. 193-202). IEEE.

Zhu, W., Luo, C., Wang, J., & Li, S. (2011). Multimedia cloud computing. *IEEE Signal Processing Magazine, 28*(3), 59–69. doi:10.1109/MSP.2011.940269.

ADDITIONAL READING

Antonopoulos, A., & Veglis, A. (2012). Technological characteristics and tools for web media companies in Greece. In *IEEE Proceedings of 16th Panhellenic Conference on Informatics* (pp. 44-50) ISBN: 978-0-7695-4825-8/12, DOI: 10.1109/PCI.2012.32.

Atzori, L., Delgado, J., & Giusto, D. D. (Eds.). (2012). Special issue on pervasive mobile multimedia. *Signal Processing Image Communication, 27*(8), 785–934. doi:10.1016/j.image.2012.05.002.

Barker, J., & Vincent, E. (Eds.). (2012). Special issue on speech separation and recognition in multisource environments. *Computer Speech & Language, 27*(3), 619–894. doi:10.1016/j.csl.2012.09.005.

Batzios, A., Dimou, C., Symeonidis, A. L., & Mitkas, P. A. (2008). BioCrawler: An intelligent crawler for the semantic web. *Expert Systems with Applications, 35*(1-2), 524–530. doi:10.1016/j.eswa.2007.07.054.

Buyya, R., Yeo, C. S., Venugopal, S., Broberg, J., & Brandic, I. (2009). Cloud computing and emerging IT platforms: Vision, hype, and reality for delivering computing as the 5th utility. *Future Generation Computer Systems, 25*(6), 599–616. doi:10.1016/j.future.2008.12.001.

Chandrasekhar, V., Sharifi, M., & Ross, D. A. (2011). Survey and evaluation of audio finger-printing schemes for mobile query-by-example applications. Paper presented at the Proceedings of the 12th International Society for Music Information Retrieval Conference, ISMIR 2011, 801-806.

Chapman, N., & Chapman, J. (2009). *Digital multimedia* (3rd ed.). Chichester: John Wiley & Sons, Ltd.

Cordara, G., Bober, M., & Reznik, Y. (Eds.). (2013). Special issue on visual search and augmented reality. *Signal Processing Image Communication, 28*(4), 309–402. doi:10.1016/j.image.2012.11.001.

Diemert, B., & Abel, M. -., & Moulin, C. (2011). Semantic audiovisual asset model - the case of TV production. *Multimedia Tools and Applications,* 1–28.

Dimou, C., Symeonidis, A. L., & Mitkas, P. A. (2008). Data Mining and Agent Technology: a Fruitful Symbiosis. In O. Maimon & L. Rokach (Eds.), Soft Computing for Knowledge Discovery and Data Mining, 327-362, Springer..

Dimoulas C, Kalliris G, Chatzara E, Tsipas N, and Papanikolaou G (2013) Audiovisual production, restoration-archiving and content management methods to preserve local tradition and folkloric heritage. http://dx.doi.org/10.1016/j.culher.2013.05.003. in press.

Domingue, J., Fensel, D., & Hendler, J. (Eds.). (2011). *Handbook of Semantic Web Technologies.* Springer. doi:10.1007/978-3-540-92913-0.

Kanellopoulos, D. (2012). Semantic annotation and retrieval of documentary media objects. *The Electronic Library, 30*(5), 721–747. doi:10.1108/02640471211275756.

Karydis, I., Deliyannis, I., & Floros, A. (2011). Augmenting virtual-reality environments with social-signal based music content. Paper presented at the 17th DSP 2011 International Conference on Digital Signal Processing, Proceedings.

Kosch, H. (2004). *Distributed multimedia database technologies: supported by MPEG-7 and MPEG-21.* CRC Press..

Liao, S. -., Chu, P. -., & Hsiao, P. (2012). Data mining techniques and applications - A decade review from 2000 to 2011. *Expert Systems with Applications, 39*(12), 11303–11311. doi:10.1016/j.eswa.2012.02.063.

Moustakas, N., Floros, A., & Grigoriou, N. (2011). Interactive audio realities: An augmented/mixed reality audio game prototype. Paper presented at the 130th Audio Engineering Society Convention 2011, 1 427-434.

Pagani, M. (2009). *Encyclopedia of Multimedia Technology and Networking* (2nd ed., pp. 1–1756)..

Preda, M., Morán, F., & Timmerer, C. (Eds.). (2013). Special issue on MPEG-V. *Signal Processing Image Communication, 28*(2), 85–196. doi:10.1016/j.image.2012.12.002.

Quénot, G., Benois-Pineau, J., & André-Obrecht, R. (Eds.). (2012). Content-based Multimedia Indexing, Special issue of MTAP following CBMI 2010. *Multimedia Tools and Applications, 60*(2), 257–482. doi:10.1007/s11042-010-0648-2.

Subashini, S., & Kavitha, V. (2011). A survey on security issues in service delivery models of cloud computing. *Journal of Network and Computer Applications*, *34*(1), 1–11. doi:10.1016/j.jnca.2010.07.006.

Tsipas, N., Dimoulas, C., Kalliris, C., & Papanikolaou, G. (2013). Collaborative annotation platform for audio semantics. *In Proceedings of the 134th Audio Engineering Society Convention 2013*, 218-222.

Turnbull, D., Barrington, L., Torres, D., & Lanckriet, G. (2008). Semantic annotation and retrieval of music and sound effects. IEEE Transactions on Audio. *Speech and Language Processing*, *16*(2), 467–476. doi:10.1109/TASL.2007.913750.

Veglis, A. (2007). Cross media publishing by U.S. newspapers. *Journal of Electronic Publishing*. Spring. 10(2). Retrieved June, 7, 2013, from http://quod.lib.umich.edu/j/jep/3336451.0010.211?rgn=main,view=fulltext

Veglis, A. (2012). From Cross Media to Transmedia Reporting in *Newspaper Articles. Publishing Research Quarterly*, *28*(4), 313–323. doi:10.1007/s12109-012-9294-z.

Vrisis, L., Dimoulas, C., Kalliris, C., & Papanikolaou, G. (2013). Mobile audio measurements platform: bringing audio semantic intelligence into ubiquitous computing environments. In *Proceedings of the 134th Audio Engineering Society Convention 2013*, 183-189.

Yick, J., Mukherjee, B., & Ghosal, D. (2008). Wireless sensor network survey. *Computer Networks*, *52*(12), 2292–2330. doi:10.1016/j.comnet.2008.04.002.

KEY TERMS AND DEFINITIONS

Augmented Interaction: Exploitation of augmented reality concepts where physical and virtual worlds are merged, offering augmented information views and interaction in the favor of mobile users.

Cloud Computing: A model of offloading data, applications and computing to a shared pool of remote and configurable computing resources (e.g., networks, servers, storage, applications and services). Typical usages include webmail, file storage, calendar services, file sharing, web publishing, etc.

Media: The main means of mass communication (television, radio, newspapers, and various internet tools and services).

Mobile-Multimedia: Interaction with multimedia content and interfaces that can be accessed through mobile terminals.

Multimedia Semantics: Intelligent content analysis usually implementing machine learning with text and multimedia features, purposing to provide semantic interpretation and conceptualization outcomes.

News-Consumers: End-users and professionals that access and consume news content.

News-Producers: Any professional or contributing user that is part of the news production chain.

News-Reporting: Information on current events which are presented in various formats (print, broadcast, Internet, or word of mouth) to a mass audience.

News Reporting Model: Logically connected processes and alternative options that can be deployed to serve generic news reporting scenarios.

ENDNOTES

1. http://www.youtube.com/
2. https://twitter.com/
3. http://www.google.com
4. http://en.publiatis.com/products_overview_uk.asp
5. http://soundation.com/
6. http://www.indabamusic.com/
7. http://www.scratchaudio.com/
8. http://www.audiotool.com/

9 http://www.irradiatedsoftware.com/dropvox/

10 http://soundcloud.com

11 http://audioboo.fm/

12 http://www.evoca.com

13 http://www.shozu.com/portal/index.do

14 http://www.flickr.com/

15 http://www.aviary.com

16 http://www.facebook.com/

17 http://www.videotoolbox.com/

18 https://www.filelab.com/

19 http://www.wevideo.com/

20 http://studio.stupeflix.com/en/

21 https://vimeo.com/

22 http://www.ustream.tv

23 http://www.adobe.com/products/creative-cloud.html

24 http://apps.avid.com/avid-viewpoint/

Compilation of References

3GPP Technical Specification 23.203. (2008). *Policy and charging control architecture* (Release 8). Retrieved April 21, 2013, from www.3gpp.org

Abdallah-Saleh, S., Wang, Q., Grecos, C., & Thomson, D. (2012). Handover evaluation for mobile video streaming in heterogeneous wireless networks. In *Proceedings of the 16th IEEE Mediterranean Electrotechnical Conference (MELECON)* (pp. 23-26).

Abid, H. A. (2011). V-cloud: Vehicular cyber-physical systems and cloud computing. In *Proceedings of the 4th International Symposium on Applied Sciences* (pp. 165-170). San Francisco, CA: ACM.

Abu-Rgheff. (2007). *Introduction to CDMA wireless communications*. London: Academic Press..

Adomavicius, G., & Tuzhilin, A. (2005). Toward the next generation of recommender systems: A survey of the state of-the-art and possible extensions. *IEEE Transactions on Knowledge and Data Engineering, 17*, 734–749. doi:10.1109/TKDE.2005.99.

Advanced, I. M. T. (n.d.). *Wikipedia.* Retrieved March 8 2013, from http://en.wikipedia.org/wiki/IMT_Advanced

Aggarwal, B., Spring, N., & Schulman, A. (2010). *Stratus: Energy-efficient mobile communication using cloud support.* Paper presented at the meeting of ACM SIGCOMM. New Delhi, India.

Agrawal, Jain, & Sharma. (2011). A survey of routing attacks and security measures in mobile ad-hoc networks. *Journal of Computing, 3*(1).

Ahlehagh, H., & Dey, S. (2012). *Hierarchical video caching in wireless cloud: Approaches and algorithms.* Paper presented at the meeting of IEEE ICC. Ottawa, Canada.

Ahlund, A., Mitra, K., Johansson, D., Ahlund, C., & Zaslavsky, A. (2009). *Context-aware application mobility support in pervasive computing environments.* Paper presented at the 6th International Conference on Mobile Technology, Application Systems. Nice, France.

Ahmad. (2005). Wireless and mobile data. London: Wiley.

Ajuriahuerra, J. (1977). Las psicosis infantiles. In Manual de Psiquiatría Infantil (4ª ed.). Barcelona: Toray-Masson..

Akan, O. B., & Akyildiz, I. F. (2006). ATL: An adaptive transport layer suite for next-generation wireless internet. *IEEE Journal on Selected Areas in Communications, 22*(5), 802–817. doi:10.1109/JSAC.2004.826919.

Akyildiz, I. F., Su, W., Sankarasubramaniam, Y., & Cayirci, E. (2002). A survey on sensor network. *IEEE Communications Magazine*, 102–114. doi:10.1109/MCOM.2002.1024422.

Alazawi, Z. A. (2011). Intelligent disaster management system based on cloud-enabled vehicular. In *Proceedings of the 11th International Conference on ITS Telecommunications* (pp. 361-368). London: ITST.

Alazawi, Z., Altowaijri, S., Mehmood, R., & Abdljabar, M. B. (2011). Intelligent disaster management system based on cloud-enabled vehicular networks. In *Proceedings of ITS Telecommunications* (ITST), (pp. 361 – 368). ITST.

Alizadeh, M., Hassan, W. H., Behboodian, N., & Karamizadeh, S. (2013). A brief review of mobile cloud computing opportunities. *Research Notes in Information Science, 12*, 155–159.

Allman, M., Paxson, V., & Stevens, W. (1999). *TCP congestion control. RFC 2581.* Internet Engineering Task Force..

Al-Omari & Sumari. (2010). An overview of mobile ad hoc networks for the existing protocols and applications. *International Journal on Applications of Graph Theory and Ad Hoc Networks and Sensor Networks, 2*(1).

AMA. (n.d.). *Treatment.* Retrieved June 29, 2012 from http://www.ama.org.br

Aman, M. G. (2005). Treatment planning for patients with autism spectrum disorders. *The Journal of Clinical Psychiatry, 66*(10), 38–45. PMID:16401149.

Amazon Web Services. (2013). *Amazon elastic compute cloud (Amazon EC2), cloud computing servers.* Retrieved 22 March 2013, from http://aws.amazon.com/ec2/

Ambike, S., Bhansali, D., Kshirsagar, J., & Bansiwal, J. (2012). An optimistic differentiated job scheduling system for cloud computing. *International Journal of Engineering Research and Applications, 2*(2), 1212–1214.

Anand. (2003). *Power aware public key authentication for Bluetooth.* (M.Sc. Thesis). University of Florida, Gainesville, FL.

Anda, J. A.-N. (2005). VGrid: Vehicular adhoc networking and computing grid for intelligent. In *Proceedings of the 61st IEEE Vehicular Technology Conference* (pp. 2905--2909). Madrid: IEEE.

Anderson, D. P., & Fedak, G. (2006). The computational and storage potential of volunteer computing. In *Proceedings of the Sixth IEEE International Symposium on Cluster Computing and the Grid* (CCGRID '06) (pp. 73-80). IEEE Computer Society.

Angin, P., Bhargava, B., & Helal, S. (2010). *A mobile-cloud collaborative traffic lights detector for blind navigation.* Paper presented at the Mobile Data Management (MDM). New York, NY.

Anh-Dung, N., Senac, P., & Ramiro, V. (2011). *How mobility increases mobile cloud computing processing capacity.* Paper presented at the Network Cloud Computing and Applications (NCCA). New York, NY.

Apple (2013). *iCloud.* Retrieved 22 March 2013, from http://www.apple.com/icloud/

Arif, S. A. (2012). Datacenter at the airport: Reasoning about time-dependent parking. *IEEE Transactions on Parallel and Distributed Systems, 23*(11), 2067–2080. doi:10.1109/TPDS.2012.47.

Armbrust, M., Fox, A., Griffith, R., Joseph, A. D., Katz, R. H., Konwinski, A., & Zaharia, M. (2009). *Above the clouds: A Berkeley view of cloud computing.* Berkeley, CA: EECS Department, University of California..

Arslan, Chen, & Di Benedetto. (2006). Ultra wideband wireless communication. London: John Wiley & Sons..

Audi. (2012). Retrieved February 14, 2013, from http://www.greencarcongress.com/2012/03/audicon-nect-20120309.html#more

Avdelidis, K., Dimoulas, C., Kalliris, G., Bliatsiou, C., Passias, T., Stoitsis, J., & Papanikolaou, G. (2001). *Multilingual automated digital talking character.* Paper presented at the International Broadcasting Convention. Amsterdam, The Netherlands.

Avdelidis, K. A. (2012). *Synchronous voice and speech analysis and synthesis techniques using visual and auditory information. (Unpublished Ph.D.).* Thessaloniki, Greece: Dept. of Electrical and Computer Engineering, Aristotle University of Thessaloniki..

Bagheri, E., Zafarani, R., & Ebrahimi, M. B. (2009). Can reputation migrate? On the propagation of retation in multi-context communities. *Knowledge-Based Systems, 22,* 410–420. doi:10.1016/j.knosys.2009.05.007.

Bahl, P., Han, R. Y., Li, E., & Satyanarayanan, M. (2012). Advancing the state of mobile cloud computing. In *Proceedings of the Third ACM Workshop on Mobile Cloud Computing and Services* (pp. 21—28). ACM.

Bahl, P., Han, R. Y., Li, L. E., & Satyanarayanan, M. (2012). Advancing the state of MCC. In *Proceedings of MCS"12.* MCS.

Balakrishnan, H., Padmanabhan, V., Seshan, S., Stemm, M., & Katz, R. (1997). A comparison of mechanisms for improving TCP performance over wireless links. *IEEE/ACM Transactions on Networking, 5*(6), 756–769. doi:10.1109/90.650137.

Balan, R. K., Gergle, D., Satyanarayanan, M., & Herbsleb, J. (2007). Simplifying cyber foraging for mobile devices. In *Proceedings of the 5th International Conference on Mobile Systems, Applications and Services* (MobiSys '07) (pp. 272-285). ACM.

Bankoski, J., Bultje, R., Grange, A., Gu, Q., Han, J., Koleszar, J., et al. (2013). Towards a next generation open-source video codec. In *Proceedings of the SPIE Conference on Visual Information Processing and Communication IV*.

Barbará, D. (1999). Mobile computing and databases-A survey. *IEEE Transactions on Knowledge and Data Engineering, 11*(1). doi:10.1109/69.755619.

Baum, J. A. C., Calabrese, T., & Silverman, B. S. (2000). Don't go it alone: Alliance network composition and startups' performance in Canadian biotechnology. *Strategic Management Journal, 21*, 267–294. doi:10.1002/(SICI)1097-0266(200003)21:3<267::AID-SMJ89>3.0.CO;2-8.

Berners-Lee, T., Hendler, J., & Lassila, O. (2001). The semantic web. *Scientific American*. doi:10.1038/scientificamerican0501-34.

Bertsimas, D., & Tsitsiklis, J. (1993). Simulated annealing. *Statistical Science, 8*(1), 10–15. doi:10.1214/ss/1177011077.

Bertucci, G. (2007). Compendium of ICT applications on electronic government: Vol. 1. *Mobile applications on health and learning*. New York: Department of Economic and Social Affairs, United Nations..

Bhamber, R. S., Fowler, S., Braimiotis, C., & Mellouk, A. (2013). Analytic analysis of LTE/LTE-advanced power saving and delay with bursty traffic. In *Proceedings of the IEEE International Conference on Communications (ICC)*. IEEE.

Bharat, K. A., & Cardelli, L. (1995). Migratory applications. In *Proceedings of the 8th Annual ACM Symposium on User Interface and Software Technology* (UIST '95) (pp. 132-142). ACM.

Biegel, G., & Cahill, V. (2004). *A framework for developing mobile, context-aware applications*. Paper presented at the Pervasive Computing and Communications, 2004. New York, NY.

Black, A. W., & Lenzo, K. A. (2013). *FLITE: A small fast run-time synthesis engine*. Retrieved March 2013, from http://www.speech.cs.cmu.edu/flite/

Blanton, E., Allman, M., Fall, K., & Wang, L. (2003). *A conservative selective acknowledgment (SACK)-based loss recovery algorithm for TCP. RFC 3517*. Internet Engineering Task Force..

Blois, A. P. T. B. (2006). *Uma abordagem de projeto arquitetural baseado em componentes no contexto de engenharia de domínio*. (Unpublished doctoral dissertation). Universidade Federal Do Rio De Janeiro, Rio de Janeiro, Brazil.

BMW. (2012). Retrieved February 14, 2013, from http://bimmermania.com/blog/2012/07/12/bmw-connected-drive-blitzkrieg-includes-lte-connectivity -android-compatibility-and-new-idrive-touch/

Bobba, R., Khurana, H., & Prabhakaran, M. (2009). Attribute-sets: A practically motivated enhancement to attribute-based encryption. In *Proceedings of ESORICS*. Saint Malo, France: ESORICS.

Bodic, G. L., Girma, D., Irvine, J., & Dunlop, J. (2000). *Dynamic 3G network selection for increasing the competition in the mobile communications market*. Paper presented at the IEEE Vehicular Technology Conference. New York, NY.

Boncella. (2002). Wireless security: An overview. Communications of the Association for Information Systems, 9.

Bonk, C. J., Olson, T., Wisher, R., & Orvis, K. L. (2002). Learning from focus groups: An examination of blended learning. *Journal of Distance Education, 17*(3), 97–118.

Bordley, L. A. (2012). Commercial motor vehicle wireless roadside inspection pilot test. In *Proceedings of the 91st Annual Meeting on Transportation Research* (pp. 6-12). IEEE.

Bosa, C. (n.d.). *Shared care and early identification of autism*. Retrieved March 14, 2012 from http://www.scielo.br/pdf/prc/v15n1/a10v15n1.pdf.

Bosma, N., Mirjam, V. P., Roy, T., & de Wit, G. (2002). *The value of human and social capital investments for the business performance of startups*. Tinbergen, The Netherlands: Tinbergen Institute..

Bourges-Waldegg, D., Duponchel, Y., Graf, M., & Moser, M. (2005). The fluid computing middleware: Bringing application fluidity to the mobile internet. In *Proceedings of the The 2005 Symposium on Applications and the Internet* (SAINT '05), (pp. 54-63). IEEE Computer Society.

Brunette, G., & Mogull, R. (2009). Security guidance for critical areas of focus in cloud computing. *Cloud Security Alliance*, 1-76.

Bujnoch, Z. (2013). Enabling collaborative workflows: Shaping the future of mobile healthcare. *Frost & Sullivan*. Retrieved from http://www.frost.com

Buyya, R., Pandey, S., & Vecchiola, C. (2009). *Cloudbus toolkit for market-oriented cloud computing*. Paper presented at the 1st International Conference on Cloud Computing. Beijing, China.

Buyya, R., Yeo, C. S., & Venugopal, S. (2008). *Market-oriented cloud computing: Vision, hype, and reality for delivering IT services as computing utilities*. Paper presented at the 10th IEEE International Conference on High Performance Computing and Communications (HPCC '08). New York, NY.

Byung-Gon, C., Sunghwan, I., Petros, M., & Mayur, N. (2010). CloneCloud: Boosting mobile device applications through cloud clone execution. *Journal of CoRR*.

C2Power. (2013). *Cognitive radio and cooperative strategies for power saving in multi-standard wireless devices*. Retrieved February 14, 2013, from http://www.ict-c2power.eu/over_objs.htm

Caini, C., Firrincieli, R., Marchese, M., de Cola, T., Luglio, M., & Roseti, C. et al. (2006). Transport layer protocols and architectures for satelite networks. *International Journal of Satellite Communications and Networking*, 25(1), 1–26. doi:10.1002/sat.855.

Çakıro, Bayilmi, Özcerit, & Çetin. (2010). Performance evaluation of scalable encryption algorithm for wireless sensor networks. *Scientific Research and Essays*, 5(9), 856–861.

Calo, S., & Lobo, J. (2006). A basis for comparing characteristics of policy systems. In *Proceedings of Policies for Distributed Systems and Networks* (pp. 188–194). IEEE. doi:10.1109/POLICY.2006.1.

Calvary, G., Coutaz, J., & Thevenin, D. (2001). Supporting context changes for plastic user interfaces: A process and a mechanism. In *Proceedings of AFIHM-BCS Conference on Human-Computer Interaction IHM-HCI* (pp. 349-363). Springer-Verlag.

Cao, J., Spooner, D., Turner, J. D., Jarvis, S., Kerbyson, D. J., Saini, S., et al. (2002). *Agent-based resource management for grid computing*. Paper presented at the 2nd IEEE/ACM International Symposium on Cluster Computing and the Grid. New York, NY.

Capera, D., Picard, G., & Gleizes, M.-P. (2004). *Applying ADELFE methodology to a mechanism design problem*. Paper presented at the 3rd International Joint Conference on Autonomous Agents and Multiagent Systems. New York, NY.

Capra, L., Emmerich, W., & Mascolo, C. (2003). Carisma: Context-aware reflective middleware system for mobile applications. *IEEE Transactions on Software Engineering*, 29(10), 929–945. doi:10.1109/TSE.2003.1237173.

Case, J., Fedor, M., Schoffstall, M., & Davin, J. (1990). *RFC 1157: The simple network management protocol*. Internet Activities Board..

Cazella, S. C., Nunes, M. A., & Reategui, E. (2013). *A ciência da opinião: Estado da arte em sistemas de recomendação*.

Celesti, A., Salici, A., Villari, M., & Puliafito, A. (2011). A remote attestation approach for a secure virtual machine migration in federated cloud environments. In *Proceedings of the IEEE 1st International Symposium on Network Cloud Computing and Applications (NCCA)* (pp. 99-106).

Chan, M., & Ramjee, R. (2004). Improving TCP/IP performance over third generation wireless networks. In *Proceedings of IEEE Infocom*. Hong Kong, China: IEEE.

Chang, H., Kang, Y., Bae, Y., Ahn, H., & Choi, E. (2012). Filtering technique on mobile cloud computing. *Energy Procedia*, 16, 1305–1311. doi:10.1016/j.egypro.2012.01.209.

Chapin, S. J., Katramatos, D., Karpovich, J., Karpovich, A. G., & Grimshaw, A. (1999). Resource management in legion. *Future Generation Computer Systems*, 15(5-6), 583–594. doi:10.1016/S0167-739X(99)00011-4.

Chen, M. (2012). *AMVSC: A framework of adaptive mobile video streaming in the cloud.* Paper presented at the Meeting of IEEE GLOBECOM. Anaheim, CA.

Chen, Y., Zhu, Z., Zeng, Y., & He, Z. (2010). UbiCloud: A cloud computing system for ubiquitous terminals based on end user virtualization. In *Proceedings of the 2010 IEEE/IFIP International Conference on Embedded and Ubiquitous Computing* (EUC '10) (pp. 363-367). IEEE Computer Society.

Chen, Y.-J., & Wang, L.-C. (2011). *A security framework of group location-based mobile applications in cloud computing.* Paper presented at the 40th International Conference on Parallel Processing Workshops (ICPPW). Taipei, Taiwan.

Chen. (2007). The next generation CDMA technologies. London: Wiley..

Chen, C. A. (2009). Fairness and QoS guarantees of WiMAX OFDMA scheduling with fuzzy. *EURASIP Journal on Wireless Communications and Networking*, 1–14. doi:10.1155/2009/512507.

Cheng, J., Balan, R. K., & Satyanarayanan, M. (2005). *Exploiting rich mobile environments.*

Chi, C., Alvarez-Mesa, M., Juurlink, B., Clare, G., Henry, F., Pateux, S., & Schierl, T. (2012). Parallel scalability and efficiency of HEVC parallelization approaches. *IEEE Transactions on Circuits and Systems for Video Technology, 22*(12), 1827–1838. doi:10.1109/TCSVT.2012.2223056.

Chikkerur, S., Sundaram, V., Reisslein, M., & Karam, L. J. (2011). Objective video quality assessment methods: A classification, review, and performance comparison. *IEEE Transactions on Broadcasting, 57*(2), 165–182. doi:10.1109/TBC.2011.2104671.

Chirigati, F. S. (n.d.). *Cloud computer.* Retrieved June 30, 2012 from http://www.gta.ufrj.br/ensino/eel879/trabalhos_vf_2009_2/seabra/index.html

Chow, R., Jakobsson, M., Masuoka, R., Molina, J., Niu, Y., Shi, E., & Song, Z. (2010). *Authentication in the clouds: A framework and its application to mobile users.* Paper presented at the 2010 ACM Workshop on Cloud Computing Security Workshop. Chicago, IL.

Christensen, J. H. (2009). *Using RESTful web-services and cloud computing to create next generation mobile applications.* Paper presented at the 24th ACM SIGPLAN Conference Companion on Object Oriented Programming Systems Languages and Applications. Orlando, FL.

Chu, D., & Humphrey, M. (2004). Mobile ogsi.net: Grid computing on mobile devices. In *Proceedings of the Fifth IEEE/ACM International Workshop on Grid Computing* (pp. 182-191). IEEE Computer Society.

Chuang, I. H., Li, S. H., Huang, K. C., & Kuo, Y. H. (2011). An effective privacy protection scheme for cloud computing. In *Proceedings of the 13th International Conference on Advanced Communication Technology (ICACT)* (pp. 260-265). ICACT.

Chu, H.-H., Song, H., Wong, C., Kurakake, S., & Katagiri, M. (2004). Roam, a seamless application framework. *Journal of Systems and Software, 69*(3), 209–226. doi:10.1016/S0164-1212(03)00052-9.

Chun, B. G., Ihm, S., & Maniatis, P. M. Naik, & Patti, A. (2011). CloneCloud: Elastic execution between mobile device and cloud. In *Proceedings of the Sixth Conference on Computer Systems* (EuroSys '11) (pp. 301-314). New York: EuroSys.

Chun, B. G., Ihm, S., Maniatis, P., Naik, M., & Patti, A. (2011). CloneCloud: Elastic execution between mobile device and cloud. In *Proceedings of the 6th Conference on Computer Systems* (EuroSys), (pp. 301-314). EuroSys.

Chun, B., & Maniatis, P. (2009). *Augmented smartphone applications through clone cloud execution.* Paper presented at the Meeting of the 12th Conference on Hot Topics in Operating Systems. Monte Verità, Switzerland.

Chun, B., Ihm, S., Maniatis, P., Naik, M., & Patti, A. (2011). Clonecloud: Elastic execution between mobile device and cloud. In *Proceedings of ACM EuroSys'11* (pp. 301-314).

Chun, B.-G., & Maniatis, P. (2010). *Dynamically partitioning applications between weak devices and clouds.* Paper presented at the 1st ACM Workshop on Mobile Cloud Computing Services: Social Networks and Beyond. San Francisco, CA.

Chun, B.-G., Ihm, S., Maniatis, P., Naik, M., & Patti, A. (2011). *CloneCloud: Elastic execution between mobile device and cloud.* Paper presented at the 6th Conference on Computer Systems. Salzburg, Austria.

Chung, D. S., Kim, E., Trammell, K. D., & Porter, L. V. (2007). Uses and perceptions of blogs: A report on professional journalists and journalism educators. *Journalism & Mass Communication Educator, 62*(3), 305–322. doi:10.1177/107769580706200306.

Cisco. (2013). *Cisco visual networking index: Global mobile data traffic forecast update, 2012-2017.* Retrieved May 30, 2013, from http://www.cisco.com/en/US/solutions/collateral/ns341/ns525/ns537/ns705/ns827/white_paper_c11-520862.html

CISCO. (2013). *MPLS whitepaper.* Retrieved May 20, 2013 from http://www.cisco.com/en/US/tech/tk436/tk428/technologies_white_paper09186a00800a4455.shtml#wp15329

Clinch, S., Harkes, J., Friday, A., Davies, N., & Satyanarayanan, M. (2012). How close is close enough? Understanding the role of cloudlets in supporting display appropriation by mobile users. In *Proceedings of the 2012 IEEE International Conference on Pervasive Computing and Communications (PerCom)* (pp. 122-127).

Cloud Security Alliance. (2009). *Security guidance for critical areas of focus in cloud computing V2.1.* Retrieved October 28, 2012, from http://www.cloudsecurityalliance.org/guidance/csaguide.v2.1.pdf

Cloud Security Alliance. (2010). *Top threats to cloud computing.* Retrieved October 28, 2012, from https://cloudsecurityalliance.org/topthreats/csathreats.v1.0.pdf

CLOUD4all. (2013). Retrieved February 14, 2013, from http://cloud4all.info/

Cohen, S. B., & Frith, L. A. (1985). Does the autistic child have a theory of mind? *Cognition, 21,* 37–46. doi:10.1016/0010-0277(85)90022-8 PMID:2934210.

Comaniciu, Mandayam, & Poor. (2005). *Wireless networks multiuser detection in cross – layer design.* Berlin: Springer Science.

Commission of the European Communities. (1995). The protection of individuals with regard to the processing of personal data and on the free movement of such data. *Official Journal of the European Communities, 281,* 31–50.

Commission of the European Communities. (1999). Directive 1999/5/EC on radio equipment and telecommunications terminal (R&TTE). *Official Journal of the European Communities, 91*(10), 1–8.

Commission of the European Communities. (2012). *European data protection regulation.* Retrieved October 28, 2012 from http://ec.europa.eu/justice/newsroom/data-protection/news/120125_en.htm

Cong, W., Chow, S. S. M., Qian, W., Kui, R., & Wenjing, L. (2013). Privacy-preserving public auditing for secure cloud storage. *IEEE Transactions on Computers, 62*(2), 362–375. doi:10.1109/TC.2011.245.

Cong, W., Qian, W., Kui, R., Ning, C., & Wenjing, L. (2012). Toward secure and dependable storage services in cloud computing. *IEEE Transactions on Services Computing, 5*(2), 220–232. doi:10.1109/TSC.2011.24.

Costa, R. A., Oliveira, R. Y. S., Silva, E. M., & Meira, S. R. L. (2009). A.M.I.G.O.S: knowledge management and social networks. In *Proceedings of Sigdoc'08.* Lisbon, Portugal: ACM..

Coyle, S. (2009). *BIOTEX–Bio-sensing textiles for healthcare.* Paper presented at Smart Textiles Salon. Ghent, Belgium.

CROSSFIRE. (2013). *Uncoordinated network strategies for enhanced interference, mobility, radio resource, and energy saving management in lte-advanced networks.* Retrieved February 14, 2013, from http://gain.di.uoa.gr/crossfire/

Cuervo, E., Balasubramanian, A., Cho, D., Wloman, A., Saroiu, S., Chandra, R., & Bahl, P. (2010). *MAUI: Making smartphones last longer with code offload.* Paper presented at the Meeting of the 8th International Conference on Mobile Systems, Applications, and Services. San Francisco, CA.

Cui, Y., Ma, X., Wang, H., Stojmenovic, I., & Liu, J. (2012). A survey of energy efficient wireless transmission and modeling in mobile cloud computing. *Mobile Networks and Applications,* 1–8.

Czajkowski, K., Foster, I., Karonis, N., Kesselman, C., Martin, S., Smith, W., & Tuecke, S. (1998). A resource management architecture for metacomputing systems. In *Proceedings of IPPS/SPDP '98 Workshop on Job Scheduling Strategies for Parallel Processing* (IPPS/SPDP '98) (pp. 62-82). Springer-Verlag.

da Autonomia, F. P. P. (1996). *Saberes necessários a prática educativa*. São Paulo, Brazil: Paz e Terra..

Dash, S. K., Mohapatra, S., & Pattnaik, P. K. (2010). A survey on applications of wireless sensor network using cloud computing. *International Journal of Computer Science & Emerging Technologies, 50*(1).

Das, S. K., Lin, H., & Chatterjee, M. (2004). An econometric model for resource management in competitive wireless data networks. *Journal Network: The Magazine of Global Internetworking, 18*(6), 20–26. doi:10.1109/MNET.2004.1355031.

de Jong, I. (n.d.). *PYRO - Python remote objects*. Retrieved 1 October 2012, from http://pypi.python.org/pypi/Pyro

Dean, J., & Ghemawat, S. (2008). MapReduce: Simplified data processing on large clusters. *Communications of the ACM, 51*(1), 107–113. doi:10.1145/1327452.1327492.

Demeure, A., Sottet, J., Calvary, G., Coutaz, J., Ganneau, V., & Vanderdonckt, J. (2008). The 4C reference model for distributed user interfaces. In *Proceedings of the Fourth International Conference on Autonomic and Autonomous Systems* (ICAS '08) (pp. 61-69). IEEE Computer Society.

Deng, B., Wang, W., & Li, Y. (2012). A novel low complexity cell search algorithm for TD-LTE advanced system. In *Proceedings of the IEEE International Conference on Wireless Communications, Networking and Mobile Computing (WiCOM)*. IEEE.

Devarapalli, V., Wakikawa, R., Petrescu, A., & Thubert, P. (2005). Network mobility (NEMO) basic support protocol. *IETF RFC, 3963*.

Dey, S. (2012). Cloud mobile media: Opportunities, challenges, and directions. In *Proceedings of International Conference on Computing, Networking and Communications (ICNC)* (pp. 929-933). IEEE.

Diaz-Sanchez, D., Sanchez Guerrero, R., Marin Lopez, A., Almenares, F., & Arias, P. (2012). A H.264 SVC distributed content protection system with flexible key stream generation. In *Proceedings of the 2012 IEEE International Conference on Consumer Electronics - Berlin (ICCE-Berlin)* (pp.66-70).

Dimoulas, C., Tsourvakas, G., Kalliris, G., & Papakis, N. (2012). Audiovisual content management for the new media environment and economic aspects. In *Proceedings of the 10th World Media Economics and Management Conference*. Thessaloniki, Greece: IEEE.

Dimoulas, C., Avdelidis, A., Kalliris, G., & Papanikolaou, G. (2008). Joint wavelet video denoising and motion activity detection in multi-modal human activity analysis: Application to video – Assisted bioacoustic/psycho-physiological monitoring. *EURASIP Journal on Advances in Signal Processing*. doi:10.1155/2008/792028.

Dimoulas, C., Papanikolaou, G., & Petridis, V. (2011). Pattern classification and audiovisual content management techniques using hybrid expert systems: A video-assisted bioacoustics application in abdominal sounds pattern analysis. *Expert Systems with Applications, 38*(10), 13082–13093. doi:10.1016/j.eswa.2011.04.115.

Dinh, H. T., Lee, C., Niyato, D., & Wang, P. (2011). A survey of mobile cloud computing: Architecture, applications, and approaches. In *Wireless Communications and Mobile Computing*. Hoboken, NJ: Wiley. Retrieved from http://onlinelibrary.wiley.com/doi/10.1002/wcm.1203/abstract

Dinh, H. T., Lee, C., Niyato, D., & Wang, P. (2013). *A survey of mobile cloud computing: Architecture, applications, and approaches*. Wireless Communications and Mobile Computing..

Dinh, H. T., Lee, Ch., Niyato, D., & Wang, P. (2011). *A survey of MCC: Architecture, applications, and approaches*. Hoboken, NJ: Wiley Online Library..

Distefano, S., & Puliafito, A. (2012). Cloud@Home: Toward a volunteer cloud. *IEEE IT Professional, 14*(1), 27–31. doi:10.1109/MITP.2011.111.

Distributed Management Task Force, Inc. (2005). *DMTF CIM specification*. Author..

Distributed Management Task Force, Inc. (2009). *DMTF CIM operations over HTTP*. Author..

Dobrian, F., Sekar, V., Awan, A., Stoica, I., Joseph, D., & Ganjam, A. ... Zhang, H. (2011). *Understanding the impact of video quality on user engagement*. Paper presented at the ACM SIGCOMM. Toronto, Canada.

Dong, Curtmola, & Nita-Rotaru. (2009). Secure network coding for wireless mesh networks: Threats, challenges, and directions. *Computer Communications, 32*, 1790–1801. doi:10.1016/j.comcom.2009.07.010.

Doukas, C., Pliakas, T., & Maglogiannis, I. (2010). Mobile healthcare information management utilizing cloud computing and Android OS. In Proceedings of Engineering in Medicine and Biology Society (EMBC), (pp. 1037 - 1040). IEEE..

Downer, S. R., Meara, J. G., & Costa, A. C. (2005). Use of SMS text messaging to improve outpatient attendance. *Med J Aust., 183*(7), 366-368. Retrieved March 14, 2012 from http://www.ncbi.nlm.nih.gov/pubmed/16201955

Elminaam, Kader, & Hadhoud. (2009). Performance evaluation of symmetric encryption algorithms on power consumption for wireless devices. *International Journal of Computer Theory and Engineering, 1*(4), 1793–8201.

Elminaam, Kader, & Hadhoud. (2010). Evaluating the performance of symmetric encryption algorithms. *International Journal of Network Security, 10*(3), 216–222.

Eltoweissy, M. A. (2010). Towards autonomous vehicular clouds. *Ad Hoc Networks, 49*, 1–16. doi:10.1007/978-3-642-17994-5_1.

ENISA. (2009). *ENISA cloud computing risk assessment*. Retrieved October 28, 2012, from http://www.enisa.europa.eu/act/rm/les/deliverables/cloud-computingrisk-assessment

Entertainment, S. (2013). *Welcome to Shazam*. Retrieved 22 March 2013, from http://www.shazam.com

Erdal, I. (2007). Researching media convergence and crossmedia news production mapping the field. *Nordicom Review, 28*(2), 51–61.

Estevez, C., Angulo, S., Abujatum, A., Ellinas, G., Liu, C., & Chang, G.-K. (2012). A carrier-ethernet oriented transport protocol with a novel congestion control and QoS integration: Analytical, simulated and experimental validation. In *Proceedings of the IEEE International Conference on Communications (ICC)* (pp. 2673-2678). Ottawa, Canada: IEEE.

Estrin, D. (2001). Comm'n sense: Research challenges in embedded networked sensing. *UCLA Computer Science Department Research Review*. Retrieved from http://lecs.cs.ucla.edu

EuroCloud. (2013). *Energy-conscious 3D server-on-chip for green cloud*. Retrieved February 14, 2013, from http://www.eurocloudserver.com/

Facebook (2013). Retrieved 22 March 2013, from http://www.facebook.com

Fall, K., & Floyd, S. (1996). Simulation-based comparisons of Tahoe, Reno and SACK TCP. *ACM SIGCOMM Computer Communication Review, 26*(3), 5–21. doi:10.1145/235160.235162.

Falub, C. V., von Käne, H., Isa, F., Bergamaschin, R., Marzegalli, A., & Chrastina, D. et al. (2012). Scaing heteroepitaxy from layers to three-dimensional crystals. *Science, 335*(6074), 1330–1334. doi:10.1126/science.1217666 PMID:22422978.

Feijoo, C., & Jos, G-L., Mez-Barroso, & Ramos, S. (2012). Mobile gaming: Industry challenges and policy implications. *Telecommunications Policy, 36*(3), 212–221. doi:10.1016/j.telpol.2011.12.004.

Fernando, N., Loke, S. W., & Rahayu, W. (2013). Mobile cloud computing: A survey. *Future Generation Computer Systems, 29*(1), 84–106. doi:10.1016/j.future.2012.05.023.

Ferraiolo, D. F., & Kuhn, D. R. (1992). Role-based access control. In *Proceedings of the 15th National Computer Security Conference* (pp. 554–563). IEEE.

Fesehaye, D., Gao, Y., Nahrstedt, K., & Wang, G. (2012). Impact of cloudlets on interactive mobile cloud applications. In *Proceedings of 2012 IEEE 16th International Enterprise Distributed Object Computing Conference* (pp. 123-132).

Fillipo, D., Raposo, A., Markus, E., & Hugo, F. (2007). Ambientes colaborativos de realidade virtual e aumentada. In SBC–Sociedade Brasileira De Computação (Ed.), Porto Alegre, (pp. 168-191). Press..

Fit4Green. (2013). *Federated IT for a sustainable environmental impact*. Retrieved February 14, 2013, from http://www.fit4green.eu/

Flexiscale (2013). *Flexiant cloud computing services, cloud software and cloud hosting provider*. Retrieved from http://www.flexiscale.com

Floyd, S. (2003). *HighSpeed TCP for large congestion windows. RFC 3649*. IETF..

Floyd, S., & Henderson, T. (1999). *The NewReno modification to TCP's fast recovery algorithm. RFC 2582*. Internet Engineering Task Force..

Floyd, S., Mahdavi, J., Mathis, M., & Podolsky, M. (2000). *An extension to the selective acknowledgement (SACK) option for TCP. RFC 2883*. Internet Engineering Task Force..

Ford. (2012). Retrieved February 14, 2013, from http://www.indiandrives.com/fords-new-mobile-app-promises-to-speed-up-car-charging.html

Forman, G. H., & Zahorjan, J. (1994). The challenges of mobile computing. *Journal of Computer, 27*(4), 38–47. doi:10.1109/2.274999

Fortin-Parisi, S., & Sericola, B. (2004). A Markov model of TCP throughput, goodput and slow start. *Performance Evaluation, 58*, 89–108. doi:10.1016/j.peva.2004.07.016.

Fowler, S. (2011). Study on power saving based on radio frame in LTE wireless communication system using DRX. In *Proceedings of the IEEE Globecom Workshop*. IEEE.

Fowler, S., & Zeadally, S. (2006). Fast handover over micro-MPLS-based wireless networks. In *Proceedings of the 11th IEEE Symposium on Computers and Communications (ISCC)*. IEEE.

Fowler, S., Bhamber, R. S., & Mellouk, A. (2012). Analysis of adjustable and fixed DRX mechanism for power saving in LTE/LTE-advanced. In *Proceedings of the IEEE International Conference on Communications (ICC)*. IEEE.

Fowler, S., Zeadally, S., & Mellouk, A. (2008). Quality of service support for MPLS-based wired-wireless domains. In A. Mellouk (Ed.), *End-to-End Quality of Service Engineering in Next Generation Heterogeneous Networks* (pp. 309–345). London, UK: Wiley/ISTE Publishing..

Fowler, S., & Zhang, X. (2012). Ubiquitous fair bandwidth allocation for multimedia traffic on a WiMAX mesh network with multi-channels. *International Journal of Ad Hoc and Ubiquitous Computing, 9*(4). doi:10.1504/IJAHUC.2012.047009.

Fox, A., Gribble, S. D., Brewer, E. A., & Amir, E. (1996). Adapting to network and client variability via on-demand dynamic distillation. In *Proceedings of the Seventh International Conference on Architectural Support for Programming Languages and Operating Systems (ASPLOS-VII)* (pp. 160-170). ACM.

Fraleigh, C., Moon, S., Lyles, B., Cotton, C., Khan, M., & Moll, D. et al. (2003). Packet-level tra c measurements from the sprint IP backbone. *IEEE Network, 17*(6), 6–16. doi:10.1109/MNET.2003.1248656.

Francisco, K. C. (n.d.). *News about phones: The approaches of newspapers*. Retrieved August 30, 2012 from http://sbpjor.kamotini.kinghost.net/sbpjor/admjor/arquivos/9encontro/CL_87.pdf

Frederking, R. E., & Brown, R. D. (1996). *The pangloss-lite machine translation system*. Paper presented at the ExpandingMT Horizons. Montreal, Canada.

Freund, R. M. (2004). Applied lagrange duality for constrained optimisation. *Lecture notes of Massachusetts Institute of Technology*.

Fuggetta, A., Picco, G. P., & Vigna, G. (1998). Understanding code mobility. *IEEE Transactions on Software Engineering, 24*(5), 342–361. doi:10.1109/32.685258.

Fuks, H., Raposo, A., & Gerosa, M. A. (2002). *Engenharia de groupware: Desenvolvimento de aplicações colaborativas*. XXI Jornada De Atualização Em Informática, Anais Do XXII 188.[Projeto E Aplicações Congresso Da Sociedade Brasileira De Computação.]. *Realidade Virtual E Aumentada: Conceitos, 2*, 89–128.

FUNEMS. (2012). *iCore demo*. Retrieved from http://www.iot-icore.eu/latest-news/88-icore-project-demonstration-receives-the-runner-up-demonstration-award-at-funems-2012-berlin-germany

Gabale, V., Dutta, P., Kokku, R., & Kalyanaraman, S. (2012). InSite: QoE-aware video delivery from cloud data centers. In *Proceedings of 20ᵗʰ IEEE International Workshop on Quality of Service(IWQoS)*.

Gadia, A. (n.d.). *Autism and pervasive development disorders*. Retrieved March 14, 2012 from http://www.scielo.br/pdf/jped/v80n2s0/v80n2Sa10.pdf

Garg, S. K., Versteeg, S., & Buyya, R. (2011). SMICloud: A framework for comparing and ranking cloud services. In *Proceedings of the Fourth IEEE International Conference on Utility and Cloud Computing*. IEEE.

Gartner. (2011). *Gartner says worldwide mobile device sales to end users reached 1.6 billion units in 2010, smartphone sales grew 72 percent in 2010*. Retrieved March 18, 2012, from http://www.gartner.com/newsroom/id/1543014

Gartner. (2012). *Gartner says 821 million smart devices will be purchased worldwide in 2012, sales to rise to 1.2 billion in 2013*. Retrieved February 9, 2013, from http://www.gartner.com/newsroom/id/2227215

Gavrilovska & Prasad. (2006). *Ad hoc networking towards seamless communications*. Berlin: Springer..

Gayathri, K. S., Thomas, T., & Jayasudha, J. (2012). Security issues of media sharing in social cloud. *Procedia Engineering*, *38*, 3806–3815. doi:10.1016/j.proeng.2012.06.436.

Gehrmann, Persson, & Smeets. (2004). *Bluetooth security*. Boston: Artech House, Inc..

Geier, J. (2007). *Wireless network industry report*. Wireless-Nets, Ltd.

Geoghegan, M., & Klass, D. (2007). Podcast solutions: The complete guide to audio and video podcasting (2nd ed.). New York: Frieds of ED..

Gerkis. (2006). *A survey of wireless mesh networking security technology and threats*. SANS Institute.

Gerla, M. (2012). Vehicular cloud computing. In *Proceedings of the The 11th Annual Mediterranean on Ad Hoc Networking* (pp. 152-155). Philadelphia: IEEE.

Germanakos, P., Mourlas, C., & Samaras, G. (2005). A mobile agent approach for ubiquitous and personalized ehealth information systems. In *Proceedings of the Workshop on 'Personalization for e-Health' of the 10th International Conference on User Modeling (UM'05)*, (pp. 67–70). eHealth.

Ghafoor, K. Z. (2010). A novel delay-and reliability-aware inter-vehicle routing protocol. *Network Protocols and Algorithms*, *2*(2), 66–88. doi:10.5296/npa.v2i2.427.

Ghafoor, K. Z. (2012). Fuzzy logic-assisted geographical routing over vehicular ad hoc networks. *International Journal of Innovative Computing, Information, & Control*, 8(7B), 1–26.

Ghafoor, K. Z. (2013a). A fuzzy logic approach to beaconing for vehicular ad hoc networks. *Telecommunication Systems Journal.*, *52*(1), 139–149. doi:10.1007/s11235-011-9466-8.

Ghafoor, K. Z. (2013b). Intelligent beaconless geographical forwarding for urban vehicular. *Wireless Networks*, 19(3), 345–362. doi:10.1007/s11276-012-0470-z.

Ghosh, M. (2010). Mobile ID fraud: The downside of mobile growth. *Computer Fraud & Security*, (12): 8–13. doi:10.1016/S1361-3723(10)70155-X.

Giurgiu, I., Riva, O., Juric, D., Krivulev, I., & Alonso, G. (2009). Calling the cloud: Enabling mobile phones as interfaces to cloud applications. In *Proceedings of the 10th ACM/IFIP/USENIX International Conference on Middleware* (Middleware '09). Springer-Verlag.

Globus Alliance Resource Management (GRAM). (n.d.). Retrieved 1 October 2012, from http://www.globus.org/toolkit/docs/2.4/gram/

GM. (2012). Retrieved February 14, 2013, from http://www.greencarcongress.com/2012/01/onstar-20120110.html#more

Gmb, H. P. I. H. (2013). *Virtualization and automation solutions for desktops, servers, hosting, SaaS - Parallels*. Retrieved 22 March 2013, from http://www.parallels.com/

Gmb, H. Z. (2011). *Zimory enterprise cloud*. Retrieved from http://www.zimory.de/index.php?id=75

Goatman, K., Amanda, C., Laura, W., & Nussey, S. (2011). Assessment of automated disease detection in diabetic retinopathy screening using two-field photography. *PLoS ONE*, 6. PMID:22174741.

GoGrid. (2013). *Deploy public, private or dedicated cloud servers in minutes*. Retrieved 22 March 2013, from http://www.gogrid.com

Goland, Y., Cai, T., Leach, P., & Gu, Y. (1999). *Simple service discovery protocol/1.0 operating without an arbiter*. Internet Engineering Task Force..

Goldberg, D., Nichols, D., Oki, B. M., & Terry, D. (1992). Using collaborative filtering to weave an information tapestry. *Communications of the ACM*, *35*(12), 61–70. doi:10.1145/138859.138867.

Gomes, P. (n.d.). *Kinect helps diagnose and treat autism review*. Retrieved August 30, 2012 from http://porvir.org/porcriar/kinect-ajuda-diagnosticar-tratar-autismo/20120612

Google App. Engine. (n.d.). Retrieved July, 2008, from http://appengine.google.com

Google. (2012). *Google terms of service*. Retrieved March 1 2012, from http://www.google.com/intl/en/policies/terms/

Google. (2013a). *Google app. engine*. Retrieved 22 March 2013, from http://developers.google.com/appengine/

Google. (2013b). *Google goggles*. Retrieved 22 March 2013, from http://www.google.com/mobile/goggles/

Google. (2013c). *Google mobile*. Retrieved 22 Mar 2013, from http://www.google.com/mobile/mail

Gough, C. (2009). *Industry brief: Healthcare cloud security*. Intel IT Center..

Govil, K., Chan, E., & Wasserman, H. (1995). *Comparing algorithm for dynamic speed-setting of a low-power CPU*. Paper presented at the 1st Annual International Conference on Mobile Computing and Networking. Berkeley, CA.

Grace, P., Blair, G. S., & Samuel, S. (2003). Remmoc: A reflective middleware to support mobile client interoperability. In *On the Move to Meaningful Internet Systems 2003: CoopIS, DOA, and ODBASE* (pp. 1170–1187). Berlin: Springer. doi:10.1007/978-3-540-39964-3_75.

Grecos, C., & Wang, Q. (2011). Advances in video networking: standards and applications. *International Journal of Pervasive Computing and Communications*, *7*(1), 22–43. doi:10.1108/17427371111123676.

Grimshaw, A. S., & Wulf, W. A. (1996). Legion - A view from 50, 000 feet. In *Proceedings of the 5th IEEE International Symposium on High Performance Distributed Computing* (HPDC '96). IEEE Computer Society.

Grolaux, D., Vanderdonckt, J., & Van Roy, P. (2005). Attach me, detach me, Assemble me like you work. In *Proceedings of the 2005 IFIP TC13 International Conference on Human-Computer Interaction* (INTER-ACT'05) (pp. 198-212). Berlin: Springer-Verlag.

Group, T. C. C. U. C. D. (2009). *Cloud computing use cases whitepaper*. Retrieved from http://www.scribd.com/doc/17929394/Cloud-Computing-Use-Cases-Whitepaper

Guan, L., Ke, X., Song, M., & Song, J. (2011). *A survey of research on mobile cloud computing*. Paper presented at the Computer and Information Science (ICIS). New York, NY.

Guang, Tao, & Wen. (2012). Parallelise encoder of HM reference software for multi-core/cluster environment. *Input Document to JCT-VC*. JCTVC-K0137.

Guilhermo, Sapiro, & Firth, N. (n.d.). *Kinect cameras watch for autism*. Retrieved August 28, 2012 from http://www.newscientist.com/article/mg21428636.400-kinect-cameras-watch-for-autism.html

Guo, Y., Zhang, L., Kong, J., Sun, J., Feng, T., & Chen, X. (2011). Jupiter: Transparent augmentation of smartphone capabilities through cloud computing. In *Proceedings of the 3rd ACM SOSP Workshop on Networking, Systems, and Applications on Mobile Handhelds* (MobiHeld '11). ACM.

Guojun, W., Qin, L., & Jie, W. (2010). Hierarchical attribute-based encryption for fine-grained access control in cloud storage services. In *Proceedings of the 17th ACM Conference on Computer and Communications Security (CCS '10)* (pp. 735-737). ACM.

Gupta, P., & Gupta, S. (2012). Mobile cloud computing: the future of cloud. *International Journal of Advanced Research in Electrical, Electronics and Instrumentation Engineering, 1*(3).

Guttman, E. (1999). Service location protocol: Automatic discovery of ip network services. *IEEE Internet Computing, 3*(4), 71–80. doi:10.1109/4236.780963.

Gu, X., Messer, A., Greenberg, I., Milojidc, D., & Nahrstedt, K. (2004). Adaptive offloading for pervasive computing. *IEEE Pervasive Computing Magazine, 3*(3), 66–73. doi:10.1109/MPRV.2004.1321031.

Gwon, Y., Funato, D., & Takeshita, A. (2002). *Adaptive approach for locally optimized IP handoffs across heterogeneous wireless networks.* Paper presented at the 4th International Workshop on Mobile and Wireless Communications Network. New York, NY.

Haas, Z., & Agrawal, P. (1997). Mobile-TCP: An asymmetric transport protocol design for mobile systems. In *Proceedings of the International Conference on Communications* (pp. 1054-1058). Montreal, Canada: IEEE.

Hakkani-Tür, D., Tur, G., & Heck, L. (2011). Research challenges and opportunities in mobile applications. *IEEE Signal Processing Magazine, 28*(4), 108–110. doi:10.1109/MSP.2011.941132.

Han, Q., & Gani, A. (2012). Research on mobile cloud computing: Review, trend and perspectives. In *Proceedings of the Second International Conference on Digital Information and Communication Technology and its Applications (DICTAP)* (pp. 195-202). DICTAP.

Han, R., Bhagwat, P., LaMaire, R., Mummert, T., Perret, V., & Rubas, J. (1998). Dynamic adaptation in an image transcoding proxy for mobile web browsing. *IEEE Personal Communications Magazine, 5*(6), 8–17. doi:10.1109/98.736473.

Harold, P. (2007). MyHeart - Fighting cardiovascular diseases through prevention and early diagnosis. *Philips Research Password, 29*, 12–15.

Harter, A., Hopper, A., Steggles, P., Ward, A., & Webster, P. (2002). The anatomy of a context-aware application. *Wireless Networks, 8*(2-3), 187–197. doi:10.1023/A:1013767926256.

Ha, S., Rhee, I., & Xu, L. (2008). CUBIC: A new TCP-friendly high-speed TCP variant. *ACM SIGOPS Operating Systems Review, 42*(5), 64–74. doi:10.1145/1400097.1400105.

Hassan, M. M., Song, B., & Huh, E. (2011). Distributed resource allocation games in horizontal dynamic cloud federation platform. In *Proceedings of the IEEE 13th International Conference on High Performance Computing and Communications (HPCC)*, (pp. 822-827). IEEE.

Haythornthwaite, C. (2009). Agrupamentos e comunidades: Modelos de produção colaborativa leve e pesada. *Estudos Midiáticos, 11*(3), 161–175. doi:10.4013/fem.2009.113.01.

Helmbold, D. P., Long, D. D. E., & Sherrod, B. (1996). *A dynamic disk spin-down technique for mobile computing.* Paper presented at the 2nd Annual International Conference on Mobile Computing and Networking. New York, NY.

Herlocker, J., Konstan, J., & Riedl, J. (2000). Explaining collaborative filtering recommendations. In *Proceedings of ACM 2000 Conference on Computer Supported Cooperative Work.* ACM.

Hess, C. K., & Campbell, R. H. (2003). An application of a context-aware file system. *Personal and Ubiquitous Computing, 7*(6), 339–352. doi:10.1007/s00779-003-0250-y.

Hirsch, B., & Ng, J. W. P. (2011). *Education beyond the cloud: Anytime-anywhere learning in a smart campus environment.* Paper presented at the Internet Technology and Secured Transactions (ICITST). New York, NY.

Hitchens, M., & Varadharajan, V. (2000). Design and specification of role based access control policies. *Proceedings of IEEE Software, 147*(4), 117–129. doi:10.1049/ip-sen:20000792.

HL7. (2012). Retrieved from http://www.hl7.org/Special/committees/mobile/index.cfm

Hoang, D. B., & Lingfeng, C. (2010). *Mobile cloud for assistive healthcare (MoCAsH).* Paper presented at the Services Computing Conference (APSCC). New York, NY.

Hobfeld, T., Schatz, R., Varela, M., & Timmerer, C. (2012). Challenges of QoE management for cloud applications. *IEEE Communications Magazine*, *50*(4), 28–36. doi:10.1109/MCOM.2012.6178831.

Holden, W. (2010). Mobile ~ ahead in the cloud. *Juniper Research*. Retrieved February 9, 2013, from http://www.juniperresearch.com/shop/products/whitepaper/pdf/Juniper%20Research%20Cloud%20WhitepaperS.pdf

Holden, W. (2013). *Juniper research - Mobile telecoms research*. Retrieved from http://www.juniperresearch.com

Holder, O., Ben-Shaul, I., & Gazit, H. (1999). Dynamic layout of distributed applications in fargo. In *Proceedings of the 21st International Conference on Software Engineering* (CSE '99), (pp. 163-173). ACM.

Hollot, C., Misra, V., Towsley, D., & Gong, W.-B. (2001). A control theoretic analysis of RED. *Infocom*, *3*, 1510–1519.

Holohan, A., & Garg, A. (2009). Collaboration online: The example of distributed computing. *JCMC*, *10*(4).

Honda. (2012). Retrieved February 14, 2013, from http://www.greencarcongress.com/2012/04/ibm-20120412.html#more

Hopfgartner, F., & Jose, J. M. (2009). Semantic user modelling for personal news video retrieval. *Lecture Notes in Computer Science*, *5916*, 336–346. doi:10.1007/978-3-642-11301-7_35.

Hopfgartner, F., & Jose, J. M. (2010). Semantic user profiling techniques for personalised multimedia recommendation. *Multimedia Systems*, *16*(4-5), 255–274. doi:10.1007/s00530-010-0189-6.

Houacine, F., Bouzefrane, S., Li, L., & Huang, D. (2013). MCC-OSGi: A OSGi-based mobile cloud service model. In *Proceedings of the IEEE 11th International Symposium on Autonomous Decentralized Systems (ISADS)*.

Hsueh, S.-C., Lin, J.-Y., & Lin, M.-Y. (2011). *Secure cloud storage for convenient data archive of smart phones*. Paper presented at the 15th IEEE International Symposium on Consumer Electronics (ISCE). Singapore.

Huang, C., Hsu, C., Chang, Y., & Chen, K. (2013). GamingAnywhere: An open cloud gaming system. In *Proceedings of ACM Multimedia Systems 2013*.

Huang, D., Zhang, X., Kang, M., & Luo, J. (2010). Mobicloud: Building secure cloud framework for mobile computing and communication. In *Proceedings of the 5th IEEE International Symposium on Service Oriented System Engineering* (pp. 27-34).

Huang, D., Zhang, X., Kang, M., & Luo, J. (2010). MobiCloud: Building secure cloud framework for mobile computing and communication. In *Proceedings of the Fifth IEEE International Symposium on Service Oriented System Engineering (SOSE)* (pp. 27-34). IEEE.

Huang, D., Zhou, Z., Xu, L., Xing, T., & Zhong, Y. (2011). Secure data processing framework for mobile cloud computing. In *Proceedings of the 2011 IEEE Conference on Computer Communications* (pp. 614-618). IEEE.

Huang, C. A. (2010). Adaptive intervehicle communication control for cooperative safety. *IEEE Network*, *24*(1), 6–13. doi:10.1109/MNET.2010.5395777.

Huang, P. (2000). *Promoting wearable computing: A survey and future agenda*. Academic Press..

Huang, Z., Mei, C., Li, L. E., & Woo, T. (2011). CloudStream: Delivering high-quality streaming videos through a cloud-based SVC proxy. *Proceedings - IEEE INFOCOM*, *11*, 201–205. doi:10.1109/INFCOM.2011.5935009.

Huedo, E., Montero, R. S., & Llorente, I. M. (2004). Experiences on adaptive grid scheduling of parameter sweep applications. In *Proceedings of 12th Euromicro Conference on Parallel, Distributed and Network Based Processing* (PDP'04). IEEE Computer Society.

Huerta-Canepa, G., & Lee, D. (2010). A virtual cloud computing provider for mobile devices. In *Proceedings of 1st ACM Workshop on Mobile Cloud Computing & Services: Social Networks and Beyond* (pp. 6:1-6:5).

Hughes, K. (2012). The future of cloud-based entertainment. *Proceedings of the IEEE*, *100*, 1391–1394. doi:10.1109/JPROC.2012.2189790.

Hunt, G. C., & Scott, M. L. (1999). *The coign automatic distributed partitioning system*. Paper presented at the 3rd Symposium on Operating Systems Design and Implementation. New Orleans, LA.

Hussain, R. A. (2012). Rethinking vehicular communications: Merging VANET with cloud computing. In *Proceedings of the IEEE 4th International Conference on Cloud* (pp. 606-609). New Orleans, LA: IEEE.

Hwang, J., & Wood, T. (2012). Adaptive dynamic priority scheduling for virtual desktop infrastructures. In *Proceedings of 2012 IEEE 20th International Workshop on Quality of Service* (IWQoS). Coimbra, Portugal: IEEE.

Hyek, P. (2013). mHealth: Mobile technology poised to enable a new era in health care. *Ernst & Young*. Retrieved from http://www.ey.com/Publication/

I2Web. (2013). *Inclusive future internet web services*. Retrieved February 14, 2013, from http://services.future-internet.eu/index.php/I2WEB

IEEE-SA. (2013). *Guide for cloud portability and interoperability profiles*. Retrieved 8 March, 2013 from http://standards.ieee.org/develop/project/2301.html

ISO/IEC. (2011). Dynamic adaptive streaming over HTTP (DASH). *ISO/IEC FCD 23001 -6*.

ISO/IEC. (2013a). High efficiency video coding. *ISO/IEC 23008-2*.

ISO/IEC. (2013b). MPEG HEVC – The next major milestone in MPEG video history is achieved. *ISO/IEC JTC 1/SC 29/WG 11 N13253*.

Itani, W., Kayssi, A., & Chehab, A. (2010). *Energy-efficient incremental integrity for securing storage in mobile cloud computing*. Paper presented at the Energy Aware Computing (ICEAC). Cairo, Egypt.

ITS-Standards. (1996). *Research and innovative technology administration (RITA)*. Retrieved January 10, 2013, from http://www.standards.its.dot.gov/about.asp

ITU-T & ISO/IEC. (2010). Advanced video coding. *ITU-T Rec. H.264 and ISO/IEC 14496-10*.

ITU-T & ISO/IEC. (2012). Joint call for proposals on scalable video coding extensions of high efficiency video coding (HEVC). *ITU-T SG16/Q6 and ISO/IEC JTC 1/SC 29/WG 11 document VCEG-AS90 and WG 11 N12957*.

Jacob, R. L., & Alan, J. S. (1997). *Software strategies for portable computer energy management* (Report No. UCB/CSD-97-949). Berkeley, CA: Computer Science Division, University of California.

Jacobson, V. (1988). Congestion avoidance and control. *Computer Communication Review, 18*(4), 157–173. doi:10.1145/52325.52356.

Jacobson, V., & Braden, R. (1988). *TCP extensions for long-delay paths. RFC 1072*. Internet Engineering Task Force..

Jakobsson, M., Shi, E., Golle, P., & Chow, R. (2009). *Implicit authentication for mobile devices*. Paper presented at the 4th USENIX Conference on Hot Topics in Security. Montreal, Canada.

Jarek, N., Jennifer, M. S., & Jan, W. (2004). Grid resource management: State of the art and future trends. In *Grid resource management* (pp. 507–566). Boston: Kluwer Academic Publishers..

Jarschel, M., Schlosser, D., Scheuring, S., & Hoßfeld, T. (2013). Gaming in the clouds: QoE and the users' perspective. *Mathematical and Computer Modelling, 57*(11–12), 2883–2894. doi:10.1016/j.mcm.2011.12.014.

Jia, W., Zhu, H., Cao, Z., Wei, L., & Lin, X. (2011). *SDSM: A secure data service mechanism in mobile cloud computing*. Paper presented at the IEEE Conference on Computer Communications Workshops (INFOCOM WKSHPS). Shanghai, China.

Jia-Ming, L., Chen, J.-J., Cheng, H.-H., & Tseng, Y.-C. (2013). An energy-efficient sleep scheduling with QoS consideration in 3GPP LTE-advanced networks for internet of things. *IEEE Journal on Emerging and Selected Topics in Circuits and Systems, 3*(1), 13–22. doi:10.1109/JETCAS.2013.2243631.

Jian, L. (2010). *Study on the development of mobile learning promoted by cloud computing*. Paper presented at the Information Engineering and Computer Science (ICIECS). New York, NY.

Jian, X., Hu, J., Zhao, H., & Zhang, S. (2009). An optimized solution for mobile environment using MCC. In Proceedings of Wireless Communications, Networking and Mobile Computing, 2009. WiCom..

Jiang, D. A. (2008). IEEE 802.11 p: Towards an international standard for wireless access. In *Proceedings of the Vehicular Technology Conference* (pp. 2036-2040). IEEE.

Jin, C., Wei, D., & Low, S. (2004). FAST TCP: Motivation, architecture, algorithms, performance. In *Proceedings of IEEE Infocom*. Hong Kong, China: IEEE.

Jing, J., Helal, A. S., & Elmagarmid, A. (1999). Client-server computing in mobile environments. *ACM Computing Surveys, 31*(2), 117–157. doi:10.1145/319806.319814.

Jorge, V. D., Silvio, C., & Jonas, L. V. B. (2010). Um serviço para recomendação de artigos científicos baseado em filtragem de conteúdo aplicado a dispositivos móveis. *Cinted-Ufrgs, 8*(3).

Jung, H., Kim, S., Yeom, H., Kang, S., & Libman, L. (2011). Adaptive delay-based congestion control for high bandwidth-delay product networks. In *Proceedings of IEEE Infocom*. Turin, Italy: IEEE.

Jung, H., Kim, S., Yeom, H., & Kang, S. (2010). TCP-GT: A new approach to congestion control based on goodput and throughput. *Journal of Communications and Networks, 12*(5), 499–509. doi:10.1109/JCN.2010.6388496.

Júnior, P. (n.d.). *Brazil is featured on world autism*. Retrieved August 14, 2012 from http://www.revistaautismo.com.br/diamundial2011

Juniper Research. (n.d.). Retrieved June, 2010, from http://www.juniperresearch.com/index.php

Kadu, C., Bhanodiya, P., & Samvatsar, M. (2012). Review of challenges in accessing cloud services through mobile devices. *International Journal of Scientific & Engineering Research, 3*(11).

Kalliris, G., & Dimoulas, C. (2009). *Audiovisual content management issues for the new media environment*. Paper presented at the International Conference on New Media and Information: Convergences and Divergences. Athens, Greece.

Kalliris, G., Dimoulas, C. A., Veglis, A., & Matsiola, M. (2011). *Investigating quality of experience and learning (QoE & QoL) of audiovisual content broadcasting to learners over IP networks*. Paper presented at IEEE Symposium on Computers and Communications. New York, NY.

Kanday, R. (2012). *A survey on cloud computing security*. Paper presented at the Computing Sciences (ICCS). Phagwara, India.

Karagiannis, G. A. (2011). Vehicular networking: A survey and tutorial on requirements, architectures. *IEEE Communications Surveys & Tutorials, 13*(4), 584–616. doi:10.1109/SURV.2011.061411.00019.

Karetsos, G. T., Kyriazakos, S. A., Groustiotis, E., Giandomenico, F. D., & Mura, I. (2005). A hierarchical radio resource management framework for integrating WLANs in cellular networking environments. *Journal of IEEE Wireless Communications, 12*(6), 11–17. doi:10.1109/MWC.2005.1561940.

Karjoth, G., Schunter, M., & Waidner, M. (2002). Platform for enterprise privacy practices: Privacy-enabled management of customer data. In *Proceedings of the 2nd Workshop Privacy Enhancing Technologies (PET 02)* (LNCS), (vol. 2482, pp. 69-84). Berlin: Springer.

Katayama, N., Mo, H., & Satoh, S. (2011). News shot cloud: Ranking TV news shots by cross TV-channel filtering for efficient browsing of large-scale news video archives. *Lecture Notes in Computer Science, 6523*, 284–295. doi:10.1007/978-3-642-17832-0_27.

Kay, M., Santos, J., & Takane, M. (2011). mHealth new horizons for health through mobile technologies. In Global Observatory for eHealth. Geneva: WHO Press.

Kelly, T. (2003). Scalable TCP: Improving performance in highspeed wide area networks. *ACM SIGCOMM Computer Communication Review, 33*(2), 83–91. doi:10.1145/956981.956989.

Kemp, R., Palmer, N., Kielmann, T., & Bal, H. (2012). Cuckoo: A computation offloading framework for smartphones mobile computing, applications, and services. [LNCS]. *Proceedings of Social Informatics and Telecommunications Engineering, 76*, 59–79.

Kennedy, J., & Eberhart, R. (1995). Particle swarm optimization. In *Proceedings of Neural Networks, 1995* (Vol. 4, pp. 1942–1948). IEEE..

Kern, S. E., & Jaron, D. (2003). Healthcare technology, economics, and policy: An evolving balance. *IEEE Engineering in Medicine and Biology Magazine, 22*(1), 16–19. doi:10.1109/MEMB.2003.1191444 PMID:12683057.

Kesavan, S., Anand, J., & Jayakumar, D. J. (2012). Controlled multimedia cloud architecture and advantaged. *Advanced Computing: An International Journal, 3*(2), 29–40. doi:10.5121/acij.2012.3204.

Khafizov, F., & Yavuz, M. (2002). Running TCP over IS-2000. In *Proceedings of the International Conference on Communications*. New York, NY: IEEE.

Khan, K., Wang, Q., & Grecos, C. (2012). Experimental framework of integrated cloudlets and wireless mesh networks. In *Proceedings of the 20th Telecommunications Forum (TELFOR)* (pp. 190-193). IEEE.

Khan, A. N., Mat Kiah, M., Khan, S. U., & Madani, S. A. (2012). Towards secure mobile cloud computing: A survey. *Future Generation Computer Systems*, *5*(29), 22.

Khan, A., & Ahirwar, K. (2011). Mobile cloud computing as a future of mobile multimedia database. *International Journal of Computer Science and Communication*, *2*(1), 219–221.

Khazaei, H., Misic, J., & Misic, V. (2012). Performance analysis of cloud computing centers using M/G/m/m + r queueing systems. *IEEE Transactions on Parallel and Distributed Systems*, *23*(5), 936–943. doi:10.1109/TPDS.2011.199.

Khorshed, M. T., Ali, A., & Wasimi, S. A. (2012). A survey on gaps, threat remediation challenges and some thoughts for proactive attack detection in cloud computing. *Future Generation Computer Systems*, *28*(6), 833–851. doi:10.1016/j.future.2012.01.006.

Khungar, S., & Riekki, J. (2004). *A context based storage for ubiquitous computing applications*. Paper presented at the 2nd European Union Symposium on Ambient Intelligence. Eindhoven, The Netherlands.

Kim, K., Lee, S., & Congdon, P. (2012). On cloud-centric network architecture for multi-dimensional mobility. *Computer Communication Review*, *4*(42), 509–514. doi:10.1145/2377677.2377776.

Kim, M. J., Yoon, H. G., & Lee, H. K. (2011). An intelligent multi-agent model for resource virtualization: Supporting social media service in cloud computing. *Studies in Computational Intelligence*, *365*, 99–111. doi:10.1007/978-3-642-21375-5_9.

Kim, S., Song, S.-M., & Yoon, Y.-I. (2011). Smart learning services based on smart cloud computing. *Sensors (Basel, Switzerland)*, *11*(8), 7835–7850. doi:10.3390/s110807835 PMID:22164048.

King, N. J., & Raja, V. T. (2012). Protecting the privacy and security of sensitive customer data in the cloud. *Computer Law & Security Report*, *28*(3), 308–319. doi:10.1016/j.clsr.2012.03.003.

Kj, M. B., Bhattacharya, S., Blunck, H., & Nurmi, P. (2011). *Energy-efficient trajectory tracking for mobile devices*. Paper presented at the 9th International Conference on Mobile Systems, Applications, and Services. Bethesda, MD.

Kj, M. B., Langdal, J., Godsk, T., & Toftkj, T. (2009). *EnTracked: Energy-efficient robust position tracking for mobile devices*. Paper presented at the 7th International Conference on Mobile Systems, Applications, and Services. Krakow, Poland.

Klein, A., Mannweiler, C., Schneider, J., & Schotten, H. D. (2010). Access schemes for mobile cloud computing. In *Proceedings of 11th International Conference on Mobile Data Management* (pp. 387-392). IEEE.

Kleinrock, L. (1975). Queueing systems: Vol. I. *Theory*. New York: Wiley..

Kleinrock, L. (1976). Queueing systems: Vol. II. *Computer applications*. New York: Wiley..

KMV. (2013). *Kernal based virtual machine*. Retrieved 22 March 2013, from http://www.linux-kvm.org/page/MainPage

Koponen, T., Gurtov, A., & Nikander, P. (2004). *Application mobility with host identity protocol*. Paper presented at the Identifier/Locator Split and DHTs. Helsinki, Finland.

Ko, S.-K. V., Lee, J.-H., & Kim, S. W. (2012). Mobile cloud computing security considerations. *Journal of Security Engineering*, *9*(2), 143–150.

Kosta, S., & Mortier, R. (2012). ThinkAir: Dynamic resource allocation and parallel execution in the cloud for mobile code offloading. In IEEE INFOCOM 2012 (pp. 945-953)..

Kotsakis, R., Kalliris, G., & Dimoulas, C. (2012). Investigation of broadcast-audio semantic analysis scenarios employing radio-programme-adaptive pattern classification. *Speech Communication*, *54*(6), 743–762. doi:10.1016/j.specom.2012.01.004.

Kottari, V., Kamath, V., Saldanha, L. P., & Mohan, C. (2013). A survey on mobile cloud computing: Concept, applications and challenges. *International Journal of Academic Research, 2*(3), 487–492.

Kovač, D., & Trcek, D. (2009). Qualitative trust modeling in SOA. *Journal of Systems Architecture, 55*(4), 255–263. doi:10.1016/j.sysarc.2009.01.002.

Kovachev, D., Cao, Y., & Klamma, R. (2011). Mobile cloud computing: A comparison of application models. *Computing Research Repository, 1009*(3088).

Kovachev, D., Tian, Y., & Klamma, R. (2012). *Adaptive computation offloading from mobile devices into the cloud.* Paper presented at the Parallel and Distributed Processing with Applications (ISPA). New York, NY.

Kovalick, A. (2011). Cloud computing for the media facility: Concepts and applications. *SMPTE Motion Imaging Journal, 120*(2), 20–29.

Kretzschmar, M., & Golling, M. (2011). Security management spectrum in future multi-provider Inter-Cloud environments — Method to highlight necessary further development. In *5th International DMTF Academic Alliance Workshop on Systems and Virtualization Management (SVM)* (pp.1-8). IEEE.

Kshetri, N., & Murugesan, S. (n.d.). Cloud computing and EU data privacy regulations. *Computer, 46*(3), 86-89.

Kumar, K., & Yung-Hsiang, L. (2010). Cloud computing for mobile users: Can offloading computation save energy?. *IEEE Computer, 43*(4).

Kumar, A. (1998). Comparative performance analysis of versions of TCP in a local network with a lossy link. *IEEE/ACM Transactions on Networking, 6*(4), 485–498. doi:10.1109/90.720921.

Kumar, K., Liu, J., Lu, Y. H., & Bhargava, B. (2012). A survey of computation offloading for mobile systems. *Journal of Mobile Networks and Applications*, 1-12.

Kumar, K., Liu, J., Lu, Y.-H., & Bhargava, B. (2013). A survey of computation offloading for mobile systems. *Mobile Networks and Applications, 18*(1), 129–140. doi:10.1007/s11036-012-0368-0.

Kumar, K., & Yung-Hsiang, L. (2010). Cloud computing for mobile users: Can offloading computation save energy? *Computer, 43*(4), 51–56. doi:10.1109/MC.2010.98.

Kun, Y., Shumao, O., & Hsiao-Hwa, C. (2008). On effective offloading services for resource-constrained mobile devices running heavier mobile internet applications. *IEEE Communications Magazine, 46*(1), 56–63. doi:10.1109/MCOM.2008.4427231.

Kunz, T., & Black, J. (1999). An architecture for adaptive mobile applications. In *Proceedings of the 11th International Conference on Wireless Communications* (Wireless 99) (pp. 27-38). IEEE.

Kwak, J. S. (2004). Infrared transmission for intervehicle ranging and vehicle-to-roadside. *IEEE Transactions on Intelligent Transportation Systems, 5*(1), 12–19. doi:10.1109/TITS.2004.825082.

La, H. J., & Kim, S. D. (2010). A conceptual framework for provisioning context-aware mobile cloud services. In *IEEE 3rd International Conference on Cloud Computing* (pp. 466-473).

Laeeq. (2011). Security challenges & preventions in wireless communications. International Journal of Scientific & Engineering Research, 2(5).

Lagerspetz, E., & Tarkoma, S. (2011). *Mobile search and the cloud: The benefits of offloading.* Paper presented at the Pervasive Computing and Communications Workshops (PERCOM Workshops). New York, NY.

Laird, J. E., Newell, A., & Rosenbloom, P. S. (1987). SOAR: An architecture for general intelligence. *Artificial Intelligence, 33*(1), 1–64. doi:10.1016/0004-3702(87)90050-6.

Lakshman, T., & Madhow, U. (1997). The performance of networks with high bandwidth-delay products and random loss. *IEEE/ACM Transactions on Networking, 3*(4), 336–350. doi:10.1109/90.611099.

Lamberti, F., & Sanna, A. (2007). A streaming-based solution for remote visualization of 3D graphics on mobile devices. *IEEE Transactions on Visualization and Computer Graphics, 13*(2), 247–260. doi:10.1109/TVCG.2007.29 PMID:17218742.

Langley, P., Cummings, K., & Shapiro, D. (2004). Hierarchical skills and cognitive architectures. In *Proceedings of the Twenty-Sixth Annual Conference of the Cognitive Science Society* (pp. 779–784). CSS.

Langley, P., Laird, J. E., & Rogers, S. (2006). Cognitive architectures: Research issues and challenges. *Cognitive Systems Research, 10*(2), 141–160. doi:10.1016/j.cogsys.2006.07.004.

Lao, F., Zhang, X., & Guo, Z. (2012). Parallelizing video transcoding using map-reduce-based cloud computing. In *Proceedings of the 2012 IEEE International Symposium on Circuits and Systems (ISCAS)* (pp.2905-2908).

Larosa, Y. T., Jiann-Liang, C., Der-Jiunn, D., & Han-Chieh, C. (2011). *Mobile cloud computing service based on heterogeneous wireless and mobile P2P networks.* Paper presented at the 7th International Wireless Communications and Mobile Computing Conference (IWCMC). New York, NY.

Lashkari, Danesh, & Samadi. (2009). A survey on wireless security protocols (WEP, WPA, and WPA2/802.11i). In *Proceedings of the 2nd IEEE International Conference on Computer Science and Information Technology*, (pp. 48-52). IEEE.

Lawton, G. (2012). Cloud streaming brings video to mobile devices. *IEEE Computer, 45*(2), 14–16. doi:10.1109/MC.2012.47.

Lazzeri, T. (n.d.). *Autism: The universe around me.* Retrieved August 30, 2012 from http://m.parc.terra.com.br/efamilynet/dev/generic/interna.php?id_cat=25&article_id=557

Lee, D., Carpenter, B., & Brownlee, N. (2010). Observations of UDP and TCP ratio and port numbers. In *Proceedings of the Fifth International Conference of Internet Monitoring and Protection (ICIMP).* Barcelona, Spain: ICIMP.

Lee, J., Feng, T., Shi, W., Bedagkar-Gala, A., Shah, S. K., & Yoshida, H. (2012). Towards quality aware collaborative video analytic cloud. In *Proceedings of IEEE 5th International Conference on Cloud Computing (CLOUD)* (pp.147-154).

Lee, W. H., & Pang, C. T. (2009). An extension of semantic proximity for fuzzy functional dependencies. In *Proceedings of the Annual Meeting of the North American Fuzzy Information Processing Society* (pp.1-6). IEEE.

Lee, C. C. (1990). Fuzzy logic in control systems: Fuzzy logic controller II. *IEEE Transactions on Systems, Man, and Cybernetics, 20*(2), 419–435. doi:10.1109/21.52552.

Lee, Z., Wang, Y., & Wen, Z. (2011). A dynamic priority scheduling algorithm on service request scheduling in cloud computing. In *Proceedings of Electronic and Mechanical Engineering and Information Technology (EMEIT).* Harbin, China: EMEIT. doi:10.1109/EMEIT.2011.6024076.

Li, H., & Hua, X. (2010). *Melog - Mobile experience sharing through automatic multimedia blogging.* Paper presented at the Meeting of ACM MCMC. Firenze, Italy.

Li, L. T., Yang, S., Kavanaugh, A., Fox, E. A., Sheetz, S. D., Shoemaker, D., & Srinivasan, V. (2011). *Twitter use during an emergency event: The case of the UT Austin shooting.* Paper presented at the ACM International Conference. New York, NY.

Li, Z., & Wang, F. (2012). Cloud transcoder: Bridging the format and resolution gap between Internet videos and mobile devices. In *Proceedings of ACM NOSSDAV'12.*

Li, Z., Wang, C., & Xu, R. (2001). Computation offloading to save energy on handheld devices: A partition scheme. In *Proceedings of the 2001 International Conference on Compilers, Architecture, and Synthesis for Embedded Systems (CASES '01)* (pp. 238-246). ACM.

Liang, H., Cai, L. X., Huang, D., Shen, X., & Peng, D. (2012). An SMDP-based service model for interdomain resource allocation in mobile cloud networks. *IEEE Transactions on Vehicular Technology, 61*(5), 2222–2232. doi:10.1109/TVT.2012.2194748.

Li, F. A. (2007). Routing in vehicular ad hoc networks: A survey. *IEEE Vehicular Technology Magazine, 2*(2), 12–22. doi:10.1109/MVT.2007.912927.

Li, J., Qiu, M., Ming, Z., Quan, G., Qin, X., & Gu, Z. (2012). Online optimization for scheduling preemptable tasks on IaaS cloud systems. *Journal of Parallel and Distributed Computing, 72*(5), 666–677. doi:10.1016/j.jpdc.2012.02.002.

Li, L. (2009). An optimistic differentiated service job scheduling system for cloud computing service users and providers. In *Proceedings of Multimedia and Ubiquitous Engineering*. Qingdao, China: MUE. doi:10.1201/9781420093391.

Lim, M. S., Hoking, J. S., Hellard, M. E., & Aitiken, C. K. (n.d.). SMS STI: A review of the uses of mobile phone text messaging in sexual health. *Int JSTD AIDS, 19*(5), 287-290. Retrieved August 30, 2012 from http://www.ncbi.nlm.nih.gov/pubmed/18482956

Lin, Y.-W. A.-M.-J. (2011). Cloud-assisted gateway discovery for vehicular ad hoc networks. In *Proceedings of the 5th International Conference on New Trends* (pp. 237-240). IEEE.

Ling, C., Chen, M., Zhang, W., Tian, F. (2011). AR cloudlets for mobile computing. *International Journal of Digital Content Technology and its Applications, 5*(12), 162-169.

Lin, K., Ge, X., Wang, X., Zhu, C., & Ryu, H.-G. (2012). Research on secure data collection in wireless multimedia sensor networks. *Computer Communications, 35*(15), 1902–1909. doi:10.1016/j.comcom.2012.03.010.

Lin, N. (2001). *Social capital: A theory of social structure and action*. Cambridge, UK: Cambridge University Press. doi:10.1017/CBO9780511815447.

Lipsky, L. R. (2006). Queuing theory: A linear algebraic approach. Berlin: Springer.

List of OnLive Video Games. (n.d.). *Wikipedia*. Retrieved March 19 2013, from http://en.wikipedia.org/wiki/List_of_OnLive_video_games

Litzkow, M., Livny, M., & Mutka, M. (1988). Condor - A hunter of idle workstations. In *Proceedings of the 8th Intl. Conf. of Distributed Computing Systems* (pp. 104-111). IEEE.

Liu, L., Moulic, R., & Shea, D. (2010). *Cloud service portal for mobile device management*. Paper presented at the e-Business Engineering (ICEBE). New York, NY.

Liu, L., Yang, F., Wang, R., Shi, Z., Stidwell, A., & Gu, D. (2012). Analysis of handover performance improvement in cloud-RAN architecture. In *Proceedings of the IEEE International Conference on Communications and Networking in China* (CHINACOM) (pp. 850-855). IEEE.

Liu, W., Liu, Z.-T., & Shi, B.-S. (2005). *AOMG environment: An environment for agent-oriented analysis and design modeling based on grid*. Paper presented at the IEEE International Conference on Software - Science, Technology and Engineering. New York, NY.

Logicworks. (2013). *Logicworks healthcare cloud*. Retrieved from http://www.logicworks.net

Lopes, I., Vaidya, B., & Rodrigues, J. P. C. (2011). Towards an autonomous fall detection and alerting system on a mobile and pervasive environment. *Telecommunication Systems*, 1–12. doi: doi:10.1007/s11235-011-9534-0.

Lopes, M. C. (2004a). *Communication*. Aveiro, Portugal: Edição Universidade de Aveiro..

Lopes, M. C. (2004b). *Playfulness*. Aveiro, Portugal: Edição Universidade de Aveiro..

Low, S. H. (2003). A duality model of TCP and queue management algorithms. *IEEE/ACM Transactions on Networking, 11*(4), 525–536. doi:10.1109/TNET.2003.815297.

LTE-BE-IT. (2013). *LTE-advanced for network behaviour, energy and intelligent transportation systems*. Retrieved February 14, 2013, from http://webstaff.itn.liu.se/~scofo47/WebPage%20LTE-BE-IT/

Ma, R. K. K., Lam, K., & Wang, C.-L. (2011). eXCloud: Transparent runtime support for scaling mobile applications in cloud. In *Proceedings of the IEEE International Conference on Cloud and Service Computing* (CSC) (pp. 103-110). IEEE.

Maes, P., & Shardanand, U. (1995). Social information filtering: Algorithms for automating word of mouth. In *Proceedings of Human Factors In Computing Systems* (pp. 210–217). IEEE..

Mahmoud. (2007). Cognitive networks: Towards self-aware networks. London: John Wiley & Sons..

Malawski, M., Kuźniar, M., Wójcik, P., & Bubak, M. (2013). How to use Google app. engine for free computing. *IEEE Internet Computing, 17*(1), 50–59. doi:10.1109/MIC.2011.143.

Malhotr, K., Gardner, S., & Rees, D. (2005). Evaluation of GPRS enabled secure remote patient monitoring system.[Riga, Latvia: ASMTA.]. *Proceedings of ASMTA, 2005*, 41–48.

Manca, M., & Paternò, F. (2011). Flexible support for distributing user interfaces across multiple devices. In *Proceedings of the 9th ACM SIGCHI Italian Chapter International Conference on Computer-Human Interaction: Facing Complexity* (CHItaly) (pp. 191-195). ACM.

Mane, M. Y. D., & Devadkar, K. K. (2013). *Protection concern in mobile cloud computing-A survey.* Paper presented at the Second International Conference on Emerging Trends in Engineering. New Delhi, India.

Mapp, G., Katsriku, F., Aiash, M., Chinnam, N., Lopes, R., Moreira, E.,... Augusto, M. (2012). Exploiting location and contextual information to develop a comprehensive framework for proactive handover in heterogeneous environments. *Journal of Computer Networks and Communications*, 1-17.

Marinescu, D. C. (2012). Cloud computing: Theory and practice. ISBN: 9780124046276.

Marques, E., Veiga, L., & Ferreira, P. (2008). Transparent mobile middleware integration for java and. net development environments. In *Proceedings of the 14th International Euro-Par Conference on Parallel Processing* (Euro-Par '08) (pp. 47 – 57). Berlin: Springer-Verlag.

Mason, R., & Kelly, W. (2003). Peer-to-peer cycle sharing via.net remoting. In *Proceedings of AusWeb 2003 - The Ninth Australian World Wide Web Conference*. Retrieved 23 April 2013, from http://ausweb.scu.edu.au/aw03/papers/mason/paper.html

Mathis, M., Mahdavi, J., Floyd, S., & Romanow, A. (1996). *TCP selective acknowledgment options. RFC 2018*. Internet Engineering Task Force..

Ma, X., Cui, Y., & Stojmenovic, I. (2012). Energy efficiency on location based applications in mobile cloud computing: A survey. *Procedia Computer Science, 10*, 577–584. doi:10.1016/j.procs.2012.06.074.

McCabe. (2007). *Network analysis, architedture, and design* (3rd ed.). London: Elsevier Inc.

MCCF. (2013). *Mobile cloud computing forum.* Retrieved from http://www.mobilecloudcomputingforum.com/

Mei, C., Taylor, D., Wang, C., Chandra, A., & Weissman, J. (2011). *Mobilizing the cloud: Enabling multi-user mobile outsourcing in the cloud* (TR 11-029). Retrieved February 10, 2013, from http://www-users.cs.umn.edu/~jon/papers/11-029.pdf

Meir, A., & Rubinsky, B. (2009). Distributed network, wireless and cloud computing enabled 3-D ultrasound, a new medical technology paradigm. *Journal of PLoS ONE, 4*(11), e7974. doi:10.1371/journal.pone.0007974 PMID:19936236.

Melchior, J., Vanderdonckt, J., & Roy, P. V. (2011). A model-based approach for distributed user interfaces. In *Proceedings of the 3rd ACM SIGCHI Symposium on Engineering Interactive Computing Systems* (EICS '11) (pp. 11-20). ACM.

Mell, P., & Grance, T. (2011). The NIST definition of cloud computing. NIST Special Publication, 800(145).

mHealth. (2012). *Wikipedia*. Retrieved from http://en.wikipedia.org/wiki/MHealth#Definitions

Miao, D., Zhu, W., Luo, C., & Chen, C. (2011). *Resource allocation for cloud-based free viewpoint video rendering for mobile phones.* Paper presented at the meeting of ACM MM. Scottsdale, AZ.

Microsoft Research. (2011). *Stratus: Energy-efficient mobile communication using cloud support.* Retrieved September 27 2011, from http://research.microsoft.com/apps/video/default.aspx?id=158653

Microsoft. (2013). *Windows Azure.* Retrieved 22 March 2013, from http://www.microsoft.com/azure

Middlesex University. (2013). *The y-comm research.* Retrieved 8 March, 2013 from http://www.mdx.ac.uk/research/areas/software/ycomm_research.aspx

Miller, F. (2004). *Wearables–Clothing with a sixth sense. Fraunhofer magazine*, 38-39.

Minjuan, W., & Ng, J. W. P. (2012). *Intelligent mobile cloud education: Smart anytime-anywhere learning for the next generation campus environment.* Paper presented at the Intelligent Environments (IE). New York, NY.

Mirusmonov, M., Changsu, K., Yiseul, C., & Jongheon, K. (2012). *Mobile cloud computing: The impact of user motivation on actual usage.* Paper presented at the Computing and Networking Technology (ICCNT). New York, NY.

Mirzaei, N. (2008). *Cloud computing.* Bloomington, IN: Indiana University..

Misra, A., & Ott, T. (1999). The window distribution of idealized TCP congestion avoidance with variable packet loss. *Infocom, 3,* 1564–1572.

Misra, V., Gong, W., & Towsley, D. (2000). A fluid-based analysis of a network of AQM routers supporting TCP flows with an application to RED. In *Proceedings of Sigcomm.* Stockholm, Sweden: ACM. doi:10.1145/347059.347421.

Mobile Phone. (n.d.). *Wikipedia.* Retrieved March 26 2013, from http://en.wikipedia.org/wiki/Mobile_phone

MobileCloud. (2013). *Future communication architecture for mobile cloud.* Retrieved February 14, 2013, from http://www.utwente.nl/ctit/research/projects/international/fp7-ip/mobilecloud.doc/

Mohiuddin, K., Mohammad, R., Raja, A., & Begum, S. (2012). Mobile-cloud-mobile: Is shifting of load intelligently possible when barriers encounter? In *Proceedings of the 2012 International Conference on Computing, Networking and Communications (ICNC)* (pp. 326-332). IEEE.

MONICA. (2013). *Mobile cloud computing: Networks, services and architecture.* Retrieved February 14, 2013, from http://www.fp7-monica.eu/

Mont, M. C., Pearson, S., & Bramhall, P. (2003). Towards accountable management of identity and privacy: Sticky policies and enforceable tracing services. In *Proceedings of the 14th International Workshop on Database and Expert Systems Applications* (pp. 377- 382). IEEE.

Montalvo, S., Palomo, J., & Laguna, P. (2010). *Bridging the gap between teaching and breaking news: A new approach based on ESHE and ICT.* Paper presented at the Procedia - Social and Behavioral Sciences. New York, NY.

Monteiro, R. F. (1994). Jogos dramáticos (3ª ed.). São Paulo, Brazil: Agora..

Moon, J., & Lee, B. (2006). Rate-adaptive snoop: A TCP enhancement scheme over rate-controlled lossy links. *IEEE/ACM Transactions on Networking, 13*(3), 603–615. doi:10.1109/TNET.2006.876154.

Moorthy, A. K., Seshadrinathan, K., Soundararajan, R., & Bovik, A. C. (2010). Wireless video quality assessment: A study of subjective scores and objective algorithms. *IEEE Transactions on Circuits and Systems for Video Technology, 20*(4), 587–599. doi:10.1109/TCSVT.2010.2041829.

Morais, J., Silva, J. N., Ferreira, P., & Veiga, L. (2011). Transparent adaptation of e-science applications for parallel and cycle-sharing infrastructures. In *Proceedings of the 11th IFIP WG 6.1 International Conference on Distributed Applications and Interoperable Systems* (DAIS' 11) (pp. 292-300). Berlin: Springer-Verlag.

Morrow, S. (2011). Data security in the cloud. In *Cloud Computing: Principles and Paradigms.* London: Wiley. doi:10.1002/9780470940105.ch23.

Morshed, M. S. J., Islam, M. M., Huq, M. K., Hossain, M. S., & Basher, M. A. (2011). Integration of wireless hand-held devices with the cloud architecture: Security and privacy issues. In *Proceedings of 2011 International Conference on P2P, Parallel, Grid, Cloud and Internet Computing (3PGCIC)* (pp. 83-88). 3PGCIC.

Moustafa, H., Marechal, N., & Zeadally, S. (2012). Mobile multimedia applications delivery technologies. *IEEE IT Professional, 14*(5), 12–21. doi:10.1109/MITP.2012.46.

Müller, C., & Timmerer, C. (2011). A test-bed for the dynamic adaptive streaming over HTTP featuring session mobility. In *Proceedings of the 2011 ACM Multimedia Systems (MMSys).*

Murarasu, A. F., & Magedanz, T. (2009). Mobile middleware solution for automatic reconfiguration of applications. In *Proceedings of the 2009 Sixth International Conference on Information Technology: New Generations* (ITNG '09) (pp. 1049-1055). IEEE Computer Society.

Mushtaq, M. S., Shahid, A., & Fowler, S. (2012). QoS-aware LTE downlink scheduler for VoIP with power saving. In *Proceedings of the IEEE 15th International Conference on Computational Science and Engineering (CSE).* IEEE.

Nabrzyski, J., Jennifer, M. S., & Weglarz, J. (2003). *Grid resource management: State of the art and future trends.* Berlin: Springer..

Nakajima, T., & Hokimoto, A. (1997). Adaptive continuous media applications in mobile computing environment. In *Proceedings of the 1997 International Conference on Multimedia Computing and Systems* (ICMCS '97). IEEE Computer Society.

Namboodiri, V., & Ghose, T. (2012). To cloud or not to cloud: A mobile device perspective on energy consumption of applications. In *Proceedings of the 2012 IEEE International Symposium on a World of Wireless, Mobile and Multimedia Networks (WoWMoM)* (pp. 1-9).

Narain, D. (n.d.). Mobile cloud computing the next big thing. *ABI Research* Retrieved July, 2010, from http://ip-communications.tmcnet.com/topics/ip-communications/articles/59519-abi-research-mobile-cloud-computing-next-big-thing.htm

Nash, J. (1950). Equilibrium points in n-person games. *Proceedings of the National Academy of Sciences of the United States of America, 36*(1), 48–49. doi:10.1073/pnas.36.1.48 PMID:16588946.

Ng, D. K. W. (1994). Grey system and grey relational model. *SIGICE Bull, 20*(2), 2–9. doi:10.1145/190690.190691.

Nguyen, A., Senac, P., & Ramiro, V. (2011). How mobility increases mobile cloud computing processing capacity. In *Proceedings of the 2011 First International Symposium on Network Cloud Computing and Applications (NCCA)* (pp. 50-55). IEEE.

Nguyen, V. (2000). *Mobile computing & disconnected operation: A survey of recent advances.* Retrieved from http://www.cis.ohio-state.edu/~jain/cis788-95/mobile_comp/index.html

Nguyen, V. M., Chen, C. S., & Thomas, L. (2011). Handover measurement in mobile cellular networks: analysis and applications to LTE. In *Proceedings of the IEEE International Conference on Communications (ICC).* IEEE.

Nicopplitidis, O. Papadimitrious, & Pomportsis. (2003). Wireless networks. Hoboken, NJ: John Wiley & Sons..

Nightingale, J., Wang, Q., & Grecos, C. (2012). Removing path-switching cost in video delivery over multiple paths in mobile networks. *IEEE Transactions on Consumer Electronics, 58*(1), 38–46. doi:10.1109/TCE.2012.6170053.

Ni, Q., Bertino, E., Lobo, J., & Calo, S. B. (2009). Privacy-aware role-based access control. *IEEE Security & Privacy, 7*(4), 35–43. doi:10.1109/MSP.2009.102.

Nitz, J. C. et al. (2010). Is the Wii fit a new-generation tool for improving balance, health and wellbeing? A pilot study. *Climacteric: The Journal of the International Menopause Society, 13*(5), 487–491. doi:10.3109/13697130903395193 PMID:19905991.

Niyato, D., Vasilakos, A. V., & Kun, Z. (2011). Resource and revenue sharing with coalition formation of cloud providers: Game theoretic approach. In Proceedings of Cluster, Cloud and Grid Computing (CCGrid). Newport Beach, CA: CCGrid..

Niyato, D., & Hossain, E. (2008). A noncooperative game-theoretic framework for radio resource management in 4G heterogeneous wireless access networks. *IEEE Transactions on Mobile Computing, 7*(3), 332–345. doi:10.1109/TMC.2007.70727.

Niyato, D., Wang, P., Hossain, E., Saad, W., & Han, Z. (2012). Game theoretic modeling of cooperation among service providers in mobile cloud computing environments. *Proceedings of IEEE WCNC, 2012,* 3128–3133.

Nogueira, a.j. (2000). methodology of scientific work. *Impresso no Brasil, 21*(1).

Nonaka, I. (1991). The knowledge-creating company. *Harvard Business Review,* 96–104.

Novaes, J. C. (1992). *Play wheel.* Rio de Janeiro, Brazil: Agir..

Oberheide, J., Veeraraghavan, K., Cooke, E., Flinn, J., & Jahanian, F. (2008). *Virtualized in-cloud security services for mobile devices.* Paper presented at the Meeting of the First Workshop on Virtualization in Mobile Computing. Breckenridge, CO.

Oguchi, N., & Abe, S. (2011). Reconfigurable TCP: An architecture for enhanced communication performance in mobile cloud services. In *Proceedings of the International Symposium on Applications and the Internet* (pp. 242-245). Munich, Germany: IEEE/IPSJ.

Ohm, J.-R., Sullivan, G. J., Schwarz, H., Tan, T. K., & Wiegand, T. (2012). Comparison of the coding efficiency of video coding standards—Including high efficiency video coding (HEVC). *IEEE Transactions on Circuits and Systems for Video Technology, 22*(12), 1669–1684. doi:10.1109/TCSVT.2012.2221192.

Okamura, H. (2007). A laser motor directly transforms light energy into mechanical energy. *SPIE*. Retrieved November 17, 2007 from http://Spie.Org/X8435.Xml

Olakanmi. (2012). RC4c: A secured way to view data transmission in wireless communication networks. International Journal of Computer Networks & Communications, 4(2).

Olariu, S. A., Weigle, M. C. (2009). Vehicular networks: From theory to practice. London: Chapman and Hall/CRC. doi:doi:10.1201/9781420085891 doi:10.1201/9781420085891.

Olariu, S. A., Khalil, I., & Abuelela, M. (2011). Taking VANET to the clouds. *International Journal of Pervasive Computing and Communications, 7*(1), 7–21. doi:10.1108/17427371111123577.

OnLive. (2013). *Mobile platforms*. Retrieved 8 March, 2013 from http://www.onlive.co.uk/mobile

Oran, D. (2013). Video quality assessment in the age of internet video: Technical perspective. *Communications of the ACM, 56*(3), 90. doi:10.1145/2428556.2428576.

Ormond, O., Murphy, J., & Muntean, G. M. (2006). *Utility-based intelligent network selection in beyond 3G systems*. Paper presented at the IEEE International Conference on Communications (ICC '06). New York, NY.

Othman, A., Dew, P., Djemame, K., & Gourlay, I. (2003). Adaptive grid resource brokering. In *Proceedings of Fifth IEEE International Conference on Cluster Computing* (CLUSTER'03). IEEE.

Othman, M., & Hailes, S. (1998). Power conservation strategy for mobile computers using load sharing. *ACM Mobile Computing and Communication Review, 2*(1), 44–50. doi:10.1145/584007.584011.

Padhye, J., Firoiu, V., Towsley, D., & Kurose, J. (1998). Modeling TCP throughput: A simple model and its empirical validation. *ACM SIGCOMM Computer Communication Review, 28*(4), 303–314. doi:10.1145/285243.285291.

Padiy, A., Riley, L., & Mapp, G. (2012). *yRFC: The simple protocol specification*. Retrieved October 30, 2012, from http://ebookbrowse.com/yrfc2-sp-protocol-v2-doc-d357544954

Padmavathi & Shanmugapriya. (2009). A survey of attacks, security mechanisms and challenges in wireless sensor networks. *International Journal of Computer Science and Information Security, 4*(1).

Paek, J., Kim, J., & Govindan, R. (2010). *Energy-efficient rate-adaptive GPS-based positioning for smartphones*. Paper presented at the 8th International Conference on Mobile Systems, Applications, and Services. San Francisco, CA.

Pageau, G. (2011). Facebook now hosts 4 percent of all photos ever taken: Report. *PMA Newsline*. September 22, 2011, from http://pmanewsline.com/2011/09/22/facebook-now-hosts-4-percent-of-all-photos-ever-taken-report/#.UI2aAMWk680

Papapetrou, O., Papadakis, G., Ioannou, E., & Skoutas, D. (2010). Efficient term cloud generation for streaming web content. *Lecture Notes in Computer Science, 6189*, 385–399. doi:10.1007/978-3-642-13911-6_26.

Park, H. S., Yoon, S. H., Kim, T. H., Park, J. S., Do, M. S., & Lee, J. Y. (2003). *Vertical handoff procedure and algorithm between IEEE802.11 WLAN and CDMA cellular network*. Paper presented at the 7th CDMA International Conference on Mobile Communications. Seoul, Korea.

Park, H. (2003). What is hyperlink network analysis? A new method for the study of social structure on the web. *Connections, 25*(1), 49–61.

Park, S., & Jayaraman, S. (2003). Enhancing the quality of life through wearable technology. *IEEE Engineering in Medicine and Biology Magazine*. PMID:12845818.

Pearson, S., Casassa, M. M., & Kounga, G. (2011). Enhancing accountability in the cloud via sticky policies. *Secure and Trust Computing. Data Management and Applications, 187,* 146–155.

Pearson, S., & Mont, M. C. (2011). Sticky policies: An approach for managing privacy across multiple parties. *Computer, 44*(9), 60–68. doi:10.1109/MC.2011.225.

Pedersen, K. I., Kolding, T. E., Frederiksen, F., Kovács, I. Z., Laselva, D., & Mogensen, P. E. (2009). An overview of downlink radio resource management for UTRAN long-term evolution. *IEEE Communications Magazine, 47*(7), 86–93. doi:10.1109/MCOM.2009.5183477.

Pedersen, M. V., & Fitzek, F. H. P. (2012). Mobile clouds: The new content distribution platform. *Proceedings of the IEEE, 100,* 1400–1403. doi:10.1109/JPROC.2012.2189806.

Pereira, R., Azambuja, M., Breitman, K., & Endler, M. (2010). An architecture for distributed high performance video processing in the cloud. In *Proceedings of 2010 3rd IEEE Third International Conference on Cloud Computing (CLOUD)* (pp. 482-489).

Perkins, C. (Ed.). (2010). IP mobility support for IPv4, revised. IETF RFC 5944..

Perkins, C., Johnson, D., & Arkko, J. (Eds.). (2011). Mobility support in IPv6. IETF RFC 6275..

Pfaltz, M. C., Grossman, P., Michael, T., Margraf, J., & Wilhelm, F. H. (2010). Physical activity and respiratory behavior in daily life of patients with panic disorder and healthy controls. *International Journal of Psychophysiology, 78,* 42–49. doi:10.1016/j.ijpsycho.2010.05.001 PMID:20472006.

Philippsen, M., & Zenger, M. (1997). JavaParty - Transparent remote objects in Java. *Concurrency (Chichester, England), 9*(11), 1225–1242. doi:10.1002/(SICI)1096-9128(199711)9:11<1225::AID-CPE332>3.0.CO;2-F.

Ponnekanti, S., Johanson, B., Kiciman, E., & Fox, A. (2003). Portability, extensibility and robustness in iROS. In *Proceedings of the First IEEE International Conference on Pervasive Computing and Communications* (Percom 2003). IEEE Computer Society.

Ponnekanti, S., Lee, B., Fox, A., Hanrahan, P., & Winograd, T. (2001). ICrafter: A service framework for ubiquitous computing environments. In *Proceedings of the 3rd International Conference on Ubiquitous Computing* (UbiComp '01) (pp. 56-75). Berlin: Springer-Verlag.

Popa, D., Cremene, M., Borda, M., & Boudaoud, K. (2013). *A security framework for mobile cloud applications.* Paper presented at the 11th Roedunet International Conference (RoEduNet). Sinaia, Romania.

Prasad, M. R., Gyani, J., & Murti, P. R. K. (2012). MCC: Implications and challenges. *Journal of Information Engineering and Applications, 2*(7).

Preeti, G., & Vineet, S. (2013). Secure data storage in mobile cloud computing. *International Journal of Scientific & Engineering Research, 4*(4).

Preston, C. (2008). Braided learning: An emerging practice observed in e-communities of practice. *International Journal of Web Based Communities, 4*(2), 220–243. doi:10.1504/IJWBC.2008.017674.

Preuveneers, D., & Berbers, Y. (2010). Context-driven migration and diffusion of pervasive services on the OSGi framework. *International Journal on Autonomous and Adaptive Communications Systems, 3*(1), 3–22. doi:10.1504/IJAACS.2010.030309.

Prttig, Szewczyk, Tygar, Wen, & Culler. (2002). SPINS: Security protocols for sensor networks, wireless networks. Dordrecht, The Netherlands: Kluwer Academic Publishers..

Puttonen, J., Virtej, E., Keskitalo, I., & Malkamaki, E. (2012). On LTE performance trade-off between connected and idle states with always-on type applications. In *Proceedings of the IEEE 23rd International Symposium on Personal Indoor and Mobile Radio Communications* (PIMRC) (pp. 981-985). IEEE.

Qi, H., & Gani, A. (2012). Research on MCC: Review, trend and perspectives. In Proceedings of Digital Information and Communication Technology and it"s Applications (DICTAP). DICTAP..

Raatikainen, K., Christensen, H. B., & Nakajima, T. (2002). Application requirements for middleware for mobile and pervasive systems. *ACM SIGMOBILE Mobile Computing and Communications Review*, *6*(4), 16–24. doi:10.1145/643550.643551.

Rackspace, U. I. (2013). *Open cloud computing*. Retrieved 22 March 2013, from http://www.rackspace.com

Rahimi, M. R., Venkatasubramanian, N., Mehrotra, S., & Vasilakos, A. V. (2011). MAPCloud: Mobile applications on an elastic and scalable 2-tier cloud architecture. In *Proceedings of Utility and Cloud Computing (UCC)*. IEEE..

Raicu, I., Schwiebert, L., Fowler, S., & Gupta, S. K. S. (2005). Local load balancing for globally efficient routing in wireless sensor networks. *International Journal of Distributed Sensor Networks*, *1*(2), 163–185. doi:10.1080/15501320590966431.

Raj, D. A. A., & Mala, T. (2012). *Cloud press: A next generation news retrieval system on the cloud*. Paper presented at the 2012 International Conference on Recent Advances in Computing and Software Systems, RACSS 2012. New York, NY.

Ramakrishnan, K., Floyd, S., & Black, D. (2001). *The addition of explicit congestion notification (ECN) to IP. RFC 3168*. IETF..

Raman, R., Livny, M., & Solomon, M. H. (1999). Matchmaking: An extensible framework for distributed resource management. *Cluster Computing*, *2*(2), 129–138. doi:10.1023/A:1019022624119.

Rao, M. (2011). *Mobile Africa report 2011: Regional hubs of excellence and innovation*. Retrieved February 10, 2013, from http://www.mobilemonday.net/reports/MobileAfrica_2011.pdf

Rao, N. M., Sasidhar, C., & Kumar, V. S. (2010). Cloud computing through mobile-learning. *International Journal of Advanced Computer Science and Applications*, *1*(6).

Raposo, A., & Fuks, H. (2002). Defining task interdependencies and coordination mechanisms for collaborative systems. *Frontiers in Artificial Intelligence and Applications*, *74*, 88–103.

Ray-Yuan, S., Michael, C., Martin, O. H., & Greg, S. (2009). *Multiagent-based adaptive pervasive service architecture (MAPS)*. Paper presented at the 3rd workshop on Agent-oriented Software Engineering Challenges for Ubiquitous and Pervasive Computing. London, UK.

Reategui, E., & Lorenzatti, A. (2005). Um assistente virtual para resolução de dúvidas e recomendação de conteúdo. In *Proceedings of XXV CSBC*. CSBC.

Rehman, A., Mustafa, M., Javaid, N., Qasim, U., & Khan, Z. A. (2012). Analytical survey of wearable sensors. In *Proceedings of BioSPAN with 7th IEEE International Conference on Broadband and Wireless Computing, Communication and Applications (BWCCA)*. Victoria, Canada: IEEE.

Rellermeyer, J. S., & Alonso, G. (2007). Concierge: A service platform for resource-constrained devices. In *Proceedings of the 2nd ACM SIGOPS/EuroSys European Conference on Computer Systems 2007* (EuroSys '07) (pp. 245-258). ACM.

Ren, F., & Lin, C. (2011). Modeling and improving TCP performance over cellular link with variable bandwidth. *IEEE Transactions on Mobile Computing*, *10*(8), 1057–1070. doi:10.1109/TMC.2010.234.

Resnick, P. E., & Varian, H. R. (1997). Recommender systems. *Communications of the ACM*, *40*(3), 55–58. doi:10.1145/245108.245121.

Reynolds, P. D. (2000). National panel study of U.S. business startups: background and methodology. *Databases for the Study of Entrepreneurship*, *4*, 153–227. doi:10.1016/S1074-7540(00)04006-X.

Ries, M., & Gardlo, B. (2010). Audiovisual quality estimation for mobile video services. *IEEE Journal on Selected Areas in Communications*, *28*(3), 501–509. doi:10.1109/JSAC.2010.100420.

RightScale Inc. (2009). *RightScale cloud management features*. Retrieved from http://www.rightscale.com/products/features/

Rimal, B. P., Choi, E., & Lumb, I. (2009). A taxonomy and survey of cloud computing systems. In *Proceedings of Fifth International Joint Conference on INC, IMS and IDC*. IEEE.

Rochwerger, B., Breitgand, D., Levy, E., Galis, A., Nagin, K., & Llorente, I. M. et al. (2009). The reservoir model and architecture for open federated cloud computing. *IBM Journal of Research and Development*, *53*(4). doi:10.1147/JRD.2009.5429058.

Rodrigues, J. J., Zhou, L., Medes, L. D. P., Lin, K., Lloret, J. (2012). Distributed media-aware flow scheduling in cloud computing environment. *Computer Communications*, *35*(15), 1819–1827. doi:10.1016/j.comcom.2012.03.004.

Román, M., Hess, C., Cerqueira, R., Ranganathan, A., Campbell, R. H., & Nahrstedt, K. (2002). A middleware infrastructure for active spaces. *IEEE Pervasive Computing/IEEE Computer Society [and] IEEE Communications Society*, *1*(4), 74–83. doi:10.1109/MPRV.2002.1158281.

Romano, L. De Mari, D., Jerzak, Z., & Fetzer, C. (2011). A novel approach to QoS monitoring in the cloud. In Proceedings of Data Compression, Communications and Processing (CCP), (pp. 45 – 51). CCP..

Rose, J. (1990). *RFC 1158: Management information base for network management of TCP/IP-based internets: MIB-II*. Internet Activities Board..

Rosenberg, D. (2009). Why mobile applications need cloud services. *Cnet*. Retrieved October 20, 2012, from http://news.cnet.com/8301-13846_3-10300564-62.html

Rosenberg, J., Schulzrinne, H., Camarillo, G., Johnston, A., Peterson, J., Sparks, R., Handley, M., & Schooler, E. (2002). SIP: Session initiation protocol. *IETF RFC 3261*.

Roveri, A., Chiasserini, C. F., Femminella, M., Melodia, T., Morabito, G., Rossi, M., et al. (2003). *The RAMON module: Architecture framework and performance results*. Paper presented at the Second International Workshop on Quality of Service in Multiservice IP Networks. New York, NY.

Rudenko, A., Reiher, P., Popek, G. J., & Kuenning, G. H. (1998). Saving portable computer battery power through remote process execution. *ACM SIGMOBILE Mobile Computing and Communications*, *2*(1), 19–26. doi:10.1145/584007.584008.

Saaty, R. W. (1987). The analytic hierarchy process—What it is and how it is used. *Mathematical Modelling*, *9*(3–5), 161–176. doi:10.1016/0270-0255(87)90473-8.

Saaty, T. L. (1990). How to make a decision: The analytic hierarchy process. *European Journal of Operational Research*, *48*(1), 9–26. doi:10.1016/0377-2217(90)90057-I.

Sabelström, K. (2001). *Information categories and editorial process in multiple channel publishing. (Unpublished Ph.D.)*. Stockholm, Sweden: Royal Institute of Technology, Department of NADA, Division of Media Technology and Graphics Arts..

salesforce.com. (2013). *Salesforce platform*. Retrieved 22 March 2013, from http://www.salesforce.com/platform

Sampaio, P., Ferreira, P., & Veiga, L. (2011). Transparent scalability with clustering for Java e-science applications. In *Proceedings of the 11th IFIP WG 6.1 International Conference on Distributed Applications and Interoperable Systems* (DAIS'11) (pp. 270-277). Berlin: Springer-Verlag.

Sandhu, R., Ferraiolo, D., & Kuhn, R. (2000). The NIST model for role-based access control: Towards a unified standard. In *Proceedings of the 5th ACM Workshop on Role-Based Access Control* (pp. 47–63). ACM.

Santa, J., Gómez-Skarmeta, A. F., Sánchez-Artigas, M. (2008). Architecture and evaluation of a unified V2V and V2I communication. *Computer Communications*, *31*(12), 2850–2861. doi:10.1016/j.comcom.2007.12.008.

Sarwar, B., Konstan, J., Borchers, A., Herlocker, J., Miller, B., & Riedl, J. (1998). Using filtering agents to improve prediction quality in the grouplens research collaborative filtering system. In *Proceedings of the 1998 Conference on Computer Supported Cooperative Work*. New York: CSCW.

Satyanarayanan, M. (1996). *Fundamental challenges in mobile computing*. Paper presented at the Fifteenth Annual ACM Symposium on Principles of Distributed Computing. Philadelphia, PA.

Satyanarayanan, M., Bahl, P., Caceres, R., & Davies, N. (2009). The case for VM-based cloudlets in mobile computing. *IEEE Pervasive Computing/IEEE Computer Society [and] IEEE Communications Society*, *8*(4), 14–23. doi:10.1109/MPRV.2009.82.

Schadow, G., Mean, C. N., & Walker, D. M. (2006). The HL7 reference information model under scrutiny. *Master of Industrial Engineering*, *124*, 151–156. PMID:17108519.

Schafer, J., Konstan, J., & Riedl, J. (1999). Recommender systems in e-commerce. In *Proceedings of ACM E-Commerce*. ACM.

Schierl, T., Hannuksela, M. M., Wang, Y., Wenger, S., & Member, S. (2012). System layer integration of high efficiency video coding. *IEEE Transactions on Circuits and Systems for Video Technology, 22*(12), 1871–1884. doi:10.1109/TCSVT.2012.2223054.

Schubert, L., Jeffery, K. G., & Neidecker-Lutz, B. (2010). *The future of cloud computing: Opportunities for European cloud computing beyond 2010*. Brussels, Belgium: European Commission, Information Society and Media..

Schulenburg, J. (2013). *GORC*. Retrieved from http://jocr.sourceforge.net/

Schwartz. (2005). Mobile wireless communications. Cambridge, UK: Cambridge University Press..

Schwarz, H., Marpe, D., & Wiegand, T. (2007). Overview of the scalable video coding extension of the H.264/AVC standard. *IEEE Transactions on Circuits and Systems for Video Technology, 17*(9), 1103–1120. doi:10.1109/TCSVT.2007.905532.

Sen. (2009). A survey on wireless sensor network security. International Journal of Communication Networks and Information Security, 1(2), 55-78.

Seshadrinathan, K., Soundararajan, R., Bovik, A. C., & Cormack, L. K. (2010). Study of subjective and objective quality assessment of video. *IEEE Transactions on Image Processing, 19*(6), 1427–1441. doi:10.1109/TIP.2010.2042111 PMID:20129861.

Shan, C., Heng, C., Xianjun, Z., & Co, H. T. (2012). Inter-cloud operations via NGSON. *IEEE Communications Magazine, 50*(1), 82–89. doi:10.1109/MCOM.2012.6122536.

Shao, D., Ding, L., Yang, F., Qian, L., & Fang, X. (2012). A novel queue scheduling scheme for video transmission over IEEE 802.11e WLAN. *Advances on Digital Television and Wireless Multimedia Communications, 331,* 355–362. doi:10.1007/978-3-642-34595-1_49.

Shayea, I., Ismail, M., & Nordin, R. (2012). Advanced handover techniques in LTE-advanced system. In *Proceedings of the IEEE International Conference on Computer and Communication Engineering* (ICCCE). IEEE.

Shi, E., Niu, Y., Jakobsson, M., & Chow, R. (2011). Implicit authentication through learning user behavior. In *Proceedings of the 13th International Conference on Information Security (ISC 2010),* (pp. 99-113). Berlin: Springer.

Shi, S., Hsu, C., Nahrstedt, K., & Campbell, R. (2011). *Using graphics rendering contexts to enhance the real-time video coding for mobile cloud gaming*. Paper presented at the meeting of ACM MM. Scottsdale, AZ.

Shi, Z., Beard, C., & Mitchell, K. (2007). Misbehavior and MAC friendliness in CSMA networks. In *Proceedings of Wireless Communications and Networking Conference, 2007*. Hong Kong, China: IEEE.

Shi, Z., Beard, C., & Mitchell, K. (2008). Tunable traffic control for multihop CSMA networks. In *Proceedings of Military Communications Conference*. San Diego, CA: IEEE.

Shi, Z., Beard, C., & Mitchell, K. (2011). Competition, cooperation, and optimization in Multi-Hop CSMA networks. In *Proceedings of the 8th ACM Symposium on Performance Evaluation of Wireless Ad Hoc, Sensor, and Ubiquitous Networks*. ACM.

Shi, Z., Zhang, H., Dong, M., Zhao, Z., Sheng, Q., Jiang, Y., et al. (2003). *MAGE: Multi-agent environment*. Paper presented at the International Conference on Computer Networks and Mobile Computing. New York, NY.

Shi, Z., Beard, C., & Mitchell, K. (2009). Analytical models for understanding misbehavior and MAC friendliness in CSMA networks. *Journal Performance Evaluation, 66*(9-10), 469–487. doi:10.1016/j.peva.2009.02.002.

Shi, Z., Beard, C., & Mitchell, K. (2012a). *Analytical models for understanding space, backoff, and flow correlation in CSMA wireless networks*. Journal Wireless Networks. doi:10.1007/s11276-012-0474-8.

Shi, Z., Beard, C., & Mitchell, K. (2012b). Competition, cooperation, and optimization in multi-hop CSMA networks with correlated traffic. *International Journal of Next-Generation Computing, 3*(3).

Shorten, R., & Leith, D. (2004). H-TCP: TCP for high-speed and long-distance networks. In *Proceedings of PFLDNet Workshop*. Argonne, IL: PFLDNet.

Silva, B. M. C., Neves, P. A. C. S., Denko, M. K., & Rodrigues, J. J. P. C. (2009). *MP-collaborator: A mobile collaboration tool in pervasive environment.* Paper presented at the WiMob 2009 - 5th IEEE International Conference on Wireless and Mobile Computing Networking and Communication. New York, NY.

Silva, J. N., Ferreira, P., & Veiga, L. (2010). Service and resource discovery in cycle-sharing environments with a utility algebra. In *Proceedings of 2010 IEEE International Symposium on Parallel & Distributed Processing (IPDPS)*. IEEE.

Silva, J. N., Veiga, L., & Ferreira, P. (2009). Mercury: A reflective middleware for automatic parallelization of bags-of-tasks. In *Proceedings of the 8th International Workshop on Adaptive and Reflective Middleware (ARM'09)*. ACM.

Silva, J., & Ferreira, F. (2004). Remote code execution on ubiquitous mobile applications. In *Proceedings of the Second European Symposium on Ambient Intelligence (EUSAI 2004)* (pp. 172-183). Berlin: Springer.

Simoens, P., De Turck, F., Dhoedt, B., & Demeester, P. (2011). Remote display solutions for mobile cloud computing. *Computer, 44*(8), 46–53. doi:10.1109/MC.2011.70.

Simpson, W. (2008). Video over IP: IPTV, internet video, H.264, P2P, web TV, and streaming: A complete guide to understanding the technology. Oxford, UK: Focal Press, Elsevier..

Singh, A., & Malhotra, M. (2012). Agent based framework for scalability in cloud computing. *International Journal of Computer Science & Engineering Technology, 3*(4).

Singh, M. A., & Shrivastava, M. (2012). Overview of security issues in cloud computing. *International Journal of Advanced Computer Research, 2*, 41–45.

Sklavos & Xinmiao. (2007). *Wireless security and cryptography: Specification and implementation.* Boca Raton, FL: CRC Press..

Sloninsky, D., & Mechael, P. N. (2008). *Towards the development of a mhealth strategy: A literature review.* Geneva: World Health Organization..

Smith, B., & Ceusters, W. (2006). HL7 RIM: An incoherent standard. *Studies in Health Technology and Informatics, 124*, 133–138. PMID:17108516.

Sodagar, I. (2011). The MPEG-DASH standard for multimedia streaming over the internet. *IEEE MultiMedia, 18*(4), 62–67. doi:10.1109/MMUL.2011.71.

Sohr, K., Drouineaud, M., Ahn, G.-J., & Gogolla, M. (2008). Analyzing and managing role-based access control policies. *IEEE Transactions on Knowledge and Data Engineering, 20*(7), 924–939. doi:10.1109/TKDE.2008.28.

Sommer, C. A. (2010). Adaptive beaconing for delay-sensitive and congestion-aware traffic. In *Proceedings of the IEEE International Vehicular Networking Conference* (pp. 1 - 8). IEEE.

Song, H., Bae, C.-S., Lee, J.-W., & Youn, C.-H. (2011). Utility adaptive service brokering mechanism for personal cloud service. In *Proceedings of IEEE Military Communications Conference* (MILCOM) (pp. 1622-1627). IEEE.

Song, W. A. (2011). Review of mobile cloud computing. In *Proceedings of the 3rd International Conference on Communication* (pp. 1-4). IEEE.

Song, W., & Su, X. (2011). Review of mobile cloud computing. In *Proceedings of the 2011 IEEE 3rd International Conference on Communication Software and Networks (ICCSN)* (pp. 27-29). IEEE.

Song, Z., Molina, J., Lee, S., Lee, H., Kotani, S., & Masuoka, R. (2009). Trustcube: An infrastructure that builds trust in client. In *Future of Trust in Computing*. Berlin: Springer. doi:10.1007/978-3-8348-9324-6_8.

SoundHound. (2013). *SoundHound - Instant music search and discovery*. Retrieved 22 March 2013, from http://www.soundhound.com

Sousa, J. P., Poladian, V., Garlan, D., Schmerl, B., & Shaw, M. (2006). Task-based adaptation for ubiquitous computing. *IEEE Transactions on Systems, Man and Cybernetics. Part C, Applications and Reviews, 36*(3), 328–340. doi:10.1109/TSMCC.2006.871588.

Spiegel, A. (2000). Automatic distribution in pangaea. In *Proceeding of the 3rd International Workshop on Communication-Based Systems* (CBS 2000) (pp. 119-129). Berlin: Springer.

Spyridou, L.-P., Matsiola, M., Veglis, A., Kalliris, G., & Dimoulas, C. (2013). Journalism in a state of flux: Changing journalistic practices in the Greek newsroom. *International Communication Gazette, 75*(1).

Sreedhar, C., Verma, & Kasiviswanath. (2010). Potential security attacks on wireless networks and their counter-measure. *International Journal of Computer Science & Information Technology, 2*(5).

Srinivasa, R., Nageswara, R., & Kumari, E. (2009). Cloud computing: An overview. *Journal of Theoretical and Applied Information Technology, 9*(1), 71–76.

Stanik, A., Hovestadt, M., & Kao, O. (2012). Hardware as a service (HaaS), the completion of the cloud stack. In *Proceedings of the 8th International Conference on Computing Technology and Information Management (ICCM)* (pp. 830-835). ICCM.

Stevens, W. (1994). TCP/IP illustrated: Vol. 1. *The protocols*. Boston: Addison-Wesley..

Stevens, W. (1997). *TCP slow start, congestion avoidance, fast retransmit, and fast recovery algorithms. RFC 2001.* Internet Engineering Task Force..

Stirparo, P., & Kounelis, I. (2012). The MobiLeak project: Forensics methodology for mobile application privacy assessment. In *Proceedings of the International Conference for Internet Technology and Secured Transactions (ICITST 2012)*. ICITST.

Stuedi, P., Mohomed, I., & Terry, D. (2010). WhereStore: Location-based data storage for mobile devices interacting with the cloud. In *Proceedings of the 1st ACM Workshop on MCC & Services: Social Networks and Beyond*. San Francisco, CA: ACM.

Subashini, S., & Kavitha, V. (2011). A survey on security issues in service delivery models of cloud computing. *Journal of Network and Computer Applications, 34*(1), 1–11. doi:10.1016/j.jnca.2010.07.006.

Sugiura, A. A., Dermawan, C. (2005). In traffic jam IVC-RVC system for ITS using Bluetooth. *IEEE Transactions on Intelligent Transportation Systems, 6*(3), 302–313. doi:10.1109/TITS.2005.853704.

Sullivan, G. J., Ohm, J., Han, W.-J., & Wiegand, T. (2012). Overview of the high efficiency video coding (HEVC) standard. *IEEE Transactions on Circuits and Systems for Video Technology, 22*(12), 1649–1668. doi:10.1109/TCSVT.2012.2221191.

Sunggeun, J., & Qiao, D. (2012). Numerical analysis of the power saving in 3GPP LTE advanced wireless networks. *IEEE Transactions on Vehicular Technology, 61*(4), 1779–1785. doi:10.1109/TVT.2012.2187690.

Sweha, R., Ishakian, V., & Bestavros, A. (2012). AngelCast: Cloud-based peer-assisted live streaming using optimized multi-tree construction. In Proceedings of 2012 ACM Multimedia Systems (MMSys)..

Symeonidis, A. L., & Mitkas, P. A. (2005). Agent intelligence through data mining. In *Multiagent systems, artificial societies, and simulated organizations series* (Vol. 14). Berlin: Springer..

Tachikawa. (2002). *W-CDMA mobile communication systems*. London: Wiley and Maruzen.

Taleb, T., & Ksentini, A. (2012). QoS/QoE predictions-based admission control for femto communications. In *Proceedings of the IEEE International Conference on Communications* (ICC) (pp. 5146-5150). IEEE.

Tamanaha, A. C. (n.d.). *The play activity in infantile autism*. Retrieved April 14, 2012 from http://www.pucsp.br/revistadisturbios/artigos/Artigo_490.pdf

Tanenbaum, A., & Van Steen, M. (2007). *Distributed systems: Principles and paradigms*. Englewood Cliffs, NJ: Pearson Prentice Hall..

Tang, J., Liu, S., Liu, C., Gu, Z., & Gaudiot, J.-L. (2012). Acceleration of XML parsing through prefetching link. *IEEE Transactions on Computers*.

Tang, J., Thanarungroj, P., Liu, C., Liu, S., Gu, Z., & Gaudiot, J.-L. (2013). Pinned OS/services: A case study of XML parsing on Intel SCC. *Journal of Computer Science and Technology, 28*(1), 3–13. doi:10.1007/s11390-013-1308-6.

Tao, G., Pung, H. K., & Da Qing, Z. (2004). *A middleware for building context-aware mobile services*. Paper presented at the Vehicular Technology Conference, 2004. New York, NY.

Taylor, C., & Pasquale, J. (2010). Towards a proximal resource-based architecture to support augmented reality applications. In *Proceedings of 2010 Cloud-Mobile Convergence for Virtual Reality Workshop (CMCVR)* (pp. 5-9). IEEE.

Teicher, J. G. (2012). The brain of the beast: Google reveals the computers behind the cloud. *WBUR*. Retrieved October 17, 2012, from http://www.wbur.org/npr/163031136/the-brain-of-the-beast-google-reveals-the-computers-behind-the-cloud

Thakker, D. N. (2010). *Prefetching and clustering techniques for network based storage*. (Doctoral Thesis). Middlesex University, London, UK.

Thang, T. C., Ho, Q.-D., Kang, J. W., & Pham, A. T. (2012). Adaptive streaming of audiovisual content using MPEG DASH. *IEEE Transactions on Consumer Electronics*, *58*(1), 78–85. doi:10.1109/TCE.2012.6170058.

Thelwall, M., & Vaughn, L. (2004). Webmetrics. *JASIST*, *55*(14).

Thompson, K., Miller, G., & Wilder, R. (1997). Wide-area internet traffic patterns and characteristics. *IEEE Network*, *11*(6), 10–23. doi:10.1109/65.642356.

Thurwachter. (2002). Wireless networking. Upper Saddle River, NJ: Prentice Hall..

TREND. (2013). *Towards real energy-efficient network design*. Retrieved February 14, 2013, from http://www.fp7-trend.eu/

Troncoso-Pastoriza, J. R., & Perez-Gonzalez, F. (2013). Secure signal processing in the cloud: Enabling technologies for privacy-preserving multimedia cloud processing. *IEEE Signal Processing Magazine*, *30*(2), 29–41. doi:10.1109/MSP.2012.2228533.

Truong, T. H., Nguyen, T. H., & Nguyen, H. T. (2012). On relationship between quality of experience and quality of service metrics for IMS-based IPTV networks. In *Proceedings of the IEEE International Conference on Computing and Communication Technologies, Research, Innovation, and Vision for the Future* (RIVF). IEEE.

Truyen, E., & Joosen, W. (2008). Towards an aspect-oriented architecture for self-adaptive frameworks. In *Proceedings of the 2008 AOSD Workshop on Aspects, Components, and Patterns for Infrastructure Software* (ACP4IS '08). ACM.

Tubaishat, M., & Madria, S. (2003). Sensor networks: An overview. *IEEE Potentials*, *22*(2), 20–23. doi:10.1109/MP.2003.1197877.

Turcu, G., Foster, I., & Nestorov, S. (2010). Reshaping text data for efficient processing on amazon EC2. In *Proceedings of the 19th ACM International Symposium on High Performance Distributed Computing*, (pp. 435-444). ACM.

Tursunova, S., & Young-Tak, K. (2012). Realistic IEEE 802.11e EDCA model for QoS-aware mobile cloud service provisioning. *IEEE Transactions on Consumer Electronics*, *58*(1), 60–68. doi:10.1109/TCE.2012.6170056.

Twitter (2013). Retrieved from http://www.twitter.com

Uzcategui, R., & Acossta-Marun, G. (2009). Wave: A tutorial. *IEEE Transactions on Communications Magazine*, *47*(5), 126–133. doi:10.1109/MCOM.2009.4939288.

Vallina-Rodriguez, N., & Crowcroft, J. (2011). *ErdOS: Achieving energy savings in mobile OS*. Paper presented at the Sixth International Workshop on MobiArch. Bethesda, MD.

Van Der Auwera, G., & Reisslein, M. (2009). Implications of smoothing on statistical multiplexing of H.264/AVC and SVC video streams. *IEEE Transactions on Broadcasting*, *55*(3), 541–558. doi:10.1109/TBC.2009.2027399.

van Rossum, G. (1997). *Python programming language*. Retrieved 1 October 2012, from http://www.python.org

Vanderdonckt, J. (2010). Distributed user interfaces: How to distribute user interface elements across users, platforms, and environments. In *Proceedings of XIth Congreso Internacional de Interacción Persona-Ordenador* (Interacción' 2010). Retrieved 23 April 2013, from http://lilab.isys.ucl.ac.be/BCHI/publications/2010/Vanderdonckt-Interaccion2010.pdf

Vaquero, L. M., Rodero-Merino, L., Caceres, J., & Lindner, M. (2009). A break in the clouds: Towards a cloud definition. *ACM SIGCOMM Computer Communication Review*, 50-55.

Vartiainen, E., & Väänänen-Vainio-Mattila, K. (2010). *User experience of mobile photo sharing in the cloud*. Paper presented at the Meeting of ACM MUM. Limassol, Cyprus.

Vasiljevs, A., Skadiņš, R., & Samite, I. (2012). Enabling users to create their own web-based machine translation engine. In *Proceedings of the 21st Annual Conference on World Wide Web Companion*, (pp. 295-298). IEEE.

Vassilaras, S., & Yovanof, G. S. (2011). Wireless going in the cloud: A promising concept or just marketing hype? *Wireless Personal Communications*, *58*(1), 5–16. doi:10.1007/s11277-011-0284-9.

Vegiris, C., Avdelidis, K., Dimoulas, C., & Papanikolaou, G. (2008). Live broadcasting of high definition audiovisual content using HDTV over broadband IP networks. *International Journal of Digital Multimedia Broadcasting*. doi:10.1155/2008/250654.

Veglis, A. (2009). *Cross media communication in newspaper organizations*. Paper presented at the MCIS 2009. New York, NY.

Veglis, A. (2010). *Modeling cross media publishing in radio and TV stations*. Paper presented at the 2nd International Conference on Advances in Multimedia, MMEDIA 2010. New York, NY.

Veglis, A., & Pomportsis, A. (2012). *Journalists in the age of ICTs: Work demands and educational needs*. Unpublished.

Veglis, A., Tsourvakas, G., Pomportsis, A., & Avraam, E. (2005). The exploitation of information technology by Greek journalists. *1st Monday, 10*(8).

Veglis, A. (2012). Journalism and cross media publishing: The case of Greece. In A. Veglis, & E. Siapera (Eds.), *The Wiley-Blackwell handbook of global online journalism*. Oxford, UK: Blackwell Publishing. doi:10.1002/9781118313978.ch12.

Velev, D., & Zlateva, P. (2011). Principles of cloud computing application in emergency management. In *Proceedings of 2011 International Conference on E-business, Management and Economics*. IPEDR.

Verbelen, T., Simoens, P., De Turck, F., & Dhoedt, B. (2012). Cloudlets: Bringing the cloud to the mobile user. –In *Proceedings of the 3rd ACM Workshop on Mobile Cloud Computing and Services*, (pp. 29-35). ACM.

Vingelmann, P., Fitzek, F. H. P., Pedersen, M. V., Heide, J., & Charaf, H. (2011). Synchronized multimedia streaming on the iphone platform with network coding. *IEEE Communications Magazine*, *49*(6), 126–132. doi:10.1109/MCOM.2011.5783997.

Visiongain. (2011). *Mobile cloud computing industry outlook report: 2011-2016*. Retrieved February 10, 2013, from http://www.visiongain.com/Report/737/Mobile-Cloud-Computing-Industry-Outlook-Report-2011-2016

Vitorino, A. J. (n.d.). *Mobile technology applied in health care and support*. Retrieved March 14, 2012 from https://docs.google.com/viewer?a=v&q=cache:mwR9kk1xCGkJ:www.faculdadeflamingo.com.br/ojs/index.php/rit/article/download/5/15+&hl=pt-BR&gl=br&pid=bl&srcid=ADGEESi1qWzMCFVrYfqykdZb7dgRmw1aoS-d0D_k7hCeJahO0a3Fdc8kiC4Z_nw-17Gzgbh8Ch63v-yhSYL6EG-oLm1UzTOQejOwZ_ejmN9_nXdagq6d_SFsHZjO__3Bsj0XCM7MU6fU-&sig=AHIEtbQwnVYJiM1UP7pETAuTxocudXGoGw

VMware. (2013). *VMWareESXServer*. Retrieved 22 May 2013, from http://www.vmware.com/products/esx

Wang & Poor. (2003). *Wireless communication systems: Advanced techniques for signal reception*. Upper Saddle River, NJ: Prentice Hall..

Wang, S., & Dey, S. (2009). *Modeling and characterizing user experience in a cloud server based mobile gaming approach*. Paper presented at the Meeting of IEEE GLOBECOM. Honolulu, HI.

Wang, S., & Dey, S. (2010). *Addressing response time and video quality in remote server based internet mobile gaming*. Paper presented at the meeting of IEEE WCNC. Sydney, Australia.

Wang, S., & Dey, S. (2010). *Rendering adaptation to address communication and computation constraints in cloud mobile gaming*. Paper presented at the Global Telecommunications Conference (GLOBECOM 2010). New York, NY.

Wang, S., & Wang, X. S. (2010). *In-device spatial cloaking for mobile user privacy assisted by the cloud*. Paper presented at the International Conference on Mobile Data Management (MDM). St. Louis, MO.

Wang, S., Liu, Y., & Dey, S. (2012). Wireless network aware cloud scheduler for scalable cloud mobile gaming. In *Proceedings of IEEE ICC 2012* (pp. 2081-2086).

Wang, S., Liu, Y., & Dey, S. (2012). *Wireless network aware cloud scheduler for scalable cloud mobile gaming*. Paper presented at the meeting of IEEE ICC. Ottawa, Canada.

Wang, W., Li, Z., Owens, R., & Bhargava, B. (2009). *Secure and efficient access to outsourced data*. Paper presented at the 2009 ACM Workshop on Cloud Computing Security. Chicago, IL.

Wang, Y., Even, R., Kristensen, T., & Jesup, R. (2011). RTP payload format for H.264 video. *IETF RFC 6184*.

Wang, C., & Li, Z. (2004). A computation offloading scheme on handheld devices. *Journal of Parallel and Distributed Computing*, *64*(6), 740–746. doi:10.1016/j.jpdc.2003.10.005.

Wang, Q., & Abu-Rgheff, M. (2003). Next-generation mobility support. *IEEE Communication Engineer*, *1*(1), 16–19. doi:10.1049/ce:20030104.

Wang, Q., & Abu-Rgheff, M. (2006). Mobility management architectures based on joint mobile IP and sip protocols. *IEEE Wireless Communications*, *13*(6), 68–76. doi:10.1109/MWC.2006.275201.

Wang, Q., Hof, T., Filali, F., Atkinson, R., Dunlop, J., Robert, E., & Aginako, L. (2009). QoS-aware network-controlled architecture to distribute application flows over multiple network interfaces. *Wireless Personal Communications*, *48*(1), 113–140. doi:10.1007/s11277-007-9424-7.

Wang, S., & Dey, S. (2012). Cloud mobile gaming: modelling and measuring user experience in mobile wireless networks. *Mobile Computing and Communications Review*, *16*(1), 10–21. doi:10.1145/2331675.2331679.

Wang, S., & Dey, S. (2013). Adaptive mobile cloud computing to enable rich mobile Multimedia applications. *IEEE Transactions on Multimedia*. doi:10.1109/TMM.2013.2240674.

Wang, X., Chen, M., Kwon, T., Yang, L., & Leung, V. (2013). AMES-cloud: A framework of adaptive mobile video streaming and efficient social video sharing in the clouds. *IEEE Transactions on Multimedia*. doi:10.1109/TMM.2013.2239630.

Weber, R. H. (2010). Internet of things – New security and privacy challenges. *Computer Law & Security Report*, *26*(1), 23–30. doi:10.1016/j.clsr.2009.11.008.

Weiguang, S., & Xiaolong, S. (2011). *Review of mobile cloud computing*. Paper presented at the 3rd International Conference on Communication Software and Networks (ICCSN). New York, NY.

Weiser, M. (1994). *Building the invisible interface*. Paper presented at UIST '94 Symposium on User Interface Software and Technology. Marina del Rey, CA. Retrieved 23 April 2013, from http://www.ubiq.com/hypertext/weiser/UIST94_4up.ps

Weiser, M. (1991, September). The computer for the twenty-first century. *Scientific American*, 94–100. doi:10.1038/scientificamerican0991-94 PMID:1675486.

Weller, D., & Woodcock, B. (2013, January). Bandwidth bottleneck. *IEEE Spectrum Magazine*.

Wells, P. N. T. (2003). Can technology truly reduce healthcare costs? *IEEE Engineering in Medicine and Biology Magazine*, *22*(1), 20–25. doi:10.1109/MEMB.2003.1191445 PMID:12683058.

Wen, Y., Zhang, G., & Zhu, X. (2011). *Lightweight packet scheduling algorithms for content uploading from mobile devices to media cloud*. Paper presented at the Meeting of IEEE GLOBECOM Workshops. Houston, TX.

Weng, C., & Wang, K. (2012). Dynamic resource allocation for MMOGs in cloud computing environments. [*th International Wireless Communications and Mobile Computing Conference][IWCMC][. IEEE.]. *Proceedings of*, *2012*, 8.

Wenwu, Z., Chong, L., Jianfeng, W., & Shipeng, L. (2011). Multimedia cloud computing: An emerging technology for providing multimedia services and applications. *IEEE Signal Processing Magazine*.

Wen, Y., Zhang, W., Guan, K., Kilper, D., & Luo, H. (2011). *Energy-optimal execution policy for a cloud-assisted mobile application platform (Tech. Rep.)*. Singapore: Nanyang Technological University..

White Paper. (2010). *Mobile cloud computing solution brief*. AEPONA.

White, H. D., Wellman, B., & Nazer, N. (2004). Does citation reflect social structure? *JASIST*, *55*(2), 111–126. doi:10.1002/asi.10369.

Wiegand, T., Sullivan, G., Bjontegaard, G., & Luthra, A. (2003). Overview of the H.264/AVC video coding standard. *IEEE Transactions on Circuits and Systems for Video Technology, 13*(7), 560–576. doi:10.1109/TCSVT.2003.815165.

Williamson, C. (2001). Internet traffic measurement. *IEEE Internet Computing, 5*(6), 70–74. doi:10.1109/4236.968834.

Winnicott, D., & Autismo, W. (1997). *Thinking about children*. Porto Alegre, Brazil: Artes Médicas..

Winnicott, W. D. (1975). *Playing and reality*. Rio de Janeiro, Brazil: Imago..

Wlodarczyk, T. W. (2011). An initial survey on integration and application of cloud computing. In *Proceedings of the Third International Conference on Cloud* (pp. 612-617). IEEE.

Worstall, T. (2013). Rumours of two new apple phones this year: iPhone 5S and a cheap iPhone for emerging markets. *Forbes Online Article*. Retrieved May 20, 2013, from http://www.forbes.com/sites/timworstall/2013/04/04/rumours-of-two-new-apple-phones-this-year-iphone-5s-and-a-cheap-iphone-for-emerging-markets/

Wu, Y., Wu, C., Li, B., Qiu, X., & Lau, F. (2011). *Cloud-Media: When cloud on demand meets video on demand*. Paper presented at the meeting of IEEE ICDCS. Minneapolis, MN.

Wu, X., Wu, G.-Q., Xie, F., Zhu, Z., Hu, X.-G., Lu, H., & Li, H. (2010). News filtering and summarization on the web. *IEEE Intelligent Systems, 25*(5), 68–76. doi:10.1109/MIS.2010.11.

XenSourceInc. (2013). *XenServer*. Retrieved from http://www.xensource.com

Xiao, C., Estevez, C., Ellinas, G., & Chang, G.-K. (2007). A resilient transport control scheme for metro ethernet services based on hypothesis test. In *Proceedings of the IEEE Global Telecommunications Conference (Globecom)* (pp. 2461-2466). Washington, DC: IEEE.

Xiao, Chen, & Yang, Lin, & Du. (2009). Wireless network security. URASIP Journal on Wireless Communications and Networking.

Xing, T., Huang, D., Ata, S., & Medhi, D. (2012). Mobi-Cloud: A geo-distributed MCC platform. In *Proceedings of Network and Service Management (CNSM)*. Las Vegas, NV: CNSM..

Xu, L., Harfoush, K., & Rhee, I. (2004). Binary increase congestion control for fast long-distance networks. In *Proceedings of IEEE Infocom*. Hong Kong, China: IEEE.

Xu, Q. A. (2004). Vehicle-to-vehicle safety messaging in DSRC. In *Proceedings of the International Workshop on Vehicular Ad* (pp. 28-38). Philadelphia, PA: ACM.

Yamauchi, H., Kurihara, K., Otomo, T., Teranishi, Y., Suzuki, T., & Yamashita, K. (2012). Effective distributed parallel scheduling methodology for MCC. In *Proceedings of SASIMI*. SASIMI.

Yang, L. A. (2008). Congestion control for safety messages in VANETs: Concepts and framework. In *Proceeding of the 8th International Conference on ITS Telecommunications* (pp. 199-203). IEEE.

Yang, L. A. (2009). Piggyback cooperative repetition for reliable broadcasting of safety. In *Proceeding of the Consumer Communications and Networking Conference* (pp. 1-5). Anchorage, AK: IEEE.

Yang, Y., & Lam, S. (2000). General AIMD congestion control. In *Proceedings of International Conference on Network Protocols (ICNP)* (pp. 187-198). Osaka, Japan: ICNP.

Yang, J., Wang, H., Wang, J., Tan, C., & Yu, D. (2011). Provable data possession of resource-constrained mobile devices in cloud computing. *Journal of Networks, 6*(7), 1033–1040. doi:10.4304/jnw.6.7.1033-1040.

Yang, T., Lee, P. P. C., Lui, J. C. S., & Perlman, R. (2012). Secure overlay cloud storage with access control and assured deletion. *IEEE Transactions on Dependable and Secure Computing, 9*(6), 903–916. doi:10.1109/TDSC.2012.49.

Yang, Y., Zhou, Y., Sun, Z., & Cruickshank, H. (2012). Heuristic scheduling algorithms for allocation of virtualized network and computing resources. *Journal of Software Engineering and Applications, 6*(1).

Yavuz, M., & Khafizov, F. (2002). TCP over wireless links with variable bandwidth. In *Proceedings of the IEEE Vehicular Technology Conference*. Birmingham, AL: IEEE.

Ye, Z., Chen, X., & Li, Z. (2010). *Video based mobile location search with large set of SIFT points in cloud*. Paper presented at the Meeting of ACM MCMC. Firenze, Italy.

Ylitalo, J., Jokikyyny, T., Kauppinen, T., Tuominen, A. J., & Laine, J. (2003). *Dynamic network interface selection in multihomed mobile hosts*. Paper presented at the 36th Annual Hawaii International Conference on System Sciences (HICSS'03). Hawaii, HI.

Youseff, L., Butrico, M., & Da Silva, D. (2008). Toward a unified ontology of cloud computing. In *Proceedings of Grid Computing Environments Workshop, 2008* (pp. 1–10). GCE.

Yu, J., Dong, Z., Xiao, X., Xia, Y., Shi, S., Ge, C., et al. (2011). Generation, transmission and coherent detection of 11.2 Tb/s (112x100 Gb/s) single source optical OFDM superchannel. In *Proceedings of the OSA/OFC/NFOEC National Fiber Optic Engineers Conference*. Los Angeles, CA: OSA/OFC/NFOEC.

Yu, W., Li, J., Hu, C., & Zhong, L. (2011). *Muse: A multimedia streaming enabled remote interactivity system for mobile devices*. Paper presented at the Meeting of ACM MUM. Beijing, China.

Yuan, S., Tao, L., & Win, M. Z. (2012). Neighboring cell search for LTE systems. *IEEE Transactions on Wireless Communications*, *11*(3), 908–919. doi:10.1109/TWC.2012.011012.100089.

Zachariadis, S., Mascolo, C., & Emmerich, W. (2003). Adaptable mobile applications: Exploiting logical mobility in mobile computing. In *Proceedings of 5th Int. Workshop on Mobile Agents for Telecommunication Applications* (MATA03) (pp. 170 – 179). Berlin: Springer-Verlag.

Zadeh, L. (1965). Fuzzy sets. *Information and Control*, *8*(3), 338–353. doi:10.1016/S0019-9958(65)90241-X.

Zawoad, S., & Hasan, R. (2013). *Cloud forensics: A meta-study of challenges, approaches, and open problems*. Retrieved from http://arxiv.org/abs/1302.6312

Zhang, D., Li, B., Xu, J., & Li, H. (2012). Fast transcoding from H.264 AVC to high efficiency video coding. In *Proceedings of 2012 IEEE International Conference on Multimedia & Expo (ICME)* (pp. 651-656).

Zhang, L., Ding, X., Wan, Z., Gu, M., & Li, X. Y. (2010). WiFace: A secure geosocial networking system using WiFi-based multi-hop MANET. In *Proceedings of the 1st ACM Workshop on Mobile Cloud Computing & Services: Social Networks and Beyond* (MSC). ACM.

Zhang, P., & Yan, Z. (2011). A QoS-aware system for MCC. In Proceedings of Cloud Computing and Intelligence Systems (CCIS), (pp. 518 - 522). CCIS..

Zhang, H., Zheng, Y., Khojastepour, M. A., & Rangarajan, S. (2010). Cross-layer optimization for streaming scalable video over fading wireless networks. *IEEE Journal on Selected Areas in Communications*, *28*(3), 344–353. doi:10.1109/JSAC.2010.100406.

Zhang, Q., Cheng, L., & Boutaba, R. (2010). Cloud computing: State-of-the-art and research challenges. *Journal of Internet Services and Applications*, *1*(1), 7–18. doi:10.1007/s13174-010-0007-6.

Zhang, X., Kunjithapatham, A., Jeong, S., & Gibbs, S. (2011). Towards an elastic application model for augmenting the computing capabilities of mobile devices with cloud computing. *Mobile Networks and Applications*, *16*(3), 270–284. doi:10.1007/s11036-011-0305-7.

Zhang, Y., & Henderson, T. (2005). An implementation and experimental study of the explicit control protocol (XCP). In *Proceedings of IEEE Infocom* (pp. 1037–1048). Miami, FL: IEEE..

Zhiguo, W., June, L., & Deng, R. H. (2012). HASBE: A hierarchical attribute-based solution for flexible and scalable access control in cloud computing. *IEEE Transactions on Information Forensics and Security*, *7*(2), 743–754. doi:10.1109/TIFS.2011.2172209.

Zhong, L., Wang, B., & Wei, H. (2012). *Cloud computing applied in the mobile Internet*. Paper presented at the Computer Science & Education (ICCSE). New York, NY.

Zhou, D., & Lo, V. (2004). Cluster computing on the fly: Resource discovery in a cycle sharing peer-to-peer system. In *Proceedings of the 2004 IEEE International Symposium on Cluster Computing and the Grid* (CCGRID '04). (pp. 66-73). IEEE Computer Society.

Zhou, F., Dun, H. B.-L., & Billinghurst, M. (2008). Trends in augmented reality tracking, interaction and display: A review of ten years of ISMAR. In *Proceedings - 7th IEEE International Symposium on Mixed and Augmented Reality 2008, ISMAR 2008*, (pp. 193-202). IEEE.

Zhou, J., & Beard, C. C. (2007). Adaptive probabilistic scheduling for a cellular emergency network. In *Proceedings of IPCCC 2007*. IPCCC.

Zhou, K., Yeung, K., & Li, V. (2005). Throughput modeling of TCP with slow-start and fast recovery. In *Proceedings of the Global Telecommunications Conference (Globecom)*. St. Louis, MO: IEEE.

Zhou, J., & Beard, C. C. (2009). A controlled preemption scheme for emergency applications in cellular networks. *IEEE Transactions on Vehicular Technology, 58*.

Zhou, L., & Wang, H. (2013). Toward blind scheduling in mobile media cloud: Fairness, simplicity, and asymptotic optimality. *IEEE Transactions on Multimedia*. doi:10.1109/TMM.2013.2241044.

Zhou, L., Wang, X., Tu, W., Muntean, G., & Geller, B. (2010). Distributed scheduling scheme for video streaming over multi-channel multi-radio multi-hop wireless networks. *IEEE Journal on Selected Areas in Communications, 28*(3), 409–419. doi:10.1109/JSAC.2010.100412.

Zhu, X., Zhu, J., Pan, R., Prabhu, M. S., & Bonomi, F. (2012). *Cloud-assisted streaming for low-latency applications*. Paper presented at the Meeting of International Conference on Computing, Networking and Communications. Maui, HI.

Zhuang, Z., Kim, K.-H., & Singh, J. P. (2010). *Improving energy efficiency of location sensing on smartphones*. Paper presented at the 8th International Conference on Mobile Systems, Applications, and Services. San Francisco, CA.

Zhu, Q., & Agrawal, G. (2012). Resource provisioning with budget constraints for adaptive applications in cloud environments. *IEEE Transactions on Services Computing, 5*(4), 497–511. doi:10.1109/TSC.2011.61.

Zhu, W., Luo, C., Wang, J., & Li, S. (2011). Multimedia cloud computing. *IEEE Signal Processing Magazine, 28*(3), 59–69. doi:10.1109/MSP.2011.940269.

Zhu, Z., Li, S., & Chen, X. (2013). Design QoS-aware multi-path provisioning strategies for efficient cloud-assisted svc video streaming to heterogeneous clients. *IEEE Transactions on Multimedia*. doi:10.1109/TMM.2013.2238908.

Zou, P., Wang, C., Liu, Z., & Bao, D. (2010). *Phosphor: A cloud based DRM scheme with sim card*. Paper presented at the 12th International Asia-Pacific Web Conference (APWEB). Busan, South Korea.

About the Contributors

Joel José P. C. Rodrigues (S'01, M'06, SM'06) is a professor at the Department of Informatics of the University of Beira Interior, Covilhã, Portugal, and researcher at the Instituto de Telecomunicações, Portugal. He received a PhD degree in informatics engineering, an MSc degree from the University of Beira Interior, and a five-year BSc degree (licentiate) in informatics engineering from the University of Coimbra, Portugal. His main research interests include sensor networks, e-health, e-learning, vehicular delay-tolerant networks, and mobile and ubiquitous computing. He is the leader of NetGNA Research Group (http://netgna.it.ubi.pt), the Vice-chair of the IEEE ComSoc Technical Committee on Communications Software, the Vice-Chair of the IEEE ComSoc Technical Committee on eHealth, Member Representative of the IEEE Communications Society on the IEEE Biometrics Council, and officer of the IEEE 1907.1 standard. He is the editor-in-chief of the *International Journal on E-Health and Medical Communications*, the editor-in-chief of the *Recent Patents on Telecommunications*, and also served several Special Issues as a Guest Editor (*IEEE Transactions on Multimedia, Elsevier Journal of Network and Computer Applications, IET Communications, Journal of Communications*, etc.). He has served as General Chair, Technical Program Committee Chair, and symposium Chair for many international conferences, including IEEE ICC/GLOBECOMs, CAMAD, MAN, ITST, ICNC, SoftCOM, among others. He participated in tens of international TPCs and several editorial review boards (including *IEEE Communications Magazine, International Journal of Communications Systems*, etc.). He has authored or coauthored over 250 papers in refereed international journals and conferences, a book, and 2 patents. He had been awarded the Outstanding Leadership Award of IEEE GLOBECOM 2010 as CSSMA Symposium Co-Chair and several best papers awards. Prof. Rodrigues is a licensed professional engineer (as senior member), member of the Internet Society, an IARIA fellow, and a senior member of ACM and IEEE.

Kai Lin is an assistant professor at the School of Computer Science and Technology, Dalian University of Technology. He received a PhD degree in computer science and a MS degree in communication engineering from Northeastern University, China, and a BS degree in electronic engineering from Dalian University of Technology, China. His research interests include wireless network, body area network, ubiquitous computing, and cloud computing. He is an associate editor of the Recent Patents on Telecommunications, and also served several journals and Special Issues as editor or guest editor. He served as General Chair, Technical Program Committee Chair, publicity Chair for many international conferences, including IEEE I-SPAN, CSE, SCALCOM, EmbeddedCom, MWNS, IWSMN, MSN, ChinaGrid. He also participated in more than forty of international TPCs. He has authored or coauthored over 100 papers in international journals and conferences.

Jaime Lloret received his M.Sc. In Physics in 1997 at the University of Valencia, and he finished a postgraduate Master in Corporative networks and Systems Integration from the Department of Communications in 1999. Later, he received his M.Sc. in Electronic Engineering in 2003 at University of Valencia and his Ph.D. in telecommunication engineering (Dr. Ing.) at the Polytechnic University of Valencia in 2006. Before concluding his PhD. Thesis, he obtained the first place given by the Spanish Agency for Quality Assessment and Accreditation for the Campus of Excellence in the New Technologies and Applied Sciences Area. He was awarded the prize of the best doctoral Student in the Telecommunications area in 2006 according to the Social Council of the Polytechnic University of Valencia. He is a Cisco Certified Network Professional Instructor of the regional academy "Universidad Politécnica de Valencia" in the Cisco Networking Academy Program (CNAP) and he is the Legal Main Contact of UPV-ADIF (local academy of the CNAP). He teaches Local Area Networks and Systems Integration in the "Escuela Politecnica Superior de Gandia" at the Polytechnic University of Valencia. He has been working as a network designer and administrator in several companies. His academic interests and research are P2P networks, Wireless Local Area Networks, Sensor Networks, and Routing Protocols. He also researches on educational approaches and strategies.

* * *

Nidaa A. Abaas received the M.Sc. degree in "Homogenous Image Compression using Quadtree" from Computer Science Dept. in University of Babylon, Iraq, in 1999, and the Doctor degree from Computer Science Dept. in University of Technology, Iraq, in 2006, with thesis titled "A Comparison among Adaptive ICA Algorithms for Blind Speech Signals Separation: Cocktail Party Problem."

Abbes Amira is a professor in visual communication at the University of the West of Scotland (UWS), Scotland. Prior to joining UWS, he took academic positions at the University of Ulster, UK, Qatar University, Qatar, Brunel University, UK, and Queen's University Belfast, Ireland. He received his PhD from Queen's University Belfast in 2001. He has been awarded a number of grants from government and industry and has published around 200 publications in the area of reconfigurable computing and image processing during his career to date. He has been invited to give talks at many universities and international conferences and being chair, program committee for a number of conferences. He is also one of the 2008 VARIAN prize recipients. He holds two visiting professor positions at the University of Nancy, France and University of Tunn Hussein Onn, Malaysia. He is a Fellow of IET, Senior Member of the IEEE, and Senior Member of ACM.

Cory Beard received the Bachelor of Science and Master of Science degrees in Electrical Engineering at the University of Missouri-Columbia in 1990 and 1992 and his Ph.D. in Electrical Engineering at the University of Kansas in 1999. He is in an associate professor of Computer Science Electrical Engineering at the University of Missouri-Kansas City. His research interests are in the areas of emergency services in wireless networks, wireless cellular opportunistic scheduling, wireless cooperative relaying, resilient networks, performance assurance for service oriented architectures, and the communications for disaster response and search and rescue.

Rosli Bin Salleh received his B.Sc. degree in computer science from University of Malaya, Malaysia, in 1994, and the M.Sc and PhD degrees from the University of Salford, United Kingdom, in 1997 and 2001, respectively. From 2001, he worked as a lecturer in the Department of Computer System and Technology, Faculty of Computer Science and Information Technology, University of Malaya, Malaysia. He was appointed as a senior lecturer at the same department since 2007. His research interests include handoff techniques and security in wireless networking.

Jorge E. F. Costa was born in Santa Maria da Feira, Portugal, in 1989. He received his BSc degree in Technologies and Information Systems from University of Beira Interior, Portugal, in 2010, and an MsC degree in Informatics Engineering from University of Beira Interior, Portugal, in 2012. His current research areas are Mobile Computing and Cloud Computing.

Charalampos A. Dimoulas was born in Munich, Germany, on August 14, 1974. He received his diploma and PhD from the Department of Electrical and Computer Engineering of Aristotle University of Thessaloniki (AUTh) in 1997 and 2006, respectively. In 2008, he received scholarship on post-doctoral research at the Laboratory of Electronic Media of the Department of Journalism and Mass Communication of AUTh. Both his doctoral dissertation and his post-doc research deal with advanced audio-visual processing and content management techniques for intelligent analysis of prolonged multi-channel recordings. He currently serves as Lecturer of Electronic Media in the Dept. of Journalism and Mass Media Communication, AUTh. His current scientific interests include media technologies, signal processing, machine learning, multimodalintelligent content analysis including multimedia semantics, audiovisual content description and management automation. Dr. Dimoulas is member of IEEE, EURASIP, and AES.

Claudio Estevez received a B. S. in electrical and computer engineering from the University of Puerto Rico, Mayaguez, PR, USA, 2001; an M.S. in electrical and computer engineering with a minor in optical engineering from the University of Alabama in Huntsville, Huntsville, AL, USA, 2003; and a Ph.D. in electrical and computer engineering and with a minor in computer science from the Georgia Institute of Technology, Atlanta, GA, USA, 2010. In 2011, he was hired as an assistant professor by the electrical engineering department at Universidad de Chile. In 2012, he obtained a Chilean national research grant (FONDECYT) to study MAC protocols in WPAN using 60 GHz. In the same year, he was appointed coordinator of the Communication Networks M.Eng. program. His research interests include: Connection-oriented transport protocols, network fairness study, MAC-layer protocols in WPAN, 60-GHz WPAN applications, cloud computing with data mining/warehousing, wireless body area networks, remote biological monitoring.

Scott Fowler received a Ph.D. from Wayne State University, USA in 2006. During 2006 – 2010, he was a Research Fellow in the Adaptive Communications Networks Research Group at Aston University, UK, where the research focused on multiple services in Next Generation Networks (NGNs) in both wireless and wired, and the project team was composed of multi-disciplinary/multi-institutional partners from industry and academia. Since 2010, he has been an Associate Professor at Linköping University, Sweden, and works with the Mobile Telecommunication (MT) group. Dr. Fowler has served on several IEEE conferences/workshops as TPC to Chair. Dr. Fowler's research interests include Quality of Service (QoS), Computer networks (wired, wireless), Energy management, Performance Evaluation of Networks and Security. In 2012, he was awarded a Visiting Professorship from the France Scientific Council to the University of Paris-Est Creteil (UPEC), France. Dr. Fowler was a host for a Fulbright Specialist from the USA in 2011.

Joel Gonçalves de Oliveira is Digital IC Designer Frontend-Verification at SMDH (Santa Maria Design House). His research focus is on the design of medium and large digital integrated systems, emphasizing the steps involved in the design flow for digital technologies in modern manufacturing He has been a finalist for the award: Siemens Student Award-2011, Batteries with ecological design. He graduated in Computer Science from the State University of Rio Grade do Norte. He is a member of the Research Group GSiD-UERN since 2009. He developed projects in GSiD with Formal Methods applied to the Semantic Web between the years 2009-2011. He is a guest columnist of topics related to innovation and technology and had even articles published in 2011 in the journal *Science Online* (Brazil).

Christos Grecos, SMIEEE, SMSPIE, is a professor in Visual Communication Standards and Head of School of Computing at the University of the West of Scotland. Before coming to Scotland, he worked at the universities of Central Lancashire and Loughborough. He has more than 120 publications, has obtained significant funding for his research from the Engineering and Physical Sciences Research Councils (UK), Technology Strategy Board (UK), European Regional Development Fund and Scottish Funding Council, and he is also in the international and technical programme committees of many prestigious conferences. His main areas of expertise are image and video compression algorithms and standards.

George Kalliris was born (1964) in Nicosia, Cyprus. In 1989, he received his Diploma in Electrical Engineering with Telecommunications from the Aristotle University of Thessaloniki. In 1995, he received his PhD from the same University. His doctoral research was carried out at the Laboratory of Electroacoustics and TV Systems. During and after completing his doctoral studies, he worked in research projects and as a part-time teacher. His current position is associate professor and director of the Electronic Media Lab at the Department of Journalism and Mass Communication. He has also taught in two Master degree programs, to the Film Studies Department and as a visiting professor of the Frederick University of Cyprus. His current research interests include audiovisual technologies for the new media, radio and television studio design, digital audio-video processing–production–broadcasting-Webcasting, multimedia content, restoration, management, and retrieval.

Tae-Gyu Lee (BSc'92, MSc'96, PhD'06) received the B.Sc. degree from Kunsan National University, Kunsan, Korea in 1992, the M.Sc. degree from Soongsil University, Seoul, Korea in 1996, and the Ph.D. degree from Korea University in 2006. He is currently an Adjunct Professor in the Department of Computer Engineering, Korea Polytechnic University, Gyeonggi, Korea. In addition, he is a Professional Researcher in Advanced Convergent Technology R&D Group, Korea Institute of Industrial Technology (KITECH), Ansan, Korea. He has also been a President in the JIGUNET Corporation, Seoul, Korea, from 1999. His research interests are in distributed systems, ubiquitous computing, middleware, networks, wearable and robot computing.

Jonathan Loo, a.k.a. Kok-Keong Loo, received his MSc degree in Electronics (with Distinction) from the University of Hertfordshire, UK, in 1998, and his PhD degree in Electronics and Communications from the same university in 2003. Currently, he is a Reader in Communication and Networking at the School of Science and Technology, Middlesex University, UK. He leads a research team in the area of communication and networking. His research interest includes network architecture, communication protocols, network security, wireless communications, embedded systems, video coding and transmission, digital signal processing, and optical networks. He has successfully supervised 11 PhDs and contributed over 150 publications (journals, conferences, book chapters, edited book) in the afore-mentioned specialist areas.

Chunbo Luo is a lecturer in networks at the University of the West of Scotland (UWS). He received the B.Eng. and M.Eng. degrees in Electronic Engineering from the University of Electronic Science and Technology of China (UESTC), China, in 2005 and 2007, respectively, and the Ph.D. degree from the University of Reading, UK, in 2011. He is with the Centre of Audio-Visual Communications and Networks (AVCN) in UWS and a member of IEEE. His research interests include wireless communication, signal processing, wireless sensor networks and Unmanned Aerial Vehicle (UAV) networks.

Shiwen Mao received Ph.D. in electrical and computer engineering from Polytechnic University, Brooklyn, NY. Currently, he is the McWane Associate Professor in the Department of Electrical and Computer Engineering, Auburn University, Auburn, AL, USA. His research interests include cross-layer optimization of wireless networks and multimedia communications, with current focus on cognitive radios, femtocells, 60 GHz mmWave networks, free space optical networks, and smart grid. He is on the Editorial Board of *IEEE Transactions on Wireless Communications, IEEE Communications Surveys and Tutorials,* and several other journals. He received the NSF CAREER Award in 2010 and is a co-recipient of The 2004 IEEE Communications Society Leonard G. Abraham Prize in the Field of Communications Systems.

Glenford Mapp received his BSc (First Class Honours) from the University of the West Indies in 1982, a MEng (Distinction in Thesis) from Carleton University in Ottawa in 1985, and a PhD from the Computer Laboratory, University of Cambridge in 1992. He then worked for AT&T Cambridge Laboratories for ten years before joining Middlesex University as a Principal Lecturer. His primary expertise is in the development of new technologies for mobile and distributed systems. He does research on Y-Comm, an architecture for future mobile communications systems. He also works on service platforms, cloud computing, network addressing, and transport protocols for local environments. He is currently focusing on the development of fast, portable services that can migrate or replicate to support mobile users.

Hero Modares is an assistant research in the Computer System and Technology department at University of Malaya. She is currently a Ph.D. student majored in Mobile IPv6 security in Faculty of Computer Science and Information Technology University of Malaya, and she obtained her Master degree in the same university in 2009. During her master degree, she was a research assistant. Her research interests are in computer and network security, cryptographic protocol, digital signature and nonrepudiation, mobile communications security (MIPv6), public-key infrastructure.

Amirhosein Moravejosharieh completed Master of Computer Science in the area of Wireless Network (bandwidth consumption and resource usage) through the coursework and dissertation program. Currently, he is studying as a PhD student in the field of wireless networks in University of Canterbury

/ New Zealand. His primary area of research includes analyzing wireless networks in terms of handover procedure, QoS during handover procedure, and security issues related to handover procedure in Mobile IPv6 wireless network.

James Nightingale is a Postdoctoral Research Associate with Centre of the Audio-Visual Communications and Networks (AVCN) in the University of the West of Scotland (UWS), UK, working on the EPSRC funded project "Enabler for Next-Generation Mobile Video Applications" (EP/J014729/1). His research interests include mobile networks, multihoming, and video streaming techniques. He is a member of the IET and IEEE. He received the BSc degree in Network Computing from Edinburgh Napier University, UK with distinction and as winner of the Napier Medal for Outstanding Achievement, and the BSc (Honours) degree in Computer Networks from UWS with First Class Honours and won the Best Honours Dissertation Prize. He received his PhD from UWS with Outstanding Progression Award.

Naeem Ramzan, FHEA, MIEEE, MIET, received M.S in Telecom from Brest, France, and PhD in Electronics Engineering form Queen Mary University of London in 2004 and 2008, respectively. From 2008 to 2012, he worked on EU projects aceMedia, PetaMedia, SARACEN, and CUBRIK in Queen Mary University of London. Currently, he is a lecturer in Visual Communication in the University of the West of Scotland. His research interest includes image and video coding, scalable video coding, multimedia search and retrieval, multimedia transmission over wireless and P2P networks. He has been a co-chair of special session in ACM MIR 2010, WIAMIS 2009, WIAMIS 2010, and WIAMIS 2011, and the co-organiser and co-chair of ACM Multimedia workshop SAP 2010, SBNMA 2011, UXeLate 2012. He has published more than 60 research publications, and served as Guest Editor of a special issue of the *Elsevier Journal Signal Processing: Image Communication* and *IEEE COMSOC E-Letter.*

Sattar B. Sadkhan is Chairman of IEE IRAQ Section at IEEE, Chairman of IEEE ComSoc. Iraq Chapter and Chair of URSI Iraq Committee. He received a Diploma in Radar Repairing in Iraq (1970-1974), B.Sc. Electrical and Electronic Engineering, Iraq (1978), MSc, Wireless Digital Communication, Czech Republick (1981), PhD, Detection of Digital Modulation Signals, Czech Republick (1984), and a Diploma, Information Security, Crypto – Switzerland (1988). He has published more than 200 papers in international conferences, journals. He is Editor in Chief of 5 international scientific journals, and Associate Editor in Chief of another 7 international scientific journals. He has supervised 125 M.Sc. and PhD Postgraduates since 1988. He is a member of Scientific Committee for more than 15 International Scientific Institutes, and more than 180 international conferences committees.

Fragkiskos Sardis received his Bachelor (First Class Honours) from Middlesex University in 2008. He received a scholarship for a Master degree in Computer Networks at Middlesex University, which he completed in 2009 with distinction. In 2010, he received a scholarship by Middlesex University for PhD in the area of Cloud computing and mobile networks. Throughout his studies, he has worked as an IT administrator, network architect, and IT consultant. His other areas of interest include network security, wireless communications, and distributed computing.

João Silva obtained the PhD in Computer and Systems Engineering (2011) by Instituto Superior Técnico, Lisbon Technical University. He is an Assistant Professor at Instituto Superior Técnico (Electrical and Computer Engineering Department) and a researcher at INESC-ID, in the Distributed Systems

Group. His research interests include mobile and cloud computing. In the area of mobile computing the research focus is on the development of middleware to allow an easy and transparent (for the programmer and user) use of the available resources. The research on cloud computing has allowed the use of the cloud to execution parallel jobs with minimal programming knowledge and efficient use of the resources.

Andreas Veglis is an Associate Professor, head of the Media Informatics Lab in the Department of Journalism and Mass Media Communication at the Aristotle University of Thessaloniki. He received his BSc in Physics, MSc in Electronics and Communications, and PhD in Computer Science, all from Aristotle University. In November of 2010, he was elected head of the postgraduate programme of the Department of Journalism and Mass Media Communication, Aristotle University of Thessaloniki. In March of 2012, he was elected Deputy Chairman of the Department of Journalism Mass Media Communication. His research interests include information technology in journalism, new media, course support environments, and distance learning. He is the author or co-author of ten books, he has published 50 papers on scientific journals and he has presented 65 papers in international and national Conferences. Dr. Veglis has been involved in 11 national and international research projects.

Luís Veiga is an Assistant Professor (2007-) in the Computer Science and Engineering Department at Instituto Superior Técnico, Lisbon Technical University. He teaches courses on Middleware for Distributed Internet Applications and Virtual Execution Environments. As Senior Researcher at INESC-ID with the Distributed Systems Group, he led two research projects financed by FCT (Portuguese Science Foundation) on P2P cycle-sharing systems, and is local coordinator of 2 others in distributed virtual machines and multicore component programming. He is the local coordinator of the Cloud4Europe FP7 project and team member of the Timbus FP7 project. His research interests include distributed systems, replication, virtualization technology and deployment, distributed garbage collection, middleware for mobility support, grid and peer-to-peer computing. He has over 60 scientific publications (Best-paper at Middleware 2007) peer-reviewed scientific communications. He was co-General Chair of ACM Middleware 2011, proceedings editor (ACM Middleware 2012, EuroSys 2007, ACM PPPJ 2007-2008, MobMid/M-MPAC 2008-2010, ARM 2012), and Steering Committee member. He was twice an "Excellence in Teaching" IST mention recipient (2008 and 2012), Best Young Researcher at INESC-ID (2012) nominated twice (2010, 2011). He is a member of IEEE, ACM, and EuroSys. He is a member of IST School Assembly, Scientific Board of Communication Networks Msc, Erasmus Mundus Master, and Doctorate in Distributed Computing.

Qi Wang is a lecturer with the Centre of Audio-Visual Communications and Networks (AVCN) in the University of the West of Scotland (UWS), UK. He is the Principal Investigator of the EPSRC project "Enabler for Next-Generation Mobile Video Applications" (EP/J014729/1) and several industry-sponsored projects. His research interests include mobile/wireless networks, cloud computing and visual applications. He has published over 40 peer-reviewed papers in these areas with over 400 peer citations. He was a winner of the IEEE ICCE 2012 Best Poster Paper Award, a finalist of the IEE 3G2003 Best Paper Award, and a recipient of a UWS 2013 STAR Award (Highly Commended) for Outstanding Research and an ORS Award by the Higher Education Funding Council for England (HEFCE). He is a Member of IEEE and on the technical programme committees of over 20 international conferences.

Runpeng Wang is with International Business School, Beijing Foreign Studies University (BFSU), China. She is a cofounder and manager of the Department of Projects of BFSU Business Incubator Centre. Her research interests focus on the business aspect of digital media and communication technologies covering social media and networking, cloud computing, mobile communications, game theory, and integrated marketing communications.

Xinheng Wang is a professor in networks at University of the West of Scotland. He has attracted a number of research grants including two EPSRC projects "A Universal PAN Architecture for Monitoring Multiple Chronic Conditions" and "Distributed and Iterative Processing for Wireless Sensor Networks with Multiple Local Fusion Centres," several TSB/KTP projects, and other nationally/internationally funded projects with overall the research grants exceeding one million pounds. Nearly 100 papers have been published, including the Best Student Paper Award for "Smartphone-Based 3D In-Building Localization and Navigation Service" on the 10th International Conference on Mobile and Ubiquitous Multimedia. Under his supervision, eight research students have been completed their study over the last five years. He is actively engaged with industry, and acting as a member of BSI (British Standards Institution) Committee in ICT, Electronics and Healthcare.

Yi Xu received the M.S. degrees in Electronic Engineering from Tsinghua University, Bejing, China, in 2010, and the B.S. degree in Electronic Information Engineering from University of Electronic Science and Technology of China, Chengdu, China, in 2007. Since 2011, he has been pursuing the Ph.D. degree in the Department of Electrical and Computer Engineering, Auburn University, Auburn, AL. His research interests include Optimization, Game Theory, MIMO, OFDM, IDMA, and Cognitive Radio Networks.

Index

A

adaptive middleware 231

agent-based resource management 118, 121, 124-129, 131-132

Analytic Hierarchy Process (AHP) 121

Application Level Throughput (Goodput) 155

applications mobility 230

Attention Deficit Disorder with Hyperactivity (ADHD) 308, 312, 318

augmented interaction 322, 342

autistic multidisciplinary software 295

C

cellulare networks 58

cloud-based video applications 158, 170, 182

cloud context awareness 182

cloud mobility management 182

cloud security 80, 83-84, 89, 99-100, 115, 182, 279, 292, 294

cloud services 15, 40, 42, 55, 63, 81, 83, 95, 100, 113-114, 136, 152, 154, 160, 164, 179, 183-188, 198-199, 203-204, 275, 300-301, 308, 322, 326, 329-330, 337

code mobility 233, 256-257, 260

Committed Information Rate (CIR) 146, 156

congestion avoidance 135, 137-138, 146-147, 152, 154-156

congestion control 130-131, 135, 137-138, 143-150, 152-155, 274

congestion intensity 135, 149-151, 153

Congestion Window Size (cwnd) 137, 156

D

data protection 92, 94, 98, 101, 110, 112-113, 115, 163, 166, 182

deficit disorder 308, 312, 318

digital garments 275, 292

Digital Imaging and Communications in Medicine (DICOM) 309, 318

E

energy efficiency 16-17, 38-39, 41-44, 46-47, 49, 51, 54, 76, 87, 132, 161, 218, 227, 254, 332

epoch regions 147, 156

Excess Information Rate (EIR) 146, 156

F

future internet 56, 79, 92

G

game theory 200, 204, 212-214

I

iCore framework 92, 95, 102-114

in-flight segments 139, 156

information life cycle 291

K

Kinect technology 295, 299-300

L

limited processing 83-84